HUMAN SEXUALITY IN
P E R S P E C T I V E

Richard A. Maier has a broad background in psychology as a clinician, researcher, and teacher. He has served as an alcohol abuse counselor and as a marriage therapist, has conducted numerous laboratory studies involving both humans and animals, and is presently associate professor of psychology at Loyola University, Chicago, where he designed and teaches the human sexuality course. Dr. Maier received his undergraduate education at the University of Michigan and holds an M.A. degree from Emory University and a Ph.D. from Kansas State University. He has published widely in scholarly journals and is co-author of two books, Comparative Animal Behavior *and* Comparative Psychology.

HUMAN SEXUALITY IN PERSPECTIVE

Richard A. Maier

Nelson-Hall
Chicago nh

TEXT CREDITS

From Kenneth Smith, ''The Homophobic Scale,'' in George Weinberg, *Society and the Healthy Homosexual.* New York: St. Martin's Press, Inc., 1972, pp. 133–34. Copyright © 1972 by George Weinberg.

''Male Responses during Sexual Intercourse'' and ''Female Responses during Sexual Intercourse'' from *The Sex Atlas: A New Illustrated Guide* by Erwin J. Haeberle. Copyright © 1978 by the author. Used by permission of the Continuum Publ. Co.

''Systematic Desensitization Hierarchy for Retarded Ejaculation'' from Tollison & Adams, *Sexual Disorders: Treatment, Theory, and Research.* Copyright © 1979. Used by permission of Gardner Press.

''The Percentages of Male and Female Homosexual Individuals Assigned to Each of Five Categories'' from *Homosexualities* by Alan Bell and Martin Weinberg. Copyright © 1978 by Alan P. Bell and Martin S. Weinberg. Reprinted by permission of Simon & Schuster, Inc.

''Sexual Orientation'' adapted from Kinsey et al., *Sexual Behavior in the Human Male.* Copyright © 1948. Used by permission of The Kinsey Institute for Research in Sex, Gender & Reproduction, Inc.

''Reports of Fantasies of Men and Women during Masturbation'' reprinted with permission of Playboy Enterprises, Inc. from *Sexual Behavior in the 1970s* by Martin Hunt. Copyright © 1974.

Excerpts from R.J. Stoller, ''Sexual Deviation,'' in F.A. Beach (ed.), *Human Sexuality in Four Perspectives* (Baltimore: Johns Hopkins Press, 1976). Used by permission of Johns Hopkins Press.

Excerpts from Shere Hite, *The Hite Report* (New York: Macmillan Publ. Co., 1976). Copyright © 1976. Used by permission.

PHOTOGRAPH CREDITS

page 243, from *The Birth Atlas* (New York: Maternity Center Association). Also from *The Child: An Introduction to Developmental Psychology* by D.L. Holmes and F.J. Morrison. Copyright © 1979 by Wadsworth, Inc. Reprinted by permission of Brooks/Cole Publ. Co., Monterey, California.

Continued on page 556

LIBRARY OF CONGRESS CATALOGING IN PUBLICATION DATA

Maier, Richard A., 1933–
    Human sexuality in perspective.

    Includes bibliographical references and index.
    1. Sex.   2. Intimacy (Psychology).   3. Human repro-
duction.   4. Sexual deviation.   5. Sexual disorders.
6. Sex therapy.   I. Title.   [DNLM: 1. Sex.   2. Sex
behavior.   3. Sex disorders.   HQ 21 M228h]
HQ21.M1943   1984   612.6   83–11478
ISBN 0–8304–1059–7

To my wife, Barbara

CONTENTS

PART 3

PART **4**

PART 5

PART 6

PREFACE

Before developing a course in human sexuality, I spent many years teaching basic social science courses. Among the goals of these courses were to increase students' understanding of research methods, present a balanced view of competing theories, and introduce the basic facts in a relatively unbiased fashion. I also attempted to share some of my enthusiasm for scientific inquiry and the learning process in general.

Human Sexuality in Perspective is a basic text with similar goals. The chapter on methodology emphasizes the advantages and disadvantages of each of several scientific approaches to sexuality (as well as ethical problems related to certain techniques of inquiry). Sections throughout the book entitled "Theoretical Perspective" deal with controversial issues and theories. An attempt is made to present a fair appraisal of both sides of a controversy and to discuss competing theories in enough detail so that students may draw their own conclusions. The basic facts are documented so that a student may verify statements or read further on a particular topic.

Courses in human sexuality are different than basic social science courses. I have tried to take this into account in several ways. In the first place, many students feel uncomfortable about their own sexuality, particularly in regard to communicating about sex with other people. Therefore, I have tried to present material in an open, relaxed fashion, which will help to desensitize individuals to sexual matters while still remaining within the boundaries of good taste. There are also several sections that discuss difficulties in sexual communication.

In response to the interests of my students—and the expressed desires of many other students surveyed nationally—I have included considerable material on the sociological and psychological aspects of sexuality. This material is included in sections labeled "Sociological Perspective" or "Psychological Perspective" and also in chapters on attraction, emotional intimacy, sexual variations, and sexual dysfunction.

Courses in human sexuality are taught in a variety of departments with an emphasis on different ideas. With this in mind, "Perspective" sections can easily be emphasized or deemphasized. For example, biologically oriented courses may wish to stress comparative and evolutionary perspectives; more practically oriented courses, medical and legal perspectives.

ACKNOWLEDGMENTS

A large number of people have contributed to this book and their help is greatly appreciated. The following colleagues reviewed parts of the manuscript in various stages of development: Tom Boyden, John Carroll, Al DeWolfe, Bob Eme, Bob Hamilton, Debbie Holmes, Homer Johnson, Jim Johnson, Tony Kopera, Paul Lavrakas, Joanne May, Dan McAdams, John Peluso, Emil Posavac, Pat Rupert, and Jan Savitz. Special thanks is due Jeanne Foley, the Psychology Department Chair, for reading parts of the manuscript, and for her continuing support.

Typing was done by Cindy Bishop, Maggie Melville, Judy Savage, and Cheryl Sporlein. I am especially grateful to Cheryl who typed the lion's share of the manuscript and showed incredible patience during the seemingly endless revisions.

Over a period of years several of my students read over various drafts of the manuscript and offered many valuable suggestions for improvement. I am particularly indebted to the following people: P. Alexander, W. Aukstolis, C. Campbell, D. Becker, T. Clewell, D. Doyle, M. Dwyer, E. Gottfried, L. Jolly, H. Kabakovich, I. Karalekas, R. King, T. Kougias, R. Maier, Jr., L. Matre, J. Näslund, L. Nurme, S. O'Callaghan, J. Panesi, W. Rose, L. Ruggero, P. Topel, T. Williams, and M. Winnega.

I have greatly enjoyed working with the people at Nelson-Hall on the production of the book, especially Dick Epler, Managing Editor, Carol Gorski, Copy Editor, Claudia von Hendricks, Production Editor, Midge Stocker, Photo Editor, Ron Warncke, Director of the College Division, Kristen Westman, Assistant Editor, and Sally A. Ireland and Julie Zolot, illustrators.

Finally, I would like to thank my wife, Barbara, for her help at numerous stages of the book's development and for her untiring encouragement and emotional support.

PART 1

Developing Ideas of Sexuality

The chapters in this part provide an overview of how ideas of sexuality have progressed from primitive notions based on folklore and tradition to more sophisticated conceptualizations grounded on scientific research and technology. Even today, however, many beliefs and feelings about sexuality reflect deep, historical roots.

CHAPTER 1

Sex in Historical and Cross-cultural Perspective

Our society has been passing through a period of massive change in conceptualizing sexuality, a change so fast and great that many refer to it as a sexual revolution. Only one or two generations ago, sex was not discussed in public, and it was censored from movies (even a married couple could not be shown in bed together). Nudity appeared in magazines, but only if the virtues of sunbathing were being extolled. Premarital sex was relatively rare, abortion was illegal, and premarital pregnancy was generally considered a crushing disgrace. A college course in human sexuality was practically unthinkable.

Today, of course, all of this is much different. But no revolution is total. There is probably more divergence in opinions related to sexuality than ever before in our history. This chapter will consider the evolution of ideas about sexuality—as well as other cultures' standards—in order to better understand the present sexual issues and controversies. Such knowledge may also help the reader clarify his or her own standards and the reasons for them, and, possibly, to experience greater communication, joy, and understanding in sexual relationships.

SEX IN HISTORY

A study of the history of sexual behavior could extend into prehistory and into every culture—it could be a book in itself. However, we will focus mainly on how our own Western culture has dealt with sexuality at various times.

Throughout known history, cultures seem to have fluctuated in their attitudes toward sexuality. At times sex has been seen as mainly good—a rewarding human activity and even a great gift from God, literally a bit of heaven on earth. In other times and places, people have tended to see sexuality as mainly an evil—required for the continuance of the

FIGURE 1.1

Attitudes toward sexuality have fluctuated greatly throughout our history. At the time of this painting—the Renaissance—sexual attitudes were generally liberal.

human race, of course, but degrading all the same. If one did find it necessary to participate, one should try not to enjoy it!

One thing has continued, however. There has rarely if ever been a society that did not think it necessary to regulate sexuality in one way or another, through rules and customs. Because sexuality is such a powerful force in human life, many societies have feared the disorder that might be brought about by its unchecked expression. They have tried, in one way or another, to prevent rivalries and jealousies that might lead to violence, and the birth of children who would not fit into the economic and social structure. But, although customs have always existed, they have never stayed exactly the same, at least in Western society.

The Ancient Hebrews

There are many reasons for these variations, of course. But it does seem to be generally true that a society tends to be most positive about sexuality when times are good. During harder times, sexual attitudes tend to become more restrictive (Nelson 1978). For example, the ancient Hebrews seem to have been fairly open to sexual enjoyment during the reigns of Kings David and Solomon, when they had a large and prosperous empire. The Song of Solomon in the Old Testament, dating from this period, is a celebration of sexual love. On the other hand, when the Hebrews returned from exile in Babylon, powerless and poverty stricken, they became more cautious about sexuality. In all cases, however, they saw it as a gift from God and not to be taken lightly. They emphasized the need for strong families and the duty to rear children.

Some of the sexual taboos discussed in the Old Testament—particularly nakedness and prostitution—may have developed by negative association. For example, these activities were practiced by the Canaanites, a group with whom the early Jews were in strong competition and conflict (Sussman 1976).

The Greeks and the Romans

Similar fluctuations in attitudes about sexuality occurred in ancient Greek and Roman life. During the Golden Age of Greek civilization, the human body was glorified in beautiful statues that still represent some of the greatest art of their kind. Many works of art depicted sexual interaction, and Greek gods were seen as sexual beings.[1] Later, as Greece suffered a decline in its political fortunes, it developed a more skeptical view of sexuality. Plato and other philosophers drew a major distinction between the things of the mind and spirit and the things of the body. They thought that mind and spirit were far superior. This way of thinking has influenced Western culture down to the present day.

These Greek thinkers also used the supposed split between mind and body to justify the greater privileges that males enjoyed at that time. They claimed that men were predominantly mental and spiritual in their makeup, and that women were mainly physical and earthy. Therefore, men had a higher nature and deserved their dominance. This notion, too, persisted for centuries. In some cases, an even more negative way of thinking about females developed. Since men felt tempted by women to express their "evil" sexual natures, the women themselves were seen as the source of the "evil." Some historians believe this kind of blaming was an important reason for the persecution of "witches."

The ancient Romans, like the early Hebrews, placed great emphasis on home and family. During the heyday of the Empire, however, sexual excesses became fairly common. For example, the wife of Emperor Claudius—Messalina—was known to promote sexual promiscuity in public. In a special room of the imperial palace she would force ladies of the nobility to have coitus with certain men, often in the presence of the ladies' husbands. During the late Roman Empire, sexually sadistic practices were performed in public as a means of entertainment for the masses. Women were sometimes tied to a bed and raped by men or animals.

At about the same time, however, there was a shift in thinking as the Empire slowly declined. For example, Emperor Marcus Aurelius, who defended the Roman Empire from the first barbarian invasion, is still known today for his *Meditations*, a sort of diary of stoic thought. Followers of the stoic philosophy distrusted passion and tended to deny sexuality. They preferred the rule of reason and self-restraint.

Theoretical Perspective: Historical Bases of Sex Biases

In the ancient civilizations we have just considered, women were generally considered second-class citizens. However, there is evidence that this was not always the case. Stone Age art from approximately 20,000 years ago suggests there was no clear differentiation between male and female social power. In fact, numerous cave paintings of large breasts, exaggerated female sex organs, pregnancy and childbirth — with a relative absence of males and male sex organs — indicate that the female's role in reproduction was particularly appreciated (Rawson 1973).

Some anthropologists believe that around 10,000 years later, two changes took place that tended to add relative power to the male sex role. The first was that plant cultivation was developed, and animals began to be domesticated. Men, with their greater physical strength and freedom from the restrictions of bearing children, were most likely to benefit from the possibility of the economic surplus associated with agriculture and animal husbandry.

The second change — the discovery that coitus was necessary for pregnancy — led to an emphasis on male sexuality. In many parts of the world, the penis was prized and worshiped. For example, the male organ appeared as a symbolic plow and a sword; among the ancient Hindus, the supreme god Shiva was represented as an erect penis. The male's role in reproduction clearly affected inheritance laws which, in most societies, favored males and added to the power differential between men and women (Janda & Klenke-Hamel 1980).

Once males gained control of the power structure of a society, biases against women tended to develop. It is only recently, as women have gained economic and political power, that our society has become concerned with inequities and further changes have started to take place.

Some of these changes in the power structure are related to technological advances. Greater availability of birth-control devices has made it possible for women to limit their fertility and competitively enter the job market. Other changes are related to economic factors such as the increasing need for women to contribute financially to the support of their families. Still others are political, especially the increased activity of feminist groups and women in government positions. One of the major lessons of history is that these various factors tend to interact with one another. Without the proper economic climate, technology does not develop. Without technological changes, the economy tends to stagnate. When the economy stagnates, social changes are not likely to occur.

The Early Christians

Christianity arose in a world that on the one hand practiced sexual excess and on the other was urging its better-educated citizens to deny sexuality and pursue ''higher'' goals of the mind and spirit. In this perspective, the views on sexuality of both Jesus and Saint Paul may be seen as radical.

Jesus insisted on the fundamental equality of the sexes. He opposed Jewish divorce law, under which women could be disposed of as property. He insisted on "the supreme importance of love and forgiveness in sexual matters as well as in every other area of life" (Nelson 1978). He also condemned lust as sexual desire without personal valuing.

Paul seems more ambivalent on sexual matters. On the one hand, he advocated the subordination of women to their husbands. On the other hand, he ringingly affirmed the basic equality of the sexes ("In Christ there is no male or female"). He praised celibacy because it freed people for complete service of God, and yet he "elevated the sexual union in marriage as a parable of . . . the union of Christ and the church" (Nelson 1978). Paul thus raised the possibility that intercourse between husband and wife could engage two persons in a union with mystical, even divine, overtones.

As Christianity became established in the ancient Mediterranean world, Christianity's sex-denying tendencies were emphasized and its affirmations of sexuality and sexual equality were suppressed. Augustine (354–430), for example, saw sex as "the bestial appetite of lust, and for a couple to copulate for any purpose than procreation was debauchery" (Nelson 1978).

The Middle Ages

The period following the fall of the Roman Empire in 476—and lasting approximately 1,000 years—is generally referred to as the Middle Ages. This period is marked by several attempts at sexual repression by various branches of the Christian church, most of which were not very successful. Celibacy was the rule for many of those in service to the church. However, there was a large gulf between church theory and actual behavior. For example, some priests kept mistresses and had illegitimate children.

There were times of romance and chivalry during the high Middle Ages. Knights went forth to do battle in order to win the love of their ladies. However, during the fourteenth century, the bubonic plague killed much of the population of Europe, and people began looking for scapegoats. Sexuality was one that they found, and special efforts were made to repress it. Some religious people wore a heavy, iron girdle and a shirt of horsehair; nuns were known to scar their faces and cut off their hair; and in France as many as 800,000 religious individuals made a practice of whipping themselves.

Another phenomenon apparently associated with sexual guilt was the fear of witchcraft. Lust was thought to be brought about by witchcraft, and the seductive woman was seen as an agent of the devil. Under the guise of religion, many women were stripped, subjected to vaginal searches, and tortured in horrible ways to extract confessions (Sussman 1976).

The Renaissance

In the early 1400s the Renaissance began in Florence, a city made prosperous by trade with Asia, and gradually spread to other parts of Italy and Europe. There was a movement toward individualism and materialism and a relaxation of restraints on sexuality. Artists enjoyed great prestige, and some expressed their sexuality exuberantly. For example, Benvenuto Cellini (1500–71) wrote an autobiography in which he discussed his need to have intercourse with his models between poses. Raphael (1483–1520) used his current mistress or a prostitute as a model for many of the fifty madonnas he painted. (Although this fact was well known, his works were extremely popular.) Perhaps the women also benefited from their increased—if ambiguous—fame.

Among the general population, there was a decline in modesty. Female breasts became more visible and, for more formal dress, women were completely bare chested. The codpiece became popular for men in the fifteenth and sixteenth centuries (see figure 1.2). This flap or bag on the front of the pants accentuated the bulge associated with the genitals. In some cases, stuffing was added to further enhance the apparent size of the organs.

There were, undoubtedly, a variety of reasons why attitudes toward sexuality became more liberal during the Renaissance. As Europe recovered from the plague, sex guilt was probably reduced. Furthermore, increased individual wealth associated with the expanding middle class gave many people more leisure time, some of which was invested in sensual pleasures. Finally, the Renaissance represented an attempt to return to the ideals of classical Greece, which in some respects were very liberal in regard to sexuality.

Reaction and Counterreaction

During the sixteenth through nineteenth centuries there were considerable fluctuations in sexual attitudes and practices. In the sixteenth century, John Calvin preached that people in general should try to overcome sinful, sexual impulses. He opposed singing, dancing, cursing and the wearing of provocative clothing. The Catholic church, responding to the success of Calvin and the growth of Protestantism, also called for sexual reforms. Among other things there was an attempt to abolish prostitution in the Papal States (which failed). There was also a papal order to paint clothing over some of the nude figures depicted on the walls of the Sistine Chapel (which succeeded). It seems that, at this time, there was a general reaction against the liberality of the Renaissance.

In the seventeenth century, Puritanism—founded on the austere

FIGURE 1.2

In this Renaissance engraving, the man wears a codpiece to accentuate his sex organs.

views of Calvin—became a dominant political force in England, and, later, North America. Laws were passed that forbade singing, dancing, the theater, and other worldly pleasures. However, not all aspects of sexuality were put down, especially marital sex. Jeremy Taylor viewed it as a means to "lighten and ease the cares and sadnesses of household affairs." Similarly, the Puritan poet John Milton reemphasized Paul's suggestion that sexual union could be "a prefiguring of the heavenly realm" (Nelson 1978).

As one might expect, not all people were as conservative as the word "puritan" might suggest. In fact, records of a church in New England indicated that one-third of couples coming to baptize their babies between 1771 and 1775 confessed to having had sexual intercourse before marriage (Calhoun 1917). The confessions were given so that baptism of the child could take place (babies conceived by unconfessed premarital intercourse could not be baptized).

Puritanism was followed by periods of liberality in various parts of the Western world. One of the most colorful of these was seen in England following the restoration of the throne (which marked the end of English Puritanism imposed by Cromwell). The first king of the Restoration period, Charles II, kept a series of mistresses. Nell Gwyn, perhaps the most popular of these women—with both the king and the populace in general—was extremely proud of her position as ''royal whore''; she had fourteen illegitimate children. John Wilmot, Second Earl of Rochester, was an accomplished writer and scholar as well as an avowed libertine. His play, *Sodom or The Quintessence of Debauchery*, was performed for the royal court in 1665 and seemed to exemplify Restoration taste. Among the characters in the play were the Buggermaster General, Queen Cuntigratia, Prince Pricket, and the Dildoe Maker to the Royal Family (Sussman 1976).

The Victorian Era

Toward the end of the eighteenth and beginning of the nineteenth centuries, the Industrial Revolution began a move toward greater prosperity based on the machine. For many, however, it also meant an uprooting from farm life, the weakening of ties to an extended family, and the beginning of ''slavery'' to the mill. When Victoria became queen of England in 1837, her virginal modesty and insistence on spotless moral character set the tone for the remainder of the century. Love was supposed to be expressed independent of sex, and sexual suppression was the ideal. Prudery reached its height at this time. Sex-related words—like breast or belly—were not to be used in public. There was even a general rule that table legs should be covered so that gentlemen would not liken them to human female ones (Trudgill 1976).

A hidden reality of the Victorian era was the proliferation of illicit sex. Brothels reached new heights of opulence. Often they were staffed by women of lower-class origins but patronized by men of the middle and upper classes.

In contrast, the Victorian era also brought an interesting reversal in traditional thinking about the nature of men and women. The Greek idea that men were not only more intelligent but also more spiritual than their earthier female counterparts had persisted for many centuries. However, the Victorians regarded women as the more spiritual of the two. Good women were seen as guardians of truth, beauty, morality, and culture, while men were supposedly influenced by animal-like lust, as suggested in figure 1.3. This interesting shift raised the relative status of women, for it made them something more than sex objects. Citing their personal value, women in the 1840s began to agitate for the right to own property (not permitted to married women in the United States at that time) and to vote.

FIGURE 1.3

During Victorian times, there was a marked differentiation of sex roles; the man typically exhibited sexual aggressiveness while the woman tended to be demure. This painting is called *The Awakened Conscience* (Holman Hunt, 1827–1910).

Author's Perspective: The Legacy of Victorianism

As we have seen, each historical period has had significant effects on succeeding generations. And although many people hold sexual attitudes far different from those of the last century, others are relatively conservative on sexual matters. In some families, different views on sexuality may create conflicts. Parents may insist on a combination of love, marriage, and sexual expression, while their children view these factors as somewhat independent. The question of censorship in regard to sexual material in movies and on television is hotly debated. Of particular relevance as a social issue is the nature of sex roles and the double standard; older individuals are more apt to conceptualize sex roles as being relatively distinct, while younger ones are more likely to reject a double standard. However, there are also many old liberals and young conservatives, and many more take a moderate position. Clearly, our society is dealing with massive changes and disagreements regarding sex roles and sexual expression, and these cannot be quickly or easily resolved. However, an understanding of historical roots may help to provide insight into the issues involved and enable those on different sides to see where the other person is "coming from."

The Twentieth Century

From the time of the death of Queen Victoria in 1901, there has been a slowly increasing movement towards acceptance of sexual expression and variety. Several factors appear to have been particularly important in the first half of the century. First, Sigmund Freud's theories—especially those pointing to sexuality as a critical factor in human development and motivation—shook the foundations of Victorianism. Second, there was a general rebellion against the conventional morality following World War I. Berlin and Paris became well-known centers of sexual "excesses," and the Roaring Twenties in the United States were associated with flappers, "red-hot mammas," and the introduction of what might be called the first sex queen, Clara Bow. Third, the automobile allowed adolescents and young adults a convenient means of escaping the supervision of parents and chaperones. Finally, the resurgence of the women's suffrage movement and rebellion against Prohibition contributed to a general mood of defiance and an increase in permissiveness.

World War II also had a strong impact on sexual attitudes and practices. Like World War I, it promoted rebellion against conventional sexual morality. Furthermore, changes in the wartime economy led many women to work outside the home for the first time, and although many returned to domestic life afterwards, others did not. Partly as a result, women's economic role began to change.

Shortly after World War II, Alfred Kinsey and his co-workers published two books that had an effect on society somewhat similar to that of Freud. The Kinsey reports shook the establishment, not only because they revealed that much ''unconventional'' sexual activity was going on, but because someone had dared to study sexuality on a scientific basis.

In the 1950s, scientific and technological advances had a strong impact. The Pill reached the U.S. market in 1960. More than ever before, people could successfully separate sexual activity from reproduction. In essence, the fear of unwanted pregnancy was greatly reduced. As a result, many people enjoyed sex more, and some enjoyed it with a variety of partners. Sexual anxiety was also reduced by the development of relatively successful treatments for sexually transmitted diseases and by the easier availability of abortions.

The reduction of sex-related anxiety led to increased emphasis on sexual pleasuring. Several magazines and books began to emphasize hedonism and sensuality. Starting in 1953, *Playboy* magazine displayed female nudes and espoused the philosophy that sensuality was among the benefits of success for males. This magazine became very popular in the United States and overseas. Other magazines—including female counterparts such as *Viva* and *Playgirl*—followed on the heels of *Playboy*'s success. In the early 1970s, two books that emphasized the mutuality inherent in sexual pleasure became tremendously popular: *Everything You Always Wanted to Know about Sex but Were Afraid to Ask* (Reuben 1969) and *The Joy of Sex* (Comfort 1972).

The pattern of liberalization seen throughout most of the earlier part of the twentieth century seems to have continued into the middle 1970s. For example, 84 percent of males and 73 percent of females in a national survey condoned premarital intercourse for males. There was also less of a double standard than was apparent at the time of the Kinsey reports; almost as many people considered premarital coitus acceptable for women as for men. Liberalization can also be seen in regard to attitudes about other sexual activities. Over 75 percent of the women and 80 percent of the men surveyed condoned oral sex, a considerable increase over comparable figures a generation earlier. These percentages were also higher for people under thirty-five than for older persons (Hunt 1974). More recent attitudes—and how these attitudes are related to sexual practices—will be discussed in the chapters that follow.

Theoretical Perspective: Reasons for Historical Fluctuations

A question frequently asked is, Do people or the spirit of the times bring about changes in sexual attitudes and practices? Obviously, certain individuals have a great influence on public attitudes: Augustine, Queen Victoria, and Alfred Kinsey left indelible marks on the history of sexuality. However, the times must also be right, or potentially great figures may be rejected. For example, one reformer—a monk named Savonarola—was excommunicated and burned for attempting moral purification in Florence during the late Renaissance.

A factor that appears to be important in ushering in a change—particularly a change toward liberalism—is war. In twentieth-century America, the two world wars and the Vietnam War were all accompanied by a decrease in sexual inhibition. In contrast, long periods between wars are often marked by relative conservatism.

Another factor that seems to be important is economic. As we have seen, economic security is usually associated with liberalism. The leisure classes of ancient Greece, Rome, the Italian Renaissance, and, to a certain extent, post–World War I America seem to have been less inhibited sexually than their poorer counterparts. It is also noteworthy that the so-called ''sexual revolution'' was most active during the economically prosperous 1960s and early 1970s. Once again, it appears that when there is energy left over from the struggle for survival, some of it tends to be invested in sexual pleasures.

Still another factor is religion. Christianity and Judaism have tended to insist that sexual energies be invested within a marriage. Thus, at times when these religions have exerted a strong influence on people's lives, sexuality is more conservatively expressed and evaluated. On the other hand, religions are no more monolithic and unchanging than the rest of society. Both Christianity and Judaism have gone through enormous evolutionary changes in their thinking and practices along with the rest of the culture.

Religious leaders of all varieties—including Roman Catholics, Jews, and liberal and conservative Protestants—are seeking to better understand how to combine love, responsibility, today's sexual climate, and the medical advances affecting reproduction. All at present tend to see sexuality as a good gift from God, within marriage. Some are also willing to consider the possibility that sex is acceptable in some cases within a caring, committed—but unmarried—relationship. Protestants, Catholics, and Jews also sponsor seminars on sexuality in an effort to help their members affirm and enrich their relationships. There is some evidence that these attempts at reevaluation have been successful.

A 1975 *Redbook* magazine survey of 100,000 women found that the more devout a woman was, the more likely she was to describe marital sex as ''very good.'' In addition, strongly religious women were the most orgasmic, and the most apt to discuss sexual feelings and desires with their husbands (Levin & Levin 1975). The Kinsey survey some twenty years earlier had found no such correlation. The *Redbook* authors speculated that the change might have resulted from the positive approach toward sexuality adopted by religious leaders in the intervening years. The leaders' point of view may have helped believers shed sexual inhibitions and anxiety.

It is difficult to predict what attitudes toward sexuality will be like in the future because economic, political, technological, and religious changes cannot be foreseen, nor can interactions between these variables be anticipated. Nonetheless, the lessons of history suggest that there will be fluctuations between liberalism and conservatism. However, it is doubtful that any future eras will resemble those of the past; each era seems to have its own character. For example, even though the Middle Ages, Puritanism, and Victorianism were all sexually conservative, each was unique in several respects. Similarly, Roman courtiers, Renaissance painters, and modern swingers all have had their special way of expressing sexual liberalism.

One thing, however, does seem to be quite certain. Each particular orientation has had definite disadvantages as well as advantages. The liberalism of the 1960s and 1970s brought an end to much sexual ignorance and prejudice associated with Victorianism, but it also made many people feel inadequate because they could not always achieve their presumed sexual potential. Others may have traded increased sexual pleasure for the rewards of a long-term relationship and later regretted it. Whatever lies ahead, it seems likely that human sexuality will continue to present problems and challenges.

SEXUALITY IN VARIOUS CULTURES

Cross-cultural analyses of sexuality, like historical analyses, have certain limitations. Biases on the part of individuals reporting behavior—and anthropologists interpreting the reports—undoubtedly exist. Nonetheless, the generalizations from studies of various cultures provide considerable insight into the basic nature of human sexuality. For example, if one type of behavior occurs in virtually all societies and another is reported only rarely, the former may be assumed to be more closely related to a biologically determined human drive. Cross-cultural studies also provide information on the relationships among such variables as climate, economy, religion, and politics on the one hand, and sexual attitudes and expression on the other.

In many areas of sexual research, early works become outdated by later contributions. However, early cross-cultural studies often have particular value because the data were most likely gathered before the societies had much, if any, contact with the outside world. Since the widespread use of air travel, it is becoming increasingly difficult to find cultures that have remained totally isolated. For example, it is probable that, by now, most of the 190 preliterate societies surveyed by Ford and Beach (1951) have been influenced by Western ideas and customs.[2]

Evaluation of Sexuality

Cultures exhibit great variability in the general evaluation of sexuality. A small island community off the coast of Ireland—called Inis Beag by the anthropologist who studied it—represents an extremely conservative viewpoint. Sex is virtually never discussed, and sex education is nonexistent. Adolescent males and females are segregated most of the time, and there is very little or no sex play or touching among teenagers. Even after marriage, there is only brief foreplay. Sexual intercourse (which occurs more rarely than it does in most societies) is considered a duty, performed in the interest of procreation. Supporting this view of intercourse, there is an unfounded belief that coitus is bad for one's health. Men never report having more than one orgasm a night, and orgasm in women is unknown, or at least considered abnormal. Following intercourse, the man quickly falls asleep (Messinger 1971).

The repression of sexual expression on Inis Beag seems to be strongly related to the acceptance of an especially rigid, fundamentalist version of Catholicism. It is also likely that the generally hard life of the community—associated with an agricultural existence derived from relatively poor soil—promotes an ascetic view of sexuality and life in general.

In marked contrast to the conservatism of Inis Beag, sexuality is viewed very liberally in Polynesia. In a group of islands that came to be known as the Friendly Islands (now the kingdom of Tonga), young women would swim out to visiting ships and have sexual intercourse with the sailors. Afterwards, they would sing songs indicating that they enjoyed giving of themselves freely and would look forward to doing so again in the future (Mantegazza 1932).

Sexual pleasure is also highly valued on Mangaia, which is one of the Cook Islands. Males are encouraged to extend their virility to the limit, and females are active partners in a relationship that emphasizes mutual gratification. The language itself includes a large variety of words describing details of sexual anatomy and functioning. Furthermore, conversations among the Mangaians often include humor that has overtones of an explicit sexual nature.

When Mangaian boys are approximately thirteen, they are given instruction in oral-genital sex, breast manipulation, coital positions, and ways of bringing females to multiple orgasm. Within two or three weeks after the ritual of manhood, an older woman provides sexual experience and gives the boy practice in withholding ejaculation in order to have orgasms simultaneously with his partner. Girls receive similar instruction, and, shortly thereafter, seek out boys who can demonstrate "satisfactory" virility as a token of their affection. Satisfactory is usually defined as intromissions that last as long as thirty minutes or more. During coitus, the female is equally active, moving her hips "like a washing machine."

In marked contrast to Inis Beag, young adult Mangaians typically have coitus at least once every twenty-four hours and usually have three orgasms per night. Virtually all women have orgasm, and mutual sexual satisfaction of partners is rated as extremely important (Marshall 1971).

Like Polynesian societies, most Oriental cultures are quite positive in their evaluation of sexuality. Taoism, a religion that began in China, includes the belief that sexual activity promotes health and longevity. Taoists conceptualize male and female sexuality as two forces, Yang and Yin, which come together to form ultimate unity. Yang—the male form—is likened to fire. It is quick to ignite, but overwhelmed and extinguished by the female Yin, a force considered similar to water (Chang 1977). Of course, it is also true that this belief emphasizes and stereotypes the differences between males and females.

Japan's positive view of sexuality may be seen in much of its art (see Figure 1.4). It is also reflected in a toy known as the surprise box, which was popular with young girls in the 1920s. When the box was opened, a bright red penis would spring up (Mantegazza 1932)—a kind of sexually explicit jack-in-the-box. It should also be pointed out that the Japanese prescribe very different male and female sex roles, in which the female definitely has the inferior position.

FIGURE 1.4

Japanese art reflects the oriental's view of sexuality in such frank portrayals of sexual intercourse.

Sexual Modesty

Generally speaking, cultures that are liberal in their views on sexuality have positive attitudes about the human body and nudity. For example, before Western missionaries arrived in Tahiti, the nude male and female bodies were considered not only erotic but works of art (Davenport 1976). In contrast, nudity is abhorred in Inis Beag. Couples invariably wear clothing during sexual intercourse. In some cases, individuals fail to learn to swim because swimming would require "scanty" clothing (Messinger 1971).

The vast majority of societies studied practice some form of sexual modesty. Even in societies where adults are nude on most occasions, there are customs that prevent a provocative display of the genitals—especially those of the women—at times considered inappropriate. For example, in the Kwoma society of New Guinea, a man is obliged to step aside and not look at a woman's pelvic area if he meets her on a path. Similarly, Kurtatchi women in the Solomon Islands are taught to sit with their legs close together in social situations. It seems that modesty is more closely associated with females than with males. Taking into account all societies in which only one sex appears without clothing in public, nudity is more commonly practiced by men than women (Ford & Beach 1951).

Pervasiveness of Sexuality

Sexuality colors many aspects of social interaction in liberal societies. It may also pervade conservative societies, but in more subtle ways. As illustrated in Inis Beag, conservative societies spend a great deal of time and energy in attempts to suppress sexual expression.

The pervasiveness of sexuality seems to be particularly great in societies that are in the process of changing from a basically conservative to a more liberal orientation. Contemporary America provides a good example. We spend a great deal of energy trying either to express or, in some cases, suppress sexuality. Sexuality in a direct or veiled form pervades our literature, painting, and music. Sexuality is also an important part of our everyday conversation, ranging from sexual jokes to serious discussions of sex and morality.

In contrast, the Dani society, located in the mountains of western New Guinea, is relatively indifferent to sex. Premarital and extramarital affairs are rare, and married couples usually wait about two years after marriage before having intercourse. After the birth of a child, there is generally a period of abstinence lasting four to six years. During these periods of abstinence—which seem to be voluntary—there are generally no other sexual outlets, such as masturbation or homosexuality. Furthermore, in spite of this sexual deprivation, the people exhibit few signs of concern or frustration.

Under such conditions, one might suspect a physiological problem. However, members of the Dani society are healthy and vigorous and show normal fertility, although the lack of sexual activity is related to an unusually low birth rate. The only clue as to the reasons for this apparent indifference to sex is a general lack of affect in the society. There are few emotional outbursts and practically no signs of general arousal. Even child-rearing practices are relaxed and largely free of stress (Heider 1976). Perhaps these people find it difficult to get excited about anything, including sex.

Male Compared to Female Sexuality

In many cultures, female sexuality is viewed quite differently than that of males. As in Victorian society, males may be allowed special privileges that are not accorded females. For example, when the Chukchee men of Siberia travel to a distant community, they typically make special arrangements with a man in that community. These arrangements allow the visiting man to have sex with the resident's wife in exchange for a similar favor when the resident is traveling. Taking a large number of societies into consideration, it is more common for men to have such sexual privileges outside of marriage than for women (Ford & Beach 1951).

There are also examples of inequality in regard to the evaluation of masculine and feminine sexuality. In some societies, sexuality is supposed to be pleasurable only for men. For example, the Chiricahua, a tribe of the Apache Indians who live in Arizona, feel that it is inappropriate for a woman to show any emotion either before or during intercourse (Ford & Beach 1951). Similarly, in the Tepoztlan village of Mexico, men try to avoid arousing their wives sexually; they assume that a passive wife is most likely to be faithful (Lewis 1960).

In contrast, many South Seas cultures value the expression of feminine sexuality. As already suggested, both Tahiti and Mangaia emphasize pleasure and freedom in female sexual interactions. In fact, on the island of Mangaia, a "good" male has been defined as one who can bring high levels of satisfaction to a female (Marshall 1971).

Political and social power appear to be major factors in regard to conceptualizations of male and female sexuality. In societies like those typical of Polynesia—where women have at least some economic power and independence—relatively great equality is seen. In contrast, societies such as the Chukchee and Chiricahua, where the hunting of big game by men is basic to the economy, tend to value male sexuality to a greater extent than that of females (Friedl 1975).

Aggression and Sexuality

Tenderness and consideration are thought of as virtues in many South Seas cultures. It is not unusual for couples to literally spend hours gently caressing one another and exchanging tender vows of love and affection. Aggression is very rare and, if it does occur, is considered highly inappropriate.

In contrast, there is a high degree of aggression associated with sexuality in some societies. The Siriono Indians of eastern Bolivia scratch and pinch, and sometimes poke each other in the eyes during foreplay. During intercourse they frequently beat each other on the chest and neck with such severity that they end up with what are referred to as lovescars (Holmberg 1946; cited in Ford & Beach 1951).

It seems that societies that are warlike—as are the Sirionos—are more likely to associate aggression with sexual expression than generally peaceful societies. Aggression apparently becomes a way of life and is likely to generalize to sexuality. (As will be seen in chapter 19, a similar explanation for the relationship between sex and aggression seems to apply to certain individuals in Western society.)

Variations in Sexual Behavior

Preliterate societies vary in the amount of tolerance they show toward individuals who deviate from the sexual norms. In some cultures, sexual deviants are ostracized or killed. In others—including many Polynesian societies—deviants are reasonably well accepted; to drive out such people is considered wasteful in the sense that they might well be good citizens in other respects (Janda & Klenke-Hamel 1980).

In many cases, there is not much correlation between the acceptance of a particular behavior and the frequency with which the behavior occurs. For example, the Mangaians report that homosexuality would be tolerated but, in fact, it is very rare (Marshall 1971). In a Melanesian culture known as East Bay, male homosexuality is actually encouraged during adolescence. A father may facilitate such a relationship by choosing an older man as a partner for his son. However, there are apparently no exclusively homosexual individuals. The adult men typically marry and report that heterosexual relationships are more satisfying than homosexual ones (Davenport 1965).

The Western world has traditionally been rather intolerant of sexual variations. For example, the coital position with the man lying above the woman came to be known as the "missionary position" because Western missionaries taught this position as the only one appropriate for intercourse. Variations in methods of stimulation, including oral-genital stimulation and anal penetration, were forbidden. They are still considered illegal in some states. As will be seen in later chapters, these types of variations are quite common in the United States despite these stigmas.

Other variations are even less widely accepted but continue to occur. Variations such as pedophilia, sadomasochism, fetishism, and voyeurism (which will be discussed in detail later in the book) occur with greater frequency in the Western world than in preliterate cultures. It seems that in the large, complex societies of the West individuals are more anonymous and can more easily evade social sanctions (Gebhard 1971). It also seems that these variations deemphasize interpersonal relationships. People who tend to become "lost in the crowd" and lack rich personal relationships may also depersonalize sexuality—which may help to explain the frequency of these variations in large, highly technological cultures such as the United States.

SUMMARY

Throughout history, there have been significant changes in sexual attitudes and practices. In the Western world, sexual attitudes have tended to fluctuate between liberal and conservative. The twentieth century has been marked by an increasing liberal trend. In the United States, two of the most important factors in this trend have been wars, which were generally followed by an increase in permissiveness; and technological advances, particularly those related to birth control and the treatment of sexually transmitted diseases.

Each particular era was, in many senses, unique. Although the Middle Ages, Puritanism, and Victorianism were all conservative, they each reflected special concerns and emphasized particular values. Despite societal attitudes, there have always been many individuals who did not follow the norm.

Sexual attitudes in different cultures range from the extreme liberalism of Mangaia to the ultraconservatism of Inis Beag. Certain warlike cultures, such as the Siriono Indians, are very aggressive in their sexual expression. In contrast, South Seas cultures exhibit little or no sexual aggression. There are also strong differences in the way cultures evaluate male and female sexuality.

The economy of a society is generally reflected in its sexual attitudes. Where basic survival is difficult, attitudes tend to be conservative; when people have excess time and reasonably comfortable living conditions, attitudes are usually liberal. Political power is also a factor. When men control most of the power, there tends to be more of a ''double standard'' than when there is equality between the sexes. Still another factor in the formation of sexual attitudes and practices is religion. Judaism and Christianity, the most influential religions of the West, have historically opposed sexual intercourse outside marriage. Their attitudes toward marital sex have tended to fluctuate with the times.

NOTES

1. A positive and rather fanciful view of sex is also presented by Plato in *The Symposium.* It was assumed that, in the beginning, humans were round and had four arms, four legs, and sex organs of both genders. At some later time, the gods split the primitive human forms into the familiar two-legged, two-armed types. Ever since, there has been a basic drive to regain wholeness.
2. It is difficult to know whether behaviors reported by anthropologists many years ago are still practiced or if, in fact, the societies in question still exist. Generally speaking, the older the date of the reference citation, the less likely that the practices still go on. However, in some cases, the publication date is much later than the time at which the data were collected. This is particularly true of the Ford and Beach (1951) survey, which includes some information collected during the early part of the century.

CHAPTER 2

The Scientific Study of Sexuality

Have you ever read an article announcing that a certain percentage of people engage in a particular sexual practice? Or seen an advertisement that claims a product can increase one's sexual satisfaction? Or heard that there are a particular number of ways to become more sexy? If you are like most people, you certainly have; you may also have wondered how much faith to put in such statements. This chapter is concerned with the ways in which sex research is conducted and the degree of confidence one can place in the results and conclusions.

In contrast to our historical interest in human sexuality, the history of sex research is very short. Although some research on sexual behavior took place in the nineteenth century, such work did not become common or well accepted until well into the twentieth century. After human sexuality became an accepted subject of study, however, research in this field skyrocketed. Especially during the last twenty years, a large variety of disciplines have become involved in this work, and each has developed its own particular research techniques. We will discuss some of the most important research methods, paying special attention to the advantages and disadvantages of each.

CASE HISTORY STUDIES

The earliest investigators of sexual behavior utilized what is called the case history method. In 1886, Richard von Krafft-Ebing, a German, broke new ground with a book entitled *Psychopathia Sexualis*, which presented over 200 unusual—even bizarre—sexual histories. These studies—although bitterly criticized by Victorian society—represented a significant first step towards a serious investigation of sexual behavior.

Beginning in 1896, an English physician named Havelock Ellis published a series of volumes entitled *Studies in the Psychology of Sex*. For his time, Ellis was remarkably tolerant of many types of sexual varia-

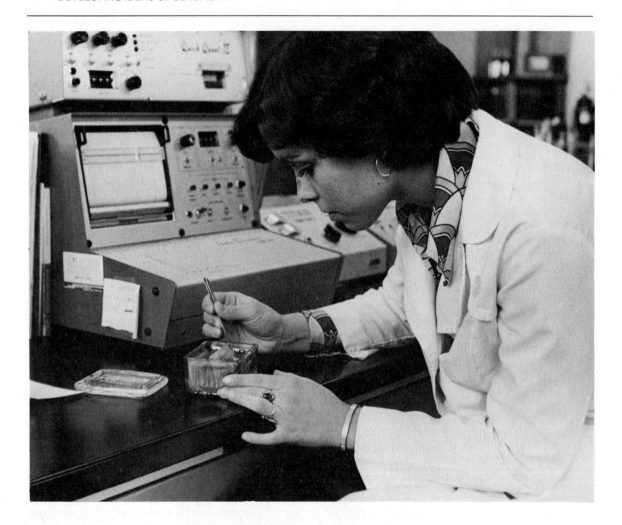

FIGURE 2.1

Research into human sexuality has increased greatly during the last generation. Several disciplines—and individuals of both sexes—are currently involved in a variety of research projects.

tions. He spent much of his life arguing against the Victorian suppression of sexuality.

The most influential figure in the study of human sexuality in the late nineteenth and early twentieth centuries was Sigmund Freud, a Viennese physician. Freud relied heavily on information provided by his patients, especially memories of early childhood sexual experiences. On the basis of case history evidence, Freud developed a theory of personality that emphasized the role of childhood sexuality in the development of adult personality characteristics (Freud 1938). Freud also stressed the importance of sexual energy, which he called *libido*; this libidinal energy was presumed to be the wellspring of many other human drives. Perhaps Freud's greatest contribution was to suggest that sexuality should be studied seriously and openly if the human personality was to be understood. He developed a complex and comprehensive theory of personality—known as *psychoanalytic theory*—which marks the beginning of modern psychiatry and still has a significant impact on psychotherapeutic techniques. (Various aspects of psychoanalytic theory will be considered in later chapters.)

Contemporary use of the case-study method often involves a comparison of case histories. For example, John Money and Anke Ehrhardt (1972) used this method to see how sexual misidentification affected the development of sexual identity. As will be seen in chapter 13, sometimes the genitals of a baby boy resemble those of a girl, or vice versa, and such babies are raised to be members of the opposite sex. By comparing the development of these children with the development of their normal brothers and sisters, Money and Ehrhardt were able to draw certain conclusions about the development of psychological maleness and femaleness.

The case-study method has also been used to identify common denominators in the histories of persons with unusual sexual orientations. For example, researchers have analyzed a large number of case histories of men who have requested sex-change operations because they felt

FIGURE 2.2

Sigmund Freud, the founder of psychoanalysis. Freud's theories stressed the role of sexuality in the development of personality and had a strong influence on later ideas about human sexuality.

strongly that they were actually women "trapped" in the bodies of men. (Such persons, known as transsexuals, are further discussed in chapter 18.)

Case history studies have provided important insights into persons who have unusual sexual variations or have experienced rare types of trauma. But the method, although fruitful, has its drawbacks. Investigator bias is a particular hazard in conducting case studies because it may affect the types of questions asked, the tolerance of the investigator for certain types of answers, and the conclusions drawn on the basis of the data. In recent years, social scientists have been trained to be aware of bias and have developed research procedures that reduce its occurrence. However, the inevitability of some bias limits the effectiveness of the case history approach.

Another problem with the method is the difficulty of finding appropriate comparison groups. For example, individuals arrested for sexual variations have been interviewed and compared to "normal" individuals. However, the individuals arrested are probably not representative of all persons showing the variation (some were smart enough not to get caught), so the comparison is not really legitimate.

SURVEYS

When Alfred Kinsey was asked to teach a course on human sexuality at Indiana University in the 1940s, he was surprised to find that there was virtually no information available on how the average person behaved sexually. Kinsey, who previously had done research on gall wasps, then began his vast and well-publicized surveys of the sexual behavior of American men and women. Since the publication of the two Kinsey reports (Kinsey et al. 1948, 1953), a large number of sexual surveys have followed. Basically, the survey approach involves questioning a sample of people about their sexual practices and attitudes and then making generalizations from the sample to a population as a whole. Two types of surveys are used: interviews and questionnaires.

Interview Studies

The interviewing techniques of Kinsey and his associates will be described in some detail because the Kinsey reports have served as models for virtually all later sexual surveys. Furthermore, many of the general problems of sex research are reflected in these studies.

Because respondents were asked detailed questions about their sexual behavior, the quality of the interviewers was most important. Kinsey did much of the interviewing himself, and he carefully selected three other interviewers from a group of social scientists. All were skilled at establishing rapport with a variety of people and conducting interviews without any sign of passing moral judgment. Many people were embarrassed

FIGURE 2.3

Alfred Kinsey. Kinsey and his colleagues were pioneers in the development of sexual surveys. Their work helped to break the barriers of resistance to research on human sexuality.

to talk about their sexual histories, but the interviewers eventually made them feel at ease. The interviewers were so skillful that less than 1 in 1,000 subjects refused to complete an interview once it was started (Pomeroy 1963).

The subjects for the Kinsey studies were recruited largely through personal contacts and introductions. In many cases, persons who had served as subjects helped to recruit other subjects. If the cooperation of some members of an organization was secured, social pressure was put on other members of the organization to participate, with a goal of 100 percent cooperation.

Kinsey was extremely careful to maintain confidentiality. All questions and answers were coded, and great care was taken to make sure that the code was virtually indecipherable. Only four persons knew the entire code, and they were prepared to defy any possible court order to reveal confidential records (Kinsey et al. 1948). Such precautions undoubtedly helped to enlist subjects' cooperation.

The subjects were interviewed in private, and the questions were asked in a frank, direct manner, using the presumed everyday language of the subject. Great care was taken to see that the subject understood the importance of the project. The questions were phrased so that the burden of denial was placed on the subject. For example, a person was asked *when* he or she first engaged in a particular sexual act, rather than *if* this act had been practiced. There were several checks on accuracy. In the first place, there were subtle cross-checks throughout the interview. Questions were interlocked in such a way that, if a subject was falsifying answers, he or she would be caught in contradictions. At this point, the interviewer would gently confront the subject and emphasize the importance of accuracy. In all cases such as this, the interview concluded successfully. Another check on accuracy involved "retakes" of the interview after a period of eighteen months or longer. Still another check was possible when both a husband and wife were interviewed separately; the investigators were able to compare reports of the same activity. Finally, the records of the principal interviewers were compared to see if there were significant differences in the frequency of sexual acts reported. It was theoretically possible that one interviewer was more likely to elicit certain types of information from subjects than the others were. However, the results were highly encouraging: there were no consistent interviewer biases, and the general accuracy of the data appeared to be high (Kinsey et al. 1948).

It is possible that responses might have been distorted, since people are generally not very honest in talking about their sexual behavior. However, the checks on accuracy and the emphasis on the serious, scientific nature of the interviews seem to cast doubts on this possibility. The Kinsey data appear to be as valid as other comparable data obtained since then.

Another possible problem concerns sampling technique. Because of the time involved and the revolutionary nature of the study, it was necessary to rely on volunteers. People who volunteer information about their sexual behavior may very well behave differently from those who are hesitant to talk about sex. Furthermore, if a sample is to be truly representative of a population, all individuals in the population should have an equal chance of appearing in the sample. Clearly, Kinsey's subjects were not representative of the total population of the United States. However, as we shall see, later research projects are open to the same criticism to varying degrees.

Several years after Kinsey's death, the institute he founded sponsored another large, interview-type study of sexuality. In this case, the subjects were homosexual. Because of the general cohesiveness of the homosexual population and the possible distrust of persons perceived as outsiders, recruiting procedures were necessarily different than in studies involving heterosexuals. About 1,500 individuals were recruited from gay bars, baths, and organizations and from personal contacts and public advertising, all in the San Francisco Bay area. In some cases those persons already interviewed suggested other contacts (Bell & Weinberg

1978). Although the sample was most appropriate for making generalizations about San Francisco—where homosexuality is somewhat more prevalent and better accepted than in other parts of the United States—there are indications that the findings apply to most large North American cities.

Author's Perspective: The Impact of Kinsey

When I was a student at the University of Michigan, I attended a debate that followed the publication of Kinsey's first report. The audience overflowed one of the largest auditoriums on campus. Clearly, the time had come to bring human sexuality out of the Victorian closet and treat it as an object of serious research and debate.

Ironically, the object of all this attention was a dedicated, hardworking scientist who had not anticipated—and did not relish—public controversy. In the 1950s, when McCarthyism swept the country, Kinsey's work was viciously attacked, and he was accused of aiding communism by "weakening" American morality. Following these attacks, the research institute which he had founded lost its financial support. The combination of overwork, stress from the attacks, and financial worries led to Kinsey's death from heart failure in 1956.

Fortunately, the influence of McCarthy waned, and the research institute regained its financing. It is still actively supporting sex research. However, it is a sad commentary that Kinsey never lived to see his work appreciated by the general public and to enjoy the fruits of his outstanding scientific contribution.

Questionnaire Studies

A large number of questionnaire studies have been published in recent years, including a rather extensive one sponsored by Playboy Foundation; information from over 2,000 individuals was collected (Hunt 1974). An attempt was made to obtain a sample that represented the U.S. population of adults. In regard to marital status, age, education, and urban-rural background, the sample was very similar to Americans in general. However, the large number of refusals (four out of five contacted) indicates that this, like the Kinsey study, did not represent a true random sample of U.S. adults.

Individuals' names were chosen at random from telephone books. They were called by the researchers and asked to participate—anonymously—in panel discussions about American sexual behavior. After the discussions, the individuals were asked to fill out questionnaires about their own behavior; this was the real purpose of the research. Since these subjects responded to written questions, the data are not directly comparable to those of the Kinsey interviews. However, the Kinsey and Playboy data provide a reasonable measure of sexual behavior during two time frames and allow for some estimates of changes in such behavior over that period.

Two more recent reports, by Shere Hite (1976, 1981), consist of responses to questions about sexuality sent in by mail, presumably by people from various parts of the United States. The first report is on females, the second on males. No attempt was made to obtain representative samples. Furthermore, there is no assurance that all the respondents were seriously answering the questions. However, many of the questions concerned preferences for various sexual activities, and some insight into satisfaction—and, on the other hand, frustration—can be obtained by analyzing the responses.

There are special problems in doing research with select populations of individuals. For example, in a research investigation of sexuality among adolescents, ethics dictate that parental consent be obtained before teenagers are given questionnaires. This means that there can be nonrespondents for either of two reasons: the parent refuses to give consent, or the adolescent decides not to participate. Therefore, obtaining a representative sample is particularly difficult. However, in one such study, 393 responses were obtained, and the nonresponse rate was only 53 percent (Sorenson 1973). This nonresponse rate is excellent under these conditions.

Interview versus Questionnaire Surveys

Both interview and questionnaire studies have suffered because it is virtually impossible to obtain a random sample of the total population for sex research. When it comes to answering questions about one's sexual experiences, there is always a high rate of refusal. Therefore, generalizations to the population as a whole should be made cautiously. Probably, the best assumption is that more sexual conservatives than liberals refuse to participate in surveys; one study indicated that liberals were more likely to volunteer information on a sex-attitude study than were conservatives (Kaats & Davis 1971).

Interviews have certain advantages over questionnaire studies. In the first place, it is possible to vary the format on the spot so as to follow up leads that develop from responses. For example, if someone with an unusual sexual orientation is found, one can then ask questions pertaining to this preference. Furthermore, it is possible to repeat interviews to check for accuracy.

On the other hand, interviews are very time-consuming and consequently expensive to conduct. It is also possible that an insensitive or poorly trained interviewer will subtly influence the responses of the interviewee. Therefore, questionnaires have certain advantages, particularly if large numbers of subjects are required.

In some studies, an attempt is made to maximize the benefits of interviews and questionnaires by using both techniques. For example,

Sorenson (1973) interviewed several adolescents while constructing his questionnaire, and as a result he eliminated several questions that proved hard to understand or threatening. Similarly, researchers in the Playboy study (Hunt 1974) conducted some in-depth interviews in order to obtain a more personal view of people's attitudes about sex and their sexual behaviors.

LABORATORY STUDIES

Although virtually all other types of human responses had been thoroughly investigated under laboratory conditions, little was known about the physiology of sexual responses until the 1950s. At this time, William Masters (later joined by Virginia Johnson) began a series of studies aimed at discovering exactly what happens to humans as they respond to sexual stimulation. Over 10,000 sexual responses were observed under laboratory conditions (Masters & Johnson 1966).

At the beginning of the project, male and female prostitutes served as subjects. However, the prostitutes turned out to be unsuitable subjects for two reasons. First, they moved from one city to another so frequently that they could not be studied over extended periods of time. Second, female prostitutes usually developed pain in the pelvic region from frequent sexual arousal without orgasm (see chapter 7), making their sexual responses different from those of most other women. It later became apparent that many individuals from the community were willing to serve as subjects. Therefore, the final sample consisted of 382 females and 312 males—none of whom were prostitutes. Most of the subjects were married couples. The potential subjects were screened to eliminate people who felt uncomfortable about sex or who had emotional problems. Furthermore, all subjects selected had normal sexual organs, an ability to communicate about sex, an apparent sexual responsiveness, and willingness to participate. As in virtually all studies of sexuality, the sample was not a random sample of U.S. citizens. In fact, there were undoubtedly even fewer sexual conservatives in this sample than in the samples chosen for sexual surveys.

The first phase of the study consisted of interviews where complete medical, social, and sexual histories were obtained. After thorough physical examinations, the subjects were introduced to the research quarters (complete with observational and recording devices). They were encouraged to initiate sexual activity in this setting. Once the subjects felt comfortable with the setting, they were then encouraged to have sexual intercourse in the presence of investigators (both a man and a woman). Finally, after the subjects felt confident and relaxed under the laboratory conditions, they were assigned to one of several specialized research projects.

Three basic types of sexual stimulation were investigated: (1) auto-

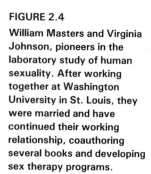

FIGURE 2.4

William Masters and Virginia Johnson, pioneers in the laboratory study of human sexuality. After working together at Washington University in St. Louis, they were married and have continued their working relationship, coauthoring several books and developing sex therapy programs.

manipulation (masturbation), (2) copulation, and (3) artificial copulation. Only females participated in the third study. They stimulated themselves with an artificial penis, a transparent mechanism containing a camera and a recording device. The artificial penis allowed the investigators to observe and record responses inside the vagina, responses that had never before been measured during sexual activity. The device could be adjusted for size as well as for depth and rapidity of thrust. For all three types of stimulation, extensive physiological measures were taken. In addition, interviews before, during, and after sexual stimulation provided data in regard to the subjects' emotions and opinions (Masters & Johnson 1966).

The contributions of Masters and Johnson to the understanding of sexual physiology have been widely heralded. Their research results eliminated many fallacies about sexual responses and have been successfully applied to the treatment of various types of sexual problems. However, the generality of some of the findings has been questioned. It is quite possible that people do not respond sexually in the same way in a laboratory setting—with various instruments attached and other people observing—as they might in the privacy of their own home.

Obviously, there are several ethical considerations involved in this type of research. A particular danger seemed to be that the laboratory experiences might adversely affect a person's sexual functioning in the future. However, follow-up contacts with the subjects indicated no harmful aftereffects (and, in some cases, certain positive effects).

Some of the strongest criticisms of Masters and Johnson have been directed at their later work on sex therapy (1970) and homosexuality

(1979). These criticisms, which are primarily concerned with evaluating psychotherapeutic approaches to sexual problems, will be discussed in chapter 19.

PARTICIPANT-OBSERVER TECHNIQUES

In a few instances, researchers have gained access to otherwise closed groups by entering into the activities of the group. For example, a male researcher and his wife exchanged sexual partners in a "swinging" group and obtained information on associated attitudes and behaviors (Bartell 1970).

In a different type of setting, an investigator posed as a "watch-queen" (someone who warns homosexuals of the approach of police or strangers) and made detailed observations of homosexual activities in rest rooms (Humphreys 1975). A follow-up involved recording license-plate numbers and tracing the identity of the participants. A year later, wearing a disguise, Humphreys interviewed the participants in their homes, stating that the interview was part of a routine survey.

The methods used in the participant-observer technique—especially those of Humphreys—raise important ethical questions. First, collecting data without the subjects' knowledge may be considered a violation of a person's right to privacy. Second, the collection of data under false pretenses (Humphreys's wearing a disguise and stating that he was conducting a "routine" survey) is definitely contrary to most people's ethical standards. Because of these types of practices, such organizations as the American Psychological Association (1973) have moved to spell out ethical standards in some detail. Furthermore, virtually all universities now have a committee that must approve all research proposals involving human subjects; the committee's major concern is the protection of subjects' rights.

Researcher bias can also be a problem in the participant-observer technique. For example, researchers participating in "swinging" sexual exchanges are likely to be sexual liberals. Therefore, an evaluation of conclusions should take this presumed orientation into consideration.

Despite the disadvantages of participant-observer techniques, they may be the only way to glean much information about certain "underground" sexual activities. As in the case of all research, disadvantages must be weighed against potential benefits.

EXPERIMENTAL STUDIES

A large variety of experimental approaches have been utilized in the study of human sexuality. Since many of the experiments will be described in later chapters, this section will consist of only a brief overview. What differentiates experiments from other investigations is the manipulation of certain dimensions or variables. A variable which is manipulated is known as an *independent variable.*

In some cases, the independent variable is a type of stimulus associated with sexuality. For example, subjects may be shown silhouettes of the human body that differ in the size and shape of certain areas, or movies that differ in their apparent degree of erotic stimulation. Other studies have had an independent variable only suspected of being associated with sexuality—for example, the degree of general emotional arousal.

Many experiments study the independent variable by using two groups: an *experimental* group and a *control* group. Both groups are treated the same except in regard to the independent variable. If emotional arousal is the independent variable, the experimental group may be asked to walk over a high, swaying bridge, presumably experiencing fear or general emotional arousal as a result. The control group may also be asked to walk over a bridge but, in this case, a low, stable one. Both groups may then be greeted by an attractive, opposite-sex person and their responses to this person measured. Differences in responses may be assumed to result from general emotional arousal and not from such factors as walking over a bridge or being out-of-doors. (See chapter 9 for more details on this technique.)

FIGURE 2.5

Sexual research.

Distinct control and experimental groups are not always necessary in an experiment. Qualities of the subjects themselves may serve as independent variables. It is often interesting to compare responses of males with females, older with younger persons, or homosexual with heterosexual individuals.

The reaction or response of subjects is called the *dependent variable*. Dependent variables are the ones measured in an experiment. The dependent variable may consist of ratings (1 for "I like it very much," 4 for neutral, and 7 for "I dislike it very much"), or a preference ("I like stimulus A better than stimulus B"). In some cases the dependent variable is indirectly measured. An attractive female experimenter may leave a telephone number; the dependent variable is the number of calls she later receives.

Certain dependent variables are physiological. For example, urine samples can be taken before and after the presentation of erotic material, and the amount of acid phosphatase measured. Acid phosphatase is known to increase following sexual arousal (Barclay 1970). Another method of measuring the physiological response of individuals is through the use of instruments known as plethysmographs. The male version—a *penile plethysmograph*—is painlessly attached to the penis. It is sensitive to the changes in circumference of the penis that accompany sexual arousal (Freund et al. 1965). A *vaginal plethysmograph* measures changes in the female that are associated with sexual arousal. This instrument is about the size of a menstrual tampon and fits in the vagina like a tampon. The vaginal plethysmograph measures the amount of blood in the walls of the vagina, an indicator of female arousal. The instrument has a light source to beam light at the vaginal walls and a light-sensing device to measure the reflection. The higher the blood volume, the more light is reflected (Sintchak & Geer 1975).

Sometimes several independent variables are measured in the same experiment. For example, experimenters may take plethysmographic measurements, ask subjects if they feel sexually aroused, and analyze the sexual content of stories written by subjects. Discrepancies between the variables may then provide useful information. If a person is apparently sexually aroused but writes a story with little sexual content, one might conclude that the individual is denying or repressing certain aspects of sexuality.

The great advantage of the experimental approach is that it allows for careful control of variables; any significant difference between control group and experimental group may be attributed to the independent variable.[1] Thus, the experimental method is superior to other methods in that cause-and-effect relationships may be clearly established.

There are, however, several limitations. In the first place, it is sometimes misleading to generalize from laboratory situations to the real world. Part of this difficulty may be solved by doing research in natural

FIGURE 2.6

Instruments that measure physiological sexual arousal.

The penile plethysmograph (left) responds to increases in the diameter of the penis that accompany erection. The vaginal plethysmograph (right), which is placed just inside the vagina, measures increases in the volume of blood in the vaginal walls, a response associated with female sexual arousal.

or seminatural settings, but it may be more difficult (or more expensive) to control variables outside the laboratory.

Similarly, since college students are usually used as subjects, there may be problems in generalizing to the population as a whole. Some experiments have used nonstudents, but, once again, certain procedural difficulties arise and expenses increase.

Experiments may also involve ethical problems. An experiment on how certain dating procedures affect sexual potency may function to condone activities not generally accepted by society, such as premarital intercourse. A more common ethical problem centers on honesty with the subjects. In some cases, it is not possible to be completely open with subjects at the beginning of an experiment. Telling subjects that their written stories will be analyzed for sexual imagery would influence their writing to the extent that the analysis would be useless. It is, however, important to weigh against the benefits of such research the possible distress or suggestion of dishonesty caused by any deceit. In most instances, subjects are told after the study exactly what was done and why (or at least given an opportunity to obtain this information). This is known as debriefing.

ANIMAL RESEARCH

In some cases, scientists have made a contribution to understanding human sexuality by studying animals.[2] On the basis of work with a large variety of mammals, Frank Beach (1965) developed a theory of how hormonal control of sexual behavior evolved in humans. J. Maynard Smith (1978) integrated research findings on a large number of lower species and made a hypothesis related to the evolution of basic sexual processes. One of the most controversial theories to have emerged in recent years has been *sociobiology*, first articulated in detail by E. O. Wilson (1975) and later elaborated by Donald Symons (1979). Relying on comparative studies of animals and also of humans in various cultures, sociobiologists have discussed the possible evolution of human behavior, suggesting that much of it has had a strong genetic basis.

In addition to generating hypotheses related to evolution, studies with animals enable one to develop a perspective on where our species stands in relation to our animal relatives. As we shall see, some aspects of our sexuality are unique, while others are shared by a variety of animals.

Animal research has an advantage in that it can be done in situations impossible or unethical with human subjects. Parts of the brain may be selectively destroyed and the resulting changes in sexual behavior observed. Animals can be reared in complete isolation from other animals—and from humans as well. (It is possible to feed the animals and clean their cages without any direct contact.) Considerable insight into the development of sexuality has been gained by raising series of monkeys in social isolation and then testing their social and sexual responses as adults (Harlow 1962).

Another advantage of animal research is that certain animals have unusual sexual physiology. Because of this, one can make experimental manipulations that would be impossible with humans, even if these manipulations were ethical. For example, certain fish normally change sex, and a complete change of gonads and other sex organs can be brought about simply by administering sex hormones. In these fish, it is also possible to produce individuals with unusual complements of sex chromosomes and observe their subsequent sexual behavior. Taking these and other situations into account, it is not surprising that animals have played a significant role in the development of an understanding of human sexuality.

Unfortunately, as Masters and Johnson (1966) have pointed out, some investigators have overgeneralized from animal studies to human sexual physiology; as we have seen, relatively little work had been done on human sexual physiology prior to the 1960s. Masters and Johnson's research—and later research by other investigators—indicated that there are significant differences in the sexual responses of humans and animals. One lesson from these findings is that evidence from animal research should always be considered tentative when applied to humans. A most favorable situation exists when a preliminary hypothesis is developed using animals and it then becomes possible to test the hypothesis in some way with human subjects. For example, a hypothesis may be developed concerning the involvement of some part of a monkey's brain in its sexual behavior. If a human with accidental damage to the same brain area is found, questions by researchers may then be directed toward possible changes in the individual's sexual behavior. Without the knowledge of the animal research, the opportunity for asking critical questions of humans might very well be overlooked.

CORRELATIONAL METHODS

Sometimes it is impossible to conduct an experiment to evaluate the effects of a variable, but information is available about the relationship between two variables. For example, there is evidence that cancer of the penis occurs less frequently in circumcised than in uncircumcised men (Hand 1970). This inverse correlation suggests that circumcision prevents cancer, possibly because a circumcised penis is easier to clean than an uncircumcised one. However, the relationship is not proven. It may be that uncircumcised males are generally from lower socioeconomic conditions and some other factor related to these conditions is responsible for the higher rate of cancer. (Today, it is generally agreed that penile cancer is not related to lack of circumcision.)

In some cases, finding a lack of correlation provides useful information. For example, Masters and Johnson (1966) found no correlation between the penis size of a man and reports of sexual satisfaction given by his female partner (small-sized penises produced as much satisfaction as large ones). This finding of no correlation helped to dispel the long-standing myth that a man with a large penis is a superior lover.

Although correlation does not prove a cause-and-effect relationship, hypotheses developed by observation (which is essentially a correlational technique) may sometimes be tested later in an experimental setting. For example, observations have indicated that men tend to talk to attractive women most often when the men are feeling positive about themselves. Self-confidence seems to overcome feelings that attractive women are unapproachable and likely to reject a man. However, this observed relationship may be due to other factors. For example, the women may find the men more attractive when they exhibit self-confidence, or men who feel self-confident may simply talk more to everyone—attractive women included. An experiment can be designed in which the attractiveness of a woman is systematically varied (by utilizing wigs and make-up) and the self-esteem of the man is experimentally manipulated (by giving him a success or failure experience prior to meeting the woman). If the results of the experiment are in agreement with the interpretation of the observed correlation (feeling positive increases approaches to attractive women more than to unattractive women), the initial hypothesis is strengthened and alternative hypotheses can be rejected.

Author's Perspective: A General Look at Scientific Research

Whether one can place much faith in scientific research on sexuality is a complex question. Some research findings have limited generality, while others apply to a large variety of people and situations. Fortunately, reputable scientific journals employ editors who evaluate the methodology of research and demand that authors spell out how far results can be generalized.

Another advantage of scientific research and reporting over popularized accounts is that science tends to be self-correcting. As new research tools, procedures, and statistical techniques are developed, older misconceptions and fruitless theories are identified and discarded or reconstructed. Ultimately, the test of great scientists should be how much research and progress they stimulated, not how many incorrect conclusions were drawn at the time. No scientist provides all the final answers in any area of research. The best that can be produced is a series of building blocks for the future.

Obviously, no one research method can be considered ''best''; each has its advantages and limitations. Furthermore, each method tends to be suited for investigating certain questions related to sexuality. In some cases, two or more methods may be applied to the same question to increase the general validity of the results.

Even in our scientific age, science cannot answer some questions related to sexuality. Research provides background information, but the most important decisions are based on one's own experience and personal philosophy.

SUMMARY

The earliest systematic investigations of human sexual behavior utilized case history studies. In the late nineteenth century, Freud began to develop his psychoanalytic theory of personality based on this technique. Later, Money and Ehrhardt provided insight into the formation of sexual identity by analyzing case histories of children whose anomalous genitals caused them to be reared as boys when they were genetically girls or vice versa. Case history studies may promote understanding of unusual sexual functioning. However, with this method it is difficult to eliminate problems of bias or to isolate causal factors.

Surveys involving interviews and/or questionnaires are often used to sample sexual attitudes and practices. A pioneering survey—one of the most extensive studies of sexuality ever attempted—was published by Kinsey and his associates in the late 1940s and early 1950s. A major problem with sexual surveys is that samples are virtually never representative of populations as a whole, and those people sampled are not always accurate or honest in their responses.

Masters and Johnson published an extensive report on the first laboratory study of the sexual response cycle. The physiological measurements were made in a precise, objective fashion and greatly added to the understanding of human sexuality. However, such studies raise certain ethical problems, and their findings may not be entirely generalizable to nonlaboratory situations.

Participant-observer techniques also raise ethical problems. However, by active participation, researchers are sometimes able to gain access to populations not normally available for research purposes.

Experimental studies of sexuality have a major advantage in that variables may be controlled and quantitative measures taken. As a result, cause-and-effect relationships can be accurately identified. However, there may be problems involved in generalizing from a laboratory situation to the real world.

Animal research contributes to an understanding of human sexuality because animals may be experimented upon in ways impossible with humans. Furthermore, it may be possible to make inferences about human evolution. Nonetheless, there may be problems in generalizing from one species to another.

Correlational methods provide measures or relationships between two or more variables, but they do not prove a cause-and-effect relationship. In contrast, a lack of correlation does present evidence against a cause-and-effect relationship.

NOTES

1. The term *significant* refers to statistical procedures or tests. Specifically, significant means that differences are not likely to be due to chance.
2. There are also concerns over the treatment of animals in research. Principles related to the care and use of animals have been spelled out by the American Psychological Association (1971).

PART 2

Biological Bases of Sexuality

The structures and concepts introduced in these chapters form a background for much of the material discussed in later chapters. Although these chapters focus on the biological components of sexuality, it is impossible to separate biology from psychology. Psychological functioning is dependent upon biological structures; emotional and psychological reactions, in turn, significantly affect structural development and physiological functioning.

CHAPTER 3

The Sex Organs

People in our society seem to have a tremendous interest in sex organs—as seen in the great variety of jokes on the subject—but by and large, they do not understand sexual anatomy and physiology very well. Even freshmen and sophomores in U.S. universities score surprisingly low on sex-knowledge inventories. Unfortunately, inaccurate information about sexual anatomy may result in anxiety, reduced sexual pleasure, and sometimes sexual dysfunction.

The purpose of the present chapter is not only to introduce the basic biological facts necessary for an understanding of later chapters, but to put this information in perspective and reduce anxiety. We hope that by gaining such knowledge and perspective, readers will enjoy increased sexual health and be able to communicate better with their sexual partners.

In many cases, people are ignorant about sexuality because they have a negative emotional attitude toward sex organs. It is not uncommon for people to perceive their sexual anatomy as dirty and to refrain even from looking at it. Such negativism is particularly common among women, probably because they are still influenced by the Victorian standard that frowns on any female enjoyment of sexuality. But males, too, may have negative feelings about sex organs. To counteract such attitudes, some sex therapists suggest that people periodically examine their own genitals in a relaxed atmosphere. (Since visual self-inspection is difficult for women, the use of a mirror is encouraged.) During such an examination, one should remember that it is an exceptional person whose sex organs directly resemble those outlined in the figures of this chapter.

FEMALE SEX ORGANS

External Organs

The external parts of the female genitals—those more or less visible on the outside of the body—are collectively called the *vulva*. The most apparent part of the vulva is the *mons veneris*, which literally means the "mound of Venus." The mons is a fatty pad of tissue, covered with pubic hair, which lies on top of the pubic bone at the front of the body.

FIGURE 3.1

Interest in sex organs develops at an early age. In our society, however, children generally learn that sexual anatomy should not be discussed with adults.

A variety of street terms refer to the mons and other parts of the vulva. One of the problems with these terms is that they are not specific. For example, at one time "bottomless" dancing was forbidden in a certain community because it was illegal to display "private" parts in public. Private parts were defined as those areas covered by pubic hair. Enterprising dancers were able to evade the law by simply shaving their pubic hair.

The *labia majora* or *outer lips* are also covered with pubic hair on their outer surfaces (next to the thigh). The outer lips extend downward from the mons. Like the mons, the labia majora have a large number of sensory nerve endings that respond to touch and pressure; this sensitivity makes the mons and labia majora primary centers for erotic stimulation.

The *labia minora* or *inner lips* are hairless folds of skin lying between and under the labia majora and running along the edge of the vaginal opening. They may fold over the vaginal opening, particularly when the woman is in a relaxed state. The inner lips contain extensive numbers of blood vessels and nerve endings. Unless a woman is sexually aroused— and has the increased blood supply associated with arousal—direct stimulation of this area may be unpleasant. However, after sufficient arousal, stimulation may be perceived as highly satisfying. There is particularly great variability in the appearance of labia minora.

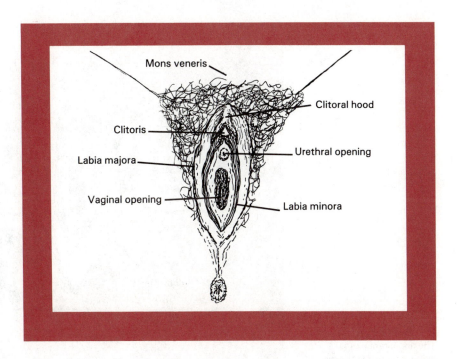

FIGURE 3.2
External female genitals.

The structure of the labia is not related to sexual attractiveness in Western cultures since they are generally covered with clothing. However, in certain African tribes the labia are considered an indication of beauty. The labia minora of young girls may be pulled regularly in an effort to increase their size (Masters & Johnson 1966).

Bartholin's glands are structures lying within the labia minora. They connect, via small ducts, to the inner surface of the labia. At one time, these glands were thought to produce important amounts of vaginal lubrication. However, it is now clear that the glands play a relatively insignificant role in vaginal lubrication and sexual arousal in general.

The *clitoris* is surrounded by the labia minora and situated above the urethral opening. The sole function of the clitoris is erotic; it has no reproductive function. Although the size and exact position of the clitoris vary considerably from woman to woman, there is no direct relationship between these variations and capacity for arousal and orgasm (Money 1970).

The clitoris has two parts: the *shaft* and the *glans*. The glans is clearly visible, but the shaft is partly covered by the *clitoral hood*, a sheath of tissue which is an extension of the labia minora. (At certain times, the glans is also covered by the clitoral hood.) The glans has an extremely rich supply of nerve endings, making it more sensitive to touch than any other part of the female's sexual anatomy. As will be seen in chapter 8,

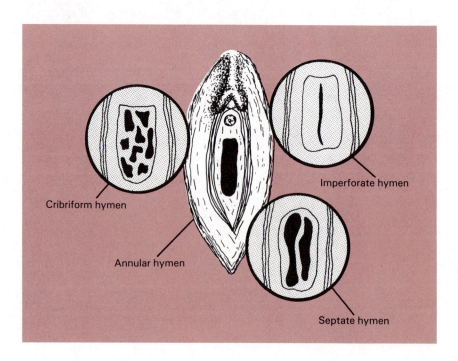

Cribriform hymen

Annular hymen

Imperforate hymen

Septate hymen

FIGURE 3.3

The appearance of various types of hymens.

some women have a clitoral glans so sensitive that they try to avoid having it stimulated directly; these women consider stimulation resulting from friction with the clitoral hood or extremely light touch the most satisfying.

Another structure surrounded by the labia minora is the *urethral opening*. Urine passes through the *urethra* and out through this opening. The urethra does not have any sexual or reproductive function. Nonetheless, the raised tissue surrounding the opening is quite sensitive to erotic stimulation.

The *hymen* is a thin membrane situated over the vaginal opening of most young girls (see figure 3.3). Typically, the hymen is broken during the first intercourse. However, some women are born without a hymen, and others accidentally tear it during vigorous exercise. On the other hand, coitus can occur without tearing a very flexible hymen. The only apparent function of the hymen is to protect internal tissues early in a female's life, but, as we shall see in the next section, a great deal of excess meaning has been attached to its presence or absence.

Historical and Anthropological Perspective: The Significance of Female Sexual Anatomy

As we have seen, some cultures have very negative views of female sexuality. In parts of Africa and the Middle East, certain tribal groups still strive to eliminate female sexual feeling surgically by removing baby girls' labia and/or clitoris (a procedure called *clitoridectomy*). Occasionally, edges of the excised vulva have been made to heal together, resulting in a vaginal opening too small for intercourse. Clitoridectomy was also practiced by certain physicians in the United States and Europe during the Victorian era. It was considered an appropriate treatment for masturbation and "excessive" sexual desire (Paige 1978). Although clitoridectomy is no longer sanctioned in the Western world, the fact of its acceptance in the nineteenth century serves as a grim reminder of the extent to which male chauvinism may be carried.

The hymen has taken on particularly great significance for certain cultures. In the Yungar society of Australia, the hymen of a young woman was inspected and ceremoniously broken—a week before her marriage—by two old women. If the hymen was found to have been broken before this time, the woman was tortured, mutilated, or even put to death. In the Kurd society of Iran and Iraq, the bedsheet or nuptial cloth was examined after the bridal night. When there was blood on the cloth—indicating that the hymen had been broken the previous night—the cloth was proudly paraded on a stick through the community. If, however, there was not an indication of virginity, the bride was publicly ridiculed (Ford & Beach 1951). Some of my students from Iran tell me this practice is still in effect in certain villages.

The unfairness of hymen inspection and evaluation is obvious, since no comparable procedure to determine virginity is undertaken with men. An added irony is that, as we have seen, the condition of the hymen is an unreliable sign of virginity.

To set the record straight, it should be remembered that not all preliterate cultures place such importance on the condition of the hymen and presumed virginity. As mentioned in chapter 1, Mangaian parents actually encourage their daughters to have sexual intercourse early and with a variety of men before marriage. Even if pregnancy does occur in a very young woman, there is no stigma attached to this event (Marshall 1971).

In Western culture, attitudes about the condition of the hymen and loss of virginity in women are intermediate between these extremes. In the first half of the century, there was a definite double standard: loss of virginity before marriage was considered taboo for women but more or less acceptable for men. By the 1970s, a female's loss of virginity before marriage was more acceptable, particularly if it was in a love relationship (Hunt 1974). However, a woman who had her first coitus in a casual relationship was still disapproved. In contrast, a male who lost his virginity in a casual encounter received social approval; in fact, more approval was given than if he had lost it in a love relationship (Carns 1973). Clearly, some aspects of the Victorian double standard still exist.

Internal Organs

The *vagina* opens between the labia minora. When it is in a relaxed state it extends 3 to 3 1/2 inches into the body and connects with the cervix of the uterus. Since the vagina is the passageway through which the baby passes at birth, it is sometimes referred to as the *birth canal*. The vagina is extremely flexible. When relaxed, the walls lie against one another, much like a deflated balloon. During sexual arousal the vagina expands, so that it can accommodate even a very large penis during intercourse.[1]

The walls of the vagina are lined with a mucous membrane that keeps the structure moist and warm. During sexual arousal, the walls secrete a substance that functions as a lubricant (this will be discussed in more detail in chapter 5).

The lower one-third of the vagina, near the vaginal opening, has more nerve endings than the upper two-thirds. As a result, the lower vagina is more sensitive to sexual stimulation. However, women differ greatly in the sensitivity of the upper vagina. As will be seen in chapter 5, certain women have in their vagina an area known as the Grafenberg spot, which is particularly sensitive.

The size and tension of the vaginal opening is controlled by the *pubococcygeal* or *P-C muscle*. When a woman is nervous and finds it difficult to relax, the muscle constricts the opening and the vagina feels "tight" or too small. On the other hand, the muscle may become stretched or generally flaccid. Contrary to popular opinion, it is not the size of the vagina but the condition of the P-C muscle that is more important to the sensations that accompany sexual intercourse. If a woman feels that she is "too loose," certain relatively easy exercises can strengthen the muscle. These exercises, called *Kegel exercises*, were designed primarily to strengthen the P-C muscle after childbirth (Kegel 1952). However, many women who have practiced the exercises for about six weeks independent of childbirth recommend them for increasing pleasurable sensations during intercourse.

The exercises involve, first of all, identifying the P-C muscle. This can be done by stopping the flow of urine and paying attention to the muscular sensation. (The P-C muscle also controls the flow of urine.) The next step is to contract and relax the muscle ten to twenty-five times. Then, the muscle should be contracted for a period of three seconds before relaxing and this procedure repeated approximately ten times. Both sets of exercises should be done three or four times a day. Since the exercises can be done without attracting attention, virtually any time a woman is sitting down is appropriate—even during classroom lectures or discus-

FIGURE 3.4

The female reproductive organs (longitudinal section).

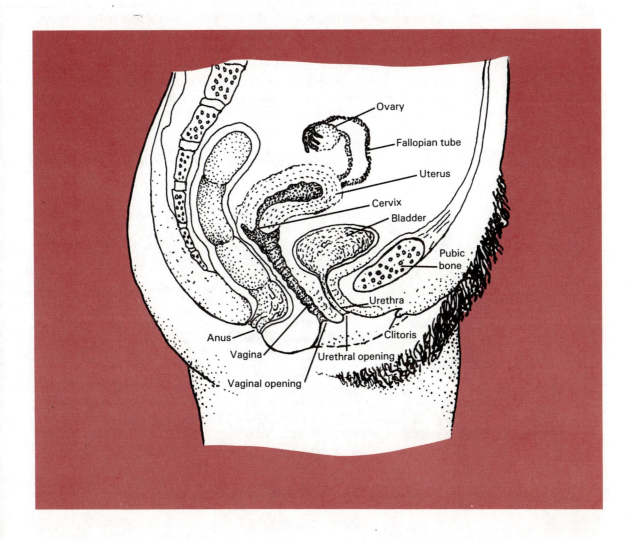

sions. In addition to increasing the sensitivity of the vagina, strengthening the muscle allows a woman to regulate the amount of stimulation she gives a man's penis during intercourse; many men enjoy variations of pressure (Barbach 1975).

The *uterus*, or womb, is shaped like a pear with its small end down. The small end, called the *cervix*, extends into the vagina. Following coitus, some sperm pass through a small opening in the cervix known as the *os* as they enter the uterus.

The uterus holds and provides nourishment for a developing fetus. There are three layers to the uterus. The inner layer, or *endometrium*, has a rich supply of blood vessels and glands. This layer is sloughed off during menstruation, forming much of the menstrual flow. The middle layer is muscular and highly elastic. The muscles stretch to accommodate a growing fetus and, during labor, contract to deliver the child. The outer layer, which is also elastic, forms a protective cover.

The paired *ovaries* are each about the size and shape of an almond. They are located to the left and right of the uterus. At birth, the ovaries contain approximately four hundred thousand eggs, more than 40 percent of which fail to survive. At puberty, some of the eggs start to mature within a capsule known as a *follicle*. Each month some of the follicles containing maturing eggs increase in size, moving toward the surface of the ovary. Every four weeks (plus or minus a few days) one of the follicles at the surface of the ovary bursts and releases its egg, a process known as *ovulation*.

An important function of the ovaries—in addition to the production of

FIGURE 3.5

The female reproductive organs (cross-section).

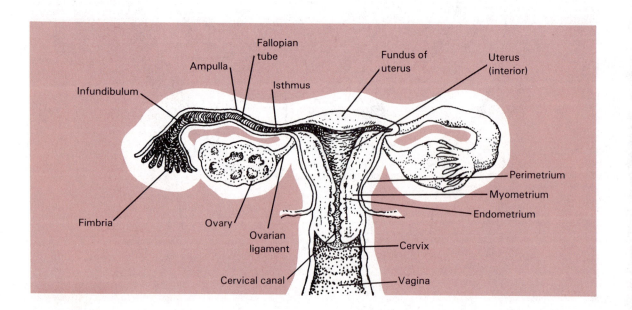

mature eggs—is the secretion of hormones. *Estrogen* is produced by ovarian tissue and *progesterone* by the follicles after they have shed their eggs. Much more will be said about these hormones in the next chapter.

When a mature egg leaves the ovary, it enters the *fallopian tubes,* or *oviducts.* However, these structures are not directly attached to the ovaries. They extend from the sides of the upper uterus and form a sort of semicircle around the ovaries. The part of the tube nearest the ovary is called the *infundibulum.* At its open end are several fingerlike projections known as *fimbriae.* Following ovulation, the egg enters the body cavity and is apparently attracted to the infundibulum by the movements of the fimbriae. Fertilization of the egg by the sperm—when it occurs—usually takes place in the infundibulum.

The Female Breasts

The breasts are, strictly speaking, secondary sex characteristics. However, because of their strong sexual significance and role in reproduction, they will be considered in this chapter. The breasts consist of fifteen to twenty clusters of mammary glands surrounded by fatty and fibrous tissue. These tissues give the breasts their soft consistency. Each of the clusters of glands has a separate duct that opens to the nipple (see

FIGURE 3.6

Internal structures of the female breast.

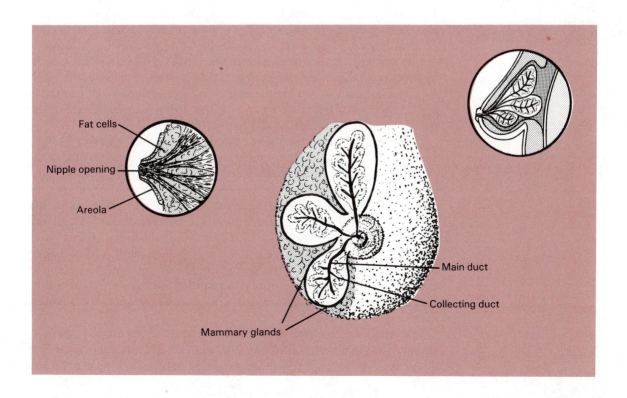

figure 3.6). The nipple consists of smooth muscle fibers; when these muscles contract, they cause an erection of the nipple. The dark area surrounding the nipple is called the *areola*. It generally becomes darker during pregnancy and remains darkened thereafter.

In many cultures, breast size and shape are associated with attractiveness. However, there are considerable variations in the standards of beauty. In some societies small, upright breasts are envied; in others, long and pendulous ones are in vogue; in still others, large breasts are considered most desirable. Despite the emphasis on female breasts in our culture and several others, there are no differences in function associated with shape or size; small breasts produce as much milk as large ones when infants are breast-fed. Similarly, small breasts and large breasts do not seem to differ in their response to sexual stimulation (see chapter 8).

MALE SEX ORGANS
External Organs

The external structure of the male sexual system consists of the *penis* and *scrotum*. Although the *testes* are contained within the scrotum, they are considered internal organs; the testes develop embryologically inside the body cavity and do not enter the scrotum until approximately five months before birth.

The penis is a complex organ consisting, externally, of the head or *glans* and a relatively long body or *shaft*. The glans is the most sensitive part, having a large concentration of nerve endings. Separating the glans from the body of the penis is a somewhat raised area known as the *corona* or *coronal ridge*. On the underside of the penis is a thin strip of skin—the *frenulum* or *frenum*—which connects the glans and the body. For many men, the corona and frenum are particularly sensitive to erotic stimulation. However, there are large individual differences in the areas and types of penile stimulation that are considered most satisfying.

The internal parts of the penis include the *urethra*, which is the tube through which the urine and semen pass, and three cylinders of sponge-like tissue that run parallel to the urethra. Two cylinders lie on top of the urethra and are called the *corpora cavernosa*. The single cylinder surrounding the urethra is known as the *corpus spongiosum*. In the flaccid or unaroused state these cylinders contain relatively little blood. However, when the male is aroused, blood fills the many spaces much like water fills a sponge, a condition called *engorgement* or *vasocongestion*. The resulting expansion and stiffening of the penis is known as *erection* or *tumescence*. Contrary to popular opinion, erection results entirely from this flow of blood; there is no direct muscular involvement.

Despite the lack of their direct involvement, the condition of the pelvic muscles does seem indirectly related to sexual responsiveness. For this reason, Zilbergeld (1978) believes that men as well as women can

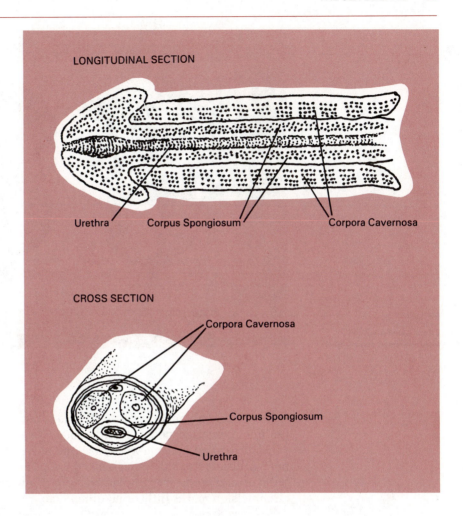

LONGITUDINAL SECTION

Urethra   Corpus Spongiosum   Corpora Cavernosa

CROSS SECTION

Corpora Cavernosa

Corpus Spongiosum

Urethra

FIGURE 3.7

Internal structures of the penis.

benefit from the Kegel exercises described earlier in this chapter. He claims that regular exercise improves the circulation of blood in the pelvis, which could facilitate erection. Furthermore, some of Zilbergeld's patients reported stronger and more pleasurable orgasms after doing the exercises.

The skin of the penis is arranged in loose folds, allowing for rapid expansion during erection. When the *foreskin* is present, it forms a kind of protective sheath over the glans of the penis. In many cases the foreskin is surgically removed, a process known as *circumcision*. When this simple operation takes place, it is typically performed shortly after birth. However, in some preliterate societies circumcision is done at puberty as part of an initiation rite. Among Jews, circumcision is generally a symbolic, religious rite performed on the eighth day after birth. There are also a number of societies in which circumcision is not practiced.

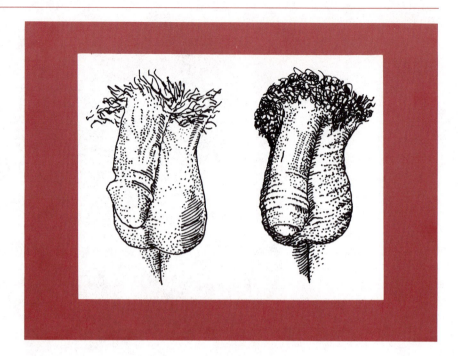

FIGURE 3.8

Circumcised penis (left);
uncircumcised penis (right).

One commonly mentioned advantage of circumcision is hygienic. In the uncircumcised penis, small glands under the foreskin produce a substance called *smegma* which accumulates on the glans. If a man does not regularly retract the foreskin and wash the glans, the smegma may build up and produce an unpleasant odor. However, with good hygiene, circumcision makes little or no difference.

The size of penises is the subject of considerable interest and conjecture, particularly among males (see Reuben 1969). Penises generally vary in length from 3 inches to $4\frac{1}{2}$ inches in the flaccid state. However, erection typically expands smaller penises more than larger ones and thus has an equalizing effect. In the Masters and Johnson sample, a small phallus (3 inches) showed a record increase of $3\frac{1}{2}$ inches in length; a large flaccid organ ($4\frac{1}{2}$ inches) increased only 2 inches in length. Although there are generally correlations between sizes of organs in the body, there is no correlation between general body size and phallus size. In fact, the largest flaccid organ in the study ($5\frac{1}{2}$ inches) belonged to a 5-foot-7-inch, 152-pound male. Of particular interest is the finding that there was no relationship between penis size and female ratings of effectiveness during intercourse. There was also no difference between circumcised and uncircumcised penises in sensitivity and excitability (Masters & Johnson 1966).

The other part of the male external genitalia is the *scrotum*, a loose pouch of skin that contains the testes. The fact that the testes are located outside the body cavity allows them to remain about three degrees Celcius cooler than the rest of the body; body temperature would kill the sperm produced by the testes. The *dartos muscle*, which forms the middle layer of the scrotum, further regulates the temperature of the testes. When the surrounding temperature is very hot, the dartos muscle relaxes, allowing the scrotum to hang down and away from the body; when the temperature is cold—or during a dip in a cold lake—the muscle contracts and brings the testes close to the body. (Cool temperatures, like warm ones, are harmful to sperm.) The testes are also brought close to the body during sexual excitement or strong emotional states.

Internal Organs

The *testes* are the male *gonads* (organs that produce reproductive cells). They have two major functions: the production of male *gametes* (sperm) and the secretion of the sex hormones known as *androgens*.[2]

The *seminiferous tubules*, which manufacture and store the sperm, take up a major portion of the testes. Each testis has about five hundred of these long, curled tubes approximately the width of a thread. They lie densely packed together, separated by connective tissue that also gives body to the testes.

The *interstitial cells*, which are located within the connective tissue, manufacture androgens. Since the interstitial cells lie close to the blood vessels of the testes, they secrete their hormones directly into the bloodstream.

Toward the surface of the testes near the top is a converging network of tubes. The sperm pass from the seminiferous tubules through these tubes into a single tube known as the *epididymis*. This tube coiled on the top and side of the testis is actually about twenty feet long. Here the sperm complete their process of maturation. Altogether about seventy days elapse from the time a sperm originates in the seminiferous tubules until it leaves the epididymis (Avers 1974).

At the end of the epididymis is the *vas deferens*, a long tube that passes out of the scrotum and around the bladder to the *prostate gland* (sometimes referred to as simply the *prostate*). This gland lies below the bladder and is approximately the shape and size of a chestnut. At the prostate, the tube narrows and is referred to as the *ejaculatory duct*. There is evidence that, if ejaculation does not take place very frequently, congestion of the prostate may result (Mobley 1975). The symptoms of this difficulty include pain in the lower back and genital region. Thus, contrary to some of the teachings of the Victorian period, infrequent sexual activity may produce some negative effects.

The glandular tissue of the prostate secretes a fluid that makes up the major part of the *semen*, or ejaculate. Another portion of the semen is

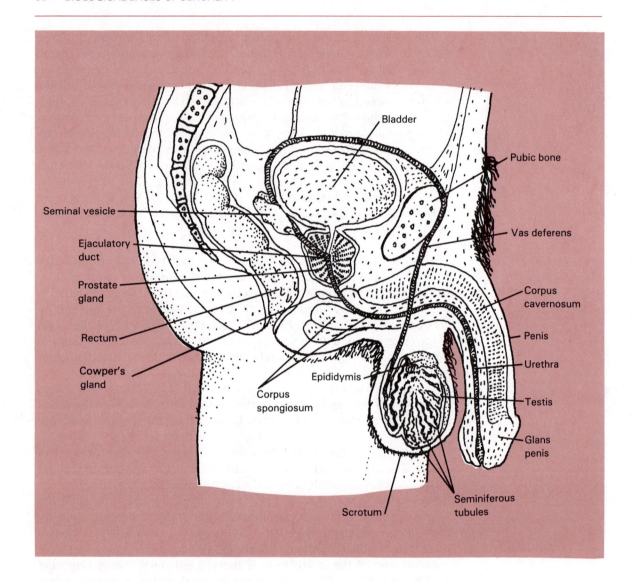

Bladder

Pubic bone

Seminal vesicle

Ejaculatory duct

Prostate gland

Rectum

Cowper's gland

Vas deferens

Corpus cavernosum

Penis

Urethra

Testis

Glans penis

Corpus spongiosum

Epididymis

Scrotum

Seminiferous tubules

FIGURE 3.9

The male reproductive organs (longitudinal section).

contributed by the *seminal vesicles,* two structures located just above the prostate. Both the prostate and the seminal vesicles empty into the ejaculatory duct.

Finally, the ejaculatory duct joins the urethra, which also serves as the outlet from the bladder. Just before ejaculation, a sphincter closes off the bladder so that no urine can be ejected.

One more pair of glands must be mentioned before the picture of the male's sexual anatomy is complete. *Cowper's glands,* which are located below the prostate, secrete a small amount of clear liquid during sexual arousal. This liquid enters the urethra and appears as a droplet at the tip of the penis before ejaculation. Apparently, the secretion helps to neutralize the urethra, which remains somewhat acidic after the passage of urine. About twenty-five percent of the time there are sperm in the clear liquid. Thus, it is possible for a woman to become pregnant even if ejaculation has not occurred.

Comparative and Evolutionary Perspective: How Did Sex Organs Evolve?

A certain amount of insight into the evolution of sex organs may be gained by comparing these structures in different groups of animals. Most primitive animals live in the water and do not have copulatory organs. Eggs and sperm are simply deposited into the water where fertilization takes place. However, as animals began to inhabit the land, there was an advantage to fertilization taking place inside the female's body (eggs and sperm deposited on the land would quickly dry out and die). But which came first, a penis or a vagina?

The answer to this question is rather complex. Evidence from different groups of living animals suggests that, in some cases, a primitive male organ evolved first; this organ functioned like a hypodermic needle, depositing sperm inside the female's body cavity. In other groups of animals, a female opening was present—associated with depositing eggs—and the male organ probably evolved as a modification of a structure with another function. (It will be remembered that the human penis conveys urine—an apparently more primitive function than conveying semen.) Thus, for some groups, a primitive male organ seems to have come first, but for others, a primitive female one. At any rate, once both organs had developed, they evolved together in the sense that changes in the size and shape of one brought about changes in the other (Maier & Maier 1970).

Today, a tremendous variety of sizes and shapes of sex organs exists. Certain mammals have developed bones inside their penises which facilitate erection. (It will be remembered that this is *not* the case in humans.) One of the largest such bones—known as an os penis—belongs to the male walrus. In adult walruses it reaches twenty-four inches in length or more; it is so sturdy that Eskimos have been known to use it as a war club. Incidentally, the walrus penis is withdrawn into the body cavity when the animal is not sexually aroused, protecting the organ from sharp objects and also reducing drag when the walrus is swimming.

Although human penises and vaginas are not as big as those of walruses, they are large compared with those of other primates—our closest living relatives. Even gorillas, whose bodies are much bigger than those of humans, have shorter, narrower phalluses, especially in an erect state.

One might wonder why many human societies have developed the idea that a large penis represents potent male sexuality. In fact, a book known as the *Kama Sutra*, which contains a summary of ancient Hindu writings on sexuality, includes a completely unfounded theory that classifies men according to their penis size and explains various personality traits on the basis of these measurements. The classification system includes the following colorful—if not meaningful—categories: The hare-man (an erect penis 6 finger breadths long); the bull-man (9 finger breadths); and the horse-man (12 finger breadths) (Vatsyayana 1963). Clearly, penis size is not related to reproduction nor, as we have seen, does a large penis produce more satisfaction in female partners than a small one. Perhaps the penis myth is the result of simple generalization. A relatively large, erect penis is associated with more sexual gratification than a small, flaccid one; people may have carried this relationship one step further and assumed that "the bigger, the better."

Another possibility is that, as sex began to take on a great deal of excess meaning for humans, the penis size of men—like the breast size of women—took on symbolic significance. Unlike animals, people have given myths, symbolisms and various types of complex cognitions extremely important roles in human sexual expression and conceptualization.

EMBRYOLOGY OF THE SEX ORGANS

Another type of insight into the sex organs and their relationship to human sexuality can be gained by taking a general look at the embryology of male and female organs. Although the genetic sex of an individual is determined at conception, there are no observable sex differences early in embryonic development. In fact, up until the fifth or sixth week, all individuals have undifferentiated gonads, two sets of ducts (*müllerian* and *wolffian*), and rudimentary external genitals known as the *genital tubercle*.

Starting about the seventh week of embryological development, sex differences become noticeable. In males, the undifferentiated gonads develop into testes. However, no changes take place in females for another four or five weeks. Then, during the eleventh or twelfth week, the ovaries develop from the undifferentiated gonads.

Following differentiation of the testes or ovaries, changes in the ducts take place. However, in this case, only one set of the original two sets of ducts develops. In males, the müllerian ducts degenerate and the wolffian ducts become the internal male reproductive ducts: the epididymis, vas deferens, and ejaculatory duct.

In females, the wolffian ducts degenerate, while the müllerian ducts develop into the fallopian tubes, the uterus, and the lower third of the vagina. The fact that the lower vagina develops from different embryological tissue than the upper two-thirds helps explain why the upper and lower vagina differ in sensitivity to stimulation.

At about the same time that the internal sex organs are differentiating, the external organs are beginning to develop. In the male, the undiffer-

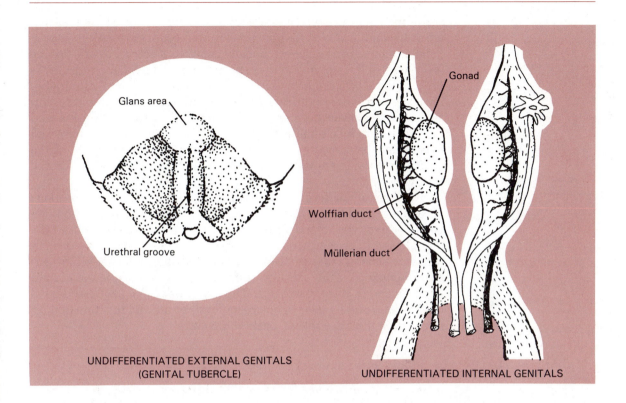

Glans area

Urethral groove

UNDIFFERENTIATED EXTERNAL GENITALS
(GENITAL TUBERCLE)

Gonad

Wolffian duct

Müllerian duct

UNDIFFERENTIATED INTERNAL GENITALS

FIGURE 3.10
Undifferentiated sex organs.

entiated external genitalia become the penis and the scrotum; in the female, this undifferentiated structure develops into the clitoris, labia minora, and labia majora.

The structures that become the ovaries or testes are located near the top of the abdominal cavity. However, by the tenth week, they have moved down to an area around the upper edge of the pelvis. The ovaries remain in this position throughout embryonic development. In contrast, the testes continue a much longer descent: they move into the scrotum via a passageway known as the *inguinal canal*. Once the testes have passed through (during about the fourth month following conception), the inguinal canal becomes too small to accommodate the enlarging testes.

A conclusion that may be drawn from the previous paragraphs is that, although men and women have very different types of sex organs, some of these organs have very similar embryological origins. When two structures have similar embryological backgrounds—such as the testes and ovaries—they are said to be *homologous*. Another example of homologous organs is the glans penis and the clitoris.

Knowledge of these homologues can be very helpful in understanding sexuality. For example, the ovaries and the testes perform functions that are quite similar. In the first place, they both produce sex cells (eggs in females and sperm in males). Second, they both secrete sex hormones (estrogens in females and androgens in males). The biochemical structures of these two sex hormones are remarkably similar. Furthermore, the testes and ovaries both secrete small quantities of what might be considered opposite-sex hormones: the testes produce some estrogens, and the ovaries produce some androgens. A third similarity can be observed in regard to the perception of pain: a kick in the testes seems to bring the same unpleasant sensation as a deep pelvic thrust that knocks against the ovaries.

A comparison of the clitoris and the penis is also of interest; the glans of each is extremely sensitive to sexual stimulation, and both organs become swollen with blood when the individual is sexually aroused (although, as will be seen in chapter 5, the clitoris does not become erect in the same fashion that a penis does). The clitoris and the penis have another homologue: the *prepuce*. In females, the prepuce is the clitoral hood; in males, it is the foreskin. Thus, despite obvious differences between males and females in regard to the structure and function of their sex organs, there are several basic similarities.

Author's Perspective: Language and Sexuality

The conflict between sexual interest and negative emotional reactions to sex organs is clearly reflected in the English language. A number of slang words for the sex organs are also used as derogatory terms for people. Similarly, the street expression for sexual intercourse is a common synonym for doing something nasty to another person or for expressing disgust. It is interesting to note that, in Nigeria, the technical words for sexual organs and sex acts were introduced by missionaries, and these technical words then became the most negative in their connotation (Money 1980). One is led to wonder if, when a Nigerian misses an easy shot in a basketball game, he or she yells "sexual intercourse!"

The types of slang words used as synonyms for sex organs also provide insight into how people conceptualize male and female sexuality. Words with an active connotation like *tool* represent the penis. In contrast, words such as *box* and *tunnel*—which have a more passive connotation—stand for female organs, particularly the vagina. Especially significant is the fact that the clitoris is not represented by a common slang word. Similar insight into male-female relationships is provided by the observation that having sexual intercourse is commonly described in street language as the male doing something to the female rather than as the couple sharing an experience or the female initiating a sex act.

Even technical words in our language sometimes reflect sex biases. For example, *pudendum,* which is a term for the external female genitals, is derived from the Latin word *pudendus,* which literally means "something to be ashamed of."

Unfortunately, language not only reflects our attitudes but tends to reinforce cultural biases. Many of the negative attitudes people have about sex—including, in some cases, sex between married couples—were probably learned at an early age by association between sexuality and "bad" words. Similarly, the idea that female sexuality is more passive than male sexuality is undoubtedly reinforced by a young adolescent's use of words like *tool* and *tunnel.*

Over a period of time, attitudes change, and so do the words that represent them. If we continue to move toward a wholesome acceptance of sexuality, perhaps synonyms for sexual organs and sexual experiences will take on more positive connotations. Wouldn't it be interesting if we essentially called people penises or vaginas and they took it as a compliment?

SUMMARY

External female sex organs are collectively called the vulva. The vulva includes the mons veneris, labia majora (outer lips), labia minora (inner lips), clitoris, urethral opening, and hymen. The clitoris is the only sexual structure whose sole function is erotic. Although the condition of the hymen is an unreliable sign of virginity, many cultures have demanded an intact hymen as a prerequisite for marriage.

Internal female organs include the vagina, uterus, ovaries, and fallopian tubes. During the middle part of the menstrual cycle, an ovarian follicle releases a mature egg. The egg then moves into the tubes, where fertilization may take place.

The size of the vaginal opening is controlled by the P-C muscle. Procedures known as Kegel exercises have been developed to strengthen this muscle and increase erotic satisfaction.

The female breasts consist of clusters of mammary glands surrounded by fatty and fibrous tissue. Externally, each breast includes the nipple and the surrounding areola. The female human breasts are unique in that they remain relatively large and soft when they are not producing milk. Breast size is not related to how much milk is produced or to responsiveness to sexual stimulation.

The male external sex organs include the penis and scrotum. The penis becomes erect when it becomes engorged with blood; there is no muscular involvement in erection. Penis size is not related to general body size, nor does it predict a female partner's satisfaction with coitus.

The scrotum contains the testes. The dartos muscle—which is the middle layer of the scrotum—regulates the distance of the testes from the body so as to protect the testes from overly high or low temperatures.

Male internal organs include the testes, vas deferens, prostate gland, seminal vesicles, ejaculatory duct, and Cowper's glands. In the testes, androgens are manufactured in the interstitial cells, while sperm are produced in the seminiferous tubules. Sperm mature in a long, coiled tube (the epididymis) and, during ejaculation, pass out through the vas deferens, ejaculatory duct, and urethra. Seminal fluid is added by the prostate and seminal vesicles.

Embryologically, the sex organs of males and females start out the same: each sex has undifferentiated gonads, a genital tubercle, and wolffian and müllerian ducts. In males, the undifferentiated gonads develop into testes, the wolffian ducts into internal sex organs, and the genital tubercle into the penis and scrotum. At a somewhat later time the female's undifferentiated gonads develop into ovaries, the müllerian ducts into internal organs, and the genital tubercle into the vulva.

Organs that have similar embryological origins are called homologous. Some examples of homologous sex organs are the testes and the ovaries, and the penis and the clitoris.

NOTES

1. It is frequently stated in textbooks that the vagina is flexible enough to accommodate not only a large penis but also a baby's head during delivery. However, intercourse and childbirth are completely different physiological processes that involve different states of vaginal expansion. For example, as will be seen in chapter 11, the hormone relaxin facilitates relaxation of muscles and pelvic ligaments needed to accommodate the passage of the child. It is misleading to compare vaginal expansion under these two conditions.

2. The sex hormones—estrogens and androgens—are biochemically related compounds known as steroids. The most important estrogen is estradiol-17b. The most important androgen is testosterone. For purposes of the general discussion in this text, it is practical to think of estrogens and androgens as being synonymous with estradiol-17b and testosterone, respectively. In many cases it has even become conventional to use the singulars—estrogen and androgen—rather than referring to *the* estrogens and *the* androgens. Nonetheless, there are some examples of different androgens having different types of effects (see Imperato-McGinley et al. 1979).

CHAPTER 4

Nerves and Hormones

The changes that take place within our bodies during sexual arousal and expression have long been a source of mystery. Both demons and deities have been held responsible for the unexplainable. However, within the last few decades, research has indicated that complex activities of nerves and hormones in the brain, sex organs, and other parts of the body are involved in sexual behavior. The interactions of these systems—along with psychological reactions to the changes—are the subject of this chapter.

THE NERVOUS SYSTEM

An arrangement of interacting nerves in the spinal cord and brain, with peripheral nerves running to and from these centers, makes up the nervous system. Two types of studies help to shed light on the functioning of the nervous system. In one type, neural areas are stimulated by minute electric currents that resemble the stimulation produced by other neurons; if sensations or behaviors result, it can be assumed that the neural area in question is normally linked to these sensations or behaviors. In the second type of study, persons or animals with neural damage are investigated. An evaluation of their behavior or feelings indicates how, in essence, the system works without one of its parts. In other words, if a behavior or sensation is lost, it can be assumed that the structure in question is critical to normal functioning of that sort.

The Spinal Cord

More is known about the spinal mechanism in males than that of females, primarily because men are more likely than women to suffer spinal injuries from war or sports accidents. Erection of the penis is controlled by both the brain and the spinal cord. Erection can result when direct stimulation of the organ activates the nerves that carry information from the penis to a center in the lower spinal cord. This spinal center responds by sending a message to the muscles around the walls of the blood vessels of the penis. As a direct result, the muscles relax; the relaxation of the blood vessels allows blood to flow into the corpora cavernosa and corpus spongiosum of the penis, inducing an erection. At the same time, valves in the veins close, preventing most of the blood from leaving (once erect, the penis has only a slow flow of blood). The degree or firmness of the erection is a function of the number of individual nerves sending messages (Weiss 1973).

However, an erection also can be facilitated or inhibited by messages coming from the brain to the appropriate spinal center. Thus, thoughts and fantasies can induce erections, or fears and anxieties can eliminate them. Men with severed spinal cords but no destruction of erection centers may be capable of erection, but they cannot feel the usual related sensations. And their erections are not responsive to thoughts and fantasies, since the connection to the brain no longer exists.

Another aspect of sexuality that is regulated by spinal mechanisms is ejaculation. Since erection and ejaculation are represented in somewhat different levels of the spinal cord, it is possible for a spinally injured man to have erections without ejaculation, or vice versa (Comarr 1970).

In women, it appears that vaginal lubrication and other genital responses are controlled by spinal mechanisms similar to those which regulate erection and ejaculation in men. However, as will be seen in chapter 16, spinally injured women are much more likely to be fertile than comparably injured men.

The Brain

The role of the brain in sexuality is much more complex—and less completely understood—than that of the spinal cord. It appears that sexual behavior is influenced by a large number of areas of the brain which interact with one another. In other words, it is more accurate to describe neural control of sexuality as depending upon a net of subsystems rather than upon a single "sex center" (Beach 1977).

The *hypothalamus* is one neural area with an important role in sexual behavior. The hypothalamus communicates directly with the *anterior pituitary*, a gland within the brain that secretes several hormones basic to sexual responses. To be more specific, the hypothalamus is linked with the anterior pituitary via a special vascular system; large quantities of blood carry chemical messages between these two structures.

A second function of the hypothalamus appears to be relatively independent of the anterior pituitary. Electrical stimulation of certain areas of the hypothalamus results in immediate superpotency. Male rats receiving such stimulation have constant erections and up to forty-five ejaculations over a four-hour period, surpassing considerably any normal performance. When the current is turned off, the sexual responses

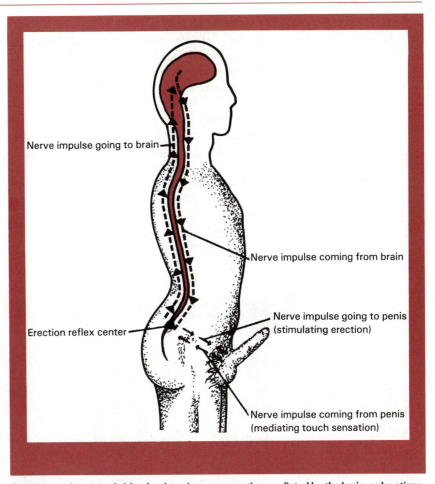

Nerve impulse going to brain

Nerve impulse coming from brain

Nerve impulse going to penis (stimulating erection)

Erection reflex center

Nerve impulse coming from penis (mediating touch sensation)

FIGURE 4.1

Erection.

Erection can be caused either by thoughts or perception mediated by the brain, or by stimulation of sensory receptors in the penis. In either case, neural impulses are sent to the erection reflex center in the spinal cord. With adequate stimulation, neural impulses are sent to the walls of the blood vessels of the penis, inducing an erection. Arrows going toward the spinal cord indicate incoming neural messages. Arrows going away indicate outgoing messages.

immediately cease (Vaughn & Fisher 1962). In rats—and probably humans as well—the hypothalamus is apparently involved in sexual motivation.

Other areas involved in sexuality include the *amygdala* of the limbic system (see figure 4.2).[1] The amygdala seems to function as an inhibitory center, as illustrated by an experimental study involving male cats. Researchers destroyed the amygdala of a group of these animals, and as soon as they were turned into a cage together, they all mounted one another. In fact, they were so uninhibited that they formed a slowly moving line of tomcats, each mounting the one ahead of him (Schreiner & Kling 1953).

Apparently, in normal animals (including humans), there is some kind of balance between the sexual motivation provided by the hypothalamus and the inhibition associated with the amygdala and other limbic structures. The common result is sexual expression with some restraints. However, when restraints are removed, dramatic changes in behavior have been known to occur. A case has been reported in which a young woman received a blow on the head—and presumable damage to the amygdala—as the result of a cable car accident. Following this, she developed an uncontrollable sexual urge which led to sexual intercourse with over 100 men in a short period of time. In addition, she lost several jobs because of her extremely strong sex drive. A court of law was convinced of the role of the brain damage in her change of behavior, and she was awarded a large monetary settlement in a suit against the cable car company (Tollison & Adams 1979).

The *cerebral cortex* of the brain is also involved in sexuality; destruc-

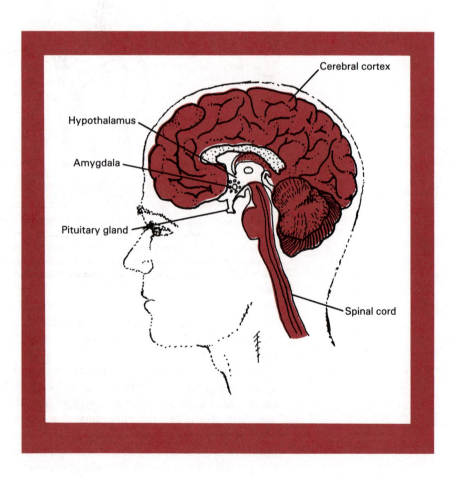

FIGURE 4.2
The brain.

tion of the cortex has been found to disrupt the organization and integration of sexual behaviors in a variety of mammals (see Whalen 1976). Part of this disruption appears to be associated with damage to sensory and motor systems located in the cortex. However, in humans, a change in sexual behavior following cortical damage is also related to losses of such higher-order functions as language, reasoning, and ideation.

Comparative and Evolutionary Perspective: The Development of the Human Brain

Generally speaking, higher animals have more individual nerves in their nervous systems and a greater complexity of interaction between nerves. In humans, neural complexity has reached its apex; it is estimated that there are 100 billion nerve cells and more than a quadrillion connections, or synapses, among these cells.

There is a clear-cut relationship between the complexity of the cortex and the variability of behavior—including sexual behavior. For example, rats have a primitive cortex, and little variation in sexual behavior; cats have a fairly well-developed cortex and more variability; and humans, with their highly developed cortex, exhibit the greatest complexity and variability of sexual behavior (Maier & Maier 1970).

Apparently, the more complex the cortex, the more sexual behavior depends on it. Rats are affected less than cats by damage to the cortex, and cats are affected less than monkeys or humans (Beach 1947). This relationship can best be understood as an analogy to a cash investment. Rats, with a poorly developed cortex, have invested little and, therefore, have little to lose if the cortex is damaged. On the other hand, humans have a large "investment," and cortical damage proves disastrous.

Fossil evidence suggests that, as humans developed from a primitive, apelike state, the cortex evolved relatively rapidly. The major survival advantage associated with a well-developed cortex was, of course, intelligence. Intelligence was particularly important because language and the use of tools were beginning to evolve at this time. It appears that the high degrees of complexity and variability of sexual behavior were a kind of by-product of cortical and intellectual development. To be more specific, as the cortex developed, humans became more and more sensitive to experience and were able to integrate information in complex ways. Correspondingly, sexual behavior became more and more open to modification as the result of experience—both cultural and individual.

THE HORMONAL SYSTEM

Hormones are chemical substances that are secreted in one part of the body and have their effects in a different part. Many hormones involved in sex and reproduction are secreted by endocrine glands located in various parts of the body. Endocrine glands are highly vascularized (have a rich blood supply) so that their hormones can quickly enter the bloodstream.

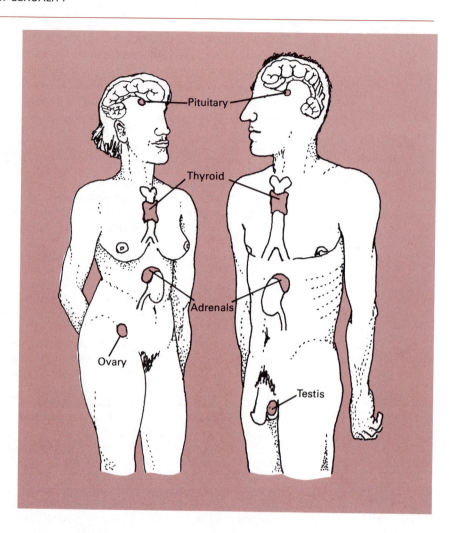

FIGURE 4.3

The location of major endocrine glands.

Hormones do not stimulate all parts of the body; they affect only certain tissues or organs, referred to as targets. The hormones exert their influence in a variety of ways. First, they may facilitate or inhibit the growth of tissues (including structures within the sexual and reproductive organs); such effects are most pronounced at the time of early embryonic development, and, much later, at the time of puberty. For example, the sex hormones are important in the development of mature, fully functional sex organs and the appearance of such secondary sex characteristics as beard growth in men and breast development in women.

A second general effect of hormones is to facilitate or inhibit the secretion of other hormones. This allows for the coordination of a variety of hormonal effects. The anterior pituitary gland secretes two hormones—

luteinizing hormone, or *LH,* and *follicle-stimulating hormone,* or *FSH*—which are known as *gonadotrophins.* (*Gonadotrophin* literally means "nourishing the gonads)''. The gonadotrophins cause the gonads to secrete their own hormones. However, gonadotrophins are not released in significant amounts until puberty. The pineal gland—a pea-sized organ that lies within the brain—regulates the timing of sexual maturity in certain animals and may do so in humans as well. For whatever reason, the anterior pituitary begins releasing gonadotrophic hormones at the appropriate age, the gonads, in turn, begin to secrete primarily androgens or estrogens, and the person then begins to develop adult sexual characteristics. The interaction between hormones and the glands that secrete them allows for a regulation of hormone levels in the blood via a feedback system. This system, which functions somewhat like a thermostat, is illustrated by the relationship between a gonadotrophic hormone—LH—and androgen secretion in the male. When androgen levels are low, the hypothalamus senses this condition and sends a chemical message to the anterior pituitary calling for more LH. Increased LH production stimulates the secretion of more androgen. The hypothalamus senses the increase in androgen and signals the anterior pituitary to secrete less LH. This system allows the male to compensate for the loss of a testis; after such a loss occurs, the output of the other testis doubles, and the androgen level in the blood returns to normal.

Conversely, injecting androgen into a normal male does not ultimately increase the sex-hormone level, since injected androgen results in reduced gonadotrophin output and lessening of androgen secretion by the testes. As a matter of fact, if androgen injections are continued, the testes will atrophy and completely cease secreting hormones (Bermant & Davidson 1974).

A third effect of hormones is to modify responses in various parts of the brain. For example, sex hormones may influence the cerebral cortex, modifying thoughts and perceptions. Sex hormones may also affect emotions via their influence on the brain and spinal cord (Broverman et al. 1980).

On the other hand, sexual behavior (or the anticipation of sexual behavior) can also affect sex-hormone output. A rather unusual type of study illustrates this relationship. A scientist (who has requested to remain anonymous) established a definite weekly pattern of activity; during the week he lived in relative isolation, but he consistently had sexual intercourse with a woman on weekends. Every day he measured the growth of his beard (beard growth is roughly correlated with the androgen level in the blood). He found that his beard growth—and presumably his androgen level—was lowest at the beginning of the week but peaked on the day before sexual relations usually began. Apparently, a pattern had been set in which the hormone level became adjusted to his sexual habits.

The Menstrual Cycle

In men, the hormonal balance is relatively stable over a period of several months or years. However, women show a complex cycle of hormonal activity that is known as the menstrual cycle. This cycle is approximately twenty-eight days in length but may vary, under perfectly normal conditions, from twenty-five to thirty-eight days. There are four phases to the menstrual cycle; each is associated with a particular hormonal balance.

The first phase—which is known as the *follicular phase*—is characterized by relatively high concentrations of one of the gonadotrophic hormones: FSH (follicle-stimulating hormone). As its name implies, FSH stimulates the growth of follicles in the ovaries and the maturation of eggs contained within the follicles. Specifically, several follicles begin to develop and bring the eggs to maturity. Ordinarily, however, only one egg develops to full maturity and is ovulated. Meanwhile, gonadotrophic hormones stimulate the ovaries to secrete estrogen. The estrogen brings about the growth of the endometrium of the uterus. This structure, by midcycle, is thick and has glands that will later secrete nourishing substances associated with pregnancy—if pregnancy indeed occurs.

The second phase of the menstrual cycle is known as *ovulation*: the release of the egg from its follicle. The gonadotrophic hormone LH, or luteinizing hormone, is responsible for ovulation. In some mammals—such as cats—LH secretion and subsequent ovulation result from vaginal stimulation during copulation. However, in most mammals—including humans—the LH surge necessary for ovulation results from increasing levels of estrogen. Although most women are not aware of any sensation associated with ovulation, some women can feel themselves ovulate; this sensation is known as *Mittelschmerz* (literally, "middle pain"). The feeling—which lasts about a day—is one of cramping in the lower abdomen and may be quite painful. (However, knowing when ovulation occurs has its advantages for women who are either trying to become pregnant or trying to avoid pregnancy.)

The third phase—the *luteal*, or *postovulatory*, *phase*—is dominated by the hormone *progesterone*. Progesterone is secreted by the follicle after it has released its egg. At this stage, the follicle has turned into a yellow glandular mass of cells; because of its yellow appearance, it is called the *corpus luteum*. (In Latin, *corpus* means "body" and *luteum* means "yellow.") A major function of progesterone is to induce the endometrium of the uterus to start secreting protein-rich substances which, if the woman is pregnant, will nourish a fertilized egg.

If fertilization does not occur, the woman enters the fourth phase—*menstruation*. Since the corpus luteum has started to degenerate near the end of the third phase (and an intact structure is necessary to maintain high progesterone levels), the progesterone level is low. For reasons that will become apparent later, the estrogen level is also low. These low hormone levels mean that the uterine lining cannot be maintained; con-

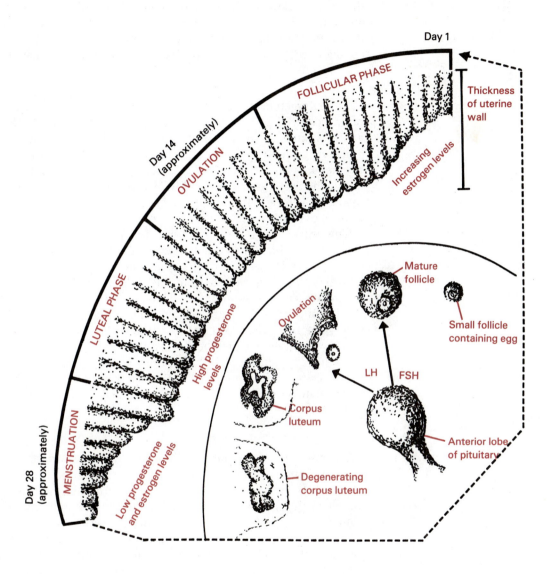

FIGURE 4.4

The phases of the menstrual cycle.

Note that rising FSH levels are associated with development of the follicle; high estrogen levels with increasing thickness of the uterine wall; high LH and estrogen levels with ovulation; high progesterone levels with the luteal phase (preparation for possible pregnancy); and low progesterone and estrogen levels with sloughing of the endometrium (menstruation).

sequently, it is shed, making up part of the menstrual flow. Specifically, the menstrual flow consists of blood from the endometrium, dead cells, and mucus from the cervix and vagina; the total volume of menstrual flow is typically between four and sixteen tablespoons. The low levels of estrogen trigger an increase in FSH, and the cycle is repeated.

Hormones and The Pill

The interactive effect of hormones is rather clearly seen in an analysis of *oral contraceptives* (often referred to collectively as *The Pill*). Virtually all brands of The Pill contain some combination of synthetic estrogen and synthetic progesterone. Estrogen inhibits secretion of FSH. In a normal menstrual cycle, FSH is secreted during and following menstruation when estrogen levels are low. However, the estrogen from The Pill lowers FSH levels and thereby blocks follicle development and the maturation of eggs.

The progesterone in The Pill prevents pregnancy in a different fashion. Progesterone inhibits the secretion of LH. In a normal menstrual cycle, LH secretion begins in midcycle, when progesterone levels are low. However, the progesterone from The Pill reduces LH levels to the point where ovulation is not induced. Thus, even if an egg happens to escape the inhibiting effect of estrogen and reaches maturity, the ovulation necessary before fertilization can take place is blocked by the progesterone.

After twenty-one days, the woman does not take The Pill for a period of seven days (or takes pills that do not have any hormones in them). As a result, estrogen and progesterone levels drop, and menstruation takes place (Hatcher et al. 1976). The Pill will be discussed in more detail in chapter 12.

Painful Menstruation

The amount and frequency of menstrual discomfort varies from one woman to another and also from one menstrual period to another. There appear to be two general categories of painful menstruation. The first, known as the *spasmodic* type, consists of cramps, pain in the lower abdomen, and sometimes nausea; generally, these symptoms disappear after the first pregnancy and childbirth. The second category, referred to as the *congestive* type of painful menstruation, includes a variety of symptoms such as a dull aching in the abdomen, headaches, breast pains, and lethargy. There is also increased water retention. As opposed to the first type of menstrual problem, the congestive type usually continues until menopause and may become more severe after each pregnancy. This increase in severity is related to an increase in vasocongestive capability which follows pregnancy (Dalton 1969).

The exact causes of painful menstruation are not known, but there is some evidence that hormonal shifts (and possibly hormonal imbalances) are involved; treatment with progesterone has produced some success in alleviating both types of symptoms (Dalton 1969). Another possibility is that cramping is related to general muscular conditioning. Menstruation causes certain muscles in the uterus to contract rather strongly. If these muscles are out of condition, sudden contractions can result in discomfort. At any rate, exercise and staying in good physical shape seem to be important in reducing the unpleasant effects of menstruation.

Painful menstruation is a good example of an interaction between psychological and physical factors. If a girl learns at a young age that menstruation causes severe pain, she is likely to experience more discomfort than if she learns to approach menstruation more positively. On the other hand, certain drugs have been successful in reducing menstrual pain, demonstrating that the discomfort also has a physical side. Among the drugs found to be successful are aspirin, some muscle relaxants, and certain anti-inflammatory drugs such as Motrin.

One of the major effects of Motrin is to inhibit the production of prostaglandins—chemical substances that induce contractions of uterine muscles and are also important in labor. An excess of prostaglandins commonly leads to the spasmodic type of menstrual pain. In this case, Motrin may bring relief. However, a small percentage of women experience unpleasant side effects—such as nausea and heartburn—from this drug.

Other types of treatments not involving the use of drugs have also met with success. The use of B complex vitamins, reduction of salt intake, a decrease in carbohydrate consumption, and chiropractic adjustment have all been recommended and found helpful to certain women. In some cases, women report that orgasm—stimulated by either masturbation or sexual intercourse—brings about relief of painful menstruation, especially the congestive type. It seems to work best if the woman expects it to work. Masters and Johnson (1966) have suggested that at least part of this relief is related to a sudden clearing of menstrual fluid from the uterus and a relaxation of uterine muscles that follows orgasm.

Anthropological Perspective: Reactions to Menstruation

In some societies, menstruation is viewed as perfectly natural. It leads to little or no change in a woman's daily routine and does not preclude intercourse. However, many cultures do place restrictions on menstruating women. Some simply prohibit intercourse at this time, but in other cases restrictions are more severe. Women may be prevented from eating certain foods or from dancing; they may also be placed in isolation from other members of the community, especially men.

Intercourse with menstruating women has been blamed for various types of problems in men, including headaches (Mataco of South America), cowardliness in battle (Thonga of East Africa), and virulent illness (Tswana of South Africa). In the Ila society of South Africa, even eating in the presence of a men-

FIGURE 4.5

In certain cultures, restrictions are placed on women during menstruation. This sign appears in Bali, an island which is part of Indonesia.

struating woman was thought to lead to impotence (Ford & Beach 1951). Taking many societies into consideration, more male than female problems have been attributed to menstruation. However, since men are traditionally in positions of power in most societies, masculine concerns are more likely to be reflected in the society's attitudes.

In the United States, there is considerable variation in the feelings about menstruation. Some individuals refer to menstruation as "the curse" or "being unclean." Orthodox Jews abstain from intercourse during the menstrual period and for seven days afterward. At the end of this time, a woman must go through a ritual, cleansing bath before resuming sexual relations.

In contrast, approximately half the individuals surveyed in one study had experienced sexual relations at least once when the woman was menstruating (Paige 1973). Some women report that coitus is more satisfying during this period than during other times of the menstrual cycle, perhaps, in part, because sexual relations help to relieve menstrual cramping.

Medical Perspective: Toxic Shock Syndrome

In 1980, it was discovered that a rare disease—toxic shock syndrome (TSS)—was linked to the use of certain types of tampons during menstruation. The symptoms of the disease are high fever, vomiting, diarrhea, and rapid drop in blood pressure. In some cases, the disease has been fatal (Price 1981). Subsequent to this discovery, the brand of tampons most closely linked with the disease—Rely—was taken off the market.

Recent studies suggest that tampons contribute to the development of TSS by providing a favorable environment for the growth and proliferation of *Staphylococcus aureus,* the bacterium causing the disease. It is also possible that the tampons damage the vaginal lining and make it easier for an infection to get started.

The Center for Disease Control (1980) suggests that women can reduce the risk of TSS by not using tampons or by using them only intermittently during each menstrual period (for example, during the day but not at night). If a woman prefers continuous use of tampons during the menstrual period, she should be aware of TSS symptoms and be prepared to notify a physician immediately if they appear.

Mood Changes and Hormones

Considerable evidence suggests that hormone levels are related to moods or emotional states as well as biological changes in the body. In women, a negative feeling, which is sometimes called *premenstrual tension,* may build up three or four days before menstruation and continue until shortly beyond the start of the menstrual flow. Premenstrual tension is characterized by anxiety, depression, fatigue, and/or low self-esteem. In some cases, more severe emotional reactions may occur. Women are more likely to abuse alcohol or drugs or to commit crimes of violence or even suicide during the premenstrual period than at other times (Ivey & Bardwick 1968, Dalton 1979).

Since premenstrual tension occurs when estrogen and progesterone levels are at their lowest, a relative lack of these hormones has been implicated in these mood changes. Independent support for the role of estrogen and progesterone comes from a study in which the hormone levels of women were experimentally manipulated by administering the hormones orally. One group of women took The Pill for twenty-eight days—and consequently had a high level of estrogen and progesterone throughout the period. Generally, their moods did not fluctuate. However, other women were given drugs that caused their balance of estrogen and progesterone to shift as it would during a normal cycle but at a higher level. These women experienced shifts in moods that corresponded to those found in women during a normal cycle (Paige 1971).

That hormones influence moods is also indicated by a study of women who had their ovaries removed for medical reasons and subsequently experienced a reduction in estrogen levels. In many cases, these women suffered a loss of energy and felt depressed. With estrogen replacement therapy, these women generally regained their energy and good spirits (Bardwick 1971). However, as we will see in chapter 16, there are certain dangers associated with estrogen replacement therapy.

Although males' sex-hormone level does not fluctuate as dramatically as that of females, there is evidence of small monthly changes in androgen levels. Furthermore, these changes have been correlated with certain mood shifts. In an extensive Danish study (cited in Janda & Klenke-Hamel 1980), androgen level was measured from urine samples and mood sampled by standardized psychological tests at the same time. Periods marked by high androgen levels were associated with high energy levels and a sense of well-being; conversely, low androgen levels were significantly correlated with apathy and a tendency to magnify small problems.

Clearly, as suggested in chapter 2, the correlational evidence presented in these studies does not prove beyond all doubt that hormones influence moods. For example, the men may have felt better with high androgen levels because they were sexually aroused more easily. Similarly, certain women may have learned to dread the arrival of the menstrual period and its associated discomforts. Some support for the theory that certain mood fluctuations are learned comes from a study of religious differences in reactions to the menstrual cycle. Roman Catholic women reported significantly more fluctuation in anxiety level during the course of the menstrual cycle than Protestant women did. Since it can be assumed that the two groups had comparable hormonal cycles, it seems that social learning was a major factor in the differences in mood fluctuation (Paige 1973).

Another study implicating the importance of social learning involved a comparison of the moods of husbands and wives over a period of time. Mood changes were highly correlated, suggesting that interaction between the spouses was the major factor in determining how the people felt (Dan 1976).

Author's Perspective: Hormones, Mood, and Communication

Although there is definite evidence that hormones affect mood, it appears that social learning is even more important in determining how a person feels (Brooks-Gunn & Ruble 1980). Most women have learned to compensate for hormone levels that are not optimal. For example, a study of the academic performance of college women indicates that competency does *not* fluctuate with the menstrual cycle (Bernstein 1977).

Unfortunately, some women have been discriminated against because people assumed that females' moods fluctuate too much for them to be successful in highly responsible positions. However, this assumption is more a reflection of society's attempt to "keep women in their place" than it is a legitimate analysis of the relationship between hormones and mood.

Of course, women differ considerably in the mood fluctuation they experience. Some women have learned to avoid dealing with emotional issues at certain times during their menstrual cycles, if possible. A young couple I worked with in a marriage counseling setting became aware that they had most of their fights just before the woman menstruated. The man did not realize that his wife experienced discomfort at this time, and the woman felt uncomfortable discussing matters related to menstruation with him. However, once they identified the potential problem and decided to avoid controversial issues at this "critical" time, they fought less and reported a more satisfying relationship.

It should be added that the improvement in their relationship was due to more than just avoiding controversy at a particular time; discussing feelings—and developing a sensitivity to them—seemed to play a large role. It would probably be equally beneficial to develop sensitivity to work-related anxieties and irritabilities in a spouse. Unfortunately, many people have a tendency to avoid discussing matters related to sexual processes such as menstruation. As we shall see again in later chapters, this avoidance can often lead to problems in a relationship.

A Comparison of Male and Female Hormonal Systems

In this chapter considerably more space has been given to female hormonal systems than to those of males. This reflects a basic sex difference: female hormonal systems are more complex and show a wide, monthly fluctuation. Furthermore, females ovulate and menstruate—processes which have no counterpart in males.

There are, however, several similarities between females and males in regard to hormonal systems. Both secrete gonadotrophic hormones which influence the output of sex hormones. In addition, the gonadotrophic hormone FSH is instrumental in the development of the gametes (eggs in females and sperm in males). Specifically, FSH stimulates the growth of the egg-containing follicles of women and the production of sperm in men. Furthermore, in both sexes, LH is involved in the full maturation and release of the gametes.

In some respects, the effects of the female and male sex hormones are comparable. Estrogen is necessary for the maturation of the female sexual system at puberty, while androgen is necessary for comparable maturation in males. Nonetheless, as illustrated in the next chapter, there are some instances when estrogen and androgen have very different types of effects.

SUMMARY

The spinal cord regulates the most basic aspects of sexuality, such as penile erection and, most probably, vaginal lubrication. This spinal reflex is influenced by neural messages coming from the brain. In contrast, higher sexual functions are regulated entirely by the brain. For example, two subcortical brain centers are involved in sexual motivation. The hypothalamus facilitates sexual motivation, while the amygdala inhibits it. The cerebral cortex is associated with the most complex aspects of sexuality. It also seems to affect the organization and integration of sexual behaviors.

Hormones influence sexuality by (1) facilitating or inhibiting the growth of bodily tissues; (2) influencing the secretion of other hormones; (3) stimulating the brain and, consequently, influencing thoughts and emotions.

The menstrual cycle in women is under complex hormonal control. The cycle occurs in four phases: the follicular phase, ovulation, the postovulatory phase, and menstruation. These phases are regulated by the interaction of four hormones: FSH, LH, estrogen, and progesterone.

Pain experienced by women during menstruation varies greatly. There are, essentially, two types of painful menstruation: the spasmodic type, characterized by cramps, and the congestive type, which features dull, aching pain and irritability. Recently, toxic shock syndrome has been linked to the use of certain types of tampons during menstruation. Presumably, the tampons provide a favorable environment for the disease-causing bacterium.

NOTES

1. The components of the limbic system are arranged like two rings surrounding the brain stem—one in each cerebral hemisphere. (The brain stem is a continuation of the spinal cord.) Several limbic system structures, and other structures nearby, are apparently related to sexuality, but the amygdala seems to be particularly important. For a general discussion of the limbic system and sexuality, see Beach (1977).

CHAPTER 5

The Sexual Response Cycle

As we have seen—and will continue to see throughout the book—there are tremendous differences in how different people experience sexual activity psychologically. However, a given individual's physiological responses during the sexual cycle remain remarkably uniform, whether a person is stimulated to orgasm by fantasy, masturbation, sexual intercourse, or oral-genital sex. There are also strong similarities in physiological response among individuals of the same sex. Perhaps the most surprising finding is that, despite the obvious differences in anatomy, the sexual response cycles of males and females are alike in many respects.

Masters and Johnson (1966) divided the human sexual response cycle into four phases—excitement, plateau, orgasm, and resolution. (Although other classification systems have been proposed, theirs is the one that is most widely accepted.) The phases are not separate or distinct; they flow from one to another in a continuous fashion and are sometimes difficult to delineate. For clarity of presentation, the female and male sexual cycles will be discussed separately. Then, a comparison will be made between the sexes.

THE FEMALE SEXUAL RESPONSE

Before considering the physiological aspects of the sexual response cycle, it should be remembered that there is a danger of overanalysis at a personal level. There are examples of people who have concentrated so much on the internal physiology of sexuality that spontaneity has been inhibited and sexual pleasure reduced. Other persons have developed anxieties about being abnormal in some respect. However, if one keeps in mind that there are individual differences in sexual responses—and that there is no "correct" or "incorrect" response—an awareness of what is going on may be liberating and can enhance sexual satisfaction.

Excitement

Effective sexual stimulation produces various physiological responses in women. Heart rate, blood pressure, and breathing rate all increase. In addition, sexual excitement leads to vasocongestion and myotonia. *Vasocongestion* refers to an engorgement of blood vessels in tissues of the body associated with sexual excitation. Normally, the arterial flow of blood into organs and tissues is balanced by an outflow in the veins. However, during the excitement phase, the dilation of the arteries in sexual areas is so great that the draining capacity of the veins becomes overloaded. The vasocongested areas appear swollen and red because of the increased blood supply, and they may feel unusually warm.

The other basic response—*myotonia*—is defined as increased muscular tension. During sexual arousal, myotonia appears in both voluntary and involuntary muscles; it may be observed in such responses as facial grimaces as well as increased hardness of certain muscles.

In many women, vasocongestion in the breasts increases their size by about 25 percent. At the same time, the nipples become erect, and the dark area around the nipples swells considerably. The amount of in-

FIGURE 5.1

People traditionally conceptualize sexuality in men and women as being quite different. However, research indicates there are several similarities in the male and female sexual response cycles.

crease in the size of the breasts depends to a certain extent on whether or not the woman has nursed babies; if more than one child has been breast-fed, there is usually no increase in size.

About 75 percent of the Masters and Johnson sample of women developed what is called a *sex flush*. This is a reddening of the skin which begins in the stomach region or the throat and spreads to the breasts. It typically becomes more intense as the level of sexual arousal increases.

The major physiological changes take place in the genitals, particularly the labia minora, clitoris, and vagina. As the woman reaches high levels of arousal, the labia minora increase two or three times in diameter (due to vasocongestion) and begin to move outward from the vagina. Next, the labia minora change color, from pale pink to deep pink or even dark red. Generally, the more brilliant the color, the more intense the woman's response.

The clitoris responds to sexual arousal by exhibiting vasocongestion and increasing in diameter, particularly in the glans. It responds most rapidly to direct stimulation. Fantasy or stimulation of other parts of the body such as the breasts causes some enlargement, but it is usually less pronounced.

The vagina shows a number of responses to sexual stimulation. There is the production of vaginal lubrication, which appears on the walls of the vagina within ten to thirty seconds of effective stimulation.[1] This secretion has two functions. First, it lubricates the vagina, allowing for easier penile penetration. (Without adequate lubrication, penetration is difficult and painful for both partners.) The second function is to promote the survival of the sperm. The secretion neutralizes the vagina's natural acidity, which would otherwise destroy the sperm.

As the excitement phase continues, the upper two-thirds of the vagina lengthens and balloons out. At first, the walls involuntarily expand and then partially contract, but shortly thereafter the vagina remains distended. This distention is apparently an adaptation for the reception of the penis. In a related move, the uterus assumes a more upright position (see figure 5.2).

The subjective reactions to these changes vary from woman to woman. Typically, there is a throbbing, congested sensation in the pelvic area accompanied by general, bodily nervousness. Adolescent women who are experiencing arousal for the first time sometimes have difficulty identifying the meaning of these sensations.

Plateau

There is not a clear-cut distinction between the excitement and plateau phases of the response cycle. In the plateau phase, most of the responses begun in the excitement phase simply reach a high level and remain there for a period of time. For example, heart rate, blood pressure, and breathing rate are maintained at a relatively high level. Myoto-

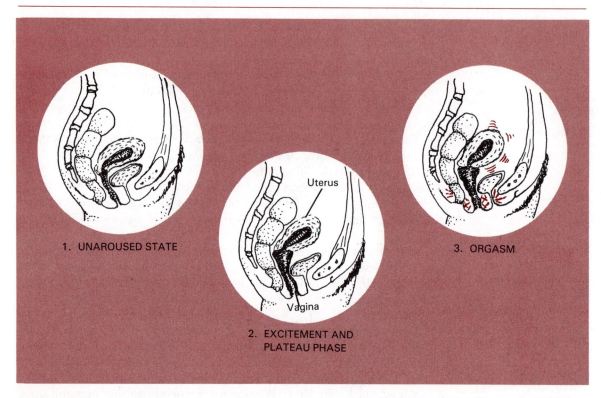

1. UNAROUSED STATE

Uterus

Vagina

2. EXCITEMENT AND
PLATEAU PHASE

3. ORGASM

Note the lengthening and ballooning of the vagina, the shift in the position of the uterus, and the build-up (followed by contractions) of the orgasmic platform.

FIGURE 5.2

Changes in the female sex organs and internal anatomy associated with phases of the sexual response cycle.

nia may be evidenced in extended neck cords and rigid muscles in the thighs and buttocks. In addition, some women make clawing and grasping movements.

The clitoris, however, rather clearly signals the end of the excitement phase and the beginning of the plateau with a response that is inconsistent with what is happening in the rest of the woman's body. It decreases in size and is retracted to a position under the clitoral hood, where it stays until after orgasm. Thus, the clitoris cannot receive direct stimulation during either plateau or orgasm.

In the outer third of the vagina, engorgement reduces the diameter of the opening by about 30 percent. Furthermore, the muscles encircling the vagina in this area contract, so that the vagina tightens around the penis during coitus. The vasocongested vaginal area and labia minora form what Masters and Johnson (1966) call the *orgasmic platform;* this area is the focus of contractions during orgasm.

Although the plateau phase is usually short in duration—lasting a few seconds to somewhat less than a minute—some women are able to prolong it for several minutes. To accomplish this, the woman or her partner may reduce stimulation just as the woman senses that orgasm is approaching. Generally, the prolonged plateau phase is reported to be very

FIGURE 5.3
The Phases of the Female Sexual Response Cycle

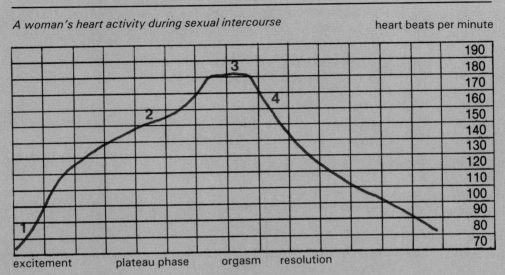

A woman's heart activity during sexual intercourse   heart beats per minute

excitement   plateau phase   orgasm   resolution

1. The heart rate quickens steadily at first   3. A high peak is reached at orgasm
2. The rise is gradual through the plateau phase   4. The fall during resolution is immediate

Female responses during sexual intercourse

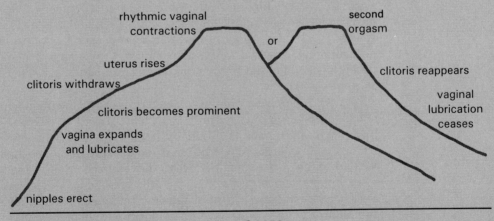

SOURCE: Erwin J. Haeberle, *The Sex Atlas,* © 1978.
Reprinted by permission of Seabury Press.

enjoyable and is usually followed by a relatively intense orgasm (Crooks
& Baur 1980).[2]

Orgasm   Climax, or orgasm, consists of specific sensations, a set of overt, observable responses, and specific physiological changes. As the sensa-
tion of orgasm begins, the orgasmic platform starts to contract and ex-

pand repeatedly. Typically, there are between three and fifteen contractions, at intervals beginning at about 0.8 seconds and then slowing down. The last few contractions tend to be less intense.

The uterus also has contractions, which are similar to those that occur in the early part of labor. They generally begin at the top of the uterus and move down the cervix. There is evidence that a woman's orgasm increases the possibility of pregnancy because the movement of sperm is facilitated by uterine contractions and the upright position of the uterus (C. A. Fox 1977).

During orgasm, the heart rate, blood pressure, and breathing rate reach their highest levels. The breathing rate in particular is a good indication of the level of arousal: the faster the rate, the more intense the orgasmic response. Masters and Johnson (1966) found that, for many women, clitorally stimulated orgasms without intercourse were more intense than orgasms accompanying intercourse.

Recently, research has indicated that some women experience a different type of orgasm—one without substantial contractions of the P-C muscle that surrounds the vagina. There is a small area in the vagina— known as the *Grafenberg spot*—that may be stimulated by deep penile thrusts during coitus.[3] When the spot is first stimulated, a woman experiences a need to urinate. However, this feeling is quickly followed by sexual arousal and pleasurable sensations. At the same time, the area becomes firm and hard, apparently due to vasocongestion.

Continued stimulation of the Grafenberg spot typically leads to orgasm and, in some women, the ejaculation of a fluid through the urethra. At first, this fluid was assumed to be urine. However, laboratory analysis indicates that, chemically, it is very similar to the semen of men. At this time, the origin of the fluid is unknown (Addiego et al. 1981, Perry & Whipple 1981).

Why has the presence of the Grafenberg spot and the phenomenon of female ejaculation only recently been scientifically confirmed? In the first place, physicians traditionally have investigated the vaginas of women in an unaroused condition, when the spot cannot be identified. Second, since the fluid emitted was assumed to be urine, many women were probably embarrassed to discuss the presence of wet spots following sexual intercourse. Third, it appears that female ejaculation is more common in women who have liberal attitudes about sexuality; in the past, sexual inhibitions may have made this event much more rare. Finally, women with strong P-C muscles are most likely to ejaculate; the recent increase in the number of women doing Kegel exercises (discussed on p. 50) may be a factor of significance (Belzer 1981; Perry & Whipple 1981).

After reading the previous paragraphs, one might naturally assume that women experience either a clitoral or a vaginally stimulated orgasm. However, it seems likely that, in many cases, women experience a combination of the two. Such a conclusion was proposed by Singer and

Singer (1972) even before the identification of the Grafenberg spot. At any rate, the reported sensations of orgasm vary greatly. In some cases, a wave of sensual pleasure begins in the clitoral area and radiates throughout the lower abdomen. The woman usually feels that the surrounding environment is unimportant. Next comes an extremely enjoyable, rapid release of tension—followed by a very pleasant serenity. The build-up and sudden release of tension are described in the following quotations, reprinted with permission from Hite (1976):

> Before, I feel a tremendous surge of tension and a kind of delicious feeling I can't describe. Then, orgasm is like the excitement and stimulation I have been feeling, increased, for an *instant*, a hundred-fold.

> It feels like a balloon in the abdomen filling up and then exploding rapidly through my body.

Behaviorally, orgasm may be accompanied by moans or rhythmic vocalizations. The whole body tends to become rigid, with the legs and feet extended and the arms making grasping movements. Often, the neck is stiffened and the face takes on a grimace. In some respects, the woman does not look as if she is enjoying herself (something that may be confusing to children if they happen to observe adults having intercourse).

Theoretical Perspective: Freud and Women's Orgasms

Freud was probably the first writer to make a distinction between vaginal and clitoral orgasms. He thought that the clitoral one was immature and associated with masturbation, while the vaginal type represented a more mature kind of sexuality, brought about by stimulation of the vagina during intercourse. This distinction was consistent with his general position that female sexuality was somewhat inferior to that of males. Freud also hypothesized women had *penis envy* as the result of a biological "deficiency." Feelings of jealousy and inferiority, which could never be completely resolved, presumably sprang from this complex. Finally, Freud believed that, as recipients of the male phallus, women were necessarily passive.

Considerably later, Masters and Johnson (1966) concluded that sexual intercourse stimulates the clitoris indirectly: the movement of the penis in and out of the vagina puts pressure on the clitoral hood, which, in turn, stimulates the clitoris. They argued that there was only one type of orgasm. The recent research on the Grafenberg spot suggests that Freud may have been right in regard to the two types of female orgasm. However, the concepts of biological deficiency and female passivity are without support. In the meantime, over a period of years, the Freudian concepts have encouraged a condescending attitude toward women, especially in traditional psychoanalysis.

In retrospect, although Freud's theories promoted discrimination against women, Freud himself should not be viewed as an extraordinary male chauvinist; he simply reflected the attitude of his time. Unfortunately, as we shall see in several examples throughout this book, scientific theories are often influenced by the predominant social attitudes of the day.

Author's Perspective: Feigning Orgasms

Many women have reported that, at one time or another, they have merely pretended to have an orgasm. Their reasons for doing so included a desire to end an unsatisfying sex act, cover up orgasmic problems, or give satisfaction to a partner who valued inducing orgasm (Rosenbaum 1970). Men may also fake orgasms. Since women cannot usually feel semen entering the vagina, women may be deceived as easily as men. Males probably feign orgasm most often because of a fear that they will not be able to ejaculate (Zilbergeld 1978).

Faking orgasm may have some temporary benefits, but it also has long-term disadvantages. Like any other deception, it threatens an open, honest relationship. It allows people to avoid facing difficulties in their sexual interaction, which may only become more difficult to handle later. Thus, although occasional faking may not cause much harm, a pattern of deception may lead to problems.

Resolution

After orgasm, there is a slow return to unaroused conditions. The last responses to occur are the first to cease. In the vagina, the orgasmic platform disappears first, next the vaginal canal returns to normal size, and finally vaginal secretion ceases. Elsewhere in the body, nipple erection is lost, next muscular tension vanishes, and finally heart rate, blood pressure, and respiration return to normal. Some women develop a thin coat of perspiration as the sex flush dissipates; there may also be heavy perspiration on certain parts of the body, such as the forehead and underarms. The amount of perspiration generally reflects the intensity of the orgasm.

A few seconds after orgasm, the clitoris reemerges from under its hood and, somewhat later, its swelling subsides. If the woman has not had an orgasm, tumescence of the clitoris may persist for a period of time, creating an uncomfortable feeling. As suggested earlier, prostitutes frequently experience abdominal discomfort as the result of frequent sexual arousal that is not followed by orgasm.

Certain changes associated with the resolution phase take place more slowly in women who have had children than in those who have not. For example, it takes longer for the uterus to return to normal size and for the labia majora to lose their swelling in women who have given birth.

It is possible to return to the orgasmic phase from any point in the resolution phase; thus women can have *multiple orgasms* in a relatively short period. If the sexual stimulation that produced the first orgasm continues, it may lead to a second or third climax or, in some cases, more. Generally, the succeeding orgasms are perceived as more intense than the first. In 1953, Kinsey estimated that only 13 percent of all women experienced multiple orgasms; however, he believed that the percentage would be higher if more women received sufficient stimulation.

Women usually report feelings of serenity during the resolution phase. Some fall asleep. Generally, they experience a feeling of closeness and a need to be held and/or gently caressed by their partners.

THE MALE SEXUAL RESPONSE

Excitement

A readily apparent indication of sexual arousal in males is penile erection. Erection occurs as blood vessels in the penis dilate and the flow of blood is increased until the sinuses within the penis are filled. During a long excitement phase, a man may lose and regain an erection several times. Loss of erection may result from such physical events as sudden light or noise or such psychological variables as fear or anxiety (which may arise from the physical changes).

The fact that sexual arousal is more apparent in males than in females may help to explain the fact that men's verbal reports of sexual excitement correlate better with their physiological state than women's do. When men say that they are sexually excited, the plethysmograph measurement almost always confirms it. However, physiological measurements often indicate excitement in a woman who does not report feeling aroused (Heiman 1975). It seems likely that, since men can observe their erections, they learn to associate erection with excitement. Since women's arousal is not reflected in a clearly observable event, they may not learn to identify the physiological changes associated with sexual excitement.

Another physiological aspect of the excitement phase in males is the contraction of involuntary muscles associated with the scrotum, pulling the sac towards the body. In addition, there is an elevation of the testes. Still other responses—increase in muscular tension, heart rate, blood pressure, and breathing rate—are similar to those of females.

Plateau

As sexual tension approaches its zenith, the penis achieves its fullest erection. There is a slight increase in the diameter of the organ—primarily in the corona—and the coloration of the glans may deepen.

The testes reach their maximal elevation during the plateau phase. (One testis may react to stimulation by elevating before the other, but both are high in the scrotum and close to the body before ejaculation takes place.) The testes also increase in size—sometimes as much as 100 percent—due to a vasocongestive response within the organs.

The Cowper's glands secrete two or three droplets of fluid shortly before ejaculation. There are often some sperm in these droplets and so, as mentioned earlier, pregnancy can occur even if ejaculation does not take place in the vagina. However, since several sperm are required for penetration of the egg (see chapter 11), resulting pregnancy is unlikely.

Orgasm   Male orgasm is linked to ejaculation, although the two processes are not the same. There are a series of contractions occurring at 0.8-second intervals (the same interval found in females). These contractions involve the vas, seminal vesicles, and prostate, and they propel the ejaculate into the urethra. The sensation associated with this reaction has been called *ejaculatory inevitability* by Masters and Johnson; it is a feeling that ejaculation is coming and cannot be stopped. When the ejaculate reaches the urethra, a neural message is sent to the lumbar section of the spinal cord. In response, another neural message is sent from this "ejaculation center" to muscles within the internal organs of the sexual system.

A second series of rhythmic contractions—of the urethra and the penis—forces the semen out through the tip of the penis. After the first three or four expulsions of semen, the contractions continue, but with less force. One study identified a group of males who were able to volun-

FIGURE 5.4

Changes in the male sex organs and internal anatomy associated with phases of the sexual response cycle.

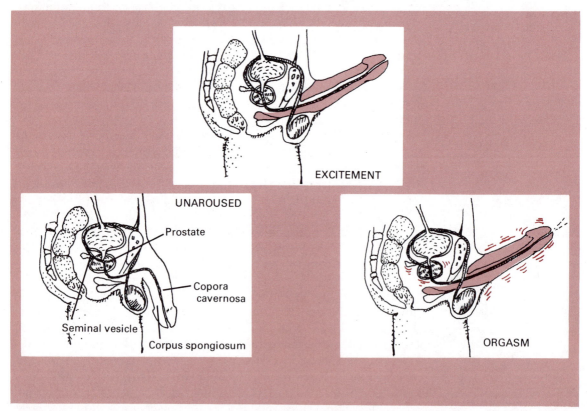

Note the blood in the corpora cavernosa and corpus spongiosum causing erection during the excitement phase. During orgasm, contractions of the vas, prostate, and seminal vesicle are followed by contractions of the penis and finally, ejaculation.

tarily stop their ejaculation while still experiencing orgasm. This relatively rare technique apparently involved learning to relax at the time of orgasmic inevitability. The men were then able to have second or third orgasms shortly after the first one (Robbins & Jensen 1977).

A man's other responses during orgasm are similar to those of women: a sudden rise in heart rate, blood pressure, and rate of breathing. There may also be muscle contractions in such places as the arms, thighs, and buttocks.

Comparative and Evolutionary Perspective: Orgasms in Animals

The adaptive value of male orgasm is rather clear: the pleasure and release of tension associated with ejaculation motivate a male to seek ejaculatory experiences and reproduce the species. And indeed, all male mammals studied show physiological and behavioral signs of orgasm. (The subjective aspects, of course, cannot be measured, since animals are unable to tell us how they feel.)

In female animals, the presence of a full-blown orgasmic response is much more difficult to identify. Some lower mammals do show evidence of sexual arousal and resolution in females. For example, female dogs exhibit a rise in blood pressure when the male achieves intromission and a drop in pressure when the penis is removed (Beach 1969). However, there are no sharp peaks comparable to those of human females when they report orgasm. It is only recently that a response comparable to human orgasm has been identified in an animal. In 1980, four Dutch scientists observed uterine contractions, heart-rate changes, and a distinctive facial expression during sexual activity in stump-tailed macaque monkeys (Goldfoot et al. 1980).

Female orgasm apparently occurs only in primates. Therefore, it must have evolved relatively late, much later than it did in males. This makes sense, since female orgasm is less closely related to survival of the species; nonorgasmic females may become pregnant.

Another observation may shed light on the evolution of orgasm. Monkeys normally copulate for a very short period of time. It seems that this brief period of stimulation is insufficient to induce a maximal response in females. Actually, the orgasmic response of the female monkeys in the study occurred when one female mounted another in homosexual fashion; this type of stimulation lasted longer than normal heterosexual stimulation. Another study—this time with rhesus monkeys—supports this interpretation. The females do not normally show much response during copulation. However, when restrained and stimulated for a relatively long time by artificial means, the monkeys exhibited an excitement phase and orgasmlike responses, such as contractions of the vagina and low-pitched grunting (Burton 1971). It may be concluded that male sexuality was important in the evolution of female orgasm. As males spent more time in sexual relations with females, responsiveness may have been heightened. Of course, as females became more responsive to males, this probably induced males to spend more time with their partners. Ultimately, then, the evolution of female orgasm most likely involved increased responsiveness of both males and females.

Author's Perspective: A Possible Overemphasis on Orgasm

Reports of multiple orgasms have typically been greeted with great interest by the general public; many people attempt to improve their sexual "performance" by having more and more orgasms. However, it is not at all clear that having several orgasms increases personal satisfaction or adds to the partner's enjoyment (Clifford 1978). Furthermore, an overemphasis on orgasm and setting high goals for sexual performance may lead to frustration and a feeling of inadequacy or failure.

Masters and Johnson (1966) suggest that overemphasis on orgasm and sexual goals may result from a generalization of the work ethic. Various work-related phrases are often applied to sexuality—"a job well done" and "using the tools of the trade" to name two. Even the phrase "achieving orgasm" implies that orgasm is a goal rather than a natural consequence of certain sexual experiences. Recent research in social psychology indicates that a substantial number of Americans have a strong belief in an equity principle—i.e., what one puts into something should be matched by a fair, measurable reward (Leventhal et al. 1980). For many of these people, this principle translates into "If I put a certain amount of time and energy into a relationship, I should receive a certain number of orgasms."

Perhaps the strong emphasis on orgasm in our society is also related to the high degree of emotional tension people experience, particularly in urban settings. With high tension, there is a premium on tension release, such as that experienced through orgasm. Philip Slater suggests that this need may be particularly great in men, who traditionally have been socialized to inhibit emotional expression. Slater believes that the strong desire many men have to induce explosive orgasm in women, particularly inhibited or resistant women, also reflects this need. Presumably, the sudden release of the woman's tension results in vicarious satisfaction for the man (Slater 1977).

Undoubtedly, people will continue to show interest in orgasms, especially multiple ones or those associated with the Grafenberg spot (which has only recently been "officially" recognized). As we shall see in chapter 21, there is also a legitimate concern for problems associated with orgasmic dysfunction. However, focusing too much on orgasm is likely to detract from two of the most important aspects of a sexual relationship: emotional warmth and intimacy. Furthermore, worrying about orgasm may actually increase the probability that orgasmic dysfunction will occur. It seems that a sensitivity to the partner's needs and what is occurring emotionally during the sexual interaction is more likely to produce a satisfying sexual relationship than a strong emphasis on orgasm.

Resolution

The final stage of the human male's sexual response cycle—resolution—is similar to that of the female. The body and its processes slowly return to the normal resting state. Even though a man may have multiple orgasms, a second ejaculation cannot occur shortly after the first: a *refractory period* takes place, during which the man is unresponsive to sexual stimulation. Second ejaculations—and even more—may be experienced, but only after a period of rest. (The length of the refractory period varies considerably from man to man and tends to increase with age.)

The return of the penis to its flaccid state occurs in two stages. The first stage involves a rapid, partial reduction in size to a state about 50 percent larger than the flaccid state. The second stage, which ultimately reduces the penis to its unstimulated state, lasts longer. Its exact duration depends upon the level of sexual stimulation. Some men are able to delay the onset of the second stage by continued intravaginal contact, which also provides continued stimulation of the woman.

The subjective reaction to the resolution phase is typically very relaxed and pleasant. Couples often enjoy engaging in expressions of warmth and tender affection during this quiet time. However, it is not unusual for one partner to become frustrated because the other abruptly leaves or turns over and falls asleep. It may be that the current emphasis on orgasm has led some people to believe that sexual interaction ends there. In contrast, other couples report that a satisfying sexual and emotional relationship does not have a well-marked beginning or end.

A COMPARISON OF MALE AND FEMALE SEXUAL RESPONSES

As already suggested, there are several similarities in the physiological responses of men and women, especially in nongenital areas: respiratory, circulatory, voluntary muscular, and perspiratory responses show similar patterns in the two sexes. Furthermore, both men and women demonstrate the sexual flush, although it develops more rapidly in women and is observed in a higher percentage of cases. Approximately 75 percent of the women in the Masters and Johnson sample developed the flush, compared with 25 percent of the men. Nipple erection was also much more consistent in women than in men. Perhaps most surprising is the recent finding that women sometimes show a response similar to ejaculation in men.

Involuntary muscle tension occurs in both sexes, but its effect on the genitals obviously differs. In women, certain muscle contractions result in expansion of the vagina; comparable contractions in men cause elevation of the testes. Similarly, both sexes experience tumescence of the genitals, but with different effects—the enlargement of the labia majora and clitoris or the erection of the penis and the swelling of the testes.

Both males and females report the sensation of orgasm to be very enjoyable. There are also similarities in the general description of orgasm given by men and women. For example, in one study, descriptions of the sensation of orgasm written by college students—with references to sexual anatomy deleted—were given to experts (medical students, gynecologists, and clinical psychologists). The experts could not identify the

FIGURE 5.5
The Phases of the Male Sexual Response Cycle

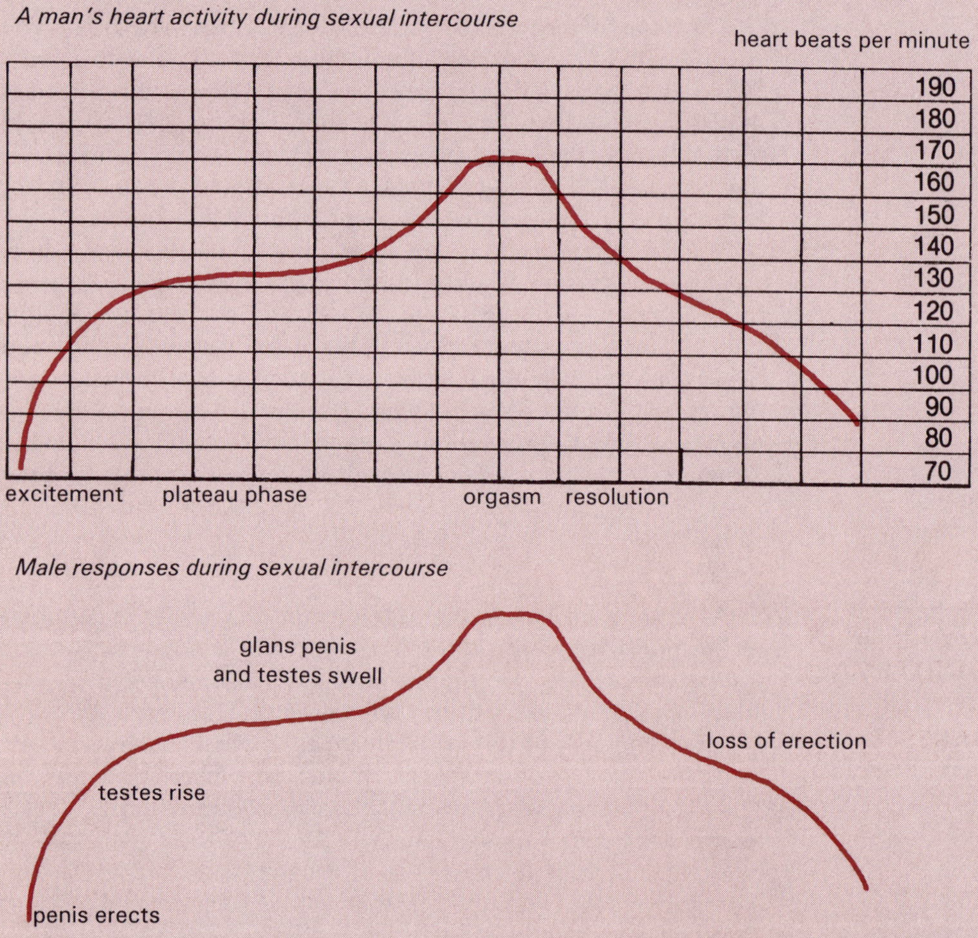

A man's heart activity during sexual intercourse

heart beats per minute

190
180
170
160
150
140
130
120
110
100
90
80
70

excitement   plateau phase   orgasm   resolution

Male responses during sexual intercourse

glans penis
and testes swell

loss of erection

testes rise

penis erects

SOURCE: Erwin J. Haeberle, *The Sex Atlas,* © 1978.
Reprinted by permission of Seabury Press.

sex of the student authors beyond the chance level (Vance & Wagner 1976). It seems that either the sensation of orgasm is similar in men and women or that the two sexes choose similar ways of describing it. (Until someone discovers a way to have an orgasm as both a genetic man and a genetic woman, one cannot be sure which explanation is correct.)

Certain sex differences are found, however, in regard to the timing of orgasm. In adult males, a vaginal penetration is usually followed by one orgasm. In females, coitus may be accompanied by one or a number of orgasms. In some cases, no orgasm occurs. Another difference between males and females is in regard to the intensity and duration of orgasms. Male orgasms are fairly similar from one time to the next. However, the same woman may show considerable variability in both the strength of an orgasm and how long it lasts. This sex difference is reflected in the subjective quality of the orgasms. Men usually perceive their orgasms to be quite similar; in contrast, women judge some of their orgasms to be much more satisfying than others.

Generally, women who have multiple orgasms find the second and third orgasms in the sequence to be more satisfying than the first. In contrast, men who have more than one orgasm during a sexual encounter report that the second or third orgasm is somewhat less satisfying than the first (Marmor et al. 1971). This difference may account, at least in part, for some women's reports that their intercourse is generally too brief to be completely satisfying (Hite 1976).

In both sexes, there are individual differences in the timing of sexual response cycles. For example, some men—particularly older men—take a relatively long time to reach the orgasmic phase, while others reach it rapidly. The shortest cycle on record was recorded by Kinsey and his associate, Wardell Pomeroy. They were conducting interviews for their book on male sexuality when they happened upon a man who bragged about an unusually fast sexual response. After they expressed disbelief at the man's claim, he masturbated to ejaculation—against Kinsey and Pomeroy's protest—within ten seconds (Pomeroy 1972). According to Pomeroy, this was the only time the Kinsey group collected data by direct observation.

There seems to be an even greater variability in the response cycles of women. Female variability is especially apparent in the number of orgasms reported: some women never have an orgasm, while others have multiple orgasms in virtually every sexual encounter.

Extreme variability is also seen in the resolution phase. Certain women show a relatively fast recovery, although it is generally slower than that of men. Other women have a considerably longer resolution phase than men, and such women are especially likely to feel frustrated if their male partner falls asleep or is unresponsive after ejaculation.

Author's Perspective: Similarities between Men and Women

Discussions of the similarities between the sexes are greeted with surprise by many people. Our Victorian tradition has tended to emphasize sex differences and minimize similarities. Perhaps even more surprising is the conclusion—based on studies of individuals' responses to erotic material—that the sexes are much alike in what they perceive to be sexually arousing. Two

German psychologists, Schmidt and Sigusch (1970), showed erotic movies depicting sexual scenes to a large number of male and female college students. A variety of tests were administered to the students to measure their responses to the movies. The results indicated no sex differences in responses, or differences so small that they were insignificant. For both men and women, the most arousing movie showed a couple undressing, caressing, engaging in oral-genital sex, and having intercourse in a variety of positions. On the other hand, both sexes found a movie much less arousing if the couple remained partially clothed, caressed and petted, but did not reach orgasm.

Of course, there are some sex differences in arousal related to the content of erotic stimulation. A story in which a man sexually exploits a woman is more likely to be arousing to males than to females. Women are particularly apt to be turned off by such a theme if they have been the target of exploitation in real life (Vogelmann-Sine et al. 1979).

There are also certain sex differences in the speed of arousal. In one study, erotic films and literature were presented over a period of an hour to married graduate students. Males became aroused more rapidly but tended to "cool down" by the end of the session; females started out slowly but continued to increase in arousal throughout the session. By the end of the hour, there were no differences between the men and the women.

Perhaps the largest difference between men and women is in what they expect to be arousing to members of the opposite sex. In one study, male and female subjects were shown a series of nineteen erotic slides. They were asked how arousing they found each slide and also the entire series, and then they were asked to assess how members of the opposite sex would react to the slides and the series. As in the previous studies, there were only very small sex differences in reaction to the slides. However, females thought males would generally become highly aroused, while males thought females would only be moderately aroused. Thus, both males and females misjudged the reaction of the opposite sex. The females were particularly inaccurate in predicting the general level of male arousal; the males were often wrong in predicting which of the slides would be most arousing to females (Griffitt 1973).

It seems that inaccuracies in the perception of sexual arousal in the opposite sex are fairly common. My experience as a marriage counselor indicates that couples often have a poor understanding of what is exciting to their partner. Part of this problem undoubtedly results from the old Victorian stereotype that males get "turned on" by one type of thing and females by another. A related problem is the Victorian belief that it is not "nice" to discuss sexual matters. At any rate, inaccurate perceptions can not only reduce sexual satisfaction but may lead to sexual dysfunction. Clearly, there is a need for open, honest communication between partners.

SUMMARY

Masters and Johnson have divided the human sexual response cycle into four phases: excitement, plateau, orgasm, and resolution. There are many similarities between the physiological responses of men and women during this cycle, especially in regard to vasocongestion and myotonia. However, there are also several responses specific to each sex.

The excitement and plateau phases in females are marked by changes in the breasts, labia minora, and clitoris. The vagina becomes lubricated, lengthened, and distended—responses associated with the possible acceptance of a penis. In males, excitement and plateau are associated with erection of the penis and elevation of the testes. Both sexes show increased heart rate, blood pressure, and rate of breathing.

Orgasm in women involves contractions of the P-C muscle surrounding the vagina as well as contractions of the uterus. There is also evidence of another type of orgasm—brought about by stimulation of the Grafenberg spot in the vagina—which includes ejaculation of a fluid through the urethra. In men, physiological accompaniments to orgasm occur in two stages: contraction of the vas, seminal vesicles, and prostate (experienced as "ejaculatory inevitability"), followed by rhythmic contractions of the urethra and penis. Despite these sex differences, descriptions of the feeling of orgasm by males and females are quite similar. In rare cases, male orgasm may occur without ejaculation, and vice versa.

The resolution phase consists of a slow return to a physiological resting state. Women can return to the orgasmic phase from any point in the resolution phase, and some women experience multiple orgasms within a short time. In contrast, orgasm and ejaculation in men are followed by a refractory period during which the individual is relatively unresponsive to sexual stimulation.

Orgasms appear to have evolved much earlier in male animals than female ones. Only female human beings and a few other primates show full-blown orgasmic responses.

NOTES

1. At one time it was thought vaginal lubrication was produced by the cervix or, as suggested earlier, Bartholin's glands. However, it now appears that the lubrication comes from the walls of the vagina (Masters & Johnson 1966).
2. Some people feel that, since the plateau phase involves dynamic changes, the term "plateau" is inappropriate. Crooks and Baur (1980) suggest that the more descriptive term "charge phase" has certain advantages. However, the Masters and Johnson terminology has become widely utilized, and some confusion would result from any change.
3. The spot, which is about the size of a quarter, was named after Ernest Grafenberg. He first described vaginally induced orgasms and female ejaculation in 1950, but for some reason his work was ignored at that time.

Sexual Functioning

The first chapter in this part—"Sexual Drive"—considers the physiological potential for sexual activity. The second and third—"Solitary Sex" and "Heterosexual Interaction"—deal with common ways in which the drive is activated and expressed. Despite this partitioning, it should be remembered that there is not a sharp line of distinction between sexual drive and sexual expression. In most cases, drives are subtly activated and expressed without a person becoming aware of when he or she passed from one stage to another.

CHAPTER 6

Sexual Drive

Georges Boulanger was one of the most respected men in France during the late 1880s. After his party had won a victory in the elections of 1889, crowds formed in the streets and demanded that he march to the presidential palace and take over the government. Despite his high political aspirations, he opted to be with his mistress, Madame de Bonnemains. Later, when he returned to his headquarters, he discovered that the moment for the coup d'etat had been lost; it was never recaptured (Shirer 1971). This account—and similar, though somewhat less dramatic, stories throughout history—dramatize the powerful role of the sexual drive in the course of people's lives. But the question remains, What is the nature of this drive? Is it primarily biological or psychological? What causes extreme variations in sexual drive? Is the drive greater in men or women?

In an attempt to address these questions, the first sections of this chapter will be concerned with biological aspects of sexual drive. The middle sections will focus on psychological contributions. Finally, individual variations and sex differences will be discussed in the last sections.

THE NERVOUS SYSTEM

A series of studies by James Olds suggests that two neural structures already mentioned—the hypothalamus and the amygdala—are involved in sexual drive. Several areas within these structures have been described as "pleasure centers." In certain experiments, the brains of rats have been wired so that, if a tiny electrical current is sent through the wires, these pleasure centers will be stimulated. The rats are then placed in what is called a *Skinner box*, where, by pressing a bar, they can send a current to these brain areas. Apparently, the stimulation is highly rewarding; rats will press bars as often as 5,000 times per hour for as long as twenty hours a day. During this "orgy" of self-stimulation, the rats

FIGURE 6.1
Sexual drive.

will forgo such normally attractive experiences as nibbling morsels of food (Olds 1956).

Some pleasure centers do not seem to be associated with any specific stimulus in ordinary life. However, others are directly related to sex. Evidence linking these centers with the sexual system comes from the observation that male rats that have been castrated—and therefore lack the normal supply of sex hormones—do not attempt to stimulate themselves when these centers are wired; in contrast, normal rats press the bar vigorously (Olds 1956, 1958). Thus, these centers apparently are not only associated with sexual pleasure but are activated by sex hormones—at least in rats.

Fortunately, from a scientific standpoint, two human subjects—one a male psychiatric patient and the other an epileptic woman—have had electrodes implanted in their brains for therapeutic purposes. Pleasure centers corresponding roughly to those of animals were identified in both subjects. The man, in fact, received such pleasurable sensations that he stimulated himself 1,500 times during a span of three hours and objected strongly when the stimulating apparatus was taken away.

FIGURE 6.2

A Skinner box. Animals learn to press the bar to obtain a food reward. Once they have learned to associate pressing the bar with the reward, their drive strength can be measured by recording the number of times they bar press for other types of reinforcement—including electrical stimulation of the brain.

When a pleasure center in the amygdala was stimulated, both subjects likened the feelings to sexual arousal and orgasm. The response of their bodies corroborated their reports—the male developed an erection and the female, vaginal lubrication (Heath 1972).

The sexual pleasure systems that have been identified lie in and around the hypothalamus and amygdala. Experiments suggest that at least part of sexual drive represents an attempt to bring about stimulation of these areas. Normally, this stimulation results from sexual activities and fantasies. Why don't children have sexual drives comparable to those of adults? It seems probable that in humans, as in rats, some of the pleasure centers must be primed by sex hormones before they are functional; these hormones are not secreted in large enough quantities to be effective until the individual reaches puberty.

In real life, repeated sexual encounters in a short period of time lead to a temporary reduction in sexual drive. A commonly accepted hypothesis is that, for males, fatigue is brought about by a loss of seminal fluid. However, experiments with animals fail to support this hypothesis. For example, an electrical current has been passed through the posterior end of a male, causing loss of seminal fluid. This procedure—termed electroejaculation—does not involve any direct stimulation of the penis or higher nervous centers. Even after repeated electroejaculations, male rats show a normal frequency of copulation and ejaculation if they are placed with females in estrus (Arvidsson & Larsson 1967). Apparently, loss of seminal fluid has little or nothing to do with sexual fatigue.

The evidence at the present time suggests that sexual fatigue is a function of the higher neural centers, which take into account a variety of factors. Such a conclusion is consistent with the findings of supernormal potency and arousal resulting from certain types of brain stimulation. In short, the saying "Fatigue is all in your head" may contain some seeds of truth.

HORMONES

As suggested in chapter 4, other biological factors—sex hormones—are also involved in sexual drive. Since there are significant differences between males and females in regard to these hormones, the two sexes will be discussed separately in this section.

Males

Long before the relationship between the gonads and sex hormones was understood, humans knew that the testes influenced sexual behavior. *Castration* was performed in ancient Rome in order to provide "safe" male protectors for Roman ladies. Apparently, the age at which castration was performed made a difference. Castration before puberty produced companions who were least likely to attempt coitus. Males castrated after puberty were able to perform sexually on occasion (Bermant & Davidson 1974). Much later, experimental studies on animals confirmed that the age of castration is an important variable. Furthermore, the amount of previous sexual experience before castration was found to make a difference; a castrated monkey that was experienced showed a slower decline in sexual performance than one that had lacked sexual experience (see Daly & Wilson 1983).

There seem to be large individual differences in the effects of castration. Some idea of these differences may be obtained from a study of 157 men legally castrated in Norway as a result of sex offenses or various psychiatric disorders. Approximately one half lost sexual interest and became impotent shortly after the operation; one sixth lost sexual desire over the course of a year; but about one third retained at least some sexual interest and/or potency for more than a year (Bremer 1959).[1]

Certain difficulties arise in interpreting studies of human castration. One cannot be sure that the resulting decline in performance is caused by the reduction of sex hormones. The stress of the operation or anxiety following the loss may contribute to a decline in sexual drive ("castration anxiety" must have been very real for the Norwegian men). One way of eliminating this difficulty is to administer sex hormones after the operation and then keep records of sexual performance. When sex hormones are replaced after castration of animals, sexual activity generally returns to about the same level as before the operation. However, if males are given unusually high doses of androgen, their sexual activity does not exceed the preoperative level (Young 1961). It may be concluded that androgens are a major factor in the male sex drive, but once an adequate hormone level is reached, additional hormones have little or no effect.

Studies of the normal, daily fluctuations of androgen support the conclusion that hormones beyond a certain level do not increase the sexual drive. There is no correlation between more than adequate androgen levels and extreme sexual activity in either humans or monkeys (Michael et al. 1974).

On the other hand, one might predict that sexual drive would decrease as soon as the sex hormone level dropped below the adequate level, as in castration. However, this is not the case. It takes weeks or even months for some castrated males to cease copulating, even though virtually no male hormone remains in the blood a few hours after castration (Resko & Phoenix 1972). Moreover, hormone-replacement therapy typically requires a series of treatments over a period of time; androgen must be injected daily for four to six weeks before potency is restored (Michael et al. 1973). It seems it is not the sex hormone per se that activates the potential for copulation but changes brought about by the hormone. For example, it may be that androgen produces and maintains certain changes in the nervous and/or muscular systems. When the androgen level drops below a certain point, the systems involved slowly lose the capability to maintain sexual interest and behavior.

Females

The role of estrogen in the sexual drive of women seems to be less important than that of androgen in men. After menopause, when the output of estrogen drops markedly, the sexual drive generally remains normal and, in some cases, increases. (The increase is probably due to a loss of the fear of pregnancy in some women.) Similarly, ovariectomy (removal of the ovaries) in young adult women does not usually result in reduced sexual drive.

The normal fluctuations of estrogen output during the menstrual cycle make possible another evaluation of the role of estrogen. There are considerable individual differences among women's reports of maximum sex drive during the cycle. Similarly, women differ in the times during the cycle that they are most active sexually. However, on the average, coital frequency shows two peaks: one in the middle of the cycle—when estrogen levels are high—and another just before menstruation—when the sex hormone level is low (Udry & Morris 1968).

If estrogen is not a major factor in female sexual drive, then what hormone is important? Somewhat surprisingly, there is evidence that androgen is an agent. It will be remembered that the adrenal glands of females produce large amounts of relatively weak androgen. Following surgical removal of the adrenals in women suffering from cancer, a decrease in sexual drive was reported, including a reduced ability to have orgasm (Schon & Sutherland 1960). In a complementary study, increased sexual gratification and orgasm resulted from treatment with androgen (Salmon & Geist 1943).

Author's Perspective: A Possible Overemphasis on the Role of Human Sex Hormones

One often reads statements in the popular press—or hears comments on television—that are misleading in regard to the relationship between hormones and sexual drive. People may complain that their juices (hormones) are no longer flowing, or they may compliment another person by saying that he or she raises their hormone level. In actuality, it is very rare that a low sex drive is caused by inadequate supplies of hormones. Furthermore, an extra dose of hormones is not likely to raise one's sex drive—nor is an attractive person liable to significantly increase the level of sex hormones.

In people, unlike animals, cultural and/or psychological factors may override the influence of hormones on sexual drive. This has important implications for both sexes. A woman who believes her menstrual cycle strongly affects her sexual drive is quite likely to feel sexually unresponsive at certain times of the month. Similarly, a man who feels that, with increasing age, his hormones and potency are decreasing rapidly may experience a loss of sexual desire.

Fortunately, the vast majority of us have enough hormones—and potential for relatively high levels of sexual drive—to last throughout most, if not all, of our lifetimes. As we shall see at several points in the book, a positive attitude about sexuality and life in general is much more significant in sexual drive and expression than are sex hormones.

APHRODISIACS

Throughout history, people have been searching for a potion, or *aphrodisiac*, to increase their sexual motivation and pleasure. In some cases, substances have been assumed to be aphrodisiacs because of their association with sexuality. For example, eating bulls' testes was thought by certain people to heighten sexual powers. In the Siwan culture of North Africa, the males have been known to conceal some of their sperm in their partner's food as part of a seduction routine (Ford & Beach 1951).

In other cases, substances have apparently developed a reputation as aphrodisiacs because they superficially resemble male sex organs. For example, oysters—which resemble testes—and rhinoceroses' horns—which look like erect penises—have a long history of demand as sexual enhancers. (Incidentally, the rhinoceros horn is consumed in powdered form.) It seems likely that the term "horny" originated from this fortuitous association.

A substance known as Spanish fly is thought by many people to increase arousal and potency. However, its major effects are an irritation of the urinary tract and dilation of the blood vessels of the genital organs. In some cases, this dilation produces prolonged erections, but it does not increase sexual drive. Furthermore, Spanish fly—which is a powder made from certain dried beetles—is poisonous and can produce serious illness (Leavitt 1974).

If these presumed aphrodisiacs have been found to be ineffective, why do the myths continue? One reason is that sexual pleasure is so important to some people that they will try almost anything. Another is that, as we shall see, when one believes that a substance will increase sexual drive, the belief itself may lead to confidence and determination.

Alcohol

A reduction of inhibitions and feelings of guilt often results from alcohol consumption. In one survey, approximately 60 percent of the people questioned reported that they enjoyed sex more after drinking (Athanasiou, Shaver, & Tavris 1970). Psychological factors associated with alcohol seem to be important in this reduction of inhibition, particularly for men. In a well-controlled laboratory study, college males were divided into four groups and given something to drink. Two of the groups received vodka and tonic, but one of these groups was told that they received only tonic. The other two groups were given only tonic, but one of them was told that they received vodka. All groups were then shown erotic films, and their physiological arousal (degree of penile erection) was measured. The greater arousal was shown by the groups who thought that they drank alcohol. (Whether or not they actually did was unimportant.) The least arousal was exhibited by the group who had consumed vodka but believed it to be only tonic (Wilson & Lawson 1976).

A comparable study was later conducted with college females. In this case, the results were quite different. The women showed the highest levels of arousal when they drank alcohol, whether they believed they were drinking liquor or not (Wilson & Lawson 1978). The reason for the sex difference in response to alcohol is not clear from these studies. However, the association between alcohol and reduced sexual inhibitions in females is consistent with the belief of males in many societies that women are easier to seduce after a few drinks.

Greater amounts of alcohol, however, have a very different effect. Alcohol is a depressant, and consumption of large amounts results in a male's inability to have an erection. The continued use of high amounts of alcohol can eventually lead to lowered levels of the sex hormones and damage to nerves involved in the sexual response (Rubin et al. 1976). In conclusion, it appears that small amounts of alcohol (or the belief that one is drinking alcohol) may reduce sexual inhibitions, but large amounts reduce sexual potential.

FIGURE 6.3

Because small to moderate amounts of alcohol tend to reduce inhibitions and sex guilt, drinking is often associated with sexual interaction.

"Pleasure-inducing" Drugs

The effects of the so-called pleasure-inducing drugs are highly varied. Heroin seems to decrease sexual desire and temporarily inhibit sexual responsiveness. In contrast, reports of cocaine users indicate that small dosages increase responsiveness to sexual stimulation. Nonetheless, continued usage ultimately reduces sexual pleasure because of such side effects as inflammation of the genital area and dryness of the vagina. Furthermore, repeated, heavy usage may lead to brain damage and psychosis (Woods 1975).

As in the case of cocaine, small amounts of marijuana reportedly increase sexual enjoyment. Touch seems more stimulating, emotional warmth between partners is enhanced, and orgasm is intensified. The relaxing effects of marijuana may reduce inhibitions, especially in women, resulting in a somewhat higher desire for sexual activity. However, there is no evidence that marijuana smoking increases the number of orgasms or the frequency of coitus (Halikas et al. 1971; Koff 1974).

Long-term, heavy usage of marijuana has certain negative side effects, including a lowering of the output of gonadotrophic hormones by the pituitary gland. In men, this may result in lowered sperm production and retarded ejaculation; for pregnant women, this deprivation of hormones may adversely affect the development of the fetus. In both sexes there is also a danger of chromosomal damage and impaired mental functioning (Jones & Jones 1977).

In the 1970s, a drug known as Quaalude (methaqualone) developed a street reputation as a pleasure enhancer and an aphrodisiac. However, this drug is a nervous system depressant and is likely to impair sexual performance. It seems likely that people taking Quaaludes experience a temporary loss of inhibition and that this has mistakenly been interpreted as an increase in sex drive (Bush 1980).

Considering all the presumed aphrodisiacs, it seems that the dangers outweigh any of the limited benefits. A good diet, regular rest and exercise, and positive attitudes about sex and interpersonal relationships in general apparently produce more beneficial results—and are less likely to bring one into conflict with the law.

Anaphrodisiacs

Substances that reduce sexual drive—known as *anaphrodisiacs*—have also been of interest throughout history. Cold baths and showers—which have rather dramatic, temporary effects—have been advocated by some since the days of the ancient Greeks. More recently, potassium nitrate, or saltpeter, has gained the reputation of an anaphrodisiac; and it has been rumored in some universities that this substance is added to the student meals on weekends. However, saltpeter does not reduce sexual desire; its only effect is, by acting as a diuretic, to increase the frequency of trips to the bathroom.

However, some other substances have been found to act as anaphrodisiacs. The drug ismelin, which is used in the treatment of high blood pressure, has been found to reduce the frequency of erections and ability to ejaculate. It also leads to stomach cramps and diarrhea in many patients. Other drugs that may act as anaphrodisiacs also have unpleasant side effects or may reduce inhibitions to a greater extent than sexual drive. At the present time, there does not appear to be a safe, reliable alternative to the cold shower.

THE EFFECTS OF SEX GUILT

References have already been made to the effect of psychological factors on sexual drive. One factor of considerable importance is *sex guilt*: a tendency to develop anxiety whenever ethical standards are violated by sexual thoughts or behaviors (Mosher 1968). An experimental study with college students has indicated that women with high sex guilt were less likely to become aroused while listening to erotic tapes than women with low or moderate guilt. The high-guilt women were also most likely to express disgust and contempt in response to the stimuli (Mosher & White 1980).

In some cases, it is not inadequate sexual arousal per se but a negative evaluation of arousal that reduces sexual drive and subsequent sexual activity. This conclusion is supported by two studies of the reactions of college students to erotic material. In the first study, students were divided into sexual conservatives and sexual liberals on the basis of their responses to attitude questionnaires (which were administered before the experiment began). All subjects were then shown a series of photographic slides depicting explicit sexual scenes; the subjects rated the degree of arousal they experienced. They also expressed their feelings about the slides. The results indicated that all subjects reported high levels of arousal. However, the sexual liberals judged the most arousing slides to be *most* entertaining; the sexual conservatives rated the most arousing slides as most offensive and *least* entertaining (Wallace & Wehmer 1972). Apparently, both groups were aroused, but they evaluated their arousal differently.

In the second study, attitudes of students toward an erotic movie were obtained and correlated with reported sexual activity. The liberal group (the group that liked the movie) admitted to more sexual activity than the conservative group (Fisher & Byrne 1976). It appears that the conservative group had a reduced drive level—or at least converted their drive into sexual activity less often—compared to the liberal group. Of course, it is also possible that the conservatives had fewer sexual opportunities or were less likely to tell about their activities than the liberals. However, the fact that the conservatives' sexual activity temporarily equaled that of the liberals (for a two-day period following the movie) argues against these explanations. Apparently, the sexual drive of conservatives is simply suppressed over greater periods of time than that of liberals.

Women seem to have greater sex guilt than men. After exposure to sexually explicit films, photographs, and literature, college women reported more negative emotional reactions than college men (Schmidt & Sigusch 1970). However, sex guilt in women appears to be on the decline. In a study of married women, Keller and associates (1978) found that sex guilt was lower in young than in older women.

There is also a decline in the amount of sex guilt among males. In 1952, Clark reported a series of studies in which college men were shown erotic slides. Considerable inhibition and sex guilt were expressed, especially when an attractive woman served as the experimenter. In comparison, the studies just discussed indicate that there were significantly fewer male sexual conservatives in the 1970s. Apparently sex guilt is decreasing in both sexes but at an especially fast rate in women. It may be that, within a short time, gender differences in sex guilt will disappear altogether.

A recent laboratory study indicates that sex guilt is related not only to how one responds to sexual stimuli, but also to how likely a person is to administer pleasurable stimuli to an opposite-sex person. The amount of sex guilt in male college students was measured on a typical sex-guilt inventory. These students were then asked to participate in an experiment in which presumably pleasurable stimulation was given by a machine as a reward to a young woman in an apparent learning context. (In actuality, the young woman was a cohort of the experimenter and was faking the pleasurable responses.) Subjects low in sex guilt administered significantly more "pleasurable" stimulation than those high in sex guilt. The low-sex-guilt subjects were particularly likely to administer high levels of pleasure if they were led to believe that they would see the young woman again (Janda et al. 1981). It seems that, for most people, giving pleasure is a rewarding experience. However, for individuals high in sex guilt, pleasure giving has negative connotations that result in some inhibition of this activity.

The apparent reduction of sex guilt in our society is viewed in different ways by different people. Some see this reduction as associated with less sexual inhibition and a resulting increase in social problems such as teenage pregnancies and venereal disease. Others see the reduction as increasing one's capacity for sexual pleasure and, perhaps, pleasure in general. Clearly, as in any large social change, the results are diverse and widespread. It is virtually impossible to evaluate the fallout as all good or all bad.

HYPERSEXUALITY

There are fairly reliable case reports of extremely high drive levels in certain individuals; these levels produce sexual activity well above the mean. Kinsey and his co-workers (1948) interviewed a thirteen-year-old boy who apparently had had twenty-six orgasms during a twenty-four-hour period. Another male—who kept a detailed notebook on his sexual experiences—reportedly averaged thirty-three orgasms per week over a thirty-year period; it took Kinsey and Wardell Pomeroy seventeen hours to obtain his sexual history. The record contained examples of orgasms achieved with a large number of individuals (both young and old) and a variety of animals, as well as through elaborate techniques of masturbation (Pomeroy 1972).

There are comparable reports of high sexual drive levels in women. A nineteen-year-old mother apparently engaged in nightly coitus which lasted for several hours. After dozens of orgasms, she was just as enthusiastic about the sexual activity as she was at the beginning of the episode (McCary 1972).

Author's Perspective: The Dynamics of Hypersexuality

My clinical experience with certain individuals reporting hypersexuality suggests that, in some cases, an unusually high drive level is associated with interpersonal difficulties. For example, one young man consistently viewed sexual relations with a woman as a conquering-type experience. The pursuit of sexual adventure was analogous to a battle in which one antagonist—the woman—was injured. Then, after the "injury," the man wanted little more to do with her. Instead, he had an intense desire for another woman the same night. Ultimately, the man's self-image was closely tied to the number and variety of sexual conquests he achieved.

Females who exhibit hypersexuality may also have intercourse with a large variety of partners without much concern for health or reproductive consequences. Several years ago, I conducted a psychological evaluation of a fifteen-year-old girl who had become pregnant after having had sexual intercourse with each of eighteen young men at a party. In response to a standard question concerning the possible father of the child, she posed another question: "If you had been shot by a machine gun, would you know which bullet killed you?"

This response illustrates the elements of self-destruction that are sometimes involved in hypersexuality. In certain respects, the consequences of hypersexual behavior—pregnancy, sexually transmitted diseases, and/or abandonment by the partner—function as punishment and alleviate guilt related to the behavior.

Traditionally, hypersexuality has been called *satyriasis* in men and *nymphomania* in women. However, these labels carry considerable excess meaning and, like other words that imply value judgments, may be misleading. For example, people who are unable to sexually satisfy their partners may label them as nymphomaniacs or satyrs and thus imply that their partners are to blame for sexual problems. In one marriage-counseling session, a man revealed that he thought his wife was a nymphomaniac because she desired intercourse twice a week. The wife had developed extreme guilt over her husband's perception, and this guilt had contributed to further marital problems.

There are also many examples of individuals who have high sexual drives, express them in socially appropriate ways, and have happy, productive lives. Much of the furor over satyriasis and nymphomania undoubtedly reflects persisting Victorian fears of sexuality, especially hypersexuality. For most people with high sexual motivation, there is no need to feel guilty or embarrassed.

SEX DIFFERENCES IN SEXUAL DRIVE

Whenever two people are interacting, the individual drives cannot be separated. However, some insight can be gained by looking at male and female sex drives independently. One way of doing this is simply to ask partners if they would prefer to have intercourse more or less frequently than they do and then compare their answers. At the time of the Kinsey report, young husbands apparently desired intercourse more frequently than their wives. However, the pattern was generally reversed in middle age (Kinsey et al. 1953). Thus, there was evidence that the male drive reached its peak in the late teens or early twenties, but the female drive did not reach its highest point until the late thirties and forties.

Recent surveys have indicated that there is practically no difference in the responses of young men and women to questions about desired frequency of intercourse. In contrast to Kinsey's findings, very few young wives wished to have intercourse less frequently than they actually did (Hunt 1974). It may be that the earlier finding of lower sexual drive in young women is related to the double standard, which tended to make women feel more guilty than men about sexual desires. As women became older—and more experienced sexually—the apparent increase in sexual drive may actually have reflected a reduction in sexual guilt and inhibition.

The studies just mentioned involved verbal reports of sexual motivation. Behavioral observations provide another indication of motivational level, but in most circumstances, these are considered unethical with humans. Once again, however, animal studies may provide some insight into the situation. In one study, a female rat in estrus was placed on a balcony-like structure overhanging a group of males. It was possible for the female to jump down and gain access to the males, but the experimenters prevented the males from leaping onto the balcony. Thus, sexual contact was strictly a matter of the female's choice (Pierce & Nuttall 1961).

A different procedure involved having one animal press a bar in order to gain access to opposite-sex animals (Larsson 1956). In both of these studies it was found that the female delayed resuming activity with males longer if she had copulated than if she had been allowed only brief contact with the males. Furthermore, the preferred time between copulation and resumption of sexual activity was somewhat shorter for fe-

FIGURE 6.4
"Wherefore art thou, Romeo?"

males than for males under comparable conditions. In a bar-pressing situation involving monkeys, the female also demonstrated a high drive level; she pressed the bar a considerable number of times, exhausting a series of males (Keverne 1976).

Author's Perspective: The Myth of Higher Sexual Drives in Men

Despite the evidence that the male's sexual drive is not stronger than that of the female — and may, in some circumstances, be weaker — a myth of male sexual superiority is prevalent in our society. The myth has probably persisted for several reasons. First, desire for intercourse with a new acquaintance has mistakenly been equated with sexual drive. Men are typically the initiators in regard to sexual advances. However, the sexually aggressive male probably represents a sex role that reflects some harsh realities. Females have a lot to lose if they engage in casual sex: they may damage their reputation, and they even risk pregnancy followed by abandonment. Males have relatively less to lose. Thus, caution on the part of females when a relationship is first developing should not be considered a reflection of sexual drive.

A second reason why the myth persists may be related to the finding that women become sexually aroused more slowly than men. It seems likely that some men have accused women of lacking sexual drive because the women failed to respond rapidly to sexual advances. (The same men may not have noticed that, once aroused, the women were relatively slow to ''cool down''.)

Finally, Mary Jane Sherfey (1972), a psychiatrist, has argued that the female capacity for multiple orgasms suggests that women have a stronger sex drive than men do. Presumably, society has acted to suppress female drives since there is need to ''socialize'' women into the structure of a ''civilized'' culture. Thus, men, who have most of the power, will not be threatened by women but will help support them and their offspring. Whether or not Sherfey's argument is correct, there is certainly historical evidence of greater suppression of female sexual drives than those of males. As we have seen, there have even been cultures in which the female's clitoris was surgically removed. However, with the gradual dissolution of the double standard, there seems to be less suppression and greater equality in the expression of male and female sexual drives and sexuality in general.

SUMMARY

''Pleasure centers'' located in two parts of the brain, the hypothalamus and the amygdala, seem to be involved in sexual drive. These centers are apparently activated by sex hormones when individuals reach puberty. Experiments with male animals indicate that fatigue or loss of sexual drive result from sexual inhibition in the brain rather than a depletion of seminal fluid.

The role of androgens in the sexual drive of males has been addressed by studies of castration and hormone replacement therapy. There is a relationship between androgen level in the blood and sexual drive, but it is not direct; the androgen effects appear to be mediated indirectly via the brain and other structures. Androgens also appear to be related to sexual motivation in females.

Up to this point, no one has discovered a true, safe aphrodisiac. Alcohol in small or moderate amounts may reduce inhibitions, but large amounts reduce sexual drive. Similarly, limited doses of marijuana seem to enhance sexual satisfaction in some people, but continued usage presents real dangers.

Sex guilt inhibits sexual drive in certain people. During the past few years, such guilt seems to be declining in both sexes but at an especially fast rate in women. Sex guilt has also been found to inhibit the tendency to induce physical pleasure in others.

Hypersexuality has been reported in both sexes. Although it is associated with personality problems in some cases, there are examples of hypersexuality in relatively well-adjusted individuals.

Some evidence suggests that males' sexual drive reaches its peak earlier than that of females. In recent years, as sexual guilt in women has been reduced, it appears that young women have sexual drives comparable to those of young men. The myth of greater sexual drive in males seems to have been derived from a combination of factors: the tendency to mistakenly equate coyness in females with lack of sexual drive; the fact that women become sexually aroused more slowly than men; and a historical tendency for cultures to suppress female sexuality.

NOTES

1. A recent study of castrated sex offenders in West Germany indicated similar types of reactions. In addition, it was found that convicted rapists were particularly likely to retain sexual drive after castration. The author concluded that castration was not an effective means of treating sex offenders (Heim 1981).

CHAPTER 7

Solitary Sex

Some of our first sexual thoughts and experiences probably occurred when we were alone or at least not interacting directly with another person. Even when one has a satisfying relationship with a sexual partner, certain forms of solitary sex—sexual fantasies, dreams, nocturnal orgasms, and/or masturbation—tend to take place. Although this chapter is concerned primarily with solitary sex, it should be remembered there is no sharp line of distinction between solitary and two-person sex.

SEXUAL FANTASIES

People apparently spend a large amount of time engaged in sex-related fantasies. In recent years, many people have also spent time reading about other people's fantasies; a large number of best-selling books and articles have been published on the subject of sexual fantasies, complete with numerous examples. The apparent interest is probably related to enjoyment of the highly erotic content of most of these accounts. In addition, exposure to other people's fantasies may allow individuals to make a social comparison; seeing that one's own fantasies are similar to those of others provides some assurance of normality. For example, a person who has had a fantasy about performing a socially unacceptable act might fear being abnormal or losing inhibitions in an embarrassing fashion. However, if it becomes apparent that such a fantasy is common, the individual may be somewhat relieved.

A major function of a sexual fantasy seems to be the induction of sexual arousal. In fact, there is evidence that some people become more aroused by fantasizing a sexual event than by viewing erotic pictures or reading erotic literature (Byrne & Lamberth 1971). Similarly, many people report higher levels of arousal when they watch a film implying that

FIGURE 7.1

Sexual fantasies may provide relief from boredom.

an erotic scene will follow than they do when they watch the same film including the erotic scene (Tannenbaum 1970).

There are, however, some people who report a reduction of arousal when they fantasize (Hensen & Rubin 1971). The fantasy may induce strong guilt or inhibition or even distract attention from physical stimulation.

Another function of fantasies is to provide a kind of rehearsal for events that may occur in the future. In this way, various types of problems may be anticipated. Commonly, fantasies involve the replay of an event involving a "missed opportunity," but with a sexually satisfying ending (Barros 1970). It seems likely that such fantasy allows the development of various contingency plans that may be utilized later in appropriate situations.

Still another function of sexual fantasies is to enrich the sexual experience at hand. Many people fantasize during intercourse, and the imagined experience often involves strangers or a series of lovers. Such fantasies do not seem to reflect dissatisfaction with a partner; rather, they provide additional excitement and variety without violating an agreement to be faithful or sacrificing certain moral standards. In support of this interpretation, one study indicated that how happy women were with their husbands was unrelated to the content of their fantasies (Hariton 1973). Similarly, women's fantasies of rape—which are fairly common—do not indicate that women actually want to be raped. These mental images seem to add an air of excitement. In some cases, rape fantasies may also function to alleviate guilt, since being taken by force indicates that one is not guilty of sexual improprieties (Friday 1973).[1] In a recent laboratory experiment, researchers varied the amount of sexual fantasizing of respondents. Results indicated that college students who fantasized freely showed the highest level of both sexual arousal and sexual behavior (Eisenman 1982).

Finally, sexual fantasies—like other daydreams—may provide relief from boredom. Many individuals report a strong tendency to fantasize during dull speeches or lectures. (It is also possible that readers will have slipped into a fantasy or two while reading this chapter.) The role of boredom—or, in contrast, concentration on a task—is indirectly illustrated by an experiment by Geer & Fuhr (1976). It was hypothesized that, as interference with thinking about sexual activity increased, sexual arousal would decrease. To test this hypothesis, experimenters played a recording of a woman's voice explicitly describing various sexual experiences—including oral-genital sex and intercourse—while random numbers were spoken by a second voice. Four different conditions were created to produce various degrees of interference. At one extreme, the subjects (all males) had to add pairs of numbers and classify them as to above or below fifty, odd or even; at the other extreme, the subjects were free to ignore the numbers; the two middle conditions involved intermediate amounts of concentration on the numbers. Sexual arousal was measured physiologically. As predicted, when interference with concentration on the female voice increased, sexual arousal decreased.

Factors Related to Persistent Fantasies

It seems that, just as people fantasize most often about food when they are hungry, persistent fantasies about sex are associated with a high sexual drive. Support for this conclusion comes from a study which indicates that men with a very active fantasy life report the highest level of general sexual activity (Giambra & Martin 1977). Similarly, women who report a high frequency of using fantasies during masturbation tend to become most sexually aroused when exposed to an erotic tape recording (Stock & Geer 1982).

There also appears to be a relationship between age and frequency of fantasies. Sexual fantasies occur most often among young men seventeen to twenty-three years of age—whose drive levels are presumably at their highest. In middle adulthood, these fantasies are less common. Then, after age sixty-five, when the sexual drive seems to decrease significantly, the frequency of sexual fantasies drops off rapidly (Giambra 1974).

Other than sexual drive and age, what factors are related to frequency of sexual fantasy? There is indirect evidence that intelligence and creativity are important. Adults who daydreamed frequently as children were found to be more creative, imaginative, and original than those who fantasized infrequently (Singer 1975). Research also shows that make-believe play facilitates the development of verbal ability in children (Pulaski 1974).

Research on the Content of Fantasies

Unfortunately, it has been difficult to study fantasies in a well-controlled fashion. An investigator must reconstruct another person's thoughts and images, and this process always leads to a certain amount of distortion. Fantasies tend to be fleeting and do not follow a logical order, but people generally try to make them more logical during the reconstruction process.

The investigator may also have an effect on the recall process. An individual may be subtly influenced to "spice up" certain details that the investigator seems to find interesting, or to leave out portions that may be embarrassing or threatening to recount to another person. Such distortions may vary from group to group—for example, between men and women or between older and younger people. As a result, intergroup comparisons may be inaccurate. One may not know for certain if there are actual differences in fantasy life or simply differences in the way fantasies are remembered and reported. Despite this problem—and the omnipresent problem of obtaining representative samples—certain tentative generalizations about the content of fantasies are possible. .

FIGURE 7.2

A fantasy common to both men and women is having sex with a stranger.

One of the major research findings is that men and women differ somewhat in the themes of their sexual fantasies. Men often imagine situations in which they express power and aggression; the sexual interaction is likely to be relatively impersonal. In contrast, women's fantasies tend to be more romantic. Probably most of these differences are related to learned sex roles. A man's image is tied in with power and aggression, and success is often measured in these terms. In contrast, a desirable woman is often pictured as being romantic and sexually attractive (Crépault & Couture 1980).

Despite these general differences, the fantasies of males and females also have many themes in common (see figure 7.3). During masturbation, for example, males most commonly imagined having intercourse with a stranger; this theme was the second most common among females. The most common theme for women was doing some things that they would never do in reality; this was ranked third by men. Another common theme (second for men, fourth for women) was having sex with more than one person at the same time (Hunt 1974). It appears that most of these themes represent an attempt to enhance the sexual experience with variety and excitement, which apparently are important for both sexes.

There is some evidence that the sexual fantasies of men and women—like other aspects of sexuality—are more similar in the 1970s than in the 1940s and 1950s. For example, Kinsey found that 89 percent of the males reported using fantasies as a source of stimulation during masturbation, while only 64 percent of the women did so; by the 1970s, the percentage for women had increased and approximated that for men (Hunt 1974).

It seems likely that there are also fewer sex differences in the themes of

FIGURE 7.3
Reports of Fantasies of Men and Women During Masturbation

Theme	Percent Reporting Theme	
	Males	Females
1. Having intercourse with a stranger.	47	21
2. Having sex with more than one person at the same time.	33	18
3. Doing things one would never do in reality.	19	28
4. Being forced to have sex.	10	19
5. Forcing someone to have sex.	13	3

SOURCE: From Hunt, 1974

sexual fantasies than there were in the 1940s and 1950s. Unfortunately, themes of fantasies were not investigated at that time. However, one would predict that, as women are encouraged to become more assertive, the amount of assertiveness in female sexual fantasies will also increase.

A final difference between male and female fantasies seems to be related to timing. Men are most likely to fantasize as a means of becoming aroused; women tend to fantasize most often after becoming aroused (Daley 1975). This heightening of arousal has reportedly been used by certain women to trigger orgasm. In contrast, there are no reported examples of men reaching orgasm through fantasy alone (Goleman & Bush 1977).[2]

Author's Perspective: Should Sexual Fantasies Be Shared?

Many people believe sexual fantasies are private property and should not be shared with one's partner. These beliefs are probably strongest in people who believe that fantasies have a generally negative function or represent the dark side of one's personality. For example, one psychiatrist, Avodah Offit (1977), sees wild fantasies as representing potential personality problems. A person who shared Offit's views would certainly see potential embarrassment in the airing of fantasies.

Even people who have positive concepts about sexual daydreams face the possibility that their partners will view certain fantasies as signs of emotional disturbance. There is always the risk that one will receive the response, "That's sick," or "That means you don't love me."

On the other hand, the sharing of fantasies may open new channels of communication. The exchange of secret thoughts may provide some of the same satisfactions and feelings of intimacy as the sharing of other very personal experiences and ideations. It is also possible that discussing fantasies will identify factors that tend to increase (or decrease) sexual and interpersonal satisfaction.

Generally speaking, if one does decide to discuss sexual fantasies, it is probably best to start with something relatively innocuous. Then, if things seem to work out well—and one's partner is willing to share something comparable—more may be risked.

Another possibility is for each person to read a discussion of the apparent functions of fantasies. If there is reasonable agreement on the subject—and a general feeling of comfort with the material—the chances of a successful fantasy-sharing discussion seem relatively good.

SEXUAL DREAMS

Apparently, most people have sexual dreams. However, because people have great difficulty reconstructing dreams, scientists have problems studying them. Dreams have less logic and are under less conscious control than daytime fantasies. Nonetheless, some experiments shed light on the function of dreams.

Most dreams take place when a person is in an REM phase of sleep (REM stands for the rapid eye movements that take place under the closed lids during this phase of sleep). REM phases appear four or five times during a normal seven-to-eight-hour sleep; each phase lasts thirty to forty minutes. It is possible to deprive people of dream time by awakening them as soon as REMs appear (the person can still obtain a full night's sleep because other stages of sleep always precede the REM stage). After REM deprivation, a person generally feels irritable. Furthermore, when given an opportunity to sleep at a later time, the individual exhibits more than the usual REM time (Dement 1965). These findings suggest that REMs—and presumably dreaming—function to release tension.

This theory is also supported by a later study. People who reported frequent daytime fantasies were compared to those who fantasized relatively little; both groups were deprived of nighttime REM sleep. It was found that frequent daytime fantasizers did not increase their REMs after deprivation. In contrast, the low-fantasy group showed a large increase in the amount of REM sleep exhibited the next night; this group also reported enriched fantasies the next day (Cartwright & Ratzel 1972). It seems that those people who normally fantasized a great deal during the day had less need than the other people for the tension release that dreams provided.

Sexual responses such as erections and vaginal lubrication may occur spontaneously during sleep, particularly during the REM phase. For ex-

FIGURE 7.4

Measuring physiological activity during sleep. Some insight into dreams may be obtained by awakening subjects during certain types of physiological activity and asking whether or not they were dreaming.

ample, partial or full erections occur in over 80 percent of the REM stages of males; these erections even occur in infants and elderly men (Kleitman 1963). However, the sexual responses do not seem to be a reliable indicator of sexual arousal. Skeletal muscles, which are tense during arousal in the waking state, are relaxed during REM sleep. Furthermore, people do not usually report erotic dreams while they exhibit the sexual responses. The function of erections and vaginal responses during sleep is not clearly understood, but one possibility is that these responses function to keep the sexual system in working order during the sleep period (Renshaw 1976).

For hundreds of years people have assumed that dreams have definite meanings. Many Shakespearian plays include scenes that apparently illustrate how dreams foretell the future. Much later, in 1900, Freud published a very influential book, *The Interpretation of Dreams*, in which he proposed that dreams do not predict future events but rather function to help the mind deal with problems of the past. In Freudian theory, unconscious—often sexual—wishes threaten to enter consciousness, create anxieties, and interrupt sleep. These wishes are then transformed into symbolic forms and experienced as relatively nonthreatening dreams. Freud believed that there are some fairly universal symbols. For example, long objects like poles and sticks or guns symbolize a penis; boxes, cupboards, and rooms represent a vagina; going up and down steps or in and out of rooms stand for sexual intercourse. In addition, he thought many symbols are unique to a person and can only be understood after months of analysis.

Unfortunately, it is impossible to systematically test theories of dream symbolism. Nonetheless, some psychoanalytically oriented therapists still rely on dream interpretation as a method of gaining insight into an individual's personality.

NOCTURNAL ORGASMS

In certain cases, an orgasm will occur during sleep, and the individual will awaken with only a hazy memory of the experience. *Nocturnal orgasms* are fairly common in males, particularly during their late teens and early twenties. Since male nocturnal orgasms are accompanied by ejaculation, they are frequently called *nocturnal emissions* or *wet dreams*. In females, nocturnal orgasms are less frequent. Approximately 40 percent of the females in the *Playboy* survey reported having a nocturnal orgasm at least once—a figure less than half that for males. In the Kinsey survey, women reported nocturnal orgasms to be most frequent during their forties, a time when, as we have seen, their sexual drives are particularly high (Kinsey et al. 1953; Hunt 1974).

During the Middle Ages it was believed that orgasms occurring after people had gone to sleep were caused by demons. For males, the demon was called succubus, and it would lie underneath the person; for females, a number of demons named incubus would lie on top of the sleeper. Individuals were warned to avoid willfully enjoying their encounters with these creatures.

By the 1950s, our society had largely rejected the demon explanation. Nonetheless, guilt and embarrassment often accompanied nocturnal orgasms, especially if young people were not told that the phenomenon was perfectly natural. By the 1970s, most people—especially boys—had experienced orgasms through other outlets, so there was less mystery surrounding the first nocturnal orgasm (Oliven 1974). Today, as with other types of sexual expression, there is considerably less anxiety about nocturnal orgasms than in the past.

When other forms of sexual expression have been drastically reduced, nocturnal orgasm tends to occur more often. For example, nocturnal orgasms in women were found to increase following imprisonment or loss of a spouse. Thus, it appears that nocturnal orgasms function as a release of sexual tension or as a kind of safety valve. However, the number of nocturnal orgasms following periods of abstinence is generally far short of the number of orgasms experienced during comparable periods of sexual activity with a partner (Kinsey et al. 1948; Hunt 1974).

In many cases, nocturnal orgasms accompany dreams; if the person awakes during the dream, he or she is aware of being sexually excited. Rather surprisingly, nocturnal emissions have occurred in men with spinal cord injuries. Since mental activity cannot affect sexual functioning in these people, the emission must have taken place independent of any dream state. Thus, although dreams may facilitate nocturnal orgasms, they do not seem to be a necessary requisite (Greenhouse 1974).

MASTURBATION

Masturbation, or self-stimulation, is a common form of solitary sex. During the Victorian period, however, any type of sexual self-stimulation was vehemently condemned. To support such condemnation, epilepsy, headaches, dark rings under the eyes, asthma, nosebleeds, and insanity—as well as other maladies—were all falsely blamed on masturbation. Early in the twentieth century, belief in the dangers of self-stimulation was strong enough that the U.S. Patent Office granted a patent for an alarm that rang in the parents' bedroom when the child's bed moved in a pattern suggestive of masturbation. Other patents were granted for metal mittens and a variety of restraining straps designed to prevent "self-abuse" (LoPiccolo & Heiman 1977).

Even what appeared to be involuntary masturbation among seamstresses was considered as an evil. Rhythmic up-and-down movements of the women's legs on the treadles sometimes led to unrestrained pumping action on the machine. In certain cases, matrons were hired to circulate among the seamstresses to detect instances where machines went out of control (Duffy 1963).

Several preliterate societies share this negative view of masturbation. In many cases, taboos are based on the same fallacies found in Western cultures—that masturbation causes weakness, illness, or proneness to some type of disaster (Davenport 1976).

Recently, some sex therapists have taken a more positive stand. They claim that masturbation may be helpful in overcoming some types of sexual dysfunction and that observing a partner masturbate may provide information about what arouses and pleases the partner; this information may then help to increase satisfying sexual interaction. In addition, it has been suggested that masturbation can be a useful aid in inducing sleep at night. Nonetheless, a substantial number of people still hold negative views. A national survey found that 50 percent of those questioned agreed with the statement that masturbation is ''always wrong'' (Levitt & Klassen 1973). In 1976, the Roman Catholic Church declared that masturbation is a ''seriously disordered act.'' Thus, it is not surprising that guilt over masturbation is fairly common, particularly among adolescents (Arafat & Cotton 1974).

Males

Despite traditional condemnation and guilt, masturbation is an almost universal experience for males. Stimulation of the genitals occurs during early childhood, but masturbation to orgasm usually begins at, or slightly before, puberty. By the age of thirteen, approximately two thirds of males have stimulated themselves to orgasm (Hunt 1974).

Although masturbation is typically done in private, many boys learn about this practice by observing their peers. In some cases, a group of boys get together in a competitive atmosphere to see who can ejaculate fastest or propel semen the farthest (Kinsey et al. 1948). In one of the most extreme examples of public masturbation, Jim Morrison of a rock group known as The Doors masturbated to orgasm in front of overflow audiences at concerts in the late 1960s.

Masturbation typically decreases in frequency by the late teens and, for some males, is replaced by coitus as a primary sexual outlet. However, many males continue to masturbate after marriage or a steady relationship with a sexual partner. Masturbation following marriage has been reported as more common in the 1970s than in the 1940s or 1950s (Hunt 1974). It may be that, in the relatively liberal atmosphere of the 1970s and 1980s, people are feeling freer to utilize masturbation as an extra sexual outlet, especially during periods when a partner is not available.

The techniques of adult male masturbation have been described by Masters & Johnson (1966). Men typically encircle the shaft of the penis with their fingers and make back-and-forth movements. At first the glans and frenum may be gently stimulated, but contact with these areas is usually avoided as they become more highly sensitive with increased arousal. The speed of rhythmic movement generally increases as orgasm is approached, and stimulation stops at the moment of orgasm; further contact would produce discomfort. A less commonly utilized method is for the man to lie on his stomach and make pelvic thrusts against a relatively soft substrate such as a bed or couch.

It is likely that some readers, especially males, will find the preceding paragraph distasteful. Research by Elaine Hatfield and associates (1978) indicates that portrayals of male masturbation are particularly upsetting to men; in contrast, depictions of females masturbating are more disturbing to women than men. Apparently, as suggested earlier, masturbation is seen by many as a generally unacceptable practice, and the natural tendency to identify with members of one's own sex brings the accounts close to home. On the other hand, masturbation by the opposite sex is probably less threatening—and may in fact have some positive erotic value.

Females

In females, the techniques of masturbation are more variable than in males. The most common method involves stroking or rubbing the clitoris and labia minora. Sometimes the shaft of the clitoris is manipulated from either side; direct stimulation of the glans is often avoided because of its extreme sensitivity. The following description is taken from *The Hite Report* (Hite 1976) with permission from the author.

> . . . usually I lie on my back, my legs apart. I almost always have my panties on, as rubbing the clitoris itself directly is just annoying. I use one hand, two fingers together, rubbing up and down in short, quick strokes right over my clitoris. As I get closer to climax, my legs tend to spread apart and my pelvis tilts up more. I don't move around too much, but sometimes during climax I roll from side to side.

A less common method is the insertion of fingers or objects into the vagina. Although this technique is one that males generally imagine when they think of female masturbation, it occurs in only 20 percent of the women who stimulate themselves to orgasm. Another technique of self-stimulation involves rubbing the genitals against an object such as a pillow or towel. Breast manipulation may also be part of female masturbation, and in a few cases breast stimulation alone is enough to bring about orgasm (Kinsey et al. 1953).

Masturbation is less frequently reported by females than by males. Fewer than two thirds of the women surveyed in the *Playboy* study indicated that they had masturbated at some time. Furthermore, among those who said they had masturbated, the median frequency was significantly lower than the comparable frequency in men (Hunt 1974). Assuming that the sex drive is no lower in females than in males (as we have seen in chapter 6), what accounts for these differences? It seems likely that learning of sex roles is a major factor. While the male sex drive is defined, more or less, as an aggressive, performance-oriented one, the female role is traditionally more modest and passive. The traditional female role is also less oriented toward self-pleasure (Gagnon & Simon 1973).

This sex-role explanation is consistent with other male-female differences as well. Females generally report beginning masturbation at a relatively late age. In contrast to boys, girls are not likely to discuss self-stimulating experiences with their friends and are more likely to masturbate in private (Kinsey et al. 1953; Hunt 1974).

At least some of the male-female differences may represent differences in an ability to recall and report early masturbatory experiences. Females are probably more embarrassed by memories of these activities—and are less likely to recall them—than males. Some support for this explanation comes from the results of a survey conducted with young children (Elias & Gebhard 1973). There was very little difference between boys and girls in the reported age of the first masturbation. For both sexes, the median age of the first masturbation was lower than that reported by adults who were asked when they first masturbated.

It is also possible that some male-female differences are related to the fact that masturbation is more difficult to define in females than in males. The penis of a male is a much more obvious structure than the clitoris of a woman. Consequently, young boys are more likely to become aware of the erotic potential of their phalluses than young girls of theirs (Heiman 1977). In several cases, women have reported that it was not until years later that they realized certain pleasurable experiences could be classified as masturbation.

As sex roles become less differentiated—as they have in recent years—it seems likely that there will be fewer sex differences in regard to masturbation. There is already some evidence that this trend is developing; young women are reportedly masturbating earlier and more frequently than women did a generation earlier (Hunt 1974).

Psychological and Sociological Variables

There is an old belief that masturbation is most likely to occur in individuals who are unstable or low in self-esteem. However, research indicates that neither emotional stability nor self-esteem is significantly correlated with frequency of masturbation (Greenberg & Archambault 1973; Abramson 1973). However, general interest in sexual matters has been found to be positively related to frequency of masturbation (Abramson 1973). High frequencies of self-stimulation are most likely to occur in sexually active adolescents who have just broken up with a partner (Gagnon, Simon, & Berger 1970). On the basis of these studies, it seems that masturbation is related to sexual drive and lack of other sexual outlets, especially in people with sexual experience.

Educational level and religiosity are also related to masturbation. The greater the amount of education, the more likely it is that an individual has masturbated (Miller & Lief 1976). This relationship is particularly pronounced in women. Highly educated women have more liberal attitudes about female sexuality in general, and it seems that these attitudes work against the traditional societal restraints (Schmidt & Sigusch 1971). In contrast, religious devoutness appears to inhibit masturbation; the greater the identification with a traditional religion (Judaism, Catholicism, or Protestantism), the less likely a man or woman is to masturbate. However, there is evidence that the inhibitory effect of religion—as well as other types of restraints—has been waning since the time of the Kinsey report (Hunt 1974).

Comparative Perspective: Masturbation in Animals

Masturbation is fairly common in mammals. In males, the method utilized is generally adapted to the manipulatory skills of the species: Old World monkeys usually stimulate themselves by hand; spider monkeys, which have a prehensile tail (one that may be utilized for grasping), often use the tip of this structure to stimulate their penises; and elephants may use their trunks in masturbation. In the case of dolphins—which have no way of manipulating themselves with their appendages—special behaviors have been observed: captive animals may hold their erect penises against the jet of the water intake or rub against objects—like brushes—on the bottom or the side of the tank. Generally, males masturbate more frequently when they do not have access to receptive females. However, some rhesus monkey males masturbate to ejaculation in the presence of receptive females (Carpenter 1942; Ford & Beach 1951).

In rare cases, animals may erotically stimulate themselves in areas other than their genitals. During the rutting (reproductive) season, male red deer have been observed rubbing their antlers gently against vegetation. Erection and extrusion of the penis from its sheath follow within a few seconds, and shortly thereafter ejaculation occurs (Darling 1937).

The masturbation of female cats and dogs is familiar to most pet owners. During the estrous period, these animals frequently rub their vulvas against objects (including the legs of their owners). This behavior not only functions to stimulate the genitals but leaves a distinctive scent mark which attracts males of the species to the area. In captive female porcupines, a rather unusual method of masturbation has been observed. Individuals in estrus hold a stick in one forepaw, straddle it, and walk about the cage in an erect position; bumps and vibrations from the end of the stick in contact with the ground apparently produce erotic stimulation of the genitals (Wallace 1980).

In conclusion, masturbation seems to have evolved in lower animals and is not a uniquely human phenomenon. For both animals and humans, masturbation appears to be a substitute for copulation or coitus. Nonetheless, there is evidence that masturbation may function as a supplement to other sexual outlets.

Theoretical Perspective: Masturbatory Aids

A variety of paraphernalia used to facilitate masturbation is sold in certain stores. For males, an inflatable, life-sized rubber doll resembling a female is available; the doll is equipped with an artificial vagina and anus. There are also various types of vacuum devices that can be attached to the penis.[3]

For females, artificial penises of various sizes can be purchased. There are even models that simulate ejaculation by permitting the passage of warm liquid through a small tube. Vibrators are also sold in a variety of shapes and sizes. (In what might be called "respectable" stores, vibrators are marketed as massagers for the muscles or face.) The vibrators may be pressed against the clitoral and mons area or inserted into the vagina.

Attitudes about these masturbatory aids differ greatly. Some of the differences can be conceptualized in light of two sociological orientations: utopian and dystopian. *Utopians* believe that a continually expanding economy will pro-

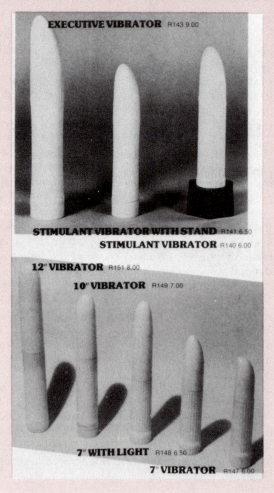

FIGURE 7.5
Vibrators.

vide for an ever-rising standard of living. This higher standard of living will usu-ally be translated into more enjoyable leisure time, probably including more sat-isfying sexual relationships. In contrast, *dystopians* claim that continued tech-nological growth is bringing about certain social problems; technology is, in a sense, becoming master instead of slave. For example, dystopians believe that technology has led to what they call the "Playboy syndrome." In essence, technological growth has produced compulsive consumption; compulsive con-sumption requires contrived scarcity; contrived scarcity has resulted in the commercialization of sex; and, with commercialization, certain aspects of sex-uality have become depersonalized (Gendron 1977).

In regard to masturbatory aids, the utopian could argue that technological advances have benefitted people sexually. They now have a greater number of options in regard to sexuality. Furthermore, technology may be helpful to those with sexual problems. For example, some sex therapists have recommended the use of vibrators in therapy for women who do not experience orgasm (see chapter 21).

The dystopians might counter by arguing that technology has interfered with the most intimate aspects of people's lives. They could claim that an activity that should be a natural, spontaneous expression of love and affection has been depersonalized and made artificial. Whatever one's personal evaluation, it appears that there has been an increase in the sales of masturbatory aids in the late 1970s and early 1980s.

SUMMARY

Sexual fantasies seem to have a large variety of functions. They facili-tate sexual arousal for many people, but they may inhibit arousal for cer-tain individuals with strong sex guilt. Fantasies may also serve to re-hearse possible future events, enrich the sexual experience at hand, or provide relief from boredom. High frequency of fantasizing seems to be related to high levels of sexual drive and to intelligence or creativity.

Sexual themes in fantasies are similar for men and women. However, males are more likely to utilize fantasies to become sexually aroused, while women tend to fantasize most after becoming aroused.

Sexuality in dreams is particularly difficult to interpret. Sex-related factors seem to affect the content of dreams, but penile erections and vaginal arousal may occur during sleep independent of sexual dreams.

Nocturnal orgasms—orgasms occurring during sleep—take place in both sexes but more commonly in males. The orgasms apparently func-tion to release sexual tension. However, the number of nocturnal or-gasms occurring following periods of sexual abstinence is relatively small.

Masturbation has been condemned historically, and many people still have negative attitudes about sexual self-stimulation. A large variety of maladies have been blamed on masturbation. However, there is no evidence to support these myths. Furthermore, some sex therapists have pointed to certain positive aspects of masturbation.

Males masturbate more frequently than females, and typically recall beginning masturbation at an earlier age. These sex differences are probably related to sex-role learning. In addition, masturbation in females may be more difficult to define and consequently is less frequently reported.

Sex surveys indicate religious devoutness inhibits masturbation, but educational level is positively correlated with likelihood of masturbation, particularly in women. In contrast to Victorian beliefs, neither emotional stability nor self-esteem is related to frequency of masturbation.

NOTES

1. As will be seen in chapter 19, rape consists of hostile and sometimes brutal aggression. In contrast, fantasies of rapelike scenes involve a more assertive type of aggression; a common theme is that the women are so desirable that men simply cannot resist them. Clearly, there is a difference between being highly desired and being brutalized.

2. I have heard of (but have not personally observed) a Hindu guru who can induce erection and ejaculation by meditation alone. However, this phenomenon has not, as yet, been reported in the scientific literature.

3. The *British Medical Journal* published a detailed report of penile injuries resulting from vacuum cleaners. Apparently, some men placed their organs in the machines in search of sexual excitement. (The explanations given to the physicians, however, were quite bizarre.) Injuries consisted mostly of severe lacerations and were painful but reparable (Citron & Wade 1980).

CHAPTER 8

Heterosexual Interaction

The majority of people in our society—and in virtually all societies—find sexual interaction with a member of the opposite sex very satisfying. It is not unusual for someone to rate a heterosexual episode as the most satisfying single experience of his or her life.

Heterosexual interaction involves a great variety of behaviors. At one time, various types of noncoital activities were classified as *foreplay*. However, coitus does not always follow sexual play, and sexual activities often continue after sexual intercourse. Furthermore, foreplay suggests a specified order of events, a suggestion that tends to reduce spontaneity in sexual interaction. Therefore, the term foreplay will be used sparingly. It should be remembered that the topics discussed in this chapter—mutual touching, oral stimulation, coitus, and anal intercourse—may occur in a large variety of combinations and orders.

TOUCHING

Various forms of touching, stroking, and caressing can be extremely arousing. In fact, several women in the Hite (1976) survey remembered the arousal resulting from mutual touching and kissing before marriage to be more exciting and satisfying than coitus following marriage. In contrast—as will be seen in chapter 21—certain sexual dysfunctions seem to be related to inadequate tactual stimulation before coitus is attempted.

Touching can have a variety of meanings. Sometimes, it may simply represent a kind of playfulness or generally positive feeling. At other times, touching communicates affection and trust. At still others, a touch promotes feelings of comfort or security, feelings that can have the deepest significance.

The meaning behind a touch is, of course, not always this positive. In some cases, a touch represents attempts at manipulation or exploi-

FIGURE 8.1

Many people rate sexual interaction between a man and a woman as one of life's greatest pleasures.

tation—for example, President Lyndon Johnson was known for his "laying on of hands" when he wanted a political favor. Another less positive aspect of touching is its use to reinforce status differential. One study found that doctors tended to touch other members of the hospital staff, but it was considered presumptuous for lower-status persons to reciprocate or initiate tactual contact with a doctor (Goffman 1967). Since a touch can carry such a variety of messages, it is not surprising that touching is sometimes ambiguous.

Although there are general similarities between the sexes in regard to perception of touching, women seem to evaluate nonsexual touching more positively than men. An attitudinal study of touching behavior suggests that part of this difference is due to fears of femininity or homosexuality in certain men. Men who have high levels of self-esteem (and presumably low fears of being feminine) have significantly more positive feelings about touching in general than men with low levels of self-esteem (Maier & Ernest 1978).

There are also certain sex differences concerning touching in sexual areas. Evidence from a study investigating reactions to hypothetical touches given to various parts of the body indicates females generally perceive a sexual touch as arousing but not necessarily pleasant; males perceive a comparable touch as arousing, pleasant, and playful (Nguyen, Heslin, & Nguyen 1975). Apparently, men are likely to consider sexual touching within a playful context. In contrast, women— who typically fear sexual exploitation to a greater extent than men—are inhibited from enjoying some of the more playful aspects of sexual touching.

Erogenous Zones

Some parts of the body which have relatively high concentrations of tactile nerve endings are very sensitive to touch and sexual stimulation; these areas are called *erogenous zones*. The glans penis, labia minora, areas between the anus and the genitals, anus, breasts (especially the nipples), mouth, ears (particularly the lobes), buttocks, and inner surface of the thighs are generally considered the primary erogenous zones. In addition to these areas, the neck, inside of the hands and feet, and abdomen and groin may be responsive to sexual stimulation in some individuals. Although there are similarities in the erogenous zones of the two sexes, certain differences exist: significantly more males than females consider their thighs to be erogenous zones; conversely, more females than males consider their breasts erotic areas (Goldstein 1976).

People of the same sex, however, differ a great deal in where and how they like to be stimulated. Most women find stroking and caressing of the breasts pleasantly arousing, and, in some cases, women can be brought to orgasm by breast stimulation alone. In contrast, certain women dislike breast manipulation. (As suggested in chapter 3, there is no relationship between breast size and satisfaction with breast stimulation.)

The type of genital stimulation that is perceived as most pleasant depends, to a great extent, on the level of arousal. Generally, light, leisurely touching of the external genital area is satisfying to a woman in the early stages of a sexual encounter. Then, as sexual arousal increases, more vigorous stimulation is preferred. A common complaint of women is that their partners place a finger or fingers in their vagina too early in their sex play (Masters & Johnson 1966). As suggested earlier, men tend to become aroused more rapidly than women and, consequently, they may overestimate their partner's need for strong tactile stimulation.

Since the vaginal lips and clitoris do not receive direct vaginal lubrication, too much stimulation—even during relatively high levels of arousal—may cause irritation. Lubrication brought from the vagina or obtained from a bottle in the form of lotion or oil may help to relieve this problem. Some women enjoy direct stimulation of the tip of the clitoris during sexual interaction. However, because of the extreme sensitivity of the clitoral glans, most women prefer manipulation of the clitoral shaft. In the majority of cases, a variety in types of stimulation and areas stimulated is perceived as highly enjoyable (Hite 1976).

Males, too, prefer light stroking and caressing at first, followed by more vigorous stimulation as arousal builds. When the penis is flaccid, strong stimulation is not arousing and, in some cases, may be threatening; a man may fear that he is not getting an erection fast enough. Many men enjoy light stroking of the inner thighs and scrotum during the early stages of arousal (Masters & Johnson 1979).

Once a firm erection occurs, strong stimulation of the penis is typically perceived as arousing. In some cases, stimulation of the frenulum (the fold of skin just below the glans on the underside of the penis) is very satisfying. As we have seen in chapter 3, this is one of the most sensitive areas of the penis (Hite 1981).

Comparative and Anthropological Perspective: Touching in Other Animals and in Other Cultures

Various forms of touching occur in other animals, especially as a prelude to copulation. A sexually ready male octopus will typically attempt to caress a female with his eight sucker-clad arms (female readers are perhaps reminded of experiences somewhat comparable to this). On certain occasions, female insects poke males in the genital area, particularly if they are occupied in nonsexual activities such as eating (Lane 1960; Wallace 1980).

Among mammals, elephants have been observed manipulating one another's genitals with their trunks, and apes sometimes grasp the penis or place a finger in their partner's vagina before they copulate (Wallace 1980). However, touching behavior—especially the touching of nonsexual areas—is much less common in nonhuman mammals than in people.

These differences between humans and other mammals are apparently related to two factors. Humans have very little hair on their bodies and have superior control of the hands and fingers. No one is sure why humans lost their body hair, but the development of hand and finger control is probably related to the development of tool use. Some other mammals—such as dolphins—have lost their body hair, and apes have fairly good control of their hands and fingers. However, humans are the only ones that have shown both developments.

Another factor related to the varieties of human touching behavior is the development of the brain. As suggested earlier, humans' great intelligence enables them to express themselves in a multitude of ways and find extreme diversity of meaning in sexual expression. Although it is impossible to compare how much animals and humans "enjoy" sex, one can be quite sure that sexual interaction takes on a greater variety of meaning for a human than for any animal.

Among various human societies, there are great differences in the emphasis placed on touching in general. It is not uncommon for a southern European to perceive a northern European as cold for not reciprocating a touch. On the other hand, touching by southern Europeans may be perceived as crude by their northern neighbors.

Touching during sexual interaction also varies considerably. As described in chapter 1, the sexually liberal Mangaians often spend hours stroking and caressing one another before engaging in sexual intercourse. In contrast, people in Inis Beag spend little or no time touching as a prelude to intercourse (Messinger 1971; Marshall 1971). Within our society, significant changes have taken place since the time of the Kinsey studies. During the 1940s and early 1950s, couples spent relatively little time touching or engaging in other sexually stimulating activities before coitus. By the time of the *Playboy* survey, couples of all educational levels reported significantly longer periods of foreplay (Hunt 1974). It seems that, as people become more liberal in their sexual attitudes, they express their sexuality in a great variety of ways, including various forms of touching.

Author's Perspective: Touching and Sexual Communication

Since there are great individual differences in what types of touching are satisfying—and the areas of the body that are most sensitive—it is important to communicate about touching with one's partner. This can be done verbally or with various kinds of nonverbal messages. Sometimes a smile or a gentle movement of the partner's hand can not only communicate information but add to the excitement of the moment. Despite the many possibilities for communicating, it was somewhat surprising for me to find, as a marriage counselor, that couples rarely understood what was tactually satisfying to one another.

There are probably several factors that inhibit communication and reduce the possibilities of a good understanding between partners. In some cases, early negative conditioning by Victorian-type parents, friends, or teachers makes it difficult for people to discuss—or even think much about—sexual matters. Guilt and embarrassment may result from even the most rudimentary attempts at communication.

Sexual communication may also be inhibited by hesitance to consider sexual "performance." This can work in two ways. People may avoid communicating what is pleasurable because they fear exposing their own "inadequacies" or because they are afraid of hurting their partner's feelings.

In still other cases, certain problems in communication may be related to the traditional male and female roles associated with erotic interaction. Men are expected to be knowledgeable and sexually competent; it is traditionally "unmasculine" for a male to inquire about what is satisfying to a woman. The traditional woman, in turn, is supposed to be sexually reserved and demure; it may be considered "unfeminine" for women to take initiatives or offer suggestions. Such traditional role-playing inhibits sexual communication even though communication about other matters may be good.

Fortunately, my experiences with couples in therapy suggest it is not too difficult to open channels of communication. If both partners are motivated to try, some positive experiences in communicating are often followed by the lessening of several other types of inhibition. For example, the discovery that one's partner enjoys a certain type of touch—followed by a successful stroke or caress in the "appropriate" fashion—may culminate in the discussion of several previously taboo topics.

The pleasure or arousal value of a touch is, of course, not the only factor to consider. As we have seen, touches carry a variety of meanings, and there is sometimes a discrepancy in the way partners interpret a stroke or caress. Particularly relevant is the finding that men are more likely to interpret a touch in a sexual area as playful than are women. This may help to explain certain misunderstandings that may emerge when a male casually caresses his female partner's breasts or buttocks. As with the association between pleasure and touching, it seems important for couples to discuss what certain kinds of touches mean to them. This complex relationship between a touch and sexual communication—and possible ways to improve it—will be considered again in chapter 21.

ORAL STIMULATION

Kissing in various forms is one of the most common types of heterosexual interaction, and many people remember a kiss as their first highly arousing sexual activity. As couples become more intimate, lip kissing is often accompanied by the deep or "French" kiss, which involves the placement of one partner's tongue in the other's mouth. Like touching, kissing has taken on a great deal of meaning not directly related to sexuality. A kiss may be a symbol of respect for authority, a sign of endearment between friends, or, in some instances, a signal for impending disaster—as in the "kiss of death" from a leader of the Cosa Nostra.

Of course, a kiss may be directed at areas other than the partner's lips. Kissing or nibbling of various body parts typically accompanies the stroking and caressing activities discussed in the last section. Since the moistness of the lips and tongue enhance erotic stimulation, it is not surprising that people respond favorably to oral contact with such areas as the earlobes, nipples of the breasts (especially those of women), and inner thighs (Hite 1976, 1981).

Oral-Genital Sex

Oral stimulation of the male's genitals is known as *fellatio;* comparable stimulation of the female's genital area is called *cunnilingus.* When simultaneous oral-genital interaction takes place, it is sometimes referred to as *sixty-nining,* or sex in the 69 position (the numbers mimic the inverted position of the couple).

Oral-genital sex, like many other forms of sexual activity, is more prevalent today than at the time of the Kinsey reports. However, some people still believe that oral-genital sex is dirty or unhealthy. In actuality, there are no health problems unless one of the partners has a sexually transmitted disease. In this case, oral-genital sex is no more likely to transmit the disease than sexual intercourse. If ejaculation takes place in the mouth of the female, the semen is not likely to cause problems, even if swallowed. (Some women dislike the taste, but others do not find it offensive.) Similarly, vaginal lubrication does not contain any dangerous or unhealthy substances.

Receiving oral stimulation of the penis is highly satisfying to many

FIGURE 8.2

Cues from the environment may function to accentuate the impact of a kiss. For many people, automobiles—sports cars in particular—symbolize sexuality.

men. A general indication of males' desire for this type of interaction comes from research into the types of activities requested of prostitutes; fellatio is by far the most popular type of sexual service performed by call girls in New York (Stein 1974).

There are large individual differences in the specific types of oral stimulation that men find arousing. However, several respondents in a survey found movements of the woman's tongue around the frenulum and glans penis highly satisfying. Another popular technique involved slow movements in and out of the woman's mouth. In several cases, men reported oral stimulation of the penis to be a successful way of inducing erection when other methods failed (Tavris 1978).

Women who engage in fellatio tend to find it satisfying, particularly after they have overcome initial resistance to this activity (as we shall see, this resistance is not uncommon). Some women report a satisfaction with oral-genital sex because it allows them to stay virgins and still participate in highly erotic activity (Hite 1976).

In many cases, women get a sensation of gagging if the penis exerts pressure against the back of the tongue or throat. (This sensation is due to a physiological gag reflex.) Gagging can be prevented if the woman controls the depth of penetration by holding onto the shaft of the penis. If stimulation in the deep throat is frequent, a woman may get used to it and no longer experience the gagging sensation (Masters & Johnson 1966).

Cunnilingus is reported as highly satisfying by many women. In fact, 62 percent of the respondents in the *Redbook* survey rated oral stimulation of their genitals as "very enjoyable" (Tavris & Sadd 1977). Particularly arousing was stimulation of the clitoris by gentle tongue movements or, in some cases, by firmer pressure from the tongue and lips. The labia minora are also very sensitive to oral stimulation. Some women enjoy having their partners blow into their vaginas or on their clitorises (Hite 1976).

Comparative and Anthropological Perspective: Oral Stimulation in Other Animals and in Other Cultures

Kissing is practically nonexistent in subhuman animals. However, there are a few examples of oral-genital stimulation. In an unusual marine worm, what might be called oral-genital sex actually results in the equivalent of pregnancy. Males develop sperm-containing segments at the tail end of their bodies at certain times of the year. When these segments are well developed, the females bite off the tail ends of the males. The females then swallow the tails, and the digestive juices liberate the sperm, which eventually find their way to the eggs. Strangely, this is the only way in which the eggs can become fertilized (Michelmore 1965).

In mammals, oral-genital stimulation occurs infrequently. Nonetheless, a large group of human spectators casually strolling by a Chicago outdoor zoo exhibit observed a female orangutan take a male's penis in her mouth. This interaction was followed by vigorous, but brief, copulation.

Why is oral stimulation so much more common in humans than animals? A major factor seems to be the great ability of humans to make subtle tongue and lip movements—and to be sensitive to minimal tactile stimulation of these areas. The area of the cerebral cortex governing the motor and sensory functions of the mouth and tongue is much larger in humans than in any other mammal (Penfield & Rasmussen 1950; Woolsey 1958). It seems that the evolution of speech was important in this development; then, the greater sensitivity and muscular control of the lips probably became related to oral stimulation associated with sexuality. Another factor, mentioned earlier, is the tendency of humans to express variability and originality in their sexual interaction.

Variability and originality are clearly seen when oral stimulation in various cultures is considered. For example, the Ford and Beach (1951) survey of information on preliterate cultures indicates that a kiss may take many forms. The Lapps of northern Scandinavia kiss with their mouth and nose at the same time. Among the Tinguians of the Philippine Islands, the partners place their lips near one another's face and suddenly inhale. Several societies found the Western method of kissing—especially the deep kiss—disgusting when they first heard of it.

The prevalence of oral-genital sex depends, to a great extent, on a culture's general attitudes towards sexuality and on its attitudes towards male and female sex roles. Cultures such as Inis Beag that are conservative in regard to sexuality do not report much oral-genital sex (Messinger 1971); male-dominated societies, like the Chiricahua Indians of the Southwest, tolerate fellatio to a much greater extent than cunnilingus (Friedl 1975); Mangaia and other sexually liberal societies that perceive males and females as having equal status report a high incidence of both fellatio and cunnilingus (Marshall 1971). Some of the liberal South Sea cultures also report interesting variations on oral-genital sex. Men of the Ponapeon culture of the Caroline Islands were known to place a small fish in a woman's vagina and then slowly remove it with their mouths (Ford & Beach 1951). Our society presents some relevant parallels to these cross-cultural comparisons; as sexual attitudes have become more liberal, oral-genital sex—and variations of oral-genital interactions—have become more common. Similarly, as attitudes towards female sexuality have become more liberal, cunnilingus has been more widely accepted (Hunt 1974).

Author's Perspective: Negative Feelings and Ambivalence about Oral-Genital Sex

In all probability, some readers thought parts of the preceding sections on oral-genital sex were gross. There are a variety of reasons for negative or at least ambivalent feelings about oral-genital sex. In the first place, the early Judeo-Christian view that any sexual act that does not lead to reproduction is "perverse" or "unnatural" is still alive. This negative view is dramatically reflected in our language: some of the most degrading slang terms refer to oral-genital sex, particularly fellatio.

Even our legal system reflects this negative view. In certain states, oral-genital sex is illegal and may be prosecuted under *sodomy* laws (*sodomy* literally means "crime against nature"). Since sodomy is considered a serious crime, there have been some controversial court decisions. In Indiana, during the 1960s, a woman became angry at her husband and charged him with sodomy, even though he did not use force. Before the case came to trial, the woman changed her mind and attempted to withdraw the charge. However, her petition was denied because sodomy is defined as an offense against the state. Consequently, the husband was tried and convicted, and he ended up spending three years in a state prison.

Clearly, there are a number of moral and constitutional problems inherent in sodomy laws. As in the Indiana case, a person may receive a long jail sentence for a behavior that is widely practiced and accepted by a large number of people. Another problem is related to collecting evidence. Since sexual acts generally take place in private, police and private detectives are encouraged to collect evidence under questionable circumstances. The gathering of evidence related to sexual behavior may also promote extortion and police corruption (Packer 1968).

Fortunately, as a result of these and other arguments, the American Law Institute (1962) prepared a *Model Penal Code* which recommended the abolition of laws proscribing or limiting sexual activities performed by consenting adults in private. Some states have revised their laws along the guidelines of this code. Furthermore, certain other states have reduced the penalties for sexual offenses between consenting adults.[1]

The "perverse" and "unnatural" arguments are not the only ones that create negative or ambivalent feelings about oral-genital sex. As we have seen, some people falsely believe that fellatio and cunnilingus are dirty or unhealthy. Extensive interviews with couples indicate that these beliefs are most commonly found in working-class individuals. Working-class women who engage in oral-genital sex often report their involvement in such activities is reluctant and accompanied by guilt. Working-class men, in return, have ambivalence about their partner's involvement in oral-genital sex; they enjoy it but somehow feel that "nice" women shouldn't do it. Professional couples have some of these same conflicts, but to a lesser extent. Differences between working-class and professional couples are most pronounced in regard to perceptions of health. Working-class individuals of both sexes tend to believe the genitals are dirty and that oral-genital sex is unhealthy (Rubin 1976).

Still other negative or ambivalent feelings are related to more specific factors, such as embarrassment at not knowing what to do or fear that one's partner will not like the odors and tastes associated with the genitals. Sex-role conflicts may emerge if a woman feels that she should adopt a traditionally passive part in sexual activities or if a man feels it is unmasculine to be concerned with a woman's sexual needs. There is also the fear, particularly in women, of losing the partner's respect.

Since such a variety of beliefs and feelings is associated with oral-genital sex, it seems particularly important that couples discuss their attitudes if they engage in—or are contemplating—fellatio or cunnilingus. Unexpected conflicts have arisen between many couples who entered a committed relationship and then found that their views on oral-genital sex differed significantly. On the other hand, if partners are able to discuss matters openly—with respect for the other person's feelings as well as the so-called facts—many disagreements can be avoided or resolved.

ANAL STIMULATION

Since the anal region is considered an erogenous zone, it is not surprising that anal stimulation of various kinds may occur as part of heterosexual interaction. (Homosexual anal stimulation will be discussed in chapter 17.) Some couples rub the rim of the anus or insert a finger into the cavity. Both male and female orgasm can result from anal stimulation in certain cases (Masters & Johnson 1979). However, many people—particularly older individuals—have strong negative feelings about this type of stimulation and prefer to avoid it (Tavris & Sadd 1977).

Placement of the penis in the anus is known as anal intercourse. In the *Redbook* survey, the majority of women who reported engaging in this activity said that anal intercourse represented an experimentation or an attempt to please the male partner. Most of the women found the experience unpleasant or unsatisfying. Nonetheless, 10 percent rated it ''very enjoyable'' (Tavris & Sadd 1977).

Anal intercourse has certain medical dangers. If the penis is inserted into the vagina after contact with the anus, there is likely to be a transfer of bacteria that can cause vaginal infections. Therefore, any vaginal contact after anal intercourse should be preceded by a thorough washing of the penis (Feigen 1975; Neubardt 1975).

When the woman is anxious and tense, she finds it difficult or impossible to relax the anal sphincter muscle. Without relaxation of this muscle, there may be damage to the anal canal and/or pain for the woman. Generally, the use of a lubricant is advised to facilitate anal entrance. In addition to these problems, many medical authorities believe that repeated anal intercourse can result in intestinal trauma or hemorrhoids (Walen et al. 1977).

SEXUAL INTERCOURSE

Coitus, or sexual intercourse, is the activity most closely identified with ''having sex.'' As we have seen, attitudes toward sexuality have been becoming more liberal since the time of the Kinsey reports, and this liberalization is reflected in several changes in coital patterns in recent years.

For several age groups, coitus is reportedly taking place more frequently than during the 1940s. This increase is probably due to a general reduction in sex guilt and a corresponding increase in sexual drive.

There is also an apparent increase in the duration of coitus. In the 1940s, most males ejaculated about two minutes after intromission (Kinsey et al. 1948). However, by 1972, the median duration had increased to ten minutes and was as high as thirteen minutes for partners under twenty-five. The increase in duration of intercourse may be an important factor in the increase in the number of women who report consistent orgasm (Hunt 1974). Support for this conclusion comes from a study identifying a strong relationship between duration of intercourse and female orgasm: only 25 percent of women interviewed reported consistent orgasm if intromission lasted one minute or less; 50 percent if intromission lasted one to eleven minutes; and 65 percent if intromission lasted longer than eleven minutes (Gebhard 1966).

Still another change since the time of the Kinsey reports involves a general shift away from coital patterns that reflect male domination. Not only has intercourse been prolonged, on the average, but coital positions that produce strong clitoral stimulation have become more common. The apparent result has been more satisfaction for women. Furthermore, there is less of a double standard for males and females regarding who initiates sexual intercourse. And at least some men seem more concerned with women's sexual needs than were men earlier in the century.

There are, as one might predict, large individual differences in the

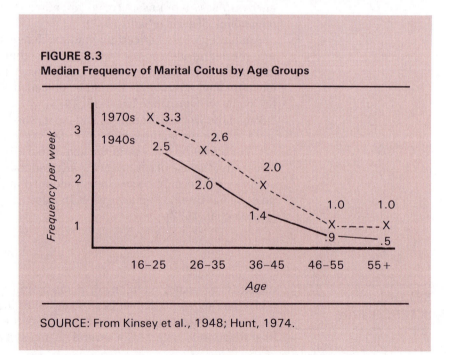

FIGURE 8.3
Median Frequency of Marital Coitus by Age Groups

SOURCE: From Kinsey et al., 1948; Hunt, 1974.

pattern of sexual intercourse. At least some of the differences may be explained in terms of general personality characteristics. Couples who have a high degree of achievement orientation tend to emphasize "achieving" orgasm or reaching high levels of sexual "performance." A couple who met with me in a marriage counseling situation recorded their sexual activity and satisfaction on charts that in many respects resembled sales charts associated with the husband's business. Another couple, who emphasized punctuality and functioning on a tight, inflexible schedule in their everyday lives, had sexual intercourse at precisely the same time every week—and with little or no variation in procedure. Of course, there are always exceptions. As suggested earlier, it is often difficult to predict the quality of someone else's sex life on the basis of external appearance.

Coital Positions

A large variety of positions for sexual intercourse have been described: the *Kama Sutra* lists over thirty-five, having such colorful names as the Lotus and the Union of the Elephant with His Mates (Vatsyayana 1963). The objective of this section is not to identify all possible positions. (Some, incidentally, are literally exhausting and are probably attempted only by acrobats.) Rather, the emphasis will be on physical, psychological, and emotional factors associated with coitus in various positions.

Face to face, with man on top is sometimes called the *missionary position* because certain nineteenth-century Christian missionaries declared

FIGURE 8.4

Face-to-face coital position, man on top.

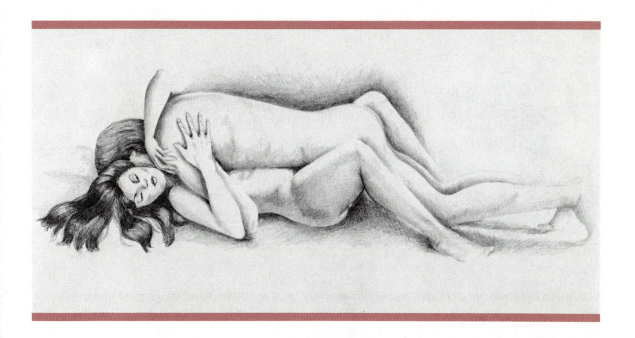

it to be the only acceptable one. It is apparently the most common in Western society. Vaginal penetration is fairly easy, especially if the female lies with her legs apart and knees bent. Often, the female guides the penis into her vagina when she has reached a sufficient level of arousal. Since the female is somewhat slower to reach a high level of excitement than the male, there are advantages to her choosing the time of penetration.

The man generally supports some of his weight on his elbows and knees to avoid crushing his partner and to direct his coital movements. Movements directed toward the top of the vulva are particularly satisfying to the woman, since they provide relatively strong stimulation of the clitoris. The woman, in turn, can regulate the amount and type of stimulation to a certain extent by shifting her pelvis and closing her legs. The latter response produces more friction against the penis and may help to produce full erection.

The missionary position has certain advantages over other positions. It allows for good communication, both vocally and visually. It also allows the male to exert more initiative and movement than the female, which some couples prefer.

A possible disadvantage of the missionary position is that the woman's movements may be somewhat restricted. Furthermore, penetration may be so deep as to cause pain in some women. Finally, if the man is very heavy or if the woman is pregnant, the man's weight may cause discomfort.

Face to face, with the woman on top appears to be the next most popu-

FIGURE 8.5

Face-to-face coital position, woman on top.

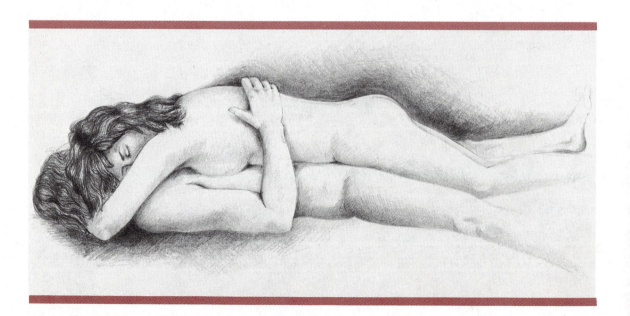

lar coital position in Western society. This position affords a better opportunity for clitoral stimulation and is more likely to produce female orgasm. Furthermore, if the woman weighs less than the man, there is not so much of a weight burden for the partner underneath.

In the United States, this position has been increasing in popularity. According to the Kinsey reports, many more couples born after 1900 had intercourse in this position than those born before 1900. Furthermore, the number of persons apparently utilizing this position in 1972 was larger than that reported by Kinsey (Hunt 1974). It seems that a greater perception of equality among sex partners reduces the psychological threat to the man of assuming a ''passive'' coital position.

Penetration is usually accomplished as the woman assumes a kneeling position and lowers her body over the man, who is lying on his back. An advantage of this position is that it allows the woman greater control and freedom of movement than the missionary position. Furthermore, penile penetration can be regulated and, if desired, can reach its greatest depth with the woman on top. The man may also find it easier to delay orgasm. Finally, this position allows the man more freedom to caress his partner with his hands.

The position does restrict the man's freedom of movement, and in some cases the penis may slip out of the vagina. Furthermore, some couples find it uncomfortable for the female to play a more aggressive role in coitus than the male.

Lying side by side, face to face is a preferred position in some societies and a common variation in Western society. Although penetration is

FIGURE 8.6
Side-by-side coital position.

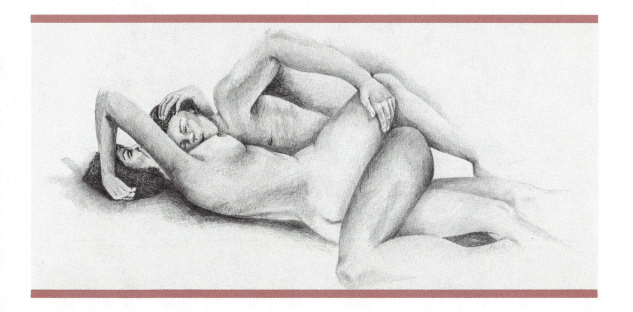

shallow and movement is somewhat restricted, there is not the problem of one partner crushing the other with his or her weight. Therefore, it is relatively easy to prolong coitus in this position. Side-by-side coitus is considered most practical when the woman is pregnant. Another advantage of the side-by-side position is that both partners can control the coital movements.

Some couples do find it difficult to achieve penetration in the side-by-side position. The position also hinders the vigorous coital movements that may be necessary in order to reach orgasm.

Rear-entry positions have been described in detail by Ellis (1960). For example, both partners may lie on their sides; the woman may kneel or lie on her stomach as the man enters; the man may sit while the woman sits on his lap. Rear-entry positions shorten the woman's vagina, making deeper penetration possible. Rear entry may be preferable for some

FIGURE 8.7

Rear-entry coital position.

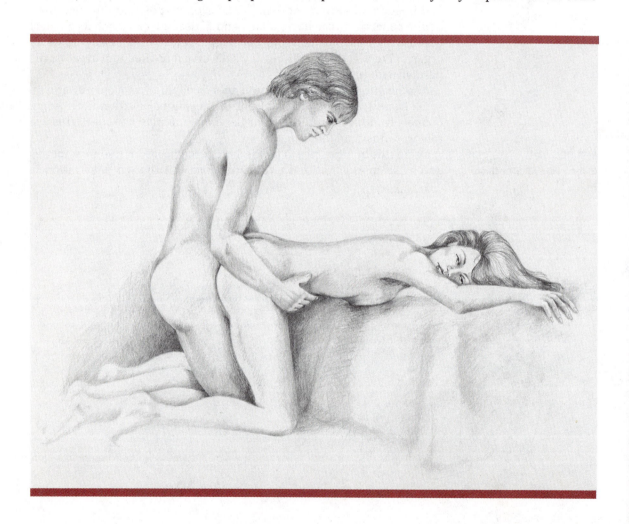

tired, older, or handicapped individuals, since it is considered less strenuous, especially side by side. However, entry may be difficult, and very heavy individuals or men with short organs have difficulty maintaining penetration (Eichenlaub 1961).

Comparative Perspective: Copulation in Animals

Copulation means basically the same thing as coitus, but the former term is preferred when considering subhuman animals. Before pursuing this topic further, it is important to note that not all animals that reproduce sexually copulate. In many fishes, sperm and eggs are shed into the water, where fertilization takes place. In contrast, all higher animals—and some lower ones as well—copulate, utilizing, as we have seen, a variety of intromittent organs and receptacles. The method of copulation is related to an animal's life-style. For example, whales mate in the sea (sometimes amid great splashes), swifts in the air (often falling a thousand feet while locked in an "embrace"), gibbons in the trees (occasionally holding onto a branch with one arm), and porcupines on the land (while exhibiting great care). In the case of porcupines, the female demonstrates her acceptance of the male by flattening her quills and pulling her tail to one side; this is crucial, since the male mounts her in typical dog fashion (Maier & Maier 1970; Wallace 1980).

The number of times an animal copulates varies greatly, especially for males. The male copulatory organ of a certain species of fly breaks off and is left inside the female after mating—blocking the female's orifice from other males and, of course, also preventing the male from initiating further encounters (Daly & Wilson 1983).

In the case of the praying mantis, the aggressiveness of the female often limits the smaller male to a single copulation. She is cannibalistic and frequently devours an unwary male. Consequently, a potentially successful male approaches slowly, with careful stalking movements that may last for hours. When the male is within range, he leaps onto the female's back, clasping her with his large front legs. The female typically shows little reaction to this; even during the copulation that follows, she may move about and devour other insects. However, if the male is discovered during his approach, or if he lands awkwardly on her back, the female wheels about, seizes him, and begins eating him head first. Despite all of this, the male—minus his head—is usually able to mount and copulate. This headless performance is possible because the neural center that controls mating is located in the body below the head. Since some inhibitory mechanisms are located in the head, a headless male may actually copulate with increased vigor before his fate is sealed (Roeder 1935).

At the other extreme, some rodents copulate at a very high rate. The animal with probably the highest level of sexual activity is a small rodent named Shaw's jird, an inhabitant of the Sahara Desert. A pair of jirds has been observed copulating 224 times in a period of two hours. Although ejaculation does not accompany each vaginal penetration in these (and most other) rodents, there were probably in excess of thirty ejaculations during this time (Maier & Maier 1970).

The duration of copulation also varies greatly. At the one extreme, monkeys, apes, and many other mammals usually remained coupled less than ten seconds. At the other extreme, a pair of sables has been observed joined together for eight hours (Ford & Beach 1951). This long period of coupling is related to the fact that sables and other members of the mink family are *induced ovulators:* vigorous and prolonged levels of sexual stimulation are necessary to induce secretion of the hormone LH, which in turn brings about ovulation. On the rare occasions when mink or sable engage in short and gentle sexual bouts, the female does not become pregnant. (In contrast, humans and most other mammals are *spontaneous ovulators;* ovulation takes place—independent of external stimulation—in the middle of the menstrual or estrous cycle.)

How does human coitus compare with animal copulation? More than any other mammals, humans exhibit variety in their choice of sexual positions—just as they show variability in many other aspects of behavior. Furthermore, the missionary position—generally the preferred position for humans—is very rare in other animals. A preference for this position may be at least partially due to the fact that human females have a vulva situated more to the front of the body than females of other species. This more ventral location of the vulva seems to have evolved in conjunction with an erect stance and bipedal method of locomotion (Morris 1967).

Humans also engage in coitus for longer periods of time than their closest relatives—monkeys and apes. Furthermore, as was mentioned in chapter 6, humans frequently have sexual relations at times when the woman is not likely to become pregnant—at the beginning and end of the menstrual cycle. As humans evolved, there was probably an increasing tendency for sexuality to become associated with interpersonal relationships transcending reproduction. Thus, as we have seen throughout the book, human sexuality involves much more than perpetuation of the species.

Anthropological Perspective: Coitus in Various Cultures

The average frequency of coitus seems to vary somewhat from culture to culture. People of the Keraki tribe of Papua and New Guinea reportedly had intercourse only once a week on the average, even as young adults. However, such low levels are rare in preliterate cultures. In most societies surveyed by Ford and Beach (1951), the average frequencies reported were approximately once a day for young couples (except during periods when intercourse was considered taboo). Higher levels of sexual activity have been reported for the Aranda of Australia, who apparently had intercourse three to five times nightly, sleeping between times. (It should be remembered that we have no way of determining the accuracy of these reports.)

There are also cultural variations in the duration of intercourse. Generally, the speed with which the male achieves orgasm and ejaculation determines the duration of the coupling. Among the Ifugao of Oceania, the males, particularly inexperienced ones, usually had orgasms very shortly after intromission, so intercourse was very brief. In contrast, Marquesan men of the South Pacific reportedly learned to control themselves to such an extent that they could maintain erection for long periods and ejaculate at will. Males on the island of Bali prolonged coitus for a rather unusual reason; they believed that brief coupling resulted in a deformed child (Ford & Beach 1951).

As in our culture, general attitudes and personality characteristics are related to coital patterns, as illustrated by a comparison of two primitive New Guinea tribes. Among the Arapesh, men and women were considered equal and this equality was seen in their approach to intercourse: either sex could initiate the activity, and emphasis was placed on mutual readiness. On the other hand, in the Tchambuli culture, the women were dominant. They went out and worked while the men stayed home with the family and gossiped with the neighbors. Women chose their mates and were considered to have a higher sex drive than men (Mead 1950).

In a similar fashion, attitudes about life in general are reflected in the manner in which people have coitus. Margaret Mead (1929) found the Samoans to be easygoing and sunny in disposition. Intercourse was approached languorously, with an emphasis upon mutual sharing and sensitivity to the overall interpersonal relationship. In contrast, the Mundugamor society of New Guinea was filled with a great deal of aggression. The aggressiveness appeared in the sexual relationship and was sometimes expressed by a couple toward a third party. For example, a couple would have sexual intercourse in a neighbor's yam garden, believing that such an act would spoil the crop. (This is an interesting contrast to the ancient Hindu belief that there was a *positive* relationship between coitus and fertility of the soil.)[2]

In conclusion, it appears that sexual intercourse, like other forms of sexual activity, is influenced by cultural learning. However, unlike other sexual interactions, every society engages in sexual intercourse to some extent—or that society would not be around for anthropologists to study and analyze.

Author's Perspective: Factors Related to Frustration or Dissatisfaction with Sexual Intercourse

Despite the extremely positive coital experiences many people have—or anticipate having—there are several types of sexual frustrations that come to the attention of marriage counselors, physicians, sex therapists, or concerned friends. In some cases, people find help in reading books and articles on sexual techniques. Inhibitions may be reduced, new channels of communication opened, and people may gain a greater understanding of their partner's sexual style. However, an overanalysis of coital positions may create problems. In extreme cases, people have been known to take books on sexual techniques to bed with them in order to improve on the details of lovemaking. Clearly the dystopians would not be impressed with such procedures. Furthermore, sexual counselors generally report that ignorance of coital positions or techniques is not a basic problem. Of much more concern are a rigid adherence to one technique and a failure to appreciate the partner's needs. Another problem seems to be a general lack of romance in a relationship, a need that is not met by having a book or a technical genius in bed.

A similar type of argument exists in regard to analyzing orgasms. Some people find it helpful to discuss factors that produce orgasm. Others report high levels of satisfaction resulting from attempts to coordinate and produce simultaneous orgasms (Ellis 1960). However, working too hard at sex can lead to what Masters and Johnson (1966) refer to as "spectating": becoming a kind of spectator at one's own performance. This state obviously detracts from the enjoyment and spontaneity of a relationship.

There are also certain technical problems associated with attempts at simultaneous orgasm. The type of movements that men and women make at the moment of orgasm tend to be somewhat incompatible: a man generally penetrates deep into the vagina and holds the position or makes relatively few powerful thrusts; a woman, on the other hand, often prefers continuous stimulation at the time of climax. Coordination, therefore, may be difficult.

It can be argued that, since the male generally becomes aroused faster, he should delay orgasm until after his partner is satisfied. Another solution is for the man to maintain penetration after his orgasm and to continue making thrusting movements until his partner is satisfied. (Since an erection is not entirely lost immediately after ejaculation, this procedure is possible for most men.)

A failure to communicate affection is seen as a problem by many couples. If one partner feels unloved or unappreciated, he or she is likely to respond, in turn, by withholding an expression of positive feelings. Eventually, both partners may withhold affection and, in some cases, each partner blames the other for starting the "merry-go-round." Some people—particularly men—feel that a free expression of affection is a sign of weakness or overly "feminine" behavior. At any rate, intercourse without apparent affection may not only be disappointing in itself but create communication problems as well.

Lack of spontaneity and originality are common problems, not only in regard to displays of affection, but in terms of the specifics of sexual interaction. Women often report that men are too mechanical and ritualistic in their foreplay. Men, in turn, frequently complain that women are not open to new approaches to arousal (DeMartino 1970). In many respects, sexual habits are formed like other habits, and it takes a conscious and concerted effort to break a well-established routine. Sometimes, a new setting—for example, on vacation—can elicit more spontaneity and originality in the sexual relationship. If a change of scene is not possible, a change in schedule may help—especially for people who plan everything, including lovemaking, by the clock.

One of the advantages of marriage counseling is that a couple may discuss such problems as dissatisfaction with coitus in a setting where a third person—the counselor—does not take sides or pass judgment. Such a setting often encourages people to speak of feelings and thoughts that had been left unexpressed because of a fear of rejection or the possibility of starting an unpleasant argument. Several of my clients have reported more satisfying sexual relations following this type of discussion. For couples outside of marriage counseling relationships, there may also be advantages in being nonjudgmental. The idea is, basically, not to find out whose fault something is, but to identify the problem and arrive at a mutually satisfactory way of dealing with it.

SUMMARY

Touching is a common form of heterosexual interaction that has a variety of meanings depending upon the setting, the type of touch, and the area touched. Parts of the body that are very sensitive to sexual stimulation are called erogenous zones. Which ways of touching these zones are most satisfying and arousing depend to a certain extent on the level of sexual arousal.

Touching is more prevalent in humans than in animals, partly because humans have relatively hairless bodies and superior control of the hands and fingers. When different human societies are compared, it appears that the more sexually liberal the culture, the more people tend to touch one another. Within our society, people tend to inhibit communication about what is tactually satisfying and the meaning associated with certain types of touches. There are certain advantages to reducing this inhibition.

Kissing, like touching, has taken on a variety of meanings. The moistness of the lips and tongue make oral stimulation of certain parts of the body appealing to many people.

Oral-genital sexual activities—fellatio and cunnilingus—are more common today than earlier in the century. For many people, these activities are very satisfying. However, some individuals falsely believe that oral-genital sex is unhealthy. Other inhibitions against oral-genital sex include embarrassment or fear, sex-role conflicts, and a feeling of unnaturalness (related to early Judeo-Christian views of sexuality).

Anal stimulation and anal intercourse are practiced by a certain number of couples, although there are generally stronger negative feelings about these activities than about oral-genital sex. Certain medical problems—including damage to the anal canal, hemorrhoids, and bacterial infections—have been associated with anal intercourse.

Attitudes toward sexual intercourse have become more liberal since the 1940s and 1950s. This liberalization is reflected in an increased frequency and duration of coitus as well as a general shift away from coital patterns that reflect male domination. A large variety of coital positions exist, and each has particular advantages and disadvantages.

Compared to our closest animal relatives, humans engage in coitus for a longer period of time, utilize a greater variety of coital positions, and tend to engage in coitus during times when the female is not likely to become pregnant.

General attitudes and personality characteristics are related to coital patterns in our culture and in other cultures as well. Among the most important attitudes and personality factors are feelings about sex roles, personality rigidity, and tendencies toward aggression.

Frustration or dissatisfaction with sexual intercourse is a fairly common problem. In some cases, an overanalysis of coital positions or attempts to achieve simultaneous orgasms may detract from the relationship. In others, failure to communicate affection or lack of spontaneity and originality may present problems. Fortunately, with the aid of marriage counseling or simply increased sensitivity to one another, some couples have improved their sexual relationship in interesting and exciting ways.

NOTES

1. Illinois, in 1962, became the first state to revise its criminal code in response to the Model Penal Code. Arkansas, California, Colorado, Connecticut, Delaware, Hawaii, Maine, New Mexico, North Dakota, Ohio, Oregon, South Dakota, and Washington later followed suit. States that have reduced offenses between consenting adults to misdemeanor status include Kansas, Minnesota, New York, and Utah.

2. A recent book by anthropologist Derek Freeman strongly suggests that some of Margaret Mead's generalizations were oversimplified and, in certain cases, incorrect (Freeman 1983). Thus, until the academic world has time to consider and debate the controversy, Mead's conclusions—especially those in regard to Samoa—should be considered tentative.

PART 4

Emotional Intimacy

The chapters in this part form a progression: Attraction may be followed by an emotionally intimate relationship and, ultimately, love. However, this is not a simple, isolated progression. Attraction does not always develop into intimacy and love. Furthermore, the physiological factors discussed in previous chapters may speed up, alter, or disrupt the progression towards intimacy. Conversely, emotional intimacy—or the lack of it—can have a great influence on sexual functioning.

CHAPTER 9

Sexual Attraction

For countless centuries, poets, novelists, and songwriters have been concerned with sexual attraction. However, it is only within the past two decades that scientists have entered the arena. In some respects, the findings of these scientists confirm what Shakespeare and other highly perceptive individuals have known all along—that physical attractiveness is very important and that there are many subtle ways in which people communicate when they are attracted to each other. However, scientific findings also point to the importance of psychological variables and the interaction between physical appearance and psychological factors. Furthermore, some progress has been made in analyzing the subtleties of communication between individuals who experience sexual attraction.

PHYSICAL APPEARANCE

In virtually all societies studied, physical appearance is important in attractiveness. Nonetheless, there are great differences in what is considered attractive; social learning seems to play a major role in the definition of attractiveness. For example, in some societies, the shape and color of the eyes is important; in others, the formation of the ears is of great significance. Generally speaking, people seem to find most attractive characteristics that are normative for the culture. In one New Guinea society, a leader told a white anthropologist that he and many members of the tribe understood why the anthropologist wore clothes; if they were white, they would probably also be ashamed of their bodies and would try to cover them up (Ford & Beach 1951).

Despite the wide variations in the definition of attractiveness, certain common principles may be identified. Good complexion and cleanliness—which are indicative of good health—are almost always considered attractive in a society; conversely, indications of disease or deformities are negatively evaluated. Another factor generally consid-

FIGURE 9.1

Sexual attraction involves a complex interaction of physical, emotional, and psychological factors. However, during moments such as the one depicted here, people tend to be unaware of—or at least unconcerned with—the nature of this interaction.

ered important is age, especially in women; relatively young women are usually seen as the most attractive. Symons (1979) has argued that attention to these factors, in the long run, has promoted survival of the human species, since healthy individuals and young women have the greatest survival rate and reproductive potential.

A factor that is less clearly related to survival and reproductive potential is plumpness. Paintings and sculptures produced prior to the twentieth century suggest that plumpness may have been seen as a feminine virtue in Western societies as well as several preliterate ones. It seems that, in cultures where food is scarce at times or where sickness is common, a slim figure comes to be associated with illness; some degree of corpulence, then, represents good health. Furthermore, since a very low degree of body fat inhibits pregnancy—and the potential to be a good breeder is highly valued in many societies—a certain amount of plumpness may be desired. In modern, technologically advanced societies, the findings of medical science—that obesity can cause health problems—may have shifted the pendulum toward slenderness. Slenderness may also be considered more attractive because there is less of an emphasis on breeding potential in societies with advanced technology.

Within most cultures, there is probably a high degree of consensus on what makes a person sexually attractive—especially a female. For example, when male and female college students were asked to rate photographs of women's faces, there was high agreement among the respondents: males and females were in strong accord on what they defined as an attractive female face (Kopera, Maier, & Johnson 1971).

There is also strong agreement, at least among men, on what constitutes an attractive female figure. In another study, college men were asked to compare silhouettes of female bodies. The sizes of various parts of the body were systematically varied, and consequently preference ratings for the various shapes could be obtained. At the same time, personality tests and biographical inventories were obtained so that the men's personality characteristics could be correlated with preferences for particular figures. Despite the general agreement on body preference, there was some variability related to personality factors. For example, men who had a definite preference for the large-breasted silhouette tended to have strong masculine interests, date frequently, and have strong needs for independence (Wiggins, Wiggins, & Conger 1968). Apparently, men who fit the stereotyped role of masculinity have a preference for the stereotyped image of female attractiveness: a slim body accentuated by large breasts.

A female's perception of male attractiveness seems to be less influenced by physical factors. When asked what factors are important in dating, college women gave physical attractiveness a lower rating than men did. Furthermore, there is a lower correlation between physical attractiveness and dating in males than there is in females (Berscheid et al. 1971).

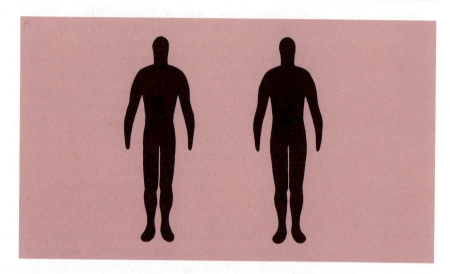

FIGURE 9.2
Silhouettes of male bodies.

The silhouettes, used as experimental stimuli, systematically differ in regard to the size of arms, upper trunk, lower trunk, and legs. Subjects are asked to express a preference for one of a pair of stimuli. By using a large number of stimuli, it is possible to identify the ideal physique for each subject and an average for all subjects tested.

The physique of a man is also of less importance than the figure of a female in the eyes of an opposite-sex person. The ultimate in sexual attractiveness has been stereotyped as an extremely muscular man. Interestingly, a study using a technique similar to that used to measure the attractiveness of female bodies found that the "he-man" body was not the most attractive to women; a more moderate body generally received higher ratings. As in the study of male preferences for female bodies, there were definite personality differences in the ratings. Women who considered themselves traditionally feminine preferred the more traditional masculine, tapering V physique. Women with a less traditional view of their sex role and a desire for more sexual equality preferred the more moderate male body. Apparently, a rejection of the traditional masculine stereotype of an ideal body is associated with the rejection of traditional male domination in heterosexual relationships (Lavrakas 1975).[1]

Author's Perspective: Beauty, Sexiness, and Sensuousness

In many people's perception, beauty, sexiness, and sensuousness are related. (Sensuousness has many connotations, but the ones implied in this discussion are relatively positive: openness to sensory gratification and warm interpersonal interaction.) The relationship among these three variables can be seen in the results of a simple, unpublished study that utilized students in an undergraduate class of mine. They were asked to rate pictures of other college students for the three variables. The rankings were moderately correlated— i.e., pictures of attractive individuals tended to be judged high on sexiness and sensuousness, and so forth.

As individuals get to know one another, however, it becomes apparent that these variables are not so closely related. Most of us have known certain physically attractive individuals whose aloofness prevents them from expressing warmth and sensuality. In a complementary fashion, persons who might go unnoticed at first because they are less physically attractive than other members in a group may become very popular, later on, as others discover their warmth and sensuousness. An often-quoted observation by Kinsey and his associates—after literally thousands of interviews with people about their sexual histories—further emphasizes how misleading physical appearance and superficial sexiness can be in predicting sexual satisfaction and fulfillment: the least likely looking people may have the most exciting sexual lives (Pomeroy 1972).

For many individuals, such observations represent good news. They suggest that physical attractiveness, although a factor in first impressions, may not consistently predict long-term satisfaction in sexual relationships. Warmth and sensuousness—which can be developed in people who were not blessed by nature with outstanding physical attractiveness or apparent sexiness—may be more important. Furthermore, although beauty may fade, warmth and sensuousness tend to remain or even increase as people grow older.

WEALTH AND STATUS

Just as it is difficult to differentiate physical attractiveness, sexiness, and sensuousness—at least through first impressions—wealth, status, and physical attractiveness tend to interact. In most societies, individuals on the higher end of the socioeconomic scale can dress more attractively and invest more in nourishing food and health care—factors that generally enhance physical attractiveness. However, when attempts are made to separate these variables, it appears that wealth and status are particularly important in the attractiveness of males. Symons (1979) has argued that, in most preliterate societies, males who are good providers are most likely to see their offspring survive and reproduce. Since wealth and status are related to being good providers, females have secured a selective advantage by paying attention to these factors in males. (Since males tend to control the wealth and have the higher status in most societies, males would derive less advantage from attraction to wealthy, high-status females.) The correlation between wealth, status, and attraction in males also helps to explain why older males may be seen as attractive (relatively more so than older women); men are likely to acquire wealth and status with age.

There are differences, of course, between modern technological societies and the more primitive ones to which Symons referred. It is now possible for women to achieve wealth and status and be good economic providers for families. Nonetheless, there still appear to be sex differences in the relative importance of various factors in sexual attractiveness. Physical attractiveness appears to be a more important factor in women, while wealth and status tend to be relatively more important in men. However, if discrepancies between the wealth and status of men and women are reduced and the sex roles become more similar, there may be fewer sex differences in the relative importance of these factors.

Comparative Perspective: Sexual Selectivity in Animals

In both animals and humans, females seem to show more care in choosing a sexual partner than males do. Turkeys are an extreme example. Female turkeys respond only to a male who presents a sequence of appropriate cues. However, males are attracted and aroused even when the only cue present is the model of a female head mounted on a stick. In fact, the males orient themselves and make copulatory movements in the air, as if the whole female were present (Schoettle & Schein 1959). One wonders if the origin of the term "turkey" as applied to a person is related to the findings of this study!

Daly and Wilson (1983) argue that female animals' greater choosiness is related to the fact that the female typically has more to lose by mating with an "unfit" partner: she "wastes" her eggs and also a large amount of time producing young who may turn out to be unfit. The male, who is generally capable of a large number of matings in a short time, wastes much less if an unfit partner is chosen. Support for this argument comes from studies of pipefish and seahorses—fishes in which the male carries and nourishes the eggs in a special pouch and the female invests little time in reproduction. In these species, the male exhibits greater sexual discrimination; the female, in contrast, is more aggressive and tends to mate with any available male (Symons 1979).

Daly and Wilson (1983) suggest that human females also have more to lose from indiscriminate matings than do males; an unwanted pregnancy is more of a disaster for the mother than the father. They point out that in virtually all societies surveyed, the female is more choosy than the male about opposite-sex companions in regard to sexual relations. Although birth control devices may reduce the possibility of pregnancy in technological societies, there is still evidence that women show more discrimination than men in our society; sexual intercourse outside of a close or loving relationship is still much more acceptable for males than for females (Peplau, Rubin, & Hill 1977).

SEXUAL ATTRACTIVENESS AND SOCIAL DESIRABILITY

As suggested in chapter 8, a major difference between humans and lower animals is that our sexuality has taken on a great deal of meaning beyond its role in reproduction. Being seen with an attractive member of the opposite sex may confer status. The "playboy" image—a male surrounded by several beautiful females—is an extreme example of the relationship between sexuality and status.

This lack of distinction between sexual attractiveness and social desirability is seen in a number of studies in which physically attractive individuals generally rated as more desirable than unattractive persons. Physically attractive people, both men and women, ranked relatively high on such positive traits as pleasantness and intelligence, a phenomenon known as the *halo effect* (Dion, Berscheid, & Walster 1972). Similarly, attractive waitresses are given significantly larger tips—even when their service is inferior—than unattractive ones (May 1979). Attractiveness also seems to be related to criminal justice. An attractive defendant is less likely to be perceived as guilty of a crime—such as cheating on an exam—and is given less punishment than an unattractive individual (Efran 1974).

As one might predict, being unattractive creates a certain amount of social pressure or stress. In some people, this is reflected in physiological changes that are associated with stress. For example, a recent study found that unattractive women have higher blood pressure than attractive ones. The relationship between blood pressure and attractiveness did not exist for men, supporting the conclusion that physical attractiveness is a more important variable for females than for males (Hansell, Sparacino, & Ronchi 1982).

Attractiveness, however, does have its disadvantages. Beautiful women may be seen as unapproachable and are less likely to be asked for help by males than unattractive women (Nadler et al. 1982). A study by Dermer and Thiel (1975) indicates that good-looking individuals of both sexes are perceived as more vain and egotistical and more likely to engage in extramarital intercourse than unattractive ones. Furthermore, older women who had been perceived as highly attractive when they were young are more likely to be unhappy than those who were perceived as less attractive. Apparently, beautiful women tend to "invest" a great deal in their appearance and, when their highly valued attribute fades, they experience a great loss (Berscheid & Walster 1972).

Recent studies have been concerned with why in some circumstances attractiveness is an advantage and in others it is disadvantageous or makes little difference. Cash, Gillen, and Burns (1977) found that, for jobs traditionally considered masculine, male physical attractiveness is an advantage. However, for females in the same jobs, attractiveness is relatively unimportant. Conversely, for traditionally feminine jobs, beautiful women have an advantage, but not physically attractive men.

Comparable findings were reported by Gillen (1981). College students rated physically attractive men high in positive "masculine" qualities but did not attribute many of these qualities to attractive women. Beautiful women—but not attractive men—were ranked high in positive "feminine" qualities. And several attributes considered positive in both men and women were influenced by either male or female physical attractiveness. Apparently, attractive persons are judged as having two types of positive attributes: sex relevant and sex irrelevant. The sex-relevant ones are those that are perceived only when one is in a sex-appropriate role (women in a feminine role and men in a masculine role). Sex-irrelevant attributes are those that are considered positive for males and females, regardless of the role they are playing.

ODOR AND ATTRACTIVENESS

One of the subtleties referred to in the introduction of this chapter appears to be odor. The perfume and cosmetics industries obviously go to great expense to promote the relationship between odor and attractiveness, and the public responds by spending billions of dollars on fragrances of various types.

There seem to be several reasons why odor and sexual attractiveness are related. In the first place, people may associate the "reward" of the pleasant odor with the person wearing it: a positive response to fragrance generalizes to the person who smells good. A less romantic possibility is that a fragrance covers up certain body odors resulting from uncleanliness that are perceived as unpleasant. Still another possibility is that there are certain natural odors that promote sexual arousal and attraction. In actuality, most expensive perfumes are made from musk, which is a natural sex attractant in musk deer. It can be argued that there are also some natural sex attractants in humans, but that these are not effective because most people have been conditioned to think of natural odors as unpleasant.

The relationship between odor and attractiveness appears to be fairly complex, as illustrated by an experiment with college students. A female accomplice of the experimenter either wore or did not wear perfume under one of two conditions: dressed informally (jeans and a sweatshirt) or relatively formally (blouse, skirt, and hose). Male subjects perceived her as most attractive when wearing perfume and informal clothing. However, the scent of perfume reduced her attractiveness when she was dressed formally. Apparently, the perfume combined with the more formal dress made the woman appear aloof and overly concerned with her appearance, thereby reducing her general attractiveness (Baron 1980; cited in Baron & Byrne 1981).

Comparative Perspective: Reproductive Pheromones

In many animals, attraction to members of the opposite sex is based upon volatile chemical substances known as *reproductive pheromones*. Sometimes both sexes secrete these substances, but in many species it is only the female. The pheromones secreted by a female may have extremely potent effects on male members of the species. For example, the pheromone from a single female sawfly in an open field has been known to attract over 11,000 male sawflies (Jacobson & Beroza 1963). Generally, the pheromones are secreted during the period when the animal is sexually receptive. In garter snakes, this is often at the time the female sheds her skin. Thus, if the skin of a female is left in a pen with other snakes after she has been removed, males find other females in the pen more attractive (Kubie et al. 1978). The critical role of the reproductive pheromone in sexual attractiveness is also illustrated in a study with rhesus monkeys. Males whose sense of smell was eliminated ignored females in heat (Michael, Keverne, & Bonsall 1971).[2]

Experiments with mice indicate a complex effect of pheromones on reproductive behavior. When a male mouse is introduced to a group of female mice, the females quickly come into heat or *estrus;* in addition, the *estrous cycles* are shorter when the females are caged with a male than when they are caged alone. This shortening and synchronization of the estrous cycle—known as the *Whitten effect*—is apparently stimulated by a pheromone in the male's urine; the introduction of male urine alone is enough to produce the effect (Marsden & Bronson 1964; Whitten, Bronson, & Greenstein 1968). The Whitten effect apparently functions to increase the fertility of mice by increasing the number of times females become estrous in situations where males are present and pregnancy can take place. Furthermore, when estrus is synchronized, many females will give birth at about the same time. Since female mice normally nurse their offspring communally, this synchronization probably leads to decreased infant mortality. (If a mother is killed or dies, other females may raise her young.)

There is some evidence of a Whitten-like effect in humans. Certain women who are deprived of male company—and presumably male odors—experience disturbances in the menstrual cycle and apparent failures to ovulate. On the other hand, women who spend considerable time with men have relatively short menstrual cycles. Another finding is that college women who are roommates show a significant synchronization of menstrual cycles; after a few months, they tend to menstruate at the same time (McClintock 1971).

An experimental study has indicated that it is indeed odor that produces at least one of these effects. A woman was recruited to function as a so-called donor. She placed cotton pads under each arm for a period of twenty-four hours. A group of women then allowed the pads to be rubbed on their upper lip just below their noses three times a week. These women showed a significant tendency to synchronize their menstrual cycle with that of the donor (Russell, Switz, & Thompson 1978).

Another example of the relationship between sexuality and smell is seen in the perception of odors. Women are able to perceive musklike male odors at the time of ovulation but are relatively insensitive to these odors at other times during their menstrual cycles. Furthermore, men and young girls are unable to detect these odors at any time (LeMagnen 1952).

Perhaps the major reason natural odors are less important to sexual attraction in humans than in most animals is that vision has become the dominant sense in humans. Other sensory information is given considerably less priority. Nonetheless, it is possible that at least some of the "magic" that takes place when certain people meet is related to subtle olfactory cues (Wiener 1966).

PROXIMITY AND ATTRACTION

It is somewhat obvious that the probability that two people will develop a friendship or become romantically involved is related to structural aspects of the environment. For example, in a classroom, individuals are most likely to become acquainted and attracted to one another if they are assigned to seats next to one another (Byrne & Buehler 1955). Similarly, the physical arrangement of housing units such as dormitories and apartments has strong effects on attraction and interpersonal relationships: the people who meet most often are most likely to become friends (Festinger, Schachter, & Back 1950).

It is less obvious, however, why proximity should effect attraction, especially when good looks and psychological variables are so influential. Perhaps the most important reason is that repeated exposure to a stimulus—almost any stimulus—generally leads to liking. Thus, one does not usually learn to love a new song or a new product on first exposure; however, as any television viewer knows, advertisers spend fortunes making certain products more familiar—and apparently better liked.

On the other side of the coin, there are strong exceptions to the relationship between familiarity and liking. The more one is exposed to a strongly *negative* stimulus, the greater one's feeling of dislike becomes (Grush 1976). Most of us do not have much difficulty recalling television commercials that illustrate this relationship. Similarly, growing accustomed to someone considered obnoxious does little to promote a romantic relationship.

PSYCHOLOGICAL AND EMOTIONAL FACTORS IN ATTRACTION

One of the things that differentiates human from animal sexual attraction is that people are greatly influenced by psychological and emotional factors. Many of us have been so emotionally involved with another person that we could hardly be objective about physical attractiveness or personality traits. In this section, several psychological and emotional factors will be considered: reward association, similarity, group pressures, emotional arousal, and the performance of a social blunder.

Reward Association

As suggested in the last section, part of the attraction process is probably a matter of simple association between something rewarding and a person of the opposite sex. If you enjoy playing tennis with a person, share a good meal, or receive a compliment from the individual, your attraction tends to increase (Lott et al. 1969). Reward association is particularly important if the other person is physically attractive. In one experiment, an attractive young woman served as an assistant, appearing either as herself or made up to look unattractive. Evaluation of a group of male subjects' performance on a task was later given by the assistant. The evaluations were prearranged to be either positive or negative, regardless of the subjects' actual performance. At the end of the experiment, subjects were asked, among other things, how well they liked the assistant. Positive evaluations produced high liking scores when the assistant was made up attractively, but relatively low scores when she looked unattractive. Negative evaluations produced low liking scores under both conditions of attractiveness (Sigall & Aronson 1969).

The effect of positive evaluations by another person is related to other factors besides attractiveness. If a compliment is too lavish, deviates rather obviously from reality, or is given by someone who stands to gain a great deal from you, the effect may be reduced or reversed (Berscheid & Walster 1969). Furthermore, if there is reason to believe that another person's evaluation of you has gone from positive to negative, your attraction to that person will probably drop to a low point—even lower than if the evaluation had been perceived as negative all along (Aronson & Linder 1965).

Similarity

Attractiveness is influenced by similarity along nonphysical dimensions—economic conditions, status, and, in particular, attitude. In one study, students were introduced to opposite-sex individuals and asked to spend thirty minutes together on a date. In half the cases, the students were matched on the basis of maximum dissimilarity; in the other half, they were matched for maximum similarity. Ratings after the dates and a later follow-up indicated that similarity was a significant factor in attraction for both sexes (Byrne, Ervin, & Lamberth 1970).

In some cases, people assume similarity when, in fact, it is not necessarily present. For example, very attractive strangers are assumed to have attitudes more similar to one's own than unattractive strangers (Schoedel, Fredrickson, & Knight 1975). In other cases, however, people assume similarity on the basis of physical characteristics that are relatively good indicators of attitude. Conservative women have been found to prefer men with short hair (at the time of the study, short hair in males was associated with political conservatism); liberal women indicated a preference for men with long hair (Peterson & Curran 1976).

Why is similarity related to liking? There seem to be several reasons. First, similarity is reflected in agreement, which tends to be reinforcing; most people find it more enjoyable to agree than to disagree. Second, when we are with someone similar, we generally assume that he or she is attracted to us; we, in turn, tend to like those who like us. Finally, similar attitudes and values allow us to make a positive social comparison: if others believe and feel the way we do, our beliefs and feelings must be legitimate.

FIGURE 9.3

Attraction is related to attitude similarity, particularly when two people know one another fairly well. One reason is that when attitudes match, there is likelihood of agreement on a variety of topics.

There are, of course, exceptions to the similarity-attraction relationship. Sometimes, disagreement may be challenging, and an interesting and informative discussion may result. And while many people prefer similarity in friends or spouses, others are more comfortable with differences in regard to a number of traits. In most studies, data are averaged across all individuals, and so these individual differences are not usually noted (Posavac 1971).

Emotional Arousal

There is some indication that emotional arousal in general increases perception of attractiveness. In one experiment, mentioned briefly in chapter 2, men were approached by a female interviewer after they had crossed one of two types of bridges: a 5-foot-wide, swaying suspension bridge 230 feet above a rapids (an adventure presumed to cause an aroused condition) or a short, sturdy bridge only 10 feet above a stream (presumed to result in a neutral condition). The men were then asked to write a short story and told that they could contact the interviewer for "debriefing." The men in the aroused condition wrote sexier stories and were much more apt to contact the interviewer than men in the neutral condition. Apparently the emotionally excited men perceived the female as more attractive. Incidentally, when a *male* interviewer approached the men under the two conditions, nobody contacted him for "debriefing" (Dutton & Aron 1974).

In another study, an attempt was made to give men the impression that a particular type of woman produced a high degree of arousal. The experimenter rigged up an apparatus that supposedly broadcast the intensity of a subject's heartbeat as he looked at pictures of nude women. Actually, the experimenter made the apparent heart rate increase or decrease when the subject looked at particular pictures but not when he looked at others. It was found that the pictures rated as most attractive were those associated with apparent heart rate changes. The preferences for these pictures lasted a relatively long time; they were still present when the men were retested four to five weeks after the original experiment (Valins 1966).

The relationship between emotional arousal and perceived attractiveness may help to explain why frustrations, such as parental disapproval, can produce the *Romeo and Juliet effect*—an increase in mutual attraction between young couples, brought on by parental or societal interfer-

FIGURE 9.4

Studies have shown that an exciting situation, such as a roller coaster ride, tends to make men see women as more desirable (and probably, vice versa). Apparently, the emotional arousal associated with the ride facilitates the perception of attractiveness.

ence. One investigation into several dating relationships in which parents tried to interfere with the romantic involvement suggests that such opposition generally leads to an increase in feelings of closeness and love (Driscoll, Davis, & Lipetz 1972).

The Performance of a Social Blunder

It seems obvious that the possession of socially desirable traits and skills enhances attractiveness—and in fact, there is considerable agreement as to which traits are socially desirable (Anderson 1968). Nonetheless, under some circumstances, committing a social blunder actually increases a person's attractiveness. A relatively high-status male is liked more when he spills coffee on himself than when he does not commit the blunder (Aronson, Willerman, & Floyd 1966). A later study suggests that there are sex differences in the effect of social blunders. Female college students rated a male more attractive and likable when he spilled a soft drink on himself than when he was depicted in a comparable situation without a blunder. However, the same blunder had no effect on the ratings of a female by male students (Maier, Lavrakas, Bentley, & Parrella 1977). Perhaps minor social blunders make a male appear less threatening and therefore more attractive to women; because of the traditional feminine role, threat may not be a comparable factor in the male's perception of the female.[3]

The reaction of the blunderer to the mistake also makes a difference. One who overreacts is liked less than a person who does not make a blunder (Mettee & Wilkins 1972). Another factor that may be important is the effect of a blunder on other people. In the examples given, no one was hurt by the incident. The evaluation of blunders that result in harm to others may be quite different.

Author's Perspective: The Role of Attraction in Heterosexual Relationships

Many of the factors discussed in the preceding sections interact with one another. As we have seen, a physically attractive person is likely to be perceived as having a pleasant personality. If an interaction resulting from this original perception gives the impression of attitude similarity, the perception of physical attractiveness and positive personality characteristics may be further enhanced. Another example of possible interaction: a person commits a blunder which produces emotional arousal and leads to a conversation about the incident. Consequently, the perception of the individual may be affected not only by the blunder but by the arousal and resulting interaction. Many of us have seen instances where a blunder livens up a party and promotes positive social interaction.

Often, after a couple gets to know and like each other, the complex interaction of several factors related to attractiveness makes it difficult to know what they like most about the other. (Nonetheless, it is fun, sometimes, to discuss what they *think* they like most.) Difficulties in identifying what factors are important in attractiveness are compounded by the development of what Levinger (1974) calls mutuality. At some point, many couples begin to perceive themselves as a ''we,'' a couple that has a sort of personality of its own. Much of the feeling of mutuality results from compatible roles that each person plays. For example, the more socially dominant person may tend to speak for the couple, while the less dominant one feels comfortable playing a less active role. At this stage, a general feeling of compatibility is probably even more important in maintaining the relationship than perceptions of attractiveness.

It is difficult to identify which factors are most important in any couple's perception of the other's attractiveness, and possibly this very mystery creates some of the magic certain people feel when they are together. At any rate, there are times when it is more satisfying to simply enjoy the magic than analyze the factors involved!

NONVERBAL CUES IN ATTRACTION

In social gatherings, most of us have little difficulty picking up certain nonverbal cues that affect the perception of attractiveness and encourage further interaction. A woman whose hand moves slowly along her thigh or brushes against her breasts while talking with a man may evoke more than casual interest in other men (and, possibly, more than mild anger in other women). Similarly, a male's swaggering gait or leaning position with the hips thrust forward may be perceived as sexy by some women—and irritating by other men (Fast 1970). However, many types of nonverbal cues are more subtle and, in certain cases, have a special meaning only for a particular couple. Some of the major categories of nonverbal cues will be discussed in the following sections.

Physical Distance

One of the easiest cues to observe is the distance between people when they are interacting. Generally speaking, the closer people stand or sit, the more intimate their communication (Hall 1959). Thus, seating arrangements or crowded conditions at a party may affect the type of verbal communication between people and ultimately their perception of others' attractiveness. Observations of couples standing together (waiting for instructions related to an experiment) indicated that the closer they stood to each other, the more they reported liking each other when they later filled out a questionnaire (Byrne, Ervin, & Lamberth 1970).

The relationship between perceived attractiveness and physical distance is not simple, however. Physical closeness, when it is considered

FIGURE 9.5
Physical distance and attractiveness are related. Persons who like one another tend to sit or stand close together. Physical closeness also promotes greater intimacy in communication which, in turn, may further increase attraction.

socially inappropriate, can have a negative effect upon communication. In a simple demonstration that was part of a social psychology class project, an attractive young woman approached male strangers, one at a time, and stood very close to them while they were looking at paintings in an art museum. Without exception, the men showed signs of feeling uncomfortable and moved away. Undoubtedly, reactions of at least some of the men would have been quite different in a party setting.

Rather clearly, the ability to judge the appropriate time to move physically close to another person is important, not only in terms of general attractiveness, but for the establishment of a relationship. Most of us, at one time or another, have experienced uncomfortable feelings when another person has moved suddenly—and inappropriately—close to us. In contrast, it can be most exciting and arousing when two people move into each other's arms at just the "right" moment.

Body Orientation

The position of the body communicates a good deal about one's attitude toward another person. Leaning or moving toward the person suggests interest and liking. In contrast, orientation away from the person or leaning back indicates lack of interest or dislike (Mehrabian 1968). In a laboratory study, a film was made in two versions. In one, an actress interacted with a man and exhibited body orientation of the type associated with liking; the other version featured body orientation associated with disliking. Subjects watching the films clearly perceived the actress as liking her partner better in the first version. Furthermore, they reported liking the actress better in the first version—in accord with the old saying "Everybody loves a lover" (Clore, Wiggins, & Itkin 1975).

Once again, however, appropriateness of expression is a key point. One can feel very uncomfortable if another person's body orientation indicates positive feelings that one does not reciprocate. Another uncomfortable feeling may result when body orientation demonstrates one type of feeling and the verbal exchange indicates something quite different (showing a possible conflict of emotions). Rather clearly, "Everybody loves a lover" has some qualifications.

Facial Expression

The face is one of the most obvious registers of emotion. People often get information about others' feelings toward them by observing such expressions as smiles and frowns. However, because facial expressions are relatively easy to control at a conscious level—and since there are social pressures against being brutally honest or completely open—people sometimes lie with their faces. The role of facial expression in deceit is illustrated in an experiment by Ekman and Friesen (1969). Silent movies were taken of a psychiatric interview in which a patient was verbally denying feelings of anxiety that she later admitted having felt. Half of a group of subjects saw a picture of only her head and face; the other half saw only her body from the neck down. The group that saw only the body was more accurate in identifying the woman's anxiety (and correctly identifying emotions in other patients as well). A person can deliberately make deceptive facial expressions, but the true feelings apparently "leak" out in general body movements that are harder to control.

Thus, of the various nonverbal cues indicating attraction or liking in general, facial expressions are probably the least reliable. Perhaps the reason that children are sometimes more accurate than adults in identifying whether or not people like them is that they pay less attention to facial expression—and fail to understand the meaning of words which are also liable to be deceiving.

The Eyes

The eyes seem to be a more accurate clue to emotion than the face in general, partly because they are harder to control. In one series of studies it was found that positive and negative reactions were reflected in the expansion and contraction of the pupils of the eyes. Males' pupils widened when they were presented with pictures of female pinups; females showed the greatest widening of the pupils when viewing male pinups—and also babies; homosexual men's pupils widened more to pictures of men than ones of women. There is also an indication that other people are aware—at least subconsciously—of the reaction of the pupils. Male subjects were shown two photographs of the same woman. In one picture, the pupils were normally constricted; in the other, the eyes were dilated. The subjects perceived the woman as more attractive and sexy in the photograph showing dilated pupils—even though most could not identify what factor made the difference (Hess 1965; Hess, Seltzer, & Schlein 1965). It seems that, in normal social settings, widened pupils are an indication that someone is interested in you, and, in turn, this "good judgment" may make the person more attractive.

Eye contact is also a good indication of attraction. Couples who say they are in love spend more time gazing into each other's eyes than couples who report little or only mild attraction to each other (Rubin 1970). People also tend to like individuals who look them in the eye better than persons who avoid eye contact (Kleinke, Staneski, & Berger 1975).

It should, however, be pointed out that looking directly at a person is not always a sign of affection: staring or gazing at someone in a continuous fashion regardless of any action on their part is usually interpreted as hostile. The effects of staring have been illustrated by a simple field study. Drivers at a stoplight were stared at by experimenters either in cars or appearing as pedestrians. Both males and females served as experimenters, and both male and female drivers were picked as "victims" of the stare. The speed at which drivers left the intersection when the light turned green was then measured for victims and also for a control group of drivers who did not receive stares. People who were stared at—regardless of the sex of the driver or the experimenter—appeared uncomfortable and left the intersection faster than drivers who did not receive stares (Ellsworth, Carlsmith, & Henson 1972). Most of us are not hard pressed to think of comparable situations where stares have made us uncomfortable.

Voice Quality

A deep male voice or a breathy woman's voice are often perceived as seductive, as any actor or singer knows. The quality of the voice is also an important clue to deception, as suggested by an experiment by N. R. F. Maier and J. A. Thurber (1968). Subjects were better able to identify persons playing the role of a liar when they heard tape recordings of an interaction (and presumably were not distracted by facial expression) than when they both saw and heard the interaction.

It was not clear from this study whether voice quality or verbal content was a more important indicator of deception. In a later experiment, however, voice quality was found to be particularly relevant to the detection of lies. Recordings were made of individuals reading a testimony. Half read a testimony that was true as far as they were concerned; the other half read the same testimony, which for them was a lie. Listeners were able to correctly identify the truthful testimonies at a better than chance level. Since the words were the same, the voice quality could be assumed to make the difference. Incidentally, there were also personality and background differences in the ability of subjects to correctly identify truths and falsehoods. Persons high in general intelligence and social intelligence and having few siblings were the best lie detectors (Lavrakas & Maier 1979).

In still another study, the effect of voice quality was measured by recording voices and then electronically filtering out the high-frequency tones, so that the speech was unintelligible but the general quality of the voice remained intact. The tapes were then played to subjects. Listeners were quite accurate in assessing whether positive or negative feelings were expressed. In fact, the experimenter concluded that whether a person feels liked or disliked depends more on voice quality than on the verbal content of a message (Mehrabian 1971).

The findings of these three studies are consistent with the observation that a great deal of information about emotions can be communicated over the telephone. The wife of a friend of mine was often able to accurately detect how he felt simply by the way he said ''hello.'' When it comes to communicating attraction or the lack of it, the old adage ''It's not what you say, but how you say it!'' contains some grains of truth.

Comparative and Anthropological Perspective: Nonverbal Cues in Other Animals and in Other Cultures

Are nonverbal cues entirely learned, or are there strong innate factors that influence nonverbal communication? One way of gaining insight into this question is to look at animal communication (most of which is unlearned) and cultural variations (which are presumably learned). Among the great apes, certain nonverbal cues bear a strong resemblance to those utilized by people. A sexually aroused male chimpanzee will sometimes approach a female with a swaggering gait much like the macho approaches of his presumably more civilized human relatives (Kortlandt 1962). Furthermore, certain chimpanzee facial expressions are similar to those of humans, particularly a prolonged stare to communicate hostility (Jolly 1972).

Certain anthropological investigations also support the conclusion that some aspects of nonverbal communication are unlearned. Ekman and his associates looked at facial expressions in widely different, independent cultures. In one study, the faces of individuals from different cultures were videotaped while they watched emotionally arousing films; the expressions associated with an emotion such as disgust were found to be remarkably similar across cultures. In another study, individuals from isolated cultures in New Guinea were asked to fantasize an emotion such as happiness. Their facial expressions were similar to those of individuals in very different cultures (Ekman & Friesen 1975; Ekman, Friesen, & Ellsworth 1972). It seems that faces reveal some basic emotional states quite independent of cultural learning.

Other aspects of nonverbal communication, however, seem to be strongly affected by cultural learning. For example, Italians tend to stand or sit relatively close to one another when talking. Many Americans visiting Italy feel threatened when native Italians approach them during a conversation. Interestingly, a recent study found that foreigners in the United States tend to sit at a different distance from one another when speaking their native language than when speaking English (Sussman & Rosenfeld 1982).

The specific meanings attached to particular gestures also seem to be culturally learned. On the island of Jaluit in the Marshall Islands, for example, Ford and Beach (1951) reported a man typically extending an invitation to coitus by rolling his eyes in a particular fashion. (It seems that women from other cultures might have found themselves in an awkward position, misunderstanding the gesture—or making a gesture in return that was misunderstood by the Jaluit man.)

In addition to gestures of various kinds, some cultures have developed the use of objects that have symbolic meaning. Ford and Beach (1951) reported that males in several Pacific Island societies would carry sticks with distinctive carvings on them. The women, in turn, learned to identify the owner of each stick. At night a man would stealthily approach his paramour's hut and thrust the stick through the wall, sometimes prodding her with it. By running her fingers over the stick, the female could identify its owner and then either accept or reject his invitation.

In conclusion, it seems that some aspects of nonverbal communication, particularly facial expressions that convey strong emotions, are unlearned. However, people learn when to express emotions openly, when to suppress them, and when to be deceitful. Furthermore, certain learned gestures have specific, culturally determined meanings (Ekman 1977). It is interesting to observe, when watching old movies, that many gestures considered sexy at the time appear ludicrous to us now. In the same vein, our grandchildren will probably laugh at the nonverbal cues given off by some of today's sex symbols.

Author's Perspective: The Perception of Nonverbal Cues

It seems when people are experiencing difficulties in a relationship there are many misperceptions in their communication. Studies indicate that unhappily married couples are less accurate in interpreting nonverbal cues from their partners than happily married ones (Kahn 1970). In fact, unhappily married couples are less able to decode the nonverbal cues from their spouses than from total strangers (Noller 1981).

Clearly, the role of the marriage counselor or psychotherapist includes being sensitive to nonverbal cues, interpreting their apparent meaning, and trying to get couples to put their true feelings into words. Many other couples could no doubt increase their marital happiness by learning to understand each other's nonverbal cues. Statements or questions like, "You seem to be upset about something" or "Are you having as good a time as it seems you are?" can sometimes open up new channels of communication. Of course, there are times when people do not feel like talking about their feelings. One of the secrets of being sensitive to nonverbal cues is to pick the right time to start such a discussion.

Most people begin to develop sensitivity to nonverbal cues at a relatively early age. Apparently, some people become more skillful than others (as illustrated in the study of lie-detecting ability). Once a person becomes an adult, however, it may be difficult to learn this sensitivity. In an unpublished study, Paul Lavrakas and I attempted to teach sensitivity to the nonverbal cues involved in lie detecting; the results indicated an actual lowering of accuracy!

As in the case of sexual interaction, too much analysis and concentration may backfire. I am reminded of a former associate who spent a great deal of time analyzing the interpersonal relationships of those around him. At social events, he was absorbed with picking up details of other people's nonverbal communication. Unfortunately for him, most people agreed that he not only lacked accuracy in his analyses, but he appeared insincere himself.

SUMMARY

There are considerable cultural differences in the definition of sexual attractiveness, but factors correlated with health and reproductive potential and the ability to provide are significant in most societies. There are also sexual differences in the relative importance of various factors in sexual attractiveness: physical attributes appear to be more important in women, while wealth and status tend to figure more importantly in the attractiveness of men.

Individuals who are physically attractive are often seen as socially desirable—an association known as the halo effect. This is especially true when they are perceived in sex-relevant roles. Nonetheless, there are certain disadvantages in being physically attractive, including being judged unapproachable and vain.

Odor influences attraction via reward association. In addition, there is evidence of a Whitten-like effect in some women—i.e., a synchronization and shortening of the menstrual cycle associated with certain odors.

It is also possible that some people perceive natural odors as subtly attractive and arousing.

Psychological and emotional factors are important in attraction, particularly after people get to know one another to a certain extent. Among the most important of these variables are reward association, similarity, emotional arousal, and the performance of a social blunder. In many cases, there is a complex interaction between these factors and the perception of physical attractiveness. Proximity is also related to attraction, probably because familiarity generally increases liking.

A variety of nonverbal cues affects the perception of attractiveness and influences the communication between individuals. Experimental studies have illustrated the importance of physical distance, body orientation, facial expression, the eyes, and voice quality. When couples are experiencing marital difficulties, problems tend to increase because the individuals become relatively insensitive to nonverbal cues from their partners. Therapists often attempt to increase sensitivity to these cues.

NOTES

1. A recent study indicates that men preferred a more stereotyped, muscular male physique than women did. The men most likely to indicate that they would like a highly muscular body were those who valued strength in sports, wanted to win at all costs (as opposed to a philosophy that emphasized sportsmanship), and had a relatively rigid personality structure (Maier & Lavrakas 1982).
2. Some insect pheromones have been artificially synthesized, resulting in certain practical benefits. Pests such as cockroaches have been lured into traps by the irresistible scent of man-made sex attractants. There are also reports of controversial Russian experiments involving pheromones: mosquito sex attractants have been sprayed on enemy troops in order to induce irritation and confusion (Baron & Byrne 1981).
3. The ratings of males by other males and females by other females were lowered by the social blunder. This was particularly true when females rated females. Apparently, raters identified with a member of the same sex, and the blunder made them feel embarrassed; the embarrassment presumably caused the lowered ratings (Maier et al. 1977).

CHAPTER 10

The Development
of Emotional Intimacy

After an initial attraction, couples often make an attempt to know one another in a more intimate way. The speed with which a relationship develops varies greatly, but there are typically a series of steps on the way to an emotionally intimate relationship. In some respects, these steps function like a series of filters that screen out "unsuitable" partners as a relationship develops. At first, such factors as similarity with regard to religion, race, and social status may be important. Thereafter, attitudes and values become significant. Those couples who are in general agreement tend to remain together, while those with widely divergent viewpoints usually break up. Then, what might be called personality matching comes into play; those people whose personalities tend to mesh continue to remain together over the longest periods and are most likely to marry (Kerckhoff & Davis 1962).

Interviews with couples who report a long and satisfying relationship indicate that the nature of this meshing process shifts over time. Factors that appear important at one point in the relationship seem to change as the relationship matures. Of greatest significance in the success of the relationship is the ability of the couple to adjust to these changes (Reedy 1978).

In this chapter several aspects of emotional intimacy will be considered, beginning with individual differences in motivation toward intimacy and ending with a consideration of love, the most intimate emotion of all. We will focus on various contemporary concepts of love, particularly as they relate to sexual behavior.

MOTIVATION FOR INTIMACY

Clearly, there are individual differences in the desire for intimate relationships. Certain people are apparently content to be loners, showing little need for close interpersonal relationships. Others interact regularly with people but seem primarily concerned with establishing power

FIGURE 10.1

Emotional intimacy tends to develop slowly, enabling a couple to know one another well before becoming seriously committed. This reduces the possibility of a mismatch and a subsequent, painful breakup.

over individuals or groups. In contrast, some people value warm, interpersonal relationships and seem to enjoy intimacy as an end in itself. One psychologist, Dan McAdams (1980), has developed a method of measuring *intimacy motivation* by responses to pictures presented in a *Thematic Apperception Test (TAT).*[1] Essentially, the pictures depict two people in an ambiguous, interpersonal situation, and respondents are asked to tell stories about the pictures. Presumably, the content of the stories reflects the storyteller's own need for intimacy.

There is impressive evidence that the analysis of the stories does, indeed, present a valid measure of intimacy motivation. In one experiment, college students were asked to write TAT stories at a sorority or fraternity initiation where the atmosphere fostered warmth, closeness, and conviviality. An equal number of fraternity and sorority members were tested in a standard classroom situation; they constituted a neutral control group. According to the TAT analysis, the students tested during the fraternity and sorority initiations displayed much higher levels of intimacy than did the controls.

In a similar experiment, students volunteered for testing at a dancing party at which they reported having a good time but were not under the influence of alcohol or drugs. The control group was the same as that used in the first experiment. Once again, the students in the situation that presumably evoked feelings of intimacy scored significantly higher on the TAT measure of intimacy than the controls did (McAdams 1980).

In the experiments just mentioned, the intimacy motivation measure was validated by demonstrating that warm settings invoke imagery related to intimacy. Later experiments were concerned with characteristics or traits of individuals who score high on intimacy motivation (I.M.) under standard test conditions. One study indicated that high-I.M. individuals are perceived by their peers to be more natural, warm, sincere, appreciative, and loving than those who score relatively low on the TAT measure. When asked to act out spontaneous minidramas in small groups, high-I.M. people are more apt to refer to themselves and their group as "we" or "us," and they position themselves physically closer to other group members than do medium- or low-I.M. individuals. High-I.M. people also tend to get other group members involved (McAdams & Powers 1981). It seems that people high in intimacy motivation express themselves in a clearly warm and caring fashion.

Preliminary research by McAdams and me indicates that intimacy motivation is also related to perceptions of sexual relationships. When asked to list factors necessary for a successful sexual relationship, high-I.M. persons name more features related to intimacy than do individuals whose I.M. scores are medium or low. Apparently, people who, in general, value intimacy feel that emotional involvement is important in satisfying sexual relationships.

FIGURE 10.2

People differ greatly in their desire for emotional intimacy. Individuals with high intimacy motivation are most likely to feel that emotional involvement is important in a satisfying sexual relationship.

Author's Perspective: The Satisfactions of Emotional Intimacy

For some people, emotional intimacy plays a very large part in their lives. Even when alone, individuals high in intimacy motivation spend considerable time thinking about others with whom they are emotionally involved. They also tend to remember, as their life's peak experiences, emotionally intimate situations—situations in which warmth, personal information, and love were shared (McAdams 1982).[2]

Emotional intimacy takes on a particular meaning for many of these people. For some, strolling with a special person in a beautiful setting—such as a garden or along a mountain trail—provides an experience of harmony, a sort of oneness with nature. Others report a feeling of timelessness associated with an embrace or looking into one another's eyes; it seems the wonderfully positive emotion will last forever. Still others experience a sense of unity—as if the two people had become one, with their strengths and positive attributes combined.

Perhaps the most important finding of McAdams's research program (McAdams & Vaillant, in press) is related to the psychosocial adjustment of people who have experienced—and have a strong need for—emotional intimacy. They tend to be significantly happier in their marriages, enjoy their jobs more, appreciate recreational activities to a greater extent, and have fewer psychiatric visits than individuals who have moderate or low intimacy motivation.

As we shall see in later parts of this chapter, becoming emotionally involved with another person has its difficulties, drawbacks, and potential for heart-break. Nonetheless, many of us feel the rewards can be great and, in some respects, make us richer human beings.

THE EARLY STAGES OF A RELATIONSHIP

Quite independent of intimacy motivation, some people, because of their social skills, find it easier to establish an interpersonal relationship than others. In the initial stages of a relationship, the ability to ask appropriate questions is useful. Questions that can easily be answered with a simple yes or no or a brief statement of fact tend to terminate conversations. In contrast, open-ended questions that are perceived as interesting or thoughtful often foster the continuance of an interaction (Arkowitz et al. 1975).

Another social skill is the ability to respond to the other person's statements in such a way that more exchanges result. This technique not only keeps a conversation flowing, but it encourages the disclosure of personal information. *Self-disclosure*, in turn, tends to encourage self-disclosure on the part of the other person. A simple experiment demonstrates this reciprocity effect. Male subjects were interviewed—one at a time—by an experimenter who took one of two approaches. In one approach (the high-intimacy condition), the experimenter gave personal, intimate information about himself; in the other approach (the low-intimacy condition), the experimenter spoke in rather impersonal, conventional terms. It was found that the high-intimacy condition evoked considerably more self-disclosure than the low-intimacy condition (Ehrlich & Graeven 1971).

A different type of experiment suggests that, if one person feels attraction towards another, self-disclosure is a means of psychologically reaching out. College women were shown pictures of a man and told he would be their partner in a study of the acquaintanceship process. The women were then asked to write a self-description that would supposedly be shown to the man in the picture. The intimacy of the disclosure was greater for pictures of attractive than unattractive men (Brundage et al. 1977).

The behaviors just discussed—asking open-ended questions, extending topics of conversation, and engaging in self-disclosure—all allow for considerable feedback. Partners usually wait for some sign of interest before continuing. Thus, if one of the individuals is not interested in pursuing the relationship, the conversation can graciously be terminated. As a result, the relationship, if it continues, tends to develop symmetrically.

Most people tend to avoid *asymmetrical relationships,* in which one person is more emotionally invested than the other. If self-disclosures are made and not reciprocated within a short time, there is a tendency to feel rejected and back off from further intimate communication (Savicki 1972). The more-interested partners in asymmetrical relationships tend to feel exploited or frustrated; they give more than they receive. The less-interested partners, in turn, may feel guilty or experience a lack of freedom.

Comparative and Anthropological Perspective: The Development of Relationships in Other Animals and in Other Cultures

Courtship is the term used to indicate behaviors preceding copulation in animals. The same word has also been used, historically, to describe interactions between people that precede marriage. There are some interesting parallels between animals and humans in regard to these interactions. In both groups, courtship functions to weed out what might be considered inappropriate mates and to coordinate sexual readiness. In some cases, male and female animals that remain together after they mate—and cooperate in the rearing of the young—court for relatively long periods. It seems the courtship establishes a pair-bond, which has some parallels in human relationships (Maier & Maier 1970).

Courtship activities in preliterate societies are, in some general respects, similar to dating activities in our society. In the United States and virtually all of the Western world, restaurants offering "intimate" dining are part of most couples' dating routine. A similar relationship between food and courtship is seen in many preliterate societies. It seems quite natural that food and courtship would become associated, since both activities are highly pleasurable. Experiments have indicated that, if food is present, another person is more likely to be perceived as attractive than if no food is associated with the interaction (Lott et al. 1969). Another possibility, first suggested by Freud, is that feeding and sex are related in some intrinsic fashion. In fact, Freud assumed that a child's first sexual experience was associated with oral stimulation during nursing.

Courtship routines are also likely to include music of one type or another. In several Indian and South Seas cultures, the men sing love songs to their women. In the Western world, too, music is almost universally associated with dating and sexual arousal. There are probably several reasons for this strong relationship. Like food, performing or listening to music is usually pleasurable, and there is a reward-association effect. Starting in the 1960s, many popular songs have had sexually explicit lyrics, which undoubtedly contribute to arousal. Even music itself—independent of the words—may be sexually arousing.

Dancing is closely related to music and, in most societies, dancing is accompanied by some form of music. The erotic aspects of dance are even more obvious than those of melody. This eroticism has been particularly emphasized in the striptease or "exotic" dance. (Although stripteases were once performed

FIGURE 10.3

Courtship shows similarities the world over. This New Guinea man is wearing a penile sheath which exaggerates the size of his genitals in the same general fashion as a Renaissance codpiece. He is playing a stringed instrument similar to the type seen in the Western world.

primarily by females for a male audience, the 1980s have seen a growth in male stripping for female audiences.)

Many preliterate societies also associated dancing with sexuality. For example, when young Alorese people were away from their elders, they engaged in dances during which females allowed their breasts to be "accidentally" touched by males (DuBois 1944). Sometimes, erotic dancing took on additional forms of social significance. Males of certain tribes in New Guinea performed a dance that can best be described as a penile display. The nude men and boys spread their thighs, grasped their genitals—which typically became erect—and made pelvic thrusts. In some groups, the beak of a hornbill or a gourd was used as a genital cover. Typically, unusually large gourds were chosen so as to exaggerate the size of the phallus. In these cases, the dancing movements included flipping the gourd from between the thighs up against the abdomen (Gajdusek 1970).[3]

In conclusion, it appears that courtship has some similar functions in animals and humans in various cultures. Perhaps some activities have roots that go back into our animal ancestry. (There are several examples of animals that "dance" together, "sing," or feed one another during courtship.) However, the specific types of activities that occur during the establishment of a human intimate relationship are strongly culturally conditioned and open to wide individual variation.

Author's Perspective: Difficulties in Establishing and Maintaining Intimate Relationships

In our society, people with poor social skills have difficulty establishing intimate relationships. A recent study suggests that satisfying heterosexual interactions develop more as the result of effective conversational skills than simply luck or convenient opportunities to meet people (Jones et al. 1982). But even persons with adequate interpersonal skills may have problems with relationships. For many, an important factor is fear of rejection. Such fear may result from a disastrous ending to an earlier relationship, or it may develop from observing other people's painful interactions, especially those of the parents.

Another cause of difficulty may be a basic lack of openness and honesty. A relationship may begin with one—or both—of the partners showing a great deal of pretense; it is then difficult to change the nature of the relationship later. For example, one individual may pretend to have a high-status job or a background filled with fascinating experiences. Although this tactic may create a favorable first impression, a crisis is likely to develop when the truth emerges, as it invariably does in a long-term relationship.

A strong need for exploitation, as opposed to sharing, may lead to a similar crisis. Some individuals establish a pattern of getting involved by pronouncing a love that they do not feel; they may have as an immediate goal sexual exploitation, increased social power, or improved status. When the partner becomes aware of the situation, the relationship is likely to end quickly.

There are some situations, however, where exploitation is tolerated because rewards are traded off. In other words, each partner exploits the other in a different way. For example, if one partner is the boss and the other is very attractive, orgasms or sexual satisfaction in general may be exchanged for economic or political advancement (Bell 1970). In certain cases, the pressures may be very subtle; nothing is communicated verbally, but there is an assumed list of obligations.

Sexual bartering presents a number of problems. In the first place, one or both of the partners may feel used (as indeed they are). If a person values affection and intimacy in a relationship, this feeling is particularly frustrating. Individuals who have had a series of relationships involving sexual bartering may come to feel that they are incapable or undeserving of love. Another problem is that sexual exploitation is incompatible with sharing sexual pleasure. Sexual takers tend to be unconcerned with giving satisfaction. Conversely, the givers may not be able to maximize their sexual enjoyment because enjoyment would indicate an imbalance in the relationship: one of the partners would be receiving both economically and sexually.

In my experience as a marriage counselor, I have known several couples who entered into a bartering type of relationship through a series of small steps. Once such a relationship has been established, dissatisfactions and frustrations tend to accumulate. Partners often do not communicate them because of a fear that favors—either sexual or economic—will be withdrawn. And if the relationship breaks down, it may be almost impossible to dissolve, especially if it is an extramarital liaison. Threat of exposure or economic punishment may serve as an effective deterrent.

Finally, a highly technological society in itself may contribute to problems in establishing and maintaining intimate relationships. Sociologists have identified a number of societal changes during the past fifty years that have tended to make intimate relationships difficult to establish and maintain. Among the most important of those are (1) increased mobility: when people move about they tend to lose friendships and acquaintanceships; (2) larger organizations: some people find it easy to become "lost in the crowd"; (3) a greater emphasis on competition on the job: there is less of the spirit of cooperation that tends to characterize small, rural communities; and (4) a reduction in the value attached to stable long-term relationships: this change may be a by-product of the first three (Middlebrook 1974).

On the other hand, emotional maturity and experience in a variety of social settings can help to overcome both personal and societal hindrances to establishing and maintaining emotionally intimate relationships. As we have seen, intimate relationships can offer extremely satisfying rewards.

INTIMACY AND SEX AMONG COLLEGE STUDENTS

The traditional intimate relationship involves different sex roles for males and females: males typically initiate sexual advances, while females set limits on the degree of sexual intimacy (Ehrmann 1959). In 1972, an extensive, two-year study of intimate relationships among college students was initiated to see if this role pattern was still present and also to investigate the relationship between patterns of sexual interaction and feelings of emotional intimacy. Three psychologists, Peplau, Rubin, and Hill (1977), recruited couples from four colleges who reported going together. The subjects were given questionnaires about their backgrounds, attitudes, and the nature of their relationship several times during the study. Some interviews were also conducted with the couples. Results indicated that there were three general patterns of relationships. A minority of couples (17 percent) abstained from coitus. These were termed "sexually conservative." The second pattern was called "sexually moderate." Intercourse took place, but only after the couple had been dating for at least a month and reported strong feelings of intimacy or love. The third pattern—"sexually liberal"—included couples who had had intercourse within a month after their first date. Forty-one percent fit into this category.

Interviews with the couples indicated that some aspects of traditional sex roles still existed. The females typically determined whether or not or at what point the first intercourse took place. However, a smaller proportion of women in the 1970s vetoed intercourse—or insisted upon a long-term relationship preceding coitus—than in the 1950s.

When the researchers compared the relationships typically enjoyed by the three groups, they found that the sexual moderates appeared to have the closest relationship and express the greatest love for one another. A combination of factors may account for the relatively high degree of love and closeness reported in the moderate group. First, many couples may delay coitus until the individuals feel emotionally close. Thus, some couples rated as conservative may simply have not yet reached sufficient emotional closeness to have intercourse; these couples would report feelings of love for each other lower than those of the sexually moderate couples. Second, the experience of coitus may heighten feelings of love for the moderate group; if love is a prerequisite for intercourse, then engaging in the activity would be an affirmation of the emotion. This would not necessarily be true for the liberals, who see less of a link between intercourse and love.

In contrast, other comparisons yielded no differences between the groups. For example, conservatives, moderates, and liberals were found to be equally satisfied with their relationship and were equally likely to continue the relationship. For all groups, approximately 46 percent broke up, 34 percent continued dating, and 20 percent of the individuals (males and females) had coitus with someone other than the dating partner during the continuing relationship.

There were certain sex differences in the reactions to loss of virginity. Women reported greater feelings of love for their partner if he was their first lover. Male perceptions were also related to a female's virginity. Typically, a man felt more love for a woman who lost her virginity with him than for someone who was not a virgin at the time of the couple's first coitus. In contrast, whether or not a male was a virgin previous to the couple's first coitus made little difference in either partner's feelings of love (Peplau, Rubin, & Hill 1977).

In some respects, intimate relationships among college students have changed considerably over a period of a generation or so. First, a wider variety of individuals seem to find one another acceptable as partners; racial, economic, and religious factors are generally considered less important in the 1980s than they were in the 1950s. Second, sex roles are less clearly differentiated. It is now considered appropriate for a woman to initiate a relationship with a man. Also, conversation between men and women can now appropriately include a number of subjects—including aspects of sexuality—that were formerly considered only feminine or masculine topics of discussion. Finally, sexual interactions generally take place earlier in the relationship than they did a generation ago.

Many other basic aspects of heterosexual relationships, however, have not changed significantly. The social skills that were crucial to the development of a relationship in the 1950s are probably very similar to those that were just discussed. Other factors—such as sensitivity, consideration, and honesty—were probably relevant for most people in the 1950s and remain so in the 1980s. It seems that some values have changed relatively little.

Author's Perspective: The Pacing of Sexual Interactions

As we have seen, some couples engage in sexual intercourse shortly after they meet and report satisfaction with this type of interaction. However, there are certain disadvantages to intimate sexual relations before couples get to know one another, especially if they are interested in developing an emotionally intimate relationship. In the first place, an asymmetrical relationship is likely to develop. One partner may simply be interested in the physical aspects of the relationship, while the other becomes both sexually and emotionally involved. In order to keep the relationship alive, then, one or both of the partners may be encouraged to be deceitful. As many people have unfortunately discovered, deceit is not a good foundation for a relationship.

Another potential problem with rapidly paced sexual interaction is related to attitudes about sexuality. As we have seen, many people have mixed feelings and conflicts about certain sexual behaviors. If sexual relations take place before a couple has had time to explore their feelings—either individually or as a couple—they may experience guilt and other unpleasant reactions. As we shall see in chapter 12, couples who have not examined their feelings about sexual interaction are also likely to put off decisions on birth control—and suffer unfortunate consequences.

Still another problem is related to a man's and woman's perceptions of one another. Once a couple has engaged in intimate sexual relations, it is difficult for them to be objective in their evaluations of their partner, and potential personality conflicts may be ignored. It is not unusual for people to discover, after they have made a serious commitment to their relationship, that they overlooked or misperceived important qualities in each other. In contrast, if two people get to know—and appreciate—each other before they have intimate sexual relations, the possibility of misperception is reduced.

Other possible advantages of deliberately pacing sexual interaction are similar to the advantages of progressive self-disclosure. There are opportunities for reciprocity at both a physical and an emotional level. Exploration of feelings about sexuality and intimacy may also take place at a relatively leisurely pace. For these and other reasons, many couples report relatively great satisfaction with sexual interactions that have proceeded in a slow, stepwise fashion.

Two obvious questions that may be raised by this discussion are, How slow is slow? and How large is a step? Several variables seem to be important in this regard. Older, experienced individuals are likely to proceed more rapidly, since they are already familiar with their own sexual attitudes and needs and know better what to look for in a partner. In contrast, young or inexperienced people should probably take more time in developing a relationship.

There are also individual differences in the way couples interact. Some couples get to know one another very quickly and are able to rapidly build mutual trust and affection. But other couples have difficulty becoming really close, for various reasons—for example, a fear of trusting anyone, or very different backgrounds and expectations. Whatever a couple decides to do in regard to sexual interaction, some advance thought should probably be given to this matter.

INTIMATE RELATIONSHIPS AND SOCIAL EXCHANGE

Some theorists perceive dating, and intimate relationships in general, as a type of exchange. Partners receive some sorts of rewards for the time, energy, and trust they invest in a relationship. *Exchange theory* assumes that the growth of the relationship depends upon (1) rewards received, (2) sacrifices made, (3) the degree to which the profits for each partner outweigh those they are accustomed to receiving, and (4) what the partners believe they could obtain elsewhere (Huston & Cate 1979).

Exchange theory is consistent with certain findings in regard to attractiveness and dating. For example, people tend to initiate social interaction with opposite-sex persons who are approximately equal to them in attractiveness. To approach a much more attractive person is likely to bring rejection; to settle for a much less attractive person would represent getting less than one deserves. Several studies have found that there is a fairly high correlation of attractiveness in heterosexual partners, a phenomenon known as *matching of attractiveness* (Murstein 1972; Huston 1973).

Of course, physical attractiveness is not the only factor involved in an exchange. Such variables as social status, wealth, pleasing personality characteristics, and self-esteem also seem to affect "exchange value," particularly that of men. A laboratory study illustrates how a male's feelings of self-esteem affect his attempts to make a date with a female. The feelings of self-esteem of a large number of males were manipulated through use of an intelligence test. All the men took the test. Some were told that they had done poorly, and others were informed that they had done very well. In reality, the "evaluations" were rigged and did not reflect the true scores.

In a second phase of the experiment, each subject was taken to a lounge area where there was a young woman who was actually a confederate of the experimenters. For half the encounters, she appeared highly attractive; for the other half, she was made up to be relatively unattractive. It was found that males who thought that they had done poorly—and presumably had temporary feelings of low self-esteem—were more likely to approach the unattractive female; males who had just received word that they were very bright were more likely to make romantic approaches to the attractive female (Kiesler & Boral 1970).

An analysis of the content of lonely-hearts advertisements also yields data consistent with exchange theory. There were significant sex differences in the factors sought and offered. Women tended to advertise attractiveness and seek financial security, usually from an older man. In a complementary fashion, men tended to seek attractiveness in a younger woman and offer financial security in exchange. It appears that these lonely-hearts advertisements reflected some of the same values apparent in the studies of initial attractiveness (Harrison & Saeed 1977).

In the dating "marketplace," like others, there is truth in the saying "Nothing succeeds like success." For example, if a man is observed in the company of a beautiful woman, he is typically attributed high status.

FIGURE 10.4

Lonely hearts ads.

Similarly, when a woman dates a wealthy or famous man, she is generally perceived as successful and admired. Thus, an attractive date can actually increase one's "exchange value" to others.

Author's Perspective: Intimacy as More than Social Exchange

Rubin (1974) has argued that exchange theory may apply to the early stages of relationships where couples do not know one another well. However, he suggests, as the relationship develops the partners develop increasing concern for what they can *do* for one another and think less about what they can *get*. Furthermore, according to Levinger's (1974) schema, there is increasing emphasis on joint rewards as the couple moves toward the mutuality stage.

It is also possible to reject exchange theory on humanistic grounds; one may dislike the idea of looking for superficial signs of quality in another person. Furthermore, the market value approach to relationships encourages phoniness and the type of dishonesty common in such places as singles bars. Several years ago I talked extensively with a student who consistently misrepresented himself in the dating market. If he was introduced to an attractive, wealthy young woman, he pretended to be from an affluent family. If he met a Jewish woman to whom he was attracted, he falsely claimed that he was Jewish. In a short time he became so entangled in falsehoods that most people perceived him as insincere and rejected him; as a result, the young man became severely depressed and attempted suicide. Eventually, after several months of psychotherapy, he was able to establish a pattern of honest relationships and was delighted to find that people basically liked him the way he was, devoid of marketing gimmicks.

The market value approach to intimacy is also marred by the fact that the market fluctuates: physical attractiveness fades, and wealth can be lost. Relationships built on such a shaky foundation are not likely to endure or continue to be satisfying.

THE BREAKUP OF AN INTIMATE RELATIONSHIP

As every twentieth-century person knows, intimate relationships do not always have a fairy-tale ending. The three psychologists who made the study of dating couples, discussed earlier, later analyzed factors related to breakups of college-student couples (Hill, Rubin, & Peplau 1979). Breakups were found to be less frequent among couples who reported being equally involved in the relationship than in couples where one person seemed to be more invested than the other. Thus, symmetry appears to be an important factor in breakups as well as development of relationships.

Certain sex differences were identified by the study. Women were more likely to initiate a breakup than men. It was also relatively easier for the woman to accept her former romantic partner as a friend. Men, on the other hand, reported more depression, loneliness, and sleeping

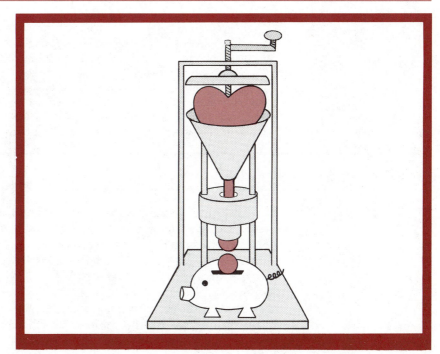

FIGURE 10.5

Some people perceive intimate relationships as a type of exchange in which emotional commitment is traded for various marketable goods and services. Others argue that as relationships develop, there is an increasing emphasis on mutuality.

problems than women (Hill, Rubin, & Peplau 1979). Even though the sex-role stereotype portrays women as more emotional and dependent than men, it appears that men generally suffer more from breakups than women do.

Part of the reason for the greater stress experienced by men is that, in most cases, it is the woman who decides to end the relationship. The initiator of the breakup feels more in control and sustains less damage to self-esteem. Another study indicates that the initiator, regardless of sex, is quicker to redefine his or her identity. Dating another person begins more quickly—or, in some cases, may have begun surreptitiously before the relationship in question was terminated (Vaughan 1979).

Author's Perspective: Recovering from a Breakup

Although some people have feelings of relief after a breakup—especially if they initiated it—most individuals experience negative emotional reactions. Among the most common are anger, depression, and loneliness—feelings that tend to come in waves. In some cases, the reactions are very intense. Another common experience is sadness at the loss of mutual friends. Usually, the couple has a number of friends in common. Some of these people find it difficult to adjust to a relationship with only one member of the former couple.

Fortunately, friends who continue to relate can be very helpful. (There is an old saying that one finds out who one's real friends are during a crisis, such as a breakup.) Friends or relatives can provide emotional support and function as a sounding board to help a person deal with the emotional impact of the breakup.

For most people, perhaps, time is the most effective healer. Although individuals may think they will never get over the shock, memories tend to fade, especially in emotional impact. Some people in fact feel stronger after recovering from the trauma. At any rate, many individuals report being better able to deal with later breakups after experiencing the first one.

LOVE

Many couples who have intense emotional relationships—and successfully deal with the many factors that are likely to lead to a breakup—come to define their feelings for one another as love. Most Americans are surprised to learn that the concept of love between a man and a woman is virtually unknown in several societies. Even in classical Greek culture, love was considered more appropriate for individuals of the same sex than as a bond between a man and a woman. Around the twelfth century heterosexual love began to appear as what has been called "courtly love" or the "romantic ideal." The distinguishing features of courtly love were its dependence upon fate, uncontrollability, irrationality, and turbulent mixtures of agony and ecstasy. This love was presumably restricted to premarital and extramarital relationships; married couples were considered too duty bound to experience romantic feelings for one another.

It was not until the late eighteenth century that the ideal of love began to be incorporated into mate selection and marriage. At this time, the inherited aristocracy was losing power to the bourgeoisie, and there was less to be gained by perpetuating the aristocracy through planned intermarriage. With the rise of industrialization, "new" families were gaining wealth, and economic factors in marriage became less predictable. In America, the pioneering spirit and emphasis on individuality seems to have had an additional effect on the growing relationship between romantic love and marriage (Rubin 1973). Nevertheless, there was, and still is, a tendency for families of wealth and power to encourage intermarriage—for example, by enrolling their young people in exclusive clubs and schools and giving debutante balls.

During the latter part of the nineteenth century and the early part of the twentieth, Victorian ideals pervaded concepts of heterosexual love. The love between a man and a woman was seen as relatively independent of sexual relations. As we have seen in chapter 1, society tended to tolerate a man (but not a woman) who gained sexual gratification with a lover or prostitute. On the other hand, it was considered unseemly for a man and his wife to enjoy their sexual relationship (Sussman 1976).

In the 1940s and 1950s, love and sex began to become more closely associated, and there were general movements away from the Victorian repression of sexuality. Since the 1960s, there have been other changes in the concept of love. A comparison of the lyrics of love songs in the 1960s with those in the 1950s indicates that love during the 1960s was less associated with fate and unpredictable emotions (Carey 1969). Similarly, an analysis of the content of romance magazines read by adolescent girls suggests that the trend was continuing into the 1970s (Hurowitz & Gaier 1976). Nonetheless, many of the concepts of courtly love and Victorianism seem to remain.

The Relationship between Love and Other Emotions

Most theorists agree that love is a complex emotion. A sociologist, Ira Reiss (1960), has described four basic dimensions of a love relationship: (1) mutual attraction, (2) self-disclosure, (3) behavioral interdependence, and (4) emotional interdependence. The various dimensions tend to interact with one another. As we have seen, when people are mutually attracted, they tend to disclose things about themselves; the self-disclosure promotes attraction and behavioral interdependence, such as enjoying certain activities together; the mutual enjoyment then leads to emotional interdependence. Finally, emotional interdependence tends to increase attraction, a tendency to self-disclosure, and behavioral interdependence. After two people have fallen in love, it is impossible to separate one dimension from another. Surely, more than one person has had difficulty answering the question "Why do you love me?"

Love and Liking

Several psychologists have attempted to study love by drawing a distinction between it and other emotions. Ellen Berscheid and Elaine Walster (1978) believe that passionate or romantic love is marked by strong physiological arousal. In many cases, there is a mixture of conflicting emotions such as love and hate. Passionate love also features extensive fantasies and idealized perceptions of the partner. In contrast, companionate love, or liking, is more rational and less emotionally intense.

Another psychologist, Zick Rubin, has also distinguished love from liking and has made an attempt to measure these two emotions. Rubin's *Love Scale* (Rubin 1970) takes into account three factors that appear to be important aspects of love: attachment, caring, and intimacy. In contrast, the *Liking Scale* taps two factors that seem to reflect liking: a favorable evaluation of the person in question and a tendency to view the person as similar to oneself.

Rubin administered the two scales to a large number of dating couples to determine if loving and liking were one and the same thing or if they

FIGURE 10.6
Nine-item versions of the love scale and liking scale

Love Scale

---

1. I feel that I can confide in _____ about virtually everything.
2. I would do almost anything for _____.
3. If I could never be with _____, I would feel miserable.
4. If I were lonely, my first thought would be to seek _____ out.
5. One of my primary concerns is _____'s welfare.
6. I would forgive _____ for practically anything.
7. I feel responsible for _____'s well-being.
8. I would greatly enjoy being confided in by _____.
9. It would be hard for me to get along without _____.

Like Scale

---

1. I think that _____ is unusually well adjusted.
2. I would highly recommend _____ for a responsible job.
3. In my opinion, _____ is an exceptionally mature person.
4. I have great confidence in _____'s good judgment.
5. Most people would react favorably to _____ after a brief acquaintance.
6. I think that _____ is one of those people who quickly wins respect.
7. _____ is one of the most likable people I know.
8. _____ is the sort of person I myself would like to be.
9. It seems to me that it is very easy for _____ to gain admiration.

People are asked to fill in the blanks with the name of the person closest to them and then rate (on a scale of 1 to 7) how much they agree with the statement. Scores are determined by totaling the ratings obtained on each scale.

were somewhat independent of one another. The results of the study indicated that, within each scale, there was a high agreement on ratings. For example, if a person scored high on one item on the Love Scale, he or she would typically score high on all other items on that scale. However, there was only intermediate agreement between scales: a person who scored high on a rater's Love Scale was only somewhat likely to be high on that rater's Liking Scale. In other words, liking and loving were found to be moderately independent.

These results were as expected. However, a rather surprising finding was that there were differences between males and females. Loving and liking were more highly correlated for women's ratings than for men's: the women were most apt to like the men they loved. Apparently, men made more of a distinction between liking and loving than did women, at least in regard to their dating partners.

Another sex difference appeared in regard to love for same-sex friends: women had higher loving scores for their same-sex friends than men did. Although women do not seem to have more friends than men, female friendship relationships appear to be more intimate, caring, and involved (Rubin 1973).

High scores on the Love Scale were reflected in eye contact. In the study of dating couples, strong lovers spent more time looking into one another's eyes than did weak lovers—couples who scored low or moderate on the scale. All couples in the study were observed while ostensibly waiting for an experiment. Experimenters measured—by means of stopwatches—the amount of time that each member of the couple looked at the other member's face. Weak lovers were just as likely to look at their partner's face, but strong lovers were more likely to look at each other simultaneously (Rubin 1973).

An attempt was also made to follow the development of the couples' feelings for each other. Early in a relationship, there were fluctuations in total scores on the Love Scale. However, as the relationship developed, the scores became more stable. One factor that apparently helped to keep Love Scale scores at a high level was the development of feelings of friendship—as well as love—for the partner.

Whether or not a relationship continued was not necessarily related to feelings of love, however. For people who described themselves as nonromantic—in the sense that they valued chiefly economic and social factors in mate selection—there was no relationship between love scores and progress in the relationship. Only those people who might be called romanticists—in that they valued love—showed a correlation between love scores and movement toward a more serious relationship (Rubin 1970, 1973).

Just as there are stages in the development of attraction in general, there appear to be stages in the development of a love relationship. According to Rubin (1974), the early stages of love are characterized by passion. If the relationship continues, the individuals develop feelings of attachment and concern for the other person's welfare. Finally, respect for the other person's abilities and personal qualities emerges and becomes important in the relationship.

Love and Limerence

Another psychologist, Dorothy Tennov (1978), makes a distinction between love and a second, related emotion, which she calls *limerence*. Limerence resembles infatuation in that it develops suddenly, is illogical, and has strong emotional overtones. However, since the term infatuation has connotations that Tennov believes are inappropriate, she coined her own term.

Limerence develops at practically any age, sometimes starting in childhood. It is most likely to occur after a period of loneliness or after the breakup of a long relationship. The "symptoms" include obsessive thoughts and fantasies about the limerent object. A large number of relatively minor conversations and gestures are remembered in great detail; even the slightest clue that the limerent object cares may evoke ecstasy. Conversely, signs of rejection may bring about severe depression.

Evaluation of the limerent object is quite irrational. Positive aspects of the personality become magnified, while negative ones are ignored. Meanwhile, strong physical symptoms predominate: an ache in the chest, fluttering in the stomach, and difficulty sleeping. Rather surprisingly, if the limerent object reciprocates the feelings, the limerence tends to disappear.

Clearly, limerence can be mistaken for love, particularly among people who are inexperienced with intimate relationships. However, the fact that limerence thrives on a lack of fulfillment suggests that it is not a good indicator of compatibility. Furthermore, since limerent objects are evaluated unrealistically, there is a poor chance that people will really get to know one another; perceptions of the partner simply reflect a fantasized ideal.

Many successful relationships begin without the symptoms of limerence. It may be a mistake to assume that nothing will happen because there were no "bells ringing" on the first date. Love has been known to grow out of friendship and develop quite independent of limerence.

How can one identify "true" love, independent of limerence? There is no certain method. However, being together under a variety of circumstances—including times when one person is upset or depressed—helps to provide a realistic setting for the development of a relationship. Unfortunately, people can spend many hours together without truly getting to know one another because they associate only on "fun" occasions when the possibility of honest self-disclosure is reduced.

Time is another factor that helps to differentiate love from limerence. According to Tennov, love is more sedate, secure, and long lasting than limerence. Unfortunately, some people, especially inexperienced ones, make a mistake by committing themselves to a relationship before they have had a chance to explore what emotions are actually involved.

Author's Perspective: Love and Jealousy

Most people feel a certain amount of jealousy when a third party seems to threaten a love relationship (Clanton & Smith 1977). The degree of jealousy seems to be somewhat culturally dependent. In societies where people value personal ownership of property in general and do not condone premarital or extramarital sex, jealousy appears to be a strong emotion. In contrast, societies that are generally liberal in their attitudes towards sexuality and are less concerned about property ownership tend to exhibit less jealousy (Hupka 1981).

Within a society, there are strong individual differences in the tendency to become jealous. The amount of jealousy people experience seems less related to how much love they feel than to how secure they are. Research has shown that highly jealous people have relatively low self-esteem and are not very satisfied with life in general (Bringle et al. 1977). Similarly, jealousy is related to emotional dependency (Buunk 1982). There are also certain sex differences in the way people react to jealousy-provoking situations. Women report they are likely to attempt repairs on the damaged relationship; men indicate they are most concerned with saving face or seeking revenge (Bryson 1977).

Jealousy can certainly be a destructive force. Arguments over another man or woman are not uncommon and may lead to the breakup of a relationship. On the other hand, discussions centered around one another's feelings of jealousy may provide insight into the dynamics of the relationship. In some cases, a not-too-vindictive expression of jealousy may function to tell one's partner that one cares. In others, discussions may touch on topics such as personal freedom, trust, and commitment—concerns that should be considered in any serious relationship.

In conclusion, it seems that the emotion of jealousy cannot be considered good or bad in itself. Rather, the way in which it is expressed—and the manner in which one's partner responds to this expression—is of major importance in a relationship.

Styles of Loving

A sociologist, John Lee (1977), has emphasized the importance of different styles of loving. He asked a variety of subjects to describe their love affairs by choosing cards from a large stack; each card described one event or feeling in a love relationship. The subjects chose the cards that described their love affairs, arranging the cards in order of events or feelings that were remembered.

By analyzing the cards chosen and the order in which they were arranged, Lee differentiated six common love styles. Eros is characterized by concern for physical attractiveness; the loved one is seen as fulfilling an ideal image. Eros is also characterized by an emphasis on self-disclosure. Generally speaking, this type of love is the one depicted in classic Hollywood movies.

Ludis is a style that can best be described as playful love. Relationships tend to be short-lived and involve only minimal commitments. There is relatively little jealousy or rivalry and, in turn, little is expected from the partner. It is not unusual for a person with this style to engage in multiple relationships.

Storge is based on a gradually developing affection and friendship; there is an emphasis on sharing of interests and activities. Self-disclosure tends to be gradual, and there is an avoidance of extreme emotions. Storge is more likely than other styles of loving to result in long-term commitments.

In contrast, mania is an emotionally intense love style featuring preoccupation with thoughts of the loved one. (In this sense, it is similar to limerence.) Persons with this style often fall in love with someone whom they disliked at first; later, they may experience strong mixed emotions. For them, love and hate may be closely related emotions.

Pragma is a style that emphasizes practical considerations. The pragmatic lover consciously takes into account such factors as socioeconomic levels, religion, age, and other demographic characteristics. Pragma is consistent with the historically common practice of arranged marriage among individuals who may not even know each other before the wedding.

FIGURE 10.7

There are many types of love or styles of loving. *Ludis* is a style associated with playful interaction.

Finally, agape implies caring, understanding, and forgiveness. This kind of love may be a sort of "overflow" from a person rich in inner resources and generous feelings. It does not depend on expectations or obligations in return. Agape is generally associated with relatively mature individuals.

Consistent with Lee's analysis of styles of loving is the observation that there are definite differences in the types of love relationships. One partner may evoke a mania reaction, while another is more likely to encourage a storge-type relationship. Furthermore, since each individual is unique, every relationship has its own special qualities.

Over a period of time, the type of relationship between two people may change. For example, ludis styles have been known to evolve into eros relationships. As suggested earlier, most couples who have been married for a number of years—and report high levels of satisfaction in their marriage—indicate that the nature of their relationship has shown some significant changes (Reedy 1978). In contrast, the failure of some relationships to survive may reflect incompatible changes in the styles of the partners.

Finally, not all people exhibit one "pure" style of loving; some people in the Lee study had a mixture of styles. For example, some relationships consisted of storge with erotic overtones. And some people showed styles different from the six mentioned. It seems likely that some aspects of love and loving will never be completely classified and analyzed—and perhaps this adds to the mystery and excitement of intimate relationships.

Comparative Perspective: The Evolution of Love

Typically, people think of love as a strictly human emotion. However, there is evidence that some aspects of love—sharing and a strong emotional attachment—exist in other animals. Among monkeys, what is known as *affectional bonding* occurs between a monkey mother and her offspring. If contact between the mother and her infant is interrupted for a short time, there is increased physical contact when the pair is reunited and for a time afterward. In many respects, the scene resembles a joyful reunion. During a separation, in contrast, the infant appears depressed and does not establish contact with other adults (Kaufman & Rosenblum 1967). Another familiar demonstration of bonding is the dog that enthusiastically greets its owner after a separation.

In subhuman mammals, affectional bonding between an adult male and adult female is rare. In most species it probably would have little survival value, since the parents do not stay together and cooperate in the rearing of the young; the female typically rears the young by herself. However, as the ancestors of humans began to combine parental efforts in protecting and feeding the young, there was clearly a selective advantage to an affectional bond between the two adults. This bond functioned to keep the pair together and facilitated cooperation in the care of the young (Mellen 1981). Thus, it seems likely that the roots

FIGURE 10.8
The rudiments of love—or
what has been called
affectional bonding—can be
seen in monkeys and other
nonhuman primates.

of love between a man and a woman are found in the need for lengthy, complex care of the human infant—requiring input from two parents.

How closely the affectional bond of animals resembles the love of humans is a matter of conjecture, but some conclusions are fairly clear. As the human brain developed—and the possibilities for abstract thinking increased—the various ramifications of love also increased. Furthermore, like sexuality in general, love took on a great diversity of meanings—a diversity reflected in the variety of ways it is defined in different cultures and for different people.

SUMMARY

The development of an intimate, emotional relationship follows a general series of steps, with each step functioning as a type of filter to screen out "unsuitable" partners. In long and satisfying relationships, factors of importance seem to change with time.

There are considerable individual differences in the motivation for intimacy. People with high needs for intimacy typically express themselves in a sincere, warm, and caring fashion. In later life, these individuals make a significantly better psychosocial adjustment than those scoring medium or low on intimacy motivation (I.M.). Recent research indicates that high-I.M. people also value emotional intimacy in a sexual relationship to a relatively great extent.

The establishment and development of emotional relationships depend upon a variety of social skills, including the ability to appropriately disclose oneself. Most individuals attempt to avoid asymmetrical relationships—situations in which one person is considerably more invested in the relationship than the other. Several factors make it difficult for some people to engage in satisfying intimate relationships: strong fears of rejection, a lack of openness, a strong need for exploitation, and/or low self-esteem. In addition, certain societal changes in the past fifty years contribute to the problem of establishing and maintaining intimate relationships.

A study of intimacy and sex among college students indicated that if or when sexual intercourse took place was not related to general satisfaction in the relationship or the probability that the relationship would continue. However, sexual moderates indicated greater love for one another than did sexual conservatives or sexual liberals.

For many couples, there is a pacing of sexual interactions, functioning to delay intimate sexual relations until the couple gets to know one another. This pacing reduces the probability of asymmetry in the relationship, ambivalent feelings or guilt associated with the sexual interaction, and unrealistic perceptions of one another.

Some theorists conceptualize intimate relationships as a type of social exchange: the growth of a relationship presumably depends upon such factors as rewards received and sacrifices made. Several studies support this theory. Nonetheless, critics of exchange theory argue that, as a relationship develops, there is a growing emphasis on joint—as opposed to individual—rewards. Furthermore, they believe that exchange theory overemphasizes superficial personal qualities.

The breakup of an intimate relationship is often a traumatic experience. Women tend to initiate a breakup more often than men. Men, in turn, usually experience more adverse emotional reactions following a breakup than women do. It seems that emotional support from family and friends—and the passage of time—are among the best healers.

Love is a complex emotion that is closely related to other emotions. Berscheid and Walster have drawn a distinction between passionate or romantic love—which is marked by strong physiological arousal—and the less intense companionate love or liking. Rubin has also distinguished love from liking and has constructed scales to measure these two emotions. He found that loving and liking are more highly correlated in women's perceptions than in men's. Women also had higher loving scores for their same-sex friends than did men.

Tennov has speculated on the difference between love and limerence, an infatuationlike emotion that is sometimes mistaken for love. Since limerence reflects a fantasized ideal and thrives on a lack of fulfillment, it is not considered a good indication of compatibility.

For most people, a certain amount of jealousy is associated with love, at least at certain times. The degree of jealousy is culturally dependent and is highest in individuals with low self-esteem. Although jealousy can be a destructive force, it may also stimulate productive discussions concerning the nature of a relationship.

Lee has analyzed different styles of loving including eros, ludis, storge, mania, pragma, and agape. Sometimes, one style evolves into another. Most couples who have had long, successful love relationships have experienced changes in the nature of their relationship over time.

NOTES

1. The TAT was developed by Henry Murray (1943) as a personality test and, over the years, has been used to measure a variety of human motives and needs.

2. In most of the studies on intimacy motivation, no sex differences have been found. However, a recent study indicated that college women spent considerably more time thinking about intimate relationships—and those to whom they felt close—than college men (McAdams & Constantian, 1982). It may be that males and females have similar needs for intimacy, but women—the more socially expressive sex (see chapter 14)—conceptualize it to a greater degree.

3. The penile display dance was also performed in several nonerotic situations. To the surprise of the anthropologist, it marked the arrival of certain visitors. The display also occurred during electrical storms and functioned to celebrate victory in battle (Gajdúsek 1970). The relationship between genital displays and battle was also apparent in some ancient societies. Etruscan and Greek infantrymen wore heavy armor but left their genitals uncovered. When they killed an enemy, they cut off his penis and kept it as a trophy. As late as the 1960s, phallic ornaments were worn on the brows of some men in southern Ethiopia. Originally, the ornaments signified that the wearer had killed an opponent in battle. However, they later became an insignia of rank (Wickler 1972).

PART 5

Sex and Reproduction

The role of sex in the reproductive process is the topic of these chapters. The first is concerned with factors which aid reproduction; the second, with attempts to prevent it.

CHAPTER **11**

Conception, Pregnancy, and Childbirth

The relationship between sex and reproduction has not always been clearly understood. Among the Trobriand Islanders, supernatural influences were considered the basic cause of conception (Malinowski 1929). The Mangaians—who were discussed earlier as an example of a sexually liberal culture—were under the impression that conception resulted from too much intercourse with the same man. Parents encouraged their young daughters to have coitus with a large variety of men in order to avoid premarital pregnancy (Marshall 1971).

In Western cultures, as well, there have been gross misconceptions of reproduction. As late as the eighteenth century, a group known as the homunculists claimed that preformed babies resided inside the head of a sperm; the mother's only role, then, was to provide a fertile environment for the infant's development (Meyer 1939). Many of the details of reproduction were not clearly understood until the twentieth century, and even today several questions remain unanswered.

The basic sexual process—conception—involves the union of two gametes: a sperm and an egg. Each of the gametes carries half the total number of chromosomes (and genes) needed to control the development of the infant. When the union takes place, there is a mixing of genetic material (*genetic recombination*). In other words, the offspring are not genetic duplicates of either parent. This fact is very important, since a population of individuals that reproduce sexually necessarily has great variability of genetic potential. As a consequence of this variability, some individuals are likely to have, by chance, the traits necessary for survival following environmental changes (such as a shift in the climate or the arrival of a new type of disease). Imagine, for a moment, what would happen if humans lost their ability to utilize sexual processes and reproduced asexually. Each offspring would then be an exact duplicate of its one parent, and so there would be much less variability. Eventually a new strain of disease-producing virus or bacterium might spring up

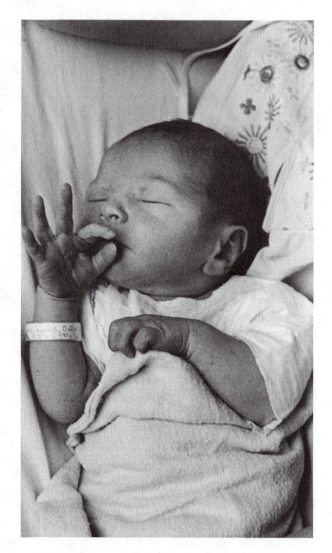

FIGURE 11.1

Although conception, pregnancy and childbirth have been considered highly significant events in virtually all cultures, there is still a great lack of education regarding the basics of human reproduction.

that would wipe out a whole group of identical humans. Furthermore, much of what makes human life interesting—variability in regard to structure, behavior, and spirit—would be lost.

Comparative and Evolutionary Perspective: The Dawn of Sexual Processes

A large number of organisms produce offspring without the direct involvement of sexual processes. For example, certain one-celled animals reproduce by simply dividing into two or more parts; sexual processes may occur at other times in the animals' lives or, in a few cases, do not occur at all. Therefore, it is possible that reproduction in the very first organisms took place without sex. Nonetheless, since sexual processes occur in extremely primitive organisms, such as bacteria, it seems likely that sex—in one form or another—has been around for an extremely long time, providing the genetic recombination so basic to life itself (Smith 1978).

Having observed sexual processes in both primitive and complex animals, some theorists have speculated on how such processes may have evolved. One-celled animals known as shelled amoeba reproduce by a process of fusion: one animal leaves its shell and enters the shell of another, resulting in a literal joining together of two individuals. Later, the new individual splits in two again, but the two new individuals have different combinations of genes than the two original parents. The first stage of sexual evolution may have been just such a process of fusion and fission, resulting in genetic variability of the new individuals.

A second stage may have provided a simple division of labor. Obviously, as animals became larger and/or multicellular, the fusion process would have become unwieldy. So, instead of having the entire body involved in reproduction, there arose specialized organs to produce sex cells, or gametes. (Such a process is seen in some primitive animals.) The gametes could then fuse with one another and, in essence, produce genetic variability without necessitating the fusion of complete animals.

A third stage may have been *gamete differentiation.* The most basic or unspecialized types of gametes—which exist today in very primitive animals—are identical; any two can successfully fuse. As animals became more complex, there seems to have been an evolutionary trend for gametes to differentiate in terms of size and mobility. The ultimate point in this trend is the condition found in higher animals, including humans: a tiny sperm and a relatively large egg. There are great advantages to differentiation of gametes based on size and structure. A small gamete—with a tail that propels it—can be highly mobile, thereby increasing its probability of finding an appropriate gamete to fertilize. On the other hand, a large gamete can retain some nutriment which may then nourish the developing organism, at least through the early stages of growth (Wendrich 1954; Dougherty 1955; Smith 1978).

Rather surprisingly, distinctly different sexes, or genders, of animals seem to have evolved *after* the evolution of basic sexual processes. There are several lower animals that are not exclusively male or female but have both male and female parts—a condition known as *hermaphroditism.* As we have seen, there are also certain animals that change sex periodically, sometimes producing male gametes and sometimes female gametes.

As animals became even more complex, they developed a distinct and stable gender. They also lost the ability to reproduce asexually; sex and reproduction became intimately associated. Finally, in the most complex animal of all—the human—sex has taken on a great many functions and meanings in addition to reproduction and genetic variability. Thus, human sexuality is used to express love, cure headaches, sell magazines, inflate egos, and gain political power—to name just a few. In fact, as we have seen throughout the book, it is difficult to separate sexuality from most aspects of our daily lives.

GAMETE PRODUCTION AND DEVELOPMENT

The production and development of eggs and sperm are complex processes in humans. Furthermore, these processes must be well coordinated for fertilization of the egg to take place. It has been estimated that conception takes place only once for every 100 or more ejaculations of sperm into the vagina—assuming that no birth-control devices are used and both male and female are normal and healthy.

Sperm Production

The primitive sperm cells start out in the seminiferous tubules of the testes with a full complement of forty-six chromosomes: twenty-two pairs of autosomes (chromosomes not governing gender) and a pair of sex chromosomes. As we have seen in chapter 4, the sex chromosomes of the male consist of one X and one Y chromosome.

By a cell-division process known as *meiosis*, two sperm cells are produced from every primitive cell. However, each of the sperm cells has only half the total number of chromosomes. Thus, each sperm cell has twenty-two autosomes and one sex chromosome; half the sperm cells contain an X sex chromosome, while the other half have a Y sex chromosome. Sperm with an X chromosome produce girl babies, and those with a Y chromosome produce boy babies. Sperm consist of a head, midpiece, and tail. The chromosomal material is found in the head; the midpiece contains mitochondria, which are involved in the energy production necessary for locomotion; and the tail propels the sperm by moving back and forth rapidly.

As the sperm mature, some remain in the epididymis, but most are kept in the vas deferens. With sexual inactivity, the sperm may be stored as long as forty-two days. While stored, the sperm are not capable of movement on their own. This immobility is related to a buildup of carbon dioxide (resulting from the sperm's own metabolism), which creates a slightly acid condition in the surrounding fluid. During ejaculation, the sperm mix with somewhat alkaline seminal fluid from the seminal vesicles, prostate, and other structures. The sperm's acidity is neutralized, and soon they are capable of movement on their own. The seminal fluid also provides nutriments for the sperm, which require large amounts of energy for their movement (Guyton 1981).

Causes of Infertility in Men

In cases where couples have difficulty in conceiving, the man's infertility is the basic cause in approximately 30 percent of the cases and may be a contributing factor in another 20 percent (Amelar 1966). One of the most common reasons for male infertility (sometimes called sterility) is a low sperm count. This may be caused by hormone disorders such as hypothyroidism or diabetes and is often treated successfully by hormone therapy.

Other causes of infertility include low sperm motility and a difficulty in penetration of the egg by the sperm (MacLeod 1971). Despite sophisti-

FIGURE 11.2
A sperm.

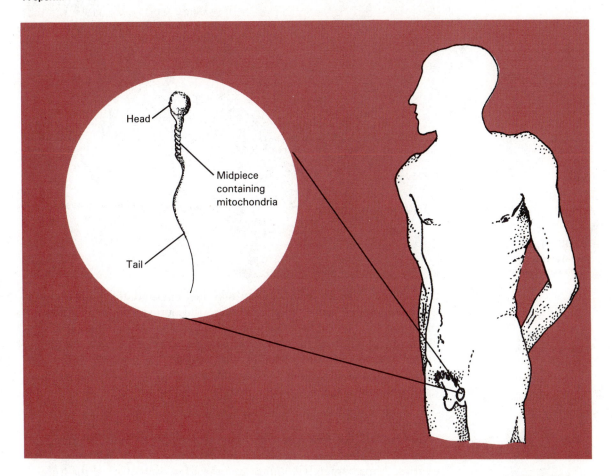

Head

Midpiece
containing
mitochondria

Tail

FIGURE 11.3
Location of testis

cated methods of analyzing sperm, predictions of fertility are often inaccurate; some people with apparent reproductive problems are fertile, while others with seemingly normal reproductive systems are infertile (Noyes 1968).

In a few cases, structural damage to part of the reproductive system makes sperm production impossible. For example, mumps in adult men may result in permanent damage to the testes.

Infertility may have a strong psychological impact upon a man. In our society, masculinity is traditionally defined in terms of the ability to fa-

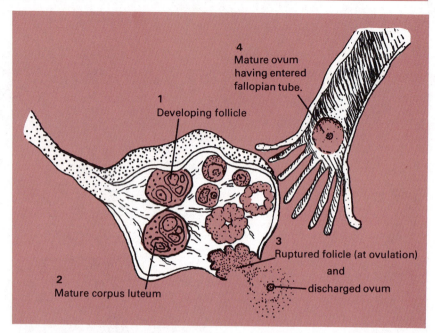

FIGURE 11.4
**Four stages of
follicle development.**

ther children, so an infertile man may feel emasculated (Debrovner &
Shubin-Stein 1975). In some societies, the derogation has been even
more extreme; an infertile Ashanti male (from the west coast of Africa)
has traditionally been described as having a "wax penis" (Ford & Beach
1951). This description probably resulted from the misconception that
infertility implies impotency. In actuality, many infertile men are able to
have erections and engage in normal intercourse.

Maturation of the Egg

In contrast to primitive sperm cells—which are continually being produced by the testes—there is a set number of primitive egg cells in the
ovaries. Approximately 400,000 are present in each ovary at the time of
birth, and by the time the female reaches puberty about half of them are
still living. However, less than one-tenth of 1 percent of these ever mature and become ready for fertilization.

As we have seen, an egg matures while encased in a follicle within one
of the ovaries. Like sperm, the primitive egg cell undergoes meiosis,
producing a cell with half the usual number of chromosomes—twenty-
two autosomes and a sex chromosome. (In egg cells, the sex chromosome is always an X.) Unlike the primitive sperm cells, however, the
primitive egg's meiotic division results in only one mature egg cell. The
excess genetic material is encased in a structure known as a *polar body*,
which is later extruded. Thus, each gamete has twenty-three chromosomes. When an egg is fertilized, the gametes combine. The resulting
zygote has the full complement of forty-six chromosomes, twenty-three
from each parent. If it has an X chromosome from each parent, it is fe-

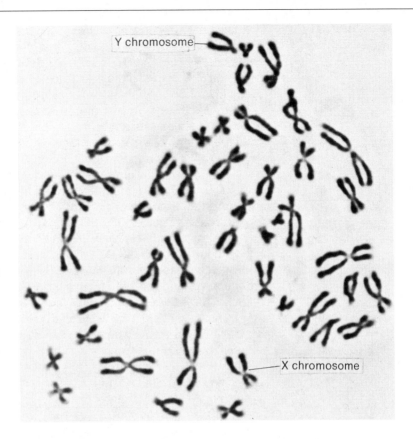

Y chromosome

X chromosome

FIGURE 11.5

A full complement of 46 chromosomes, including an X, a Y, and 22 pairs of autosomes. When cell division is not taking place, the chromosomes are wound around each other in complex ways. It is only during one of the phases of cell division that the individual chromosomes are separated. For this photograph, a chemical substance was used to arrest the cell division process at this critical point so that individual chromosomes could be seen.

male. If it has an X chromosome from the mother and a Y from the father, it develops into a male.

In addition to the chromosomal material, the egg contains fat droplets, protein, and a fluid containing nutrients. It is surrounded by a thin, gelatinous layer known as the *zona pellucida*. As will be seen shortly, it is this layer which must be penetrated by the sperm if fertilization is to take place.

At the time of ovulation, the follicle that contains a mature egg creates a bulge at the surface of the ovary; the egg itself floats in a fluid within the follicle. As a result of stimulation from the hormore LH, the follicle bursts and the egg is carried out with the fluid.

Exactly how the egg manages to get to the fallopian tube is not clear. (In some rare cases, an egg may even find its way from an ovary on one side to the tube on the opposite side.) At any rate, once in the tube, the egg is moved slowly toward the uterus—a journey that usually takes about three days but may be accomplished in considerably less time. The movement of the egg is brought about by the beating of hairlike structures called cilia that line the inside of the fallopian tube.

Causes of Infertility in Women

Female infertility may be related to a variety of factors, the most common of which is failure to ovulate. Lack of ovulation can be brought on by physical factors—such as vitamin deficiency and general malnutrition—or psychological stress. Since ovulation is accompanied by a rise in general body temperature, a chart of morning temperatures will often indicate if and when ovulation occurs.

Another common cause of infertility is a structural blockage of the fallopian tubes, which prevents passage of the egg. This can be caused by infections, congenital malformations, or tumors. A test for blockage of the tubes—known as *Rubin's test*—involves forcing carbon dioxide into the uterus through the cervix. If the tubes are obstructed, there will be a detectable rise in the pressure within the uterus; otherwise the gas will escape through the tubes into the abdominal cavity (Evans 1971).

It is also possible that an obstruction blocks passage of the sperm. The most common site of such an obstruction is the cervix, where thick mucus may prevent sperm from entering the uterus. An analysis of the cervical mucus provides a test for such a problem.

Women, too, may suffer severe psychological stress as a result of infertility. In many societies, a couple's failure to produce children is automatically blamed on the woman. In fact, it was common for a woman in the Longo tribe of East Africa to commit suicide if she failed to become pregnant (Ford & Beach 1951). Even among contemporary Orthodox Jews in the United States, a failure to conceive gives a man grounds for divorce. Fortunately, recent technological advances have facilitated the identification and treatment of infertility problems and also reduced the tendency to blame *all* infertility on women.

Methods of Increasing the Chances for Conception

There are a number of ways in which a couple may improve the chances that conception will take place. One method involves determining when the woman ovulates. A woman's temperature drops a small amount on the day of ovulation and then rises as much as one degree Fahrenheit on the day following ovulation. By taking and recording her temperature each morning for a month, she can get a good indication of when she ovulated during one menstrual cycle. Since a woman's own pattern of ovulation is usually quite consistent, she can then estimate on what day of succeeding menstrual cycles she will ovulate and plan intercourse on or just before that day. (She will probably have to take her temperature during several cycles in order to accurately establish the pattern.) Women who experience Mittelschmerz—cramping pain at ovulation—have an even easier way of knowing when their fertile period occurs.

When there is a failure to ovulate at regular intervals, hormone therapy, vitamins, improved nutrition, or reduction of emotional stress may be therapeutic. Some women have taken what are called "fertility drugs," which induce ovulation. However, one side effect of fertility drugs is that they may cause the ovulation of several eggs at once, which may, in turn, lead to a multiple birth.

Other methods of increasing the chances for conception are related to the male. Since a high sperm count is important for fertilization—and it takes a day or so to build up such a count—ejaculations should not occur more than once every twenty-four to forty-eight hours.

It should be remembered that fertility is not an all-or-nothing phenomenon. There are several examples of couples who were unable to conceive together but, in subsequent marriages with different partners, each had one or more children. As suggested earlier, problems with infertility are still incompletely understood.

FERTILIZATION OF THE EGG

Fertilization of the egg can take place if intercourse has occurred sometime during a period beginning a day and a half before and ending a day and a half after ovulation. Sperm remain fertile for about thirty-six hours after ejaculation, and eggs can be fertilized for about thirty-six hours after ovulation, for a total fertile period of roughly seventy-two hours.[1]

There are about 300 million sperm in a typical ejaculate. Many of them die or fail to reach the uterus. However, within less than an hour, a group of sperm typically makes its way through the uterus to the openings of the fallopian tubes. The sperm swim at the rate of approximately an inch an hour, not fast enough to make the journey in that period of time. Their progress may be helped by muscular contractions in the uterus; these contractions increase during orgasm, so, as we have seen, orgasm may indirectly facilitate conception. Contractions of the uterus may also be increased by prostaglandins contained within the sperm. (A woman's own body also makes prostaglandins; these substances are involved in the induction of labor, and sometimes cause menstrual cramps as well.)

Some of the sperm swim up the "wrong" tube, where there is no egg to be found. However, approximately two thousand (less than one-tenth of 1 percent of the original number of sperm) find their way into the tube that contains the egg, and soon a group of these sperm reach the egg itself.

The sperm that have reached the egg secrete an enzyme known as hyaluronidase which chemically weakens the zona pellucida surrounding the egg and permits one sperm to enter. Although it takes only one sperm to fertilize the egg, the hyaluronidase from several seems to be necessary to allow for penetration of the zona pellucida. Thus, as suggested earlier, a high sperm count is often necessary for conception to occur.

Once one sperm penetrates the egg, no more can enter. Microscopic studies indicate that many sperm attempt to pass through the latticelike structure of the zona pellucida, but all but one are inactivated while only partway through. Apparently, some substance released by the egg prevents penetration once the first sperm has entered. As a result, fertilization involves the union of only one sperm and one egg.[2] Once inside the egg, the twenty-three chromosomes of the sperm combine with the twenty-three of the egg to produce, as we have seen, the full forty-six chromosome complement (Guyton 1981).

Artificial Insemination and Conception in a "Test Tube"

Two somewhat controversial methods of inducing pregnancy have been developed. In the first—*artificial insemination*—the male ejaculates into a receptacle that contains a sperm preservative. A male with a low sperm count may build up the count by combining several ejaculates; the sperm may be frozen and stored for as long as two years. Then the sperm is artificially injected into the woman's vagina. For a man previously incapable of inducing pregnancy, the probabilities of success are increased but are still relatively low—approximately 5 out of 100 women become pregnant within a year (Lehfeldt 1961).

Sperm from anonymous donors may also be utilized. It is estimated that in 1970 almost 100,000 women attempted to become pregnant through artificial insemination with anonymous donors or donors other than a husband (Smith 1970). The rate of pregnancy under these conditions is around 80 percent within a year (Lehfeldt 1961).

Several groups—including the Roman Catholic Church—have opposed artificial insemination on the grounds of its artificiality. Additional moral questions are raised when one considers the question: Who has a right to decide what constitutes a fit donor and a fit recipient?

The other controversial procedure—*conception in a test tube*—was accomplished for the first time in the late 1970s. In this case, the mother could not become pregnant because of blockage in the fallopian tubes. However, physicians were able to remove an egg from an ovary just before ovulation would have taken place. The egg was then introduced to sperm under laboratory conditions. Shortly thereafter, the fertilized egg was placed in the uterus via the cervix. In 1978, the first "test-tube baby" was born, having developed in her mother's uterus after conception outside the woman's body.

As in the case of artificial insemination, moral objections have been raised on the basis of artificiality. As technology becomes more advanced, it seems that moral and ethical questions also increase in complexity.

Psychological Perspective: Reactions to Conception

Until recently, there were strong cultural pressures for couples to have children. However, a number of societal changes have apparently increased the number of people who feel negatively about conception. As the sex role of females has been changing, some women have rejected traditional ideas about motherhood. For example, one survey indicated that 88 percent of the women did not agree with the proposition that women who don't want children are selfish or unnatural (Hare-Mustin & Broderick 1979).

The attitudes of males are also changing. Nonetheless, the same survey indicated that men were less likely to reject traditional views about motherhood; a lower percentage of males disagreed with the above proposition. Furthermore, more males than females accepted the statement that women who want more respect should try to be better mothers.

Some couples are afraid that the arrival of children may put a damper on their relationship. And in fact, there is some evidence that stress is greater and overall satisfaction reduced when young children are present. Practical considerations are also important for many people. According to projections made by the Department of Agriculture in 1983, it would cost between $80,000 and $90,000 to rear a child to age eighteen. This does not take into account income lost if one of the parents is unable to work during certain periods of pregnancy and child rearing—a consideration that has been increasing in importance in recent years. One survey indicated that 14 percent of pregnancies were unwanted and, for another 27 percent of the prospective parents, children had not been desired until sometime in the future (Anderson, Morris, & Geshe 1977).

Despite these general changes in attitudes about conception, a large number of couples are very happy and excited to discover that they are going to become parents. For others, early doubts and negative feelings give way to more positive emotions as the pregnancy progresses. In some cases, women who are single and must face the stigma of being an unwed mother still feel positive about conception. Fortunately, many communities offer free or inexpensive services for people who are experiencing problems or conflicts regarding conception and pregnancy.

THE ESTABLISHMENT OF PREGNANCY

Contrary to what many people think, conception and the establishment of pregnancy are not the same thing. Conception refers to fertilization of the egg, whereas pregnancy occurs when the fertilized egg becomes implanted in the lining of the uterus. (The process of implantation will be discussed shortly.) Since fertilized eggs sometimes fail to become implanted, conception is not always followed by pregnancy.

Between twenty-four and sixty hours after conception, the fertilized egg, or zygote, typically divides into two cells; shortly thereafter, there is a division into four, and so forth. For the first few days, there is no significant change in the size of the zygote; it is simply a ball of very small cells. Then, somewhere between the third and fifth days, a fluid-filled cavity develops in the center of the ball.

At the same time that the first few cell divisions are taking place, the zygote moves through the fallopian tube on a journey to the cavity of the uterus. The zygote is carried in a slight current generated by the beating of hairlike structures called cilia on the sides of the tube. Weak contractions of the fallopian tube may also aid the movement. On this journey, the zygote is nourished by secretions of fallopian cells.

After about three or four days, the zygote enters the uterus. It now receives nutrients from cells lining the uterus. Cell divisions continue to take place, and after approximately four more days the developing ball of cells begins the process of *implantation*: attachment and burrowing into the endometrium, or lining, of the uterus. During this process, certain cells on the surface of the zygote secrete enzymes that digest and liquify some cells of the endometrium. At the same time, cords of cells grow from the zygote, extend into the deepest layers of the endometrium, and become attached. Once implantation has taken place (and pregnancy established), the developing individual—which is called an *embryo* during approximately the second to eighth week—receives nutrients from the maternal blood vessels (Bodemer 1968; Guyton 1981).

On rare occasions, the zygote implants itself somewhere other than the uterus, a condition called ectopic pregnancy. Most ectopic pregnancies occur in the fallopian tubes and are referred to as tubal pregnancies. Tubal pregnancies are invariably fatal to the fetus and, if the fetus is not surgically removed, may stretch the tube until it ruptures, causing hemorrhage and even death for the mother. In very rare cases, ectopic pregnancies have taken place in the abdominal cavity.

Under normal circumstances, a structure known as the *placenta* develops. The placenta—which reaches full maturity at about five months—is a round, flat structure about seven inches in diameter. It serves as a medium of exchange for nutrients and waste products between the mother and *fetus*. (The developing individual is known as a fetus after about eight weeks of pregnancy.) The placenta's blood vessels are in contact, via a semipermeable membrane, with the blood vessels of the uterus; the placenta, in turn, is attached to the *umbilical cord,* which communicates directly with the fetus. The umbilical cord is essentially the "life line" of the fetus.

The placenta also secretes hormones basic to pregnancy. At first it produces a hormone that keeps the corpus luteum producing progesterone. (As we have seen, when pregnancy does not occur, the corpus luteum disintegrates and progesterone levels drop.) Later in pregnancy, the placenta itself produces large amounts of progesterone.

During prenatal development, the fetus is enclosed in a thin, transparent membrane known as the *amnion*. Besides the fetus, the amnion contains a fluid known as the *amniotic fluid*. Thus, the fetus is suspended in fluid, attached to the placenta by the umbilical cord. The fluid has several functions. First, it protects the fetus from injury that might result from jolts or pokes. Second, it prevents the fetus from coming into contact with the amnion; this contact could result in an adhesion that would interfere with fetal development. Third, it allows the fetus to move about somewhat within the amnion. Finally, it may aid in the dilation of the cervix in childbirth as uterine contractions squeeze the fluid outward.

By the eighth week of fetal development, virtually all the major structures and organs of the body have become differentiated. Growth at the head end of the body takes place most rapidly. Starting about the fourth week, facial features—the eyes, ears, nose, and mouth—begin to develop; they become recognizable about two weeks later. It is not until after the sixth week that more peripheral structures such as fingers and toes begin to appear. During the embryonic period, a tail-like structure develops. However, it practically disappears by the eighth week (Guyton 1981).[3]

There are considerable variations in the length of time a successful pregnancy may last. Premature infants born about the twenty-eighth week may live and develop normally with special postnatal care. At the other extreme, United States courts have ruled that pregnancy may last as long as fifty weeks. (The longest possible pregnancy is of legal interest because, in cases of extended sexual abstinence between husband and wife, the legitimacy of the child may be at stake in some states.) On the

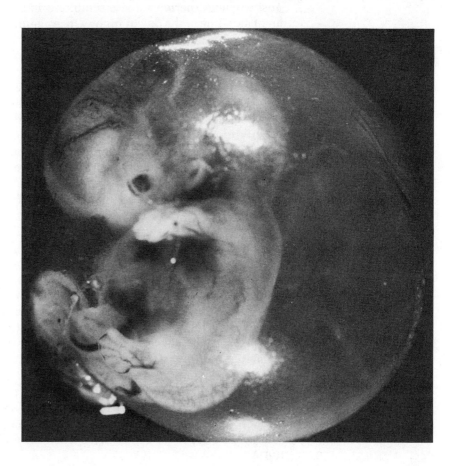

FIGURE 11.6
A fetus at eight weeks.

average, pregnancies last approximately forty weeks, or nine months. For purposes of discussion, a pregnancy is divided into three trimesters, each lasting approximately three months.

Symptoms of Pregnancy

A missed menstrual period is a sign of pregnancy but not a very accurate one. Various illnesses or emotional traumas may also result in late or missed periods. Furthermore, some women—especially those under twenty or over forty—have irregular menstrual cycles.

Another symptom of pregnancy is enlargement and tenderness of the breasts. Many women report a sense of fullness and/or a sensation of tingling in the breasts. These sensations are often related to hormonal changes that take place after conception.

A third sign is what has been called "morning sickness." This consists of a queasy feeling or nausea, sometimes accompanied by vomiting. The smell of food may also be perceived as unpleasant. Although most women experience these symptoms in the morning, they may occur at any time of the day or night. Once again, hormonal changes seem to be responsible for these reactions.

Finally, fatigue and frequent need for urination are fairly common in the early stages of pregnancy. Increased pressure from the swelling uterus causes the urinary problem. However, as the uterus enlarges and rises in the abdomen, this symptom usually disappears.

Various laboratory tests have been developed that are quite accurate in identifying pregnancy in its early stages. Most of these tests are designed to detect the presence of *human chorionic gonadotrophin (HCG)* which is produced only by pregnant women. HCG is produced in small quantities at first but in increasingly large amounts following implantation. A recently developed blood test is able to detect HCG as early as eight days following conception (even before the woman misses her period). This test can be made within minutes but is fairly expensive (Hoffman-LaRoche 1981).

An older and more commonly used test for pregnancy involves analysis of the woman's urine. Since this test is less sensitive to the presence of HCG, pregnancy cannot be detected until approximately two weeks after conception, and the test is most accurate after at least four weeks (two weeks after the woman misses her period).

In recent years, do-it-yourself pregnancy test kits have appeared on the market. The tests done in the home are virtually the same as those made in the laboratory: urine is tested for HCG. Although the tests have proven to be highly accurate in confirming a pregnancy (97 percent of women with positive tests are pregnant), they are less accurate in denying one (the false negative rate is 20–25 percent). Thus, the do-it-yourself kits appear to be of only limited value (Nass, Libby, & Fisher, 1981).

From a medical and legal viewpoint, pregnancy cannot be positively confirmed until around the third month or later. One method of positive identification is an X-ray image of the fetal skeleton or an image produced by reflection of ultrasound. Another technique involving ultrasound is used in the detection of fetal heartbeats. A high-pitched sound wave is directed at the uterus; movements of the fetal heart cause changes in the pitch of the reflected sound, which can be detected and amplified by a receiver (Goodlin 1971). Thus, technological advances allow physicians to identify pregnancy much earlier than they could a generation ago.

Pseudocyesis

One of the reasons that the usual early symptoms of pregnancy are unreliable is a phenomenon known as *pseudocyesis* or *false pregnancy*. This occurs in roughly one out of a thousand women who consult obstetricians. False pregnancy may have symptoms such as morning sickness, a cessation of menstruation, a swollen abdomen, and the sensation of fetal movements. In some cases, women with pseudocyesis may even experience labor pains. During the Middle Ages, a certain number of nuns in convents were known to have experienced pseudocyesis; they believed that they had been impregnated by Christ (Taylor 1954).

Often, the women who experience false pregnancies are young and have a strong desire for children. However, there have also been false pregnancies in older women who do not report a wish for children. There have been instances when animals exhibited pseudocyesis (Parkes & Bruce 1961). Thus it appears that a strong psychological need for pregnancy is not the only factor of importance.

Author's Perspective: Choosing a Physician

As we shall see in the next section, pregnancy involves several potential problems. Therefore, it is important that a woman consult a physician early in her pregnancy and set up regular medical examinations. The choice of physician is sometimes difficult, since there are many variables that should be considered. It is especially important that doctor and mother agree in their philosophies about childbirth—for example, about natural childbirth or home delivery, if such procedures are being considered. Other factors that may enter into the choice are fees and type of practice (obstetrician or family-practice physician; clinic, medical group, individual in private practice, or hospital). Of particular importance also is the physician's personality and style. If a woman feels uncomfortable relating to her doctor, she may fail to communicate significant information or refuse to follow certain suggestions. It is usually possible for a woman to meet with the physician in order to get a rough idea of procedures and personality before making the final choice. Even after the decision has been made—and there have been several examinations—it is still possible to switch physicians if there is dissatisfaction or conflicts cannot be resolved.

One of the best ways to obtain information about physicians is to consult family, friends, or one's regular doctor. Other sources include hospitals and local medical societies. Fortunately, for many women the relationship with the physician turns out to be very positive; an emotional closeness tends to develop during this unique physical and emotional experience defined as pregnancy.

POTENTIAL PROBLEMS OF PREGNANCY

During pregnancy, the circulatory systems of the mother and the fetus are completely separate. However, nutrients, wastes, and other substances pass between them by crossing the semipermeable membrane that separates the two circulations. Some harmful substances are filtered out by this placental barrier, but others are able to cross it. In this section, we will consider problems related to substances transmitted from the mother to the fetus, as well as certain other problems of early pregnancy.

Drugs

A number of substances have been found harmful to the human fetus. One of the most highly publicized has been a drug known as thalidomide. This over-the-counter medication was used as a sleeping aid, a nausea reducer, and a relief for morning sickness in the 1960s. Unfortunately, it was later discovered that, when the drug was taken in early pregnancy, severe deformities of the baby resulted. Many were born with hands and feet attached to the body by short stumps.

Experiments with rabbits indicated that even the sperm could be affected by thalidomide. Males given large doses of the drug fathered abnormally small, underweight offspring with some of the thalidomide abnormalities. Apparently, the sperm was coated with thalidomide, which was transmitted directly into the zygote during fertilization (Lutwak-Mann 1973).

Another substance that has been found to affect fetal development is nicotine. Nicotine absorbed by smoking has been shown to increase the incidence of miscarriage and produce infants with significantly lower birth weights; some of these smaller infants are prone to various medical problems (Fabro 1973). Generally speaking, the larger the number of cigarettes smoked, the greater the danger.

For several years it has been known that excessive intake of alcohol results in alcohol dependency and withdrawal symptoms in newborn babies (Streissguth 1977). Recently, research has indicated that even relatively moderate drinking by a pregnant woman may result in abnormalities—known as the *Fetal Alcohol Syndrome (FAS)*—in the developing individual. FAS infants have smaller heads, are less responsive to stimulation, and are more irritable than normal infants. One of the reasons for this syndrome is that, because of the immaturity of the fetus's organs, it metabolizes alcohol much more slowly than an adult. In essence, regular drinking by the mother results in an almost constant state of toxicity in the fetus. Although not all infants of drinking mothers develop FAS, the rate is around 70 percent among heavily drinking mothers, and the syndrome has even been reported with light or occasional drinkers. On the basis of this evidence, the Fetal Alcohol Syndrome Work Group (1980) advises expectant mothers to refrain from drinking completely.

Diseases

Certain maternal diseases have been found to affect prenatal development. For example, rubella (German measles) contracted by the mother during the embryonic period (two to eight weeks after conception) causes blindness, deafness, and/or heart damage in some cases (Sheridan 1964). As will be seen in chapter 22, sexually transmitted, or venereal, diseases may also be passed on to the fetus and cause serious damage.

Rh Incompatibility

In some circumstances, the Rh factor in the fetus's blood is positive, while the Rh factor in the mother's blood is negative. During the first pregnancy, this is not usually a problem. However, with subsequent pregnancies involving Rh positive babies, there is a danger that the child will be born with an unusually low red-blood-cell count, also known as severe anemia. This is because the mother may become "sensitized" by the first child and produce antibodies, or agglutins, that attack the red blood cells of the later fetuses (Guyton 1981).

Fortunately, two types of treatment have greatly reduced the incidence of this problem. A substance known as anti-D gamma globulin can be given to a woman shortly after delivery. This reduces the formation of maternal antibodies that could affect later pregnancies. The second type of treatment involves a blood transfusion for the fetus, either while it is in the uterus or immediately after it is born (Douglass 1972). Therefore, serious problems resulting from Rh incompatibility are now rare.

Maternal Stress

Some researchers believe that the mother's emotional reaction affects the fetus, as biological (particularly hormonal) reactions to stress may be passed on to the fetus in much the same way as drugs or diseases. Among the problems that seem to be caused by maternal stress are complicated deliveries, miscarriages, and feeding problems in the infant (Holmes & Morrison 1979).

It is difficult to evaluate the effects of maternal stress. In the first place, one must rely on mothers' after-the-fact reports, which are not always accurate. Furthermore, the same mother who was stressed during pregnancy is often stressed while rearing the child; therefore, the prenatal and postnatal effects are hard to separate. However, studies with rats have been conducted that have relatively fewer methodological problems. These studies indicate that maternal stress during pregnancy significantly affects emotionality, learning ability, and general behavior of the offspring (Joffe 1969).

Malnutrition

Contrary to what is popularly believed, the fetus does not have first priority on nutriments taken in by the mother. If the mother is receiving poor nutrition, the fetus is even more likely to suffer than the mother; malnutrition—especially during the last months of pregnancy—results in low birth weights and high mortality rates (Holmes & Morrison 1979).

Prenatal malnutrition along with poor nutrition shortly after birth can have an especially serious effect on neural development. Up to 60 percent reduction in the number of brain cells has been reported, along with resulting mental retardation (Winick 1975). Clearly, adequate nutrition is an important part of a healthy pregnancy.

Testing for Abnormalities

After reading the preceding sections, one is likely to get the impression that the hazards of pregnancy are very great and that the pregnant woman should spend much time worrying about herself and her body. Although there are very real risks, many adaptive responses occur quite naturally. For example, a woman is generally less inclined to smoke or drink when she is pregnant. Furthermore, she has a larger appetite, so she is likely to eat adequately (particularly if she had good dietary habits before pregnancy). It should also be remembered that there are large individual differences in the susceptibility of the fetus to drugs, diseases, and maternal stress; some fetuses are quite resistant to factors that may cause serious problems to others (Joffe 1969). Thus, caution—as opposed to extreme worry—seems to be the best practice.

A procedure known as *amniocentesis* enables physicians to detect certain genetically related problems in the fetus. The doctor inserts a long needle through the woman's abdomen into the amniotic sac, removing a small amount of amniotic fluid. Some cells from the fetus float in this fluid, and an analysis of their chromosomal structure can identify at least sixty different types of genetic defects. Amniocentesis is used only after the sixteenth week of pregnancy and then only if there is reason to suspect fetal abnormalities (Holmes & Morrison 1979).

A recently developed technique allows for a more direct examination of the fetus and enables physicians to identify a wider range of abnormalities. Pulsed sound waves are used to locate the exact position of the

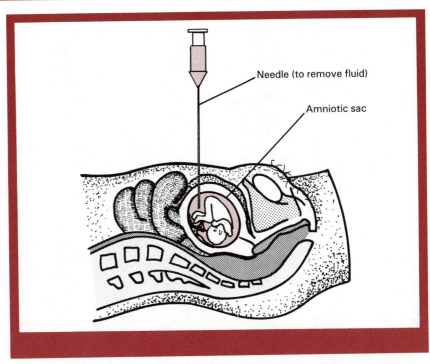

Needle (to remove fluid)

Amniotic sac

FIGURE 11.7
Amniocentesis.

Fluid is removed from the amniotic sac and the chromosomal structure of cells floating in the fluid is then analyzed. A variety of genetic defects can be identified by this method.

fetus, umbilical cord, and placenta. Next, a tiny incision is made in the mother's abdomen, and a physician inserts a thin tube in one of the fetal blood vessels of the placenta and withdraws blood for analysis. It is also possible to insert an endoscope with fiberoptic bundles that transmit light; using this technique, one can actually view tiny areas of the fetus (Mahoney & Hobbins 1980).

In the early 1980s, technological advances made it feasible to remove a fetus from the uterus, perform surgery, and then replace the fetus without ill effects. Thus, the techniques of prenatal diagnosis have made it possible to save fetuses that would not have survived under normal circumstances.

THE SECOND AND THIRD TRIMESTERS OF PREGNANCY

A pregnant woman becomes more aware of the fetus during the second trimester; she can feel the fetal movements, and her waistline begins to spread. The greatest expansion takes place in women who have previously given birth. Generally, the second trimester is more pleasant and peaceful than the first. In most cases, the symptoms of morning sickness disappear, and there are fewer concerns about miscarriage. Except when there are complications, there is no need to stop working or drastically reduce the activity level.

It is not until the third trimester that women usually experience discomfort. There may be difficulty sleeping due to the vigorous movements of the fetus. A complication known as *toxemia* develops in from 8 to 20 percent of the pregnant women who receive no prenatal care. A toxic substance causes high blood pressure and a retention of fluids in the body. Although toxemia is not serious if detected and treated early, it may be fatal to the mother if untreated (Dennis & Hester 1971). Recent research has identified a small wormlike organism which apparently causes toxemia (Lueck et al. 1983). It now looks as though the dangers of toxemia can be further reduced with early diagnosis and treatment.

Excessive weight gain during the third trimester may produce problems such as high blood pressure and strain on the heart. Most obstetricians believe that the optimal weight gain during pregnancy is around twenty-four pounds. The physician typically sets a schedule of weight gain for each few weeks and encourages the woman to stay close to this schedule.

As the end of pregnancy approaches, the fetus typically shifts and assumes a head-down position, in preparation for birth. This shift—which is known as *lightening* or *engagement*—may increase the woman's fatigue and produce unaccustomed aches.

Sexual Drive and Coitus During Pregnancy

During the first three months of pregnancy, the incidence of sexual intercourse generally remains about the same as it was before pregnancy. However, decreased sexual interest has been reported in about 25 percent of women surveyed. Factors that seem related to the lower drive are nausea associated with morning sickness, general fatigue, and anxiety about the fetus. (In actuality, there is no evidence that sexual relations endanger the fetus.) In some cases, women report that sexual arousal can result in pain in the breasts; this is most likely if the breasts were tender before pregnancy (Wagner & Solberg 1974).

The second trimester does not usually bring any significant change in sexual drive or frequency of coitus. In fact, women who experience nausea and fatigue during the first trimester may exhibit renewed sexual interest during the second three months of pregnancy. However, there is usually a shift in preference for sexual positions; the missionary position—if it is the preferred one—is generally replaced by coital positions more comfortable for the woman (Butler, Dale, & Wagner 1979).

By the seventh month of pregnancy, the woman's sexual drive begins to decline significantly, and it continues declining throughout the remaining months (White & Reamy 1982). Some physicians suggest that if the woman does not have a prior history of problems such as vaginal bleeding during pregnancy, intercourse without danger is still possible.

However, recent research indicates that amniotic-fluid infections are significantly more frequent among women who engage in coitus in the final month before delivery than among those who abstain (Naeye 1979).

Psychological Perspective: Emotional Reactions to Pregnancy

Women usually experience a wide variety of emotional reactions during pregnancy. Some of these are related to the physical and physiological changes already discussed, while others spring from physical sensations, awe at the sig-

FIGURE 11.8

Pregnancy and childbirth involve a complex series of physical, physiological, and psychological events. This nine-month period is typically seen as one of the most significant in a couple's life.

nificance of life within their bodies, and anticipation of the impending role of mother. Some women are reminded of long-forgotten feelings about their own mothers and their childhood. A sense of power in creation of a new life may be mixed with feelings of powerlessness as the pregnancy governs their bodies, distorts their figures, and promises loss of freedom after the birth of the child. It is not unusual for pregnant women to display a wide range of conflicting emotions: joy and sorrow; confidence and fear; excitement and depression (Rich 1976).

Expectant fathers also show a variety of emotional reactions, many of which are similar to those of a pregnant woman. This is especially true if the man has been involved in preparation for natural childbirth. A common conflict among expectant fathers is a feeling of closeness to the woman who is carrying ''their'' child accompanied by separateness because only she is experiencing the physical changes of pregnancy. Another ambivalence is pride at becoming a father—and passing on his bloodline—along with fear that, in some fashion, he will not be a good father or a good provider (Dailey 1978).

Although there are large individual differences in the way people react to pregnancy, most agree on one thing: pregnancy and the anticipation of birth provide a unique emotional experience for both a woman and a man.

CHILDBIRTH

The onset of labor is apparently caused by a variety of factors. At the time of fetal maturity, the hypothalamus secretes hormones (cortical steroids) that trigger mechanisms related to labor. A drop in progesterone levels also seems to be involved in the onset of uterine contractions. Animal studies indicate that withdrawal of progesterone at a time when estrogen levels are rising stimulates labor. Other chemical substances—known as *prostaglandins*—also appear to bring about contractions of the uterus. Finally, a hormone known as *oxytocin* is apparently important in the last stage of labor; oxytocin stimulates the more powerful uterine contractions required for the final expulsion of the fetus (Reeder et al. 1983). This combination of factors seems to ensure that, under normal conditions, labor occurs at the appropriate time.

There are certain signs that labor is about to begin. One may be a small discharge including some blood; this discharge represents a plug of mucus that was blocking the cervix. Shortly before onset of labor, the amnion ruptures and suddenly releases its fluid. This ''breaking of the water'' is a fairly reliable indication that labor will start within twenty-four hours if it has not begun already.

Labor itself is divided into three stages. The first stage—which may last fifteen or more hours in the first pregnancy and about half as long in later ones—includes regular uterine contractions that dilate the cervix. The contractions begin at intervals of fifteen minutes or more and increase in frequency and intensity. (When the intervals are regularly four or five minutes apart, the woman is usually admitted to the hospital.)

The second stage of labor begins when the cervix is completely dilated—about four inches in diameter—and includes the uterine contractions that expel the fetus from the uterus. This stage may last from a few minutes to a few hours. In many cases, some type of anesthetic is given a short time before the second stage begins. Early in the century, a general anesthetic was regularly given during labor. However, general anesthetics are not popular today because they slow labor and suppress the infant's activity. A spinal anesthetic—inserted by needle into the spinal cord—is used most often; this produces a temporary loss of feeling below the waist but allows the mother to remain conscious throughout delivery. In about 98 percent of the cases, the baby is delivered head first (other types of deliveries are known as *breech* deliveries). As the head of the fetus is pushed along the lower vagina, muscle reflexes help expel the fetus.

When the head of the baby emerges, the obstetrician or midwife holds it and gently guides it downward; there should be no pulling or forcing. Blood or amniotic fluid that may have collected in the nose or mouth of

FIGURE 11.9
The moment of birth.

the baby are removed with a syringe. The sudden changes in pressure and temperature that occur at birth or the buildup of carbon dioxide generally induces the baby to start breathing. However, in some cases the baby is held upside down and slapped on the buttocks, an action traditionally thought to facilitate the process.

The third and final stage of labor involves the expulsion of the placenta and fetal membrane (known as the *afterbirth*). This generally occurs about fifteen minutes after delivery of the baby. During this stage, the uterus shrinks in size and the placenta detaches from the uterine wall. In rare cases, the obstetrician or midwife must use a hand to follow the umbilical cord into the uterus and peel the placenta from the uterine wall (Reeder et al. 1983).

Medical Perspective: Episiotomy

As the head of the baby emerges during the second stage of labor, many physicians perform an *episiotomy:* an incision is made in the mother's perineum—the skin just behind the vagina. The advantage of such a procedure is that the baby's head may pass through easily without tearing the perineum. Shortly after birth, the incision is stitched closed.

It has been argued that, if an episiotomy is not performed—and a tear occurs—deep tissue may be damaged and healing will be relatively slow (Reeder et al. 1983). On the other hand, some people have suggested that episiotomies are usually performed for the convenience of the physician and are not really necessary (Hahn & Paige 1980). In Western Europe and in some U.S. hospitals, gentle massaging and stretching of the perineal area enable the baby to pass through the vagina without much difficulty. The questioning of a need for episiotomies is consistent with a recent trend away from traditionally accepted surgical procedures.

Natural Childbirth

In the early twentieth century, childbirth took place in a setting that resembled one utilized for major surgery. A variety of instruments were used in the delivery, the mother was kept in ignorance about the process, and the father was completely excluded from the procedure. However, in the early 1930s, an English physician named Grantly Dick-Read coined the term natural childbirth. He attempted to reduce the fear and muscular tension associated with childbirth by educating the parents about the birth process before delivery (Dick-Read 1944).

In 1951 a French physician, Fernand Lamaze, emphasized specific training for delivery as well as general education. The woman practiced muscle-control and breathing-technique exercises during her pregnancy. Furthermore, the man was encouraged to assist the woman in her exercises and be prepared to help during delivery. The presence of the man presumably helped to build up the woman's confidence and al-

FIGURE 11.10
Stages of childbirth.

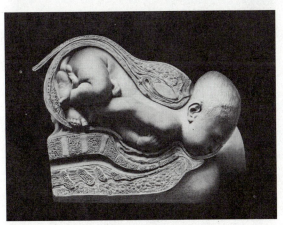

lowed for a greater sharing of the emotions associated with birth (La-maze 1970).

Another Frenchman, Frederick Leboyer (1975), developed a technique designed to reduce the baby's pain and trauma. Traditionally, the newborn suddenly enters a world of bright lights, harsh sounds, and a whack on the bottom. The Leboyer method involves gently introducing the infant into a quiet, dimly lit room; after delivery, the child is placed for a time on the mother's abdomen to reduce the shock of separation. Finally, the baby is given a warm, soothing bath. The result of this non-violent birth procedure is a more relaxed and sometimes smiling infant.

These methods of natural childbirth have become increasingly popular in the United States and have had a general effect on hospital procedures. For example, it is becoming more and more acceptable for the father to be present during labor and delivery. In many cases, newborn babies may be kept in the room with their mothers instead of in separate nurseries.

Another trend is the increased use of midwives and home deliveries

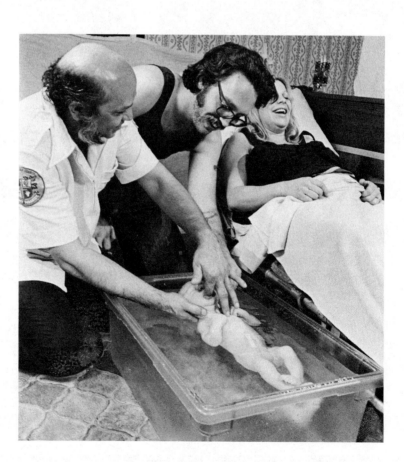

FIGURE 11.11

The Leboyer method of nonviolent delivery. An attempt is made to reduce the trauma of birth.

(with provisions made for emergencies that require hospitalization). These arrangements provide a more homelike, family-oriented atmosphere and are also less expensive than hospital deliveries.

Caesarean Section

In some cases, it is necessary to remove the infant from the uterus via an incision in the abdomen, a procedure known as *Caesarean section*.[4] This procedure is most generally used when (1) the baby's head is too large to pass through the woman's pelvis; (2) the baby is suffering from severe toxemia or another type of distress; (3) there is a premature separation of the placenta. Caesarean section is also suggested for older women having their first pregnancy. The dangers of this operation are not much greater than those of the usual, vaginal delivery. Furthermore, it is possible for a woman to have several children by Caesarean section, although it is somewhat more difficult with each succeeding delivery (Reeder et al. 1983).

Psychological Perspective: Parental Reactions to the Birth of a Child

Typically, a great variety of strong emotional reactions accompany the initial meeting of parent and child. Klaus and Kennell (1976) suggest that the first few hours after birth are a sensitive period for the development of the parent-infant relationship and refer to this process as "bonding." These authors claim that exposure to the infant during this relatively short period is necessary for the optimum development of a parent-infant relationship, particularly one between the mother and the infant.

Following its introduction, the concept of bonding has remained controversial, since it is ethically impossible to conduct well-controlled experiments during the first meeting of mother and infant. However, researchers have observed an important development in parent-infant interaction beginning shortly after the first meeting. Parents' behaviors tend to be exaggerated, repetitive, and rhythmic; infants, in turn, generally respond with relatively prolonged attention, coos, and smiles (Wasserman 1980).

If the newborn child is premature, sick, or deformed in some way, parents may have ambivalent or negative feelings and have difficulty interacting with the infant (Widmayer & Field 1980). There may be several reasons for this difficulty. Some hospitals may not allow the mother to see such an infant for a while after delivery. Clifford and Crocker (1971) found that the longer the delay, the more negative (or less positive) the feelings of the mother towards her infant.

Another factor appears to be the physical appearance of the infant. Full-term, healthy babies tend to have high, protruding foreheads, round faces, large eyes placed in the middle of the face, and relatively fat cheeks. These characteristics—perhaps innately—are attractive to adults and therefore facilitate the survival of the species (Hess 1967). Recent research indicates that premature infants differ significantly in regard to many of these characteristics and are seen as considerably less attractive than full-term infants (R. Maier, Jr.

1983). Thus, the appearance of premature babies—and sick and deformed ones as well—may have a negative effect on parents.

Still another factor may be that premature or sick babies tend to be unresponsive. They spend a great deal of time crying and sleeping and consequently are less responsive to parental attempts at stimulation (R. Q. Bell 1974). Clearly, counseling services may be helpful in encouraging the parents to come to grips with their negative or ambivalent emotional reactions and function effectively as parents of premature or less than healthy infants.

Multiple Births

The delivery of more than one child from a single pregnancy occurs about once in every eighty births. Twins are the most common type of multiple birth. *Identical twins* develop from a single, fertilized egg; the first cell division takes place and then each of the two resulting cells develops into a separate individual. Identical twins have identical heredity and consequently are always of the same sex. They are encapsulated in separate amniotic sacs, have separate umbilical cords, but share the same placenta.

In contrast, *fraternal twins* develop from two separate eggs, usually fertilized at about the same time by two separate sperm. Fraternal twins are more common than identical ones. Such twins have separate umbilical cords, amniotic sacs, and placentas. Since they develop from separate fertilized eggs, they are no more alike than other siblings; they may be of either the same sex or different sexes.

The birth of more than two babies at a time is rare but does occur, especially if the mother has taken fertility drugs. Triplets usually comprise a pair of identical twins plus a fraternal sibling; one egg separates while another does not. In the case of quadruplets, there are generally two eggs that each separate, producing two sets of identical twins. The chances of all quadruplets surviving are not great, since the infants are usually born prematurely and are very small at birth.

Lactation

Shortly after delivery, production of milk, or *lactation*, begins. Lactation seems to be initiated by the sudden change in the proportion of estrogen and progesterone that results from the delivery of the placenta. Specifically, lactation is brought about by the release of *prolactin*, a hormone secreted by the pituitary gland (Reeder et al. 1983).

Immediately following delivery, the woman's breasts are filled with *colostrum*, a high-protein liquid that apparently transmits to the child whatever immunity the mother has acquired to several infectious diseases (Steen & Montagu 1959). This immunity lasts for several months. Two or three days following delivery, colostrum is replaced by true milk.

Although milk production is induced by prolactin, another pituitary hormone already discussed—oxytocin—is necessary for the "letting down" of milk into the nipple area and the ejection of milk when the nipples are stimulated. Continued prolactin and oxytocin secretion are dependent upon stimulation of the nipples. Therefore, at the time of weaning, when the nipples are no longer stimulated (or if the mother does not nurse), the production and letting down of milk cease.

During the period of nursing, the relatively high levels of prolactin may inhibit ovulation and menstruation. Consequently, women who breast-feed their babies usually do not become pregnant again for a period of time. This natural birth control may last nine months or longer

FIGURE 11.12

As attitudes toward sexuality become more liberal, women are again finding the experience of breast feeding their infants emotionally satisfying. Although most nutritional needs of the baby can be met satisfactorily by bottle feeding, breast feeding has the advantage of providing natural immunization against some diseases.

(Jackson 1976), but it should not be regarded as completely reliable.

Whether or not to breast-feed the infant is a complex decision in which the father should generally be involved. Certain physical conditions in either the mother or infant may make breast-feeding difficult or impossible, but otherwise the nutritional needs of the infant can be met almost equally well with breast milk or formula. Psychological factors appear to be most important in the decision. Some women consider nursing unappealing or too time consuming; others find breast-feeding emotionally satisfying and sensual. Generally speaking, women with liberal attitudes about sexuality are more likely to nurse their babies and find the experience satisfying than those with conservative attitudes (Newton 1973; Reeder et al. 1983).

Resumption of Sexual Intercourse

Most women continue to have a low sexual drive for three or four weeks following delivery. In any case, couples generally are advised to refrain from coitus until a physician sees that the vagina and uterus have been restored and the episiotomy (if any) healed. The waiting period is usually four to eight weeks. During the period of abstinence, many couples utilize alternate means of sexual expression.

SUMMARY

Conception—the basic sexual process—involves the union of a sperm and an egg, each carrying half the total number of chromosomes in an ordinary human cell. It is possible for reproduction to take place in some animals without the direct involvement of sex. However, the genetic variability that is crucial for survival of a species over a period of time is dependent upon sexual processes.

In men, the process of meiosis produces sperm cells; half the sperm contain X chromosomes, which produce female babies; the other half contain Y chromosomes, which produce male offspring. The sperm are stored, in an inactive state, in the epididymis and vas deferens. During ejaculation, seminal fluid is added from the seminal vesicles and prostate; this fluid activates and nourishes the sperm.

Infertility in men usually results from a low sperm count, which in many cases is successfully treated by hormone therapy. Other causes of male infertility include structural damage to the reproductive system and low sperm motility.

In women, an egg matures in an ovary while encased in a follicle. During ovulation, the follicle of a mature egg bursts—as the result of LH stimulation—and the egg moves into one of the fallopian tubes.

Infertility in women may be caused by a variety of problems, including failure to ovulate, structural blockage of the fallopian tubes, and "hostile mucus," which obstructs the passage of sperm at the cervix. For both men and women, infertility may induce psychological stress.

Fertilization of the egg can take place if intercourse occurs within a day and a half before or after ovulation. The sperm typically surround an egg in one of the fallopian tubes. One—and only one—sperm penetrates the zona pellucida of the egg. Once inside, the twenty-three chromosomes of the sperm combine with the twenty-three of the egg to produce the full forty-six chromosome complement.

Pregnancy—beginning with implantation—is typically divided into trimesters, each approximately three months in length. At the beginning of the first trimester, the zygote (fertilized egg) moves through the fallopian tube—while increasing in size—and becomes implanted in the endometrium of the uterus. The embryo then develops a placenta. This round, flat structure serves as a medium of exchange with the blood vessels of the mother, providing the embryo with nutrients and removing its wastes via the umbilical cord, an extension of the placenta. Until the end of pregnancy, the fetus is enclosed in the amniotic sac.

Early, somewhat unreliable signs of pregnancy include a missed menstrual period, enlargement and tenderness of the breasts, morning sickness, and fatigue. The sixth week of presumed pregnancy is the earliest that reliable laboratory tests can be run.

There are a variety of potential problems during pregnancy. Several types of drugs—including nicotine and alcohol—pass through the placental barrier and may affect the development of the fetus. Similarly, certain types of sexually transmitted diseases, Rh incompatibility, maternal stress, and malnutrition may have adverse effects. Recently developed procedures, such as amniocentesis and ultrasound imaging, make it possible to identify several types of fetal abnormalities.

The second trimester of pregnancy is usually more pleasant and peaceful than the first. It is not until the third trimester that women typically begin to experience discomfort related to the growth and movement of the fetus. During this period, there is also a significant decline in the sex drive.

The onset of labor is apparently stimulated by a variety of chemical changes in the woman's body. Labor is divided into three stages: (1) dilation of the cervix (which is brought about by uterine contractions); (2) delivery of the fetus (associated with very strong uterine contractions); and (3) expulsion of the placenta and fetal membrane (called afterbirth).

Natural childbirth has been increasing in popularity in the United States in recent years. Of particular significance is the Lamaze method—which emphasizes education and training for both parents—and the Leboyer technique—associated with nonviolent birth procedures.

Lactation, or production of milk, begins shortly after delivery, stimulated by the pituitary hormone prolactin. Another pituitary hormone—

oxytocin—is necessary for the letting down of milk into the nipple area. Continued production of prolactin and oxytocin depends upon stimulation of the nipples. The decision on whether or not to breast-feed the baby is usually more related to psychological variables than to medical or nutritional factors.

NOTES

1. Sperm can remain alive for up to seventy-two hours. However, after approximately the twenty-fourth hour, they start to lose their fertility and, after thirty-six hours, a significant number of sperm have lost their ability to fertilize an egg (Guyton 1981).

2. On very rare occasions, penetration of the egg by more than one sperm takes place. However, development is abnormal and the zygote is spontaneously aborted (Newth 1973).

3. In rare instances, individuals are born with tails, which are then surgically removed at birth. However, there is a documented case of a twelve-year-old boy who had a tail nine inches long (Katchadourian & Lunde 1980).

4. The term Caesarean section is derived from the belief that Julius Caesar was delivered by this method. In fact, it seems unlikely that this was true. In ancient Rome, babies were delivered by "Caesarean" section only if the mother died late in pregnancy. Caesar's mother lived following his birth.

CHAPTER 12

Birth Control

Attempts to limit fertility go back to antiquity. Four-thousand-year-old Egyptian documents suggest that women used a pastelike substance made up of crocodile dung and honey in their vaginas to prevent conception (Suitters 1967). Among the ancient Chinese, passivity on the part of a woman was advised. The Chinese believed that her enjoyment of intercourse was evil and that pregnancy was a type of punishment (Finch & Green 1963).

Conflicts over these and other attempts at birth control have developed and continued through the ages. In the United States, a conflict between advocates and opponents of birth control reached its height during the early twentieth century. Margaret Sanger, a nurse working in the poor tenements of New York City, became convinced that great suffering resulted from a lack of contraceptive knowledge. In the face of strong opposition, she disseminated information on birth control and, in 1916, opened the first birth-control clinic in the United States. After a series of arrests and trials, she left the United States and lived in England for a number of years (Sanger 1938).

Although the laws regarding dissemination of birth-control information were softened in 1918, it was illegal to use birth-control devices in some states up until 1965. Then, in the case of *Griswold* v. *Connecticut*, the U.S. Supreme Court ruled that laws prohibiting birth control were unconstitutional because they interfered with the right to marital privacy. After this decision, it also became legal to sell and advertise birth-control devices in all states. (Before 1965, in some states condoms were sold from automatic dispensers in the rest rooms of gas stations. However, the dispensers were clearly marked "for the prevention of disease only.")

Although there are not the legal barriers that there were in the early 1900s, birth control has remained a controversial issue. The Roman

Catholic Church and certain other religious and political groups have declared that contraception violates "natural law" in that it destroys life or the potential for life. A variety of organizations in favor of birth control have countered this argument on a number of grounds. Among the factors frequently mentioned are (1) reducing the number of unwanted and/or illegitimate children, (2) allowing for family planning, (3) avoiding health risks to the mother, (4) curbing population growth, and (5) acknowledging the affectional—rather than purely procreative—value of intercourse.

Despite the controversy, the number of people practicing birth control has increased greatly during the past twenty-five years and is now at a high level in the Western world. Among married couples in the United States, over 90 percent practice some type of contraception. The greatest increase in recent decades has been among Roman Catholics. The number of Catholic women using a contraceptive method other than the rhythm method (which is the only one approved by the church) was approximately 30 percent in 1955; of the Catholic women married between 1970 and 1975, about 90 percent reported practicing some type of method other than rhythm (Westoff & Jones 1977).

Today a variety of birth-control devices are available. Which, if any, is chosen depends upon a variety of factors, including medical safety, whether or not the male is involved, amount of planning ahead required, effectiveness of the technique, and various moral and psychological factors. A recent series of interviews conducted on three midwestern college campuses indicates that psychological factors are of particularly great importance, at least among college students (Herz 1983). These will be discussed in detail when the advantages and disadvantages of the various contraceptive devices are considered.

For each technique, statistics known as failure rates have been calculated. The failure rate refers to the estimated number of women out of 100 who would become pregnant in a period of a year if the technique in question was the only one used. Actually, there are two failure rates: the first assumes that the birth-control technique is utilized properly (the "theoretical" rate); the second reflects the actual failure rate, taking into account mistakes and misuse (Hatcher et al. 1978).

WITHDRAWAL

The removal of the penis from the vagina before ejaculation—known as withdrawal or coitus interruptus—is undoubtedly one of the oldest methods of birth control still practiced. The failure rate of this method is theoretically about 9 percent, due primarily to the fact that, as mentioned earlier, some sperm may enter the vagina before ejaculation actually takes place. In practice, the failure rate is over 20 percent since it is difficult for the man to show restraint around the time of ejaculation. Furthermore, sperm ejaculated around the vulva may find their way into the vagina.

Other disadvantages of this method include anxiety on the part of both partners that withdrawal will not occur before ejaculation. Furthermore, there may be frustration that coitus must be interrupted at an emotionally critical time. An advantage of the withdrawal technique is that it does not require preplanning or the use of what might be considered artificial devices.

THE RHYTHM METHOD

Since the 1930s, when it was discovered that conception could occur only shortly after ovulation, the *rhythm method* has been utilized as a method of contraception. This method involves abstention from intercourse during the predicted "fertile period." If a woman's menstrual cycle is irregular, this method is ineffective or uncertain at best. When the cycle is quite regular, however, it is possible to approximate the time of ovulation. As we have seen, ovulation occurs about fourteen days before menstruation. If the cycle is regularly twenty-eight days, a period of abstinence is required from about day ten to day seventeen.

The time of ovulation can be estimated more accurately by determining the basal body temperature each morning. It will be remembered that the temperature drops on the day of ovulation and then rises on the next day. Thus, the "safe" period two or three days after ovulation may be predicted. However, other factors can cause shifts in temperature, so this method has definite limitations (Moghissi 1976).

Another method of identifying the time of ovulation involves an invention known as the ovutimer. The ovutimer is a long, plastic device which, when inserted into the vagina, determines viscosity (the degree of thickness) of the cervical mucus. The mucus becomes thin and watery at the time of ovulation, and this condition can be fairly easily identified.

Even when the time of ovulation is identified with reasonable accuracy, there are disadvantages to the rhythm method. Failure rates are relatively high: the theoretical rate is 13 percent and the actual rate, 21 percent. Furthermore, anxiety over the possible failure of the method may create problems; more than 40 percent of couples using this method report anxiety over pregnancy, restricted enjoyment of intercourse, and/or difficulty with periods of abstinence (Marshall & Row 1970). An advantage of this technique is that no medical examination is required and no foreign objects are involved. For Roman Catholic couples, there may be fewer guilt feelings associated with rhythm than with other types of contraceptive methods (Herz 1983).

BARRIERS AND SPERMICIDES

A number of contraceptives involve some type of barrier to the movement of sperm into the uterus, or an agent that immobilizes or kills sperm. In some cases, both a barrier and a spermicide are utilized.

Condoms

The *condom*, or penile sheath, seems to have been originally used in the sixteenth century to prevent the spread of syphilis. The device of that time was made of linen (Tietze 1965). Modern condoms are generally made of latex rubber and have a variety of designs, including a prelubricated model, some with space at the end to contain the ejaculate, and some with various projections at the end that are supposed to increase stimulation in the vagina. Most women, however, report that they are unable to feel any stimulation from the projections because, as we have seen, the inner vagina and cervix are not very sensitive.

Condoms come rolled up and are unrolled onto the erect penis before entry into the vagina. After ejaculation, the condom should be held at the rim as the penis is withdrawn. If withdrawal takes place before the erection is completely lost, the possibility of the condom slipping off in the vagina is reduced.

The failure rate of condoms is relatively low (3 percent) if they are consistently and properly used. In actuality, however, the failure rate is

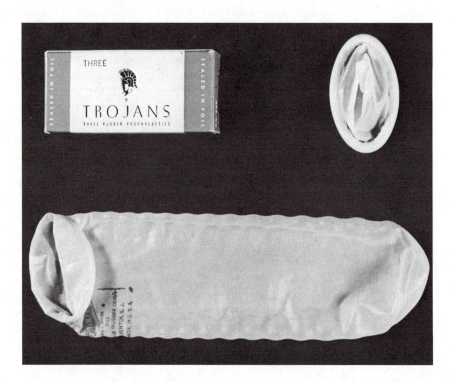

FIGURE 12.1

The condom, rolled (as it comes in the package) and unrolled (as it fits over the penis).

around 10 percent due mainly to problems of slippage or leakage. One advantage of condoms over other types of contraceptives is that they offer protection against sexually transmitted diseases. A possible disadvantage is that condoms reduce sensation in the penis. Some women also feel intercourse is less intimate without direct contact with their lover's penis. However, reduced stimulation for the man may delay ejaculation and enable couples to prolong intercourse if this is desired.

Some couples report that taking time to put on a condom interrupts sexual activity. Others, however, have found that the procedure can be effectively integrated into foreplay. The interviews with college women revealed that a perceived advantage was ease of use and relatively small expense. Some women also liked the fact that it was typically the man who took responsibility for obtaining and using this contraceptive device (Herz 1983).

Spermicides

A variety of foams, jellies, and creams that kill sperm—known as *spermicides*—are available without prescription. If used independent of a diaphragm, vaginal foam from an aerosol dispenser is generally considered the most effective of these substances; the foam is most likely to be evenly distributed deep in the vagina (Hatcher et al. 1976).

Spermicides are most effective if inserted less than thirty minutes before intercourse while the woman is lying down; she should remain in this position until after intercourse. If coitus is repeated, an application should be made before each ejaculation. When used properly, the best spermicides are approximately as effective as condoms: their theoretical failure rate is 3 percent. However, the actual failure rate is about 22 percent. If both a spermicide and a condom are used, effectiveness approaches 100 percent.

A possible disadvantage of spermicides is that couples may perceive them as messy; in a few cases, one of the partners is allergic to the chemical agents. The spermicide has a somewhat unpleasant taste, which may be a factor of significance if oral sex follows intercourse. In contrast, some couples enjoy the added lubrication provided by the foam. Like condoms, spermicides give some protection against sexually transmitted diseases and also against vaginal infections.

Diaphragms

Devices used by women to block the passage of sperm also have a rather long history. In the eighteenth century the Italian playboy Casanova supposedly placed half a hollowed-out lemon in a woman's vagina. Incidentally, this method may have been effective not because of sperm blockage but because the citric acid in the lemon immobilized the sperm (Allen 1968). Modern *diaphragms* consist of a thick rubber dome attached to a flexible, rubber-covered outer ring. They come in various sizes—around three inches in diameter—and must be individually fitted by a physician. The inner surface (the surface in contact with the cervix) should be coated with contraceptive jelly before the diaphragm is inserted into the vagina (and repeated before each intercourse). The jelly functions as a spermicide and also as a seal.

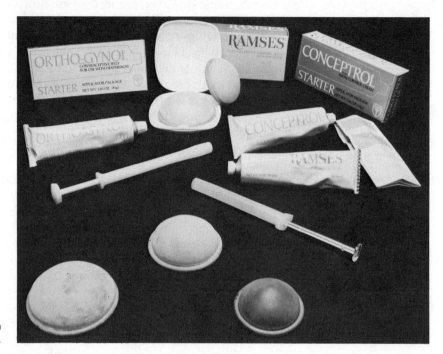

FIGURE 12.2

The diaphragm. A variety of creams and jellies are available which function both as a seal and as a spermicide.

A diaphragm and jelly may be inserted just before intercourse or up to two hours preceding it. After intercourse, it must be left in place for at least six hours and not more than twenty-four for maximum effectiveness. One advantage of the diaphragm is that it can be utilized to hold the menstrual flow in the uterus for a period of time; this makes coitus during the menstrual period more attractive to some people.

A possible disadvantage of the diaphragm is that, like the condom, using it may interrupt the spontaneity of sexual activity. However, the diaphragm may be inserted privately by the woman shortly before sexual interaction is anticipated, and some couples report that placement of the diaphragm is arousing and heightens the excitement of the sexual interaction. A few women are allergic to the latex of the diaphragm or a particular cream or jelly. Using a plastic model or changing the brand of cream or jelly, however, typically remedies the problem. Another disadvantage of the diaphragm is that the woman must plan ahead. Some women find the insertion and removal of the device inconvenient or distasteful (Herz 1983).

The failure rate of the diaphragm used properly is about 3 percent, the same as that of the condom. However, the diaphragm may become dislodged during coitus, particularly if it does not fit well or if the woman is on top of the man. Multiple withdrawals and reentries by the male also increase the chances that a diaphragm will slip out of place. These difficulties raise the actual failure rate to 17 percent.

INTRAUTERINE DEVICES (IUDs)

Devices placed in the uterus to prevent pregnancy have a long history. For centuries Arab camel drivers have been known to place round stones in the uteri of their camels before undertaking a long journey. Although the exact effect of *intrauterine devices* (IUDs) is not known, it seems that these devices make the uterus resistant to implantation.

Intrauterine devices were in disrepute in the first half of the twentieth century; it was believed that damage to the uterus might result from continued IUD usage. In the late 1950s, studies by German and Japanese physicians reported that use of metal or plastic IUDs did not produce se-

FIGURE 12.3
The insertion of a Lippes Loop IUD.

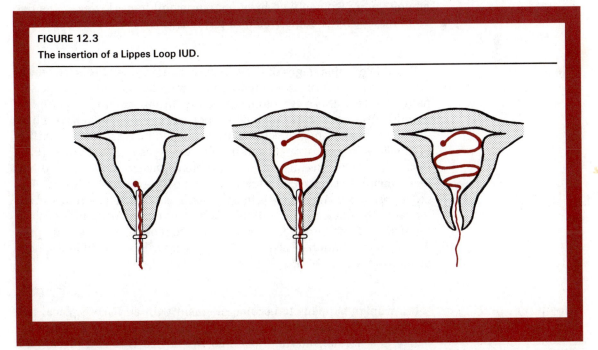

When in the plastic tube, the IUD is stretched into an approximate linear form. As it is expelled from the tube, the device assumes the shape shown.

rious complications. By the mid-1970s, 5 to 8 million women in the United States and over 50 million Chinese women were using IUDs. However, some controversy still exists concerning their safety.

These devices come in a variety of forms; however, the most popular seems to be the Lippes Loop. The device is inserted into the uterus via a plastic tube. The loop can be flattened out so as to slide through the tube; once in the uterus, the device returns to its original shape. A small nylon thread hangs down into the vagina, allowing the woman to make sure the device has remained in position. (This thread does not interfere with vaginal stimulation.)

A recently developed IUD contains progesterone which is released at a slow rate over a period of time. This small amount of the hormone alters the lining of the uterus so that implantation is presumably less likely to take place. Whereas regular, plastic IUDs may be effective for several years, these progesterone-releasing devices must be replaced every twelve months.

The failure rate of IUDs is lower than that of the other contraceptive devices considered so far—its theoretical failure rate is approximately 1 to 3 percent, and its actual rate about 5 percent. Spontaneous expulsion of IUDs may be a problem, especially during the first year of use and among young women who have not borne children. However, the devices may easily be reinserted by a physician.

Side Effects

Possible disadvantages of IUDs include certain side effects. Between 10 and 20 percent of users report some irregular bleeding and pelvic pain. However, these symptoms generally disappear after two or more months. A more serious problem is reported in women who have a history of uterine or tubal infections. IUDs seem to increase the possibility of infection in these women and in a few cases result in infertility (Piotrow et al. 1979). Because of these problems, many physicians do not recommend IUDs, especially for women who have not had children. Another possible disadvantage is the pain associated with insertion and removal of the device. And individuals who oppose abortion may reject the IUD on moral grounds: since the device most likely works by preventing implantation of a fertilized egg, its use can be considered a form of abortion (Herz 1983).

Advantages and Disadvantages

If a woman happens to become pregnant with an IUD in place, the chances of an ectopic pregnancy increase. Furthermore, if the pregnancy is a normal, uterine one—and the device is left in place—the chances of spontaneous abortion are about fifty-fifty. Nonetheless, there are several cases in which normal pregnancy has taken place with an IUD still in place. It is also possible to remove the IUD after pregnancy has been detected.

Despite the health risks, there are certain advantages of the IUD over other types of contraceptive devices. Some women like the convenience of not having to make plans or take contraceptive measures before each intercourse. In many cases, an IUD causes no discomfort. It is also possible that an IUD may be inserted within a few days after unprotected intercourse. In such cases, the device seems to be quite effective in preventing pregnancy (Lippes et al. 1979).

ORAL CONTRACEPTIVES

First put on the market in 1960, oral contraceptives—collectively known as *The Pill*—have become widely accepted. As mentioned in chapter 4, The Pill works by preventing ovulation through the use of synthetic progesterone and/or inhibiting follicle growth and egg development with synthetic estrogen. In addition, changes in the cervical mucus brought about by the synthetic hormones function as a barrier to sperm (Hatcher et al. 1976).

The various brands of oral contraceptives differ in exact dosages of the hormones. However, most have considerably more synthetic progesterone than synthetic estrogen. Generally, the pills are taken for twenty-one days, starting on the fifth day after menstruation. Thereafter, the woman goes for seven days without taking a pill. Since this sequence may be confusing (or the woman may forget to start taking pills again),

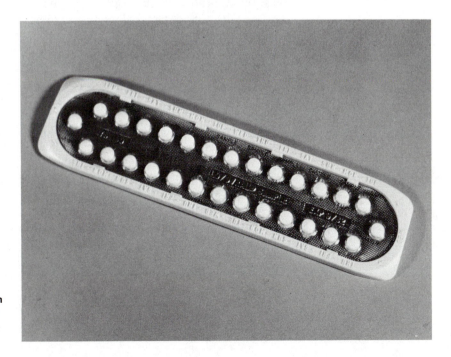

FIGURE 12.4

Birth control pills, to be taken every day. Seven of the pills contain no synthetic hormones.

some drug companies market pills to be taken every day. Seven of the pills are actually "blanks" that have no physiological effect but help the woman keep her medication on schedule.

The failure rate of pills, taken regularly, is less than 1 percent. The rate drops to near zero after the second month of usage. If a woman forgets a pill on one day, she can usually retain contraceptive effectiveness by taking two pills the next day. However, the possibility of failure increases significantly if pills are skipped for two or more days. Forgetfulness raises the actual failure rate of oral contraceptives to between 2 and 4 percent.

Side Effects

Because there are certain side effects of oral contraceptives, The Pill is not available without prescription. Some type of unpleasant side effect has been reported by about 40 percent of the women taking the pill (Hatcher et al. 1976). However, it is difficult to evaluate the effects of The Pill on the basis of these data; certain symptoms may very well be psychological in origin. In a study in which a large number of women thought they were taking The Pill—but were actually taking placebos— nearly two-thirds reported "side effects," including loss of sex drive, headaches, and nervousness (Bragonier 1976).

At any rate, the most common side effects reported by oral-contraceptive users are nausea, mild gastrointestinal disturbances, headaches, and irregular vaginal discharges. Most of these symptoms diminish and then disappear within two or three months. However, the altered chemical composition of cervical mucus brought about by The Pill makes the vagina more susceptible to fungus infections (Rinehart & Piotrow 1979).

Another possibly irritating side effect is a gain in weight, particularly in the areas of the thighs and breasts. Weight gain is most common with high-dosage pills and may be countered with a switch to lower-dosage pills and/or diuretic drugs, which reduce water retention (Potts et al. 1975).

The most serious side effects, though quite rare, may be fatal. A study has indicated increased incidence of blood clotting and resulting complications in pill users. The danger is greater among women over thirty-five and especially those with histories of blood-clotting problems (Beral & Kay 1977).

Another group of women who run a certain health risk are smokers. Users of The Pill who smoke fifteen or more cigarettes a day are three times more likely to die of heart attacks than women who do not smoke but use The Pill. Other factors that increase the risk of heart attacks in pill users include high blood pressure, obesity, and diabetes (Rinehart & Piotrow 1979).

Finally, two other groups of women are generally advised to avoid

The Pill: females who have not reached physical maturity and those who are nursing babies. For girls under sixteen or seventeen, the artificial hormones may inhibit normal growth and maturation (Cherniak & Feingold 1973). For nursing mothers, the danger is that some of the hormones will enter their milk; there is some evidence that these hormones have a feminizing effect on a male baby (Curtis 1964).

Advantages and Disadvantages

The Pill has several advantages. No foreign objects need be inserted into the vagina, and many women perceive The Pill as inexpensive and easy to obtain (Herz 1983).

Some couples report that sexual relations are more spontaneous and pleasurable because preparations need not be made before each intercourse. The increase in breast size of certain women may also be perceived as a beneficial side effect. In addition, The Pill may relieve some physical problems, including irregular menstruation, painful menstruation, pain associated with ovulation (Mittelschmerz), premenstrual tension, and the presence of ovarian cysts (Cohen 1976; Hatcher et al. 1978).

Recently published research, conducted at the Federal Centers for Disease Control, indicates that the incidence of ovarian and endometrial cancer is reduced by taking The Pill. In addition, an earlier report—that The Pill may increase the probability of breast cancer—did not gain any support.

A major disadvantage of The Pill is the increased risk of certain medical problems discussed earlier. In addition, some women may gain unwanted weight. There is also a fear that taking The Pill may cause difficulty in having children later. (No long-term decrease in fertility has been shown, although a woman has to wait approximately three months after getting off The Pill before conception may take place.) A number of women perceive The Pill as an unattractive alternative because they must remember to take it every day; this objection is most common in women who engage in sexual intercourse infrequently (Herz 1983).

The Morning-after Pill

Researchers have developed a pill containing *diethylstilbestrol (DES)*, which functions as a contraceptive "after the fact." If the first dosage is taken within seventy-two hours after unprotected intercourse, the DES is apparently quite effective in preventing pregnancy. However, the woman may experience nausea and vomiting, and there are also more dangerous side effects.

If pregnancy does occur, the fetus is liable to be damaged. There is even a risk that children of future pregnancies will be harmed. Thus, DES is administered only in extreme emergencies and, in many hospitals and clinics, DES will not be considered even in cases of rape (Hatcher et al. 1978).

CONTRACEPTIVES OF THE FUTURE

Several new contraceptive methods are currently being developed and show some promise for the future (Hatcher et al. 1978; Djerassi 1979). As a possible alternative to The Pill, rings containing progesteronelike substances (progestins) may be easily inserted into the vagina and do not interfere with intercourse. The progestins are slowly released and prevent ovulation. An encouraging early finding is that there are relatively few side effects.

Another alternative is an injection of progesterone potent enough to prevent ovulation for ninety days. Although this method is used in some parts of the world, there are indications of undesirable side effects in certain women.

A different type of injection essentially immunizes women to the substance that normally inhibits menstruation after pregnancy. If or when this vaccine becomes available, women could prevent pregnancy by menstruating each month—whether conception had taken place or not.

New types of sperm barriers are also in the process of development. *Cervical caps*—invented by a dentist and a gynecologist—can be made to fit precisely over the woman's cervix. An impression of the cervix is taken and then, in a dental laboratory, an accurately fitting cap is fashioned. The cap rides on a film of mucus and has a one-way valve for the release of menstrual flow. Although the concept of a cervical cap is not new, a possible advantage of this recent device is that it is not likely to slip off and it can be worn for relatively long periods of time.

A new type of spermicidal contraceptive is also being developed and, if everything goes according to plan, should soon be widely available. This device—known as the *spermicidal sponge*—resembles a powder puff and fits into the vagina. Each sponge contains one gram of the same spermicide found in most contraceptive foams, jellies, and creams. An advantage of this device over types of spermicides is that it is effective for 24 hours, regardless of the number of times the woman has intercourse. The sponge also absorbs the ejaculate and, to a certain extent, acts as a barrier by blocking the entrance to the cervix. In contrast to the diaphragm, the spermicidal sponge does not need to be fitted by a physician.

There are also promises of male contraceptives. In China, an extract of cottonseed has been found to inhibit sperm production. However, there are toxic side effects, including fever and burning sensations. A recent study indicates that another substance—known as a *gonadotrophin antagonist*—interferes with sperm production but does not have the toxic effects. The disadvantage of this substance is that it produces impotence in some men. Nonetheless, it is hoped that administering this new drug in combination with androgen will eliminate the potency problem (Linde et al. 1981). At any rate, extensive testing is needed for most of these new contraceptives before they become available.

Psychological Perspective: Factors Related to the Practice (or Nonpractice) of Contraception

One might think that the major reasons people who do not want a baby omit contraception would be moral objections or an inability to obtain contraceptives. However, several studies indicate that psychological factors are of greater importance. People with high sex anxiety are less inclined to communicate with their partners about birth control and are also less likely to use contraceptive devices that require touching the genitals. Furthermore, sex anxiety seems to reduce the ability to plan ahead for sexual activity (Byrne 1977).

Timidity—especially among women—also appears to inhibit contraceptive practices. Compared to women high in assertiveness, timid women are less likely to use birth control. There seem to be several reasons for this difference. Women who score high on tests of assertiveness are more likely to seek out information about contraception, to initiate discussions about birth control with their partners, and to consistently prepare for occasions of possible intercourse (Fox 1977).

In some cases, a failure to use contraception reflects a confusion of responsibility; the male may expect the female to take the initiative and vice versa. In one study, approximately half the teenage boys interviewed expected their female partners to be responsible for contraception (Finkle & Finkle 1975). It appears likely that a comparable number of women expected their partners to take the responsibility.

A confusion of responsibility seems to be especially prevalent at the time of the first intercourse. Sixty percent of teenage nonvirgin women surveyed reported that they did not use any contraceptive measure during their first coitus (Zelnik & Kantner 1978). Furthermore, contraception is less commonly practiced by adolescent women who have intercourse infrequently than by those who report regular intercourse (Kantner & Zelnik 1972). These findings may reflect the fact that there is generally less communication about contraception with new or occasional partners than with regular partners. It may be that, with a new partner, the emphasis is on seduction and romance, while thoughts of the future are put aside.

Finally, there is an indication that certain people fail to use contraception because of simple ignorance; they have misconceptions about how contraceptive devices work or have mistaken ideas about the probability of pregnancy following coitus. It has been noted that many premaritally pregnant women say such things as "I only did it a few times!" (Kantner & Zelnik 1972).

The several factors discussed in this section add up to a very high rate of pregnancy among young, unmarried women; more than one-third of sexually active, unmarried teenaged women become pregnant at least once before they are nineteen (Zelnik, Kim, & Kantner 1979). Furthermore, a comparison of the sexual activities of and use of contraceptives by college women in 1978 and 1973 indicated an increase in sexual activity but a decrease in contraceptive use (Gerrard 1982).

Author's Perspective: Discussions of Sex and Contraception

Many people believe that the high rate of pregnancy among unmarried teenagers is a serious social problem. In some cases, providing information about contraceptives may prevent pregnancies. However, if parents or other adults in positions of authority exhibit sex anxiety, discussions with adolescents are less likely to convey useful information than to transfer this anxiety (which works against using contraceptives). On the other hand, if authority figures provide contraceptive information casually, young people may perceive their manner as permission to engage in premarital intercourse (with or without contraceptives).

Rather clearly, the studies just discussed suggest that information about contraceptives (or the lack of it) is not the major factor in teenage pregnancy. Sex anxiety, lack of assertiveness, and a general failure to accept responsibility seem to be relatively more important. My experience counseling unmarried adolescent parents referred by a family court suggests that rebellion against parental authority and a search for adventure are other factors of significance. Still another consideration for teenagers appears to be peer pressure towards premarital sex.

It seems that discussions between adolescents and parents or other responsible adults about contraception and abstinence should include a consideration of these and other variables. In order to reduce sex anxiety and resistance to authority, the discussions should be relaxed and open, with an emphasis on exchange of information as opposed to one-sided proclamations. For example, a parent or teacher might ask, "Under what conditions do you think your friends consider sexual intercourse appropriate?" or "Is the male or the female usually responsible for contraception?" If discussions begin within such a nonjudgmental framework, teenagers are likely to ask questions in return. Perhaps even more important, they are going to be stimulated to think about contraception before—rather than after—a pregnancy occurs.

STERILIZATION

Surgical procedures which make it virtually impossible to reproduce have been gaining in popularity in recent years. Voluntary sterilization is a particularly common contraceptive method for married couples in which the wife is over thirty.

Female Sterilization

The most common sterilization method for women is *tubal ligation*. This method generally involves cutting and tying the fallopian tubes, thereby preventing sperm from reaching the eggs, and eggs from reaching the uterus. Thereafter, eggs are harmlessly reabsorbed by the body after ovulation.

Tubal ligation was originally performed by abdominal surgery. Today, fiber-optic instruments enable surgeons to view internal body structures through a very small opening. As a result, tubal ligations can be done with much smaller abdominal incisions ("Band-Aid surgery") or via an incision in the closed end of the vagina. Both procedures eliminate the need for general anesthesia, shorten hospital stays, lower costs, and decrease (but do not eliminate) the risks of the surgery.

Tubal ligation is close to 100 percent effective. Moreover, in some cases, the tubes can be reconnected and fertility restored. In one study, a pregnancy rate as high as 80 percent was reported after reconnection procedures (Silber & Cohen 1978). But not all results have been as good, and one should not count on being able to reverse the procedure. Furthermore, the psychological effect of such a final procedure may be difficult for some women to handle.

There are other surgical sterilization techniques, but these are not usually performed unless there are complications such as tumors in the reproductive organs. One of these—*hysterectomy*—involves the removal of the uterus. Another operation involves removal of the fallopian tubes; this is known as *salpingectomy*. Each of these is a more serious operation than tubal ligation and has a longer recovery period.

Male Sterilization

Vasectomy, the operation that induces sterility in males, is much simpler than any of its counterparts in females. A vasectomy can usually be performed in about fifteen minutes with a local anesthetic. A small incision is made on each side of the scrotum in order to expose the right and left vas deferens (which conduct the sperm from the testes). Approximately one inch is then cut and removed from each vas, and the cut ends are tied so that sperm transport is blocked (see figure 12.5). The sperm, which continue to be produced by the testes, now degenerate and are reabsorbed by the body.

After a vasectomy, the ejaculate may still contain sperm for a while, since some sperm are stored in the reproductive system beyond the point of vasectomy. However, these sperm may be eliminated by means of a spermicide introduced during the operation. The period of recovery from a vasectomy is quite short and simple: approximately two days of relative inactivity. Thereafter, the sexual response and orgasm are completely normal.

An advantage of the vasectomy procedure—in addition to its simplicity—is that it is close to 100 percent effective. The rare failures in effectiveness are typically associated with a spontaneous growing together of the vas deferens (Hatcher et al. 1976).

A disadvantage of vasectomy is that the effects are generally permanent; there is a high failure rate in attempts to surgically reverse the ste-

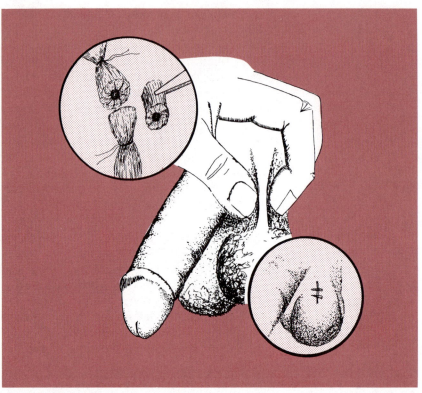

FIGURE 12.5
Vasectomy.

A small incision is made in the scrotum and a section of the vas removed. The ends of the vas are then tied to block passage of the sperm. This operation is performed on both sides of the scrotum.

rility. The tubes may be rejoined, but sperm count often remains so low that the probability of pregnancy is low (Silber & Cohen 1978).

Another possible disadvantage of a vasectomy is psychological. A study indicated that some men felt this surgery had threatened their masculinity to a certain extent. However, after four years, this anxiety had virtually disappeared (Ziegler, Rodgers, & Prentiss 1969).

Comparative Perspective: Birth and Population Control in Animals

Animals exhibit a variety of ways of controlling their birth rate and ultimately their population size. The territoriality that many animals display is one factor that limits the population. Only adults who win territories can breed. When there is overpopulation, many animals cannot establish territories and therefore do not reproduce (Maier & Maier 1970).

Another mechanism that limits population size is a tendency to produce fewer young when the food supply is short. (In many instances, food shortage accompanies overpopulation.) For example, when the quality and quantity of food have been poor in late winter, red grouse lay fewer eggs, more of the eggs fail to hatch, and an unusually large number of chicks die.

In a few animals, when conditions are crowded and food is short, not only are fewer young produced, but the offspring develop more slowly. For example, mosquito larvae raised in overcrowded conditions produce a chemical that inhibits the growth and development of younger larvae.

Among mammals, a variety of factors reduces the number of young that are produced and survive when there is overcrowding. Compared to normal conditions, overcrowded conditions produce an increase in pseudopregnancies, stillbirths, cannibalism, and poor maternal care in rats and mice. Females are also slower to come into estrus. Many of these reactions seem to result from hormone imbalances brought about by the stress of overcrowding. One line of research has attempted to reduce stress in the animals by experimentally organizing them into social subgroups. Under these conditions, which apparently help the animals cope with overcrowding, the negative effects on reproduction seem to be reduced (Maier & Maier 1970).

In humans, there apparently have been natural checks on population growth that operated for thousands of years. The world population seems to have been fairly stable from 6000 B.C. up until A.D. 1800. However, in recent years, advances in medical technology have greatly reduced infant mortality and increased the life expectancy of adults. Many scientists—including Ehrlich and Ehrlich (1972)—have argued that contraceptive practices must compensate for the vast reduction in natural population checks, or the world will soon be faced with extreme human overpopulation.

INDUCED ABORTION

Termination of a pregnancy by induced abortion[1] has a very long history. Such a procedure was described in a Chinese document over 4,000 years old. For thousands of years, abortions were performed with a variety of crude instruments. In the United States up until 1860, induced abortions were legal and fairly common. However, during the 1860s, laws against abortion were enacted; these laws were passed primarily to protect women from dangerous procedures attempted without the benefit of antiseptics or anesthesia. The laws were not very effective; ninety years later Kinsey and his associates (1953) found that almost 25 percent of the women in their sample had had an illegal abortion by the time they had reached midlife.

By the late 1960s, several states had made abortion legal. Then, in 1973, the U.S. Supreme Court declared that all remaining state laws prohibiting abortion were unconstitutional. Furthermore, states were prevented from enacting new laws restricting a woman's right to have an abortion during the first three months of pregnancy. (Abortion operations during this first trimester are relatively safe and uncomplicated.) For abortions between the third and sixth months, when there is a higher health risk, it was permissible to enact some restrictions, but only to protect a woman's health. Finally, abortions after the sixth month of pregnancy were prohibited unless the pregnancy presented a serious health threat to the mother; a fetus has a chance of surviving outside the mother during this period.

Abortion Procedures

There are three general types of abortion procedures (Shapiro 1977). The simplest and safest is *vacuum aspiration* (also known as vacuum curettage and the suction method). Essentially, it utilizes a source of suction to draw fetal tissue out of the uterus. If the woman decides on an abortion within one or two weeks after the expected time of the menstrual period, the cervix does not usually need to be dilated. Parts of the uterine lining, menstrual fluid, and possibly a fertilized egg are extracted via a small tube inserted into the uterus. (Since pregnancy tests cannot be performed at this early date and the egg is too small to identify, there is no way of knowing for certain if the woman had been pregnant.)

If the woman waits more than three weeks after the expected menstrual period, the uterus typically must be dilated. As the pregnancy

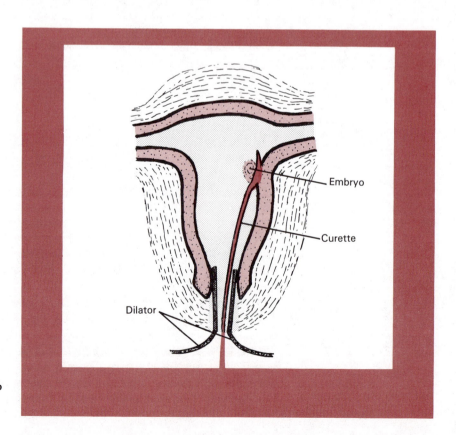

FIGURE 12.6

D & C abortion procedure. Following dilation of the cervix, the curette is used to scrape the embryo or fetus from the uterus.

FIGURE 12. 7
Summary of Methods of Birth Control

Method	Theoretical Failure Rate	Actual Failure Rate	Major Advantages	Major Disadvantages
Withdrawal	9%	20%	No preplanning or artificiality	Frustration or lack of fulfillment
Rhythm	13%	21%	Acceptable to Roman Catholic Church	Anxiety; difficulties with periods of abstinence
Condom	3%	10%	Protection against diseases; ease of use	Reduced sensitivity of penis; interruption of sexual activity
Spermacide	3%	22%	Ease of use; added lubrication	Allergic reactions in some women
Diaphragm	3%	17%	May hold menstrual flow	Allergic reactions in some women; inconvenience
IUD	1–3%	5%	Little attention required after insertion, possible after-the-fact effectiveness	Side effects, including bleeding and possible infections
Oral contraceptive	1%	2–4%	Ease of use; relief of some menstrual problems	Side effects, especially in very young women, women over thirty-five, and smokers
Female sterilization	Close to 0	Close to 0	Permanent effectiveness	Restoration of fertility not always possible
Male sterilization	Close to 0	Close to 0	Simple procedure, permanent effectiveness	Restoration of fertility unlikely
Induced abortion	—	—	After-the-fact procedure	Health risks; moral implications

progresses, a larger suction tube and stronger suction are required. Usually, the procedure takes less than ten minutes, and only a local anesthetic is necessary.

Contractions of the uterus immediately after the operation may cause painful cramps, but most women are able to leave the clinic within a half hour. The vacuum aspiration method can be used up until the end of the first trimester of pregnancy. After this, the fetus is too large and the uterus too soft for a safe operation.

A second type of abortion procedure—known as *dilation and curettage (D&C)*—is performed in a hospital under general anesthesia. After the cervix is dilated, the embryo or fetus is scraped from the uterus using a spoonlike instrument known as a curette. This procedure is also limited to the first trimester of pregnancy. Since D&C is more discomforting and has a somewhat higher rate of surgical complications than the vacuum aspiration method, the vacuum technique has largely replaced the D&C.

The third type of procedure is known as *intrauterine instillation*. It is typically used in abortions performed during the second trimester, the period when other techniques are unsafe. Intrauterine instillation involves injecting a liquid through the uterine wall into the amniotic sac; the solution induces uterine contractions, which expel the fetus.

Several years ago, saltwater was regularly used in the injection. However, complications such as salt poisoning and uterine infection sometimes resulted. At the present time, prostaglandins are generally preferred. (As we have seen, prostaglandins normally induce labor.) These substances may be injected into the uterus or into the mother's bloodstream. About 50 percent of women suffer side effects from prostaglandins, including headaches, nausea, and vomiting. Usually, these are temporary and not serious. However, in some abortions induced by prostaglandins or saline, the placenta is not expelled, and it must be removed by curettage. If it is not, severe infection can result.

Generally speaking, the health risks of abortions increase as pregnancy progresses, especially after the first trimester. During the second trimester, the mortality risk of an abortion is about that of childbirth. (Tietze 1977).

Theoretical Perspective: The Abortion Controversy

The moral controversy surrounding abortion centers on whether or not an embryo or young fetus is considered a human life. Opponents of legal abortion argue that human life begins at conception, and therefore abortion is murder. This position is most clearly identified with the Roman Catholic Church. In 1869, Pope Pius XI condemned all abortions as a form of murder. Previous to that time, the church had imposed no penalties for abortions within the first forty days of pregnancy (Westoff & Westoff 1971).

Antiabortion, or *right-to-life,* groups also contend that tolerance for the murder of unborn children will imply tolerance for assisted suicide, death by neglect, or actual murder of other categories of helpless or "undesirable" people, such as the retarded, seriously ill, or deformed. Finally, some opponents of abortion suggest that legal abortion encourages sexual permissiveness and irresponsibility.

In contrast, those who support legal abortion argue that an embryo or young fetus represents the potential for human life but should not be considered a human at that time. They view abortion as a type of surgery necessary for the physical and psychological well-being of certain women. People who believe the woman should be allowed a choice (*pro-choice* advocates) argue that legal abortions reduce the number of mutilations and deaths associated with illegal abortions. Furthermore, they argue that legal abortions help to reduce the number of unwanted children, forced marriages, and economic stresses placed on some families.

There is also a third position, intermediate between the first two: abortions should be allowed, but only when the life of the pregnant woman is in danger or in cases involving rape.

Public opinion on the morality of abortions is split fairly evenly in the United States. A 1977 survey indicated that 44 percent believed that abortion was morally wrong while 48 percent believed abortion not morally wrong (Yankelovich 1977). However, if the question of abortion is phrased in terms of who should make the decision about an abortion, the results are quite different. Seventy-three percent of those surveyed believed that the decision about an abortion in the first trimester should be made by the woman and her physician and not by law (Harris 1979). Apparently, many people believe that abortion is immoral but think that the critical decision should be made by the individuals involved in each situation.

NOTES

1. Induced abortion refers to expulsion of the embryo or fetus brought about deliberately. This is in contrast to a spontaneous abortion, or miscarriage, which occurs without human intervention in as many as 60 percent of all pregnancies (W. H. James 1970). In most cases, when the word abortion alone is used, it means induced abortion.

PART 6

The Development
of Sexuality

The four chapters in this part are concerned with the development of sexuality during the lifespan and changes or adjustments which take place following physical illness or injury. Contrary to what was once thought, sexuality does not have definite beginning and end points. It is more appropriate to consider sexuality as being with us from birth and undergoing changes in conceptualization and expression.

CHAPTER 13

Infancy and Childhood

During the Victorian era, people generally believed infants and children were devoid of sexuality. This belief was reinforced by the need to perceive children—like women—as "pure" and "untainted." However, there is now considerable evidence that sexuality in all its ramifications begins very early in life. We have already discussed the development of reproductive sexuality and sexuality related to emotional intimacy. In this chapter, the development of gender identification and erotic sexuality in the formative years will be considered.

SEX DIFFERENTIATION

The beginnings of gender sexuality occur at the moment of conception. As suggested in chapter 11, the sperm of the father may contain either an X or a Y sex chromosome. However, the egg produced by the mother can contain only an X chromosome. If a Y sperm fertilizes the egg, the offspring is male (46,XY); if an X sperm penetrates the egg, the individual is female (46,XX).[1] This interaction at conception is referred to as the *chromosomal* or *genetic factor* (Money & Ehrhardt 1972).

Although there is still some controversy, it appears that X- and Y-bearing sperm (hereafter referred to as Xs and Ys) are produced in equal numbers. Since Ys are faster swimmers, they are more apt than Xs to reach the egg first. Nonetheless, the Y advantage is nullified since fewer XY than XX eggs survive the early stages of development. As a result, the ratio of male to female infants born is very close to fifty-fifty (Daly & Wilson 1983).

Sex differentiation, however, is not as straightforward as it may first appear. If a Y chromosome is present, the undifferentiated gonads develop into testes. Without a Y—as in the case of the genetic female (XX)—the gonads become ovaries, although ovaries develop later than

FIGURE 13.1

Sexual feelings, needs, and roles tend to develop early in a person's life.

testes. This developmental interaction involves what is known as the *gonadal factor* (Money & Ehrhardt 1972).

In most cases, of course, either testes or ovaries develop. However, there are very rare cases in which a tiny piece of a Y chromosome is attached to another chromosome of a genetic female. The piece is large enough to direct production of some testicular tissue, but not large enough to suppress the later development of ovaries (Wachtel et al. 1976). Individuals having gonadal tissue of both sexes are known as *hermaphrodites*.

These findings suggest that the Y chromosome normally directs the gonads to develop into testes and, at the same time, inhibits the development of ovaries. Furthermore, it is clear that the sex of an individual is not completely determined at conception: gender depends on a combination of the chromosomal and gonadal factors.

Later in fetal development, still another variable—the *hormonal factor*—comes into play. If the individual has developed testes, these glands will produce large quantities of androgens; if ovaries have developed, only insignificant amounts of androgens will be produced (Money & Ehrhardt 1972).

Essentially, the hormonal factor is related to one of two principles. In normal potential females, the *Eve principle* operates: without androgens, the individual develops female organs. Specifically, the Eve principle states: without sufficient androgen stimulation, the müllerian ducts develop into female internal organs and the genital tubercle develops into the female external sex organs.[2]

In contrast, normal potential males develop according to the *Adam principle*: with androgens present, male organs develop and the development of female ones is suppressed. In more specific terms, the Adam principle states: With androgen stimulation at the critical time, the wolffian ducts develop into internal male sex organs and the genital tubercle develops into external male genitals (Mazur & Money 1980).

As in the case of hermaphroditism, things do not always go according to plan; a look at certain types of developmental abnormalities provides insight into the role of the hormonal factor. In a rare disorder known as *adrenogenital syndrome*, the adrenal glands of XX individuals produce an overabundance of androgen during the prenatal period. (It will be remembered the adrenals normally secrete small amounts of androgen.) At birth the reproductive system of the baby with this syndrome shows sexual ambiguity. The clitoris is very large (approaching the size of a small penis), the labia majora and minora are at least partly fused, and there is no vaginal opening. Often, the physician and parents are uncertain of the sex of the baby.

The opposite type of reaction occurs in a rare condition, found in XY individuals, referred to as *androgen-insensitivity syndrome*, in which the prenatal hormone system is normal, but the body is insensitive to

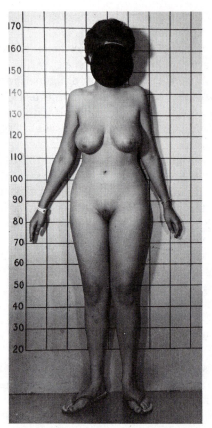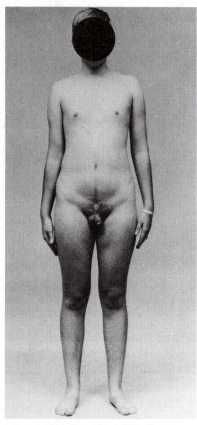

FIGURE 13.2 (left)

An androgen-insensitive XY individual. Normally, XY individuals have unambiguous male characteristics. However, because of a lack of sensitivity to androgen during an early stage of development, this person has definite female characteristics.

FIGURE 13.3 (right)

An androgenital syndrome XX individual. Because of exposure to a large amount of androgen in an early stage of development, this person exhibits male characteristics.

—From J. Money and A.A. Ehrhardt, *Man and Woman, Boy and Girl.* Copyright © 1972. Used by permission of Johns Hopkins University Press.

androgens. In the absence of effective stimulation from male sex hormones, the reproductive system develops in the female pattern. The individual is born with a vagina that lacks depth and may be only a dimple, a clitoris, and undescended testicles; as in the adrenogenital syndrome, there may be some confusion in regard to the baby's sex (Money & Ehrhardt 1972).

In conclusion, the three factors influencing sex differentiation—genetic, gonadal, and hormonal—typically work in concert to produce an unambiguous male or female baby. However, the studies of hermaphroditism and sexual ambiguity suggest these factors are not unequivocally linked to one another. Normal sex differentiation involves a sequence of events that must occur with a certain timing.

GENDER IDENTITY

One might assume that, once sex differentiation occurs, XY individuals naturally come to think of themselves as boys and XX persons clearly adopt a female sexual identity. However, this is not always the case. Some apparent males conceptualize themselves as females, and, similarly, some apparent females think of themselves as males "trapped" in the body of the wrong sex. (Individuals in this type of sex identity crisis—referred to as transsexuals—will be discussed in more detail in chapter 18.)

Further evidence regarding the development of gender identity comes from studies of the ambiguously sexed children discussed in the last section who were assigned the "wrong" sex at birth. Money & Ehrhardt (1972) have reported a case in which the sex of a child with adrenogenital syndrome was not correctly identified until age 3½. Up until that time the child had been called a boy. A decision was then made to maintain the masculine identity by administering male sex hormones and creating artificial testes for cosmetic purposes. The individual showed normal masculine sex identification and was sexually oriented toward females.

In contrast, there have been cases in which the discovery of a mistake in gender identity led physicians to suggest a sex reassignment—e.g., persons raised as boys were informed that they were really girls. This reassignment almost always led to serious sex identity problems if the child was more than three years old. Such data have led Money & Ehrhardt (1972) to conclude that gender identity is learned sometime before the age of two or three.

Still another case report supports this conclusion. One of identical male twins suffered an accidental surgical loss of the penis during an attempt at circumcision. Shortly thereafter, a decision was made to reassign him as a girl and to surgically create a vagina. Thus, at seventeen months of age, the child was given a feminine name, girl's clothing, and female genitals. (Female sex-hormone therapy was planned at a later age.) Money followed the development of the twins until age seven and reported that, in contrast to her brother, the girl had a definite female sex identity (Money & Ehrhardt 1972; Money 1975).

Perhaps the only piece of evidence at variance with Money and Ehrhardt's conclusion comes from a study of ambiguously sexed individuals in four rural villages in the Dominican Republic (Imperato-McGinley et al. 1979). These people had normal male chromosomes but, because of an enzyme deficiency, their genitals at birth appeared female. However, at puberty, increased secretion of male hormones caused their voices to deepen and male-pattern muscles to develop. Their "clitorises" became penises capable of erection and intercourse, and previously undescended testicles moved into the "labia," forming a scrotum.

Of eighteen of these persons who had been raised as females, seventeen adopted a male gender identity and sixteen a male role during or after puberty. However, the change may have been eased by the great social advantages accorded males in that society. Thus, the trauma of sex-role change may have been compensated for by an improvement in social status.

Thus, the Dominican Republic study does not prove that nature, rather than nurture, determines sexual identity, but that the two interact. In societies such as ours—which value males and females more or less equally—the gender identification process begins with the pronouncement "It's a boy" or "It's a girl" at birth. For the vast majority of people, the socialization process is consistent with the genetic sex, and gender identity is well established and irreversible by the time a child is $1\frac{1}{2}$ or 2 years of age.

SEX ROLES

Once gender identity is established, individuals begin to develop sex roles. Although there seem to be some biological factors involved, the socialization process is by far more important. The development of a sex role is somewhat like learning to represent a character in a play. With practice, the delivery of lines becomes more consistent and polished. Nonetheless, as in the case of actors, there is a tendency to develop one's own interpretations. Some of these nuances are based on the special abilities and interests that make each person unique.

The first few subsections that follow are concerned with socialization processes in sex-role development; the final ones deal with the possible influence of biological factors and the interaction between biological and socialization processes.

Differential Treatment by the Family

Parents respond differently to baby girls than they do to baby boys. From a very early age, girls are spoken to and smiled at more during feedings than boys. On the other hand, newborn boys are touched more than newborn girls. Similarly, parents decorate the rooms of boy infants differently from those of girls. Boys' rooms contain significantly more animal furnishings, educational toys, and sports equipment (see Weitz 1977).

It is difficult to know if parents treat boy and girl babies differently because there are some perceptible sex differences or because of parents' expectations of differences. One way of experimentally investigating the latter hypothesis is to present to subjects a baby who does not definitely look like either a boy or a girl and alternately label it male or female. In one study involving this procedure, a baby was offered more dolls as toys when she was said to be a girl (Seavey et al 1975).

In another study, a three-year-old child—dressed neutrally—was videotaped in a number of activities. Half the adult subjects were told that the child was a boy, while the other half were told that she was a girl. Ratings of the child's behaviors were then obtained from the subjects. There were some small overall differences in ratings for the perceived boy as compared to the perceived girl. However, the major differences found involved the sex of the raters. Women were most positive when they thought the child was a boy; men gave the most positive ratings when the child was believed to be a girl (Gurwitz & Dodge 1975).

Parents' expectations of boys and girls are reinforced by certain real differences between male and female babies. For example, Moss (1974) found that male infants fuss and cry more than female ones. These differences are probably increased by the fact that fussy male infants tend to be given close physical contact while fussy female ones are generally spoken to, imitated, and looked at. At any rate, the differential treatment of babies—combined with other factors—results in rather clear-cut sex differences by the time children are two years old.

Social Learning in the Family

Probably even more important than differential treatment by the parents is social learning; the parents (and other family members) act as role models for children. Jerome Kagan (1971) has described the possible development of social learning. The child learns to discriminate between the categories ''male'' and ''female'' at an early age. This discrimination is aided by the heavy emphasis placed on differences between males and females by our society. Children then begin to imitate the behaviors of

FIGURE 13.4

Much of sex-role development involves social learning. In this case, the father is functioning as a role model for his son.

the same-sex parent (or parent substitute). Appropriate imitations are generally rewarded, while inappropriate ones are discouraged. For example, parents are likely to say such things as "That's a good girl" or "Little boys don't do things like that."

The child also identifies with the same-sex parent because of a desire to obtain attractive rewards. For example, there is the promise that, if a boy behaves like his father, he will some day be able to drive a car and leave for a fascinating-sounding place known as work. Similarly, a girl copying the behavior of her mother will presumably be able to have children—and may also have a job like her mother has.

There is considerable support for a social-learning explanation for sex-role development. Both experiments and casual observations demonstrate the many ways in which children identify with the same-sex parent, even when the parent is not well liked. If the same-sex parent is weak or absent, other family members and/or significant persons outside of the family take on a larger role in the social-learning process.

The School Environment

A teacher transmits sex-role expectancies in much the same way as a parent does. In the context of occupational guidance counseling, teachers often convey sex stereotypes by encouraging girls to pursue marriage and child rearing, and boys to seek professional careers. In addition, the educational material available may support traditional sex roles. For example, women are rarely mentioned in history lessons, and when they are, the women generally have gained fame as wives and mothers.

A 1972 analysis of children's books revealed that girls were presented as passive while boys engaged in exciting and adventurous activities. Furthermore, women were generally depicted as full-time mothers. When they did work, females were shown in lower-status jobs. For males, there was an emphasis on accomplishment; fathers were rarely seen helping with child care (Weitzman et al. 1972). In the last decade, however, many publishers have become aware of this problem and have made an effort to present both males and females in nonstereotyped as well as traditional roles.

Even the assignment of schoolroom tasks may reflect sex-role expectancies if boys are asked to perform "masculine" tasks such as moving furniture while girls are instructed to dust. In some instances, sex-role expectancies are communicated in very subtle ways. For example, when a girl fails in a traditionally masculine task like hammering nails, the teacher is likely to complete the task for her; when a boy fails, he is often told to do it again (Harrison 1974). As a result, boys learn to persist, while girls may develop what is called "learned helplessness" (Boyd 1982).

The way in which teachers and students interact also reflects subtle sex differences. Teachers use relatively more attention-getting and controlling features in their speech when addressing boys. Generally, the norms of the classroom—quiet and conformity—tend to be more in accord with the traditional feminine role. It has been hypothesized that this type of atmosphere makes it more difficult for boys to adjust in their early school years and accounts for the fact that boys of this age have more academic and behavioral problems than girls (Saxton 1970).

Peer Groups

Beginning at early school age and continuing into adolescence, children are typically identified with same-sex peer groups. These groups generally emphasize traditional sex roles. For example, little girls may become involved in playing with dolls, jumping rope, or playing house. In contrast, boys' groups often compete with each other in sports and war games. Individuals are strongly encouraged to abide by the group rules, since violations of norms can lead to rejection and loss of valued friendships.

A study of peer groups among children and adolescents indicated that, for girls, physical attractiveness, clothes, and dating success were of the greatest importance. For boys, athletic ability and success in finding attractive opposite-sex partners were of primary importance (Coleman 1961). Although there are regional and socioeconomic differences—and changes from the time the study was completed—the general differences between male and female groups are clearly still in effect. Thus, the differentiation of male and female sex roles that was first associated with the family and later with the school is perpetuated and in some cases increased by peer-group pressure.

Television

Still another factor in the development of sex roles is television. TV heroes and heroines appear to be role models for children. An analysis of children's TV programs in the early 1970s indicated that males were likely to be depicted as more aggressive and active than females. The males were also more frequently rewarded for their behavior. In contrast, females tended to be shown following directions and having less influence than males (Sternglanz & Serbin 1974).

Television commercials also tend to support traditional sex roles. McArthur and Resko (1975) analyzed television commercials and found that 70 percent of the men were shown as authorities who had the "facts"; only 14 percent of the women who appeared as central figures were depicted as authorities. On the other hand, women were much more likely to become "sold" on the product than men. The promises of benefits were also different for men and women. Men advanced socially or in their careers; women spent their time pleasing men in general or members of their family.

A question of considerable importance is, How much effect does this type of biased commercial have on actual attitudes and behavior? An experiment by Walstedt, Geis, and Brown (1980) attempted to provide an answer by showing groups of college women two different types of commercials: (1) skits that depicted a woman in a traditional sex role, attempting to please a man and showing compliant behavior; and (2) the same type of skit, except with the sex roles reversed—in this case, the man was subservient to the woman. After viewing the commercials, subjects were asked to perform tasks during which their self-confidence and degree of independence could be rated by the experimenters. It was found that women exposed to the first type of commercial showed significantly less independence and lower self-esteem than those having viewed the second type. Quite probably the effects would have been greater if children had been the subjects. Considering the large amount of time that most people spend watching television, it seems that the electronic age has a major impact on sex-role development.

Biological Factors

Although socialization processes are clearly the major factor in sex-role development, biological factors may also be involved. For example, sex differences in general aggressiveness seem to be related, in part, to the greater size and strength of men and also to the presence of relatively large amounts of androgen in males. Studies involving the injection of androgens into both female animals and castrated male animals indicate that an increase in aggressiveness follows (Beach 1965; Deaux 1976).

The studies of sexually ambiguous children also indicate that biological factors affect behavior to a certain extent. Money found that girls with adrenogenital syndrome (AGS) were likely to be tomboyish in their behavior and interests; they were relatively uninterested in dolls, had a greater preference for boys than girls as playmates, and exhibited a high level of rough play (Money & Ehrhardt 1972). Although the role of sex hormones was strongly implicated, the social environment cannot be ruled out as a factor of importance in this investigation. A later study attempted to partially control for the effects of environmental factors by comparing girls with AGS and their normal sisters. Presumably, the siblings were being raised in more or less the same manner by their parents. In this study, tomboyishness was again found to be greater among the AGS girls. Furthermore, these girls showed less interest in jewelry, makeup, and frilly clothes than their non-AGS sisters (Ehrhardt & Baker 1974).

Another type of study provides some additional indirect support for the influence of biological factors in the formation of sex differences. For some time it has been known that visuospatial functions, which are generally better developed in males, are associated with the right cerebral hemisphere. Conversely, certain aspects of verbal communication, in which females have the advantage, are associated with the left hemisphere (Levy 1981). Recent studies with rats indicate that the male's right hemisphere is thicker than the left one; in females, the left hemisphere is thicker, although the difference in hemispheric thickness is less pronounced. In another study, removal of the ovaries in newborn female rats resulted in a hemispheric pattern identical to that of males (Diamond 1980).

There is some recent evidence that comparable sex differences exist in the brains of humans (DeLacoste-Utamsing & Holloway 1982). These findings suggest that males' better-developed right hemisphere accounts for the fact that, on average, they are superior in spatial abilities and that females' better-developed left hemisphere provides their superiority in verbal abilities. In addition, the findings implicate the role of early hormonal influence in these sex differences (Levy 1981).

Interaction between Biological Factors and Socialization Processes

It may be concluded, after considering the many studies in this section, that there is an interaction between biological and psychological or socialization processes. For example, boys are more likely to engage in rough-and-tumble play, due partly to the biological differences in aggressiveness discussed earlier. Over periods of many generations, the vast majority of societies come to expect males to be more aggressive, and so they reinforce male aggression more than comparable behavior in females. The strong role of reinforcement is illustrated in the following laboratory study. Children of both sexes were shown movies of adults punching a bobo doll. When the children were then placed in a room containing a bobo doll, they behaved aggressively towards it, with the boys showing more aggression than the girls. However, if the children were reinforced for aggressive behavior, the girls behaved just as aggressively as the boys (Bandura, Ross, & Ross 1963).

Another example of interaction may be seen in regard to the development of mathematical and visuospatial abilities, which are related to jobs such as engineering. As we have seen, there is evidence that males in general have a higher aptitude in this area than women. Perhaps as a result, society finds engineering careers more acceptable for men than for women, and even women with high aptitudes for the work are generally not encouraged to enter it. The great difference in the number of men and women in the field of engineering is probably much more a reflection of social attitudes than of any possible biologically determined difference in ability.

Author's Perspective: Teaching Sex-role Stereotypes and Biases

It has become apparent, from several of the studies just presented, that our society teaches children there are large differences between males and females. In actuality, however, there are many fewer basic sex differences than most people believe (Maccoby & Jacklin 1974). A good illustration of our socie-

FIGURE 13.5

In recent years, more and more women have been functioning in roles that were traditionally defined as masculine. However, there is still sex discrimination in our society which prevents many women from having equal opportunity to obtain certain jobs.

ty's poor perception of sex differences in children is given by the results of a study by Lott (1978). Teachers and parents filled out a questionnaire to determine how they thought the boys and girls in a kindergarten class differed in regard to certain behaviors and emotional responses. Then, Lott and several trained observers unobtrusively noted the interaction of the kindergarten children during a number of recess periods. Although there were a few sex differences, they were not nearly as great as those indicated by the parents and teachers. Furthermore, the differences found by the observers were not the same as those noted by the parents and teachers.

Perhaps more disturbing than the tendency to exaggerate sex differences is our society's bias against the female sex role. A number of studies illustrate the nature of this bias. McKee and Sherriffs (1957) asked male and female subjects to select one set of traits pertaining primarily to men and another set of traits pertaining primarily to women. The subjects selected more favorable than unfavorable traits for men, but just the opposite for women. This bias against women was reflected by both male and female subjects (McKee & Sherriffs 1957).

Another study suggests that people generally perceive the male role as more prestigious than the female one. College students were given descriptions of

FIGURE 13.6
Some Mythical Sex Differences

Myth	Research Findings
1. Females are basically more dependent than males.	There are no sex differences in the dependency of young children.
2. Females are more social than males.	Women may express more emotionally than men, but they are not more socially oriented.
3. Females are more nurturant than males.	There are no sex differences in amount of helping behavior.
4. Males are more competitive than females.	When appropriate tasks are chosen, there are no sex differences in degree of competitiveness.
5. Males are more logical than females.	There is no difference between men and women in logic and analytical ability.
6. Males are less moody than females.	Women and men are similar in the degree of mood fluctuation.

SOURCE: Summarized from Maccoby & Jacklin, 1974; Middlebrook, 1980

five traditionally male occupations: architect, lawyer, physician, professor, and scientist. They were led to believe that the percentage of women in some of these fields was increasing—and that women would soon form a majority. For each occupation, half the students were told that there would be an increase in women, while the other half were not. When an increase in women was anticipated, an occupation was rated lower in prestige than when male domination was expected to continue. As in the first study, the results were the same for both male and female raters (Touhey 1974).

Still another experimental study involved having college women rate a number of manuscripts. In some cases, the author was identified as a man; in others, the students were led to believe the author was a woman. Regardless of the topic of the manuscript, it was given a lower rating when the author was perceived as female (Goldberg 1968).

In the last several years there have been attempts to reduce sex bias. Publishers have worked to eliminate sexist language in grade-school readers, and some children's television programs—such as "Sesame Street"—support fewer sex-role stereotypes than traditional programs aimed at children. Some research suggests that, indeed, sex bias has decreased. Recent studies show less tendency for males to be ashamed of emotional expressiveness, and in fact, expressiveness is given a more favorable rating than in earlier studies (Der-Karabetian & Smith 1977). Generally speaking, the average woman receives more favorable ratings, and there is less tendency to overvalue the average man (Frieze 1974).

The increasingly large number of working mothers seems to be a factor of considerable importance in this reduction of bias. When women are employed, there tends to be less distinction in sex roles, and this relative lack of distinction is readily perceived by the children. In one study it was found that the grown son or daughter of a working mother has a less stereotyped view of sex roles (Vogel et al. 1970).

Despite the changes, there are still many biases against women and unfounded stereotypes of gender characteristics. Prejudice against women is strongest in situations where they are invading traditional male bastions. It may be that studies utilizing college students give an exaggerated view of liberal attitudes towards sex roles; blue-collar workers are clearly less liberated. Furthermore, there is evidence that many men who proclaim liberal attitudes actually behave in a very sexist manner (Spence, Helmreich, & Stapp 1975). Clearly, much work on reducing sex biases remains to be done. (Sex biases in regard to work will be discussed in the next chapter.)

SEXUAL EXPRESSION

The previous sections have been concerned with gender sexuality and how it develops. In this section, we will turn to erotic sexuality—how it develops and how it is expressed.

Infancy

As suggested earlier, there is evidence that erotic sexuality begins very early in life. In fact, male babies are sometimes born with erections, and females are known to exhibit vaginal lubrication within a short time of birth (Martinson 1980). As the infants grow older, sexual responses occur as apparent reactions to affection. For example, pelvic thrust movements have been observed in both sexes at about nine months as the infant holds onto and nuzzles the parent. Nonetheless, as the infant becomes older and more mobile, these responses tend to diminish.

Infants also appear to be responsive to stimulation of the genital area. After the third or fourth month, genital stimulation may be accompanied by smiling and/or soft vocalizations (Lewis & Kagan 1965; Kelley 1981).

There are also some reports of apparent orgasms in infants. Boys as young as five months have been observed making thrusting movements that become more rapid and vigorous, terminating in general body spasms (Kinsey et al. 1948). A similar observation has been made of a young female. A three-year-old was seen by her mother to lie on a bed with her knees drawn up, making a series of rhythmic pelvic thrusts. There were intense concentration, rapid breathing, and abrupt jerks as apparent orgasm approached. After the presumed climax, there was noticeable relief and relaxation (Kinsey et al. 1953). However, observations such as these appear to be rare.

Kinsey and his associates (1948) have estimated that more than half of boys aged three to four experience orgasm without ejaculation. (Comparable percentages were not given for females, but presumably they were much lower.) Obviously, it is difficult to know what meaning the child attaches to these very early experiences; when these individuals become adults, they usually do not even remember them. However, sexual experiences of later childhood—discussed in the next section—appear to have a strong impact on sexual development.

Middle and Late Childhood

Masturbation is fairly common during the latter part of childhood. The first masturbatory experiences generally involve absent-minded self-stimulation of the genitals, but as the child grows older such stimulation tends to become more systematic. There seem to be general sex differences in the way in which children learn to masturbate. Boys hear about it from their peers or observe other boys masturbating. In contrast, girls tend to learn about masturbation through accidental discovery or popular literature. Girls also learn masturbation at a later age than boys. In several cases girls have reported beginning the practice following heterosexual petting; after experiencing orgasm as the result of manipulation by a male, women may adapt comparable methods of self-stimulation (Kinsey et al. 1953).

Social aspects of sexual behavior develop by the time children reach four or five. Boys and girls often hug one another and talk about getting married, behaviors which are probably more an imitation of adults than anything else. A common game among preschool children is "playing doctor." Genitals are exposed, with occasionally a little touching or fondling. It seems that this type of sex play is motivated largely by curiosity.

As children approach adolescence, they tend to socialize in same-sex groups. By the time they are ten to thirteen, most of their friends are individuals of the same sex. During this period, some children—particularly boys—have homosexual or quasi-homosexual experiences. In one survey, it was found that 52 percent of the boys and 35 percent of the girls reported some homosexual or homosexual-like activity by age fourteen (Elias & Gebhard 1969). The types of experiences reported most frequently involve masturbation, exhibitionism, and stimulation of others' genitals. However, these experiences are not predictors of later homosexual behavior; the majority of preadolescents who have engaged in some type of homosexual contact do not continue homosexual play into adolescence and adulthood (Kinsey et al. 1953). Nonetheless, many people experience considerable shame and guilt over experiences that, by definition, are clearly normal.

In most families, parents are generally anxious and restrictive about childhood sexual experiences. Even when parents are relatively progressive and permissive, there tend to be social pressures from school-teachers and neighbors to curb children's sexual curiosity and experimentation. In general, there seems to be a fear that "premature" sexual information will be emotionally harmful to children (Libby & Nass 1971).

It is difficult to evaluate the effects of specific childhood practices because one cannot isolate a single behavior from a host of other behaviors. For example, if parents in certain societies stimulate a child's genitals and the child later becomes highly active sexually, one cannot be sure that the stimulation was a causal factor; the activating factor may have been the sexually permissive attitudes of the parents.

One study attempted to investigate the effects of parental attitudes upon genital play of four-year-old children in an English, urban setting. There were strong differences in the parent's attitudes toward this play and in the degree to which the children were punished for it. However, there was no correlation between parents' attitudes (or the degree of punishment) and the incidence of genital play (Newsom & Newsom 1968). Apparently, the parents had little or no effect on the actual behavior of the children at that time.

Other investigations, however, have demonstrated that parental attitudes (and punishment) affect the amount of sexual guilt that children experience. Furthermore, this guilt influences later sexual behavior and attitudes (Mosher & Cross 1971). The guilt may even affect sexual behavior after marriage (when sex is supposed to be acceptable). As suggested in chapter 6, when sex-related guilt increases, desire for sex, sexual responsiveness, and number of orgasms decrease (Kutner 1971).

Research in general has indicated that later sexual behavior is influenced not by specific childhood incidents, but by general patterns of interaction with parents or parent substitutes. Sociologists Broderick and Bernard (1969) have emphasized three developmental conditions that seem related to healthy adult sexuality: (1) the parent or substitute of the same sex must encourage identification by being relatively strong but not overly punishing; (2) the parent or substitute of the opposite sex must not be overly seductive or punishing, but stable enough so that the child may develop a feeling of trust in the opposite sex; and (3) the parents must not attempt to teach cross-sex behavior or reject the child's biological sex.

Comparative Perspective: Biological and Experiential Factors in the Development of Sexual Expression

We have already discussed the role of innate, or biological, and experimental factors in the development of gender sexuality. In this section, we will discuss the relative effects of these factors on erotic sexuality. The ultimate experiment would be to rear humans in isolation and then test them to see how they respond to sexual stimuli, but such an experiment is obviously unethical and impossible to perform. However, such experiments have taken place with animal subjects. Harlow (1962) reared rhesus monkeys in isolation from other monkeys and from humans as well. Both their physical and hormonal development seemed normal. Both sexes engaged in autoerotic activities, and the males sometimes masturbated to ejaculation. However, when the monkeys were introduced to sexually experienced monkeys of the opposite sex, none of them were capable of normal mating. The deprived monkeys had abnormal social responses, and this problem seemed to prevent the contact necessary for copulation. The males became aroused but groped about aimlessly, or brutally assaulted normal females; the females fled from or attacked normal males, despite the fact that the males showed patience and tolerance.

Even after long periods of exposure to normal animals, the socially deprived monkeys failed to show anything approaching normal sexual behavior. However, two females were finally impregnated by extraordinarily patient, normally reared males. When the females delivered their young, there was a severely abnormal maternal response: the infants were struck, beaten, and pushed into the wire-mesh floor (Harlow 1962).

In contrast, comparable studies with lower mammals indicate that the sexual responses of these animals depend very little on experience. Rats or guinea pigs reared in isolation show normal mating responses as adults, and for the most part the females are able to nurse their young (Beach 1965).

It may be concluded that, as the mammalian brain has become more complex, the role of experience has taken on increasing importance. Monkey brains are more complex than rats' and less complex than humans'; apparently, the importance of experience in monkeys' sexual expression is also intermediate. (Numerous clinical reports of human children reared in partial isolation by disturbed parents illustrate—in a disturbing fashion—the extreme dependency of humans on experiential factors.)

One may also conclude that many of the play patterns of monkeys—and undoubtedly, of humans—are crucial to the learning of adult social and sexual behavior. If the social responses are not learned in childhood, they are difficult or impossible to learn in adulthood. (Severely disturbed monkeys and humans are extremely difficult or impossible to retrain as adults.) For monkeys—and, to an even greater extent, humans—erotic sexuality is a complex pattern that develops out of the normal social and affectional responses of infants and children, and it is highly dependent on early social experience.

SEX EDUCATION

If human sexuality is so dependent upon experience, it might seem that one generation would pass on important information to the next. However, this is not generally the case, at least in our society. A study of 1,400 representative parents and children indicated that less than half the parents had ever mentioned sexual intercourse to their eleven-year-old offspring. Only about 50 percent of preadolescent daughters had been told about menstruation, and virtually none of the sons had heard about wet dreams from parents.

Some parents were willing to discuss sex with their children but delayed discussions until the appropriate time had passed. For example, several parents in the study believed it was best to discuss a sexual topic only when a child asked about it. Typically, the question was never asked, or it was put down because parents felt the timing was not right (Roberts, Kline, & Gagnon 1978).

In some cases, parents believe that giving children sex information will have negative effects, such as stimulating them to experiment with early sexual intercourse. However, research findings indicate just the opposite. When parents are the main source of sex information, young people are less likely to have premarital coitus at an early age than are individuals who gain most of their sex knowledge from their peer group (Spanier 1977).

Since adequate sex education does not take place in most homes, it can be argued that part of the responsibility belongs to schools. Nonetheless, there has been considerable controversy over school sex education. Certain people have claimed that factual material about sex destroys its "mystery" and "sacredness," thereby decreasing one's chances of enjoying it in the future. However, as we have seen, ignorance tends to have just the opposite effect, making the enjoyment of sex more difficult. Furthermore, it is unlikely that the information children inevitably pick up from their peers will emphasize the positive, sacred aspects of sexuality.

Another argument against sex education in the schools is similar to that directed against parental discussions of sex: Sex information may increase a child's tendency to experiment with sexual relations. However, one study found that sex instruction significantly *reduced* the incidence of premarital pregnancy (Guttmacher 1969).

Perhaps the most legitimate criticism of sex education in the schools is related to the quality of the teaching. Like some parents, certain instructors have so much sexual anxiety that they can hardly deal openly with the subject matter. Others have strong prejudices that make it difficult for them to be objective. Still others may promote a philosophy of extreme permissiveness, which brings them into conflict with the school's and the parents' values. However, these possibilities are not unique to the teaching of human sexuality; they exist in regard to the teaching of any subject. The real problem seems to be in selecting and training qualified people to teach sex-education courses.

To be most effective, sex education should probably take place before children obtain inaccurate or misleading information from their peers. Stephen McCary (1976) asked a large number of students when they had first heard of various sex-related terms and concepts. Most of the infor-

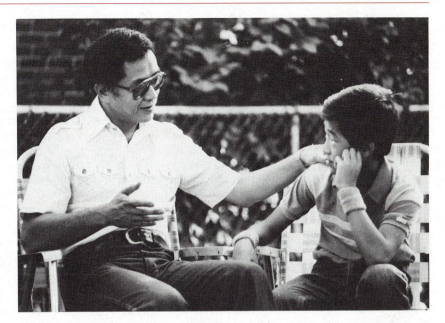

FIGURE 13.7
Many people believe that sex education is the responsibility of the parents. However, parent-child discussions of sex are often either delayed until the appropriate time has passed or are marked by the anxiety of the parents. Because of this difficulty in communication, children often learn about sex from their peers, obtaining inaccurate information and/or distorted views of sexuality.

mation was obtained from peers before the concepts were presented in sex-education classes or discussed by parents. McCary suggests that sex information should be presented at various times during the school years, with an attempt made to introduce material a year or so before students normally hear of it from their peers. He argues that this would reduce the learning of inaccurate information and the tendency to view sex as a taboo subject. Of course, it could also be argued that this procedure would simply lower the age at which children obtained sex information from their peers.

Author's Perspective: Sex Education as a Classic Example of Poor Communication

There are probably a number of reasons why American parents (or parent surrogates) fail as effective sex educators. In many cases, the same sexual guilt and anxiety that makes it difficult for the parents to communicate about sexual matters with each other inhibits or distorts communication with their children. The children learn, in essence, more sex anxiety than sexual information. This is clearly illustrated in the results of a study that compared the sexual attitudes and sex knowledge of children from a second-grade class in Pittsburgh, Pennsylvania, with similarly aged children in Sweden. (Swedish grade schools have an extensive, relatively anxiety-free program of sex education.) All children were interviewed and asked to make a number of drawings about reproduction. The American children exhibited relatively high sex anxiety. Furthermore, fearful scenes surrounding birth were depicted in the drawings. For example, many American children drew pictures of doctors with long knives ready to cut the baby out of the mother. In contrast, the Swedish children had much more accurate information and exhibited significantly less sex anxiety (Koch 1978).

Another reason parents generally fail as sex educators is related to uncertainty or misconceptions about what types of information should be presented. Parents tend to focus on reproductive sexuality. Children, however, seem to be much less interested in physiology than in emotions and sensations associated with sexual relations (Rubenstein et al. 1976). It is somewhat ironic that parents spend less time talking about the nature of intimate relationships with their loved ones than the impersonal function of reproductive organs. This overemphasis on reproduction probably reflects our society's general belief that sex and reproduction are invariably related.

In some cases, the relevant issues are not covered because the atmosphere surrounding the discussion is not free and open. Parents may lecture rather than discuss matters in a give-and-take fashion. (Generally speaking, people tend to be most authoritarian over matters about which they are uncertain or about which they feel uncomfortable.) And for most people, it is difficult to initiate self-disclosures in regard to sexual matters.

Fortunately, if there is basically good communication between parents and children, some of these difficulties are not too hard to overcome. One possibility is for parents to read books or articles on human sexuality and discuss the material with each other. During these discussions, they are likely to discover where there are feelings of guilt and anxiety — and sometimes just talking about a subject functions to reduce anxiety. The reading and discussion may also provide general knowledge and help to identify common myths or misconceptions. Still another advantage of the discussion between parents is it may serve as an effective model; if the parents themselves can have a good discussion about sex, this experience can support a fruitful parent-child discussion.

Parents are often disappointed because their children do not volunteer much information about their sexual feelings and experiences. This failure to self-disclose is not surprising, however, since parents do not generally confide in their children about sexual matters. (It will be remembered that self-disclosure tends to be evoked by comparable disclosures on the part of the other person.) Obviously, one way for parents to encourage children's self-disclosure is to volunteer some personal feelings or experiences in regard to sexuality. As in the case of most emotionally intimate exchanges, such disclosure may begin with a discussion of something relatively innocuous — such as a piece of sexual misinformation obtained by the parent as a child. Once the door is opened, it is not unusual for some open exchanges of feelings and experiences to follow. Subsequently, the child is more likely to come to the parent when he or she has questions or problems. This is, perhaps, the most important benefit of all.

SUMMARY

Sex differentiation involves a number of variables. The genetic factor depends on whether a Y sperm or an X sperm fertilizes the egg, to produce a male (XY) or a female (XX) individual. The gonadal factor refers to the differentiation of the gonads (Y chromosomes stimulate development of testes). The hormonal factor refers to the amount of androgen produced (testes produce relatively large amounts). With large amounts of androgen, the sex organs develop as male (the Adam principle); with small or negligible amounts of androgen, female sex organs develop (the Eve principle). In rare cases, sexual ambiguity results from a combination of Adam and Eve principles.

Gender identity apparently results from a socialization process during which children learn to identify with same-sex individuals. Studies of children who have undergone sex reassignment in the United States suggest that, once a child is old enough to develop a stable self-image, gender identity has been permanently established.

Sex-role development starts sometime after the gender identity is established. Socialization processes associated with differential treatment by the family, social learning in the family, the school environment, peer groups, and television are of primary importance. However, there is some evidence that biological factors interact with socialization processes to affect sex-role development.

There are apparently fewer sex differences than most people think. Many assumed differences result from individual attempts to fulfill prescribed sex roles or from misperceptions resulting from sex bias. In recent years there have been attempts to promote more accurate and equal assessment of the sexes, but much sex bias still exists in our society.

Erotic sexuality, like gender sexuality, starts to develop at a very early age. Infants are responsive to genital stimulation and in some cases may experience orgasm. By middle childhood, masturbation, heterosexual play, and homosexual or quasi-homosexual experiences are not unusual. Parental attitudes have relatively little effect on the sexual play of young children. However, the sex guilt that children develop in response to negative parental attitudes strongly affect later sexual behavior.

Experiments with animals indicate that, as the brain has increased in size and complexity, experience has played a larger role in sexual development. In monkeys and humans, erotic sexuality is highly dependent on early social and affectional experience gained during normal play.

Most people believe parents should be the primary source of sexual information. However, for a variety of reasons, parents typically fail as sex educators. Consequently, many people have argued that schools should take over some of the function. Selecting and training qualified people to teach sex-education classes is a major problem.

NOTES

1. The 46 in 46,XY and 46,XX refers to the autosomes (non-sex chromosomes). In some cases, the 46 is assumed, but left out of the notation.
2. Evidence suggests that progesterone counteracts the effect of the small amounts of androgen present in female fetuses. Thus, part of the Eve principle may be associated with progesterone (Ehrhardt & Meyer-Bahlburg 1981).

CHAPTER 14

Adolescence

There is not a clear line of distinction between childhood and adolescence; many of the processes related to gender and erotic sexuality discussed in the last chapter continue into adolescence. The period of adolescence—which is considered a transition from childhood to adulthood—is relatively long in our culture. With the increased amount of education required, this transition period has lengthened during the past seventy-five years and now corresponds roughly with the teenage years. In contrast, in many preliterate cultures—where little if any formal education takes place—the concept of adolescence is unknown. Rather, a ceremony marks the passage from childhood to adult maturity.

In this chapter, several aspects of sexuality during adolescence will be discussed: the physical and physiological changes of puberty, continuing sex-role development, and sexual expression following puberty. Finally, the development of sexuality during adolescence will be considered in a theoretical framework.

PUBERTY

The period of biological change from sexual immaturity to maturity is known as puberty. There are considerable individual differences in both the onset and the duration of this process, which lasts from 1½ to as many as 6 years (Grumbach 1980). Since there are marked sex differences, males and females will be discussed separately.

Females

The first signs of female puberty generally occur in late childhood, between the ages of eight and twelve.[1] Gonadotrophins from the pituitary stimulate the ovaries to produce estrogen. The estrogen, in turn, induces changes in the breasts, including elevation of the areola (the pigmented areas around the nipples) and general enlargement of the breasts. The

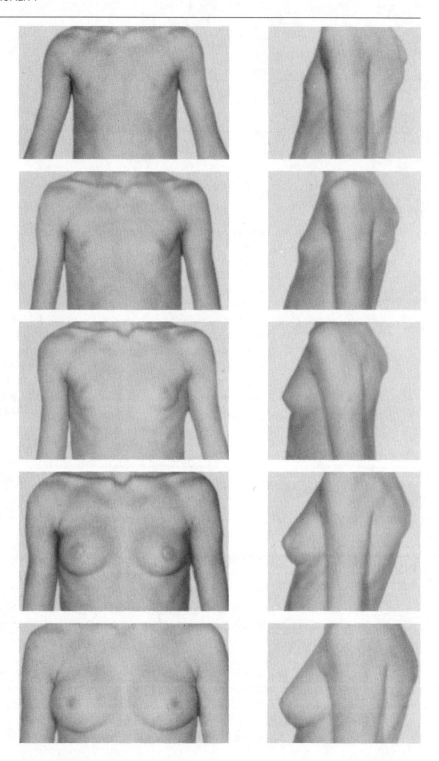

FIGURE 14.1

Breast development in a female. Enlargement is due primarily to increases in fatty tissue.

enlargement results from development of ducts in the nipple area and increases in fatty tissue, connective tissue, and blood vessels in the other areas of the breast.

Comparable changes occur in the hips and buttocks. Growth of fatty and supporting tissue in these areas—as well as skeletal changes in the hips—produce the rounded contours associated with adult femininity. There are large individual differences in the distribution of fatty tissues in the hips and buttocks, just as there are in the female's breasts.

Other changes take place in the pelvic area. There is a thickening of the walls of the uterus, and the development of blood supply to the clitoris. The pelvic bone grows, resulting in a larger pelvic opening. This enlargement is important in that it creates a passageway large enough for the infant during birth.

The changes described above are all associated with estrogen. However, some changes in girls' bodies during puberty are the result of an increase in the androgens secreted by the adrenal gland. The androgens are responsible for the growth of pubic hair and axillary hair (hair under the arms). They may also be responsible for acne, a fairly common problem during puberty for both girls and boys. Acne results from the clogging of oil-producing (sebaceous) glands. Although it usually presents only a temporary, cosmetic problem, acne can be severe enough to require medical treatment, particularly if it is accompanied by infections of the skin.

One of the most significant events of a girl's puberty is the menarche— the first menstruation. In many cultures of the past, the menarche marked the beginning of a period of seclusion. For example, in an area of Mozambique, Thonga girls made an announcement to an older woman—whom they had previously selected—that they had "come of age." When three or four girls had reached menarche, they were shut up together in a hut and secluded for a month. Every morning the girls were led—with veils covering their faces—to a pool where their bodies were immersed in water up to the neck. The girls were always accompanied by older women who sang obscene songs and drove away any men in the area with sticks; no man was allowed to see the girls during this initiation period. If a man did happen to see one of the initiates, it was believed that he risked blindness. During the time in the hut, the girls were teased, pinched, and given instruction in sexual matters. At the end of the month, a feast marked the return of the girls and their transformation into womanhood.

In general, menarche or puberty ceremonies functioned to announce to others that the females had become adults: in some cases, the rites marked the time when sexual intercourse became acceptable; if coitus was considered acceptable in younger girls, the ceremonies announced eligibility for marriage (Ford & Beach 1951).

In Western societies, the average age of the first menstruation has declined over a period of years. For example, it was 16.6 years of age in Germany in 1795, but 14.5 years of age in 1920. Today, in the United States the average age is around 13; indications are that the trend has finally leveled off (Tanner 1967). The earlier age for the first menarche seems to be related to improved nutrition.

In the United States, there is a wide range of reactions to the first menstruation. If the girl has not been prepared, she may feel fear or disgust. Negative reactions from others—including the use of phrases such as "having the curse" or being "unclean"—also contribute to a negative reaction (Holmes & Morrison 1979). On the other hand, with some forewarning and understanding, menarche may evoke generally positive feelings such as pride and a sense of maturity.

Males

For boys, puberty usually begins at around age ten or eleven, an average of two years later than for girls. It is ushered in by increased production of the gonadotrophic hormones. One of these hormones—LH—stimulates the production of androgen, which is mainly responsible for the several changes associated with male puberty.

Among the first visible changes is the rapid growth of the testes and scrotum. Pubic hair begins to appear at the same time. Approximately a year later, the penis thickens and lengthens. In another year, facial and underarm (axillary) hair starts to grow. The facial hair has the appearance of fuzz at first; the typical adult beard—as well as hair on the chest—does not appear until late in puberty or early in adulthood.

Ejaculations start at about age thirteen or fourteen, and erections increase in frequency. However, the ejaculate does not contain mature sperm for another year or so. The mature sperm, it will be remembered, are produced as the result of the joint stimulation of the two gonadotrophic hormones, FSH and LH.

Early in puberty, the larynx, or "voice box," begins to enlarge. When this growth reaches a certain point—at around thirteen or fourteen—the voice starts to change to a lower register. During this period of transition, there may be frequent shifts between the higher and lower registers, particularly when the individual is excited. Such shifting—which is sometimes referred to as the voice "cracking"—can be a source of temporary embarrassment.

There is a great spurt in body growth from about eleven to sixteen. This growth is stimulated by a pituitary growth hormone (somatotrophic hormone) in conjunction with androgen. The male-typical changes in body contour and increases in muscle mass are strongly influenced by androgen. Although there is a comparable spurt in females, body growth in girls terminates sooner.

As in the case of girls, several cultures mark male puberty by initiation rites. Although nothing quite as obvious and definite as the first men-

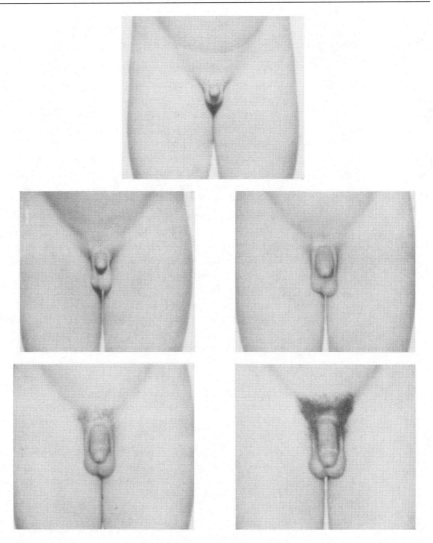

FIGURE 14.2

Genital development in a male. The first apparent change is the enlargement of the testes and scrotum. Later, the penis thickens and lengthens.

struation marks puberty in boys, the first ejaculation or the appearance of facial and/or pubic hair may be taken as a symbol of male maturity. In preliterate societies, the initiation rites often involved ordeals of various kinds. Among the Keraki of Papua and New Guinea, the boys had to submit to a blow on the back with a large banana stalk. The boys also spent a period of time when they were forced to play the passive role in anal intercourse with older men.

Initiation rites in other societies were less extreme. For example, on the island of Truk, a boy celebrated his maturity by starting to wear a red loincloth and living in the men's dormitory. In many societies, including those that included ordeals, sexual instruction was included in the rites.

Author's Perspective: Age of Puberty Related to Later Self-concept

Variations in the time at which an individual reaches puberty are not significantly related to physical health. However, the time of maturation may have a psychological effect. Early-maturing girls are sometimes ridiculed, but older males generally encourage them to date at a relatively young age. By the beginning of high school, such a girl's mature physique is an advantage in the competition for dates. In contrast, late-maturing girls generally have less prestige among classmates and tend to have less-adequate self-concepts than early-maturing ones. Furthermore, the late-maturing girls generally have poorer relationships with their parents and peers than their early-maturing classmates (Weatherly 1964).

A comparable situation exists for boys. Individuals who mature early experience definite social advantages. They tend to be regarded as attractive and mature in character. On the other hand, late-maturing individuals tend to be less successful in sports, have poorer self-concepts, and behave in a more immature, attention-seeking fashion than early-maturing ones. Some of these differences have been found to persist into adulthood, even though physical differences no longer exist (Mussen & Jones 1958).

Fortunately, the frustrations of being a late developer do not usually have a lasting effect. In some cases, people who were late developers and subsequently became successful function as positive role models and supply inspiration. In other cases, the development of special skills in areas such as music, writing, or mechanics—areas which do not depend on physical development—provide needed success experiences.

Parents, teachers, and friends can be particularly helpful to adolescents. It is often important to encourage teenagers to talk about their frustrations and disappointments—not only in relation to late development, but in other areas as well. All too frequently, adults shuck responsibility by saying such things as "Chris is just going through a phase and will get over it." My experience in counseling suggests most teenagers strongly need an adult whom they trust and respect, not necessarily to supply brilliant solutions to problems, but to provide warmth, understanding, and encouragement.

SEX ROLES

Adolescents typically spend a large amount of time in school and/or college and, in many cases, enter the work force on a full- or part-time basis. Therefore, sex roles related to academics and the job situation will be emphasized in this section.

Success in academic situations reflects sex roles in a somewhat surprising fashion. Even though women's performance in academic areas is generally equal to that of men, females have a lower expectation of success. For example, when asked to guess what scores they would receive on an examination, women tend to underestimate their performance to a greater extent than men (Berg & Hyde 1976). Furthermore, when some success is reached, women are more liable to attribute their success to luck than to ability. This doubt about success is especially likely to occur when women are competing in tasks that are considered traditionally masculine (Deaux 1976).

Another factor related to women's relatively low striving for mastery in academia seems to be what has been termed a *fear of success*. This fear is illustrated in a study conducted by Matina Horner (1972). Female college students were asked to write a story based on the statement, "After first-term finals, Anne finds herself at the top of her medical class." Sixty-five percent of the women wrote stories that reflected conflict or fear of success; in contrast, less than 10 percent of the stories written by college men reflected such conflicts or fears. (For the men, the name John was substituted for Anne in the initial statement.) Many of the women who expressed fear of success wrote of anxiety over loss of femininity.

Later studies of fear of success have indicated that it is not always higher in women than in men. One of the most important factors seems to be whether or not the area in which performance is evaluated is a traditionally masculine one (Zuckerman & Wheeler 1975).[2]

Turning to the job situation, we find sex biases in many hiring practices. For example, strength may be considered a requisite for a job, even though physical strength has little or nothing to do with job performance. In some cases, mythical qualities—such as heightened moodiness in females—may be cited as a reason for not hiring women. The end result is a large gap in the earning potential of males and females—a gap that may be increasing. In 1955, the typical female worker was paid 64 percent of what the typical male earned; in 1977, the percentage dropped to 59 percent, despite increased concern over sex biases.

Sex stereotypes, sex biases, and sex discrimination all contribute to the discrepancy in earning potential of men and women. Nonetheless, another factor must be taken into consideration. There is some experimental evidence that females "shortchange" themselves, or are less sensitive to underpayment than are males. In the first of two experiments, Callahan-Levy and Messé (1979) asked male and female college students to perform a task and then to estimate how much they should be paid for their work. The females' estimates were significantly lower than were the males'. In the second experiment, a similar situation was set up, but this time the subjects were children at various grade levels. For each grade level, the amount of money requested—or, in the case of first graders, the number of pieces of candy asked for—was less for females than for males. Apparently, starting at a very young age, females perceive relatively less of a relationship between work and money. This may be because, traditionally, feminine activities such as housework and child care are not linked with pay. At any rate, these sex differences in pay expectancy may account for at least part of the discrepancy between male and female earning potential.

Theoretical Perspective: Factors That Promote Sex Biases

In many preliterate societies, the greater size and strength of men has helped to determine their role as hunters and miners. Since hunting and mining bring in highly valuable products, men have tended to control the wealth. In addition, men's greater size, strength, and general aggressiveness—plus the fact that women are often restricted by pregnancy and child rearing—have typically helped them attain the most powerful social positions. As suggested in chapter 1, when men control the power, women are generally given lower-status roles.

Anthropological studies in general indicate that societies which put a premium on physical strength (and resultant male power) tend to make a relatively great distinction between male and female sex roles (Barry, Bacon, & Child 1957). It seems that much of this distinction probably developed as a means of maintaining sex differences in power and status. In other words, the negative stereotype of women functions as a justification for keeping them in their place.

Once traditional sex-role differences have become established, they tend to be self-perpetuating. An examination of humor expressed by professional comics of both sexes in the United States illustrates one way this is accomplished. Male comics express a great deal of aggression toward others but are not likely to put themselves down. In contrast, 63 percent of female comics' recordings include self-disparagement. Since the development of a comic routine is highly dependent upon feedback from the audience, it is easy to understand how general conceptions of sex roles affect the routine, and, in turn, how the routine reinforces sex biases (Levine 1976).

Even our language tends to perpetuate sex biases. Terms such as his, he, and man refer to males but are also used as supposedly gender-neutral words, referring to either sex. An experiment indicates that, in situations that are clearly gender-neutral, a male pronoun causes subjects to think first of males. For example, when responding to the sentence "In a large coeducational institution the average student will feel isolated in *his* introductory courses," most subjects respond as if the student is male. If "his or her" is substituted, then the male bias is significantly reduced. Undoubtedly, over a period of time, the male bias in language leads people to feel that males are the "real people" who "belong" in certain contexts, particularly high-status ones (Moulton et al. 1978).

Clearly, some people are more likely to promote sex biases than others. Research indicates that, among males, negative attitudes toward women are correlated with general authoritarian attitudes and a "win at all costs" attitude in sports (Maier & Lavrakas 1981). For both males and females, sex biases against women are strongest among those who hold traditional beliefs about sex roles (Spence, Helmreich, & Stapp 1975). It seems that people who are rigid in their personality structure and beliefs are most likely to be biased.

Since the late 1960s several of the sex biases discussed in this and the pre-

FIGURE 14.3

An example of sex role differentiation or sex typing which is strongly associated with Victorian times. Many people now believe it is most satisfying to be androgynous, i.e., to develop positive qualities which are both masculine and feminine in the traditional sense.

vious chapter have been challenged and, in some cases, become less widespread. There have also been considerable changes in conceptions of sex roles, many of them stimulated by technological advances and pressures applied by the feminist movement. Juanita Williams (1980), a leading feminist, has outlined some of the changes that took place in the 1970s, particularly in sex roles related to marriage. Educational and employment opportunities have given women more social and economic independence. These opportunities have reduced the need to get married or remain in unhappy marital situations. In addition, the availability of other types of male-female relationships—including nonmarital cohabitation—has provided options to traditional marriages; until recently, traditional marriage was one of the few socially acceptable alternatives for women. Finally, more egalitarian relationships between women and men have become possible; both females and males can be freed from the restrictions of prescribed power and dominance roles. These changes associated with the feminist movement have also brought about changes in the law. For example, the man in a marriage is not automatically assumed to be the head of a household; women can be made to pay alimony to men; and men are frequently able to win court battles over custody of children.

It is difficult to know if trends toward greater equality in sex roles will continue in the 1980s and 1990s. There is some evidence of a backlash effect on the part of conservative elements. How strong this reaction will be depends on many of the same factors that influence attitudes about erotic sexuality: economic, political, and technological. However, it seems unlikely there will be a return to sex-role differentiation resembling that of the Victorians or even the 1950s.

Author's Perspective: Androgyny as an Alternative to Traditional Sex Roles

In the past, it was assumed that biological males were high on psychological masculinity and biological females were high on psychological femininity. There were exceptions (women who were high on masculinity, or men who were high on femininity), but these individuals were considered poorly adjusted. Another assumption was that femininity and masculinity were at opposite ends of a scale. These assumptions were supported by studies utilizing tests that were, in essence, biased; the tests were constructed in such a fashion that, if a person scored high on one end of the scale, he or she necessarily scored low on the other end. However, in the early 1970s, Sandra Bem (1974) constructed a scale that had separate measures of masculinity and femininity. On this scale, known as the Bem Sex Role Inventory (BSRI), it was possible to score high on both measures, low on both measures, or exhibit any combination of the two. People who scored approximately equal on masculinity and femininity were called *androgynous*.[3] Since this time, the BSRI has been used in a large number of psychological studies.

Androgynous people who score high on both parts of the BSRI presumably have the positive qualities associated with each traditional role. For example, they may be traditionally masculine in the sense that they are aggressive and assertive; at the same time, they can be affectionate and love children, tendencies traditionally identified with the female role. Laboratory research supports the assumption that androgynous people are more flexible than traditionally sex-typed individuals. Male and female subjects were confronted with two types of situations, one requiring independence and the other involving the expression of warmth or affection. It was found that androgynous subjects were able to express "masculine" independence when under pressure to conform and "feminine" warmth when given the opportunity to play with a young kitten. In contrast, the nonandrogynous subjects were restricted in their behavior: strongly sex-typed males did not express warmth, and markedly sex-typed females did not assert independence (Bem 1975).

In another study, Bem and Lenney (1976) found that androgynous individuals performed cross-sex behavior with few problems; in contrast, markedly sex-typed persons avoided a task such as nailing two boards together or winding a package of yarn simply because one of these activities was deemed appropriate for the opposite sex. Furthermore, if pressured into performing an "inappropriate" task, sex-typed individuals experienced marked discomfort and loss of self-esteem.

It seems clear, from the results of the studies just mentioned, that there are certain advantages to androgyny. Nonetheless, there may also be disadvantages. Conversations with women who have both a career and a family suggest that it is very difficult to find enough time to do justice to both, especially when problems arise. Traditionally, a woman would be viewed as successful if she was a good homemaker. Today, some women feel pressured to be competent in both "masculine" and "feminine" areas. There are even examples of women who feel that they must apologize for being "just a housewife."

A similar type of situation exists for males. A study of married men who are extensively involved in taking care of their children indicates that they spend less time working outside the home than a comparable group of more traditional men (Wolfson 1982). Clearly, reduced time on the job may result in fewer promotions and less success in the traditional sense. As Bem (1981) has stated, androgyny may not be for everyone, especially those who feel very comfortable in traditional male or female roles.

Perhaps the best thing that has resulted from studies of androgyny and nontraditional sex-role orientation is a realization that there are now reasonable alternatives available. Girls who show interest in sports or mathematics and boys who are artistic or emotionally expressive need not feel embarrassed or pressured to alter their life-styles. The available sex-role choices may be complex and confusing, but the rewards associated with increased freedom can be truly great.

SEXUAL EXPRESSION

Adolescence in the United States and the Western world in general is often conceptualized as a time of stress. Some of the factors contributing to this stress—adjustments to physical and psychological changes following puberty and pressures associated with school and work—have already been discussed. In this section, we consider what is often viewed as the major stress of adolescence: the emergence of a strong sexual drive and the need to express this drive in a society with conflicting standards.

Noncoital Activities

During adolescence, the frequency of masturbation tends to increase. By the end of the teen years, nearly 100 percent of males have masturbated to orgasm an average of two or three times a week. During periods when they are engaging in sexual intercourse, however, the frequency tends to be lower (Sorenson 1973; Hass 1979).

Adolescent girls also show an increase in the tendency to masturbate. However, only about two-thirds of them do so to the point of orgasm. Of those who do masturbate, the average frequency is about once a month, considerably lower than that for boys. Another sex difference is seen in the relationship between masturbation and coitus. In contrast to boys, adolescent girls tend to masturbate more frequently during periods when they are engaging in coitus (Sorenson 1973; Hass 1979). As suggested in chapters 7 and 8, at least some of these sex differences are probably due to discrepancies in the traditional sex roles, especially as they apply to sexual satisfaction. Another explanation is probably related to the relatively late development of the female sex drive, which continues to increase well into adulthood.

Heterosexual petting typically begins and shows an increase in frequency during the adolescent years. Petting includes a variety of activities in varying degrees of sexual intimacy. Less intimate interactions, such as kissing and embracing when fully clothed, may give way to stimulation of the genitals and female breasts as couples get to know each other and become more emotionally involved. Essentially, interaction during petting provides an opportunity to experience sexual sharing and communication without the commitments or "dangers" of coitus. Thus, it is an important learning experience on the road to adult heterosexuality. According to the *Playboy* survey, approximately one-half of the females and two-thirds of the males questioned engaged in petting to the point of orgasm during their adolescent years (Hunt 1974).

Some adolescents engage in homosexual contacts; 11 percent of the males and 6 percent of the females in the teenage survey reported at least one homosexual experience. In almost all these cases, the first such experience was with another teenager. Thus, there is no evidence that adult homosexuals contribute to adolescent homosexuality by seduction (Sorenson 1973).

Not all individuals who have homosexual experiences as adolescents continue a homosexual orientation. For some, the adolescent behavior is an expression of curiosity or experimentation and does not continue until adulthood. On the other side of the coin, some individuals do not begin a homosexual life-style until they are adults. Consequently, like childhood practices, adolescent homosexual experiences—or the lack of them—are not good predictors of a later homosexual life-style.

Coitus

A large number of individuals experience their first sexual intercourse during their teen years. Approximately 60 percent of males and close to 50 percent of females in the adolescent study were unmarried nonvirgins (Sorenson 1973). These figures are up considerably from those of the Kinsey reports of the 1940s and 1950s (Kinsey et al. 1948; Kinsey et al. 1953), and females have changed their behavior more than males. In one study, approximately twice as many women had lost their virginity by the end of their nineteenth year as had in a comparable survey taken five years earlier (Kantner & Zelnik 1972; Zelnik & Kantner 1977).

There seem to be several reasons for the increase in premarital coitus among teenagers. The general trend toward sexual liberalism in our society is certainly one. Another seems to be the increasing incidence of female-headed families. Shah and Zelnik (1980) found much less likelihood of premarital coitus in adolescent women if a father or stepfather was present in the home than if one was not. Apparently, a female head-of-family has relatively greater difficulty in repressing sexual activity in an adolescent, especially an adolescent daughter. Another factor may be that a girl is so much in need of masculine attention that she engages in sexual activity to get it.

Despite the general availability of willing sex partners, most people in the early 1970s were not highly promiscuous during their adolescent and early adult years. The average male had about six premarital sex partners; selectivity was even greater for females. Among women who had premarital experience, approximately half had only one partner, whom they later married (Hunt 1974).

It appears that the general increase in premarital sexual relations for both men and women represents not so much an increase in casual and impersonal sex as a shift in standards. At the time of the Kinsey report, most people believed that intercourse should be limited to marriage. However, in the 1970s many people, particularly adolescents, adopted a standard that has been described as permissiveness with affection: intercourse is acceptable if it takes place in a stable relationship that includes love and some kind of commitment. It is interesting that this same shift in standards often takes place as individuals reach adolescence: eleven-year-olds generally believe that the first intercourse should be delayed until marriage, but sixteen-year-olds tend to think that intercourse is appropriate if the people are in love (Schoof-Tams, Schlaegel, & Walczak 1976).

Even though most adolescents do not find sex with a variety of partners satisfying, some have a large number of partners. In certain cases, males gain recognition from friends and associates by discussing sexual

FIGURE 14.4
Incidence of Premarital Coitus

	Males	Females
1950s	71%	33%
1970s	97%	67%

SOURCES: Kinsey et al., 1948; 1953; Hunt, 1974

exploits. Unfortunately, many females experience sexual coercion during casual dating with these men (Kanin & Parcell 1977).

There are also some females who have many sexual partners. Research indicates that the age of the first intercourse is a factor in predicting the number of partners. The earlier a woman loses her virginity, the larger the number of premarital partners. Generally, sex with a variety of partners is more common in older, unmarried females than among adolescents (Hunt 1974; Tavris & Sadd 1977).

For some men (but very few women), the first intercourse is with a prostitute. However, the percentage of men who had their first sexual contact with a prostitute is lower—according to the *Playboy* report—than it was during the Kinsey era. As a matter of fact, sex with prostitutes is generally on the decline (Hunt 1974). Apparently, more women are willing to participate in sexual intercourse, and this is reducing the need for paid sexual partners.

Psychological Perspective: Emotional Reactions to the First Coitus

Most individuals consider the first sexual intercourse a highly significant event. Nonetheless, females generally react to the first coitus in a negative way: emotions such as guilt, sorrow, and disappointment are fairly common. In contrast, males typically react with feelings of joy and pride. Positive feelings are reported approximately twice as frequently by males as by females (Sorenson 1973). The reactions of the sexes are in line with the way our culture responds to their loss of virginity. There is often peer approval when males have their first coitus, especially if it is in a casual relationship. (Even the phrase "loss of virginity" has humorous overtones when applied to males.) In contrast, loss of virginity is not considered a laughing matter for females and is liable to meet with strong disapproval if it occurs in a casual context or one without feelings of intimacy (Carns 1973).

These sex differences are probably related, at least in part, to the fear of unwanted pregnancy—which is obviously more relevant to females. Whereas males are generally concerned with possible difficulties in sexual performance, females have to fear the possibility of both sexual failure and reproductive success (Eme 1979).

Pain associated with the penetration of the intact hymen or a constricted P-C muscle was probably a contributing factor for some women. Approximately 30 percent of women reported severe pain; another 50 percent, brief or moderate pain (Oliven 1974).

Still another factor of importance may be related to self-concept. Becoming sexually experienced rather than inexperienced is perceived as a large step for women (Waterman & Nevid 1977). The transition from virginity may be justified by believing that intercourse took place in a love relationship. However, if the relationship breaks up, women may go through a period of doubting their self-worth (Kleinman 1978). Nonetheless, the Sorenson study indicated that negative emotional reactions of women to the first coitus are not long lasting; a majority of the women surveyed reported an increase in satisfaction with intercourse, particularly if it continued with their initial partner (Sorenson 1973).

Is the first coitus more stressful for women if it occurs before marriage than if it occurs on the wedding night? A study conducted in England attempted to answer this question by interviewing a large number of women. Positive and negative feelings were similar for groups of women who lost their virginity either before or after marriage (Schofield 1973). However, the conclusion that marriage makes little difference must be considered tentative; those women who waited until marriage were clearly sexual conservatives. As we have seen, sexual conservatives tend to enjoy coitus less than liberals under any circumstances.

Theoretical Perspective: How Does Human Sexuality Develop?

In the previous chapter and the preceding sections of this chapter, we have been concerned with a description of changes associated with the development of sexuality. We have also looked at evidence suggesting the role of experience in this development. Nonetheless, some controversy exists among theorists as to just how much of sexual development depends on experience and how much is biological or innate. In this section, we will look at three theories that place differing degrees of emphasis on the roles of experiential and biological, or innate, factors.

Sociobiology is representative of a theory that stresses innate factors. Theorists such as E. O. Wilson (1975) and Donald Symons (1979) have suggested that many aspects of human sexuality are carried in our genes. Presumably, human sexuality became genetically adapted—via natural selection—to the environment of early humans. (It has not become particularly adapted to modern conditions because the modern era has lasted only a few thousand years, whereas significant genetic changes require millions of years.) According to sociobiologists certain sex differences may be explained in relation to different biological functions of males and females. For example, male orgasm is reproductively necessary, whereas female orgasm is not. The fact that a failure to reach orgasm is more common in females than in males is consistent with a reduced selective advantage for orgasm in women; men cannot generally impregnate without orgasm, but women can become pregnant without experiencing orgasm.

Freud's (1938) psychoanalytic theory is an example of an approach that stresses the interaction between innate and experiential factors. All people presumably go through certain biologically determined stages of development. However, one's personality and sexual development depend upon the experiences associated with these stages. For example, during the first stage of development—known as the *oral stage*—libidinal or sexual energy is centered in the mouth area. According to Freud, adults retain some elements of this stage; oral needs are apparently reflected in such activities as licking ice cream cones and kissing. If a person experiences severe frustrations at an early stage of development, part of his or her libidinal energy remains focused on the unfulfilled needs of this stage. Such a problem, called a fixation of infantile sexuality, may result in one or more of the sexual variations discussed in chapters 17–19.

Freudian theory attempts to explain several of the differences between males and females in terms of *identification;* children attempt to be like their same-sex parents (or parent substitutes). Furthermore, boys and girls develop different types of complexes while resolving their sexual identity at about ages four to six. Males develop an *Oedipus complex* (sexually desiring their mothers); females have a comparable *Electra complex* (falling in love with their fathers). How these complexes are resolved is presumably important in the achievement of mature sexuality. Theoretically, one should renounce the parent as lover, identify with the same-sex parent, and put one's own sexuality on the "back burner" while developing the social and academic skills of middle childhood.

Learning theorists place a strong emphasis on experiential factors (see Hilgard & Bower 1975). In some cases, sexual responses may develop as the result of simple *operant conditioning.* For example, a young woman may become pleasantly sexually stimulated by riding a horse or a motorcycle. The learning theorists suggest that the tendency to repeat these types of activities is increased by the sexual reinforcement.

Presumably, responses—including emotional responses—may *generalize* from one situation to another. For example, it is assumed that the positive responses that develop during sex therapy will generalize to sexual experiences outside the therapeutic environment. Of course, it is also possible that negative responses will generalize. Parents punishing a child for an "unacceptable" sex act such as masturbation may find that the child develops some negative feelings towards them as well as—or perhaps instead of—toward the sex act.

It appears that some types of learning related to sexuality are more complex than those just discussed. Of particular importance is imitational or social learning: the copying of behaviors and attitudes exhibited by another person. Relevant, accessible adults—particularly parents—tend to be models of behavior. For example, girls develop many behaviors and concepts of femininity by observing their mothers. Television and movie heroes and heroines also become what are referred to as role models. It seems that many of the subtle nuances of sex-role behavior are learned through imitation rather than through operant conditioning or punishment. (In some respects, this observation is similar to Freud's concept of identification.)

One finding of particular significance is that a person does not need to be a rewarding figure—or even admirable—in order to function as a role model. For example, an aggressive, sexually abusive father may be hated by his children; however, the children still tend to mold some of their behavior after his. Similarly, some television villains may function as negative role models (Bandura & Walters 1963).

Clearly, each theory provides thought-provoking insights into the development of sexuality, and it is difficult to make a clear-cut determination of which is "best." Of course, one does not want to rule out biological factors—without sex hormones, where would one be? It is also important to remember how interwoven are biological and experiential factors. As we have seen, people's feelings of self-confidence depend to a certain extent on how physically attractive they are and how others have reacted to their attractiveness. Nonetheless, as a psychologist and former psychotherapist, I tend to be most sympathetic with the learning theory approach, since it follows that therapy is a learning experience that can have an important effect on one's feelings and behavior. (As we shall see in chapter 21, there is considerable evidence that therapy based on learning theory does indeed produce significant effects.)

Author's Perspective: Adolescents, Parents, and Personality Development

My experiences with clients in psychotherapy have strongly convinced me of the importance of adolescent sexual experiences and conflicts in the development of adult sexuality. And it seems that these experiences and conflicts also have a great influence on the formation of adult personality structure in general. For example, basic feelings of self-confidence, trust, and security depend a great deal on how successfully an individual learns to deal with male and female sex roles as a teenager. A similar situation exists in regard to intimacy. If people are unable to establish satisfying emotional relationships as children or adolescents, it is very difficult for them to do so as adults. The establishment of a mature ethical system serves as still another example. Adolescents who have trouble arriving at a consistent moral decision in regard to sexuality usually find it difficult to make moral judgments on a variety of issues as adults.

Parents or parent substitutes play a critical role in the sexual development of adolescents, particularly in regard to the teenager's increasing need for independence. Some parents tend to be overprotective or overcontrolling, preventing the adolescent from gaining important growth experiences and a sense of independence. At the other extreme, parents may exercise too little control, creating an atmosphere that fosters reckless abandon. (Most adolescents actually feel uncomfortable in situations where there are no restrictions.) It seems that the best course is the middle-of-the-road approach, which allows an adolescent to test developing feelings of independence within certain guidelines.

Perhaps, as suggested several times earlier in the book, good communication is of primary importance. Open discussions about such issues as curfews, privacy, and use of the car may result in decisions satisfactory to both parents and adolescents (or at least a better understanding of the other person's point of view). Furthermore, when adolescents have been active in the decision-making process, they are more inclined to abide by the decision—and less apt to look for ways to break the rules.

Another advantage of open discussions—if they are successful—is that the communication skills developed tend to transfer to other areas. Parents and adolescents who are able to comfortably discuss the use of the family car are more likely to discuss feelings associated with sexuality (feelings that, as we have seen, are often poorly communicated). Furthermore, both adolescents and parents may sharpen the skills necessary for effective communication within the context of an intimate relationship.

SUMMARY

Puberty generally begins between ages eight and twelve in girls. Gonadotrophins stimulate the ovaries to produce estrogen, which, in turn, brings about breast development and changes in the hips, buttocks, and pelvis. Increased androgen output from the adrenals induces growth of pubic and axillary hair. At about age thirteen, menarche (the first menstruation) occurs.

In males, puberty starts about two years later than in females. Physical changes include an increase in size of the testes, scrotum, and penis, as well as growth of facial and axillary hair. Later, ejaculations start, and mature sperm are produced. A relatively rapid increase in body size is stimulated by a growth hormone that works in conjunction with androgen.

Certain psychological effects are related to the age of puberty. Late-maturing girls and boys generally have less-adequate self-concepts and poorer social relationships than early-maturing ones. Fortunately, parents, teachers, and friends can be helpful in dealing with these problems.

Sex biases have a significant effect on sex roles related to academics and work. The development of these biases seems to be related to the fact that, in most societies, men control the power. Once established, sex biases tend to be self-perpetuating. However, in recent years, the feminist movement has initiated a reduction in sex biases in certain areas.

People who score approximately equal on measures of masculinity and femininity are called androgynous. Laboratory research indicates that androgynous individuals are relatively flexible in their definition of male and female sex roles and perform "inappropriate" sex-role tasks with little difficulty. Despite apparent advantages of an androgynous orientation, there are still many societal pressures that tend to keep individuals in traditionally feminine or traditionally masculine roles.

The emergence of a strong sexual drive during adolescence is reflected in increases in masturbation and heterosexual petting. In some cases, teenagers have homosexual experiences, but these are not good predictors of a later homosexual life-style.

In the last several years, premarital coitus has become more common among adolescents, with a greater relative increase reported in females. Despite the general increase in coitus, most adolescents do not have a large variety of partners.

Coitus within a casual relationship is considered, by our society in general, more appropriate for males than females. A related fact is that most women consider the loss of virginity a highly significant event and are more likely than males to have negative emotional reactions to the first coitus.

Several types of theories attempt to explain the development of sexuality; sociobiology is representative of a theory that emphasizes innate factors; Freud's psychoanalytic theory is an example of an interactionist approach; and learning theorists point to the importance of experiential factors. Each type of theory is particularly effective in explaining certain aspects of sexual development.

Such factors as self-confidence, trust, need for intimacy, and a mature ethical system all seem to depend in part on how successfully one deals with developing sexuality during adolescence. Parents or parent surrogates are particularly important during this critical period of development.

NOTES

1. In a very few cases, females are sexually mature in infancy. A Peruvian girl began menstruating around one month of age and gave birth—by Caesarean section—to a normal child at age five.
2. The review article by Zuckerman and Wheeler (1975) also pointed to other problems with the *fear of success* measure. It seems that, generally speaking, this concept has not proven to be as fruitful as was originally anticipated.
3. The noun androgyny and the adjective androgynous are derived from two Greek words: *andros* means "male"; *gynos* means "female."

CHAPTER **15**

Adulthood

Just as there is no clear line of distinction between childhood and adolescence, it is difficult to point to an exact age at which people become adults. In fact, it is not hard to think of people we have known who lived to an old age without ever really becoming adults in an emotional or psychological sense. In this chapter, we will consider sexuality in the adult years in relation to four life-styles: never married, married, divorced, and widowed.

NEVER-MARRIED ADULTS

In the past several years, there has been an increase in the number of people who are not married as adults. This trend toward a singles life-style is due to a combination of factors: people are marrying at a later age than they did in the 1950s and 1960s; more marriages are ending in divorce; and people are waiting longer to remarry following a divorce (Glick & Norton 1979).

Although some of the never-married individuals are cohabiting or have an exclusive sexual relationship with one other person, many are unattached. Peter Stein (1976) conducted in-depth interviews with a sample of twenty singles of each sex who were in their late twenties or early thirties. Both males and females tended to prefer multiple sexual relationships to exclusive ones and felt generally positive about their life-style. Other factors mentioned as attractive were high levels of mobility, self-sufficiency, psychological autonomy, and freedom to sustain a variety of friendships.

Generally speaking, studies indicate that single adult women experience relatively more satisfaction and better adjustment than single adult men. For example, Knupfer, Clark, and Room (1966) found that single adult women over thirty were less depressed and maladjusted than a control group of married women. In contrast, single men in the same age

FIGURE 15.1
Sexual interaction in adulthood is traditionally considered the ultimate expression of human sexuality.

group showed poorer social and psychological adjustment than their married counterparts. In another study, generally positive factors such as high intelligence and a successful career were associated with the singles life-style in women. However, single men tended to have a relatively large amount of difficulty in interpersonal relationships (Spreitzer & Riley 1974). Thus, the motivation for remaining single may be somewhat different for the two sexes.

Cohabitation

Recent changes in adolescent and adult sexuality are not restricted to patterns of coitus. There are also significant changes in living arrangements. An unmarried male and female living together and having a sexual relationship was rare a generation ago, but the practice is becoming more and more common. The U.S. Bureau of the Census has indicated that the number of people cohabiting increased 700 percent between 1960 and 1970 and has more than doubled between 1970 and 1979 (U.S. Bureau of the Census 1979). This group includes individuals in several categories: adolescents, divorced and widowed individuals, people married to someone else but waiting for a divorce, and single, never-married adults. Most of the research on cohabitation involves college students, probably because this population is readily available to researchers at universities.

One study of cohabiting students indicates that most individuals do not look at their relationship as a trial marriage, nor do they definitely plan on later getting married. However, they do feel committed to an exclusive, intimate relationship (Macklin 1972). In fact, a later study indicated that cohabiting students were as committed to remaining monogamous as were engaged couples (Lewis et al. 1977).

A variety of reasons are given for wanting to cohabitate. Certain people desire a more emotionally intimate relationship than is provided by conventional dating, but they wish to avoid marriage. Some couples simply want to continue a sexual relationship under more convenient conditions. In most cases, couples do not consciously plan to cohabitate but simply drift into the relationship. They sleep together increasingly often and then eventually move in together (Cole 1977).

An apparent advantage of cohabitation over marriage is that the couple may not feel the pressure of a binding legal contract. Furthermore, if the relationship eventually proves unsatisfactory, there is less stigma associated with the failure than there is with divorce. Nonetheless, research comparing breakups after cohabitation and after marriage indicates that the resulting emotional traumas are very similar (Yllo 1978).

Certain disadvantages of cohabitation are related to a general lack of acceptance of the arrangement, especially among older people. Parents, landlords, or employers may disapprove, thus putting a strain on the re-

FIGURE 15.2

Cohabitation has become increasingly popular during the past two decades. Most cohabiting couples feel committed to an exclusive, intimate relationship.

lationship. However, cohabitation is generally accepted by college students, even among those who have not lived with an opposite-sex person; more than 70 percent of students surveyed on two campuses approved of cohabitation (Silverman 1977).

In 1979, a landmark court decision helped to establish some of the legal aspects of property and financial rights related to cohabitation. Michelle Triola Marvin filed suit against her former cohabitor, actor Lee Marvin.[1] The court ruled that certain oral and written agreements may be binding. Following this decision—which became known as the *palimony decision*—many cohabiting couples have made legal contracts in an attempt to protect against unfair division of property when or if the relationship breaks up.

Celibacy

Up to this point in the book it has been implied that everyone who is capable has sexual intercourse at one time or another. However, a small minority of individuals choose to abstain completely from coitus. In the case of certain religious leaders—such as Buddhist monks and Roman Catholic priests and nuns—celibacy is required.[2] In other cases, individuals may abstain from sexual intercourse in order to avoid the entanglement of sexual relationships. Sandra Coyner (1976), a feminist, suggests that periods of celibacy may be important for self-exploration and recuperation from some of the struggles of intimate relationships.

Although some people find abstinence to be very difficult, others experience it as satisfying and conducive to good health. There is, in fact, some evidence of health benefits; in a study of 13,000 Canadian nuns, no cases of cancer of the cervix were found (Novak, Jones, & Jones 1975). As we shall see in chapter 22, between 2 and 3 percent of women who engage in coitus develop this type of cancer at some time during their lives.

MARRIAGE

The vast majority of people are married for at least part of their lives. Despite the high divorce rate, many surveys indicate that married people report consistently higher levels of satisfaction with their lives than those who never marry, are widowed, or are divorced (Glenn 1975). (On the other hand, as we have seen, other surveys find single women to be happier than wives.)

There appears to be a close relationship between sexual satisfaction and marital satisfaction in general, particularly for men. This close rela-

FIGURE 15.3

Most people wish to marry at some point in their lives. Generally, married people report higher levels of satisfaction in their lives than those who are single.

tionship is at least partly due to males' relatively high expectations of sexual pleasure associated with marriage.

In contrast, women have traditionally tended to focus their expectations on an emotionally gratifying relationship; for them, sexual fulfillment has generally followed emotional satisfaction (Udry 1968). However, a more recent investigation indicates that sexual gratification is also highly correlated with overall marital satisfaction for women. Of the women who reported satisfaction in their marriages, 80 percent were pleased with their sexual relations; only 14 percent of those who reported dissatisfying marriages rated their sexual lives comparably well (Tavris & Sadd 1977). Of course, the results of this study do not necessarily detract from the role of emotional factors. It is still possible that emotional satisfaction from the marriage preceded the gratifying sexual relationship for the women surveyed. Nonetheless, sexual satisfaction—primarily or secondarily—is clearly an important factor.

Generally speaking, people report satisfaction with marital sex. The *Playboy* questionnaire asked married men and women how they would rate sexual intercourse with their spouses and found that the vast majority rated it as "very pleasurable" or "mostly pleasurable." The ratings given by the men were generally higher than those of the women. For men, satisfaction was highest in the younger age groups and decreased slightly as the men got older. However, for women, satisfaction was highest in the thirty-five to forty-four-year-old group (Hunt 1974). These findings are consistent with the observation reported in chapter 6 that a man's sex drive reaches its peak at a relatively young age, while that of a woman tends to peak in her late thirties or early forties.

The results of the studies of frequency of sexual intercourse tend to be more consistent with the apparent sex drive of the man than that of the woman. In the United States, the average frequency of marital coitus is between two and three times per week when the individuals are in their twenties; the rate slowly declines to about once a week in couples over forty-five (Hunt 1974). However, there is evidence that marital sexual intercourse for all ages increased somewhat during a relatively short period from 1965 to 1970 (Westoff 1974). This increase in the frequency of coitus is consistent with findings of studies that show a reduction in sexual inhibition.

Some studies have focused on the nature of the marital relationship. One compared the satisfaction of marriage partners who shared many activities and interests, and the feelings of couples who were relatively independent of one another. Couples in sharing relationships reported more sexual satisfaction than those in independent relationships. In particular, the wives in independent marriages reported sexual frustration (Rainwater 1965).

Another study examined the effects of a wife's job on sexual satisfaction. The evidence suggests that it is not so much a question of whether or not the wife is working as it is her motivation for holding a job. Women who have a job because they wish to work report a higher frequency of marital intercourse (and presumably sexual satisfaction) than either nonworking wives or wives who work out of economic necessity (Westoff 1974).

Parenthood and Sexual Satisfaction

The arrival of children produces many satisfactions for the majority of husbands and wives. However, research indicates that children do not change an unhappy marriage into a happy one; rather, both the satisfactions and the feelings of obligation of parenthood may function to maintain some unsatisfying marriages (Luckey & Bain 1970).

For some couples, the birth of the first child produces difficulties, particularly if the pregnancy was unplanned. Wives typically experience

FIGURE 15.4

Having children together is often reported as one of the major goals of marriage. However, the arrival of a baby presents many challenges which if not met may reduce sexual satisfaction.

the most stress. They are likely to be concerned about changes in their physical attractiveness, experience fatigue as the result of extra responsibilities, and feel neglected by their husbands because husband-and-wife social activities diminish (Russell 1974; Hobbs & Cole 1976).

It is not surprising, then, that parents questioned shortly after the birth of their first child report less sexual satisfaction on the average than comparable couples without children. There is also less overall satisfaction with the marriage among the new-parent group (Feldman & Feldman 1977).

The arrival of more children does not usually reduce problems related to sexual activity. In fact, one study indicated that the frequency of sexual intercourse is negatively related to the number of children in a family. Contrary to popular belief, the highest rate of coitus occurs in childless couples. It seems the presence of children in the household generally functions as an inhibition to sexual relations (James 1974).

The finding that the presence of children generally reduces sexual activity and gratification should not be interpreted as meaning that parenthood is a negative experience. Most parents report that their role as father or mother is one of the most rewarding of their adult life. Of particular significance are the enjoyment of seeing the children develop, a pride in performing parental roles, and a focus of common interest (Russell 1974). Furthermore, as parents become older, the children typically provide emotional and, in some cases, financial support.

Another factor presumably related to satisfaction in parenthood is knowing that one's bloodline or genetic characteristics will be perpetuated through the children. This factor has been emphasized by sociobiologists who suggest that immortality via one's offspring is a very basic human drive (Wilson 1975).

It is naive, however, to believe that the arrival of children will increase the general quality of a marital relationship. There are a number of pressures and problems associated with parenthood in modern, Western society, particularly as the cost of raising children increases faster than does the typical family income. It seems that family planning and realistic expectations of family pressures—as well as family satisfactions—are of greater importance than ever before.

Author's Perspective: Maintaining a Good Sexual Relationship

The high divorce rate as well as the results of several surveys suggest that it is not easy to maintain a satisfying sexual relationship. One inhibiting factor seems to be poor communication. During periods when communication is good—and there is a sharing of interests and ideas—sexual relationships are generally at their best. In contrast, when there are problems in verbal communication, there are usually problems in sexual communication and sexual satisfaction. In a study of twenty-seven married couples, it was found that frequency of arguments was *negatively* correlated with frequency of coitus (Howard & Dawes 1976).

The results of the survey conducted by *Redbook* magazine also seem to support the relationship between communication in general and sexual satisfaction, particularly for women. The more women talked about sex with their husbands, the better they rated their sex lives (Tavris & Sadd 1977).

Of course, it is difficult to know what is the cause and what is the effect of these situations. However, it seems that there is an interaction: an increase in communication and sharing in nonsexual areas induces more sexual sharing and concern for the partner; as sexual satisfaction increases, more general communication may result. A similar interaction may take place in regard to satisfaction in general; a person who is sexually satisfied is generally more effective in interpersonal relationships on the job than a sexually frustrated person; conversely, a person who has experienced good interpersonal relationships on the job is relatively confident and sensitive in the sexual area.

As suggested in chapter 8, a lack of concern for one's partner may develop if one begins to take the other person for granted. The early stages of a relationship are often marked by excitement and expressions of warmth and appreciation. However, as the relationship continues, couples may get into ruts and fail to express the same positive feelings. My experiences as a marriage counselor indicate that, many times, couples don't tell each other, "I love you," explaining that they were sure the other person knew this. Often, both partners then confess that they would like to hear such expressions more often but never got around to mentioning it.

On the other hand, an unexpected gesture of appreciation may sometimes add sparkle. Care expressed through a special telephone call, a thoughtful gift, or a surprise invitation to a favorite restaurant or other romantic spot often conveys a very meaningful message.

If couples have been together long enough to have aged significantly, it is not unusual for one or both persons to feel they have lost attractiveness or sexual appeal. As we have seen in chapters 9 and 10, physical attractiveness is not a major factor, once a basic relationship has been established. Nonetheless, the *feeling* of being less attractive may lower self-confidence and function as an inhibiting factor. In many cases, exercise programs, diets, or the development of new interests may function to increase self-confidence, and this good feeling—more than actual changes—may have beneficial effects. Furthermore, people almost always like to know that their partners are concerned about being attractive to them.

At one time or another, virtually all couples experience periods when the sexual relationship is frustrating or unsatisfying, and/or there are problems of sexual dysfunction. Some of these difficulties are associated with illness, fatigue, anxiety, or anger. In other cases, it may not be possible to identify a cause. At any rate, a great deal of patience and understanding may be needed. Fortunately, couples who have weathered such crises generally feel that their relationship is stronger than before. In fact, people with happy, long-term marriages often report that working through and surviving crises of various kinds has strengthened their relationship (Reedy 1978).

Since, as we have seen, sexual satisfaction is closely correlated with satisfaction with a relationship in general, several nonsexual factors are important in the maintenance of a good sexual relationship. The partners both have to want to make the relationship work and be willing to make sacrifices at various times. Because perceptions of what is a fifty-fifty split invariably differ (ask any divorce lawyer), it is probably best for each partner to be willing to go more than halfway. Sometimes, just knowing that one's partner is willing to make sacrifices is important in ending an argument or crisis.

Another nonsexual factor related to sexual satisfaction is a respect for the other person's independence. It is unrealistic to think that any other person can meet *all* of one's needs—even though it may appear this way early in the development of a relationship. My counseling experiences indicate a common problem is the feeling of extreme restriction some people associate with their partner. On the other side of the coin, the study of happy, long-term relationships suggests that respect for the other person's point of view and different lifestyle is of major importance (Reedy 1978).

Clearly, fairy-tale endings of falling in love and living happily ever after—without stress or sacrifice—are, indeed, fantasy. Nonetheless, many couples who have lived together more than half their lives say that their relationship was their major source of life satisfaction.

Anthropological Perspective: Sex and Marriage in Non-Western Societies

In most Western societies, having more than one spouse at a time is illegal. However, taking a large number of independent societies into consideration, *polygamy* is the general rule. As a matter of fact, out of 849 human societies surveyed, 84 percent included polygamous marriages, at least for individuals who were wealthy enough to afford several spouses (Murdock 1967). There are three types of polygamy: *polygyny* (one man with more than one wife), *polyandry* (one woman with more than one husband), and *polygynandry* (two or more men living with two or more women, with all the men considered married to all the women).

One man married to two or more wives is by far the most common type of polygamous arrangement. Generally, the wives do not have equal status: the first wife is of highest rank and the other wives share secondary roles within the family. In a few cases of polygynous relationships, the man has one legal wife but a number of concubines who are only loosely attached to the family (Ford & Beach 1951). It may seem that there would be jealousies and conflicts between wives. However, among the Ibo of Nigeria, a sole wife is often lonely and reports feelings of humiliation; the husband is often encouraged to take on more wives (Egboh 1972).

There are relatively few data on the sexual behavior of individuals in polygynous societies. However, the Chagga men of East Africa have been reported to display a high level of sexual activity: an individual may have intercourse with each of three or four wives during the night (Ford & Beach 1951).

Obviously, not all men in a polygynous society can take on multiple wives: the number of women available soon would be exhausted. Polygyny is generally a privilege of the wealthy and, indirectly, functions to distribute some of the wealth via the offspring.

In contrast to polygyny, families of one woman with several husbands are very rare: less than 1 percent of the 849 societies surveyed are polyandrous (Murdock 1967). In one of these societies—the Tre-ba of Tibet—polyandry has a function opposite that of polygyny: the elite class keeps its wealth within the family. Sons may take on a common wife and remain in a single household. Although the men reportedly do not like to share a wife, they prefer such an arrangement to partitioning the land, and, in the process, meeting large tax obligations. Other classes of Tibetans, lacking such property, are almost exclusively monogamous (M. C. Goldstein 1971, 1976).

In a few societies, a married woman who takes on a lover is condoned. However, once again economics and politics seem to be important factors. Among the Birom of northern Nigeria, marriage is arranged, but the woman chooses one or more lovers. Each lover pays the husband for the right to visit his wife. Furthermore, the lover and husband are deemed allies. Thus, a man with an attractive wife or wives may gain considerable economic and political power (Smedley 1976).

Polygynandry is the rarest form of polygamy. In fact, in only one known society—the Pahari of north India—is this arrangement the practice of the majority. Brothers typically buy a series of wives, one at a time, and the group lives in a common household. The arrangement reportedly produces satisfaction for both the males and females and is preferred to other types of marriages (Berreman 1962).

EXTRAMARITAL SEXUAL RELATIONSHIPS

Sexual intercourse with someone other than the spouse is apparently more frequent among men than women. According to the Kinsey report, approximately 50 percent of males had experienced extramarital coitus compared to 25 percent of females by the time the two groups reached forty. However, certain changes appear to have taken place since that time. The percentages reported have remained about the same for men but have increased for women. The more recent *Redbook* survey indicates that about 40 percent of the women have had extramarital intercourse. This increase seems to be most pronounced among young women (Kinsey et al. 1953; Hunt 1974; Tavris & Sadd 1977). It appears likely that, if this trend continues, there soon will be little or no sex difference in the rate of extramarital coitus.

Despite the rather high incidence of extramarital sex, most Americans have negative attitudes about the practice. Seventy-two percent of people surveyed indicated that extramarital sex is "always wrong," while another 14 percent regarded it as "almost always" wrong (Levitt & Klassen 1973). Apparently, there is a discrepancy between many individuals' sexual attitudes and their sexual practice, at least in regard to extramarital sex.

There are some differences in extramarital activity related to age. For males, the frequency of extramarital coitus decreases with age. However, for females, the frequency tends to increase with age, at least up to age forty (Harper 1961). Once again, these sex differences seem to reflect differences in the peaking of the sex drive, which is earlier for men than for women.

Another factor related to the frequency of extramarital intercourse is employment of the wife. The Redbook survey indicated that wives with full-time jobs were more likely to have extramarital affairs than housewives (Tavris & Sadd 1977). In this case, the chance to meet a variety of men not known by the husband—under relatively unrestricted conditions—is probably a factor of importance.

Some surveys have inquired into the reasons why a sizable number of people have avoided extramarital sex, despite its apparent availability. The most common reason given was that it is a betrayal of trust in the love relationship. Another frequent response is that extramarital sex hurts the spouse or damages the relationship. Furthermore, some people feel that the probable rewards of extramarital sex are not worth the investment of time, money, and attention (Hunt 1974; Sprey 1972).

On the other side of the fence, people become involved in extramarital affairs for a variety of reasons. In some cases, a deprivation of sexual activity resulting from lengthy separations, illness, or sexual dysfunction is a factor. In other cases, marital sex may be unsatisfactory; the extramarital affair represents an attempt to compensate for what is missing in the marriage. For still others, extramarital involvements are an attempt to satisfy curiosity, find excitement, or gain enrichment of some kind. Finally, an affair may represent an attempt to punish the spouse—perhaps for loneliness or lack of appreciation—or even to flout societal standards (Greene, Lee, & Lustig 1974). In most cases, extramarital affairs seem to be stimulated by a combination of factors, many of which are not understood by the individual at the time of the involvement.

Despite the fairly high incidence of extramarital sex, the Playboy survey found that this activity is generally less satisfying than marital sex. For example, more than half of wives sampled by Playboy reported reaching orgasm "almost always" with their husbands, but only 39 percent did so in extramarital affairs. Similarly, two-thirds of husbands reported marital intercourse as "very pleasurable," but less than half the men who had experienced extramarital affairs gave this high a rating to extramarital coitus (Hunt 1974). The relatively low satisfaction in extramarital coitus is probably related, in many instances, to fear and guilt. Furthermore—as in the case of acting out a sexual fantasy—the reality of an affair may be disappointing in comparison to the expectations.

Surreptitious Extramarital Sex

In most cases, extramarital affairs are carried on—or at least attempted—in secret. There are a variety of social environments that are conducive to such extramarital liaisons. Bars are one of the most common meeting places. A study of bars and cocktail lounges indicated that encounters most frequently involve married men and single or divorced women. Usually, the encounters do not develop into long-term relationships since one or both of the partners wish to avoid emotional involvement (Roebuck & Spray 1967).

Another common place for transient extramarital sex is at a convention. Since conventions are usually out of town, there is a reduced chance of discovery. There is also a relatively small probability that long-lasting emotional commitments will be the result.

Longer-lasting affairs tend to develop among people who work together. However, the sexual activity is often rushed, limited by the work schedules and time expected home. Perhaps the time pressures experi-

FIGURE 15.5

Bars and cocktail lounges are commonly used as meeting places for singles and also for extramarital liaisons. Despite strong cultural mores against extramarital sex, it is fairly common in our society.

enced by the couples help to account for their generally reduced satisfaction with extramarital sex (Hunt 1974; Roy 1974).

Author's Perspective: Reactions to the Discovery of a Spouse's Affair

A wide variety of reactions may follow the discovery of a spouse's affair. Much of the following material is taken from my own experience as a marriage counselor and from a published report by a group of marriage counselors (Mead et al. 1975).

Among the most common feelings expressed by a spouse after such a discovery are anger and a sense of being deceived and betrayed. In addition, the affair is often seen as a symbolic insult to the spouse's affection and sexual adequacy. Certain subcultures consider it appropriate to seek some type of revenge or retribution.

In many cases, discovery of an extramarital affair leads to divorce proceedings. One study indicates that extramarital affairs are the major issue of contention in couples seeking divorce (Weiss 1975). Of course, it is not known for how many couples extramarital affairs were the source of the discord and for how many they were the result. It is likely that sex outside of marriage is used as an excuse to dissolve some otherwise unhappy marriages.

Generally speaking, isolated sexual experiences are less disturbing to spouses than prolonged extramarital affairs. Brief sexual encounters can sometimes be written off as temporary reactions to sexual frustrations; however, longer affairs are seen as greater threats to the marital love relationship.

The discovery of an extramarital affair does not always destroy a marriage. The spouse may have suspected or known that there was something wrong with the marriage. Bringing the affair to light can stimulate a couple to deal with certain basic interpersonal problems—nonsexual as well as sexual. It is possible that the result will ultimately be a relationship built on a firmer foundation.

Some people seem to accept their spouse's affairs without showing much response. Among the reasons no action is taken is that divorce tends to be very expensive and socially degrading, especially among the affluent. Instead, the marriages may become devoid of emotional attachment and more like alliances of convenience (Cuber & Harroff 1965).

Finally, as will be seen in the next section, a few couples decide to enter into consensual extramarital relationships after the discovery that one or both of the partners has had or is having an extramarital affair. Such a choice is seen by them as preferable to divorce.

Consensual Extramarital Sex

A relatively small number of couples have marital arrangements that permit—and may even encourage—extramarital sexual relations. One type of arrangement has been described as *group marriage*. Some members of group marriages are never-married or divorced individuals. However, a number of couples in the group may be legally married. The group may be a commune that is quite large, but it usually consists of three or four people. Although sexual intimacy takes place among all members of the group, the primary reasons given for group marriages are usually nonsexual. Group members commonly rank such rewards as intimacy, a sense of attachment, and commitment as being most important (Ramey 1976).

The term *open marriage* was coined by a couple—George and Nena O'Neill—to describe an arrangement that included freedom to pursue extramarital relationships. The O'Neills believed that it was difficult or impossible for one partner to satisfy all the needs—social and sexual—of the other. If jealousies could be overcome, an open marriage was presumed to be enriching (O'Neill & O'Neill 1972); however, interviews with seventy-one people who were involved in an open marriage—or who had become separated after attempting such an arrangement—indicated a variety of reactions. Most of the separated or divorced couples were pessimistic about open marriages and subsequently chose monogamous relationships. (Incidentally, the O'Neills are now divorced and presumably less enthusiastic about their "open" relationship.) In some cases, couples believed that the experience of an open marriage was a growth experience, after which they moved to a more committed relationship. In virtually all the cases, whether the relationship was perceived as successful or not, the couples felt it was destructive to talk to their spouses in detail about their outside affairs (Watson 1981).

Swinging or *mate swapping* is another type of extramarital arrangement, one that encourages sexual activities with a large variety of partners. Most swingers try to avoid emotional involvement with their temporary partners. It is generally felt that too much involvement will create problems within the marriage (Gilmartin 1975).

A considerable amount of data on swinging were gathered by Gilbert Bartell (1970), using the participant-observer technique. Swinging couples typically make contact with other interested individuals at bars or at clubs organized for the purpose of arranging exchanges. In some cases, advertisements are placed in papers or magazines sympathetic to the swinging philosophy. Generally, these ads are not very accurate, overemphasizing the positive physical attributes of the couples and underestimating ages.

Several types of swinging affairs are described by Bartell. In the simple closed arrangement, two couples meet and exchange partners, each new couple retiring to a separate place in order to have sexual relations. In the simple open condition, the couples spend at least part of the time having sex in the same room, with various combinations of partners. Swinging parties or complex swinging arrangements also take place. At some of these, nudity is permitted anywhere in the house, and large numbers of people participate in group sexual activities.

Swinging is usually initiated by husbands; wives tend to react to the idea with revulsion and resistance. However, once initiated, some women report enthusiasm for the affairs. Since the male's sexual capacities are limited compared to the female's, the men are often very tired by the end of a swinging party. However, women frequently remain active and may end the evening with homosexual activities. In fact, 65 percent of the women interviewed by Bartell reported that they preferred the homosexual encounters to heterosexual ones (Bartell 1970).

How do swinging couples compare with those involved in a traditional marriage? Most swingers report that their parents' marriages were unhappy and ended in divorce. Compared to nonswingers, a high percentage of swingers reported unhappy childhoods and a high sex drive. Both male and female swingers reported earlier dating and premarital intercourse than a comparable group of nonswingers (Gilmartin 1977).

It is difficult to tell how many couples are swingers. However, the *Playboy* survey in the early 1970s led to estimates that between 1 and 5 percent of married couples had been involved in at least some swinging affairs. Later reports indicate that the incidence of swinging is on the decline (MacNamara & Sagarin 1977).

Psychological Perspective: Personality Characteristics of Swingers

Most people seem to have preconceived notions of what swingers are like; they are conceptualized as exciting, dynamic people, full of life and adventure. However, the Bartell study indicated that individuals who engage in swinging have relatively few outside interests or hobbies; they spend a large amount of time watching television. Furthermore, they tend to be politically conservative. The swinging events—which typically take place once every other week—seem to represent the main focus of excitement in an otherwise somewhat boring way of life (Bartell 1970).

Another image of swingers is that they are very different from other married persons in terms of their emotional stability and the value they place on their marriages. A study indicates that this image is also a myth. Swingers are similar, on the average, to conventionally married persons in regard to emotional health. Furthermore, there are no significant differences between swingers and nonswingers in regard to marital happiness (Gilmartin & Kusisto 1973).

Comparative Perspective: The Coolidge Effect

Some men in swinging groups report greater potency with a variety of sexual partners than with a single partner (Denfield & Gordon 1970). However, there are obvious problems associated with conducting controlled experiments on this multiple-partner effect. Fortunately, of course, animal experiments can be conducted without fear of such ethical problems. In experiments involving bulls and cows, a definite multiple-partner effect has been demonstrated. An average bull will copulate with a cow about ten times, resting for increasing periods of time between copulations and finally exhibiting signs of exhaustion.

However, if different cows are presented to the bull, he may have up to seventy ejaculations in a twenty-four-hour period (Maier & Maier 1970). This multiple-partner effect has been termed the *Coolidge effect* because President Calvin Coolidge is said to have made a remark about the unusually high potency of roosters in the presence of many hens (Bermant & Davidson 1974).

The reasons for a Coolidge effect are not clear from the experiment. However, at least part of the effect may be related to novelty or need for variability. In another experiment, bulls that had become sexually satiated with a cow showed renewed vigor when the cow was moved to a new stall or even a distance of only a few feet (Almquist & Hale 1956). A similar novelty effect has been demonstrated in rats. A sexually exhausted male's interest in a female was rejuvenated when researchers provided a discolike atmosphere with flashing lights and intermittent tones (Peters 1980).

It seems that male animals, such as bulls, that in the wild keep a harem of females benefit biologically from the Coolidge effect; they can produce more offspring. However, there is no indication that females produce more offspring if they mate with a variety of males. And in fact, there is little or no evidence of a Coolidge effect in female animals (Daly & Wilson 1983).

What can be concluded in regard to humans? First, the presumed increase in potency of men with multiple sex partners may be, as in the case of bulls, partly a response to novelty. The very high rate of sexual intercourse right after marriage—particularly if the couple did not previously have intercourse—is probably also related to novelty (James 1981). Second, the Coolidge effect—if, indeed, there is one in humans—may be partially related to cues given by the women. Studies with animals indicate that at least part of the increased mating of the males is stimulated by the high level of receptivity of the new females. Nonetheless, it has been found that many mammals do not exhibit a Coolidge effect. Thus, there does not seem to be a strong evolutionary link between the Coolidge effect in animals and increased sexual potency with multiple partners in humans (Dewsbury 1981).

DIVORCE

It has been estimated that close to 50 percent of marriages contracted in the 1980s will end in divorce, with an even higher divorce rate among individuals in a second or third marriage (Nass, Libby, & Fisher 1981). Whether the breakup is rapid, or slow and drawn out, a very difficult emotional trauma typically follows. Napolitani and Pellegrino (1977) have described a series of stages that are often experienced. Shortly after a divorce—or during the period when a separation is being considered—individuals go through a stage known as "active bleeding." Persons in this stage tend to see themselves as failures, constantly relive the relationship and think about how it might have been saved, and feel jealous of people who seem to have good marriages. "Running" is another stage common to divorced persons. They feel compelled to get out more than usual and be around large groups of people. They have difficulty concentrating and often become exhausted and physically run-down. In some cases, newly-divorced persons run from their troubles through an all-work, no-play attitude. Usually, these unpleasant stages are interrupted by periods of euphoria. There may be feelings that everything is rosy, that others are too pessimistic, and that nothing is worth worrying about. However, the euphoria is typically short-lived.

Napolitani and Pellegrino believe that it is natural and, in most cases, necessary to go through these various stages before one can get to a point where the divorce is accepted and personal growth can occur. Since friends and family may have difficulty understanding and accepting a person's diverse reactions to divorce, many counselors recommend psychotherapy or emotional-support groups made up of other divorced persons.

In some cases, the divorce—and working through reactions to it—have resulted in positive personal growth. Individuals may feel that they know themselves better and understand more about what they find satisfying in a relationship. In fact, research indicates that second marriages are reported at least as satisfying as marriages in general and, as one might expect, more satisfying than the first marriage (Bernard 1968).

Predicting Divorce

Two psychologists, Bentler and Newcomb (1977), tested and interviewed a group of 162 newly married couples and then, four years later, followed up to see if they were still married. At the end of the period, 77 couples were located. Of these, 53 were still married, and 24 were divorced. One of the variables found to be important in the durability of the relationship was similarity of the partners. (It will be remembered that similarity was also found to be important in initial attraction.) Specifically, more similar values were placed on attractiveness and outgoingness by the married than the divorced group.

Certain factors in the individuals' backgrounds were also found to be predictors. Parental divorces were more common for the divorced than for the married group. The parental-divorce factor was significant for both males and females.

Perhaps of equal interest is a consideration of some of the factors that did not make a difference. Whether or not the individuals had a liberated or a traditional sex-role orientation was not related to marital longevity. The compatibility of a couple's attitudes about sex roles was probably more important than whether they were liberated or traditional. Another factor that failed to be significant was whether or not the couple cohabited before marriage.

It should be kept in mind that none of the variables by themselves are strong predictors; only when several are taken together is it possible to make very accurate forecasts. It should also be remembered that the criterion used in this study—remaining married—may not be the best measure of a successful marriage. It seems likely that some of the couples who stayed together would not necessarily rate their relationship a success.

Sex following Divorce

Most divorced men have an active sex life. In fact, when matched for age, previously married men have a slightly higher frequency of intercourse than married men. Divorced men also have a relatively large variety of partners, averaging around eight per year (Hunt 1974).

In women, the incidence of postmarital sex is somewhat lower. However, 90 percent of divorced women return to an active sex life. The active number of partners is approximately half that of divorced men. Generally speaking, sexual relationships are perceived as satisfying. The *Playboy* survey indicates that the majority of women report a higher frequency of orgasm than they experienced in marital sex (Hunt 1974). This comparison should not be taken to mean that sex among the divorced is generally more satisfying than sex among the married. Results of other studies indicate that satisfaction with the sexual relationship is low among individuals with marital problems; therefore, people who eventually get divorced would be expected to give relatively low ratings of marital coitus.

It appears that divorced people—both men and women—have more liberal views on sexuality than their counterparts several years earlier. Divorced individuals are more likely to enter into new sexual relationships, exhibit more spontaneity in their sexual adventures, and are less concerned about hiding their activities from their children than were divorced people a generation ago (Hunt & Hunt 1977).

WIDOWHOOD

The emotional traumas experienced after the death of a spouse appear to be similar in some respects to those of a divorced person. In other respects, the stages of adjustment resemble those reported by terminally ill patients after they have been informed of their impending death (Kubler-Ross 1969). Recent research indicates that widowhood is, in some respects, more traumatic for men than for women. Mortality rates are higher for widowed men than for a comparable group of married men. However, there is no significant difference in mortality for widowed and married women. At least part of the difference seems to be related to the relatively great stress experienced by single men; widowed men who remarry have a much lower death rate than those who do not (Helsing & Szklo 1981).

The initial reactions to widowhood are typically denial and anger. These reactions tend to be more prolonged if the death is sudden than if it followed a long illness. Apparently, some psychological preparation takes place during the period of illness.

Most young widows and widowers wear their wedding rings for a time after the death of their spouses. The removal of the ring is often symbolic of the final acceptance of the death and a desire to begin a new life, including dating relationships. Typically, it takes about a year for widows to complete the basic mourning process. During this period, each significant date—birthdays, wedding anniversary, Christmas, the anniversary of the death—brings its own occasion for reliving grief. Widowers, on the other hand, are usually ready to date again after a shorter period of time, for reasons that will be discussed shortly.

Starting to date again generally evokes considerable anxiety. For most people, the dating customs have changed since the last time they dated. Furthermore, there is often considerable guilt associated with starting a new relationship. Guilt and anxiety are particularly strong if or when sexual relations are resumed. In many cases, there are fantasies of the spouse's presence.

Fortunately, emotional-support groups seem to be very helpful for some people during the difficult adjustment following widowhood. Sharing experiences and feelings with caring and understanding people not only reduces the pain but appears to shorten the period of grieving.[3]

For widowers, entering into a new sexual relationship appears to be more common than it is for widows. Around 90 percent of widowers are sexually active. However, less than half of widows reportedly have sexual relationships (Gebhard 1968).

There are probably a number of reasons for these sex differences. First, it seems to be generally easier for males to rapidly enter into sexual relationships. According to the traditional sex roles, males may have sexual intercourse with less emotional commitment than that required of females. In addition, widows tend to have more emotional support from family and friends than widowers; consequently, they may be less inclined to start new relationships in general. Finally, widows are more likely to believe that they should be true to their deceased spouses; sex following widowhood is likely to be perceived as disloyalty, not only by the widow, but also by the family. Such perceptions are less common in widowers and their families.

SUMMARY

Among never-married adults, women are generally more satisfied and show better psychological adjustment than men. A generation ago, cohabitation was rare, but it has become increasingly common in the past several years. Among the reasons given by couples for wanting to cohabit are desire for emotional intimacy—without the long-term commitment of marriage—and sexual interaction under convenient circumstances. Despite the lack of a legal contract, the breakup of a cohabiting relationship is very traumatic for most couples.

Celibacy is practiced by a small minority. There is no evidence that sexual abstinence is adverse to one's health.

Most individuals are married for at least part of their lives, and surveys indicate that marriage is rated as more satisfactory, on the average, than the singles life-style. There is a close relationship between a person's sexual satisfaction and satisfaction with the marriage in general.

Several variables are related to sexual satisfaction with a marriage. Couples who describe their relationship as "sharing" report greater satisfaction than "independent" couples. One of the most important factors in satisfaction appears to be communication.

Extramarital sexual relationships are more common in males than females, but in recent years the gap has been closing. Generally, extramarital sex is reported as less satisfying than marital sex, probably due to fear and guilt. Most extramarital affairs are surreptitious, but some partners agree to an "open" marriage that allows sexual freedom.

Swinging, or mate swapping, is an arrangement that encourages extramarital relationships for both partners. Studies of the personalities of swingers suggest that they are a relatively conservative group in regard to political philosophy and rather conventional in terms of emotional stability and the value they place on their marriages.

From a cross-cultural perspective, polygamy is common, especially in preliterate societies. Polygyny (one man married to two or more wives) is much more prevalent than polyandry (one woman married to two or more men). Among monogamous societies, there are considerable differences in regard to extramarital sexual relationships.

Divorced persons are becoming a more significant part of the singles population as the divorce rate continues to rise. In some cases, the trauma of divorce may result in personal growth. It is possible to generalize—but only to a very limited extent—about what factors in a marriage are likely to lead to a divorce.

Becoming a widow or widower is a very traumatic experience, especially if the death of a spouse is sudden or unexpected. A study of mortality rates following widowhood indicates that widows make a better psychological or emotional adjustment than widowers.

Most men enter into a new sexual relationship following either divorce or widowhood. However, fewer women have sexual relationships after their marriage ends, and this is especially true for widows. Family pressures and traditions apparently account for these sex differences.

NOTES

1. Michelle legally changed her last name to Marvin, although she never married Lee.
2. One religious group, the Shakers, required celibacy for all members of the church. Predictably, within a generation or two, the group died out.
3. Much of the material on widowhood is taken from discussions with Patricia Martin, founder of one of the first support groups for young widows.

CHAPTER 16

Developments following Maturity

As individuals pass through their adult years, sexual feelings and expression continue to change. However, sexuality is never really lost. The two groups of people considered in this chapter—older adults and those who are handicapped—are clearly different in many respects. Nonetheless, they are similar in the sense that they must adjust to physical changes that modify the expression of their sexuality. Furthermore, society tends to underestimate or misunderstand the sexual needs of both. An increased understanding of sexuality in the elderly and handicapped may not only reduce such biases but increase appreciation of the variety of ways in which sexuality may be expressed.

ADVANCING AGE

In movies and on television, romance and passion are often depicted in young persons, while older individuals are rarely shown as sexually aroused except for comic effect. This distorted portrayal of older people is similar to college students' perceptions of sexuality in their parents. When students were asked to estimate how often their parents engaged in intercourse, the figures were very low. In fact, the mean estimates of frequency were approximately half those found by Kinsey and his associates for comparable age groups. Furthermore, the students generally saw their parents' happiness in marriage as having little to do with sex (Pocs & Godow 1977). As we shall see, the perception of older persons as sexless is as inaccurate as the pre-Freudian notion that children are asexual. In this section physical changes with aging will be discussed first, followed by a consideration of the interaction between physical and psychological factors.

The Climacteric and Menopause

The period in a woman's life during which she slowly loses reproductive potential and finally becomes incapable of pregnancy is known as

FIGURE 16.1

Sexual activity in older people is sometimes considered ludicrous and its importance and frequency are underestimated by the younger generations. In some cases, this societal attitude produces sex guilt and brings a premature end to sexual activity in senior citizens. However, even when sexual intercourse no longer takes place regularly, satisfaction associated with caressing and other expressions of emotional intimacy remains high and may even increase.

the *climacteric*. This transition period lasts about fifteen years—from approximately forty-five to sixty. The most noticeable process during this time is *menopause:* the cessation of menstruation.

Menopause is ushered in by several changes. As the ovaries age, they become less responsive to the pituitary hormones FSH and LH. This lack of responsiveness results in a chain of events. Fewer eggs mature and are released. Consequently, there is less output of progesterone (it will be remembered that progesterone is produced by the corpus luteum following the release of the egg). The lower level of progesterone results in less output of estrogen (it will also be remembered that progesterone stimulates estrogen production). Since progesterone and estrogen normally inhibit the secretion of FSH and LH, there is less inhibition, and greater quantities of FSH and LH are secreted. To put matters simply, menopause is marked by a general hormonal imbalance.

In addition, there are changes in organs receptive to estrogen. Recent evidence indicates that these organs start to lose responsiveness to estrogen several years before the onset of menopause (Eskin 1980). Thus, the events of the climacteric reflect not only hormonal changes—especially reduced output of estrogen—but also reduced sensitivity to critical hormones.

The symptoms of menopause vary from woman to woman. The most common complaints are headaches, dizziness, heart palpitations, and "hot flashes." Hot flashes are sudden waves of heat from the waist up, usually accompanied by perspiration and followed by chills. About 80 percent of the women in one survey reported hot flashes during menopause. For some reason, the more hot flashes a woman reported, the less likely she was to have other menopausal symptoms (Bates 1981).

Psychological problems are also fairly common during menopause. These include depression, irritability, anxiety, and feelings of suffocation. One study found differences in the way certain groups of women responded to menopause. Women who strongly identified with the mother role suffered more depression than women who were more closely identified with their careers outside the home (Bart 1971). Apparently, in some women, part of the stress of menopause is tied in with the "empty nest" syndrome: the departure of children from the home and inability to have more offspring.

Estrogen replacement therapy has been reasonably successful in treating both the physical and psychological symptoms of menopause. However, since there is evidence that the end-organ response is significant in menopause—and that psychological factors are important in some women's reactions—it is not surprising that hormone treatment by itself is sometimes ineffective (Bardwick 1971). There is also evidence that estrogen-replacement therapy is linked to cancer. Women undergoing this type of treatment were much more likely to develop cancer of the endometrium than a control group of women not taking estrogen. The risks appear greatest among women receiving estrogen over long periods (Antunes et al. 1979). Because of these findings, some physicians stress nonhormonal treatment of the symptoms of menopause, including physical exercises and good nutrition, both found to have significant, positive effects (Seaman & Seaman, 1978).

Males undergo changes that are similar in some respects to female menopause. The production of sperm and androgen shows a gradual decline during the period from forty-five to sixty. A fairly common problem apparently related to the hormonal shift is an enlargement of the prostate, resulting in some urinary problems. Removal of part of the gland by surgery is generally successful in relieving pressure against the urethra and alleviating the symptoms.

There may also be psychological problems for middle-aged men. These are related to a variety of factors, including anxiety about virility, a career crisis, and problems associated with a wife who is going through menopause. In certain cases, physicians recommend androgen shots for middle-aged men who are tired and/or depressed; some success has been reported.

Other Physical Changes

A number of other physical and physiological changes are related to a general decline in sexual activity in later years. These changes take place slowly, and there are large individual differences in when and how fast they develop. In both sexes, the time necessary to reach orgasm is increased and the duration of orgasm is decreased. However, the experience of orgasm is reported to be as pleasurable as ever (Silny 1980).

Many changes are sex specific. In women, there is less fatty tissue around the vulva, a thinning of the vaginal walls, a shrinking in the width and length of the vagina, a constriction at the entrance of the vagina, and a reduction in the amount of vaginal lubrication. However, regular sexual intercourse tends to minimize the physical problems associated with these changes.

In men, the testes become more flaccid, and the prostate gland grows larger while its contractions become weaker. These prostate changes are related to a decrease in the volume of semen and the force of ejaculation. Moreover, erections develop more slowly and occur less frequently. Although these changes may seem depressing, certain advantages also come with age. Older men have better control of ejaculation, so that they can prolong the duration of intercourse.

Sexual Activity

As we have noted, there is a steady decline in sexual drive of males from young adulthood to old age. However, within each age group there is considerable variability in the frequency of intercourse. This is particularly true of older age groups. For example, in a sample of men over seventy, most individuals said that they no longer engaged in sexual intercourse. Nonetheless, 4 percent reported coitus at least twice a week. Thus, a few of the men approximated the potency of men half their age (Rubin 1965).

Obviously, physical health is a major variable in sexual expression; periods of abstinence are common following illness or trauma. However, once reasonably good health has returned, it may be difficult to regain normal sexual functioning. In women, periods of abstinence typically result in some shrinkage of the vagina and a longer time required to reach plateau levels of arousal; men have more difficulty reaching and maintaining erection (Masters & Johnson 1966). Moreover, difficulties in regaining normal functioning may lead to anxieties that make coitus even more difficult; as a result, one or both partners may give up their quest to regain sexual functioning. Problems associated with the illness may be gone, but people may be convinced that they are "washed up" and, in essence, play out a self-fulfilling prophecy (Burnside 1975). Since our society generally believes that sexuality is lost in old age, the tendency to stop trying is reinforced. One study indicates that, after a period of sexual inactivity, only 14 percent of older couples returned to coitus (Pfeiffer et al. 1968).

Another source of difficulty may lie in the couple's relationship with their physician. Many doctors refrain from discussing sex with older patients, partly because they perceive the elderly as asexual and partly because, like most people, physicians have difficulty discussing sex with older individuals. More serious problems may result from mistakes by surgeons who, in some cases, have needlessly severed nerves essential for sexual functioning. Apparently, the surgeons had mistakenly assumed that their patients were no longer sexually functional (Rubin 1965).

Frequency of sexual activity among the elderly may be affected by the common view that sex in older persons is perverse or ridiculous. This belief may trigger sex anxiety or a fear that being sexual is "abnormal" for them. Negative attitudes toward sexual behavior in senior citizens may be related to the association between sex and reproduction: many people believe that once reproductive potential has passed (especially in women), sexual interest should drop markedly. However, as we have seen in previous chapters, an important characteristic of human sexual behavior and interest is that they are not strictly tied to reproduction.

Sexual activity, of course, refers to more than coitus. One of the most encouraging findings in regard to sexuality in old age is that appreciation of caressing and physical closeness seems to increase with age. Interviews with married couples indicate that caressing is more prevalent in older couples (over fifty-seven) than in younger ones, especially those in their early twenties. A factor of particular significance is that the older men seem to be the most sensitive; they tend to score higher on a "caressing scale" than the younger men (Foster 1979).

Unfortunately, there is a general scarcity of older men in our society. Since women generally live longer—and marry older men—the number of widows is particularly large; 70 percent of the women over seventy-five are widowed. Furthermore, healthy and financially successful older men tend to court younger women, so the number of potential marriage partners for older women is low. And strong societal norms prohibit sexual relations outside of marriage for these women (Rubin 1965). The family, and particularly the children, are usually instrumental in discouraging sexual involvement outside of marriage. It is somewhat ironic that this inhibition by the children represents a kind of reversal. The same children who were sexually inhibited as adolescents by their parents may turn the tables as adults and inhibit their widowed parent.

For older people living in nursing homes and some retirement centers, the general atmosphere tends to be even more sexually repressive. In many settings, patients are not given the courtesy of a knock before someone enters the room. Furthermore, couples are generally prevented from getting together in situations where sexual activity might occur. In certain cases, not even married couples are allowed privacy (White 1982).

Individuals involved in sex education have proposed that lectures and discussions about sexuality may help to counteract sexual repression and ultraconservatism among the aged. Following two-week sex-education sessions, more than 50 percent of older couples participating reported that their sex lives improved. Since senior citizens were born and raised in an era when sex was not discussed, they may have many misconceptions about sexuality in general and sex roles in particular (Rowland & Haynes 1978).

Love in the Aging

If couples stay together, they report high levels of satisfaction with their relationship during their later years. Marital satisfaction is found to be highest among newlyweds, to drop somewhat during the years when children are young, to reach a low point just before teenage children leave home, and to rise again after the children are gone. It appears that once the partners are alone again they have more time for each other and less responsibility; these factors often lead to a better relationship (Rollins & Feldman 1970).

In another study, an attempt was made to investigate more specifically the factors related to a good love relationship in older couples. Thirty-four couples with an average age of sixty-five were recommended by friends and associates as having a good love relationship; the couples then gave written answers to questions about their relationship (Reedy 1978).

Five factors were found to be particularly important. At the top of the list was emotional security: being able to depend upon and trust one another was of primary concern. Respect was rated second most important. Third was the ability to communicate and be honest with one another. The fourth-ranking factor was spending time together in both work and play. Finally, sexual intimacy was the fifth dimension of importance. Obviously, there are interactions between these factors. For example, when communication is good, there is more satisfaction in spending time together; when sexual satisfaction is high, there is apt to be more emotional security; when there is mutual respect, honesty in the relationship tends to be high.

There is considerable similarity between marital happiness in young adult years and in old age: the five factors are ranked in the same order of importance by both young couples and older ones. However, emotional security seems to take on even more importance for older couples. Furthermore, when asked how their love relationship has changed since

FIGURE 16.2

Couples who have been together for many years often report a mellowing in their relationship. Although the extreme passion tends to dissipate, satisfaction with sharing, warmth, and closeness remains high or may even increase.

they first met, the older couples suggest that the relationship has become closer and deeper; they say that life experiences—both good and bad—have drawn them together. Greater tolerance for one another is another factor reported by the older couples. Finally, many of the couples talked about a mellowing of love: although extreme passion may have dissipated, tenderness, affection, and warmth have increased (Reedy 1978).

Comparative Perspective: Sex in Older Animals

We have already seen how the potency of rams is affected by the presence of other males. In rats, competition rejuvenates old males that have not responded to females in estrus during several mating tests. When younger males are introduced—presumably offering competition—the older males copulate with youthlike vigor (Larsson 1958).

In another laboratory, a different type of rejuvenation was demonstrated in old male rats. Degeneration of the testes, penis, and accessory sex glands normally associated with advancing age was reduced when the males were allowed to cohabit and have sexual relations with females. Most surprising of all, the old males that associated with females lived longer than "bachelor" males. Possibly, copulation stimulated the secretion of androgen, and the presence of this hormone contributed to the maintenance of the reproductive system and the enhancement of general health (Driori & Folman 1964).

So far, there is no evidence that coitus is directly related to long life in humans. However, as we have seen, an active sex life may provide beneficial exercise and facilitate positive interpersonal attitudes in some older people (Hellerstein & Friedman 1969).

Author's Perspective: Aging, Sexual Attitudes, and Sexual Functioning

Reduced sexual drive and/or temporary loss of potency in aging individuals may have a variety of causes, as we have seen. Such declines may come at the same time one is moving towards retirement or trying to adjust to children leaving the home and becoming more independent. The net result is often a drop in self-esteem and feelings of adequacy—a decline that may further contribute to sexual problems. Unfortunately, children and other younger persons who may normally provide emotional support are reluctant to talk about sex—and so are many an older couple's contemporaries, who grew up with Victorian standards. Thus, older individuals with problems or anxieties related to sexuality often feel lonely and isolated.

Children and friends may help by being sensitive to these feelings and by encouraging older people to dress up or participate in social events. Especially important are activities that contribute to a sense of self-improvement— intellectual, artistic, or physical. The feeling of progressing in some way is closely related to feeling good about oneself. I have a friend over sixty-five who is an excellent tennis player and consistently beats players one-third his age in tournaments. Most significant is the fact that he is constantly focusing on improving his game—rather than reflecting on how well he used to play. As you might predict, women of several different age groups find this man interesting and attractive.

Studies consistently indicate that attitudes about oneself and sexuality in general are of major importance in maintaining an active and satisfying sex life. In one study, these psychological factors were better predictors of an active sex life in old age than were physical ones (Pfeiffer & Davis 1972). Even in very old persons who are unable to engage in sexual intercourse, sexual feelings are present. In a survey of people over eighty, 22 percent reported continued sexual desire (Rubin 1965). Finally, we must remember, no one gets too old for a hug or other expression of emotional intimacy.

PHYSICAL HANDICAPS

A substantial number of people become physically handicapped or are born with handicaps that affect their sexual functioning. The sexuality of these individuals has often been ignored, even by physicians who treat them (Comfort 1978). Recently, however, there has been interest in the sexual needs and capabilities of the handicapped, and some of the research findings are encouraging.

Spinal-cord Injury

The extent of sexual disability associated with spinal-cord injury depends upon where the cord is injured. If the erection reflex center in the lower part of the male's spinal cord is destroyed, erection is not possible. However, in many cases, accidents sever the spinal cord at some level other than the erection center. Then, men are generally able to have erections, elevate the testes, and show other evidence of sexual arousal. Some of these men can also ejaculate.

Erections in spinal-injured men generally occur in response to direct stimulation of the penis. However, since there is no connection between the brain and spinal cord, thoughts or visual cues do not result in erectile responses. Furthermore, the men are unable to feel the stimulation that resulted in erection and are typically unable to experience orgasm. Nonetheless, some men with spinal-cord injuries have learned to concentrate on a neurologically intact portion of their bodies and, in essence, assign the sensation to their genitals. Using this technique, some men are able to experience single or even multiple orgasms (Cole 1979).

Less research has been done on spinally injured women, partly because fewer women experience this type of problem as the result of a war injury or sports accident. However, spinally injured women generally

FIGURE 16.3
Physically handicapped people—and the people interacting intimately with them—must make physical and psychological adjustments to their handicaps. However, if these adjustments are successful, as they are in many cases, handicapped individuals can have satisfying emotional and sexual relationships.

exhibit signs of sexual arousal, and, in many cases, they can enjoy sexual relationships and experience orgasm. In fact, sexual interests are similar to those exhibited before the injury. The major complaint of the women is that they can no longer experience genital sensations (Cole 1979; Fitting et al. 1978).

A unique opportunity to study changes in the sexual response of a woman as the result of spinal injury was afforded scientists at the Masters and Johnson Institute in St. Louis. The woman had participated in studies at the institute prior to an automobile accident. Then, twelve months after the accident, she returned for an evaluation of the sexual-response cycle. Originally, she had experienced relatively little erotic excitation as the result of breast stimulation. However, after her spinal-cord injury—and the subsequent loss of sensation in the genital area—she reported increasingly greater erotic sensitivity in the breasts. As the result of breast stimulation she experienced orgasm, exhibiting the changes in breathing and heart rate normally associated with this phase of the sexual cycle (Kolodny et al. 1979). This case not only supports the earlier report that some spinally injured men experience orgasms, but it suggests that certain physiological adjustments can be made after an injury.

Generally speaking, spinally injured women have a normal menstrual cycle. In contrast to spinally injured men, who are typically sterile, these women are usually capable of becoming pregnant; in several cases, perfectly normal babies have been delivered (Cole 1979).

As the result of extensive studies of the handicapped, Cole has suggested that spinally injured individuals should be encouraged to make major readjustments in sexual attitudes and behavior. Specifically, he suggests a willingness to experiment with various sexual options, an emphasis on foreplay or petting techniques, a freer use of fantasy, and open and relaxed communication with the partner. As suggested in the introduction of this chapter, there is also a message here for able-bodied persons.

Blindness

Visually handicapped people do not differ from sighted individuals in regard to sexual motivation or expression, but blind women often experience irregularities in the menstrual cycle. Apparently, the normal light-dark cycle is important in the timing of hormonal output and the occurrence of ovulation and menstruation (Zacharias & Wurtman 1964). These irregularities, however, do not pose significant problems.[1]

Conversations with blind persons indicate that some of their greatest frustrations are related to dependency upon others; they cannot drive a car and must be led by someone else when in an unfamiliar environment. Contrary to what one might think, physical attractiveness in a partner is important to blind people, especially those who were once

FIGURE 16.4

Blind people have the same sexual interests as sighted people and, in many cases, are concerned about their partner's physical attractiveness.

sighted. (They can determine another person's attractiveness simply by asking for a friend's perception.)

Because they are unable to utilize visual cues, blind people are particularly sensitive to auditory and tactual communication. Intonation and inflections in the voice carry a great deal of meaning for them. For example, one of the author's students—a blind male—was quite accurate in determining the attractiveness of females by simply talking to them. Apparently, he had learned to discriminate subtle cues that indicate self-confidence or some other variable related to attractiveness.

Deafness

Like blindness, deafness does not impair sexual drive or functioning. However, a person who has been deaf from birth typically is fairly ignorant in regard to sexual matters. Responding to various societal pressures, schools for the deaf have been concerned primarily with helping individuals reach economic independence and have neglected sex education. Furthermore, even deaf persons who can lip-read effectively can comprehend only about one-quarter of speech content (Kolodny et al. 1979).

Communication problems also make it difficult for deaf persons to develop social skills. However, many deaf people—especially those who first experienced deafness in adolescence—have developed extraordinary sensitivity to facial expressions and body gestures. Even people with normal hearing have little difficulty thinking of social or sexual situations in which a great deal of communication can take place without a word being spoken!

Heart Disease

Until recently, little was known about the reactions of cardiac patients to sexual activity. Both doctors and patients often assumed that sex was dangerous, and abstinence out of fear resulted. However, programs of systematic exercise have been developed to improve the overall conditioning and the heart function of persons who have suffered heart attacks or had coronary bypass operations. Sex with a spouse places about the same strain on the heart as climbing two flights of stairs, and as the patient's conditioning improves to this point, sexual activity may be resumed gradually (Masur 1979; McLane, Krop, & Mehta 1980). Masturbation is sometimes suggested as a first step (Wagner 1975).

Certain recommendations in regard to sexual intercourse have been made to minimize health risks. Extremes of temperature, large amounts of alcohol, or digestion of large meals places a strain on the heart. Therefore, heart patients should generally avoid coitus after heavy drinking, large meals, or after having been out in very hot or very cold weather (Mackey 1978).

Another recommendation may be made as the result of a study conducted in Japan. It indicated that men were more likely to have heart attacks during intercourse with unfamiliar partners in unfamiliar settings—such as motels—than with wives in the familiar setting of the home. Apparently the added stress of an ''illicit'' affair seems to present some physical dangers (Ueno 1968; Hellerstein & Friedman 1970).

Diabetes

Approximately 50 percent of male diabetics are impotent. Another condition—which is much more rare—involves ejaculation without orgasm; a man expels semen in the normal way but without the usual intense pleasure. Although little research has been done on female diabetics, it appears that many of them experience less vaginal lubrication and lower sexual desire than nondiabetic women (Dormont 1975; Renshaw 1975).

The reasons for sexual problems among diabetics are not clear. However, neurological damage appears to be an important factor—probably more important than a hormonal imbalance. Psychological factors also seem to play a significant role. For example, depression associated with the disease—and the fear of loss of sexual function—may contribute to sexual difficulties (Renshaw 1975).

Despite the strong association between diabetes and sexual dysfunction, many diabetics report a satisfying sexual life. Furthermore, sexual problems are not related to the severity or duration of the disease. Thus, diabetics need not worry about problems necessarily getting worse over time (Renshaw 1975).

Mental Retardation

Two stereotypes are commonly applied to developmentally handicapped or mentally retarded persons. They are perceived either as relatively asexual or as unable to control their sexual impulses. In actuality, studies indicate that mentally retarded individuals have about the same sexual drive as developmentally normal people (Gebhard 1973). Furthermore, there is evidence that many retarded individuals can be trained to express needs for affection and physical contact in a socially appropriate fashion (Johnson 1971).

Generally speaking, relatives and institutional caretakers have taken an extremely repressive attitude about sexual expression in the developmentally handicapped. This attitude has instilled a large amount of guilt over such sexual behaviors as masturbation (Mitchell, Doctor, & Butler 1978). Certain liberal-minded researchers, such as Kolodny and his associates (1979), have suggested that training programs should emphasize the private nature of sexual expression rather than rely on attempts at sexual suppression.

When the reproductive potential of the mentally retarded is considered, obvious human-rights issues arise. Historically, many governments have prevented these individuals from marrying and attempted some type of sterilization procedure. However, if an individual is incompetent to give consent, it is difficult to decide who has the right to make such a decision. Although the issue is still unresolved in most cultures, the United Nations passed a bill in 1970 supporting the right of mentally retarded persons to marry and to obtain information about contraception.

Author's Perspective: The Disenfranchisement of Handicapped Individuals

While working as a psychologist in a rehabilitation institute, I had a chance to talk with a large number of people with various types of handicaps. An experience many of them shared was of being rejected or ignored by ablebodied persons. One of the most dramatic examples involved a young woman, confined to a wheelchair, who found herself stuck in the snow. Several people actually crossed the street in an apparent attempt to avoid coming into contact with her. When she waved from a distance—as a signal that she needed help—some people waved back in a friendly fashion but did not offer assistance. Fortunately, she eventually got help and was later able to perceive other people's avoidance as their failure to come to grips with the psychological aspects of handicaps. (She was even capable of repeating the story as a humorous anecdote.)

The tendency of many people to ignore or avoid the handicapped is probably motivated by several factors. In some cases, this tendency may represent a need to avoid something threatening—a person does not usually like to consider the possibility that he or she might some day be handicapped. Other people may avoid a handicapped person because they feel that they cannot make a socially appropriate response. At any rate, handicapped people have to learn to adjust to the social responses of others as well as to their handicaps.

The period of adjustment to a handicap is often quite lengthy and, as one might expect, accompanied by depression and low self-esteem. These emotional reactions typically contribute to sexual problems. Nonetheless, many handicapped persons are able to recover their self-esteem and make a good adjustment. Rehabilitation counselors believe the emphasis should be on what can be done sexually and in other aspects of life rather than on how one is limited (Comfort 1978). Even when sexual intercourse is impossible and mobility is greatly limited, many people are able to have satisfying sexual relationships. Reports such as the ones about persons with spine injuries who have been able to compensate for neurological damage and experience orgasm represent, in my thinking, a real tribute to human resourcefulness.

SUMMARY

Older persons are often depicted as devoid of sexuality, but sexual feelings tend to transcend various physical changes that take place with aging. In women, menopause (the cessation of menstruation) usually takes place between forty-five and sixty. Symptoms of menopause vary but often include headaches, dizziness, and hot flashes as well as such psychological reactions as depression and irritability. In men, the production of sperm and androgen shows a gradual decline between forty-five and sixty and, in some cases, there are psychological reactions referred to as "middle-age crisis." For both sexes, hormone treatment may be helpful.

There is considerable variability in the sexual activity of older persons. Some sexual inhibition is associated with illness or physical trauma, but much of it is related to nonphysical factors. Nonetheless, positive attitudes about sexuality—and the availability of a willing partner—may allow one to enjoy sexual relationships into extreme old age. Even when coitus is rarely or no longer practiced, sexuality associated with caressing and physical closeness tends to be very important.

There are certain similarities in the factors related to marital happiness in the young adult years and marital happiness in old age. However, emotional security apparently takes on added importance as years go by. For couples identified as having successful marriages, affection, tenderness, and warmth have apparently increased over the years.

Various types of physical handicaps affect sexuality, but the extent of sexual debilitation has probably been overemphasized in the past. Spinally injured persons are typically unable to feel sensations coming from the genitals. Nonetheless, some men are capable of erection, ejaculation, and even orgasm. In contrast to spinally injured men, who are typically sterile, spinally injured women usually have normal menstrual cycles and are capable of bearing children.

Other types of disabilities present problems to various degrees. Nonetheless, the extent to which certain individuals are able to compensate for their handicaps may provide a positive role model for many able-bodied people.

NOTES

1. Some individuals do experience sexual dysfunctions following the loss of vision. In most cases, however, the problem is associated with severe depression or neurological damage such as that resulting from a brain tumor. Blindness per se cannot be considered a causal factor (Fitzgerald 1973).

PART 7

Atypical Sexual Behavior

Sexual behaviors practiced by a minority of people are considered in this part. Historically, many of these have been described as abnormal, perverse, or deviant. However, these terms are difficult to define, and, in addition, have taken on a great deal of negative, superfluous meaning. Therefore, the words "atypical" or "variant" will be used.

CHAPTER 17

Homosexuality

At the height of the classical Greek era, homosexual relationships between men were considered a high form of emotional and affectional expression. Many ancient Greeks believed that love between two men represented greater good and beauty than that between a man and a woman. In fact, Plato's famous work *The Symposium* was actually a dialogue about the beauty and origin of homosexual love.

Homosexuality also was well accepted in ancient Rome, and several Roman emperors were known to engage in homosexual behavior. A Roman senator described Julius Caesar as "every woman's man and every man's woman" (Leiser 1979). Emperor Heliogabalus, who began his reign in A.D. 218, practiced homosexual activities in public on several occasions. He was also known to have male subjects demonstrate their respect for him by kissing his genitals (Karlen 1971).

In contrast to the ancient Greeks and Romans, the ancient Hebrews were strongly antihomosexual. Much of this attitude was related to the nonprocreative nature of homosexuality. According to one Jewish tradition, the flood in Noah's time was brought about, in part, by homosexual practices (Leiser 1979).

Following in the Hebrew tradition, early Christian writers condemned homosexuality. In the First Letter to the Corinthians, Paul wrote that men who "abused themselves" with other men would not inherit the kingdom of God. Similarly, Augustine (354–430) described homosexuality as "perverted lust."

And in 538, Byzantine Emperor Justinian I, who was a Christian, declared that cities which harbored homosexuals would be visited by earthquakes, famine, plague, and other catastrophes (Karlen 1971).

From the Middle Ages to the modern era, the Western world has been generally negative in its attitudes towards homosexuality.[1] However, there have been—and still are—considerable culture differences in these attitudes. For example, only 5 percent of the individuals sampled in

FIGURE 17.1

The pleasures associated with a homosexual relationship seem to be very similar to those reported in heterosexual relationships.

Amsterdam, Holland, agreed with the statement that homosexuality is vulgar and obscene. In Copenhagen, Denmark, the rate of agreement was somewhat higher—about 12 percent. In large American cities, nearly 50 percent of those sampled agreed with the statement (Weinberg & Williams 1974).

Despite the high incidence of negative feelings about homosexuality, there is some evidence that attitudes are changing, at least among younger people. Among male, white-collar workers *under* thirty-five, 65 percent thought that homosexuality among consenting adults should be legal. In contrast, only 43 percent of white-collar workers *over* thirty-five expressed the same belief (Hunt 1974).

Homosexuality is difficult to define because there is not a clear line of distinction between a homosexual and a heterosexual person. Kinsey and his associates (1948) found a continuum extending from persons with exclusively homosexual experience to exclusively heterosexual persons. They devised a scale from 0 to 6 that categorized an individual in terms of percentage of homosexual and heterosexual experience (see figure 17.1). Obviously, the percentage of people in the population who are defined as homosexual depends upon where one draws the line between categories. If individuals who fall into either category 5 or 6 are included in the definition, then between 5 and 10 percent of the U.S. population may be described as homosexual, with males outnumbering females two or three to one. If only people who exhibit exclusively homosexual behavior are included (category 6), then around 2 percent of the males and less than 1 percent of the females would be considered homosexual (Hunt 1974).

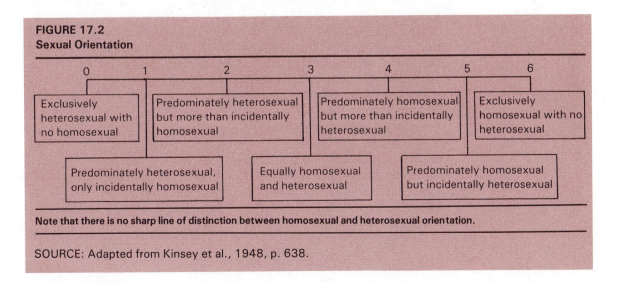

FIGURE 17.2
Sexual Orientation

| 0 | 1 | 2 | 3 | 4 | 5 | 6 |

| Exclusively heterosexual with no homosexual | Predominately heterosexual but more than incidentally homosexual | Predominately homosexual but more than incidentally heterosexual | Exclusively homosexual with no heterosexual |

| Predominately heterosexual, only incidentally homosexual | Equally homosexual and heterosexual | Predominately homosexual but incidentally heterosexual |

Note that there is no sharp line of distinction between homosexual and heterosexual orientation.

SOURCE: Adapted from Kinsey et al., 1948, p. 638.

Another problem in the definition of homosexuality involves a failure to distinguish behavior from feelings. There are some individuals who engage exclusively in homosexual relationships but may be aroused sexually by opposite-sex persons. Conversely, certain people engage only in heterosexual behaviors but have strong homosexual feelings. Thus, the term homosexuality is far from precise and includes a variety of patterns. The following sections will consider the various degrees and patterns of homosexuality as well as factors related to their development.

HOMOSEXUAL LIFE-STYLE

Some of society's negative feelings about homosexuality are based on misconceptions about homosexual relationships. For example, people generally believe that homosexual people are preoccupied with sex. However, the Bell and Weinberg (1978) survey indicates that the frequency of sexual relations is no higher among homosexuals than heterosexuals.

Another common belief is that homosexuals are looking for something very different than usual in an interpersonal relationship. Recent research utilizing questionnaire data indicates that this idea is also false. Homosexual males apparently desire the same general traits in a partner as heterosexual males do. Such qualities as sincerity, honesty, and competence seem to be universally attractive (Boyden, Carroll, & Maier, in press).

Still another misconception is that homosexuals are easy to identify because the males are feminine in their looks and manners, while the females tend to be masculine in appearance and behavior. Although some do fit these stereotypes, the vast majority do not. In fact, Kinsey estimated that only about 15 percent of homosexuals could be identified from casual observation (Kinsey et al. 1948). A recent study indicates that, on measures of masculine and feminine attributes, homosexuals in general do not differ from heterosexuals (Storms 1980).[2]

A related fallacy is that, among homosexual couples, one partner is generally masculine while the other is typically feminine. In fact, the questionnaire study mentioned earlier indicated that homosexuals tend to pick similar, not contrasting, partners. For example, relatively masculine homosexual men are attracted to males scoring high on masculinity; feminine men are generally attracted to men who have many feminine characteristics. As in the case of heterosexual couples, similarity appears to be the general rule in regard to attraction (Boyden, Carroll, & Maier, in press).

Sexual Activities

Other types of misconceptions center on the sexual relationships of homosexuals. The stereotype is that one partner plays a "masculine" role in the sexual interaction while the other partner functions in a submissive or "feminine" role. In reality, homosexual individuals frequently shift roles (Hooker 1965).

As in the case of heterosexuals, there is considerable variability in sexual activities. Most couples engage in foreplay activities such as hugging, kissing, and petting. Among male homosexuals, fellatio and mutual masturbation are the most common methods of inducing orgasm; anal intercourse is less frequently practiced. The activities that are reported as most satisfying are receiving fellatio and playing the active role in anal intercourse (Bell & Weinberg 1978).

Among lesbians,[3] the most common sexual practices are mutual masturbation and cunnilingus. Contrary to popular opinion, the use of an artificial penis is quite rare. Another relatively rare practice is for one partner to lie on top of the other and make thrusting movements with the genitals. Generally speaking, lesbians report longer periods of foreplay and caressing in general than do either homosexual male couples or heterosexual couples (Rosen 1974).

Kinsey and his associates (1953) found that lesbian women had orgasms in a greater percentage of sexual encounters than did women in heterosexual relationships. This is probably related to their extensive foreplay. In addition, Kinsey suggested, it may be related to the partners' better understanding of the sexual responsiveness of another member of the same sex.

Variety of Partners

Some homosexual men remain in monogamous relationships, at least for a certain period of time. However, many engage in a large variety of relationships. It is not unusual for homosexual men to report relationships with over a hundred partners, a considerably higher number than that reported by heterosexuals (Weinberg & Williams 1974). It may be that society's antihomosexual attitudes create anxieties that make it difficult for individuals to sustain lasting relationships. Another possibility is that partners are readily available in the homosexual world. It could be argued that, if willing women were as available to heterosexual men, there might very well be a comparably large variety of sexual partners for heterosexuals. Still another possibility is that, since homosexuals are generally excluded from heterosexual society, they tend to reject society's sexual standards and set up standards of their own.

Compared to homosexual men, homosexual women are less likely to have a large variety of partners. The majority of lesbians surveyed report being currently involved in a monogamous relationship and having had fewer than ten different sexual partners (Rosen 1974). It seems that, like heterosexual women, lesbians are more likely to value the romance and emotional satisfaction of a monogamous relationship than are their male counterparts.

Meeting Places

Homosexuality is found in virtually all social classes, occupations, and geographic areas. Therefore, it is not surprising that there are a variety of ways in which homosexual individuals meet. Most cities have a number of clubs and social organizations that function to introduce homosexuals to one another. As will be seen later in the chapter, these organizations may also serve political functions.

One of the most common public meeting places is the gay bar. Some individuals' social and sexual lives revolve around the bar and activities associated with it (Warren 1974). Generally speaking, homosexual males go to gay bars to meet new partners; lesbians are more likely to go to the bars to talk and socialize. Although some gay bars cater to both male and female homosexuals, most are associated primarily with either male or female patrons (Rosen 1974).

FIGURE 17.3

A gay bar. As is the case for many heterosexuals, a bar may function as a meeting place or center for social activities.

Gay baths are visited almost exclusively by male homosexuals. These clubs usually include a swimming pool or whirlpool and a number of small rooms furnished with beds. Sexual relationships are often impersonal; individuals may not exchange names or enter into a conversation during an encounter (Bell & Weinberg 1978).

Rest rooms, or "tearooms" as they are sometimes called, may also function as centers for homosexual encounters. Such meeting places are mainly used by males, and the sexual relationships are highly impersonal. Laud Humphreys (1975), whose controversial research technique was discussed in chapter 2, found that several of the individuals who engaged in the "tearoom trade" identified themselves as heterosexual married men. (Individuals who engage in both heterosexual and homosexual relationships will be discussed in more detail later in the chapter.)

Careers

Homosexual men, like their heterosexual counterparts, invest a large amount of energy in their jobs. Most of the men in the Bell and Weinberg study (1978) reported that their homosexuality did not affect their careers. Nonetheless, some individuals lost their jobs when employers discovered their homosexuality. In contrast, a few men felt that their homosexuality helped their careers. In regard to job stability, homosexual males were similar to heterosexual males; both groups switched jobs with about equal frequency.

Lesbians, however, tended to change employers more often than heterosexual comparison groups. It is possible that lesbians, having already experienced rejection based on their homosexuality, were particularly sensitive to general discrimination against women and reacted to it more strongly than heterosexual women (Bell & Weinberg 1978). It seems likely that, if discrimination against women in the job market is reduced or eliminated, differences between lesbians and heterosexual women in regard to job stability will also disappear.

Patterns of Homosexual Relationships

One of the major contributions of Bell and Weinberg (1978) was to differentiate several types of homosexual relationships and relate the type of relationship to the general adjustment and satisfaction of the individuals. The system of classification is based on a statistical procedure known as factor analysis. Essentially, this procedure identifies variables that are relatively independent of one another. The five variables that were found to be most important—and the percentage of individuals falling into each category—are indicated in figure 17.4.

The close-coupled category includes individuals living with another person of the same sex relatively monogamously. They have few sexual problems and do not spend much time looking for other sexual partners. These people have few worries or regrets over their homosexuality.

The open-coupled group consists of people who cohabit with one partner but who spend considerable time looking for new partners. Generally, they have sexual relations with a variety of people. These individuals have more regret about their homosexuality.

The third category, called functionals, includes "singles" who have a large number of sexual partners and little regret over their homosexual-

FIGURE 17.4
The Percentages of Male and Female Homosexual Individuals Assigned to Each of Five Categories

	Males	Females
1. Close-Coupled	14%	38%
2. Open-Coupled	25%	24%
3. Functional	21%	14%
4. Dysfunctional	18%	8%
5. Asexual	22%	16%

SOURCE: Bell & Weinberg, 1978.

ity. Compared to the other groups, they tend to be more overt, have a higher level of sexual interest, and are younger, on the average.

Dysfunctionals are "singles" who have many sexual partners, sexual problems, and regrets over their homosexuality. These people tend to concern themselves with sexual adequacy as well as finding and maintaining a relationship with a partner.

The asexuals are "single" and exhibit low levels of sexual activity. These individuals report many sexual problems and a large amount of regret over their homosexuality. They tend to be older and more secretive about their homosexual identity than other respondents.

On the basis of these findings, Bell and Weinberg suggested that it is misleading to use only one word—homosexuality—to describe same-sex attraction. Clearly, several distinct patterns emerge—what they call "homosexualities." An awareness of these different patterns makes it easier to understand the development and psychological adjustment of homosexual individuals.

Anthropological Perspective: Homosexuality in Preliterate Cultures

Although exclusively homosexual behavior was not common, it was generally accepted in the preliterate societies studied. Among the seventy-six societies for which information was available to Ford and Beach (1951), 64 percent considered homosexual behavior more or less normal. In contrast to the situation in Western society, exclusively homosexual men typically exhibited feminine behavior. For example, certain men from the large culture of East Africa dressed as women and even simulated menstruation. They became one of the wives of another man and were believed to have been affected by some supernatural power. However, they did not have much prestige in the society.

In contrast, a man who played a feminine role in the Chukchee society of Siberia was afforded high status and became known as a shaman, or medicine man. The Siberian shaman exhibited feminine mannerisms and sometimes became the wife of another man. Sexual behavior consisted of anal intercourse, with the shaman always playing the ''female'' role.

Lesbianism has been reported in only a few preliterate societies. In the Azande culture of Africa, women were sometimes known to tie a banana or sweet potato around their waists and simulate coitus with other women. Lesbianism was also described in Haiti; in this case, the women were said to be frigid in heterosexual relationships (Ford & Beach 1951).

It may be concluded that, in both preliterate and industrialized societies, there are fewer lesbians than male homosexuals. Furthermore, homosexuality in both sexes is more common in industrialized societies. It seems that, as societies have become larger, more complex, and more highly industrialized, more individuals have deviated from the norms of the society in general. Persons who deviate—as in the case of homosexuals—can find emotional support in social subsystems or subcultures sympathetic to their attitudes and behaviors. In contrast, small, preliterate societies tend to be relatively homogeneous, and there are fewer subcultures. The norms of the society in general are more influential, even if there are not strong sanctions against homosexuality.

Comparative and Evolutionary Perspective: Homosexual Behavior in Animals

Partial sexual responses of a homosexual nature are quite common among animals. For example, when rats are caged in groups, a male often mounts another male and then, within a few seconds, copulates with a female in estrus. However, a complete sexual response directed by one animal towards another animal of the same sex is quite rare. Nonetheless, a male fish (*Tilapia macrochir*) has been observed courting another male; after the two became sexually excited, they both deposited their spermatophores (Wickler 1972). Similarly, movies have been taken of a bull mounting another bull, achieving anal penetration, and ejaculating during retraction (Pomeroy 1972).

There are certain parallels between animals and humans in regard to homosexual activities: these activities are more frequent among males than among females; homosexual responses are more common among young adults or adolescents than among older adults; and homosexual behaviors appear more often in captivity or incarceration than in the wild or under conditions of freedom (Ford & Beach 1951). On the other hand, stable homosexual preferences in animals are virtually never observed, especially if an opposite-sex member of the species is available. Thus, although the rudiments of homosexuality or bisexuality are present in certain animals, exclusive homosexuality seems to be found only among humans (Maier & Maier 1970).

The finding that only humans exhibit exclusive homosexuality is consistent with the evolutionary trend away from the close relationship between sex and reproduction. As we have seen throughout the book, many human sexual behaviors occur in a manner not likely to result in reproduction. Another way of conceptualizing homosexuality is that it represents a further example of human variability in behavior. Humans exhibit more variability than any other animal, and this variability includes choice of sexual partners as well as manner in which sexuality is expressed.

THE DEVELOPMENT OF HOMOSEXUAL PREFERENCES

Two types of theories have arisen in an attempt to explain homosexuality. Biological theories have generally emphasized the role of sex hormones. Some support for the biological explanation comes from studies that indicate lesbians have a higher concentration of androgen in both the blood and urine than heterosexual females (Griffiths, Merry, & Browning 1974; Gartell, Loriaux, & Chase 1977). However, it is difficult to interpret these results; it is possible that playing a nontraditional sex role stimulated the female's adrenals to secrete more androgen (Kreuz, Rose, & Jennings 1972).

Among males, there does not appear to be a difference between homosexuals and heterosexuals in regard to testosterone levels (Rose 1975). Again, there are difficulties in interpreting these results. It is possible that there were sex-hormone differences at an early stage of development of homosexual males but that these differences are no longer present in adults. Thus, for both males and females, the role of hormones in the development of homosexuality is uncertain.

A number of theorists have suggested that psychological factors are of greater importance in the development of homosexual preferences than biological ones. In 1910 Freud hypothesized that homosexuality represented a fixation at an early stage of development. Later theorists emphasized the role of the family. For example, Irving Bieber and his associates (1962) believed that male homosexuals were influenced by a dominant, seductive mother and a weak or passive father. The mother's overprotectiveness—nurtured in part by jealousy over the boy's attention to other females—might discourage heterosexual relationships. Furthermore, the mother's seductiveness might generate anxiety (since sexual desire for the mother would be accompanied by guilt associated with the incest taboo), and this anxiety might generalize to relationships with other women. Finally, the desire for the father's love and approval that was frustrated might generalize and create an especially strong need for love and approval of other men.

Bieber's research comparing male homosexuals with male heterosexuals in psychoanalysis has generally supported the hypothesis of a dominant mother and a passive father (Bieber et al. 1962; Bieber 1976). However, his sample was necessarily biased; it did not include homosexual males who were not seeking to change their life-style. (Presumably, the males in the sample were seeking a change, or they wouldn't be in therapy.) Furthermore, the therapist may have been biased toward perceiving mothers of homosexual males as dominant and overprotective.

An unbiased study of homosexual development clearly argues against Bieber's theory, particularly when it concerns relationship between a child and its mother. Interviews with over 900 homosexual individuals—including many who were not in psychotherapy—indicate there is *no* relationship between the dominance or seductiveness of mothers and the sexual orientation of their children (Bell et al. 1981).

Recently, a theory of development of homosexual preference has been formulated that places less emphasis on parental influences and more on peer relationships. Storms (1981) hypothesizes that erotic orientation tends to become stable at puberty, when the sex drive is increasing at a rapid rate. Two types of situations might lead to homosexual preferences: (1) the sex drive may develop early, during the time when most close friendships are with members of the same sex; (2) individuals may have an unusually close, same-sex friendship that continues through the period when the sex drive is increasing rapidly. There are some data consistent with this theory, but more research is necessary before it can be thoroughly evaluated.

Perhaps more illuminating than attempts to identify causes are the results of two studies that suggest factors *not* involved in the development of homosexuality. Sociologist Robert Sorenson (1973) looked at the sexual preferences of children who had been molested or seduced by homosexuals. He found that these children were no more likely to become homosexual than children who had not had such an experience. Psychiatrist Richard Green (1978) investigated the sexual preferences of children whose mothers had atypical sexual orientations. Of thirty-seven children raised by homosexual or transsexual mothers, none showed indications of homosexual behavior at the time of adolescence or in later life. Thus, two popular folk theories of homosexuality may be laid to rest. It seems that neither a single traumatic experience nor having a homosexual mother is an important causal factor in homosexual development. (In contrast, it is interesting to note that both of these findings are consistent with Storms's theory.)

Why, after so many years of research and theorizing, do the origins of homosexuality remain obscure? There seem to be several reasons. First, it is not altogether clear what causes an opposite-sex preference. Until this matter is better understood, it will probably be difficult to draw a distinction between heterosexuality and homosexuality. Second, as we have seen, there is great diversity among homosexual individuals. It seems likely that one pattern of homosexual preference has very different causes than another pattern. Finally, much of the research has been oriented around the question, What went ''wrong'' in the past? When a question is phrased in this way, answers necessarily tend to be biased.

Sex Differences

Despite difficulties in understanding causes of homosexuality, some progress has been made in identifying the general development of homosexual preferences. There appear to be some fairly consistent sex differences. The typical male homosexual or prehomosexual pattern starts at a relatively early age. Compared to heterosexual males, homosexual males were much more likely to have played with toys considered appropriate for girls, joined girls in various types of activities, and been considered ''sissies.'' These behaviors were identified even among several homosexual men who became quite masculine in appearance and behavior as adults. Generally, homosexual males recognized a sexual preference for men by the time they were seventeen, and often by the time they were thirteen (Whitam 1977).

In contrast, the homosexual pattern generally develops at a later age in females. There are a relatively large number of cases in which women developed homosexual preferences in adulthood after establishing a basic heterosexual orientation (Saghir, Robins, & Walbran 1969; Feldman & MacCulloch 1971). Often, lesbian relationships begin as strong friendships with a great deal of affection expressed. There may be a period of a year or more before an affectionate relationship develops into a sexual one (Wolf 1979).

Another difference between males and females is in regard to acceptance of a homosexual identity; men generally have more difficulty admitting to themselves that they are homosexual than do women. Apparently, the heterosexual, masculine sex role is much more closely tied in with feelings of individual self-worth than is the heterosexual, feminine sex role (Blumstein & Schwartz 1977).

Admitting One's Homosexuality

As we have seen, the stigma of homosexuality makes it very difficult for people to ''come out of the closet,'' or admit that they are homosexual. For example, male homosexuals wait an average of six years between a first awareness of their homosexual orientation and admitting to others that they are homosexual (Dank 1971). For some, there is never a time when they feel comfortable enough to come out. It is particularly difficult to discuss homosexuality with family members. In approximately 50 percent of the cases, the matter is never discussed with parents. When there is a disclosure to the family, a period of stress and severed communication is likely to result. Nonetheless, many homosexuals do reestablish a relationship with the family and report feeling better than before the disclosure was made (Bell & Weinberg 1978).

There are a variety of reasons for wanting to come out of the closet. For some, living outwardly as a heterosexual seems false or dishonest. Others find that their pretense essentially isolates them from other homosexuals—individuals with whom they would be most likely to feel at ease. For still others, a public announcement is seen as a way of influencing the public towards greater tolerance of homosexuality (Ponse 1978; Humphreys 1979).

One of the most difficult aspects of coming out of the closet is, reportedly, to psychologically accept in oneself what society condemns. This typically involves an agonizing reappraisal, especially since many of society's attitudes have become internalized. In other words, homosexual individuals must learn to accept qualities in themselves that they have generally devalued for most of their lives. During this period of reappraisal, gay organizations and political groups can be particularly helpful in providing emotional support.

Author's Perspective: Negative Stereotypes and Homosexuality

The mass media usually try to avoid supporting racial, ethnic, and sex stereotypes. However, television and radio tend to promote homosexual stereotypes. Lesbians are generally portrayed as hard and masculine in appearance, and male homosexuals are almost always depicted as effeminate. In our language, the word ''homosexual'' and its slang synonyms carry a great deal of excess meaning which undoubtedly contribute to the negative stereotyping. A simple demonstration in one of my classes illustrates this tendency. Half the class was told that there was going to be a guest lecturer and that this person was intelligent, perceptive, warm, friendly, and sensitive. They were then asked to rate the person on likability. The other half of the class was given the same adjectives plus one more: homosexual. The latter group gave the individual significantly lower ratings. It seems that, once a person is perceived as homosexual, he or she is generally liked less. Furthermore, positive traits—such as warmth and friendliness—may take on negative connotations once the homosexual label is applied.

Irrationally strong negative attitudes towards homosexuality are called *homophobia*. These reactions apply to a variety of situations. People with rigid sex-role stereotypes typically express a relatively large amount of homophobia (MacDonald & Games 1974). Apparently, intolerance of different sex roles generalizes to include intolerance towards individuals with different sexual preferences. Other factors correlated with high scores on a homophobic scale are lack of education, strong, traditional religious beliefs, and residence in small towns or rural areas (Lehne 1976; Nyberg & Alston 1976). These factors are often found to be correlated with a lack of tolerance for people who are perceived as different. It is also possible that homophobia develops in some people as an attempt to deny homosexual feelings in themselves. Thus, several of the men who engaged in homosexual behaviors in rest rooms later expressed strongly antihomosexual attitudes (Humphreys 1975). Furthermore, a recent

FIGURE 17.5
The Homophobic Scale

A researcher has developed the following scale to identify homophobia.
Respondents answer yes in agreement or no in disagreement to the
following statements:

1. Homosexuals should be locked up to protect society.
2. It would be upsetting for me to find out I was alone with a homosexual.
3. Homosexuals should be allowed to hold government positions.
4. I would not want to be a member of an organization which had any
   homosexuals in its membership.
5. I find the thought of homosexual acts disgusting.
6. If laws against homosexuality were eliminated, the proportion of
   homosexuals in the population would probably remain the same.
7. A homosexual could be a good President of the United States.
8. I would be afraid for a child of mine to have a teacher who was
   homosexual.
9. If a homosexual sat next to me on a bus, I would get nervous.

SOURCE: Smith, 1973, pp. 129-30

study indicates that individuals who are most threatened or stressed by homosexuality have the most negative attitudes toward homosexuals (Leitner &
Cado 1982).

Unfortunately, when homophobic individuals gain positions of power or influence, they may express a great deal of prejudice toward homosexuals. For
example, a well-publicized antihomosexual movement supported by singer
Anita Bryant resulted in considerable discrimination against homosexuals in
housing and employment. Although Bryant later retracted many of her strongly
antihomosexual statements, it appears that her stand increased homophobic
reactions in many people.

In 1983, the rapid increase in the incidence of AIDS (which will be discussed
in chapter 22) contributed to homophobia and discrimination against homosexuals. Many people feel that homosexuals are "getting what they deserve."

Several organizations have attempted to provide support for homosexual
victims of discrimination. In the 1950s, primarily secretive organizations such
as the Mattachine Society and Daughters of Bilitis provided some programs of
education about homosexuality. Then, in the late 1960s there was a shift toward political activism. Gay liberation movements tried to deal more directly
with negative stereotyping and discrimination. During this period, the gay
groups gained support from a number of other organizations, including civil-
liberties groups, feminist groups, and liberal church organizations. Although
some progress has been made in reducing the number of violations of the civil
rights of homosexuals, a great deal of prejudice and discrimination still exist.

PSYCHOLOGICAL ADJUSTMENT

Traditionally, it has been assumed that homosexuals are psychologically disturbed. However, several studies have reported similarities between homosexual and heterosexual individuals in general psychological adjustment. For example, an analysis of the Rorschach (ink-blot) test produced no differences between homosexual men and a matched group of heterosexual men (Hooker 1957). Similarly, comparisons of lesbians and heterosexual women have generally indicated no differences in terms of overall psychological adjustment (Rosen 1974).

Nonetheless, homosexual and heterosexual men do differ in some specific aspects of adjustment. Homosexual men tend to be less accepting of themselves, be more depressed, and have more psychosomatic problems; also, they are more apt to have contemplated or attempted suicide (Bell & Weinberg 1978). It seems likely that many or perhaps all of these differences can be explained in terms of society's rejection and, in some cases, persecution of homosexuals. In other words, the stress of being a homosexual in a heterosexual society may account for the relatively high incidence of the problems just mentioned.

In support of the stress hypothesis is the finding that homosexual individuals who have become comfortable with their homosexuality appear to be as well adjusted as heterosexuals. For example, the *functional* group of homosexual men did not differ from heterosexuals in terms of self-acceptance, psychosomatic symptoms, or depression. Similarly, the *close-coupled* group appeared psychologically healthy and, as a matter of fact, reported being even happier than heterosexuals in general.[4] In contrast, the group that appeared least well adjusted was one of the groups that reported a great deal of regret over being homosexual— the *asexual* group (Bell & Weinberg 1978).

When male and female homosexuals are compared, the women seem, on the average, to be somewhat better adjusted than the men. In fact, the Bell and Weinberg study reported that the lesbian group did not differ from female heterosexuals in most of the measures of adjustment.

Why do gay females seem to be psychologically healthier than gay males? Part of the answer may be related to the relatively greater ease with which lesbians can blend into our society. Generally speaking, it is much more acceptable for two women past college age to live together than two men. Furthermore, masculine behavior in women is condoned more than feminine behavior in men. For example, the word sissy has more negative connotations than the word tomboy. Similarly, masculine clothes for women are more accepted than feminine clothes for men.

Another factor related to adjustment may be the fact that lesbians are more likely to be involved in a stable love relationship than homosexual men. As suggested earlier, stable relationships seem to promote happiness and may also be related to psychological adjustment in general. Supporting this conclusion is the finding that the *dysfunctional* group of lesbians—who, by definition, were not "coupled"—were more disturbed than the other groups of lesbians (Bell & Weinberg 1978).

Obviously, it is impossible to know with certainty what causes the differences in adjustment between homosexuals and heterosexuals. However, the American Psychiatric Association and American Psychological Association have evaluated the evidence against classifying homosexuals as disturbed, and they found it strong enough to remove homosexuality from the classification of mental disorder. At the present time, homosexuals are considered to be in need of help only if they experience distress over their sexual orientation.

BISEXUALITY

Individuals who engage in sexual relationships with members of both sexes—and with approximately equal frequency—are often called *bisexuals*. (The quotation at the beginning of this chapter indicates that Caesar was probably a bisexual.) Kinsey and his associates (1948) found that bisexual behavior (category 3 on the continuum) was actually more common than exclusive homosexuality.

Recent research indicates that many bisexuals have high degrees of both heterosexuality and homosexuality in regard to their erotic fantasies. These results suggest that bisexuals in general should not be conceptualized as halfway between homosexuals and heterosexuals; rather, bisexuals should be considered as a distinct category in a two-dimensional model (Storms 1980).

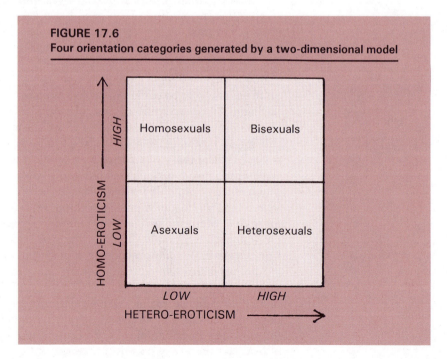

FIGURE 17.6
Four orientation categories generated by a two-dimensional model

Certain people with a bisexual orientation appear to be homosexuals who engage in heterosexual behavior primarily to avoid being stigmatized. Many homosexuals who have spent part of their lives in marital situations seem to fit into this category. Recent research by Tollison and Adams (1979) also supports this interpretation of bisexuality. Three groups of male subjects—heterosexuals, homosexuals, and bisexuals—were shown two films. One of the films depicted a male and female embracing, removing one another's clothes, caressing, and engaging in intercourse. The other film showed two males in similar activities culminating in oral-genital sex. The penile responses of the subjects were measured during their viewing of the films.

As expected, the heterosexuals showed significant penile responses during the heterosexual film, while the homosexuals exhibited comparable responses during the homosexual film. Rather surprisingly, the bisexuals' responses were the same as those of the homosexuals. However, the bisexuals reported that they were equally aroused by the homosexual and heterosexual scenes. Tollison and Adams concluded that these reports of equal arousal represented attempts to appear more socially acceptable; bisexuality is generally more acceptable—and less threatening to an individual—than homosexuality.

Another cause of bisexual behavior appears to be isolation from individuals of the opposite sex. In certain settings—such as prisons—homosexual behaviors appear in people who are normally heterosexual. Studies of sex in men's prisons indicate that, in addition to satisfying sexual needs, homosexual acts—or the threat of being "used" in homosexual acts—function as a means of bartering social power. An individual known as a "punk" may gain favors by submitting himself to the sexual desires of higher-status individuals (Kirkham 1971).

Homosexual behavior is also relatively common among female prisoners. However, the character of the lesbian prison relationship seems to be different from that of males. The female relationships apparently are based more on affection, are more stable, and are less associated with power relationships (Tittle 1969). Nonetheless, a few newspapers during the late 1970s reported that female prisoners were "using" other females in homosexual acts as a way of bartering social power.

Finally, McCaghy and Skipper (1969) found that many female striptease dancers engage in homosexual activities with other strippers. They regard their bisexuality as a reaction to difficulties in establishing lasting, affectionate relationships with men. A comparable type of dual orientation is reported among male homosexual street prostitutes. The vast majority of these men engage in homosexual activity for money but maintain a basic heterosexual self-identity (Reiss 1961).

In conclusion, bisexuality seems to have a variety of causes. It is probably just as inaccurate to stereotype bisexuals as it is to stereotype homosexuals.

Legal Perspective: Laws Relating to Homosexuality

In many states, homosexual acts are illegal, and violators are subject to prosecution under sodomy laws. (It will be remembered that sodomy is defined as an ''unnatural'' sex act and includes oral-genital sex and anal intercourse.) Some people believe that laws against homosexuality are useful in that they protect society's standards and reduce the incidence of homosexual acts. However, the Great Britain Committee on Homosexual Offenses and Prostitution (1963) concluded, on the basis of a ten-year study, that antihomosexual laws did not reduce homosexual behavior and that influencing private morality is not the proper function of the law. The committee recommended that homosexual acts between consenting adults in private should not be illegal.

Another controversy centers around the requirement, in some states, that convicted homosexuals register with city or county law-enforcement agencies. This requirement makes convicted homosexuals susceptible to questioning whenever a sex crime is committed in the area of their residence. Furthermore, it generally prevents homosexuals from obtaining jobs that require security clearance. Proponents of the requirement suggest that homosexuals are likely to commit violent sex crimes and are particularly open to blackmail.

FIGURE 17.7
**A gay protest march,
Fifth Avenue, New York.**

Those against the requirement conclude that, on the basis of available data, homosexuals are no more likely to commit violent sex crimes than heterosexuals. Furthermore, homosexuals do not appear to be any more open to blackmail than people having heterosexual affairs or individuals with gambling problems (Leiser 1979).

Finally, a controversy has developed around a police practice of using decoys who entice homosexuals. One policeman—dressed in plain clothes—attempts to elicit a proposition, while another waits nearby ready to make an arrest. Arrests have even been made on the basis of evidence obtained during concealed observations in public rest rooms (Weinberg & Williams 1974). This borders on entrapment, which is illegal; and conflicts between homosexuals and police are typically aggravated by such practices. (Traditionally, police tend to have very negative attitudes about homosexuality.)

The various homosexual organizations mentioned earlier have been concerned with many of these controversies. In some cases, the groups have been joined by civil-rights organizations. Within recent years, pressure from these groups has resulted in certain changes in the legal status of homosexuality, particularly the elimination of sodomy laws in several states. It seems likely that reappraisals of the legal rights of homosexuals will continue during the 1980s.

PSYCHOTHERAPY

A fairly large number of homosexual and bisexual individuals at one time or another seek psychotherapy. Therapists use essentially two types of approaches in dealing with them: (1) to try to help them become heterosexual and (2) to help them live more happily with their homosexuality.

The classic approach to converting a homosexual to heterosexuality involves an effort to change the individual's underlying personality structure. The method employed, which was originated by Freud, is *psychoanalysis*—a long and expensive procedure. Therapist and patient explore the individual's past, particularly childhood, and attempt to gain insight into the reasons for the homosexuality. For example, Bieber and his associates (1962) believed that male homosexuality was associated with early incestuous wishes for the mother and a fear of rivalry with the father. The analysis concentrated on resolving these childhood conflicts.

A more recently developed approach is known as *behavior modification therapy* or, simply, *behavior therapy*. In this approach, discussion centers on the patient's behavior patterns and/or imagination; no attempt is made to gain insight into the individual or his relationships with other people. One aspect of the behavior therapy typically involves attempts to reduce homosexual arousal by associating negative or noxious events with it. For example, homosexual males may be repeatedly asked to picture a naked man in their minds; they are then instructed to follow this image with that of horrible-looking sores and scabs all over the man's body and a terrible stench associated with the scene (Cautela 1967).

In many cases, there is also an attempt to increase heterosexual arousal by simple reward association. In a therapy utilized by Quinn, Harbinson, and McAllister (1970), clients were deprived of liquid for a period of time. They were then rewarded with a drink each time they reported a heterosexual fantasy. They were also rewarded for having erections (these were measured by the use of a plethismograph) in response to pictures of nude females.

The second general approach to therapy emphasizes acceptance of one's homosexuality; no attempt is made to convert the individual to a heterosexual orientation. *Client-centered* or *supportive therapy* is commonly associated with this approach. The focus is on current feelings and behaviors rather than childhood experiences or "roots." The therapist tries to provide a climate in which the client may ventilate and explore feelings, not only about other individuals and events, but about himself or herself and the relationship with the therapist. By being warm and accepting, the therapist is sometimes able to reduce guilt and anxiety. Furthermore, the atmosphere of the therapeutic relationship encourages the learning of interpersonal skills and the development of trust as well as movement toward greater self-awareness (Rogers 1951).

In some cases, two homosexuals involved in a relatively monogamous relationship may enter therapy together. Basically, the therapeutic approach—sometimes called couples therapy—is similar to marriage counseling with heterosexual couples. There is often an emphasis on improving communication, particularly in regard to feelings about one another. There may also be an attempt to help the individuals overcome sexual dysfunctions in much the same way that this is done with heterosexuals (see chapter 21).

Author's Perspective: Should Homosexuals Consider Psychotherapy?

As mentioned earlier, homosexuality is no longer classified as a mental illness, and consequently it should not be assumed that all homosexuals need to enter psychotherapy. If an individual is happy and productive, there does not seem to be a need for change.

On the other hand, depression, low self-esteem, sexual dysfunction, or low productivity suggest an attempt at therapy. As society becomes more tolerant of homosexuality, it seems that therapy to help patients accept their own homosexuality will become relatively more common than conversion therapy.

There are, of course, certain people who feel uncomfortable about their homosexual orientation and wish to become heterosexual. Before entering conversion therapy, however, they should consider its success rate. If success is defined as an improvement in only one of several categories (e.g., decreased homosexual urge, decreased homosexual behavior, increased heterosexual urge, or increased heterosexual behavior), then the success rate may be 50 percent or greater. However, if a stable, lasting conversion is the desired outcome, then the success rate is much lower (Adams & Sturgis 1977; Bancroft 1974).

Individual differences among the persons requesting therapy are also important in predicting success. The probability of success appears to be greatest (1) in young individuals (below thirty-five years of age); (2) in those who had their first homosexual encounter after the age of sixteen; (3) in persons who are more bisexual than homosexual in their erotic responses; and (4) in individuals who are not transsexual as well as homosexual (Marmor & Green 1977).[5]

In conclusion, it seems that questions concerning psychotherapy represent another parallel between homosexuality and heterosexuality. No matter what one's erotic preference, therapy is most reasonably considered when there are problems with which one cannot effectively deal alone. For all types of difficulties, the probability of success should be considered before entering therapy. And difficulties in evaluating the success of therapy are similar for both heterosexuals and homosexuals.

SUMMARY

Sexual orientation may be described along a continuum, with 0 being exclusively heterosexual and 6, exclusively homosexual. In the United States, between 5 and 10 percent of the population appear to fall into categories 5 and 6, with male homosexuals outnumbering females approximately three to one.

Several popular conceptions of homosexuality have recently been tested in surveys or laboratory experiments: (1) homosexuals are preoccupied with sex; (2) compared to heterosexuals, homosexuals are looking for something different in a relationship; (3) homosexuals are easy to identify because of their inappropriate femininity or masculinity; (4) among homosexual couples, one partner is generally feminine while the other is masculine in appearance or behavior. None of these conceptions have been supported by the research data.

In regard to sexual behavior, three generalizations can be made: (1) considerable variability exists, and couples frequently shift roles; (2) oral-genital sex is probably the most frequent form of sexual interaction; (3) homosexual men are more likely than lesbians to have a variety of sexual partners.

A large survey of homosexuals—including investigations of their behavior and emotional responses—indicates that there are several general categories of homosexuals: close-coupled, open-coupled, functional, dysfunctional, and asexual. General satisfaction and overall adjustment were found to be highest in the close-coupled category; dissatisfaction and emotional problems tended to be greatest among the dysfunctionals and asexuals.

Despite the fact that homosexuality is accepted in many preliterate cultures, it is less common than in industrialized societies. It appears that the higher incidence of homosexuality in industrialized societies is related to a greater tendency for individuals to deviate from societal norms in general.

Factors involved in the development of homosexual preferences remain obscure. There is no solid evidence that hormones or other biological factors are directly involved. Similarly, neither child molestation by a homosexual male nor being raised by a homosexual mother seems to cause homosexuality. There are, however, certain sex differences in the development of homosexuality. Males tend to develop homosexual patterns earlier and have more difficulty accepting their homosexuality than females.

Homophobia—an irrationally strong negative reaction to homosexuality—is exhibited by some people. Variables found to be associated with homophobia include rigid sex-role stereotyping, lack of education, and strong traditional religious beliefs. It is also possible that some homophobic reactions represent an attempt to deny homosexual feelings within oneself.

There do not appear to be significant overall differences in the psychological adjustment of homosexuals compared to heterosexuals, especially when comparisons are made within the female population. However, male homosexuals have a higher rate of depression and attempts at suicide than male heterosexuals. These differences are generally explained by the relatively great stress of living in a society that tends to reject male homosexuality.

Bisexuality—sexual relations with members of both sexes—is more common than exclusive homosexuality. There appear to be several routes to this orientation. Some bisexuals may be basically homosexual but engage in heterosexual behavior to avoid being stigmatized. Others may temporarily exhibit homosexual patterns when isolated from opposite-sex persons. Still others may develop bisexuality because of a dissatisfaction with exclusive heterosexuality or homosexuality.

In many states, homosexual acts are illegal. However, there is a recent trend to change the legal status of homosexuality. Professionals no longer maintain that all homosexuals should seek psychotherapy. Nonetheless, when psychotherapy is of possible benefit, two general approaches exist: an attempt to help individuals accept themselves and their sexual orientation, and a possible conversion to heterosexuality.

NOTES

1. Although Christian writers had negative evaluations of homosexuality, it was not until the thirteenth century that homosexuals were actively persecuted. At this time, the Western world showed great intolerance towards many

groups who were considered different—including heretics, Moslems, and Jews. Thus, Boswell (1980) has argued that it was not the Christian doctrine but the medieval spirit of intolerance that was historically responsible for rejection of homosexuals, which in turn led to modern antihomosexual feelings.

2. Certain earlier studies had indicated that homosexuals did differ from heterosexuals on measures of masculinity and femininity. However, Storms (1980) pointed out that these studies used inappropriate measures and must be considered less valid than the more recent studies.

3. Homosexual women are often called lesbians, a term derived from the Greek island of Lesbos. In the seventh century B.C., Sappho lived on this island and wrote poems about the joys and beauty of female homosexuality.

4. Perhaps the main reason that the close-coupled group was happier than the heterosexual group is that the heterosexual group included many men who were not in a stable love relationship. By definition, the close-coupled group included only stable couples. Stable relationships—whether homosexual or heterosexual—seem to be very important in producing happiness.

5. Masters and Johnson (1979) reported relatively high rates of conversion from homosexuality to heterosexuality. However, Zilbergeld and Evans (1980) point out that several of the individuals in the therapy program were not really homosexuals. For example, certain males seemed to be heterosexuals who experienced sexual problems with females and turned to males for sexual relief; they did not exhibit a clear pattern of preference for males. As with many studies, there were also problems in obtaining data following the termination of therapy. Thus, the Masters and Johnson data probably represent an exaggerated success rate.

CHAPTER 18

Sexual Variations

As we have seen throughout the book, human sexuality is characterized by its extreme variability. Not only are there great cultural differences in the way sexuality is expressed, but within each society people tend to have different sexual preferences. Thus, it is virtually impossible to draw a distinction between normal and abnormal sexual behavior. Furthermore, if a distinction is attempted, there is a tendency to assume normal means good and abnormal, bad. Even though certain sexual variations have clearly negative effects on our society, such a dichotomy represents an oversimplification and is unfair to certain individuals with unusual but harmless sexual preferences.

Some of the variations discussed in this chapter may seem quite bizarre and unappealing. However, others do not differ greatly from those commonly expressed by people during sexual interaction. For example, foreplay often includes exhibiting and looking at one another's genitals, activities that superficially resemble those classified as exhibitionism and voyeurism. Perhaps the major difference between so-called normal persons and exhibitionists or voyeurs is that, for the latter people, the variation itself tends to become more important than the interpersonal relationship.

Just as there is not a sharp dichotomy between normal and variant, no clear line of distinction can be made between the various categories of variation; some individuals engage in a combination of variations or exhibit behaviors that fall halfway between two categories. Thus, the major purpose of this chapter is not to develop a scheme for pigeonholing people, but rather to gain some insight into the dynamics of these variations.

EXHIBITIONISM

Many women have, at one time or another, been subjected to the "flashes" of an *exhibitionist*. The following is the case history of a man (the great majority of exhibitionists are male) who was brought to the attention of legal authorities for exhibitionism:

> This married man in his 40s has always been shy with women, and after 15 years of marriage still is passive around his wife. During their infrequent intercourse (every 6 weeks to 2 months) he has difficulty getting or maintaining an erection. While his wife constantly bullies him, he does not complain, believing that she is right to do so. In the last five years, he has succumbed to the urge to exhibit his penis to passing girls or women. This occurs on the street, in the daytime, under circumstances when he realistically runs great risk of arrest. In fact, he does this in the neighborhood where he lives, not even going to strange areas or cities.
>
> He will stand to the side of a street and show his exposed penis to women passing in cars or to women walking on the other side of the street. He has an erection at these times. If he believes he was not noticed, he will shift his position or otherwise attempt to get their attention and when he has done so, he will not flee when he senses they are upset and might call for help.
>
> On one occasion, he exposed himself to two teenage girls, who began chuckling and advanced toward him as if interested; this is the only time he has precipitously left the scene.
>
> He has been arrested six times and has already spent time in prison. His reputation is ruined, his family is humiliated, and his professional status is in terrible disrepair. Nonetheless, he says he will probably repeat the act [reprinted with permission from Stoller (1976)].

Exhibitionists use a variety of strategies to make their displays. Some drivers pull up to a woman or group of women and open the car door, displaying their nude bodies. Others ride subways and buses or stand on street corners in long coats; they periodically open their coats and "flash" their genitals. Still others may suddenly appear at a window with their genitals exposed. The penis may be in either a flaccid or erect condition. In some instances, the man masturbates during the exposure; in others, he masturbates later while remembering it (MacDonald 1973).

In most cases (over 90 percent), exhibitionists do not make further sexual advances. They are especially unlikely to make physical advances if they have exposed themselves at a distance of more than three feet from the audience. Apparently, most flashers do not intend to initiate direct sexual involvement; the reaction of fear or indignation on the part of the viewer seems reinforcing enough (MacDonald 1973).

The viewer is typically an adult woman who is alone. However, some exhibitionists prefer child audiences, usually a group of children. Homosexual exposures rarely occur (Lester 1975). One might predict that exhibitionism would take place during the warm months. However, a study of exhibitionists in Denver indicates that there are no seasonal variations, despite obvious problems associated with cold-weather exposure. The "prime time" for flashing was found to be during rush hours—between eight and nine in the morning and three and five in the afternoon (MacDonald 1973).

VOYEURISM

A *voyeur*, or "Peeping Tom,"[1] is the complement of an exhibitionist; he or she derives sexual pleasure from watching a member of the opposite sex in the nude or during a sexual act.[1] Generally, the viewing is stealthy, and its secretiveness apparently contributes to the peeper's sexual arousal. The following example is a fairly typical case.

> This single man, in his early 20s, drives to a different residential neighborhood each night and surveys homes to find rooms where he can observe women undressing, while he is safely hidden in the bushes outside the window. When he finds a room in which a young woman is undressing, he becomes excited and masturbates. Although he can exhaust himself sexually after a couple of such experiences a night, he never satisfies his desire to peep, which is an insatiable hunger.
>
> He also goes out on dates and occasionally has intercourse without problems of potency. He enjoys this intercourse but less than the masturbating while peeping. He is not especially aroused watching a girlfriend undress. No matter how closely her nude body conforms to his ideal, looking at her under these permissive circumstances is fairly casual. He says, however, that if he were to watch her undressing when she did not know he was looking, her nudity would then arouse him as much as does any unknown woman's [reprinted with permission from Stoller (1976)].

A study of male voyeurs who have been arrested has indicated that they generally have a history of poor relationships with females and inadequate heterosexual sex lives; most are single. They tend to be shy, and in a few cases have been arrested for exhibitionism (Gebhard et al. 1965). The shyness of voyeurs is illustrated by a case history reported in Tollison and Adams (1979). A young woman noticed a neighborhood male peeping in her bedroom window. Partly as a joke, she "paraded" around the room nude, engaging in sensual poses and fondling her breasts. Finally, she went to the window and invited the man to come into the house. In apparent terror, the man ran and avoided her on subsequent occasions.

As in this case, voyeurs usually watch their subjects through windows and do not make sexual approaches. However, if a voyeur enters a building or the subject's house or if he draws attention to the fact that he is watching, there is a greater probability of a rape attempt (Yalom 1960).

Contrary to what one might expect, voyeurs rarely go to strip shows, look at pornography, or attend nudist camps (Yalom 1960; Sagarin 1973). Viewing under forbidden circumstances seems basic to their sexual arousal.

Psychological Perspective: Stripteasers, Nudists, Exhibitionists, and Voyeurists

Superficially, stripteasers, or "strippers," resemble exhibitionists. However, studies of the personalities and personal histories of female strippers suggest that they are quite different. Strippers are not loners, nor do they have a history of exhibitionism. In many cases, they started working as bar girls and took up striptease dancing as a lucrative alternative (Lester 1975; Skipper & McCaghy 1970). Starting in the late 1970s, male strippers have become popular in certain nightclubs that cater to women. As in the case of their female counterparts, it appears that money is a factor of overriding importance in the choice of this occupation.

Nudists also act like exhibitionists, but once again, the resemblance is only superficial. A study of the personality characteristics of nudists indicated that they were very similar to a control group of nonnudists. The few differences that did appear between the groups seem related to the fact that people who join nudist clubs are social nonconformists (Blank 1969; Lester 1975). It seems that, within the confines of a nudist club, the naked body simply becomes part of the social scene. A certain amount of modesty is maintained by social rules that limit staring and prohibit body contact or alcohol consumption (Weinberg 1965).

FIGURE 18.1

A nude beach. In contrast to what some people believe, people who visit nudist colonies and nude beaches do not psychologically resemble exhibitionists and voyeurs.

ENGAGING IN OBSCENE CONVERSATION

In Chicago, during the early 1970s, two enterprising female sociology students established a business in which, for a fee, they would talk in obscenities to male clients. By 1983, something known as "phone sex" had arrived. A large number of businesses advertised in adult entertainment magazines, promising to provide explicit sexual conversations for up to an hour. In many instances, customers were billed via credit cards.

These examples may appear offensive to most people, but they do not represent illegal acts. In contrast, explicit sexual conversations with unwilling listeners are illegal and, for the recipients, the experience can be very unpleasant.

Obscene conversation with an unwilling listener most commonly takes place via the telephone. In many cases, the caller masturbates during the conversation. Although the number of men who make obscene phone calls is probably not large, the callers make a great many contacts. One survey indicated that 75 percent of the undergraduate females at a college had received obscene phone calls (Murray & Beran 1968).

Most obscene telephone calls are to women selected at random from the telephone directory (Gebhard et al. 1965). However, one report indicated a high incidence of obscene phone calls to female counselors at a suicide-prevention center (Brockopp & Lester 1969).

A study of the personalities of such callers apprehended by the police indicates that the offenders had low self-esteem and were angry at women in general. The hostility apparently developed from a poor rela-

FIGURE 18.2

As in the case of exhibitionists, studies reveal that most obscene callers are expressing a basic hostility toward women rather than simply a strong sexual drive.

tionship with the mother. For many individuals, the use of the telephone eliminated the anxiety they would have felt using the same language in a face-to-face relationship (Nadler 1968).

TRANSVESTISM

Dressing as a member of the opposite sex is sometimes referred to as eonism, a term derived from a Frenchman named Chevalier d'Eon. This nobleman had created some confusion by dressing sometimes as a woman and at other times as a man. It was not until after his death in 1810 that an inspection of the body allowed for an accurate identification of his gender.

Recently, the term *transvestite* has become more widely accepted for individuals who wear clothing of the opposite sex. Some have complete outfits, and others use only certain items of opposite-sex clothing—for example, underwear. Transvestites are typically males who have heterosexual orientations. Some enjoy masturbating while observing themselves in the mirror dressed in female clothing. Others appear in public dressed as a woman and gain excitement from admiring glances. Later, they may masturbate to fantasies and memories of these adventures (Tollison & Adams 1979).

FIGURE 18.3

In contrast to what most people think, most transvestites are heterosexual males. Many report that they have a feminine side that is expressed in a satisfying fashion only when they dress in female clothing.

Prince and Bentler (1972) surveyed over 500 subscribers to a transvestite magazine in order to gain insight into transvestism.[2] There were several interesting findings. Most of the men who identified themselves as transvestites were or had been married; only 22 percent were never-married singles. Many of the men viewed themselves as normal males, but with a feminine side seeking expression. When dressed as females, they perceived themselves as having a distinctly different personality. Although they were fully aware of society's disapproval, most of the men were not motivated to seek counseling or therapy.

The most common clothing preference was for lingerie. Many of the men liked to wear it, or other types of female clothing, while having heterosexual intercourse. Obviously, a large number of the wives were aware of their husbands' transvestism; the women showed a wide variety of reactions ranging from disgust to acceptance.

A few of the subscribers described themselves as homosexuals. However, in contrast to some homosexuals who cross-dress in order to present a caricature of women (these men are typically called ''in drag''), the transvestite homosexuals generally tried to appear as feminine and attractive as possible (Prince & Bentler 1972).

Robert Stoller, a psychiatrist, conducted interviews with several mothers of transvestites and observed that most of these women had sexual problems. Furthermore, the women tended to express a great deal of hostility toward men. Stoller concluded that early parental treatment—especially by the mother—was important in the development of transvestism (Stoller 1976). Several case studies seem to illustrate the significance of the mother's role. London (1957) reported a case in which a mother punished her six-year-old son by forcing him to wear girl's clothing. At first the boy was humiliated and hid under the table when visitors came. However, he later developed an interest in cross-dressing and frequently engaged in the activity on his own. Another fairly typical example is presented in more detail:

> This biologically normal man in his 20's is married, with children. He is a construction foreman.
>
> Until he was three years old he lived with his mother and father, but his mother died, and then responsibility for his care fell upon his stepmother.
>
> When he was four years old, she dressed him in girl's clothes to punish him for getting dirty. He had not cross-dressed spontaneously. She did this several times subsequently, and within two years he had arranged with a neighbor girl to dress him up regularly during their after-school play. The dressing up died away for several years, but at age 12, he did it once again, almost casually. On starting to put his stepmother's panties on, he suddenly became intensely sexually excited and masturbated for the first time. For several years thereafter, he would only put on his stepmother's underwear and either masturbate or spontaneously ejaculate. Then, in mid-teens, he began taking underwear from the homes of friends' sisters, and in a year or so increased this activity to stealing women's un-

derwear whenever he could find it. Aside from the moments when he put on these garments, he was unremarkably masculine in appearance, in athletic interests, and in daydreams of what he would wish to be in the future. He was attracted to girls and went out on dates, but, being shy, he had less sexual experience than some of his friends.

He proposed to the first girl with whom he had a serious affair, confessed his fetishistic cross-dressing to her, and was surprised and relieved when she not only was not upset but assisted him by offering her underwear and by purchasing new pairs for him as he wished. Starting within a year after marriage, he found it more exciting to put on more of his wife's clothes than just her underwear, and now he prefers dressing completely in her clothes and having her assist him in putting on makeup and fixing his wig.

He feels completely male and is accepted by all who know him as a masculine man. He does not desire sex transformation. He has never had homosexual relations and is sexually attracted only by women's bodies [reprinted with permission from Stoller (1976)].

Legal Perspective: Public-nuisance Offenses

A variety of behavior—including exhibitionism, voyeurism, and transvestism—is prosecuted under the general category of public-nuisance offenses. Although there is no physical contact between perpetrator and victim, these behaviors are assumed to offend public decency, violate community standards, and/or corrupt public morals.

Prosecutions for exhibitionism or indecent exposure reflect a wide variety of interpretations of the law. At the one extreme, individuals have been convicted of indecent exposure following swimming in the nude or sunbathing, even though no one gave testimony to being aroused or offended (Boggan et al. 1975). At the other extreme, "bottomless" dancers in California have escaped prosecution by shaving certain parts of their bodies; "private parts" were defined in the statutes as those areas covered by pubic hair (Katchadourian & Lunde 1980).

In most of the fifty states, persons repeatedly convicted of public-nuisance offenses such as indecent exposure may be labeled *sexual psychopaths.* In many cases, this labeling results in long stays in jails or in hospitals for the criminally insane. There is a belief among legal officials and society in general that, over time, sexual psychopaths are likely to progress from nonviolent offenses such as voyeurism and exhibitionism to rape and other violent sex crimes. However, research suggests that such progression is extremely rare (Gebhard et al. 1965). Thus, these individuals are probably less likely to commit violent crimes than other convicted criminals who spend less time in confinement.

As will be seen later in the chapter, some of the public-nuisance offenders, such as voyeurs and exhibitionists, seem to respond well to psychotherapy. Nonetheless, relatively few states have facilities for therapy. An exception is California, where Atascadero State Hospital was established for the treatment of sexual offenders. It will be interesting to see how effective such a treatment program proves to be and whether other states will adopt similar programs in the future.

TRANSSEXUALISM

Transsexuals are individuals who believe they are "trapped" in the body of the wrong gender. Many of them wish to have their sex surgically altered. They may be either male or female, but males wishing to be biological females are the more common.

Transsexuals differ from transvestites in that transsexuals have a desire to actually *be* members of the opposite sex, not just cross-dress for purposes of sexual arousal. (Related to this, transsexuals are sometimes considered to be individuals having sex-identity problems, not a sexual variation.)

Dissatisfaction with or confusion about one's gender has been documented for thousands of years. The Roman emperor Heliogabalus is reported to have offered half the empire to anyone who could change him into a woman, complete with female genitals. In the sixteenth century, King Henry III of France wished to be known as Her Majesty; there is a report that he appeared before the Deputies dressed in a low-cut gown and a long pearl necklace (Green 1976).

One of the first sex-change operations on record involves a person who appears to have been an innocent bystander. Allegedly, Nero killed his pregnant wife in a fit of rage. Then, filled with remorse, he looked for someone to replace her who had similar facial features. A male ex-slave named Sporum was chosen. Nero's surgeons were then ordered to trans-

FIGURE 18.4

Renée Richards as a male and after her sex-change operation. Transsexuals typically believe they were born with the body of the "wrong" sex and, in many cases, seek sex-change operations.

form the boy into a female. Following the operation, Sporum and Nero were formally married (Green 1976).

A rather large amount of research has been conducted with contemporary transsexuals, since the major hospitals that have sanctioned sex-change operations require extensive psychological tests and psychiatric evaluations before surgery is approved. Persons with severe psychiatric problems or depression are quickly identified and rejected as sex-realignment candidates. Those who are tentatively accepted as reasonable candidates are then given a thorough explanation of what is involved in the transformation. Since there are rather basic sex differences in the procedures, males and females undergoing transformation will be considered separately.

About three times as many men as women request sex-change surgery (Green 1975). The first step in the procedure is hormone therapy. Men receive estrogen regularly from this point on. It gradually reduces the number of erections and ejaculations and induces breast enlargement, rounding of the hips, and other forms of feminization. In many cases, the transsexual is told to dress and live as a female during this period (which typically lasts six months or so). This is done to help the person adjust to the new sex role and also to put the transformation decision to a test.

The next step is the surgical operation. The penis and testes are removed and, in many cases, the skin from these organs is utilized to construct an artificial vagina as well as the labia majora and minora. The advantage of using the skin from the male organs is that it has nerve endings responsive to sexual stimulation. Cosmetic surgery may also be performed. The size of the Adam's apple may be reduced, and silicone may be implanted to build up the bust or hipline. After a period of recovery from the surgery, most individuals report being able to engage in coitus as a female, even experiencing orgasm (Lester 1975).

The steps preceding surgery for females are comparable. Hormone treatment—with testosterone in this case—stimulates development of a beard, deepening of the voice, and enlargement of the clitoris. Some individuals choose to have only the hormone treatment. Others have their breasts, uterus, and ovaries removed.

For some of these persons, male genitals are constructed. A scrotum is fashioned from the labia and filled with plastic implants to simulate testicles. The development of a penis takes place in stages. First, an artificial urethra is created. The urethra is then enclosed in a tube fashioned from skin taken from the abdominal wall. Finally, the clitoris is embedded in the newly created organ, allowing for the possibility of orgasm. Despite modern technology, the artificial penis is not very realistic in appearance and is incapable of erection (Pauly 1974b). In certain cases, artificial penises have been fashioned using a rigid silicone tube as a framework. With such an organ, vaginal penetration is easy. However, physiological orgasm cannot be triggered by stimulation of the penis, and detumescence is impossible (Tollison & Adams 1979).

Studies of female transsexuals indicate certain similarities between males and females. A long history of wanting to be a male was typical of females and, in several cases, the young girls invented a masculine name for themselves (Stoller 1972). An apparent difference—as suggested by a recent Danish study—is that transsexual women (women wanting to be men), report higher levels of sexual interest and sexual activity than transsexual men (Sorensen & Hertoft 1982).

Author's Perspective: Causes of Transsexualism and the Moral Issue in Sex-change Surgery

The cause of gender-identity confusion is unclear at this point. On the one hand, Diamond (1974) has argued that transsexualism is caused by some variation in prenatal development. This biological interpretation is indirectly supported by the finding that psychotherapy is notoriously unsuccessful in treating transsexuals. On the other hand, Socarides (1975) has concluded that transsexualism is a delusion resulting from psychological factors. Much of the psychiatric literature on early childhood is consistent with this interpretation. Furthermore, there do not appear to be hormonal differences between transsexual and nontranssexual men (Aiman & Boyar 1982).

The controversy over causation is of more than theoretical interest. Until those espousing a biological interpretation can muster firm experimental support for their position, sex-change operations should be considered morally reprehensible. It is clearly a much different matter to perform surgery on a child suffering from AGS (see chapter 13) than on a person who may simply have a delusion.

There is also evidence from another source that sex-change operations are unjustified. Meyer and Reter (1979) conducted an extensive study in which a group of transsexuals who had undergone surgery were compared with a roughly comparable group not operated upon. All individuals were rated on four categories of adjustment: legal, economic, marital (or cohabitational), and psychiatric. The ratings were made on two occasions: at the beginning of the study (before the one group received surgery) and after a period of two or more years. As anticipated, the adjustment scores for both groups were low initially. However, definite improvement was shown over time. The most important finding was that, at the end of the follow-up, there was no significant difference between the subjects who had undergone surgery and those who had not.

The Meyer and Reter study had some unavoidable methodological flaws. For example, the operate and inoperate groups were not precisely comparable, and only 50 percent of the subjects could be located for follow-up. However, as a result of the study, the Johns Hopkins Hospital has stopped performing sex-change operations on transsexuals. Unless there is future evidence to the contrary, such a decision appears sound and will probably be followed by other hospitals in the United States and Europe.

INCEST

Virtually all societies studied have *incest taboos* forbidding sexual intercourse with close relatives. However, the definition of what constitutes a close relative differs among cultures. In some societies, only parent-child or sibling relationships are forbidden. Others prohibit sexual relationships between relatives by marriage—such as stepparents and in-laws. When family groupings are extensive, a large proportion of the available population may be off limits to one another as potential partners. There have occasionally been exceptions to the incest taboo for persons of special rank. For example, brother-sister marriages in the royal family of the ancient Egyptians were condoned. Similarly, among the Azande of Africa, chiefs were permitted to have sexual relations with their daughters. Nonetheless, the incest taboo applied to all other members of these societies (Ford & Beach 1951).

Incest taboos probably developed for a variety of reasons. First, many preliterate societies have noted that inbreeding often has negative effects on offspring (Segner 1968). These problems have been well documented. For example, in Japan, children from marriages between cousins talk at a later age, are physically inferior, and score lower on intelligence tests compared to children of conventional marriages (Schull & Neel 1965). Similarly, in the United States, research indicates that a greater incidence of major defects and early death occurs in the children of brother-sister and father-daughter pairings than in a comparable group of noninbred children (Adams & Neel 1967).

A second factor involved in the incest taboo may be a lowering of sexual attraction, which apparently results from close interaction before puberty. It was found that individuals raised together in Israeli kibbutzim virtually never had sexual relations or married one another (Shepher 1972). Apparently, a taboo develops similar to that usually found between brothers and sisters.

A third reason for the development of the taboo may be related to disruptive effects of incest on the family structure. Incest creates sexual rivalries and jealousies within the family. Furthermore, role confusion exists: a person must function, for example, as both father and lover, a situation that inevitably creates conflicts (Coult 1963). Since family structure was probably basic in the survival and evolution of humans, rules that reduced family disruption would tend to develop and become important in a society.

Finally, there are social and political benefits that result from marriages outside the family. Cooperation between groups is especially important in the survival of many preliterate societies. For example, an alliance resulting from a "good" marriage may allow two tribes to cooperate and gain an advantage over other competing tribes. Even in highly industrialized societies, emphasis is often placed on marrying into the "right" family. It seems likely that the possible social and political benefits of marrying outside the family encouraged the establishment of incest taboos.

Comparative Perspective: "Incest" Inhibition in Animals

Certain factors seem to reduce the probability of inbreeding among lower animals. In one study, male rats were reared with their sisters and then given a chance to mate with their sisters and unrelated females; the males were less sexually active with their sisters than with the other females (Segner 1968). As in humans, siblings reared together seem to have diminished sexual attraction for one another. Under normal conditions, the tendency to inbreed is further reduced because mother rats drive offspring away before they mature sexually.

In free-ranging rhesus monkeys, copulation between mother and male offspring rarely occurs. A variety of factors seems to inhibit this type of incest. First, males usually leave the social group that includes the mother. Second, high-ranking males (which are typically the older ones) tend to inhibit copulation of young ones. Finally, mothers generally remain dominant over their sons, and this dominance relationship inhibits mating (Sade 1968).

It seems that the roots of the incest taboo extend rather far back into our animal heritage. At least some of the advantages of avoiding matings between close relatives seem to be similar for both humans and animals. Then, as humans evolved—and their societies became more sophisticated—it seems likely that additional advantages of avoiding incest developed, and the incest taboo became even stronger.

The Incidence of Incest

Despite the taboos, human incest does occur. In the United States, approximately 4 to 7 percent of the population has had sexual intercourse with a close relative, and, with petting included, the figure rises to 15 percent (Gebhard et al. 1965; Hunt 1974).

The most common type of incest seems to be that between brother and sister. However, most of these cases are not reported to authorities. In families where brothers and sisters share bedrooms, the probability of incest increases. In contrast, incest between mother and son appears rarely, despite its popularization in certain plays and novels (Tollison & Adams 1979).

Incest between a father and daughter is apparently less common than that between a brother and sister, but it is more likely to be reported to authorities. Usually the daughter reports it, even though the wife may be aware of the relationship. The wife may deny or overlook the incest for a variety of reasons. In the first place, the incestuous relationship may be viewed as a result of the wife's failure to satisfy her husband (Weinberg 1976). A study of the wives of incest offenders suggests another reason for failure to report father-daughter incest. Many of the wives seemed to have a strong feeling of social and moral superiority over their husbands. The incest offense probably reinforced this feeling of martyrdom (Garrett & Wright 1975).

A study of fathers involved in incest indicated that, as might be expected, the men who had contact with young daughters (under twelve) were psychologically disturbed. They tended to be passive, socially inept, and ineffective as workers. However, men who had incestuous relations with older daughters did not seem to differ greatly from fathers in nonincestuous families (Gebhard et al. 1965).

One reason for the failure to find severe psychological disturbance among the latter group of fathers may be related to the daughter's role. In more than half the cases investigated, the daughter actively encouraged the father, or she showed no resistance (Gebhard et al. 1965). Thus, many of the men could probably be categorized as having a lack of inhibition rather than an unusual sexual preference.

Reactions to Father-Daughter Incest

A disproportionate number of young females involved in incestuous relations are likely to become runaways, drug addicts, or prostitutes (James & Meyerding 1977). Among women who experienced incest as children, guilt and long-lasting fears are common. Furthermore, the women are likely to have a negative self-concept and a lack of sexual responsiveness to men (Herman & Hirshman 1977). Of course, it is not clear whether the incest itself or unfavorable family conditions in general are responsible for these problems. There is little doubt, however, that father-daughter incest contributes to serious psychological and emotional difficulties for a number of women.

PEDOPHILIA

In most societies, sexual relations between adults and children are strongly forbidden, and adults who encourage such relationships—*pedophiles*—are harshly punished. However, there have been certain exceptions. The Lepcha of India believed that girls would not mature sexually if they did not experience sexual intercourse. By the age of eleven or twelve most girls engaged in coitus regularly, and older men sometimes had intercourse with eight-year-old girls. Although such behavior was unusual, the Lepcha considered it more amusing than amoral (Morris 1938). Even in the United States there are certain underground groups that encourage childhood coitus.[3]

Pedophilia is considered a serious crime in the United States. The following example illustrates male pedophilia, which is the most common type:

The subject is a married man in his 30's. His wife was the first adult woman with whom he had sexual relations, and from the beginning to the present, these have been joyless, with little erotic pleasure, and marred by his difficulty in getting an erection and by premature ejaculation. His wife's body never appealed to him because it is an adult female's; he avoids seeing her because to do so provokes feelings ranging from uneasiness to disgust. An extramarital experiment with another adult woman produced the same effects.

Several times a year, he has found himself suddenly, unexpectedly, intensely excited and preoccupied with wanting a prepubertal girl to fondle. He has never experienced such excitement with, or thinking about, an adult woman. When he can get close to such a little girl he seeks only to massage her body and fondle her genitals; he has never attempted penetration. On a few occasions he has had a cooperative child touch his penis but, because of fear, has never permitted this to advance to ejaculation. When he leaves the child, he masturbates.

When trapped into needing an erection with his wife, he fantasizes fondling a little girl [reprinted with permission from Stoller (1976)].

An investigation of convicted pedophiles by Cohen, Seghorn, and Calmas (1969) indicates that the offenders are generally socially unskilled men who avoid interaction with others, especially adults. These men generally fall into one of three categories. The first category, "personally immature offenders," consists of persons with a long history of difficulties in dealing with adults, both men and women. They are comfortable only with children. Usually, they know their victims beforehand and "court" them for a period of time before making sexual advances.

The second category, "regressed offenders," includes men who apparently had a normal adolescence. However, the stresses associated with either a marriage or their job during their adult years seem to have driven them toward relationships with children. In some instances, the men were drunk during the sexual episodes. In a large number of cases, the pedophilia began after the discovery that their girlfriend or wife was having an affair with another man.

"Aggressive offenders" make up the third category of pedophiles. These men assault children—either girls or boys—both aggressively and sexually. The penis or some elongated object may suddenly be thrust into the child's mouth or anus. Sexual excitement seems to be related to the aggressive aspects of the act. This type of pedophile generally has a long history of antisocial acts, sometimes starting with the torturing of animals.

In most cases, girls between six and twelve are approached by pedophiles; the interaction typically consists of genital exposure and fondling. Masturbation may accompany the interaction, but the man usually masturbates in private after the incident. When girls over fourteen

FIGURE 18.5

A scene from the movie *Lolita,* which illustrates a type of incest. Unfortunately, the victims of incest often experience severe psychological and emotional problems as adults.

are involved, coitus typically takes place. However, this is generally with the girl's permission. In some cases, the "victim" actually initiates the sexual interaction (Mohr et al. 1962; Vetter 1972).

Pedophiles choose boys as sex objects in approximately 20 percent of cases reported. According to one study, many cases of homosexual pedophilia do not come to the attention of authorities because sexual relations take place with young prostitutes (Rossman 1973).

Although the number of pedophiles is not large, one of them may approach many different children. As a result, a fairly large percentage of children have had some sexual contact with adults. Kinsey and his associates (1953) estimated that between 20 and 40 percent of children under fourteen have had some type of sexual experience with an adult.

Reactions to Pedophilia

In contrast to incest, children's reactions to pedophilia are not long lasting. In one study, less than 1 percent of women who had contact with pedophiles as children reported severely damaged adult lives attributable to the experience; the vast majority simply remembered the experience as unpleasant (Gagnon 1965). Of course, reactions to attacks by aggressive offenders tended to be the most severe.

The difference in reactions to incest and pedophilia is probably related to several factors. First, incidents involving incest are usually repeated, whereas contact with a pedophile is often an isolated experience. Second, the incestuous relationship virtually always involves someone with whom there is emotional involvement, and so guilt feelings are particularly likely to result. In contrast, at least some pedophiles are strangers or not well known by the child. Third, pedophilia, by definition, involves children; incest includes relations with adolescents and older individuals. As we have seen, children are less likely to exhibit long-lasting reactions to sexual traumas. Finally, incidents of incest that are reported generally include coitus; most reports of pedophilia only involve petting.

One of the greatest dangers to the victim of a pedophile is that anxiety and guilt developed during the incident will generalize and affect sexual feelings when the child becomes an adult. Extreme reactions of the parents upon discovering the incident may accentuate these feelings and essentially cause more harm than the incident itself (McCaghy 1971). Clearly, it is important that parents adopt a calm, reassuring attitude to help their children deal with the aftermath of a pedophilic experience.

Legal Perspective: Sexual Crimes against Children

Several types of laws attempt to prevent the sexual exploitation of children. *Statutory rape* laws prohibit a male over the age of seventeen or eighteen from having coitus with a female under a specific age; the age of consent varies from twelve to seventeen, depending upon the state. These laws apply even if the minor has given consent or works as a prostitute (Slovenko 1965).

Child-molestation laws are aimed at noncoital sexual behaviors that involve children. They generally apply to such behaviors as genital fondling, the use of obscene language, exhibitionism, or showing pornography to a child. However, the wording of these laws is often vague and open to a variety of interpretations.

The child sex laws that generally carry the most severe penalty are those against incest, particularly cases which involve a father and daughter. In certain states, incest offenses may carry penalties of as many as fifty years in prison. The definition of incest varies from state to state: in some instances incest refers only to immediate family members; in others, cousins, aunts, and uncles are also included (Slovenko 1965).

In cases involving sexual crimes against children, interrogations by police officers and courtroom procedures may produce a great deal of fear and anxiety in the children. In fact, the legal system may help to imprint a sexual incident on a child's mind that otherwise would easily be forgotten (Gagnon 1965). Similarly, the reporting of incest to the police and the resulting incarceration of a father may simply compound the distress of the family. A daughter may be faced with feelings of loss during imprisonment of a parent as well as guilt over presenting evidence against her father (Lester 1975). Thus, families in which incest occurs experience a dilemma: Not reporting incest constitutes failure to report a crime; reporting the incident may create more disruption in the family than the incident itself, especially since certain courts appear to be highly prejudiced against incest offenders. Clearly, the needs of the children in cases of child molestation and incest should be given high priority in both legal procedures and sentencing.

ZOOPHILIA

The choice of animals as sex objects—*zoophilia* or *bestiality*—occurs more commonly among individuals raised on farms than among those from urban areas. According to Kinsey, approximately 17 percent of rural males experienced some sort of contact with animals that resulted in orgasm; for city-dwelling males, the percentage was less than half that large. The percentage of females reporting animal contacts was relatively small—less than 4 percent for both city and rural dwellers. In most cases, the animal contacts took place during adolescence and seemed to reflect temporary experimentation rather than the establishment of a stable pattern of preference (Kinsey et al. 1948, 1953).

In some cases, a real preference for animals develops and lasts into adulthood. Occasionally, sadistic tendencies combine with bestiality. For example, an animal may be mutilated as the individual masturbates. As in cases involving sadism and aggressive pedophilia, there is usually a history of torturing animals that goes back into early childhood (Stoller 1976).

Perhaps the most common type of zoophilia involves a preference for animals that is seen in socially withdrawn individuals. The following is an example.

> A single man, a farm laborer in his late 20s, has been having intercourse with animals since puberty. Being very shy, he has never gone with a woman. Although in his late teens he would have liked to, he now has no conscious desire for women. Two attempts with prostitutes found him impotent; these were his only heterosexual experiences. He has had no homosexual relations [reprinted with permission from Stoller (1976)].

Several examples of zoophilia have been recorded in European history. In most cases, the acts were strongly condemned, and even the animals were held responsible. For example, in the fifteenth century, a man was arrested for having coitus with a cow and a goat; all three were found guilty and burned at the stake (Katchadourian & Lunde 1975).

In some societies, bestiality is or was associated with various myths. Among the Copper Eskimos of Arctic North America, there is a legend that a woman once copulated with dogs and the dogs made her pregnant. The resulting offspring were the first white men and the beginnings of the Caucasian race. In the Fez society of Morocco, animal contacts were associated with virility. It was said that a certain magical rite was so effective that, afterwards, a man could "deflower 72 virgin cows" (Ford & Beach 1951).

Theoretical and Comparative Perspective: Animals Sexually Attracted to Humans

Certain animals that have been raised by humans exhibit a sort of zoophilia in reverse. If a ring dove is reared in isolation and fed entirely by humans, it will reject ring doves of the opposite sex when it is sexually mature; instead, it will make sexual advances toward humans (Klinghammer & Hess 1964).

A similar type of cross-species attraction has been observed in apes raised by humans. A female gorilla named Congo sometimes grasped men's hands and pulled them into contact with her vulva, making masturbatory movements at the same time. In one instance, the famous animal psychologist Robert Yerkes barely escaped rape by Congo (Yerkes 1928).

One explanation for this unusual type of sexual attraction is that some animals develop a strong preference for a class of stimuli as a result of early experience during a critical period of development. This process is called *imprinting* (Hess 1964). Whether or not imprinting occurs in humans is not clear. However, some theorists suggest that a phenomenon of this sort is involved in the development of certain types of human sexual variations (see Money & Ehrhardt 1972).

FETISHISM

A person characterized by *fetishism* becomes sexually aroused by an inanimate object, some feature or quality of an object, or some part of the body that is not usually associated with sexuality. In some cases, the fetish becomes more important than any person, and orgasm is impossible without the sexually valuable item. Common fetish objects include shoes, stockings, underwear, or other articles of clothing that are worn close to the skin and tend to pick up body odors. In cases where sadism and masochism are involved, such paraphernalia as boots and whips may become fetish objects.

For some individuals, not the object itself but some quality of the object becomes a fetish. Fur, leather, and rubber are often associated with sexual arousal in fetishists or individuals with fetishist leanings. Many X-rated movies and sex magazines feature scenes with these objects' qualities.

Almost any part of the body—including feet, hands, and hair—may become a fetish. (Breasts, thighs, and genitals do not qualify as fetish items because they are traditionally associated with sexuality.) Accord-

FIGURE 18.6

Fetish items. In some cases, individuals rely strongly on such items to become sexually aroused. Most theorists believe that associative learning is basic to the development of fetishes.

ing to one police report, a man was arrested for sneaking up behind a young girl and cutting off a lock of her hair. Upon entering the offender's home, authorities found plaits of hair in five different colors, as well as seventy-two hair ribbons.

Another police case involved a young man who was known, according to the newspapers, as the "phantom female foot fondler." Several women reported that the man grabbed their feet, removed their shoes, and then passionately kissed and caressed their toes. The man was finally apprehended and charged with stealing a shoe (Tollison & Adams 1979).

Although it is rare, there are reports of individuals who develop fetishes for persons with amputated limbs. For example, a Vietnam War veteran collected pictures of mutilated bodies; he also cut off one of the arms or legs from *Playboy* photographs. These pictures were used in order to obtain erection prior to intercourse with his wife (Tollison & Adams 1979).

Some theorists believe that kleptomania—stealing objects that are not needed—is related to fetishism. There are cases in which touching an object (usually something made of cloth) with the intent to steal triggers orgasm. Others steal large amounts of material, and the satisfaction derived is described as erotic (Socarides 1960; Stoller 1976).

A few studies have been made of the personalities of fetishists, especially male fetishists. Generally, these people lack warmth and emotional expression, and they are emotionally dependent. Fantasies center around the fetish, and sexual fears tend to be unusually strong. There is also evidence that fetishist activities increase when the fetishist experiences interpersonal rejection (Weissman 1957; Epstein 1960).

Most theorists believe that associative learning is very important in the adoption of fetishes. At a time before an individual has had any heterosexual experience, he or she may come into contact with a random stimulus that is inadvertently associated with sexual arousal. Later, the memory of the erotic event becomes part of a masturbation fantasy. Repeated masturbations associating the stimulus with orgasm help to reinforce the stimulus-response relationship. Finally, the fantasy—including what could now be called the fetish—becomes more important than other types of arousal or fantasies (McGuire, Carlisle, & Young 1965).

Indirect support for this learning-oriented explanation of fetishism comes from a study in which a similar reaction was induced in normal males by a simple learning procedure. A woman's boot was presented to subjects along with pictures of nude women. After several pairings, the boot alone produced erections in the subjects (Rachman 1966). Of course, this demonstration does not prove that real-life fetishes are adopted in this way; however, it suggests that the first step—the development of a strong sexual preference—can be developed through simple, associative learning.

It is also interesting to note that some experiences in the Vietnam War veteran's personal history seem to explain the learning of the mutilization fetish. The young man had his first coitus with a Vietnamese prostitute who had lost one leg. He also remembered becoming sexually excited upon viewing partially nude and mutilated bodies of Vietnamese women who had been killed during bombing attacks (Tollison & Adams 1979).

MISCELLANEOUS VARIATIONS

Certain variations are quite rare, or little is known about their dynamics. Some of these will be briefly discussed in this section.

Frottage involves pressing or rubbing against a sex object. Frotteurs are typically men who become sexually aroused by rubbing their penises against the buttocks of strange women under crowded conditions such as those found on a bus or subway. Although some men supplement sexual intercourse with occasional rubbing behavior, the bona fide frotteur is impotent in most sexual interactions (Tollison & Adams 1979).

Saliromania is a predominantly male variation in which there is a desire to soil a woman. In some cases, saliromania may be expressed by the destruction of a statue or painting of a woman. The well-publicized attack on the Michelangelo statue *Pieta* in St. Peter's Church in Vatican City was apparently the work of a saliromaniac. In many cases, the man may get sexually excited to the point of ejaculation while engaging in a soiling or destructive act.

Urophilia is a variation involving urine. Urophiles typically urinate upon or wish to be urinated upon by their sex partners. In some cases, urophilia is associated with the drinking of urine or the stimulation of the urethra by some object. Underground newspapers have been known to run advertisements for urophiles, utilizing such phrases as "water sports" and "golden showers" (Tollison & Adams 1979).

A somewhat comparable variation—but related to feces—is known as *coprophilia*. Coprophiles report high levels of sexual excitement from defecating upon another person or watching the act of defecation. Variations involving the feces appear to be more rare than those involving urine (Solomon & Patch 1974).

The anal region is also the focus of a variation known as *klismaphilia*. In this case, erotic satisfaction is gained from receiving an enema. A prostitute named Georgina has described a role that she repeatedly played with a client. Georgina dressed herself as a nanny and "reprimanded" the man as if he were a small child. After some childlike play, the man would be brought to orgasm by being given an enema (Barros 1970; Denko 1976).

Finally, a variation involving the mouth—referred to as *erotic vomiting*—has been recently identified. In one case history, the act of vomiting was likened to a sex act: a sensation of tension, a rush or flood of good feelings, and a quiet, warm glow when finished. In another case, a woman reported orgasm triggered by vomiting (Stoller 1982).

Theoretical Perspective: Sex Differences in the Incidence of Sexual Variations

Not only are males more likely than females to commit sexual crimes, but they are also more commonly involved in sexual variations in general. Psychoanalytically oriented theorists explain some of the sex differences in terms of identification with parents. For both sexes, identification is initially with the mother. However, the male must later switch his identification to the father or a father substitute. This additional hurdle increases the chances that there will be problems in sex identification. Psychoanalysts believe that sex identification is basic to "normal" heterosexual development (Green 1974).

Another theory also suggests that males must overcome more hurdles than females. However, in this case, the hurdles are biological. As pointed out in chapter 13, all fetuses start out essentially the same. If no androgen is present at about the sixth week of prenatal development, the individual develops as a female. With androgen, primitive sexual structures develop into the penis and scrotum. Even in the later stages of sexual development in puberty, the male changes are more extensive than those of the female. Thus, biologically speaking, there is more opportunity for things to go "wrong" in a male than in a female (Eme 1979; Baumrind 1980).

Still another explanation for the greater number of males than females that develop sexual variations involves sex-role development. It could be argued that the female role undergoes less of a change at puberty than that of a male. A young girl typically develops patterns of interacting with men that remain appropriate after puberty. For example, the little girl who flirts with her father may successfully use some of the same tactics with boyfriends at a later age. In contrast, a boy's tactics of attracting attention at a young age are rarely successful if attempted by a man. Once again, it appears that a male's adjustment is more complex than that of a female. However, it seems likely that, as male and female sex roles change in our society, there will be fewer sex differences.

In addition to these developmental factors, our society may create certain problems for males. Television and magazine ads for bras and pantyhose are often blatantly erotic. This eroticization of clothing may help to establish some of the first steps in the development of certain fetishes. Some support for this explanation comes from the observation that fetishism rarely or never exists in preliterate societies that do not eroticize clothing (Gebhard 1976).

Traditionally, only female clothing has been advertised in an erotic fashion. However, within the past few years, some ads have eroticized male underwear. It will be interesting, from a theoretical viewpoint, to see if these ads and changing sex roles result in a relative increase in fetishism in females.

PSYCHOTHERAPY

Individuals who exhibit the variations discussed in this chapter sometimes become involved in psychotherapy. In certain cases, psychotherapy has been recommended by the courts after a conviction for some type of sex offense; in others, individuals seek therapy on their own.

One type of approach that has been fairly successful in the modification of sexual variations is group therapy. A small number of people meet with one—or in some cases, two—therapists. Many of the techniques that therapists use to work with individuals may also help the group, but there is generally an emphasis on interaction among group members. One of the advantages of this type of therapy is that the group provides some support for people who may feel uncomfortable or threatened when alone with a therapist. Another advantage is that this method provides an opportunity to develop interpersonal skills in a setting that is relatively free from rejection. Finally, the sharing of experience by some group members may serve to convince others that their problems are not unique. The optimum size of the group seems to be from six to ten individuals in an institutional setting and from ten to fifteen on an outpatient basis (Sadock & Spitz 1976).

The most successful therapeutic approach to the treatment of sexual variations has been behavior therapy. Since a variety of techniques are utilized, several examples will be given. A treatment of several exhibitionists involved five steps designed to provoke shame and anxiety: (1) the subject undressed before a mixed-sex audience of from five to twelve people; (2) while undressed, the subject talked about previous exhibitions and how he felt about them; (3) videotapes of the subject's disrobing were played back to him; (4) noncondemning questions about exposure experiences were asked, such as how he and the "victim" felt; (5) the naked subject was asked to stand very close to the audience (usually, it will be remembered, subjects expose themselves at a relatively great distance from the audience). Self-reports of fifteen male exhibitionists following treatment indicated that the procedure induced shame and disgust and apparently reduced the incidence of genital exposure (Jones & Frei 1977).

Shame and anxiety were also utilized in the treatment of an incestuous offender. A fifty-two-year-old man who had a history of fondling and mutual masturbation with his seventeen-year-old daughter was asked to imagine a number of scenes. In one scene, the family priest and the man's wife entered and caught him caressing his daughter's bare breasts. The daughter jumped up and left along with the wife. The man remained alone with the priest, who questioned him at length about his behavior. The scene ended with the daughter crying hysterically. After imagining scenes such as this for fifteen days, the man apparently did not engage in incest for a period of at least six months (Harbert et al. 1974).

A different strategy was employed in therapy with a voyeur. The man was presented with eleven slides showing words or phrases related to voyeuristic activities. Each stimulus was followed by an electric shock to the right ankle. Interspersed were eleven slides showing words or phrases related to boredom or frustration—feelings that apparently evoked the voyeurism. These stimuli were followed by the so-called relief stimulus, words referring to sexual excitement from the man's wife. The twenty-two slides were randomly presented during the treatment sessions. At the end of treatment—and at an eight-month follow-up—there was an apparent improvement in sexual relations with the wife and an absence of voyeuristic behavior (Gaupp, Stern, & Ratliff 1971). It should be remembered that this report involves only one case, and it requires more validation before the results can be generalized.[4]

Often, therapy involves a multidimensional approach, especially in the treatment of pedophiles. The first goal is generally to eliminate sexual arousal related to children. This involves such procedures as giving electric shocks associated with pictures of children or having the pedophile imagine a child vomiting during attempts at masturbation. Typically the therapy program focuses next on increasing sexual arousal in response to adults. This may be attempted by rewarding arousal associated with pictures of adults. Finally, an attempt may be made to improve social skills. (It will be remembered that pedophiles usually have poor interpersonal relations.) Modeling and response practice with a variety of adults may be effective in this respect (Tollison & Adams 1979).

Taking a large number of therapy cases into consideration, it may be concluded that some procedures are successful with certain individuals but not with others. Often, it is simply a matter of trying several techniques until a successful one is found. Nonetheless, a certain number of people with sexual variations remain, for one reason or another, unresponsive to any therapeutic approach.

SUMMARY

Most of the individuals who engage in variations of sexual behavior are males. Exhibitionists expose their genitals to an unwilling individual or group. The exhibitionist is typically a loner who has difficulty relating to people. Contrary to popular opinion, stripteasers and nudists should not be classified as exhibitionists.

Voyeurs derive sexual pleasure from watching a member of the opposite sex in the nude or during a sexual act. Sexual arousal is enhanced by the illicit nature of the viewing.

Engaging in lewd conversation, particularly obscene phone calls, is arousing to some individuals. Such callers apprehended by police have been found to have low self-esteem and considerable anger towards women in general.

Transvestites become sexually aroused by dressing in opposite-sex clothing. Many transvestites are heterosexually oriented but perceive themselves as having a feminine side that seeks expression.

Persons expressing the variations discussed above may be prosecuted as public nuisances and, after several convictions, labeled sexual psychopaths. Although some sexual psychopaths spend long periods in prison, research indicates that they are not likely to progress to more serious crimes such as rape.

Transsexuals are individuals who have inappropriate gender identity: they believe that they are "trapped" in the body of the wrong sex. Some transsexuals undergo sex-change operations, but recent research has questioned the advisability of such surgery. Transsexualism is more common in males than in females.

Incest taboos exist in virtually all societies studied and similar inhibitions are found in certain animals. Nonetheless, sexual intercourse with a close relative occurs in approximately 4 to 7 percent of the U.S. population. The most commonly reported type of incest—that between father and daughter—can create serious psychological and emotional problems for the daughter.

Pedophilia—sexual relations between an adult and a child—is considered a serious crime in most societies. In the United States, convicted pedophiles appear to be socially unskilled individuals who generally fall into one of three categories: personally immature offenders, regressed offenders, or aggressive offenders.

Sexual crimes against children are generally prosecuted under statutory rape, child molestation, or incest laws. Unfortunately, responses of the court—as well as those of parents and police—may heighten the trauma and make it difficult for a child to deal with the emotions associated with the incident.

Zoophilia refers to sexual contact between humans and animals. In many cases, it represents an adolescent experimentation and does not continue into adulthood.

Fetishism is a strong sexual response to an inanimate object or some part of the body not usually associated with sexuality. Fetishists are often cold and lacking in emotional expression. Some evidence suggests that early associative learning experiences are important in the development of fetishism.

Several types of psychotherapy have been attempted with individuals exhibiting sexual variations. The most successful appears to be behavior therapy. Nonetheless, certain individuals do not respond favorably to any type of therapeutic approach.

NOTES

1. The name Peeping Tom originates from the story of Lady Godiva. Tom of Coventry was the only one who "peeped" as the nude lady rode through town on horseback. Legend has it that he became blind after his experience.
2. One of the researchers, Charles Prince, was the founder and editor of the magazine *Transvestia.* Prince—a transvestite himself—wrote several articles for the magazine under the name Virginia Prince.
3. The René Gunyon Society of California has, as one of its slogans, "Sex by eight, or else it's too late" (Tollison & Adams 1979).
4. The use of electric shock as an aversive stimulus in psychotherapy raises certain ethical problems. It has been argued that techniques that involve pictures of unpleasant scenes or the use of imagination (cognitive aversion) are preferable to physically painful stimulation (Brownell & Barlow 1976). However, if cognitive techniques are not effective or seem to require an extraordinary amount of time, aversion therapy may be preferable to long jail sentences or ineffective therapy.

CHAPTER 19

Aggression, Sex, and Mental Illness

The large number of aggressive crimes, especially those involving a combination of sex and aggression, has generated much concern in our society. Consequently, within the past dozen years, considerable research has been conducted—and several influential books and articles published—on the link between sex and aggression. Similarly, a steady rise in the incidence of mental illness has triggered social interest in its causes, including the possible role of sexuality. In this chapter, the relationship between aggression, sex, and mental illness will be considered, with a special emphasis on the psychological and sociological factors involved.

SADISM

A strong relationship between sex and aggression is illustrated by the *sadist*, a person who derives sexual pleasure from inflicting pain and/or humiliation. The word sadism comes from the name of the Marquis de Sade, an eighteenth-century Frenchman who wrote about the satisfaction he derived from torturing women.

Among the most lurid examples of sadism are cases in which individuals have been tortured and murdered. A study of sadistic killers—such as Ian Brady, who committed the ''Moors Murders,'' and Albert DeSalvo, who was known as the ''Boston Strangler''—indicated that their childhood was filled with violence. For example, DeSalvo apparently observed his father severely beat his mother on many occasions (Chesser 1971). In my own experience as a psychologist at a family court, I noted that individuals who commit severely sadistic acts usually have a long history of violence. Of course, many persons with violent childhoods do not become extreme sadists, but exposure to aggression—especially at an early age—seems to be a strong contributing factor.

In some cases, sadistic activities do not involve inflicting pain so much as expressing domination. *Bondage* is a variation in which one person ties up another or places the partner in restraints of some sort. A similar variation consists of a master-slave relationship. The persons involved often dress the parts, and the drama concludes with the slave yielding sexually to the master. In some cases, the slave is led around on a dog's leash.

The following is an example of sadism that involves both pain infliction and domination.

> This married man in his 20s requested psychiatric help because he feared he would soon commit murder. Since adolescence, he has been excited by fantasies and pornography depicting women bound and tortured. During courtship of his wife, he introduced mild versions of his fantasies into their sex play, and in this manner only was able to proceed on to intercourse. Now, after 8 years of marriage, they invariably have intercourse by his first binding her tightly with ropes and then, with her still bound, having intercourse. She has noticed that gradually the binding has been less and less symbolic and more and more painful. On two occasions in the last year, binding around her neck choked her into unconsciousness [reprinted by permission from Stoller (1976)].

As suggested in the example, sadistic patterns may begin with the consent of the partner; some individuals may be content with mock violence. However, as in the example, it is also possible that the violence will increase over time (Tollison & Adams 1979).

There are probably a variety of reasons why people become sadistic. As indicated earlier, some aggression associated with sex may be the result of modeling or imitation; we tend to do the kinds of things that our parents or other people of significance do to us. There may even be rewards associated with aggression, and the aggressive responses generalize to sex. Some sadism may reflect a deep-seated dislike or hatred of the opposite sex or of people in general.

MASOCHISM

Masochists obtain sexual pleasure from being hurt or humiliated. The term is derived from the name of Sacher-Masoch, a nineteenth-century Austrian; he wrote novels describing joys associated with elaborate torture and abuse. Masochistic tendencies may involve little more than fantasies and symbols of humiliation. A number of stores sell a large variety of sadomasochistic, or S-M, paraphernalia, including whips, gags, and chains. Probably, most buyers use these items in a symbolic fashion. However, in some cases, masochism becomes reality oriented. The following case illustrates a more extreme masochistic response:

The wife of the man described above, under "*Sadism*," found, during her courtship, that their first intercourse, under cramped conditions in a car, where her husband fixed her arms and legs so that they could not move, was at first uncomfortable but soon aroused in her a feeling of "interest." In time, this progressed to mild excitement, and now, several years later, she is appalled to find herself greatly excited by being bound. She is frightened by her experiences of unconsciousness while being bound. She believes that her husband is dangerous, and at the same time she feels deeply that he loves her [reprinted by permission from Stoller (1976)].

In certain cases, masochism involves verbal abuse. Tollison and Adams (1979) report a case in which a young woman could achieve orgasm only when she was insulted in the worst possible manner. In other cases, masochists endure trampling, semistrangulation, switching, spanking, or sticking with pins.

A study of a small group of male masochists by Litman and Swearington (1972) indicated that several of these individuals gained erotic pleasure from being rendered helpless. There were differences in their reactions to pain: some enjoyed it, while others disliked it. Most of the men were impotent if they were not allowed to play a masochistic role. Although they typically disliked playing the sadistic role in a relationship, about half the men had played such a role to please another masochistic partner.

Although extreme masochistic reactions are rare, erotic responses to mild pain are not unusual. Kinsey and his associates (1953) revealed that more than 25 percent of those interviewed reported some erotic response to being bitten during foreplay. The *Playboy* study found that sexual pleasure associated with pain was more frequent in females than males and in individuals under the age of thirty-five (Hunt 1974).

The finding that masochistic reactions are more common in women is, in a sense, consistent with a recent report that masochistic fantasies of bondage are fairly frequent in male transvestites when they are dressed as women (Buhrich & Beaumont 1981). It may be that, since the female role is traditionally defined as somewhat passive and long-suffering, pain and restrictions are considered more "feminine" than "masculine."

As in sadism, there seem to be a variety of causal factors. In some cases, punishment may serve to alleviate sex guilt. In other cases, masochism may develop through experiences in which pain is associated with sexual excitement; there are instances in which parents have spanked children while caressing their genitals (Rimm & Somerville 1977). I am familiar with a case in which abuse was practically the only attention given to a female patient by her parents. It seems that being hurt by another person came to be the only sure sign of love or acceptance for this woman.

Comparative Perspective: Extreme Aggression in Animals

Several types of male animals express high levels of aggression while courting or copulating with females. Aroused bulls may paw and horn the ground and/or make snorting sounds with the head lowered and nostrils distended. It will be remembered that a female mink will not ovulate unless she experiences long periods of coupling accompanied by some pain inflicted by the male (see chapter 8). The role of pain in the ovulation process is further illustrated by the fact that females sometimes ovulate after a painful struggle with the male even when copulation does not take place (Ford & Beach 1951).

Just as sexual arousal increases aggressiveness, the reverse sometimes holds. Anger in chimpanzees may increase sexual arousal. When males in their natural setting become irritated and angry, they often race about with erections and mount several members of the group (including less-dominant males), and may engage in copulation with one or more females (Wickler 1972).

Some experiments with animals have suggested that learning is an important factor in the association between aggression and sexuality. Male laboratory rats were given successful fighting experiences by pairing them with males who were restrained and had difficulty fighting back. The unrestrained rats soon increased the amount of aggression they displayed, apparently as the result of the rewards they experienced. Most interesting was the finding that the unrestrained rats also inflicted more pain on females during sexual activity than normal males (Tollison & Adams 1979). Such findings tend to support the aggression-generalization explanation of sadism in humans.

In conclusion, studies of animals generalized to people suggest that there may be some primitive relationship between sex and aggression, perhaps a holdover from times when the most aggressive males had the most success in obtaining a female and reproducing. However, psychological factors seem to be of relatively greater importance in determining whether or not aggression increases sexual arousal. Learning when to exhibit and inhibit aggression is perhaps the most important variable of all.

RAPE

Rape—especially forcible rape—involves an extreme expression of violence and coercion. In ancient civilizations, a woman was generally considered a man's property, so a forcible rape was viewed as an insult to a husband or father (Brownmiller 1975). Certain preliterate societies have maintained this conceptualization until relatively recent times. For example, in the Bala culture of Africa in 1959, a man who was convicted of rape was forced to pay the husband or father a fine of approximately ten dollars (Merriam 1971).

In some cases, the woman who was the victim of forcible rape was punished even though she did nothing to encourage the attack. According to the ancient code of Hammurabi, both the rapist and the victim were sentenced to death, although a husband had the option to save his wife. In fifteenth-century England, punishment for a rape incident could be avoided only if the rapist married the woman he raped (Medea & Thompson 1974). Although modern views of rape have changed greatly, particularly in the Western world, some aspects of these primitive notions still exist. As we shall see, society still tends to foster guilt feelings in the victims of rape.

Rape generally implies sexual intercourse by the use of force or threat.

FIGURE 19.1

In contrast to the beauty of this statue, rape is one of the ugliest of crimes. Victims may carry the emotional and psychological scars for a lifetime.

However, rape can also mean that one of the partners is not competent to give consent. Such incompetence may be due to mental illness or retardation, being drunk or under the influence of a drug, some sort of trickery, or being underage (statutory rape).

One of the most difficult things to define, from a legal standpoint, is the giving of consent. For example, if a woman has been drinking heavily on a voluntary basis before coitus takes place, it is not clear whether or not she has legally given her consent. Another difficulty in the definition of consent involves intercourse between married couples. Consent is generally implied by marriage, even if the wife is forcibly attacked. In most states, not even wives who are legally separated from their husbands may charge rape. However, certain states have recently made spouse rape a crime.[1] Nonetheless, it is much more common for an estranged wife to charge her husband with assault or battery after forced intercourse than to charge rape.

The rape of a man by a woman is very rare. One of the reasons is, of course, that penile erection and penetration usually cannot be produced under duress. Nonetheless, there are reports from an island in Melanesia that groups of women have raped men from other villages, using a combination of subtle stimulation and force (MacDonald 1971). There is also a recent U.S. study verifying eleven cases in which women raped men. Despite strong feelings of anger or fear, the men showed a normal sexual response. Some of the victims underwent a posttraumatic reaction similar to the feelings commonly experienced by raped women (Sarrel & Masters 1982).

Somewhat more common are homosexual rapes. This type of assault is most likely to take place in prisons. A man known as a "wolf" in prison slang may gain status and/or establish a territory by forcing victims to perform fellatio and/or submit to anal intercourse (Kirkham 1971). Homosexual rape of women is much less prevalent but has been reported in women's prisons. In these instances, the forced acts include manual stimulation, cunnilingus, and, in more violent cases, vaginal insertions with foreign objects (Tollison & Adams 1979).

By far the most prevalent type of rape is that of a woman by a man. The definition of heterosexual rape is couched in sexual terms—forced penetration by the penis beyond the introitus, or entrance to the vagina. However, this type of rape generally has more aggressive than sexual characteristics. Women are often beaten and humiliated. Furthermore, a study of convicted rapists indicated that about one-third of the men were unable to ejaculate during the rape. This dysfunction seems to have increased the man's expression of violence (Groth & Burgess 1977).

Characteristics of Rapists

Most convicted rapists in the United States are unmarried men between the ages of eighteen and twenty-five. They tend to come from lower socioeconomic backgrounds (Amir 1971; Schram 1978). It seems likely that certain cultural attitudes foster sexual assault by men against women. Rape is most prevalent in cultures or subcultures where physical violence is justified and/or sexual interaction represents an expression of male power. Other factors that seem important are a lack of empathy among males for females and male-female hostility in interpersonal relationships (Victor 1980). In the United States, there has probably been a general reduction in the perception of sexual interaction as representing male power and an increase in male empathy towards females during the last twenty years. However, an increase in the acceptance of violence and hostility has probably counteracted these positive factors.

Most investigations of the personalities of rapists have suffered from methodological problems. Researchers have studied only *convicted* rapists and/or failed to employ a comparison group of nonrapists. However, a recent experimental study used more sophisticated procedures. Subjects included many individuals who had not been arrested but were self-admitted rapists undergoing psychotherapy. Furthermore, a group of nonrapists was included for purposes of comparison. In the experiment, three audiotapes were played for all subjects: one describing mutually pleasurable sexual intercourse, another portraying forced coitus, and a third presenting a scenario of aggression without sexual activity. During these presentations, the sexual responses of the men were measured by means of a penile plethysmograph (which measures the degree of erection).

Results indicated that the nonrapists were aroused by the mutually enjoyable coitus tape but little or not at all by the tapes including aggression. In contrast, most of the rapists were highly aroused by the forced-coitus tape. Of special interest is the finding that rapists with a history of sadistic behavior were most aroused by the tapes of aggression, including the one describing aggression without sex (Abel et al. 1977).

The study just described indicates an association between sexual pleasure and physical aggression in rapists. Furthermore, it suggests that some rapists place more emphasis on aggression than others. Studies of the modes of operation of rapists support these conclusions. A type of rapist known as the "aggressive-aim rapist" attempts to humiliate and injure the victim. Sexual satisfaction appears to be less important than aggression. The breasts or genitals of the woman may be violently attacked and/or objects inserted into the vagina. The rapist seems to be driven by anger.

Another type of individual, described as the "sexual-aim rapist," places more emphasis on sexual satisfaction. He typically subdues the woman but uses relatively little brutality. In many cases, he imagines the victim falling in love with him.

Still another category of rapist, the "sex-aggression-fusion" rapist, utilizes violence to achieve sexual arousal. In fact, the rapist may be impatient if the victim does not resist. Some rapists of this type justify their aggression by claiming, extremely unrealistically, that women get sexually aroused by their brutal attacks (Cohen et al. 1971).

Sometimes a relationship between a man and a woman begins with no indication of sexual coercion or aggression by the man but develops into what has been termed date rape. In a survey of college students, 32 percent of the women reported having had sexual intercourse with a man who used some type of offensive force (Kanin & Parcell 1977). If forced breast and genital fondling were included, the percentage would probably be even higher.

Defending against Rape

Studies of rapes have resulted in a number of suggestions for preventing or reducing the possibility of sexual assault. Some of these seem rather obvious, but they may be overlooked and are worth summarizing (see Medea & Thompson 1974 and Hyde 1976 for more details). When walking, women should avoid dark areas at night or, if this is impossible, carry a whistle. A confident walk and manner tend to put off some potential attackers. Similarly, if a potential rapist should approach, a brief and straightforward refusal may discourage further interaction. Walking near the curb makes it more difficult for a person to approach suddenly from behind shrubbery or the corner of a building.

At home, it is important to lock windows and doors. A peephole in the door makes it possible to check the identity of a caller. People who say they have come to read a meter or make a repair should be required to show identification cards before entering.

A woman driving alone at night should take well-lighted and familiar routes. Doors should be locked and windows rolled up. If a car is following, a woman should take down its license number and then blow the horn vigorously.

If a woman is attacked, she should first attempt to talk her way out of the situation. Fighting physically may be dangerous, especially if the attacker is armed. If fighting back or fleeing is attempted, it is generally most effective after the woman pretends to go along with the rapist and then catches him off guard. One of the most effective places to strike an attacker is in the genitals.

Vomiting on oneself and/or the assailant may function as a deterrent, and placing a finger down the throat may help to induce this reaction. Also, one can carry capsules that create a foul strench when broken. This odor may not only discourage the attacker but help to identify him later.

If rape becomes inevitable, the victim should try to remain as calm as possible to reduce the probability of physical harm. However, avoiding physical injury, such as cuts and bruises, does not always reduce the trauma of a rape. Society tends to identify more with a victim who shows outward signs of abuse. Rape victims who do not have visible injuries after an attack may be taken less seriously or receive less sympathy. At any rate, rape victims almost always report that the psychological scars resulting from abuse and humiliation are much more painful than the physical injuries.

After the rape, it is important to check with a physician for injuries, pregnancy, or sexually transmitted diseases. Many communities have rape crisis intervention centers which can provide medical services and offer psychological counseling. Even if a woman decides not to report the rape to legal authorities, it is important that she have a physical checkup—which can be done in confidence.

Conversations with rape victims indicate that they feel that some of these suggestions are relevant but, in a real sense, represent an inequity. Why should women live in fear of rape and restrict their movement when rape is actually a male problem? Rather surprisingly, the fear is not always highest in the areas where the probability of rape is greatest. Clearly, there is a need for communities to cooperate not only in reducing the incidence of rape but in alleviating this debilitating fear (Riger, LeBailly, & Gordon, in press).

The Victims of Rape

In many cases, rapists are indiscriminate in their choice of victims. The rapist may simply decide to assault the next female who comes along. Thus, individuals ranging from infants to elderly women have been raped. However, the majority of victims are between the ages of fifteen and twenty-five.

Sutherland and Scherl (1970) studied the emotional reactions of several rape victims following an assault. They found that women generally go through several phases during the period of readjustment. The first phase, known as the "acute reaction," is characterized by shock and dismay. Often, it is difficult or impossible for the woman to talk about the incident or describe the assailant. There may be periods of composure followed by emotional breakdowns as the incident is remembered. This period may last from a few days to a few weeks.

A second phase is termed "outward adjustment." Anger and resentment are suppressed in an effort to return to the normal daily routine. The woman may feel that the painful, acute reaction is over.

A third phase—called "integration and resolution"—typically begins a little later. Often, there is a sense of depression; concerns that have been dealt with only superficially begin to resurface. Generally, it takes six months or more before feelings about the rape incident are resolved and the woman feels normal again. However, a four- to six-year follow-up of rape victims indicated that 25 percent did not feel that they had recovered by the end of this period of time (Burgess & Holmstrom 1978).

Many rape victims actually feel guilty. The feeling seems to be related to a belief that, somehow, the world is just. According to this *just-world hypothesis*, people get what they deserve (Lerner, Miller, & Holmes 1975). Therefore, victims may feel guilty even though there is every indication that they did nothing to provoke an assault. This feeling may be reinforced by other people who, at some level, also believe that victims must deserve what they get. Obviously, belief in the just-world hypothesis increases the difficulty of a rape victim's readjustment.

Sexuality presents another common problem for rape victims. It is not unusual for women to be sexually unresponsive for some time after the rape. In some cases, sexual advances by husbands or boyfriends evoke extreme anxiety. Psychotherapy can be particularly important in this area of the woman's readjustment (Burgess & Holmstrom 1974).

Reactions of Family and Friends

Discussions with rape victims and representatives of Chicago Women Against Rape indicate that family and friends often fail to understand a rape victim's reactions and conflicts. For example, a father or husband typically focuses anger on the rapist while ignoring the feelings of the woman. However, understanding and acceptance by a man is especially important in order to reestablish a feeling of trust in men in general. A father, boyfriend, or husband may demonstrate concern in a positive way by going with the victim to rape counseling sessions and/or trying to understand her problems in adjustment.

In many instances, loved ones also experience guilt in regard to the incident. They feel as though they should have done something that would have prevented the attack. To compensate, they may become overprotective, and this reaction tends to reinforce the guilt that the victim experiences. Focusing on how the victim feels at the present time and what she is doing to cope with these feelings is much more helpful in the adjustment process.

Family and friends may also foster guilt feelings on the part of the victim by suggesting that the victim did something to provoke the attack. For example, they may ask such questions as "What did you do?" or "What were you wearing?" In actuality, the majority of rapes are not related to any behavior on the part of the woman (Amir 1971). If family and friends can accept this, it is much easier for the victim to work through any feelings of guilt.

Sometimes, associates are so disturbed by the trauma of a rape that they avoid seeing or talking to the victim. They may justify this reaction by believing that nothing can be done to help or that in some way their friend deserved what she got (an example of the just-world hypothesis). Clearly, friends can be helpful in providing emotional support and understanding. However, they should remember that most victims do not like to be asked details of the rape, especially soon after the incident. It is generally preferable to ask open-ended questions, allowing the woman to discuss aspects of the attack as she feels emotionally ready to deal with them. Finally, simple expressions of concern and a willingness to help have a great deal of meaning for rape victims, just as they do for any other persons who have experienced severe trauma. In fact, the four- to six-year follow-up study of rape victims indicated that family and friends were a major factor in how successfully the woman adjusted (Burgess & Holmstrom 1978).

Legal Perspective: Rape Charges and Rape Trials

Forcible rape is one of the fastest-growing crimes against a person. In 1972, it was up 27 percent from the previous year, and only murder ranked as a crime more feared by the public. In 1973, somewhere between 100,000 and

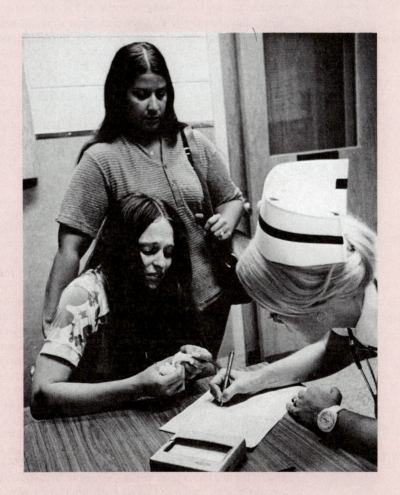

FIGURE 19.2
Rape crisis advocate assisting rape victim.

reported to authorities (Offir 1975). The major reason for not reporting or pressing charges in rape cases is the victim's desire to avoid the stress and ordeal of courtroom testimony (Holmstrom & Burgess 1978). A rape may also go unreported because a victim is hesitant to testify against someone she knows. One study indicated that in only 53 percent of rape cases was a rapist a total stranger (Mulvill 1969).

Still another reason for not reporting rape is that the conviction rate is known to be very low. There are several reasons for the low conviction rate. First, evidence that a rape occurred may inadvertently be destroyed if the victim douches or washes her clothes after the attack. Second, if there is no evidence of physical abuse, it is difficult to establish a legal case for rape. Bruises and contusions are least likely to occur as the result of group rapes, since several participants are easily able to restrain a woman. In actuality, group rapes make up a large percentage of all rapes reported—43 percent. However, the conviction rate in group rapes is much lower than in single-person rapes (Amir 1971).

Rape victims have told of many instances of callous treatment by law-enforcement agencies. Police officers have asked leading questions implying consent, such as "Did you enjoy it?" and "Did you have an orgasm?" In other instances, the victim's privacy has been invaded by questions about her virginity, her relationships with boyfriends, and her sex life in general. Fortunately, encouraged by the woman's movement and various organizations, there have been rape crisis reforms in many communities. This has reduced the possibility that, as Susan Brownmiller has suggested, a woman may be raped a second time by the legal process (Brownmiller 1975).

The availability of a *rape crisis advocate* is a major reform that has been widely instituted. During the period when the victim must respond to police questions and undergo physical examination, the advocate (who is typically a woman) provides comfort and support. Furthermore, she explains various alternatives and the reasons for certain procedures. The advocate is also available when the victim experiences some of the traumas associated with emotional adjustment to the rape.

The trial process has also undergone some reform. Before 1975, a large number of states allowed the victim's prior sexual history to be brought up in court. This sometimes resulted in essentially putting the victim on trial (Brownmiller 1975). Since 1975, forty states have enacted "rape shield" statutes that exclude from evidence the rape victim's prior sexual history except with the rapist. An experiment utilizing a mock jury trial illustrates that the admission of prior sexual history does, indeed, unduly affect a jury's decision. In one set of circumstances, prior sexual history was permitted as evidence; in another, it was not. Jurors in the former situation were more likely to find the alleged rapist not guilty. Furthermore, those jurors who reported that they placed great emphasis on sexual history and overall moral character of the victim were most likely to support a not-guilty verdict for the rapist (Borgida & White 1978). It seems that to allow prior sexual history to be used as evidence is not only embarrassing and insulting to a rape victim, but it biases the jury.

Author's Perspective: Factors Related to the Increasingly High Rate of Sexual Aggression

Several laboratory studies have investigated the effect of sexual arousal on aggression. Subjects are exposed to erotic material and then supposedly allowed to regulate the intensity of electric shocks given to another person. (In actuality, no shocks are given. The "receiver" of the shocks is a confederate of the experimenter who simply pretends to be shocked, while the "level" of shock set by the subject is automatically recorded.)

In many of these experiments, erotic material has been found to increase the amount of aggression expressed. One explanation is that emotional arousal related to sexuality—especially strong arousal—intensifies other emotional responses, including aggression. Another explanation involves the concept of *disinhibition,* or lack of inhibitory cues. The subjects in these experiments may have delivered larger "shocks" after exposure to the erotic material because they felt that if sex (a taboo subject) was condoned in a laboratory situation, then aggression (another taboo subject) must also be condoned (Malamuth, Feshbach, & Jaffe 1977). The possible effect of disinhibitory cues may be seen in regard to other taboos as well. If illegal drugs are present at a party, more sexual activity and aggression may take place, not necessarily because of a direct drug effect, but because of a general disinhibition.

Some experiments, however, have found a *negative* relationship between sex and aggression: aroused subjects administer lower levels of "shock" than nonaroused subjects, especially when only mildly arousing material is presented. It may be that mildly arousing material induces generally positive feelings that are inconsistent with anger and aggression—one doesn't usually aggress when feeling good. In contrast, highly explicit erotica may induce some negative reactions, including annoyance and sex guilt, which are apt to promote aggression (Baron 1977; White 1979).

Although psychological factors appear to be of greatest importance, there is some evidence of biological influences on aggression. The administration of androgen to either female or castrated male monkeys significantly increases their aggressive behavior (Edwards 1971; Herbert 1970).

Whatever the explanation, the amount of aggression expressed within existing sexual relationships has increased rapidly during recent years. The incidence of wife beating is particularly high and has gained a great deal of media attention (Straus et al. 1980). One might assume that much of the violence within the family is accentuated by the couple's feelings of being trapped in an intolerable situation. However, a recent survey of dating couples indicates that, even when individuals are relatively free to terminate the relationship, the incidence of violence is high (Makepeace 1981). Since biological factors have presumably remained constant over the last several decades, it appears that psychological factors—particularly disinhibition—are most responsible for this recent rise in violence.

There does not seem to be an easy solution to the problem of sexual violence in our society. However, certain changes might help. Decreasing the violence shown on television and in the movies could reduce disinhibition toward aggression in general and provide young people with fewer models of violent individuals (Comstock et al. 1979). Although TV producers have argued that violence in the media pays off, independent research indicates there is *not* a relationship between violent content and program popularity (Diener & DeFour 1978). Thus, there is no good reason to depict extreme aggression—particularly aggression associated with sexuality—on TV or in the movies.

Another possible solution is to provide better law enforcement. As we have seen, many rapists are not caught or, if apprehended, are not convicted. Even convicted rapists serve relatively short terms and are often on the streets again—committing further violent sexual crimes—before their last victim has recovered emotionally or physically (Brownmiller 1975). A similar type of situation exists in regard to wife beating (Straus, Gelles, & Steinmetz 1980).

Since individuals convicted of violent sex crimes almost invariably return to society at one time or another, it seems that therapy should be attempted, especially if methods can be developed that identify persons likely to benefit. There is already evidence that the types of behavior therapy discussed in the previous chapter are successful with certain violent sex offenders (see Tollison & Adams 1979). Furthermore, the use of antiandrogen drugs—especially in conjunction with behavior therapy—holds some promise of success, despite the ethical problems associated with "forcing" individuals to take the drugs (Money 1980).

Finally, it seems more should be done to aid the victims of sexual violence. The availability of rape crisis advocates and hot lines for victims of wife beating and child abuse certainly represents a start.

SEXUAL VARIATIONS AND MENTAL ILLNESS

Some individuals who engage in sexual variations have personality disorders classified as mental illness. However, most of the variants discussed so far are not considered mentally ill—from either a psychological or a legal standpoint. In contrast, the sexual variations discussed in this section are usually associated with either psychosis or neurosis.

Psychoses

Individuals diagnosed as *psychotic* show inappropriate emotional responses, exhibit disorganized or illogical thinking, and are generally out of contact with reality. Alan DeWolfe, who has conducted research with psychotics for several years, characterizes psychotic sexual behavior as bizarre and disorganized—which is true of most of their behavior. A *schizophrenic* (the most common type of psychotic) may express sexuality at the most unexpected times by, for example, suddenly exposing the genitals at a gathering of friends or relatives. (It will be remembered that most exhibitionists avoid people they know.) Similarly, a fairly common psychotic reaction is to disclose a large amount of intimate sexual information to a complete stranger or someone who has just been introduced.

FIGURE 19.3

A schizophrenic man. Mentally ill people classified in this category exhibit bizarre and disorganized sexual behavior and thought processes.

Psychotic patterns of thinking are revealed in unusual conceptualizations, such as a belief that the vagina has teeth that will bite the penis when it is inserted. Another example of psychotic thinking is illustrated by a thirty-three-year-old man who believed that he was pregnant. He experienced morning sickness and felt movement in his abdomen. Over a six-week period his waist expanded from thirty-two to thirty-seven inches. Despite medical evidence to the contrary, he persisted in his delusion for almost two months (Knight 1960).

Sometimes psychotics exhibit extreme sexual arousal—and even orgasm—in socially inappropriate or surprising circumstances. A twenty-five-year-old woman diagnosed as schizophrenic reported a number of spontaneous orgasms that varied in strength. During one period of hospitalization, she suddenly, without any forewarning, had an orgasm accompanied by such violent trembling that several people had to help her back to her ward (Polatin & Douglas 1953).

In extremely rare circumstances, psychotics are sexually attracted to dead persons, a condition known as *necrophilia*. Necrophiles may have sexual intercourse with a corpse and, in some cases, mutilate the body afterwards (Thorpe et al. 1961).

Some necrophiles visit prostitutes who play the role of dead persons. The prostitutes may use powder or wax on their skin to give it a lifeless appearance and remain absolutely motionless in a coffin (Solomon & Patch 1974). Most prostitutes are very careful in making arrangements with necrophiles and other individuals who may have serious mental problems. There is a case reported in which a client started to nail down the coffin lid while shouting, "You're dead now, god damn you to hell" (Young 1970). Typically, the prostitute makes plans to have someone nearby to deal with any such occurrences.

Neuroses

The *neuroses* are characterized by overwhelming anxiety. In some cases, the anxiety is obvious: the person is outwardly worried or apprehensive. In other cases, anxiety is dealt with—apparently unconsciously—by certain mechanisms that create problems for the individual or for society.

The *conversion reaction* is a type of neurotic response in which anxiety is manifested in physical symptoms. For example, an attractive young woman complained of headaches and nausea that had no apparent physical causes. The symptoms were most intense whenever she felt attracted to a man who expressed sexual interest in her. Apparently, the anxiety she experienced over sexuality—which was related to an extremely strict upbringing—was "converted" into the headaches and nausea (Sanford 1965).

Another type of neurotic response is known as an *obsessive-compulsive reaction*. Obsessive thinking involves constantly recurring ideas; compulsiveness means repeating behaviors in a rigid, stereotyped fashion. A man who, over and over again, played the same role with a prostitute illustrates this type of reaction. The prostitute discussed in chapter 18, who was named Georgina, would dress as a little girl and serve tea while the man would imagine himself as her uncle. The two of them would then look at an album of pornographic pictures, and she would pretend to be shocked. Suddenly the man would expose himself and "persuade" Georgina to do the same. Ejaculation would be accompanied by verbal abuse of the "little girl" for being naughty (Barros 1970).

A very rare type of neurotic reaction is *multiple personality*. An individual develops separate personalities and may shift dramatically from one to another. A 1950s movie—*The Three Faces of Eve*—was a reasonably accurate portrayal of an actual case study. Eve White was an extremely puritanical woman who dressed conservatively and acted very shy and inhibited. Sometimes, quite suddenly, a second personality called Eve Black would emerge, exhibiting blatant sexuality and wildly uninhibited behavior. (Eve White was not aware that the Eve Black personality existed.) After some time in psychotherapy, a third personality named Jane developed. Jane represented a sort of compromise between the two Eves and, apparently, was better integrated and adjusted (Thigpen & Cleckley 1957).

FIGURE 19.4

Eve Black, the sexy and uninhibited personality portrayed in *The Three Faces of Eve,* a case study of multiple personality. Both in the movie—and in real life—there was a sudden shift from one personality to another.

Theoretical Perspective: The Role of Sexuality in the Development of Neuroses

Mental illness, especially neurosis, has been conceptualized in a variety of ways. Two contrasting viewpoints—psychoanalysis and learning theory—will be considered in this section.

Psychoanalysis hypothesizes that the personality consists of three basic parts: the *id, ego,* and *superego.* The id centers on the basic sexual drive, or libido. Freud believed the libido provides the basic energy that fuels the personality, and that all basic emotions spring from libido. The ego—which develops as the child learns that gratification must sometimes be delayed—follows the reality principle. It is the part of the personality that governs one's actions so that they work out well in reality. As such, it puts restrictions on libidinal expression. The superego, or conscience, develops somewhat later in childhood; it also suppresses the id, but it does so in the service of moral precepts rather than pragmatic goals.

A hypothetical interaction between the three parts of the personality might be as follows: A young person in a class has an id impulse to grab an attractive individual in the front row. The ego says, in effect, "not during class." The supergo then adds, "you should direct your energy towards your studies and stop this nonsense." Basically, psychoanalytic theory assumes that a healthy personality reflects a good balance between the three aspects of the personality.

In neurotics there is presumably some type of imbalance, especially too much blocking of id impulses or denying their existence altogether. For example, Freudians would say the conversion symptoms discussed earlier came about because id impulses were repressed so much that they eventually built up force—much like steam in a kettle—and were then expressed as physical symptoms. In other words, the headaches and nausea were reactions to a damming up of sexual energy. A similar explanation might be given in the case of Eve White. Extreme denial of sexual impulses presumably led to an explosion of sexual energy in the personality of Eve Black. Once energy was released, there was a return to Eve White, accompanied by a repression of the sexual events— the memory of which would have caused excessive guilt.

As is suggested in these examples, one of the basic assumptions of psychoanalytic theory is that neurosis is intimately tied in with sexual development. Consequently, treatment involves attempts to gain insight into aspects of sexuality, including sexual wishes, desires, fears, and feelings of guilt, many of which were developed in childhood (Freud 1938).

The second school of thought that we will consider here is learning theory. It explains the development of neurosis somewhat differently. Rather than look for total patterns of personality, it emphasizes specific learning situations in the development of the neurotic pattern. For example, the conversion reaction might be explained in terms of a conflict involving a need to express sexual desires and unpleasant reactions of guilt associated with the desires. Assume the woman grew up in a home where illness immediately entitled one to withdraw and give up responsibility. Headaches and nausea, then, conveniently removed the woman from her sexual conflict and therefore were rewarding in certain respects.

The psychoanalysts and learning theorists also differ in regard to the emphasis placed on sexuality. Psychoanalysts believe that sexuality is at the root of most personality problems and that therapy cannot treat neurosis without dealing with sexuality. In contrast, learning theorists generally believe that sexual problems can be treated as distinct from personality problems and, in turn, some personality disorders do not involve sexuality.

Author's Perspective: When Should One Seek Psychotherapy?

It is often difficult to decide when psychotherapy is indicated. Since many types of mental illness do not differ in a qualitative way from the so-called normal personality pattern, mental illness may simply be considered a matter of degree with an uncertain borderline. Furthermore, there are great individual differences in the way people express their symptoms. Mental illness may practically destroy one person's life, while an equally severe illness may goad another person—such as Vincent van Gogh—to great artistic achievements.

The most important factors in determining the need for psychotherapy are probably subjective. If a person is dissatisfied with his or her life and reasonably well motivated to invest energy, time, and money in an attempt to change, therapy should probably be considered. The choice of therapist depends, among other things, on whether one is interested in a long-term personality evaluation (psychoanalytically oriented therapy) or a more specific treatment of symptoms (behavior therapy). Other factors important in the choice of therapist—particularly a sex therapist—will be considered in chapter 21.

SUMMARY

Laboratory studies indicate that, in many situations, sexual arousal increases the amount of aggression expressed. However, mild sexual arousal—which often induces generally positive feelings—may reduce the level of aggression. Men, in general, are more likely to express physical aggression than women.

Sadism refers to gaining sexual satisfaction from inflicting pain or humiliation on others. Exposure to aggression—especially at an early age—seems to be a strong contributor to sadistic tendencies. It is also possible that sadism reflects a deep-seated dislike of opposite-sex persons.

Masochism means enjoying abuse and pain in a sexual sense. Some individuals are impatient if they do not play a masochistic role in a sexual relationship. Among the factors apparently related to the development of masochism are extreme sex guilt, an early association between pain and sexual arousal, and family situations in which abuse is practically the only attention given to a child.

Rape is defined in a variety of ways but generally means sexual intercourse by the use of force or threat. Most rapists are young adult males who come from lower socioeconomic backgrounds. Studies of the modes of operation of rapists suggest varying degrees of emphasis on aggression: aggressive-aim rapists seem to be driven by anger and attempt to humiliate the victim; sexual-aim rapists place relatively more emphasis on sexual satisfaction and use relatively little brutality; and sex-aggression-fusion rapists utilize violence to achieve sexual arousal.

Victims of rape are usually women between fifteen and twenty-five years of age. They typically go through a long period of emotional readjustment following the attack. Many victims suffer unjustified feelings of guilt and difficulties readjusting to sexual interaction with husbands or boyfriends. Family and friends can be very helpful in providing emotional support during this period of adjustment.

Forcible rape has rapidly increased in frequency during the last decade. Although law-enforcement agencies and the courts have traditionally given callous treatment to rape victims, some improvements have taken place in recent years. The availability of a rape crisis advocate and the enactment of ''rape shield'' statutes are among the most significant steps forward.

Mentally ill people may exhibit sexual variations as well as other variations in behavior. Psychotic individuals typically engage in the most bizarre sexual behaviors and fantasies. Neurotic persons may develop conversion reactions, obsession-compulsive tendencies, or multiple personalities, any of which may influence their sexual expression.

Psychotherapists differ in their approaches to the understanding and treatment of the mentally ill. Psychoanalytically oriented therapists emphasize childhood development of sexuality and personality, while learning or behavior therapists focus on the present sexual problem or symptom.

NOTES

1. The first trial of a husband for rape took place in Oregon, beginning in 1978. In this well-publicized case, the husband was acquitted and, rather surprisingly, the couple was reconciled shortly after the trial (but later divorced). The first conviction in a case of marital rape occurred in Massachusetts in 1979. James Chretien was sentenced to three to five years in prison plus three years of probation.

CHAPTER 20

Illegal, Commercialized Sex

Sex has become highly commercialized in American society. In some professions, individuals make it to the top by having sexual relations with influential persons. In other cases, direct sexual interaction is not involved, but "interesting" opposite-sex persons are present to increase the likelihood that a client will find a setting attractive. For example, there have been several reports of coeds being used to help induce potential college athletes to decide to attend particular universities.

One of the most apparent commercializations of sex is in the advertising business. A product may promise to make one more sexually attrac-

---

FIGURE 20.1
Some Advertisements Having Sexual, Double Meanings

"My men wear _____, or they wear nothing at all." (Men's cologne ad)

"Take it off. Take it *all* off." (Shaving commercial)

"Reaching up. Feeling up." (Soft drink commercial)

"We'll make you feel good all over." (Travel ad)

"A silly millimeter longer." (Cigarette ad)

"We really move our tails for you." (Airline ad)

---

tive or, on the other hand, a product is linked with a pleasant feeling of sexual arousal. As Vance Packard pointed out in his book *The Hidden Persuaders,* much of this association is subtle or at a subliminal level. Advertisers hope that people will feel good while using a product without consciously realizing why. (If the reasons were understood, many individuals might reject the product out of guilt or because they would resent attempts at manipulation.)

These and many other examples of commercialized sex may be considered offensive, but there are no laws that effectively prohibit this sort of association between sex and business. In contrast, the two types of commercialized sex considered in this chapter—prostitution and pornography—are illegal in most contemporary societies, or have been until recently.

PROSTITUTION

The provision of sexual services for financial profit has a long history, dating back many years before Christ. In 550 B.C., the Greek official Solon established what appears to be the first licensed house of prostitution. Taxes from this and other brothels were used to build an elaborate temple to Aphrodite, the goddess of love (Henriques 1962). Today, in most countries throughout the world and in all of the United States (with the exception of certain counties in Nevada), prostitution is illegal.[1] Prostitutes, pimps, procurers, and operators of houses of prostitution are all subject to arrest under state laws. In addition, a federal law—the Mann Act—prohibits the transportation of women across state lines for an "immoral and illegal purpose."

Most arrests are made by plainclothes police officers as prostitutes solicit customers. However, experienced professionals are careful to word their offers in vague ways so that solicitation cannot be proven. They refer to having a "good time" or "some fun" instead of mentioning sexual acts. Furthermore, rather than speak of money for sexual services rendered, they may say a particular sum is needed to obtain champagne, pay the rent, or buy food. As a result, to prove an illegal act is difficult and prosecution is largely unsuccessful (Tollison & Adams 1979).

In actuality, there are several different categories of prostitutes. These categories—as well as some of the sociological and psychological variables involved in the profession—will be considered in more detail in the following subsections.

Female Heterosexual Prostitutes

Women who provide sexual services for men in exchange for money or other economic considerations make up the largest category of prostitutes. They conduct their business in a variety of settings. *Streetwalkers* and bar girls are generally the lowest on the socioeconomic scale. They typically approach men in certain areas of the city, especially in bars. Some of these women also solicit business in X-rated movie houses. Once an arrangement has been reached, the couple generally retires to a hotel or apartment. However, in some cases, they engage in sexual behavior in the darkened movie theater or bar.

Many streetwalkers have pimps. Pimps are men who function as a sort of protector and employment agent; they provide drugs and help the prostitute avoid arrest and conviction. They also share in the woman's earnings and make it difficult for her to leave the profession or move to another location (Young 1970).

Brothels, or *whorehouses*, are generally found in areas of a city known as "red-light districts." Prostitutes who work in brothels share a percentage of their fee with the owner of the establishment. Typically, a woman known as a madam oversees the operation, including the hiring and firing of the prostitutes. The madam may also make "arrangements" with city offices and law-enforcement agents.

FIGURE 20.2

A prostitute. Surprisingly, studies indicate that prostitutes in general are conservative in their sexual attitudes.

In many brothels, there is a sitting room in which a client makes his choice of women available at the time. Typically, the fee depends upon services required and time allotted for the activities.

Massage parlors are another setting for prostitution. Although some customers may be interested only in a massage, in many establishments it is generally understood that sexual services are available upon request. The most common activities in massage parlors are fellatio and manual stimulation to ejaculation; intercourse is relatively rare since the law prohibits beds in the parlors. Typically, a flat rate is charged for the massage, and the parlor gets half the fee. Any additional money for sexual services is usually kept by the masseuse (Tollison & Adams 1979).

Call girls are the most prestigious type of prostitute. Generally, they have regular clients and accept new ones only by personal referral. In some cases, a call girl will ask a prospective client for his name and place of business. This enables her to screen out members of the vice squad and also gives her protection against being brutalized. Brutal treatment by clients is one of the prostitute's greatest fears (Tollison & Adams 1979).

As mentioned earlier, call girls are sometimes used by corporations to promote business deals. Besides providing direct sexual services, call girls may serve as dates for important dinner parties or accompany men on short vacations (Winick & Kinsie 1971).

Entering the Profession

There are a variety of reasons why women become prostitutes, the most obvious of which are economic. For some women, prostitution is the easiest way to finance an expensive drug or alcohol habit. For others, prostitution provides a chance to live a glamorous life and associate with men of the higher socioeconomic level. Husbands or boyfriends encourage some women to enter the profession as a means of obtaining financial security for both the man and the woman. In a few cases, women of very high sex drives are apparently attracted to the combination of sexual and financial satisfaction (Tollison & Adams 1979).

Most women who enter prostitution come from lower-class or lower-middle-class homes. Usually, they have an unstable family background and a history of sexual promiscuity during early adolescence. Relatively few women have been forced into prostitution. A more common procedure seems to be to receive some sort of gift or advantage for sexual favors and then, little by little, enter the business. Certain occupations connected with restaurants, cocktail lounges, or hotels seem to be conducive to this sort of drift into prostitution (Young 1970; Coleman 1972).

In the case of the call girls, one study indicated that the vast majority of women entered the business through contacts with another call girl. In some instances, the girls had been friends or homosexual partners (Bryan 1965).

Attitudes of Prostitutes

The majority of prostitutes interviewed in one study were satisfied with their profession; over 60 percent reported that they had no regrets about their choice of work (Gebhard 1969). However, in-depth interviews of call girls in another study revealed high degrees of emotional conflict and self-destructive behavior (Davis 1978). Of course, it is not clear whether these apparent negative emotions and behaviors were the result of the women's professional experiences or if they were related to the unstable family conditions in which the prostitutes were typically raised.

Most prostitutes seem to dislike their clients, especially ones who demand unusual sexual service. For streetwalkers, the sexual interaction is usually brief and businesslike, with virtually no emotional attachment (Young 1970). In contrast, some call girls develop feelings of friendship toward their clients. In fact, one study reported that call girls generally liked and trusted their clients more than they liked and trusted other call girls (Bryan 1965).

As might be expected from the results of studies discussed in previous chapters, sexual gratification among prostitutes is related to their feelings about their male partners. A sizable percentage—about 20 percent—report that they never have orgasms with their clients. This figure is rather high in that prostitutes are generally more orgasmic with husbands and boyfriends than a comparable group of women not in the profession (Gebhard 1969). The prostitutes who seem most likely to have orgasms with their clients are call girls (Bryan 1965).

It might also be expected that, since prostitutes work outside the mainstream of American life and spend so much time involved in sex, they would have liberal or even radical attitudes about sexuality. However, this does not appear to be the case. A survey revealed that prostitutes held fewer liberal attitudes toward premarital sex and sexual intimacy than a sample of college women (Tollison, Nesbitt, & Frye 1975). Apparently, the prostitutes viewed their behavior simply in the context of a money-making proposition, and their basic attitudes toward sexuality were not radically shifted by their work.

Social psychologists might explain this finding in terms of cognitive dissonance theory (Festinger 1957). If people behave in a way that is contrary to their basic standards, they tend either to change their standards or to justify the behavior in some way. Most people—including college students—who engage in nonmarital intercourse are likely to change their standards in order to make their behavior more acceptable to themselves. However, since prostitutes get paid for their sexual behavior, they can justify it as being economically necessary. Furthermore, prostitutes are likely to say that what they do is no more immoral than marrying for money or getting a promotion by granting sexual favors. Thus, unlike common sense, cognitive dissonance theory would have predicted that prostitutes' sexual attitudes do not tend to change as the result of their behavior.

The Clients of Prostitutes

Up to this point, we have considered only half of the prostitution scene; a study of sex and prostitution is not complete without a look at the clients of prostitutes and their motivation. Sociologist Jennifer James (1977) has identified a wide variety of reasons why men visit prostitutes. As suggested in chapter 19, some men desire a variety of sexual partners and also a range of activities. In many communities, prostitutes are readily available and willing to engage in any number of sexual acts.

Some men develop impotence with their wives or regular sex partners. Prostitutes may be able to help these men relax and achieve erection by the use of such techniques as fellatio. Some prostitutes provide braces for the penis to assist men in gaining vaginal penetration. Prostitutes may also bolster a sagging ego by faking orgasm and telling a man that he is a superior lover. Sometimes a prostitute functions as a sort of therapist, listening to troubles or simply providing companionship for dinner or a movie.

Some men seem to desire release of sexual tension without becoming involved in an intimate relationship. Prostitutes provide sexual services without much risk that a wife or girlfriend will discover the relationship. Furthermore, there is little or no danger that marriage or other obligations will be expected to follow the sexual interlude.

A large number of men who travel regularly engage the services of prostitutes. Loneliness, in addition to sexual deprivation, seems to be a major motivating force for these men. In some circles, businessmen provide prostitutes for their important visitors.

Some men who are disabled or disfigured turn to prostitutes for sexual gratification. Often, these men fear rejection from attempts to date or develop serious heterosexual relationships. Similarly, older men who wish to have sexual relations with young women—but are anxious to avoid being labeled "dirty old men"—may surreptitiously visit prostitutes.

Finally, some prostitutes cater to men who desire what are referred to as "special" services. We have already discussed prostitutes who are asked to act out unusual fantasies or engage in bizarre acts. Obviously, most women would be less than enthusiastic about some of the special requests. Therefore, these prostitutes charge unusually high rates for such services.

Other Categories of Prostitutes

Although female heterosexual prostitutes are by far the most common type in virtually all cultures, there are other categories of prostitution in Western society. Male homosexual prostitutes seem to make up the second-largest category. As we have seen in chapter 16, some of these individuals do not think of themselves as homosexual, but rather as opportunists. The method of contacting customers varies considerably. Some function as highly paid "call boys." Others hang around truck stops and make arrangements to perform sexual services in the cab sleeper. Still others function as "street hustlers," soliciting business in areas that have a high percentage of homosexuals. Typically, these men go through certain rituals that function to differentiate potential customers from other men and vice officers. A key phrase is often "Would you like a beer?" Finally, some homosexual prostitutes work in homosexual brothels that are advertised as massage parlors (Corzine & Kirby 1977; Ginsburg 1977).

Male heterosexual prostitutes, or gigolos, appear to be in less demand than homosexual prostitutes. It seems that there are a large number of males who engage in sex with women free of charge. However, certain types of businesses—including dance studios, escort services, modeling agencies, and boutiques—may provide male prostitutes upon request. In some cases, males place nude pictures of themselves along with their phone numbers in women's rest rooms. Since it is difficult for a man to have intercourse with a large number of women in one evening, many male prostitutes utilize vibrators and/or cunnilingus (Hageman 1979). The majority of male prostitutes work only part-time, pursuing other, more conventional occupations between visits with clients (Allen 1980).

Theoretical Perspective: Should Prostitution Be Legalized?

Because prosecution of prostitution generally fails—and because prostitution may be considered a victimless crime—some people have argued in favor of legalizing it in the United States. Additional supporting arguments are that taxes on prostitution, and prostitutes' income taxes, would increase revenue; that sexually transmitted diseases could be more readily controlled; and that the nuisance of solicitation would be eliminated from many neighborhoods.

In contrast, those against legalized prostitution argue that prostitution is immoral and should not be sanctioned by law. Some women's-rights advocates have added that prostitution is degrading to women, and, by legalizing it, one promotes an image of women as sex objects. Finally, it is argued that legalized, regulated prostitution would not drive out the illegal variety—especially the use

FIGURE 20.3
Although prostitutes may be arrested many times, few spend much time in jail.

of runaway minors by experienced pimps. (See Babcock et al., 1975 for arguments both pro and con legalized prostitution.)

In most areas of the United States, public sentiment is against legalization of prostitution. In addition, the Model Penal Code (American Law Institute 1962) supports the concept of prostitution as a crime. Therefore, it does not seem likely that there will be major changes in the legal status of prostitution in the near future.

Attitudes about childhood prostitution are even more negative. Several states have proposed legislation related directly to the use of children as prostitutes; anyone who received money earned by a person under eighteen from acts of prostitution would face a long prison sentence. Few people seem to disagree with this proposal.

PORNOGRAPHY

Pornography is another example of illegal sex that is difficult to prosecute. The main reason for this difficulty is the vague definition of the term. Pornography literally means material intended to cause sexual arousal. How is it possible to clearly identify the intent of a book or movie? Over the years, antipornography laws have changed considerably.

One of the first effective laws was the 1873 Comstock Act, which made it illegal to deposit any obscene, lewd, or lascivious publication in the U.S. mail. Several books later considered literary classics—such as D. H. Lawrence's *Lady Chatterley's Lover* and James Joyce's *Ulysses*—were effectively banned under this act.

In 1933, pornography laws were made somewhat more lenient. In the case of *United States* v. *Ulysses*, the Joyce classic was declared worthy of shipment through the mails because it had literary merit and was not written to "deprave." In other words, a publication must be judged on its overall purpose and effect. In 1966 another stipulation was added as the result of a case involving the eighteenth-century novel *Fanny Hill* (*Memoris* v. *Massachusetts*). In order to be declared pornographic, a work must be shown to lack redeeming social value.

Since it is virtually impossible to legally establish literary merit, attempts to deprave, and redeeming social value, there were few convictions on obscenity charges following the 1966 decision. However, in 1973, the U.S. Supreme Court ruled (in *Miller* v. *California*) that local communities could judge—according to their own standards—what was pornographic. As a result of this decision, actors in movies judged

FIGURE 20.4

As in the case of prostitution, laws against pornography are difficult to enforce. Since 1973, local governments— rather than the federal government—establish the definition of what is pornographic. Contrary to what many people believe, research suggests that depictions of violence may have more socially undesirable effects than sexually arousing, nonviolent material.

pornographic have been convicted on obscenity charges, even though the movie was produced in a state other than the one involved in the prosecution. The 1973 decision seems to have increased effective censorship since many individuals are apparently afraid of prosecution by district attorneys in distant, conservative communities.

There has also been recent legislation against erotic material utilizing children as models or actors. In 1977, Congress made it illegal for individuals under sixteen to participate in the production of sexually explicit material. Anyone associated with the production—including a consenting parent—is open to prosecution.

The Effects of Pornography on Behavior and Perception

Before drawing any conclusions about the influence of pornography on our society, it was necessary to systematically investigate the effects of erotic material. In 1967, the Commission on Obscenity and Pornography was established by Congress and, in the years that followed, a large number of studies by scientists were conducted. Three questions about the effects of erotica were of principal concern: (1) Are undesirable or illegal behaviors like rape and other sex crimes increasing? (2) Is there a general increase in the frequency of sexual behaviors? (3) Are women more likely to be perceived as predominantly sex objects?

In regard to the first question, there is no available support for the hypothesis that erotica causes an increase in sex crimes. In fact, it has been found that sex offenders have had *less* exposure to erotic material during adolescence than nonoffenders (Goldstein, Kant, & Hartman 1974). Similarly, males, on the average, are fourteen years old when first exposed to a picture of a couple having coitus; for sex offenders, the average age is eighteen (Eysenck 1972).

The reason for the difference between offenders and nonoffenders in regard to erotica is not clear. On the one hand, offenders may be social misfits who did not get ''in'' on the activities of their peer group—activities that might have included looking at and/or reading erotica. On the other hand, it is possible that sex offenders were sexually repressed as children and adolescents, and the repression ultimately resulted in sexual ''explosions.'' Interestingly, there is some indirect support for the repression hypothesis. In Denmark during the 1960s, restrictions on hard-core pornography were lifted, so that all types of explicit sexual material was available. Immediately following this, the occurrence of sex crimes decreased dramatically (Commission on Obscenity and Pornography 1970).

The second concern—that erotica will significantly increase the frequency of sex acts—has only qualified support. The typical approach to the question of frequency is to obtain detailed information about a subject's sexual behavior, to present the subject with erotic material, and then to inquire about sexual practices again. In a study of married males, it was found that there was greater likelihood of marital intercourse taking place on the night following a presentation of erotic slides than following a presentation of geometric forms (Cattell, Kawash, & DeYoung 1972).

In another study involving presentations of erotic movies to married couples over a period of a month, there was an increase in sexual activity on nights following erotica, but not on other nights. Furthermore, there was no residual effect beyond the one-month period of the experiment (Mann et al. 1974). It seems that, at least for married males, erotica has no lasting effect.

In regard to the third question, there is some evidence that males' perceptions of females are temporarily altered following arousal induced by erotica. Aroused males tend to rate women as more amorous, sexually receptive, and uninhibited than do unaroused males (Stephan, Berscheid, & Walster 1971). However, at least part of this altered perception may be due to the fact that both positive and negative responses seem to be heightened by sexual arousal. A later study indicated that aroused subjects find a good-looking member of the opposite sex more attractive, but an unattractive opposite-sex person even worse looking (Weidner, Istvan, & Griffitt 1979). Thus, it is unlikely that erotica has any significant long-term effects. The actual experiences of males with females undoubtedly have a more enduring effect than fantasy representations. Moreover, there is no indication that a temporary change in perception is translated into seductive behavior. In fact, sexually conservative men tend to avoid looking at or sitting close to women after becoming sexually aroused by erotica (Griffitt, May, & Veitch 1974).

Author's Perspective: Does Pornography Have Undesirable Effects on Our Society?

Research suggests pornography is less harmful than some people have feared. For more-or-less-normal adults, exposure to erotic material does not seem to increase the likelihood of sex crimes, is not related to a permanent increase in sexual behavior, and does not significantly change males' perceptions of females. However, it is not clear what kinds of effects pornography has on psychologically disturbed individuals.

Some people have argued that the presence of X-rated movie theaters and adult book stores contributes to the general decay of a neighborhood. However, the Supreme Court decision of 1973 gave local communities considerable power to block the opening of such establishments—or close existing ones—if opposition is strong and well organized.

Although erotic material in itself does not seem to have detrimental effects on adults, the depiction of violence—particularly sexual violence—may very well have negative social consequences. One recent study indicates that exposure to a slide-audio show of a rape induced violent sexual fantasies in males (Malamuth 1981). Other studies demonstrate that exposure to pornography with aggression increases the tendency of men to aggress against women (Donnerstein, in press). Perhaps censors should be at least as concerned with the amount of violence in films and on TV shows as with the degree of sexual explicitness.

Finally, of great concern to many is the recent increase in what is referred to as "kiddie-porn": the use of child models or actors in erotic material. In many states, it has been difficult to prosecute individuals who have exploited children in this way. However, at the present time, there is a movement in most of these states to legislate tougher child pornography laws. Polls indicate considerable support for this movement, as well as attempts to restrict exposure to pornographic material in general to consenting adults (Gallup 1978).

SUMMARY

Sex has been commercialized in a variety of ways. People may go to great expense to be associated with attractive, opposite-sex persons; business arrangements may be facilitated by sexual relationships with influential people; and sex is commonly utilized in advertising.

Prostitution represents a more direct relationship between sex and financial profit. Throughout history—and in many different types of societies—the most prevalent type of prostitute has been a female who caters to males. In the United States, female prostitutes work in a variety of settings: streetwalkers and bar girls solicit business in certain areas of a city, often under the "protection" of a pimp; brothels employ prostitutes who share their earnings with the management; massage parlors generally provide sexual services in addition to conventional massages; and call girls—who are the most prestigious type of prostitute—provide services only by appointment.

Although prostitutes often report general satisfaction with their work, most of them dislike their clients and, according to one study, have high levels of emotional conflict. Rather surprisingly, prostitutes have been found to have conservative attitudes about premarital coitus and sexual intimacy.

The second-largest category of prostitution consists of male homosexual prostitutes. Like female prostitutes, these individuals contact potential customers in a variety of ways. A third category—male heterosexual prostitutes, or gigolos—is in relatively small demand.

Prostitution is illegal in most countries throughout the world. Although fairly reasonable arguments have been put forth to legalize prostitution in some parts of the United States, public sentiment is generally against such proposals. Attitudes against childhood prostitution are particularly strong.

Erotic material has existed since earliest times, but it is only recently that investigators have systematically evaluated the effects of erotica on society. Contrary to some popular opinion, research indicates that exposure to erotic material does not increase the incidence of sex crimes. Even though viewing erotica may temporarily raise the level of sexual activity of adults, there do not seem to be any long-term effects on frequency of sexual interaction. Similarly, there is no evidence that exposure to erotica increases the tendency of men to view women as sex objects, at least beyond the short term. However, it is possible that erotica depicting violence towards women can spur certain men to increased levels of aggression.

Public opinion is generally liberal in regard to viewing of erotica by consenting adults. Nonetheless, most people believe that children should be prevented from viewing erotica and from appearing in "kiddie-porn."

NOTES

1. Countries that have legalized prostitution include Great Britain, West Germany, Holland, Korea, and Sweden, as well as many smaller nations. In some countries—including Great Britain—prostitution is legal, but solicitation for prostitution is not.

PART 8

Sexual Problems

446

Some of the behaviors discussed in Part 7 may create problems for a society. However, many of the individuals who exhibit these behaviors do not consider them to be problems, at least not in the sense that they require change. In contrast, the phenomena covered in this part are seen as problems by virtually everyone.

CHAPTER 21

Sexual Dysfunction and Sex Therapy

Since the prefix "dys" means impaired, an approximate synonym for dysfunction is malfunction. However, malfunction is seldom used in regard to sexuality because it connotes a machine that doesn't work properly; people with sexual problems have trouble enough without thinking of their genitals as machinery. The exact definition of sexual dysfunction depends on the culture. Many behaviors considered normal during Victorian times—including rapid ejaculation in males and a lack of orgasm in females—are usually classified as problems in the 1980s. Even by today's standards, there are large individual differences in people's reactions to sexual impairments. In light of these differences, the American Psychiatric Association's classification system (DSM III) does not classify an impairment as a dysfunction unless an individual is concerned about it.

A sexual problem that upsets one or both of the partners can cause a great deal of disharmony. In many cases, communication is disrupted, and other members of the household are affected by the anxiety, anger, and/or guilt associated with the problem. Although some relationships are satisfying in spite of sexual dysfunctions, the quality of a relationship is generally improved if sexual problems are reduced (Tavris & Sadd 1977).

Virtually all individuals have had sexual frustrations or disappointments at one time or another. Too much alcohol, certain drugs, fatigue, or work-related anxieties are common causes of temporary problems. However, in most cases, normal functioning returns in a short time. Only when problems persist or recur a high percentage of the time are they classified as dysfunctions.

Sexual dysfunctions are generally divided into two categories. *Primary dysfunctions* include cases in which the individual has never functioned normally; *secondary dysfunctions* refer to problems that began after a period of normal functioning or that occur only in a certain

449

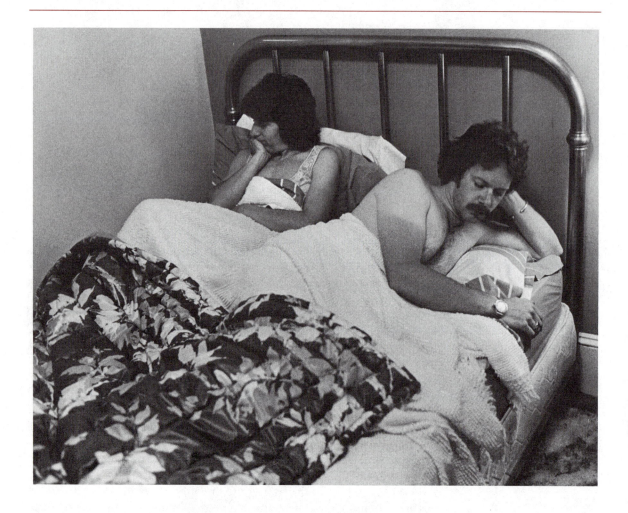

FIGURE 21.1

Sexual dysfunctions may be both the cause and the result of disharmony in a relationship.

percentage of interactions. (The critical percentage varies depending upon the type of problem considered.)

When there is a problem in a sexual relationship, it is difficult to separate the roles of the partners; an impairment on the part of the male may lead to a problem for the female and vice versa. However, for the purpose of discussion, male and female dysfunctions will be considered separately in the first two sections of this chapter. The interaction will be considered when sex therapies are discussed in the third section.

MALE DYSFUNCTIONS

Sexual dysfunction in males may cause them great frustration and anxiety, since sexual performance is closely tied to the image of masculinity. Furthermore, it is much more difficult for a man to fake a sexual response. A man's premature ejaculation or failure to obtain an erection can be quite obvious; in contrast, a woman may effectively pretend to be sexually aroused or mimic an orgasm.

Erectile Dysfunction

One of the most common types of sexual problems in males is *erectile dysfunction* or *impotence:* the failure to have or to maintain an erection. *Primary erectile dysfunction*—which is relatively rare—refers to cases in which an erection and sexual intercourse have never taken place. Men who suffer this type of impotence often come from family backgrounds of severe sexual repression, where sex is viewed as highly immoral or sinful. Among certain men who have difficulty with interpersonal relationships, the fear of intimacy involved in sexual intercourse may inhibit the development of erections (Marmor 1976a).

Secondary erectile dysfunction has been defined as a failure to obtain erection in at least 25% of the attempts at intercourse. Secondary erectile dysfunction occurs about 7 times as often as the primary type (Masters & Johnson 1970). Some of the same psychological variables that are related to primary erectile dysfunction are involved in secondary problems. For example, emotions such as shame, anger or disgust may inhibit the development of an erection. This erectile dysfunction may then lead to a general fear of failure in a large percentage of sexual interactions (Lazarus 1974).

Another factor that can cause secondary erectile dysfunction is a failure to engage in effective foreplay. In this case, communication with one's partner is particularly important; an understanding and patient partner can often alleviate anxieties and provide effective stimulation. On the other hand, if there are resentments or misunderstandings between partners, these can aggravate the problem (Wabrek & Wabrek 1976).

Although many erectile problems are psychological, they may be initiated by illness or fatigue. For example, a man may be very tired one night and fail to maintain an erection. The next time he wishes to have intercourse, he may be afraid of another failure and the anxiety he experiences may inhibit erection. Repeated failures can raise anxiety levels and the problem could become chronic.

For a long time, physicians believed that only a small percent of the cases of secondary erectile dysfunction were due to organic causes (Masters & Johnson 1970).[1] However, in the 1980s improved methods of diagnosis enabled physicians to detect physical reasons for impotence in many men whose problems had been seen as psychological. For example, a team at Harvard Medical School examined 105 impotent men and found physical causes for the problem in 70. Half the physical causes were related to problems with the hypothalamus, pituitary, or gonads. Nine other categories of physical disorder were also involved. Fifteen cases were attributed to emotional illness, and twenty were not diagnosed. Not all the problems that were diagnosed could be cured, however (Spark, White, & Connolly 1980).

Premature Ejaculation

The tendency to ejaculate too soon—or to be unable to postpone ejaculation—was the second most common sexual problem for males seeking sex therapy from Masters and Johnson. However, the incidence of *premature ejaculation* among individuals not in therapy may be quite high, so that this may actually be the most common male sexual dysfunction. Obviously, the exact number of men having this problem depends upon how "too soon" is defined. In extreme cases, ejaculation may take place before complete vaginal penetration is achieved.

In most cases, the causes of premature ejaculation are psychological. One hypothesis is that premature ejaculators have not learned to identify sensations that immediately precede ejaculation and therefore are unable to regulate the process. A probable factor in this failure to learn is anxiety associated with early sexual experiences (Kaplan 1974).

Many of the premature ejaculators in the Masters and Johnson study appeared to have low regard for women; the satisfaction of the female partner did not seem important to them. Once the habit of disregard for the woman was established, it became difficult to change the pattern of intercourse and delay ejaculation (Masters & Johnson 1970).

In some cases, early ejaculation and erectile dysfunction have become associated with one another. For example, a man may have had several encounters with his partner during which he ejaculated prematurely, evoking her frustration or anger at his "inadequacy." On subsequent occasions, his feelings of inadequacy or attempts to try too hard are likely to lead to anxiety and erectile dysfunction.

Retarded Ejaculation

A relatively rare problem—*retarded ejaculation*—is the reverse of premature ejaculation. The man finds it difficult or impossible to ejaculate during coitus. The problem may be caused by various diseases attacking the nervous system, including malfunctioning nerves of the genitals, and Parkinson's disease, which attacks the brain. Certain drugs used in the treatment of hypertension may also inhibit ejaculation (Munjack & Kanno 1979).

The most common reasons for retarded ejaculation, however, appear to be psychological. Among the most important factors are fear of impregnating the woman; anxieties about the fantasized contamination of the vagina; and a neurotic association between ejaculation and a frightening loss of control. In the last case, the man may be such a rigid, compulsive personality that ejaculation represents a symbolic giving of himself to a partner, something that is intolerable (Marmor 1976a).

Secondary retarded ejaculation is generally related to less severe types of problems. A loss of feelings of attraction for the partner, or feelings of hostility toward her, may cause this problem. In many cases of secondary retarded ejaculation, the man will be able to ejaculate following masturbation more easily than during coitus (Masters & Johnson 1970).

The prolonged duration of coitus associated with retarded ejaculation may initially please the female partner. However, once she realizes that he cannot ejaculate, she typically becomes concerned about the reasons why. Many women also become resentful of what they perceive as excessive sexual demands (Munjack & Oziel 1980).

Once again, it should be remembered that occasional problems are normal and quite distinct from the chronic problems discussed above. Most men have had difficulty ejaculating at one time or another when they were very fatigued, had many sexual encounters in a brief period, or were overly tense. In such cases, the problem is usually only temporary.

Inhibited Sexual Desire

A lack of responsiveness to sexual stimulation, absence of erotic feelings, and failure to enjoy sexual activities is referred to as *inhibited sexual desire (ISD).*[2] Psychological factors appear to be of greatest importance in this problem. In some cases, depression, extreme hostility, or a very low self-image may inhibit sexual excitement. Other individuals with ISD may have difficulty recognizing early signs of arousal. Having failed to respond sexually—in their own perception—they essentially give up and label themselves nonsexual (LoPiccolo 1980).

In a minority of cases, physical factors may inhibit sexual desire. Hormone deficiencies, drug addiction, alcoholism, and chronic illness have all been found to contribute to the problem. Recently, a number of men with ISD were found to have pituitary tumors that resulted in the secretion of excessive amounts of prolactin. Since prolactin inhibits the secretion of androgens, the resulting hormonal deficiency seems to have been an important causal condition (Schwartz & Bauman 1981).

FEMALE DYSFUNCTIONS

Women vary more than men in their reaction to sexual dysfunction. Some apparently accept it without much concern. However, more and more women today are becoming concerned with sexual fulfillment and, in turn, are more distressed by sexual dysfunctions.

Inhibited Sexual Desire

ISD in women is comparable to its counterpart in males. The inhibition is marked by a lack of vaginal lubrication, no expansion of the vagina, and a failure to establish an orgasmic platform. Inhibited sexual desire has been called frigidity in the past. However, this term is less acceptable today because it is ambiguous and has certain negative connotations.

The same types of factors associated with this problem in males are often involved in female ISD: repression of sexuality in childhood, or a general fear of intimacy. In many cases, negative experiences with males are contributing factors—for example, interaction with a man who insists upon sexual practices that are unacceptable to the woman. Similarly, a male who degrades or rejects a woman for apparently enjoying sex or taking an active role in coitus may produce inhibiting feelings or guilt. Finally, a man's forcing himself upon a woman or behaving sadistically may create strong fears of sexual intimacy (Tollison & Adams 1979).

In contrast, a male may have a very positive effect on a female's sexual responsiveness. There are many examples of women who seemed to have had a general sexual dysfunction but who became highly fulfilled when the "right" man came along. As suggested earlier, women in general appear to be relatively discriminating; female sexual fulfillment may be quite dependent upon feelings of love and trust.

Although most cases of inhibited sexual desire are related to psychological factors, one cannot rule out such physical causes as vaginal infections and illnesses that produce general apathy. A thorough physical examination by a physician is usually recommended before drawing any conclusions about causes.

Orgasmic Dysfunction

A normal sexual interest and drive but an inability to experience orgasm is referred to as *orgasmic dysfunction*. Unlike the individuals considered in the previous section, these women experience genital lubrication, swelling, and strong feelings of arousal. The problem seems to be restricted to the orgasmic phase of the sexual response.

Usually a distinction is made between primary and secondary orgasmic dysfunction. Primary dysfunction refers to cases in which orgasm has never been experienced. Approximately 10 percent of the women interviewed in the *Playboy* study had never had an orgasm, suggesting that this is a fairly common sexual problem (Hunt 1974).

Secondary, or situational, orgasmic dysfunction means that a woman has had orgasmic experiences but is having them infrequently or not at all at the present time. In some cases, a woman can obtain orgasm by masturbating but not during intercourse; in other cases, the opposite is true (Masters & Johnson 1970).

Situational orgasmic dysfunction is probably the most common type of sexual problem among women. An important political issue is raised, however, when such dysfunction is labeled a female problem. As we have seen in chapter 8, many coital positions provide inefficient forms of stimulation for the woman. Furthermore, a lack of foreplay or a male's tendency to ejaculate prematurely may make it difficult for a woman to reach sufficiently high levels of arousal. Thus, many cases of situational orgasmic dysfunction in females could be classified as results of male "clumsiness." While keeping this in mind, the remainder of the discussion will focus on problems from the female standpoint.

Just as there are great individual differences in the way a woman responds to inhibited sexual desire, there are strong differences in response to orgasmic dysfunction. Some women show very little reaction; they generally claim that the closeness, affection, and general arousal associated with coitus are rewarding enough. Other women become frustrated and feel angry toward their partners. Some become so upset that they find it more difficult to become aroused on subsequent occasions (Tollison & Adams 1979).

Orgasmic dysfunction is often associated with psychological factors. In some cases, orgasm is inhibited because the intensity of the response is frightening to the woman; orgasm may represent a vulnerability or lack of control (Friedman 1973). Other factors that may inhibit orgasm are hostility or ambivalence toward the partner, fear of abandonment, guilt about sexuality, and reluctance to assert independence (Kaplan 1974).

In general, anxiety appears to be a very important factor in orgasmic dysfunction. A woman may become aroused to a certain extent, but an anxiety reaction can then inhibit the peaking of arousal necessary to trigger orgasm. Masters and Johnson (1970) have reported that anxiety was apparently involved in almost 50 percent of their cases of orgasmic dysfunction among women.

Vaginismus

Vaginismus is a relatively rare disorder in which there is an involuntary contraction of the P-C muscle and muscles surrounding the outer one-third of the vagina. Sexual intercourse is then very difficult and painful and, in certain instances, impossible.

In some cases, painful intercourse associated with internal, physical problems may result in severe anxiety. The anxiety may then result in a type of phobia related to vaginal penetration (Tollison & Adams 1979).

In other cases, extreme guilt or marital discord may promote vaginismus. Whatever the cause, the results are often most unpleasant. After a period of time, the male partner often becomes impotent. The female typically feels embarrassed and humiliated and has fears of being abandoned by her partner (Marmor 1976b).

It is extremely rare for a severe vaginismus response to occur after penetration has occurred. However, Reuben (1969) reports a case in which a man's penis became temporarily locked in a woman's vagina. After an embarrassing experience—during which the girl's roommates as well as police arrived at the scene—the woman finally relaxed enough for the man to obtain his release.

Dyspareunia

Painful intercourse is called *dyspareunia*: the pain may be momentarily sharp, resemble intermittent twinges, or consist of a prolonged aching sensation. These reactions may occur just prior to, during, or following coitus (Abarbanel 1978). As just suggested, severe dyspareunia may eventually result in vaginismus.

Although occasional pain associated with coitus is fairly common, persistent dyspareunia is rare. Painful intercourse, whether intermittent or persistent, is usually caused by physiological or anatomical disorders, such as an intact hymen or irritated hymenal remnants; irritations of the clitoris; infections of or scarring of the vagina; allergic reactions to birth-control paraphernalia such as creams, jellies, or diaphragms; and tumors or cysts in the pelvic region (Marmor 1976b).

However, psychological factors may also contribute to dyspareunia. Insufficient foreplay may result in such low levels of sexual arousal that there is a lack of vaginal lubrication and a tightening of vaginal musculature. There are even several cases reported in which ignorance of sexual anatomy and physiology have perpetuated anxieties which, in turn, have caused coital discomfort (Tollison & Adams 1979).

Author's Perspective: Reducing the Likelihood of Sexual Dysfunctions

Several general conclusions may be drawn from the preceding section. If one is a parent, older sibling, or someone else in close contact with a child, it is important to avoid instilling strong sex guilt. As suggested earlier, sexual activities may be discussed in terms of their consequences without labeling sex in general as something evil.

In regard to one's own sexual activity, it seems that setting performance goals often results in feelings of failure. Similarly, becoming a spectator or analyst of one's own performance may result in disappointment and also detract from the quality of the sexual interaction. In contrast, a relaxed attitude and openness to spontaneity may reduce performance anxiety and focus attention on the quality of the interaction.

Situations that produce high levels of anxiety should be avoided as much as possible. As we have seen, anxiety learned in one situation tends to generalize to others. On the other hand, good sexual experiences also generalize; a sexual interaction in a relaxed, romantic atmosphere can provide lasting benefits. Similarly, a partner who is warm, understanding, and sharing may open the door to new emotional experiences. It is not unusual for a person to experience sexual dysfunctions for years but then, with a new partner, reach unanticipated levels of satisfaction.

Communication between partners seems to be a particularly important fac-

FIGURE 21.2
Poor communication in a relationship increases the possibility of sexual dysfunction. Also, sexual problems may lead to hostility and more communication blockage. Fortunately, when there is improvement in one area of a relationship, it tends to generalize to other areas.

tor in the development of sexual dysfunction. Harsh, critical comments concerning attractiveness or sexual performance can be devastating and tend to destroy the possibility of open communication. In contrast, positive reinforcement can greatly facilitate sexual interaction. Furthermore, an open discussion of what is enjoyable or what may present a problem may not only decrease the likelihood of a sexual dysfunction but add to the quality of the relationship as a whole.

SEX THERAPY

In some cases, individuals with sexual dysfunctions enter psychotherapy. There are several schools of thought as to the best way to treat such problems. Psychoanalysts in the Freudian tradition have tended to focus on the presumed dynamics of sexual dysfunction: unresolved Oedipal conflicts and penis envy. Emphasis is placed upon gaining insight into conflicts within the personality. Other types of psychotherapy have emphasized exploring feelings in a supportive atmosphere in which mutual trust between client and therapist is established. Attempts are generally made to reduce anxiety and increase the acceptance

FIGURE 21.3

A couple in sex therapy. When both partners are positively motivated toward entering therapy, there is notable success or improvement.

of one's sexuality. Still other therapies involve sessions with both sexual partners. This approach—often referred to as marital therapy—emphasizes communication between the partners. Couples are encouraged to talk openly about their sexual conflicts, feelings, and wishes. Although there are strong proponents of each of these approaches, there is little evidence to support the effectiveness of any of these therapies in the treatment of specific sexual dysfunctions (Tollison & Adams 1979).

In contrast, behavioral therapy techniques have enjoyed considerable success in the treatment of sexual problems. In the first part of this section, behavioral theory will be discussed as a general approach to sexual dysfunction; then, the application of techniques developed for the treatment of specific dysfunctions will be considered.

A Comprehensive Approach to Sex Therapy

One of the best-known and most influential treatment programs for sexual dysfunctions has been developed by Masters and Johnson (1970). It is a two-week program that includes both the male and female partners. Simple education is one of the first steps; there is thorough instruction on the anatomy and physiology of the sex organs. In addition, many myths and misunderstandings about sexuality are cleared up. A physical examination including laboratory tests is performed to identify any physiological problems. After interviews—including two interviews during which sexual histories are taken—there is a round-table discussion. Both a male and female, who function as cotherapists, interact with the couple during the discussion. The presumed advantages of having cotherapists are several: (1) There is always a same-gender person who may be especially sensitive to particular problems. (2) Neither member of the couple has to face a majority of opposite-sex individuals. (3) The possibility of getting sex-biased information is reduced. (4) The "danger" that one member of the married couple will develop a sexual-emotional attachment to the opposite-sex therapist is less likely. During the discussion, possible causes of the sexual dysfunction are brought up, and the attitudes about the dysfunction—and prescribed treatment—are considered.

An exercise known as *sensate focusing* is a basic part of the Masters and Johnson therapy program. The assumption behind the exercise—which is practiced by the couple on their own—is that touching and being touched are important forms of sexual expression and communication that are often neglected or misunderstood. In sensate focusing, the partners take turns being the "giver" and the "receiver." Let us assume that the female starts as the "giver." After removing their clothes, the couple lies in bed. The woman strokes or fondles the man in nonsexual areas such as the head or feet. During this interaction, the man discusses what he finds pleasurable, while the woman expresses her reaction as pleasure giver. The woman moves to various parts of the body, varying the type of touch or stroke. However, in this initial session, sexual areas are avoided. After a period of time, the two switch roles, and the man becomes the "giver."

The next time that the sensate focusing exercise is performed, the couple may begin to include the breasts and genitals. However, the instructions are to avoid intercourse. The reason for this avoidance is so that the two can focus on sensuous pleasuring without anticipating coital performance—or nonperformance. Another advantage of the technique is that the couple usually learns to achieve high levels of arousal during these exercises. As we have seen, many people with sexual dysfunction fail to reach sufficient arousal.

After each day's (or night's) exercise, the couple discuss their reactions with the cotherapists. Near the end of the first week, techniques and exercises for specific dysfunctions are assigned. These will be discussed in the following subsections.

Therapy for Erectile Dysfunction

Treatment of erectile dysfunction has a long history. In the fifteenth century, impotence was thought to be caused by sorcery and witchcraft. However, burning suspected witches at the stake and/or special supplications to the gods apparently brought little relief. Later, when masturbation was suspected as a cause, prescribed periods of abstinence seemed to be no more successful in restoring potency. However, recent techniques have brought much more favorable results, even though the success rate is somewhat lower for erectile dysfunction—especially primary erectile dysfunction—than for most other sexual problems.

Behavioral therapy programs usually focus on helping the man relax, since, as we have seen, high levels of anxiety inhibit erection. One method is called *imaginal desensitization*. After training in muscle relaxation, the man is given a description of various scenes, beginning with fairly neutral scenes and becoming progressively more erotic. Each time the man feels anxious, he indicates this to the therapist and there is a return to deep muscular relaxation exercises. Eventually, the man learns to associate relaxation with scenes that previously provoked anxiety, and, in most cases, he generalizes his new-found equanimity to real-life situations (Wolpe 1958).

Sensate focusing is another way to reduce anxiety, particularly anxiety connected with sexual performance. Since intercourse is not prescribed in the early stages, the couple can focus on relaxation and arousal. Many men tend to concentrate on whether or not they have a firm erection, and they become spectators at their own performance. In response to this tendency, the therapist discourages spectating and redirects concentration on giving pleasure to the woman, independent of intercourse.

Therapists generally emphasize the importance of open, honest communication. In some cases, a failure to communicate fears and anxieties may lead to tension between sexual partners; this tension may then result in erectile dysfunction. As a hypothetical example, suppose a man comes home after experiencing frustration and rejection at work. In the evening he is less responsive than usual to his partner. She suspects him of being unfaithful but doesn't say anything. In bed, he may be impotent (primarily because of the anxiety generated at work); this impotence may function to confirm the woman's hypothesis of infidelity, and she responds with exaggerated anger. Her anger may then create performance anxiety in the man—and so on and on. Obviously, good communication at the beginning could have prevented the problem.

A device known as an inflatable penile prosthesis has been developed for cases of impotency that have failed to respond to conventional therapeutic methods. Two balloonlike cylinders are implanted into the corpora cavernosa of the penis via an incision in the abdomen or scrotum. The cylinders are connected to a small, fluid-filled reservoir placed under the abdominal muscles. A pump in the scrotum forces the liquid into the cylinders, distending the penis. Thus, to achieve erection, the man simply squeezes a part of his scrotum several times. To make the penis flaccid again, the man presses a release valve near the pump (see figure 12.4). Follow-up interviews with patients who received the prosthesis indicate that the vast majority are satisfied with the device. In most cases, orgasm and ejaculation are possible. Twenty-eight out of thirty wives involved expressed complete satisfaction with the results of the implantation procedure (Scott, Fishman, & Light 1980).

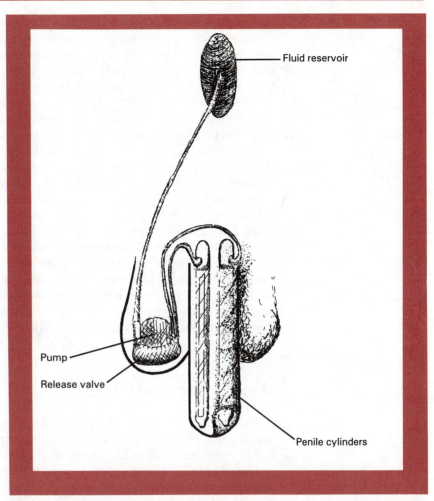

Fluid reservoir

Pump

Release valve

Penile cylinders

FIGURE 21.4
An inflatable penile prosthesis.

The man gains an erection by pressing the pump. He returns to flaccid condition by tripping the release valve.

Therapy for Premature Ejaculation

The treatment of premature ejaculation has a very high rate of success (Masters and Johnson 1970). However, people who do not strictly follow the rules laid out by the therapist are much more apt to fail. Therefore, the couple should follow instructions carefully and not try to advance more rapidly than suggested. Furthermore, the partners should be strongly committed to the program and avoid cancelling appointments.

An approach known as *start-stop technique* has been developed by Semans (1956). In this technique, the man signals the woman when he approaches ejaculation; she withdraws from contact with his genitals until the urge is reduced. Then she resumes stimulation. The number of stops required to delay ejaculation decreases each time the method is used; eventually, the man is able to maintain penetration for a period of time without any pauses. Generally, the most preferred coital position for this technique is the female above the male.

Masters and Johnson (1970) have developed what has been called the *squeeze technique.* After stimulating the man to erection, the woman takes the tip of his penis in her hand. The thumb is placed against the frenulum, and the first two fingers are placed on the opposite side, one above the coronal ridge and the other just below it. When the man feels that he is about to ejaculate, he tells the woman, and she squeezes moderately hard for three to four seconds. He loses his urge to ejaculate and, in some cases, his erection. (The squeeze is not painful.) After waiting about half a minute, the couple repeat the process, usually up to four times. Finally, the woman abandons the procedure and allows the man to ejaculate. This technique, like the start-stop procedure, usually teaches the man to delay ejaculation, and the couple may move on to penile-vaginal insertion. It should be pointed out, however, that this technique can be overdone, creating new fears and eventually producing problems of erectile dysfunction. Obviously, caution and moderation are important.

Therapy for Retarded Ejaculation

The treatment for retarded ejaculation varies depending upon the apparent cause of the problem. If a man is able to masturbate to ejaculation but experiences difficulties having orgasm in the presence of the woman, the following approach may be utilized. At first, the man is encouraged to masturbate to orgasm with the woman present. The next time, the woman masturbates the man to orgasm after nonorgasmic coitus. This procedure establishes a strong association between the woman and orgasm. Finally, through a combination of coitus and masturbation of the man by the woman, most men become able to ejaculate in the woman's vagina (Masters & Johnson 1970).

If the problem of retarded ejaculation seems related to anxiety associated with orgasm, a systematic desensitization approach is usually recommended, similar to that utilized in the treatment of orgasmic dysfunction. After practicing deep muscle relaxation, the man is asked to imagine each of a series of scenes that are increasingly erotic. Each time anxiety is experienced, there is a return to deep muscle relaxation exercises (Tollison & Adams 1979). Eventually, anxiety tends to abate, and the man is able to relax enough for ejaculation to take place. This technique is also helpful in cases where a cooperative partner is not readily available.

FIGURE 21.5
Systematic Desensitization Hierarchy for Retarded Ejaculation

1. You and your wife have turned out the lights and are lying in bed talking before going to sleep.
2. As you continue talking she places her head on your shoulder and you pull her closer to you.
3. You feel very close to her at this moment as you begin to kiss her.
4. She places her arms around your neck and pulls you to her breasts.
5. You feel your penis becoming erect as you continue kissing and begin to fondle her breasts.
6. She responds warmly to your caresses by rubbing your inner thigh.
7. You now feel your penis becoming hard and elongated as you manually stimulate her genitals.
8. She slides her hands around the waistband of your pajama bottoms and gently lowers them freeing your erect penis.
9. You reach to the bedside table and take out the electric vibrator you know gives her pleasure and begin to stimulate her genitals as she massages your penis.
10. She moves her body to you and presses your penis against her stomach while whispering how much she wants you.
11. You remove her gown and position yourself between her legs.
12. As your penis penetrates her vagina you experience very pleasurable sexual sensations.
13. You both begin thrusting, gradually at first, enjoying the sensations of intercourse.
14. As you continue thrusting you notice your wife increasing the tempo of thrusting as she nears orgasm.
15. As you meet the tempo of your wife's thrusting she reaches orgasm while holding you tightly.
16. You continue thrusting and feel the sensations of approaching climax.
17. You speed the tempo of thrusting as your wife meets every thrust.
18. You feel your muscles tensing as you continue thrusting while your wife verbally encourages you toward ejaculation.
19. Your muscles tighten and you feel a wave of sensations radiating through your body as you ejaculate into your wife's vagina.

SOURCE: From Tollison & Adams.

A sexually dysfunctional man is asked to imagine a relatively non-anxiety-producing scene and then progresses until he can imagine more explicit scenes without too much anxiety. In between times, he engages in relaxation exercises.

Therapy for Inhibited Sexual Desire

Since inhibited sexual desire is more common in females than males, the examples of treatment procedures will be directed toward women. However, some comparable techniques may be utilized for the treatment of men with inhibited sexual desire.

Sensate focusing is a particularly effective procedure for treating inhibited sexual desire because there are no demands for sexual performance that might create anxiety. However, in some cases, even the initiation of sexual pleasuring evokes inhibiting anxiety. In these situations, imaginal desensitization is often helpful. The woman is asked to imagine increasingly sensuous scenes, and deep muscle relaxation is introduced each time she feels anxious (Husted 1975). If the male partner learns to administer imaginal desensitization and muscle relaxation, communication between the partners may improve, and generalization of sexual arousal to the man is apt to take place. In addition, the man feels less like an outsider in the therapy process (Walen, Hauserman, & Lavin 1977).

Up to the point in the therapy program where the woman is relaxed and experiencing some level of sexual arousal, most therapists discourage coitus. When intercourse is introduced into the program, it should be what is referred to as "nondemand"; the woman should initiate it, and the thrusting movements should be slow and exploratory (as opposed to forceful and orgasm-oriented). It is also suggested that the woman experiment with contracting the P-C muscles at this time (Kaplan 1974). The nondemand coitus is generally attempted with the female above the male; this allows the woman relatively great freedom and allows her to disengage if and when she feels anxious or threatened. Finally, the woman is encouraged to engage in fantasies, especially those that may have been previously conditioned to elicit arousal without anxiety (Walen, Hauserman, & Lavin 1977).

Therapy for Orgasmic Dysfunction

LoPiccolo (1978) has described a treatment procedure for orgasmic dysfunction in women that involves four components. First, there is a program of masturbation training. This training is presumably important because masturbation enables a woman to feel the sensations that precede and accompany orgasm under nonthreatening conditions. Furthermore, the exercise may be less anxiety provoking than stimulation by a partner because it is under self-control. Finally, masturbation is more likely than coitus to produce orgasm in most women.

The masturbation program involves a series of steps which include self-examination with a mirror, tactile exploration of the genitals to locate especially sensitive areas, and the Kegel program of exercises. The woman is also encouraged to stimulate erotic areas while engaging in sexual fantasies or viewing erotica. If she is unable to reach orgasm using these procedures, the use of a vibrator is encouraged.

The second component of the treatment procedure involves skill training for the male partner. It is suggested that he watch his partner masturbate to become familiar with the types of stimulation most effective for her. Then the male is encouraged to manipulate the female to orgasm, and finally, this type of manipulation is paired with intercourse.

The third component involves reducing the female's inhibitions. If she is embarrassed about showing intense arousal in the presence of her partner, she may be encouraged to role-play an exaggerated orgasmic response in front of him. Acting out violent convulsions, screams of delight, and other uninhibited behaviors often helps to reduce inhibitions (Lobitz & LoPiccolo 1973).

The fourth component involves training in behaviors that usually occur involuntarily during intense orgasm; the voluntary expression of these patterns facilitates orgasm. Included in the list of behaviors are pelvic thrusting, tensing the thigh muscles, throwing back the head, and contracting muscles in the vaginal area.

The LoPiccolo four-component program appears to be most suitable for the treatment of primary orgasmic dysfunction. Secondary dysfunction usually requires a less extensive program. The nature of the program recommended depends upon the apparent cause of the problem. If the problem is primarily due to insufficient arousal, sensate focusing and techniques directed at increasing arousal are suggested; if the problem involves a troubled interpersonal relationship, some attention should be given to interpersonal conflicts.

Another approach to orgasmic problems resulting from insufficient arousal is the utilization of what might be called the teasing technique. The couple is instructed to interrupt coitus and return to foreplay activities at several points during the sexual interaction. In addition, it is suggested that the male make slow thrusting movements in a somewhat teasing manner. In some cases, manual clitoral stimulation can be alternated with periods of slow penile thrusting (Kaplan 1974).

There is recent evidence, from a well-controlled study, that nonorgasmic women can benefit from self-administered treatment and avoid the expense (and possible embarrassment) of sex therapy. The treatment tested was masturbation training similar to that utilized by LoPiccolo in the four-component program; treatment was self-administered using either videotapes or booklets of instructions. Vibrators were also given to the subjects.

At the end of the six-week program, 60 percent of the previously nonorgasmic women had achieved orgasm. (There was essentially no difference in the effectiveness of the videotape and written instructions). In many—but not all—cases, orgasm was reached during intercourse as well as masturbation. After a period of a year, all the women retained their orgasmic response and, in addition, four additional women had become orgasmic. Furthermore, four additional women reported transferring orgasm to coitus. In contrast, none of the women in the control group (who did not receive instruction) became orgasmic (McMullen & Rosen 1979).

Therapy for Vaginismus

The therapy for vaginismus usually requires two processes: (1) reduction of the anxiety associated with the vagina (women may have a phobia about virtually anything that involves the vagina); and (2) elimination of the spastic vaginal response. In the majority of cases, both aspects of treatment may be carried on at the same time. However, it is sometimes necessary to reduce anxiety connected with treatment before an attempt is made to deal with the spastic response.

Therapy aimed at reducing anxiety related to treatment usually involves systematic desensitization. Wolpe (1973) has suggested that, after relaxation exercises, the woman be asked to imagine shallow penetration with a wire-thin rod. Then, little by little, the width of the imagined rod and the supposed depth of penetration are increased. After the woman can tolerate the thought of larger rods, imagined movement of the rod is introduced until she can visualize a penis-sized rod making thrusting movements.

The second part of treatment involves the actual insertion of a rod or catheter. At first, a very small catheter is inserted and rotated gently. After this is tolerated without pain or anxiety, the size of the catheter and amount of movement are gradually increased. It is sometimes suggested that the woman practice voluntarily tensing and relaxing the vaginal muscles during these treatments. After a relatively large catheter can be inserted without pain or anxiety, coitus is suggested. However, the woman should be responsible for guiding the penis into the vagina, and the man should refrain from making overly active thrusting movements during attempts at penetration (Tollison & Adams 1979).

In contrast to the apparent success of these techniques, older, surgical techniques have produced discouraging results. Surgically enlarging the vaginal opening may allow for penile penetration, but genital friction during coitus is reduced to the extent that neither partner is sufficiently stimulated. Furthermore, surgery often compounds the woman's anxiety connected with the vagina, so that her sexual responsiveness may actually be reduced (Kaplan 1974).

Author's Perspective: Evaluating the Effectiveness of Sex Therapy and Choosing a Sex Therapist

The apparent success of the Masters and Johnson sex therapy program has been remarkable. However, a critique of Masters and Johnson's (1970) evaluation techniques by Zilbergeld and Evans (1980) suggests that methodological flaws have led to an exaggeration of its effectiveness. According to Zilbergeld and Evans, the criteria for success and failure were not clearly spelled out. Furthermore, Masters and Johnson did not take into account various degrees of change. Presumably, if there were unambiguous definitions of success and failure, several cases would fall in between these two extremes. Another criticism was that the process used to select the sample for full treatment was not well defined; it was not stated whether or not persons asked to leave the therapy program were counted as failures. The data on five-year follow-ups were particularly suspect. Clients who could not be located for follow-up were considered successes, when, in fact, they could very easily have been failures.

Masters and Johnson are not alone in their failure to meet high standards in evaluation of research. However, because of their great reputation as sex researchers, the general public and professionals alike have been more hesitant to criticize Masters and Johnson's therapy evaluation. One basic message from the Zilbergeld and Evans critique is that well-designed research is necessary before definite conclusions regarding the effectiveness of therapy can be drawn. Nonetheless, a preliminary conclusion is that, when the motivation of clients is good and when therapists are well qualified, the chances for improvement are very good—probably better than for any of the other types of therapy discussed in the previous chapters.

Before choosing a sex therapist, one should be very careful to check on the therapist's qualifications. Most physicians or psychologists can provide a list of professionally qualified individuals. However, even qualified therapists may prescribe practices that certain individuals find distasteful. It is entirely appropriate to inquire into exactly what procedures are utilized during the therapy.

Certain practices in particular raise ethical questions. For example, some therapists recommend the use of sexual surrogates—individuals (usually women) who make themselves available as sexual partners during treatment when other willing partners are not available. Although the use of surrogates in therapy has several supporters—and there is even an organization known as the International Professional Surrogates Association—others view this practice as nothing more than "thinly veiled prostitution" (Holden 1974).

A few therapists advocate some form of sexual contact between the patient and therapist. Nonetheless, the vast majority of qualified therapists and psychologists in general do not condone such interaction (Holroyd & Brodsky 1977). Furthermore, sexual contact between patient and therapist is grounds for expulsion from the therapists' professional organization and may lead to criminal prosecution. Generally speaking, well-qualified therapists have made a strong, effective attempt to maintain high ethical standards.

SUMMARY

Sexual dysfunction may cause men great frustration and anxiety, especially if they have associated sexuality with masculinity. One of the most common problems is erectile dysfunction—the failure to have or maintain an erection. Premature ejaculation is also quite frequent in males; the incidence of this problem depends upon how one defines "premature." Retarded ejaculation is probably less common than the other two types of dysfunctions. Medical problems may contribute to male dysfunctions, but many of the causal factors appear to be psychological.

Female sexual dysfunctions may also cause considerable frustration and anxiety for the women who experience them. Among the most common female sexual problems are inhibited sexual desire (the absence of erotic feelings and failure to enjoy sexual activities); orgasmic dysfunction (the failure to experience orgasm); vaginismus (involuntary contraction of the muscles surrounding the vagina); and dyspareunia (painful intercourse). Psychological factors are usually the cause of the first three dysfunctions, but medical problems are often involved in dyspareunia. In some cases, there is an interaction between psychological and medical factors.

A variety of approaches to sex therapy have been formulated. In the Masters and Johnson program there is a series of steps, including simple education, physical examination, interviews and discussions, and exercises involving tactual stimulation, such as sensate focusing. Somewhat different treatments are then utilized for specific dysfunctions. For erectile dysfunction, imaginal desensitization and sensate focusing usually help to reduce anxiety. (Inflatable penile prostheses have been developed for men who do not respond to conventional therapies.) Premature ejaculation is typically treated by the start-stop or squeeze technique. In the case of retarded ejaculation, imaginal desensitization or masturbation training may be utilized.

Many of these same general approaches are found in the treatment of female dysfunctions. Some of the more specific techniques used with women are nondemand coitus initiated by the female; training in the use of vibrators to induce orgasm during masturbation; and the use of rods or catheters during the treatment of vaginismus. For both men and women, discussion with and possible training of the individual's partner is encouraged whenever this is possible.

Unfortunately, there are a few poorly trained and/or unethical "therapists" who practice sex therapy. It is important to check a therapist's credentials and discuss the specific treatments utilized before becoming involved in a sex-therapy program.

NOTES

1. One of the most successful methods for differentiating organic from psychological causes is simply to observe the man while he is asleep. If erections occur during sleep, the cause of the erectile dysfunction is quite clearly psychological (Marshall, Surridge, & Delva 1981).
2. The ISD category may include two more-or-less-distinct dysfunctions: sexual apathy and sexual aversion. Apathy refers to a lack of interest in sexuality, while aversion implies negative feelings about sex and sexual interaction (Kaplan 1974, 1979). Since these dysfunctions are quite similar in terms of development and treatment, only the general term ISD will be used in this chapter.

CHAPTER 22

Sexual Diseases and Disorders

Sexual diseases have had a major effect upon history. During the late fifteenth and early sixteenth centuries, syphilis spread throughout Europe, greatly influencing military battles and causing many people to be banished from such cities as Paris and Edinburgh. In England, the first four children of Henry VIII and Catherine of Aragon all died, apparently of congenital syphilis. Henry's disappointment at this—and at not having a male heir—led to the breakup of his marriage and attempts to legalize his subsequent marriages. Henry argued with the pope over the legality of his second marriage. As a result of this quarrel—and general politico-religious changes of the age—England broke from the Roman Catholic Church, and the Church of England was formed (Catterall 1974).

Although there have been a number of medical breakthroughs in the treatment of sexual diseases and disorders during the second half of the twentieth century, such diseases remain common, and some are on the increase. Thus, sexual diseases continue to have a strong impact on public health—and also on how sexuality is expressed and conceptualized.

A number of medical specialists treat sexual disorders. Gynecologists specialize in female diseases while urologists generally deal with male problems. Dermatologists typically become involved with diseases that cause rashes and other skin problems. In most communities, free and confidential diagnosis and treatment of these diseases and disorders are provided in an attempt to provide relief from their symptoms and check their spread throughout the population.

In this chapter, a variety of sexual diseases and disorders will be discussed. This is not intended to be a do-it-yourself medical guide, but to help the reader identify early symptoms of any problems and also to gain a general perspective on sexual diseases and disorders.

FIGURE 22.1
Sexual diseases and disorders

A. Sexually transmitted diseases

	Cause	Early symptoms	Treatment	Comments
Gonorrhea	Bacterium	Males: burning sensation; discharge from penis; females: symptoms less noticeable, sometimes pain during urination or in pelvic region	Penicillin or tetracycline	Quite prevalent in the United States; some strains are resistant to treatment
Syphilis	Bacterium	Painless, hard-rimmed chancre where the bacteria entered the body, usually in the genital region	Penicillin or tetracycline	Occurs in four stages; if untreated, very dangerous
Genital herpes	Virus	Genital blisters or small bumps; fever	No known cure	Symptoms last 2–4 weeks; at other times, the virus remains dormant and disease is not contagious
Chancroid	Bacterium	Painful chancre with soft rim	Sulfonamide drugs	Rare
Lymphogranuloma venereum	Virus	Swelling and pain in groin	Sulfa drugs or tetracycline	Rare; if untreated, can cause elephantiasis
Venereal warts	Virus	Warts on genitals	Painting infected area with caustic solution	Rare
Granuloma inguinale	Bacterium	Small, red lumps on genitals	Antibiotics	Found mainly in tropics

B. Other sexual diseases

	Cause	Symptoms	Treatment	Comments
Monilia	Yeast fungus	Thick, white vaginal discharge	Combination of antibiotic and antifungal drugs	Most likely to occur in obese or undernourished women
Trichomoniasis ("trich")	Protozoan	Soreness of vulva; smelly discharge	A drug toxic to the trich organism	Males show no symptoms but can transmit the disease

Cystitis	Bacterium	Pain during urination	Sulfa drugs	Sometimes associated with frequent intercourse in females
Prostatitis	Congestion of prostate gland; bacteria	Pain in genital region; thin, mucous discharge from penis	Antibiotics, massage, and long, warm baths	Fairly common in older men

C. Cancer of the sex organs

	Cause	Symptoms	Treatment	Comments
Breast cancer	Virus (?)	A lump in the breast	Surgery; radiation, chemical, or hormone therapy	Breast surgery may create emotional problems for some women
Cervical cancer	Virus (?)	None for 5–10 years	Surgery	Few, if any, long-term effects after cervical surgery
Cancer of the prostate	?	Frequent urination; difficulty emptying bladder	Hormone treatment; surgery	More common in older men

D. Chromosomal abnormalities

	Cause	Symptoms	Treatment	Comments
Klinefelter's syndrome	An extra X chromosome (XXY)	Small penis, prominent breasts	Androgen treatment	Individuals are sterile males
XYY males	An extra Y chromosome (XYY)	Very tall; high rate of violent crime	None	Reasons for aggressiveness are controversial
Turner's syndrome	A missing X chromosome (XO)	Very short; deficiency in secondary sex characteristics	Hormone therapy	Individuals are sterile females

E. Miscellaneous disorders

	Cause	Symptoms	Treatment	Comments
Priapism	Tumors; causes of some cases unknown	Constant erection	Surgery to increase venous flow from penis	Erection is not associated with sexual desire
"Jock itch"	Fungus	Itching in genital area; rash	External treatment with fungicide	Common among athletes
Pubic lice	Parasitic lice	Itching in genital area; rash	Antiparasitic cream or lotion	May be transmitted during intercourse

SEXUALLY TRANSMITTED DISEASES

The term venereal disease, or VD, has taken on such a negative connotation over the years that most health practitioners try to avoid using it. Within the past few years, sexually transmitted disease (STD) has become the more widely accepted term. STD may be transmitted by sexual intercourse, oral-genital sex, anal intercourse, or, in rare instances, by kissing.

Gonorrhea

Of the sexually transmitted diseases, gonorrhea is the most prevalent. In fact, of all the communicable diseases, only the common cold occurs with greater frequency in the United States. Gonorrhea is also the oldest-known sexually transmitted disease; symptoms of it are described in the Old Testament and by the ancient Greek physician Hippocrates (Fiumara 1971).

In 1879 the bacterium that causes gonorrhea was identified. However, an effective method of treating the disease was not discovered until 1943, when penicillin became widely available. In the meantime, gonorrhea reached near-epidemic proportions during the two world wars, when it spread rapidly among servicemen and prostitutes (Blau 1961).

During the 1950s the incidence of gonorrhea dropped, and the disease was almost eliminated. However, as can be seen in figure 22.2, the

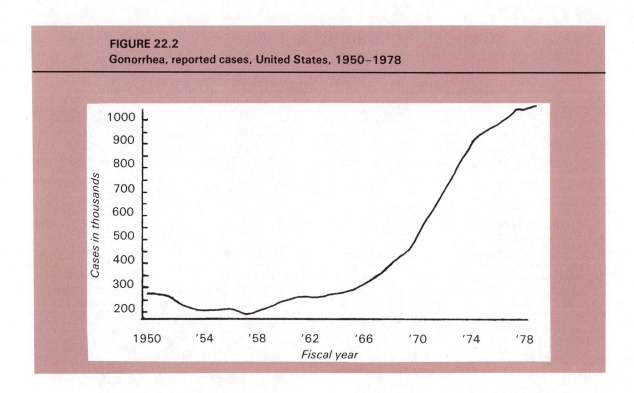

FIGURE 22.2
Gonorrhea, reported cases, United States, 1950–1978

number of reported cases increased dramatically during the 1960s and 1970s. In 1976, one million cases were reported, and it is estimated that four times that many cases go unreported (U.S. Public Health Service 1976).

Several factors seem to be involved in the recent increase in the incidence of gonorrhea. First, The Pill has, to a great extent, replaced the condom as a method of birth control. The condom provides some protection against the disease, whereas The Pill actually increases a woman's susceptibility to gonorrhea. Second, veterans of the Vietnam War brought back many cases of gonorrhea from Asia. Third, an increase in sexual permissiveness has probably been a contributing factor. Finally, a new strain of gonorrhea bacterium has recently evolved that is resistant to penicillin and other treatments (Piemme 1974).

One of the highest rates of increase in gonorrhea (and other types of STD) is among homosexual males. Because of the negative attitudes about homosexuality in our society, gonorrhea contracted through homosexual practices is particularly likely to go unreported. Another reason for the high rate among male homosexuals is that 70 percent of individuals with rectal gonorrhea have no symptoms (Handsfield 1974). In contrast, cunnilingus is less likely to spread STD; the incidence of gonorrhea among lesbians is relatively low (Unger 1975).

The symptoms of gonorrhea are more easily identified in males than females. Men feel a burning sensation when urinating, and the urine may contain pus or blood. A discharge also seeps out of the meatus (the opening at the tip of the penis). The discharge starts out as a clear, mucous substance but after a day or so becomes thick and creamy. These symptoms usually appear three to seven days after infection. If treatment is neglected, pain during urination worsens, the whole penis becomes sore, and eventually the epididymus is invaded by the gonorrhea infection. When this happens, sterility may result (Schofield 1979).

In women, there are usually no readily observable symptoms. The gonorrhea bacterium typically attacks the female's cervix. Pus discharges, but in so small an amount that it usually goes unnoticed. The urethra may also be affected, and in this case there is pain during urination. If not treated, the disease may move up into the uterus during the menstrual period. (This takes place in about 50 percent of the untreated cases.) Shortly thereafter, the fallopian tubes become infected. This results in pain within the pelvic region and, in some instances, painful or irregular menstruation. If treatment is still neglected, the fallopian tubes may become blocked with scar tissue, causing sterility. Another possibility is partial blockage of the tubes; the sperm can get to the eggs, but the eggs cannot move down the tube. Ectopic pregnancy may result.

If a pregnant woman has gonorrhea, the infection is often transferred to the baby's eyes from the mother's cervix during birth. Most states require that silver nitrate or an antibiotic be put in all newborn infants' eyes. If left untreated, gonorrhea of the eyes usually blinds a baby (Blau 1961).

Although the symptoms of gonorrhea are fairly distinct, at least in males, diagnosis is not definite until laboratory tests are made. A swab containing the suspected bacteria is rubbed on a culture plate. The bacteria are then grown, or "cultured," for 24 to 48 hours. Suspect bacteria are given as many as three chemical tests to ensure correct identification. Thus, individuals must wait for a few days before a definite diagnosis can be made.

The treatment of gonorrhea is relatively simple. Two large doses of penicillin are administered by injection into the buttocks. For individuals who are allergic to penicillin, tetracycline is generally given orally.

Syphilis

The name syphilis comes from a 1530 Italian poem about a shepherd boy named Syphilus. The boy was punished by the gods for insulting Apollo and became infected with the disease. Previous to that time, the disease had acquired several ethnic slurs: the French called it the Naples disease; the Italians called it the French disease; and the English called it the Spanish disease.

Syphilis was unknown in Europe until Columbus returned from the West Indies in 1493. Since syphilitic damage to the bones has been found in skeletons of pre-Columbian Indians, it is assumed that Columbus and his crew carried the disease to Europe from the New World.[1] Incidentally, Columbus himself seems to have died from complications of syphilis, in 1506.

In 1905 the cause of syphilis was identified as a spiral-shaped bacterium. A year later, a diagnostic blood test—known as the Wassermann test—was developed. In contrast to the great increase in gonorrhea, the incidence of syphilis has not increased significantly in the past few decades. However, syphilis still ranks as the fourth-most-common communicable disease in the United States. Furthermore, it is highly contagious; the probability of contracting it from a single act of coitus is one in two (Fulton 1974).

The most easily recognized early symptom of syphilis is a chancre, which usually appears in the genital region ten to forty days after contact with an infected person. The chancre is a painless, round lesion with hard, raised edges (see figure 22.3). In males it usually appears on the penis or scrotum. Females may have a chancre on the vulva, but it is most likely to develop on the internal sex organs, where it generally goes unnoticed.

Because the chancre is found at the point where the bacteria have entered the body, the lesion can also appear in the mouth or the rectum if a person has had oral-genital contact or anal intercourse with an infected individual. It is also possible (though unlikely) that the bacteria may en-

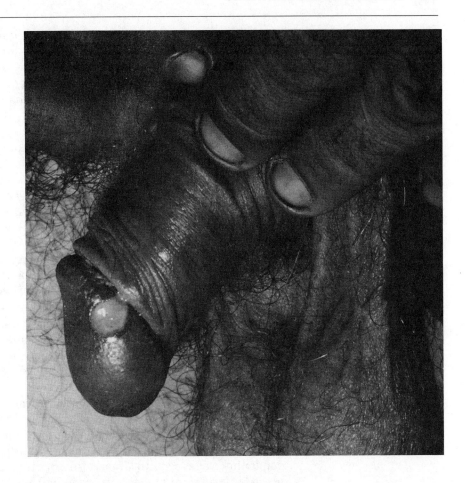

FIGURE 22.3
A syphilitic chancre.

ter the body through a cut. One man in his late sixties was found to have syphilis of the scalp. It turned out that a woman riding in an elevator with him in a cheap hotel had kissed him on a cut on his bald head, saying, "You are too old for anything else" (Johnson 1978).

Syphilis develops in four stages. The primary stage is marked by the appearance of the chancre and, after one to five weeks, its spontaneous disappearance. Some people have been fooled into thinking that the disease is gone after the chancre disappears. However, its absence simply means that the bacteria have entered the bloodstream, ushering in the secondary stage. In this stage—which begins to show symptoms one to six months after the first stage—a rash appears on various parts of the body. There may be other symptoms as well, including headaches and a low-grade fever. Within a period of months or perhaps a year, these symptoms disappear and the syphilis enters the third, or latent, stage. During this period there are no symptoms, and the disease is not infectious. However, a pregnant woman may pass the infection along to the fetus. During this latent period, the bacteria burrow into the blood vessels, central nervous system, and bones, leading up to the highly destructive fourth, or late, stage of syphilis.

The late stage of syphilis—which does not develop until several years after infection—generally takes one of three patterns. In what is referred to as *benign late syphilis*—because it is still possible to treat—the skin, muscles, liver, eyes, or endocrine glands are infected; there is a large, destructive ulcer on the organ that is attacked. In *cardiovascular late syphilis*, the heart and blood vessels are affected; this type of syphilis can be fatal. *Neurosyphilis*, or *general paresis*, is the third type of late syphilis. Brain damage resulting in paralysis and loss of mental faculties are the symptoms of this condition. The results are almost always fatal.

Another form of the disease is *congenital syphilis*; the bacteria, which are passed on by the mother, are present at birth (and during late fetal development). If congenital syphilis is detected and treated before the fourth month of pregnancy—as it often is since blood tests have become routine—the child will not be affected. However, if untreated, the child is likely to die before birth or within a short time afterwards.

The most effective tests for syphilis are blood tests. The early blood test for syphilis was known as the Wassermann test, and, although the tests have changed somewhat, the diagnostic technique is still commonly referred to as the Wassermann. The tests are very accurate in detecting syphilis in the secondary stage. However, the early stages of syphilis are difficult to diagnose; identification of the chancre is the most accurate means of detection during this period.

The treatment of syphilis is relatively simple: syphilitic bacteria are quite effectively killed by penicillin or tetracycline. The latent, late, and congenital stages require larger doses, but treatment is still effective unless a large amount of tissue or organ damage has occurred previous to the detection of the disease.

Genital Herpes

Genital herpes is caused by a virus closely related to that which causes coldsores or fever blisters in the area of the mouth.[2] This disease was very rare in the United States before 1965, but, since that time, its incidence has increased dramatically. In the 1970s, genital herpes had become the second-most-common type of sexually transmitted disease (Hatcher et al. 1978).

The symptoms of genital herpes are blisters or small bumps on the genitals, which can rupture and be quite painful. During this symptomatic period, the person usually runs a fever and exhibits the signs of a generalized systemic infection. Genital herpes typically remains active and symptomatic for a period of two to four weeks. Only when active may it be transmitted to another person. The rest of the time, the virus remains dormant in the nervous system. Symptomatic episodes typically recur when the person is emotionally upset, fatigued, or under some type of tension (U.S. Department of Health, Education, and Welfare 1980).

In addition to the physical problem, genital herpes can cause considerable psychological stress. A person must live with the anxiety that the symptomatic stage may return at any time. It is also difficult to explain to a sexual partner—or a prospective one—that one has a sexually transmitted disease that is incurable. In some areas of the country, support groups are available to help people deal with these problems. Fortunately, many people have learned to adjust to the psychological stress of herpes. They have also learned that by refraining from intercourse during flareups of the disease, they can greatly reduce the likelihood of transmitting it.

One of the most dangerous aspects of genital herpes—although relatively rare—is that in some cases it is transmitted to the fetus of an infected woman. The fetus may then be aborted or develop a serious—and sometimes fatal—brain infection after birth. A more likely possibility is that herpes will be transmitted to the baby during delivery; as a result, delivery should be by Caesarean section if the mother has active herpes at the time. Still another danger is that women with herpes may run an increased risk of cervical cancer. However, the relationship between cancer and herpes is still controversial (Kessler 1979).

In 1981, a drug was introduced that is effective in reducing the symptoms of genital herpes. This drug, acyclovir, does not kill the herpesvirus. However, at the time of publication of this book, there is some hope that an effective cure for herpes will be found in the near future.

Nonspecific Urethritis

Nonspecific urethritis (NSU) refers to an inflammation of the male urethra that is caused by something other than gonorrhea. In about half the cases, an organism called *Chlamydia trachomatis* is the villain, but a variety of other organisms have been identified as probable causes. There are also situations in which the inflammation results from allergic reactions (Barlow 1979; Feldman & Nikitas 1981). In the latter case, of course, the NSU is not transmitted during sexual relations.

The symptoms of NSU are a thin, clear discharge and mild discomfort during urination. These symptoms are similar to those of gonorrhea and, in the final diagnosis, NSU is not identified until the culture for gonococcus proves negative. Treatment consists of the administration of tetracycline or other antibiotics. (Since penicillin is not effective, a correct diagnosis is important.)

The incidence of NSU has been increasing rapidly in the last twelve years—especially among college students—and it may now be more common than gonorrhea (Feldman & Nikitas 1981). However, the law does not require that cases of NSU be reported to the government, as it does with other STDs. Therefore, it is difficult to compare the incidence of the diseases.

Relatively Rare Sexually Transmitted Diseases

A disease known as chancroid is caused by a bacterium. The major symptom is a chancre that superficially resembles that associated with syphilis. However, the chancre is painful and the rim is soft (as opposed to the painless, hard-rimmed chancre of syphilis). Sulfonamide drugs are usually effective in treatment (Blau 1961).

Lymphogranuloma venereum, or *LGV*, is a disease of the lymphatic system caused by a virus. The most obvious symptoms are swelling and pain in the groin region. The disease progresses in three stages and, if left untreated, may cause extreme enlargement of the genital organs, a form of *elephantiasis*. In a few cases, the male genitals have weighed over 100 pounds, and individuals were forced to transport them in a wheelbarrow. The treatment, which is most effective if the disease is diagnosed early, is tetracycline or sulfa drugs (Berkow 1977).

Venereal warts are warts or, more correctly, noncancerous tumors on the genitals. These tumors are caused by a virus believed to be transmitted during intercourse. The treatment, usually external, includes painting the infected area with a caustic solution. After application, the tumors dry up and fall off within a few days.

Granuloma inguinale is a disease found mainly in the tropics. The symptoms are small, red lumps, usually on the genitals. As the lumps enlarge and spread, they tend to form one large area of infection. Treatment is generally by administration of antibiotic drugs (Blau 1961).

In many cases, two or more sexual diseases occur at the same time. Consequently, when one disease is suspected, tests are usually made for several of the others.

Medical Perspective: Preventing STD

There are a variety of things that can be done to prevent or reduce the possibility of getting a sexually transmitted disease. The most obvious is to avoid sexual intercourse or, at least, intercourse with a large variety of partners. Sexually transmitted disease is much more prevalent among individuals who have multiple partners than those who are relatively monogamous (Hart 1977).

Washing the genitals before and after intercourse helps to remove bacteria, particularly those causing gonorrhea. One can also reduce the possibility of bacteria entering the urethra by urinating both before and after intercourse.

Looking at one's partner's genitals for telltale signs of STD can also be important. This can usually be done unobtrusively during the process of undressing or as a part of foreplay. Another precaution, as suggested earlier, is for the man to use a condom. Although it is not 100 percent effective, it greatly reduces the possibility of transmitting diseases, especially gonorrhea. Chemical birth-control methods—the use of foams, creams, or jellies—may also help to kill sexually transmitted bacteria.

Early diagnosis and treatment of STD are of great importance. Embarrassment and fear should not be inhibiting factors, especially since all procedures are confidential and are not painful. If STD is diagnosed, then the task of informing past partners (or prospective partners) is crucial because, as explained earlier, some infected people do not show any symptoms. Straightforward communication between partners is one of the most effective ways of controlling the spread of STD.

OTHER SEXUAL DISEASES

Several types of infectious diseases can attack sexual and reproductive organs. Although some of these diseases are transmitted via intercourse or oral-genital sex, they are often passed on in other ways; therefore, they are not usually classified as sexually transmitted diseases.

Monilia

Monilia is a type of *vaginitis* (inflammation of the vagina). It is caused by a yeast fungus, normally in the vagina, which multiples rapidly under certain conditions. Monilia may become a problem after menstruation, childbirth, or long-term use of The Pill. It is most likely to affect women who are obese or malnourished (Fiumara 1976).

The symptoms of monilia include a thick, white vaginal discharge that may appear on the lips of the vagina. This discharge can cause extreme itching and discomfort. Treatment generally consists of a drug that has both antibiotic and antifungal activity.

Trichomoniasis

Trichomoniasis, or *trich*, is another form of vaginitis, caused by a single-celled organism. Trich may be passed back and forth between a man and a woman, but the man does not usually show any symptoms. Trich may also be transmitted via swimming pools, bathtubs, or toilet seats (Tanowitz 1974).

The symptoms of this disease are a white or yellowish, smelly discharge from the vagina. The vulva is usually sore, and it itches or burns. Treatment usually involves oral administration of a drug that is toxic to the trich organism. The male partner must also be treated; otherwise, the female will be reinfected. Both trich and monilia—which may occur together—can be sexually inhibiting and are a frequent cause of the dispareunia (painful intercourse) discussed in the previous chapter.

Cystitis

Cystitis refers to an inflammation of the bladder that occurs in either men or women. It is caused by bacteria normally found in the genital area. The symptoms include a frequent need to urinate and pain during urination. The urine may also be somewhat red due to small amounts of blood from the bladder. Irritation of the bladder and ensuing cystitis in females may be prompted by frequent intercourse, since the bladder is somewhat displaced during penile thrusting. Thus, this inflammation is often referred to as "honeymoon cystitis."

The treatment of cystitis generally includes a sulfa drug. Often, the drug contains a dye that turns the urine bright red-orange; the drug helps to relieve the pain associated with urination.

Prostatitis

An inflammation of the prostate gland—known as *prostatitis*—is fairly common in men, particularly older men. Prostatitis is often caused by bacteria that invade the prostate. However, there is also evidence that very infrequent ejaculation may lead to congestion of the gland and symptoms of prostatitis (Mobley 1975).

The symptoms of prostatitis include a thin, mucous discharge. There may also be pain in the lower back and the genital region, and, in some cases, pain associated with erection. The treatment usually involves prostatic massage, antibiotics, and long, warm baths. Baths seem to help bring about drainage of the congested gland.

Medical Perspective: Preventing Sexual Infections

There are several health measures that may help prevent the aforementioned diseases. First, avoid overfatigue and maintain a good diet; extreme overweight or underweight lowers the body's natural resistance. Second, if cystitis is suspected—or if it tends to recur—drink large amounts of liquid and urinate frequently. This flushes out bacteria from the bladder and urethra. Third, wash and dry the genitals thoroughly. Moisture encourages the growth of fungus and bacteria.

The following suggestions are specific to the prevention of female genital infections. (1) Avoid feminine hygiene deodorant sprays; they tend to irritate the vagina. (2) Be careful of following anal intercourse with vaginal penetration; bacteria from the anus may enter the vagina and cause vaginitis. (3) Douche moderately with a mildly acidic solution (one to two tablespoons of vinegar in one quart of water). Douching too frequently or with a stronger solution can kill bacteria that have positive effects, thus reducing resistance to vaginitis. (4) Avoid pants that are extremely tight in the crotch or prevent the loss of perspiration (especially pants made entirely of synthetic fibers). They can be irritating and/or lead to a buildup of moisture (Crooks & Baur 1980).

Although these suggestions may be helpful, some people appear to be particularly susceptible to infections in the genital area. Thus, the frequent occurrence of sexual infections does not necessarily mean that a person has been negligent or unhygienic.

CANCER OF THE SEX ORGANS

Cancer can occur in almost any part of the body. However, the most common cancers occur in sexual or reproductive organs.

Breast Cancer

Approximately 7 to 9 percent of American women have breast cancer at some time in their lives, and this type of cancer is a major cause of death in women. Although the cause of breast cancer is unknown, a virus is suspected (Lanson 1975, Silverberg 1981).

As in all cases of cancer, an early diagnosis is crucial to successful treatment. The diagnosis of breast cancer usually involves several steps. An early indication is a lump in the breast, which can be detected by self-examination. A series of procedures then provide more information. *Thermography* can detect small changes in the amount of heat generated in various parts of the body. Since cancer cells multiply rapidly, there is a relatively large amount of heat in an area with malignant cells. Another diagnostic technique is *mammography:* taking refined X-ray photographs of the breast. Even very small tumors can be identified by this method. The most accurate technique is to perform a *biopsy,* in which a portion of the suspected lump is removed and examined directly. This is often done through a hollow needle inserted into the lump.

Treatment for breast cancer also involves a variety of approaches, including radiation therapy, chemotherapy, and hormone therapy. However, the most common treatment is *mastectomy*—surgical removal of the breast. The extent of the operation varies from the removal of the lump and some surrounding tissue (partial mastectomy or "lumpectomy") to removal of the entire breast as well as underlying muscle and nearby lymph nodes (radical mastectomy). The radical procedure is performed to guard against the spread of cancer through the lymphatic system. Such severe surgery can have strong psychological effects; many women experience a serious threat to their sexual identity and suffer extreme depression (Ervin 1973). In some communities, the American Cancer Society has organized psychological support groups for mastectomy patients and, in some cases, counseling for the male partner.

Fortunately, there is encouraging news for women who have undergone mastectomies. There are now several techniques for reconstructing breasts after surgery. For example, a plastic surgeon in Atlanta, Dr. Carl Hartrampf, developed a technique whereby a section of muscle and fatty tissue from the abdomen is excised and placed in the cavity formed after the breast or breasts are removed. (Microsurgical techniques allow for a connection of nerves and blood vessels.) In addition to a reshaping of the breasts, the woman benefits from a reduction of fatty tissue in the abdomen (Hartrampf, in press).[3]

Cervical Cancer

Cancer of the cervix is the second-most-common type of cancer; about 2 to 3 percent of American women develop it at some time. As in the case of breast cancer, a virus is suspected.

Diagnosis of cervical cancer is relatively simple. A sample of cervical mucus is obtained with a cotton swab, and a microscopic examination is conducted—a procedure called the Pap smear. If abnormal cells are found, a biopsy is usually performed for more accurate diagnosis. In this case, a biopsy consists of the surgical removal of a small part of cervical tissue.

The treatment of cervical cancer generally consists of removal of a section of the cervix. Although this is a relatively serious operation, the woman is still able to bear children and does not usually suffer any negative long-term effects. More advanced cervical cancer may require a hysterectomy, which of course causes infertility.

Cancer of the Prostate

Prostate cancer is the most common cancer in men. However, it is a less severe problem than female cancers because it develops slowly and does not usually cause difficulties until after age sixty. Nonetheless, as the life expectancy has increased, prostate cancer has become a more serious problem.

The symptoms of prostate cancer are similar to those of prostate enlargement, which is common among aging men. Both lead to frequent urination and difficulty in emptying the bladder because the enlarging prostate partially obstructs the urethra. Diagnosis of prostate cancer is usually made by a rectal examination; the physician (wearing a glove) inserts a finger in the rectum and feels the prostate for abnormalities.

Treatment is either hormonal or surgical (prostatectomy). There is some danger of a man losing his potency after prostate surgery, since nerves near the prostate may be damaged (Silverberg, 1981). Another reason for impotence may be psychological; a man is warned that he could be impotent and consequently may develop debilitating anxieties about sexual functioning. Thus, prostate surgery is considered a last resort.

Medical Perspective: Detecting Cancer at an Early Stage

There is a good chance of recovery if cancer is detected in its early stages. However, many people put off checkups or delay reporting symptoms because they wish to avoid thinking about possible problems. It should be remembered that many "signs" of cancer turn out to be false alarms; a checkup is likely to provide relief rather than increased worry.

For the majority of cancers, yearly checkups by a physician are sufficient. An exception is breast cancer, which can be identified in its early stages by a self-examination prescribed by the American Cancer Society. First, while in the tub or shower, a woman should move her hands gently over each breast, checking for lumps or hard knots (wet skin makes this procedure relatively easy). Second, she should inspect her breasts while her arms are at her sides in front of a mirror. Then, raising her arms, she should check again. Irregularities in contour—such as a swelling or unusual sign in the nipples—are relatively easy to spot using this procedure. The third step involves lying down and checking each breast with small, circular motions of the fingers. Finally, she should gently squeeze each nipple to determine if there is any discharge. Reports to a physician of any irregularities discovered with this simple examination can save much grief at a later time.

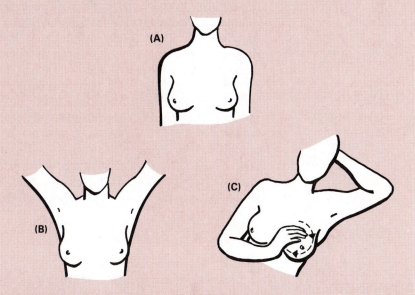

FIGURE 22.4
Self-examination for breast cancer.

Breasts are inspected while a) arms are down, b) arms are raised. Circular motions of the fingers should be used to check each breast while c) lying down with a towel under the shoulder.

CHROMOSOMAL ABNORMALITIES

Normally, people have forty-six chromosomes, but some persons are missing one or have one extra. These chromosomal abnormalities may affect sexuality in a variety of ways.

Klinefelter's syndrome is a rare male disorder in which there is an extra X chromosome, giving the individual an XXY complement of sex chromosomes. Individuals with Klinefelter's syndrome have underdeveloped testes, a small penis, and prominent breast development. They are sterile and, in most cases, impotent. Obviously, such factors have a strong impact on one's self-concept. Although nothing can be done about the extra chromosome or the problem of sterility, androgen therapy sometimes increases potency (Bermant & Davidson 1974; Raboch, Mellan, & Starka 1979).

Another chromosomal abnormality involves males with an extra Y chromosome—XYY. These men are typically taller than the average male. XYY males have been of considerable interest because they have been found to represent an unusually high percentage of men convicted of crimes involving violence (Jacobs, Brunton, & Melville 1965). For a period of time following this discovery, it was assumed that the extra Y chromosome somehow drove men to violence. However, a later study indicated that it was not hyperaggressiveness that marked the behavior of XYY males so much as lack of impulse control and long-term planning ability (Money 1975). Part of this lack of planning ability may be related to a lower level of intelligence; XYY males score lower on standard intelligence tests than normal men. Perhaps XYY men are not predisposed to indulge in violence but, if they do commit a crime, they are more likely to be arrested and convicted (Witkin et al. 1976).

Turner's syndrome is a female disorder associated with a different type of problem: there is only one sex chromosome instead of the normal two, and this is an X. Thus individuals with Turner's syndrome are represented as X0. (Y0 males sometimes occur, but they invariably die before birth.) The symptoms of Turner's disease are a very short stature, a lack of ovaries, and a deficiency in secondary sex characteristics. Treatment with sex hormones induces menstruation and breast development. However, as in the case of Klinefelter's syndrome, sterility is irreversible (Winchester 1973).

CONGENITAL ABNORMALITIES OF THE SEX ORGANS

A variety of congenital abnormalities of the sex organs have been known to occur. There may be problems associated with the uterus and fallopian tubes and, in some cases, these structures are absent altogether. The vagina has been known to develop in a double form, to be closed, or to be missing completely. Fortunately, vaginal anomalies can be corrected by surgery and, in cases where the vagina is absent, surgeons can construct one that is fully functional—at least in regard to intercourse and even orgasm (TeLinde 1953).

In males, a fairly common problem is a failure of the testes to descend into the scrotum by the time of birth. (It will be remembered that the testes normally descend shortly before birth.) In some cases, only one testis descends. Sometimes descent takes place within the first year or two of birth; if not, minor surgery is needed to open the inguinal canal. If both testes are allowed to remain inside the body cavity, sterility results, because the high temperature inside the body inhibits sperm production.

Abnormalities of the penis may also occur. One of the most common problems is for the opening of the urethra to be on the underside of the penis instead of at its tip. Another problem results when the penis curves to one side during erection. All of these problems are correctable by surgery (Culp 1974).

MISCELLANEOUS DISORDERS

The disorders included in this section involve the sex organs, but cannot be classified in any of the previous sections. The causes may be unknown or related to a variety of factors.

Priapism

This disorder is named after the Greek god, Priapus, who was depicted as a small, smiling man with a huge, erect penis. However, *priapism* does not usually evoke pleasant reactions; it is a condition of constant erection accompanied by pain and a lack of sexual desire. Although priapism is sometimes associated with tumors or inflammations, the cause is frequently unknown. Operations that increase the venous blood flow from the penis have been fairly successful in restoring normal functioning (LaRocque & Cosgrove 1976).

Dermatosis

Skin disorders in the genital region are quite common and have a variety of causes. A skin rash caused by a fungus is known as *jock itch*. The fungus thrives in dampness associated with sweating and/or inadequate drying of the genital region. Therefore, it is common in athletes. External medication is quite effective in treating jock itch.

Rashes and itching may also indicate *pubic lice*, or "crabs." The lice are pinhead-sized animals that attach themselves to the base of pubic hairs and feed on human blood. Since the lice may be transmitted during sexual intercourse, this disorder is sometimes considered a sexually transmitted disease. However, pubic lice may also be contracted from toilet seats or bed clothing. Treatment of the lice consists of external application of an antiparasitic cream or lotion and a thorough cleaning of all clothing and personal bedding (Newcomer 1976).

AIDS

In the early 1980s, a rapidly growing number of people became infected with a disease known as Acquired Immune Deficiency Syndrome (AIDS). At the time this book is going to press, the cause is unknown, but a virus is suspected. According to officials at the Federal Centers for Disease Control, the disease seems to be spread by sexual contact or contact with the blood of an affected person. The highest risk groups are homosexual males, drug abusers (who tend to inject drugs with unsterile needles), Haitians, and hemophiliacs. However, approximately 6% of the victims of AIDS do not fall into any of these categories.

The effects of the disease can be very serious and, in some cases, fatal. The body's natural immune system is rendered ineffective to the extent that a person falls prey to diseases not common in healthy individuals, especially certain types of cancer and pneumonia. At the present time, no cure is known, but officials are optimistic that one will be found in the near future.

NOTES

1. A competing, but less generally accepted, theory states that syphilis had been present in the Old World since antiquity but was originally less virulent. Then, in the late fifteenth century, the bacterium presumably mutated and took on its present form.
2. The cold sore-causing virus (herpes type I) may infect the genitals, and type II (which is usually associated with the genitals) may be found in the mouth area. However, this is relatively rare (U.S. Department of Health, Education, and Welfare 1980).
3. In some cases, if a woman's breast had been fairly large—or if there is not much fatty tissue in the abdomen—a silicone implant is also included.

EPILOGUE

Sexuality in the Future

During Victorian times, ''appropriate'' sexual behavior was clearly defined. Today, there are many sexual life-styles, and it seems that, with the continuing development of effective contraceptive techniques and dissemination of information about sexuality, this trend toward greater diversity in sexual expression will continue, at least for a while. Similarly, concepts of masculinity and femininity were relatively unambiguous in the age preceding ours. At present, there are realistic alternatives to the traditional male and female sex roles. As androgynous approaches to sex roles receive more media attention—as they have in recent years—many people may come to define masculinity and femininity in a more liberal fashion.

There are also new alternatives in regard to reproduction. As we have seen, some women who had been classified infertile can now bear children. ''Test tube'' babies are now a reality, and infertile women may receive *embryo transplants* in the near future. As a matter of fact, embryos have already been taken from one cow and placed in the uterus of another. It has been possible to freeze a cattle embryo at a very early stage of development and ship it halfway around the world. Recently, an embryo transplant has been accomplished in a monkey, suggesting that the possibility of a human embryo transplant is not far off (Kraemer, Moore, & Kramen 1976). One can only imagine the number of moral and legal issues a human transplant would raise, including questions of what constitutes true motherhood.

There is even a chance that human reproduction may someday take place completely independent of sex. A genetic duplicate of a mouse has been produced by an asexual process called *cloning*. This process involves replacing the nucleus of an unfertilized egg with that from a cell of the "parent." If such a process becomes possible in humans, further ethical questions will obviously be raised. Clearly, responsible citizens should be aware of possible consequences of cloning, including the production of a veritable army of genetic duplicates (Galston 1975).

If nothing else, it is the author's hope that this book has stimulated readers to digest new information and seriously consider many different perspectives on human sexuality. As we have seen, sexuality is one of the central features of our lives and our relationships with those closest to us.

GLOSSARY

acquired immune deficiency syndrome   An infectious disease involving a failure of the body's natural immunization system.

Adam principle   With androgens present, male organs develop and the development of female organs is suppressed.

adrenogenital syndrome   (a drē′ nō jen′ i tul) The production of an overabundance of androgen during the prenatal period in an XX individual (genetic female), resulting in sexual ambiguity.

affectional bonding   Sharing and strong emotional attachment found in some animals; presumably the forerunner of love in humans.

afterbirth   The placenta and fetal membrane, expelled by the woman after delivery of the baby.

AGS   *See* adrenogenital syndrome.

AIDS   *See* acquired immune deficiency syndrome.

amniocentesis   (am′ nē ō sen tē′ sis) A procedure whereby a small amount of amniotic fluid is removed by a long needle in order to check for possible genetic abnormalities in the fetus.

amnion   (am′ nē on) A thin, transparent membrane enclosing the fetus.

amniotic fluid   (am′ nē ot′ ik) Fluid in which the fetus is suspended within the amnion.

amygdala   (a mig′ da la) Structure located beneath the cerebral cortex that is related to sex drive.

anaphrodisiac   (a naf rō dēz′ ē ak) A drug that presumably lowers sex drive.

androgen-insensitivity syndrome   Insensitivity to androgens, resulting in sexual ambiguity in XY individuals (genetic males).

androgens   (an′ dro jinz) A class of sex hormones produced primarily by the testes but also by the adrenal glands in both sexes.

androgynous   (an droj′ i nus) Having the positive characteristics traditionally associated with both sexes; neither strongly masculine nor strongly feminine.

anterior pituitary gland   A gland located under the hypothalamus, within the brain but not part of the brain. It secretes a variety of hormones, many of which influence other glands.

aphrodisiac   (af′ rō dez′ ē ak) A drug that presumably increases sex drive.

areola   (a rē′ o luh) The reddish area surrounding the nipples of the breasts.

artificial insemination   Introduction of sperm into the vagina by artificial means.

asymmetrical relationships   Interpersonal relationships in which one person is much more invested emotionally than the other.

Bartholin's glands   (bahr′ to linz) Small glands located on either side of the vaginal opening.

behavior modification therapy   A therapy aimed at changing behavior patterns through the use of such basic learning principles as reward association and generalization.

behavior therapy   *See* behavior modification therapy.

bestiality   *See* zoophilia.

biopsy   The surgical removal of a small piece of tissue for the purpose of direct examination.

birth canal   *See* vagina.

bisexuals   Individuals who engage in sexual relations with members of both sexes.

bondage   A sexual variation involving the tying-up or physical restraint of another person.

breech delivery   Delivery in which the child

emerges from the uterus in a position other than headfirst.

brothel   House of prostitution.

Caesarean section   Removal of the baby from the uterus via an incision in the abdomen and uterine wall.

call girl   Prostitute who schedules appointments with her clients.

castration   Surgical removal of the testes.

celibacy   Living in abstention from sexual intercourse.

cerebral cortex   The convoluted layer of gray tissue covering the cerebral hemisphere of the brain.

cervical cap   Contraceptive device that fits over the cervix; may be worn for relatively long periods of time.

cervix   The narrow portion of the uterus that opens into the vagina.

child molestation   A legal term for a variety of noncoital sexual behaviors involving an adult and a child.

chromosomal factor   The genetic determination of the sex of the individual at conception. Persons with XX chromosomes are genetically female; XY persons are genetically male.

circumcision   The surgical removal of the foreskin.

client-centered therapy   A therapeutic approach aimed at increased acceptance of one's behavior patterns and feelings.

climacteric   The period in a woman's life during which she slowly loses the capacity to become pregnant; approximately 45 to 55 years of age; also, a corresponding period of declining powers experienced by some males, often at a later age.

clitoral hood   (klit' o rul) A sheath of tissue that partly covers the clitoris when the female is not sexually aroused.

clitoridectomy   (klit-oruh' dek tuh mē) Surgical removal of the clitoris.

clitoris   (klit' oris) A small, extremely sensitive organ located in front of the vaginal entrance.

cloning   Producing a genetic duplicate of the parent by replacing the nucleus of an unfertilized egg with that from the cell of the parent animal.

coitus   (kō' ēt əs) Sexual intercourse. Derived from the Latin *coire*, which means "to go together."

coitus interruptus   See withdrawal

colostrum   A high-protein liquid found in the woman's breasts following delivery; replaced by milk within two or three days.

conception in a "test tube"   The introduction of sperm to egg under laboratory conditions.

condom   A male contraceptive consisting of a sheath to be drawn over the penis.

congestive, painful menstruation   A variety of symptoms including dull aching in the abdomen, headaches, and breast pain.

control group   The group that, in an experiment, is compared to the experimental group. The control group does not receive the critical experimental manipulation.

conversion reaction   A type of neurosis featuring the conversion of anxiety into physical symptoms.

Coolidge effect   Greater sexual potency with a variety of partners than with a single partner.

coprophilia   (kup ruh fēl' ē uh) Sexual arousal associated with the feces or the act of defecation.

copulation   (cop' u lā' shun) Sexual intercourse.

corona   A rim of tissue separating the glans from the shaft of the penis.

coronal ridge   See corona.

corpora cavernosa   (kor' po ruh kav ur nō' suh) Two cylinders of spongelike tissue running parallel to the urethra.

corpus luteum   (kor' pus lew' tē um) An ovarian follicle after it has released its egg. The corpus luteum secretes progesterone.

corpus spongiosum   (kor' pus spon' jē ō' sum) One of the three cylinders of erectile tissue found in the penis.

Cowper's glands   Glands that secrete a clear alkaline fluid into the male urethra. This fluid forms part of the ejaculate and helps to neutralize the acidity of the urethra.

cunnilingus   (kun′ i ling′ gus) Oral stimulation of the female genitals.

cystitis   (sis tī′ tis) Inflammation of the bladder.

D&C   See dilation and curettage.

dartos muscle   The middle layer of the scrotum. By contracting and relaxing, it regulates the distance of the testes from the body.

dependent variable   The variable that, in an experiment, is measured by the experimenter. It presumably depends upon the independent variable.

dermatosis   Disease of the skin.

DES   See diethylstilbestrol.

diaphragm   Contraceptive device that fits over the cervix and blocks the passage of sperm.

diethylstilbestrol   (dī eth ul stil′ bes trul) The active substance in the morning-after pill.

dilation and curettage   (kyur e tazh′) A procedure that involves dilating the cervix and scraping the uterine lining. May be used as an abortion procedure or after a spontaneous abortion.

disinhibition   A lack of inhibitory cues, resulting in the expression of behaviors that might normally be suppressed.

dyspareunia   (dis′ puh roo′ nē uh) Painful coitus.

dystopians   (dis′ tō pē un) Sociologists who believe that continued technological advancements lead ultimately to worsened social relationships.

ectopic pregnancy   (ek top′ ik) Pregnancy occurring in some part of the body other than the uterus.

ego   According to Freudian theory, a part of the mind that functions to put reality-oriented restrictions on id impulses.

ejaculate   See semen.

ejaculation   Ejection of semen from the penis.

ejaculatory duct   (ē jak′ you luh to′ rē) The passageway for sperm between the prostate and the urethra.

ejaculatory inevitability   The sensation that ejaculation is about to occur; it precedes ejaculation itself.

Electra complex   According to Freudian theory, a sexual desire (mostly unconscious) that girls develop for their fathers.

elephantiasis   (el uh fuhn′ tī uh sis) An extreme enlargement of the genitals, caused by LGV.

embryo   Term applied to the prenatal individual from the second to the eighth week of development.

embryo transplant   Implanting an embryo removed from one animal into the uterus of another.

endometrium   (en′ dō mē′ trē um) The inner lining of the uterus, shed each month as part of the menstrual flow.

engagement   See lightening.

epididymis   (ep′ i did′ i mis) A long, convoluted duct in which sperm complete the process of maturation.

episiotomy   (e piz′ ē ot′ uh mē) An incision in the perineum of the mother, often made before delivery.

erectile dysfunction   The failure to have or maintain an erection.

erection   A state in which the penis becomes large and firm as the result of vasocongestion.

erogenous zones   Areas that are maximally sensitive to erotic stimulation.

erotic vomiting   Sexual arousal associated with vomiting.

estrogen   (es′ tro jin) Class of sex hormones produced primarily by the ovaries.

estrous cycle   The reproductive cycle of subhuman female mammals; similar in some respects to the menstrual cycle.

estrus   The period during which a female mammal is sexually receptive and fertile; also known as heat.

Eve principle   Without androgens, the fetus develops female sex organs.

exchange theory   A social-psychological orientation that views interpersonal relationships in terms of such things as rewards gained and sacrifices made.

exhibitionist   A person who derives sexual pleasure from displaying his or her nude body or genitals to an unsuspecting audience.

experimental group   The group that, in an experiment, is manipulated by the experimenter.

fallopian tubes   (fuh lō′ pē un) Structures connected to the uterus that provide passage for the mature egg following its ejection from an ovary.

false pregnancy   See pseudocyesis.

FAS   See fetal alcohol syndrome.

fear of success   A concept developed to explain a relatively low striving for mastery observed in certain people.

fellatio   (fe lā′ shē ō) Oral stimulation of the penis.

fetal alcohol syndrome   Abnormalities in the baby that result from the mother's alcohol intake during pregnancy.

fetishism   A tendency to become sexually aroused by an inanimate object or a part of the body not usually associated with sexuality.

fetus   Term applied to the prenatal individual from the eighth week of development until birth.

fimbriae   (fim′ brē ā) Fingerlike projections from the fallopian tubes, which help gather in the egg after it is ejected from an ovary.

follicle   (fol′ i kul) A small vesicle in the ovary that contains a maturing egg.

follicle-stimulating hormone   An anterior-pituitary hormone that, in the female, stimulates the growth of follicles and, in the male, stimulates the production of sperm.

follicular phase   (fol ik′ ū lar) The first phase of the menstrual cycle, characterized by growth of the ovarian follicles.

foreplay   Sexually arousing interaction that precedes sexual intercourse.

foreskin   The skin covering part of the glans penis.

fraternal twins   Two individuals who develop from separate eggs fertilized at about the same time.

frenulum   (fren′ ū lum) A thin strip of skin on the underside of the penis that connects the glans and the shaft.

frenum   See frenulum.

frottage   (fruh tazh′) A tendency to obtain sexual arousal by rubbing up against strangers.

FSH   See follicle-stimulating hormone.

G spot   See Grafenberg spot.

gamete differentiation   (gam′ ēt) The evolutionary process resulting in two distinct types of gametes: eggs and sperm.

generalize   To respond in the same or a similar way to stimuli perceived as similar.

genetic factor   See chromosomal factor.

genetic recombination   The mixing of genetic material from the mother and the father when fertilization takes place. As a result, the offspring are not genetic duplicates of either parent, but have some of the characteristics of both.

genital herpes   An STD caused by a virus.

genital tubercle   An embrionic structure that develops into either male or female external genitals.

glans   The tip or head of the penis or clitoris.

gonadal factor   (gō nad′ ul) The development of either testes or ovaries; depends upon the chromosomal factor.

gonadotrophins   (gō nad′ ō trō′ pin) Hormones secreted by the anterior pituitary that influence the gonads and their secretions.

gonads   The structures that produce sex cells; ovaries and testes.

gonorrhea   An STD caused by a bacterium.

Grafenberg spot   A small area identified in the vagina of some women; when it is stimulated, the woman has a type of orgasm qualitatively different than that induced by clitoral stimulation.

granuloma inguinale   (gran′ ū lō′ muh in′ gwuh nal ē) An STD, found mainly in the tropics.

group marriage   An arrangement whereby sexual intimacy may openly take place between any members of a group.

halo effect   A generalization of positive attributes such as physical beauty to other aspects of the person and his or her personality.

HCG   See human chorionic gonadotrophin.

hermaphrodite   (hur maf' rō dĭt) Individual having the gonadal tissue of both sexes.

hermaphroditism   The condition of producing both male and female gametes, or in some other way having both male and female characteristics.

homologous   (hō mahl' uh gus) Developing from the same type of embrionic tissue.

homophobia   An irrationally strong negative attitude toward homosexuality.

hormonal factor   The production of either a large or an insignificant amount of androgen; depends upon the gonadal factor.

human chorionic gonadotrophin   (kōr-ē'-on ik gō nad' ō trō' pin) A hormone produced shortly after the woman becomes pregnant; its presence in the blood provides a reliable test of pregnancy.

hymen   A membrane partly covering the entrance to the vagina. It is usually intact—at least partially—prior to the first sexual intercourse.

hypothalamus   A part of the brain below the cerebral cortex; it is associated with sexual drive as well as other hormone-related functions.

hysterectomy   Surgical removal of the uterus.

id   According to Freudian theory, the seat of the basic sexual drive or libidinal energy.

identical twins   Two individuals who develop from the same egg.

identification   An attempt to be like someone else in a psychologically important way.

I.M.   See intimacy motivation.

imaginal desensitization   A sex-therapy technique in which a person learns to associate relaxation with anxiety-provoking memories and thoughts.

implantation   The attachment and burrowing of the developing ball of cells into the endometrium of the uterus.

impotence   See erectile dysfunction.

incest   Sexual intercourse with a close relative; the definition of ''close'' varies from culture to culture.

incest taboos   Inhibitions against sexual intercourse with close relatives.

independent variable   The variable that, in an experiment, is manipulated by the experimenter.

induced ovulators   Certain mammals, such as cats and rabbits, that ovulate only as the result of stimulation during copulation.

infundibulum   (in fun dib' yuh lum) The part of the fallopian tube nearest the ovary.

inguinal canal   (in' gwuh nal) A passageway through which the testes descend from the abdomen to the scrotum; this usually occurs shortly before birth.

inhibited sexual desire   An inability to become sexually aroused.

inner lips   See labia minora.

interstitial cells   (int ur stish' ul) Cells within the connective tissue of the testes; they manufacture androgens.

intimacy motivation   A need for warm interpersonal relationships; measured by analyzing responses to TAT pictures.

intrauterine device (IUD)   A contraceptive device usually made of plastic or stainless steel that is inserted into the uterus to prevent implantation.

intrauterine instillation   An abortion procedure that involves injecting a liquid into the amnion, thereby inducing uterine contractions.

ISD   See inhibited sexual desire.

IUD   See intrauterine device.

jock itch   A dermatosis in the genital region caused by a fungus.

just-world hypothesis   A belief that, since there is justice in the world, people get what they deserve.

Kegel exercises   A series of exercises designed to strengthen the pubococcygeal muscles.

Klinefelter's syndrome   A rare male disorder in which there is an extra X chromosome.

klismaphilia   Sexual pleasure gained from enemas.

labia majora   (la' bē uh muh jor' uh) Two elongated folds of skin that surround the vaginal opening.

labia minora   (la′ bē uh mi nor′ uh) The inner and smaller folds of skin that surround the vaginal opening.

lactation   The production of milk in female mammals.

lesbian   A homosexual woman.

LGV   See lymphogranuloma venereum.

LH   See lutinizing hormone.

libido   (li bē′ dō) According to Freud, sexual energy that acts as an important driving force in the development of one's personality.

lightening   A shift in the position of the fetus to a head-down position; occurs as childbirth approaches.

Liking Scale   A scale that attempts to measure the components of liking that are somewhat independent of those measured by the love scale.

limerence   An emotion similar to infatuation but lacking any negative connotation.

Love Scale   A scale that attempts to measure the three components of love: attachment, intimacy, and sharing.

luteal phase   (lū′ tē ul) The phase of the menstrual cycle that follows ovulation; characterized by high levels of progesterone.

luteinizing hormone   (lū′ tē in îz′ ing) A hormone secreted by the anterior pituitary; in females it causes ovulation, and in males it stimulates androgen production.

lymphogranuloma venereum   (lim fō gran yuh lō′ muh vuh nir′ ē um) A rare STD of the lymphatic system, caused by a virus.

mammography   The use of X rays to check for tumors of the breast.

masochist   (mas′ ō kist) A person who becomes sexually aroused by pain and/or humiliation.

massage parlor   Typically, setting for prostitution. Sexual services are generally available upon request.

mastectomy   (mas tek′ tuh mē) Surgical removal of the breast.

matching of attractiveness   The tendency for people to become romantically involved with other people who are similar to themselves in terms of physical attractiveness.

mate swapping   See swinging.

meiosis   (mî ō′ sis) Cell division basic to sexual reproduction; as a result of it, each sperm and egg has half the total number of chromosomes needed by the fertilized egg—and the developing individual.

menarche   The onset of menstruation.

menopause   The cessation of menstruation.

menstruation   The periodic (approximately monthly) discharge of blood and tissue comprising the endometrium.

missionary position   Coital position in which the male and female face one another, with the male on top.

Mittelschmerz   (mit′ tul shmairts) Cramping in the lower abdomen of some women; associated with ovulation.

monilia   (muh nil′ ē uh) A type of vaginitis caused by a yeast fungus.

mons veneris   (mōnz ven′ e ris) A mound of fatty tissue, covered with pubic hair, just above a woman's vulva.

morning-after pill   A pill that functions as a contraceptive if taken shortly after unprotective intercourse; known to have dangerous side effects.

müllerian ducts   (mew ler′ ē un) A pair of embrionic structures that develop into part of the female reproductive system.

multiple orgasms   Orgasms that occur in succession without a resting state separating them.

multiple personality   A rare psychological disorder in which a person shifts rapidly from one personality to another, typically not realizing that the many personalities exist.

myotonia   (mî′ ō tō′ nē uh) Increased muscle tension associated with sexual arousal.

necrophilia   (nek′ ruh fēl′ ē uh) Sexual arousal associated with a dead body; sometimes involves sexual contact with a corpse.

neurons   Cells specialized to transmit information in the form of electrical impulses.

neurosis   Psychological disorder in which the person is in contact with reality but overwhelmed in some fashion by anxiety.

nocturnal emission   Nocturnal orgasm in males; accompanied by ejaculation of semen.

nocturnal orgasm   Involuntary orgasm that occurs during sleep.

nonspecific urethritis   (yuhr i thrît' us) An inflammation of the male urethra caused by something other than gonorrhea.

NSU   *See* nonspecific urethritis.

nymphomania   (nim' fō ma' nē uh) High sex drive in women.

Oedipus complex   (ed' i pus) According to Freudian theory, sexual desire (mostly unconscious) that boys develop for their mothers.

obsessive-compulsive reaction   A neurotic reaction in which the person experiences constantly recurring thoughts and behaves in an abnormally rigid, repetitive fashion.

open marriage   An arrangement that includes freedom to pursue extramarital relationships.

operant conditioning   A type of learning in which reinforcement is manipulated to alter a person's response tendencies or feelings.

oral contraceptives   Pills that, when taken regularly, prevent pregnancy. They generally contain synthetic estrogen and progesterone.

oral stage   According to Freudian theory, an early stage in psychological development during which libidinal, or sexual, energy is centered in the area of the mouth.

orgasmic dysfunction   An inability to experience orgasm.

orgasmic platform   Vasocongestion of the outer third of the vagina and labia minora which develops prior to orgasm.

os   (ōs) A small opening in the uterus that allows passage between the uterus and the vagina.

outer lips   *See* labia majora.

ovaries   (ō' vur ēz) The pair of reproductive glands in the female that produce ova.

oviducts   (ō' vuh dukt) *See* fallopian tubes.

ovulation   (ōv u lā shun) Producing and discharging ova.

oxytocin   (ahk' sē to' sin) A posterior pituitary hormone which stimulates contraction of the uterine muscles during labor; it also stimulates the letting down of milk during lactation.

P-C muscle   *See* pubococcygeal muscle.

palimony decision   A court decision relating to cohabitating couples, stating, essentially, that oral and written agreements between partners may be binding.

pedophilia   (ped ō fil' ē uh) Sexual relations between an adult and a child.

penile plethysmograph   (pē' nîl pleh thiz' muh graf) An instrument used to measure physiological sexual arousal in males.

penis   The male sex organ.

perineum   (per i nē' um) Skin just behind the vagina, often cut by the physician preceding delivery.

phallic symbols   Objects that represent the penis, typically in an erect state.

The Pill   *See* oral contraceptives.

placenta   (pluh sen' tuh) A flat, round structure that serves as a medium of exchange between the mother and fetus.

polar body   A structure associated with a developing egg that contains excess genetic material; eventually extruded.

polyandry   (pa' lē an' drē) A type of polygamy in which one woman has more than one husband.

polygamy   The state of having more than one spouse.

polygynandry   (pa' lē jin' an drē) A type of polygamy in which two or more men are living with two or more women, with all the men considered married to all the women.

polygyny   (pa lij' uh nē) A type of polygamy in which one man has more than one wife.

postovulatory phase   *See* luteal phase.

premature ejaculation   The inability to postpone ejaculation or the tendency to ejaculate too early.

premenstrual tension   A negative emotional state that may build up in some women three or four days before menstruation.

prepuce   (prē' pi oose) Skin covering part of the glans penis in the male (foreskin) or clitoris in the female (clitoral hood).

priapism (prî a′ pizm) A condition of constant erection, accompanied by pain and lack of sexual desire.

primary dysfunction Sexual dysfunction that has, essentially, always existed; the individual never functioned normally.

Primates The order of mammals that includes monkeys, apes, and humans.

prochoice Phrase adopted by many groups that believe abortion decisions should be made by the woman and her physician, not by law.

progesterone (prō jes′ tur ōn) Class of sex hormones produced primarily by ovarian follicles after they have shed their eggs.

prolactin (prō lak′ tun) A hormone, secreted by the anterior pituitary, that stimulates milk production.

prostaglandins (pros tuh glan′ dun) A class of chemical substances, some of which bring about contraction of the uterine muscles and are also believed to be related to painful menstruation.

prostate gland (pros′ tāt) A structure located below the bladder that secretes the major part of the semen.

prostatitis (pros tuh tī′ tis) An inflammation of the prostate.

pseudocyesis (sue′ dō si ē′ sus) False pregnancy; a nonpregnant woman may have many symptoms of pregnancy, including cessation of menstruation and a swollen abdomen.

psychoanalysis The therapeutic technique developed by Freud.

psychoanalytic theory A theory of personality developed by Freud and his followers. It is based on the assumption that psychological disorders are related to rejection by the conscious mind of impulses found in the unconscious.

psychotic Psychologically disturbed to the extent that one is out of contact with reality.

pubococcygeal muscle (pew′ bō kock sij′ ē ul) A muscle (or, more technically, a system of muscles) that surrounds the vagina, anus, and urethra. When the muscle is not in tone, the vagina appears loose.

pubic lice Pinhead-sized animals that live attached to the base of pubic hairs.

rape-crisis advocate A person (typically a woman) who provides emotional support and advice to a rape victim.

refractory period The period of time following orgasm during which the individual is unresponsive to sexual stimulation.

reproductive pheromones (fer′ uh mōn′) Chemical compounds that facilitate reproduction. In many cases, one sex secretes a pheromone that attracts the other sex.

retarded ejaculation Difficulty in ejaculating during coitus; in some cases, a complete inability to ejaculate.

Romeo and Juliet effect An increase in the seeming attractiveness of a member of the opposite sex that results when one's parents reject this person.

rhythm method Abstention from coitus during the woman's apparent fertile period.

right to life Phrase adopted by many antiabortion groups.

Rubin's test A diagnostic test for blockage of the fallopian tubes.

sadist (sā dist) A person who becomes sexually aroused by inflicting pain and/or humiliation.

saliromania (sal′ i rō mān′ ē uh) Soiling women or symbols of womanhood in order to gain sexual arousal.

salpingectomy (sal′ pun jeck′ tuh mē) Surgical removal of the fallopian tubes.

satyriasis (sat′ i rī′ uh sis) High sex drive in men.

schizophrenia (skit′ sō frā′ nē uh) The most common type of psychosis; it features inappropriate emotions, disturbed thought processes, and bizarre behavior.

scrotum The sac or pouch that contains the testes.

secondary dysfunction Sexual dysfunction that occurs after a period of normal functioning or only a certain percentage of the time.

self-disclosure Revealing personal and intimate information about oneself.

semen   Whitish fluid produced by the prostate and seminal vesicles. When ejaculated, it normally contains sperm.

seminal vesicles   (sem' uh nal ves' e kulz) Paired structures that produce a portion of the semen.

seminiferous tubules   (sem' i nif' ur us tū' bewls) Coiled tubes in the testes where sperm are produced.

sensate focusing   A sex-therapy exercise in which partners take turns stroking one another, discuss feelings and sensations, but avoid sexual intercourse.

sex flush   A rash sometimes associated with sexual arousal.

sex guilt   A tendency to feel anxiety in regard to sexual matters.

sex roles   Ways in which males and females are expected to behave according to a society's standard.

sexual psychopath   Person repeatedly convicted of public-nuisance offenses. Voyeurs, exhibitionists, and transvestites are frequently included in this category.

sexually transmitted diseases   Infectious diseases transmitted primarily by coitus, oral-genital sex, or anal intercourse.

shaft   The body of the penis or clitoris.

sixty-nining   Simultaneous oral-genital sex.

Skinner box   Apparatus equipped with a bar that an animal can press to receive some type of reinforcement.

smegma   (smeg' muh) A strong-smelling substance formed between the foreskin and the glans penis.

sociobiology   The study of biological bases of social and sexual behavior; the discipline commonly emphasizes evolution.

sodomy   A term that refers to certain sexual acts defined as illegal in some states; may include bestiality, fellatio, and/or anal sex.

spasmodic, painful menstruation   Cramps, pain in the lower abdomen, and, sometimes, nausea.

spermicides   Agents that kill sperm.

spontaneous ovulators   Mammals, such as humans, that ovulate at a fairly regular period of time during their estrous or menstrual cycles.

squeeze technique   A sex-therapy technique developed to treat problems of premature ejaculation; the penis is squeezed just as the man feels he is about to ejaculate.

start-stop technique   A sex-therapy technique developed to treat problems of premature ejaculation; the penis is withdrawn from the vagina just as the man feels he is about to ejaculate.

statutory rape   Legal term for sexual intercourse between an adult male and a female considered under the age of consent; this age varies from state to state.

STD   See sexually transmitted diseases.

streetwalkers   Prostitutes who solicit customers in public places or on the street.

superego   According to Freudian theory, the conscience, or idealistic restriction on libidinal expression.

supportive therapy   See client-centered therapy.

swinging   An arrangement that encourages sexual relations with a large variety of partners.

syphilis   An STD caused by a bacterium.

TAT   See Thematic Apperception Test.

testes   (tes' tēz) Male gonads, contained within the scrotum.

Thematic Apperception Test   A personality test that presumably measures motives and needs.

thermography   (thur' mog' ruh fē) A cancer-detecting method that involves identifying changes in the amount of heat generated in various parts of the body.

toxemia   A dangerous complication of pregnancy involving high blood pressure and retention of fluids, mainly seen during the third trimester.

toxic shock syndrome   A rare disease caused by a bacterium which is linked to the use of certain types of tampons.

transsexuals   Individuals who believe they are the "wrong" gender and wish to alter their biological sex.

transvestite   A person who derives sexual pleasure from dressing—either partially or completely—in the clothing of an opposite-sex person.

trich *See* trichomoniasis.

trichomoniasis (trick o muh nî' uh sis) A type of vaginitis caused by a protozoan.

trimester A period of three months. Pregnancy is typically divided into three trimesters.

tubal ligation A method of sterilization that involves cutting and tying the fallopian tubes.

tumescence (tew mess' uns) Swelling, as in the case of penile erection.

Turner's syndrome A rare genetic disorder of females, in which the person has only one X chromosome.

umbilical cord The structure that joins the fetus and the placenta; the "lifeline" of the fetus.

urethra (u rē' thruh) The tube that carries urine in the female and both urine and semen in the male.

urethral opening (u rē' thral) Opening through which urine passes from the female's body.

urophilia (urō fē' lē uh) Sexual arousal associated with urine or the act of urination.

uterus (ū' tur us) The pear-shaped female organ within which the fetus develops; also known as the womb.

utopians Sociologists who believe that continued technological advancement leads ultimately to better social relationships.

vacuum aspiration An abortion procedure that utilizes suction to draw fetal tissue out of the uterus.

vagina (va jî' nuh) A barrel-shaped organ that receives the penis during sexual intercourse and through which the baby passes during birth.

vaginal plethysmograph (vaj' i nul pleh thiz' muh graf) An instrument used to measure physiological sexual arousal in females.

vaginismus (vaj in iz' mus) A rare disorder in which contractions of muscles surrounding the vagina make sexual intercourse painful or impossible.

vaginitis (vaj in î tis) An inflammation of the vagina.

vas deferens (vas def' ur enz) A long tube that conveys the sperm from the epididymis to the prostate.

vasectomy A sterilization procedure that involves cutting and tying the vas deferens.

vasocongestion (vas' o kun jes' chun) Engorgement of blood vessels during sexual arousal.

venereal warts Noncancerous tumors on the genitals; caused by a virus.

voyeur (voî yur') A person who derives sexual pleasure from surreptitiously observing others who are nude or having sexual relations.

vulva The female's external sex organs.

wet dreams *See* nocturnal emission.

Whitten effect The shortening and synchronization of estrous cycles of several mammals, stimulated by reproductive pheromones.

whorehouse *See* brothel.

withdrawal Retraction of the penis from the vagina before ejaculation.

wolffian ducts (wool' fē un) Embrionic structures that develop into part of the male reproductive system.

zona pellucida (zō nuh pe lew' sē duh) A gelatinous layer surrounding the mature egg.

zoophilia (zō' uh fil' ē eh) Sexual interaction between a person and an animal.

zygote (zî' gōt) The result of a union of an egg and a sperm.

REFERENCES

Abarbanel, A. R. Diagnosis and treatment of coital discomfort. In J. LoPiccolo and L. LoPiccolo (eds.), *Handbook of sex therapy.* New York: Plenum Press, 1978.

Abel, G. G.; Barlow, D. H.; Blanchard, E. B.; & Guild, D. The components of rapists' sexual arousal. *Archives of General Psychiatry,* 1977, *34,* 895–903.

Abramson, P. R. The relationship of the frequency of masturbation to several aspects of personality and behavior. *Journal of Sex Research,* 1973, *9,* 132–142.

Adams, G. R., & Huston, T. L. Social perception of middle-aged persons varying in physical attractiveness. *Developmental Psychology,* 1975, *11,* 657–658.

Adams, H. E., & Sturgis, E. T. Status of behavioral reorientation techniques in the modification of homosexuality: A review. *Psychological Bulletin,* 1977, *84,* 1171–1188.

Adams, M. W., & Neel, J. V. Children of incest. *Pediatrics,* 1967, *40,* 55–62.

Addiego, F.; Belzer, E. G.; Comolli, J.; Moger, W.; Perry, J. D.; & Whipple, B. Female ejaculation: A case study. *Journal of Sex Research,* 1981, *17,* 13–21.

Aiman, J., & Boyar, R. M. Testicular function in transsexual men. *Archives of Sexual Behavior,* 1982, *11,* 171–179.

Alexander, R. D., & Brown, W. L., Jr. Mating behavior and the origin of insect wings. Occasional Papers of the Museum of Zoology, University of Michigan, 1963, no. 628, 1–16.

Allen, C. The long history of birth control. *Sexology,* 1968, *5,* 276–278.

Allen, C. *A textbook of psychosexual disorders.* London: Oxford University Press, 1969.

Allen, D. M. Young male prostitutes: A psychosocial study. *Archives of Sexual Behavior,* 1980, *9,* 399–426.

Almquist, J. O., & Hale, E. B. An approach to the measurement of sexual behavior and semen production of dairy bulls. *Proceedings of the 3rd International Congress of Animal Reproduction,* 1956, 50–59.

Altman, I., & Taylor, W. *Social penetration: The development of interpersonal relationships.* New York: Holt, Rinehart & Winston, 1973.

Amelar, R. D. *Infertility in men.* Philadelphia: Davis, 1966.

American Law Institute. *Model penal code: Proposed official draft.* Philadelphia: F. A. Davis, 1962.

American Psychological Association. *Principles for the Care and Use of Animals.* Washington, D.C., 1971.

American Psychological Association. *Ethical principles in the conduct of research with human participants.* Washington, D.C., 1973.

Amir, M. *Patterns in forcible rape.* Chicago: University of Chicago Press, 1971.

Anderson, J.; Morris, L.; & Geshe, M. Planned and unplanned fertility in upstate New York. *Family Planning Perspectives,* 1977, *9,* 4–11.

Anderson, N. Likeableness ratings of 555 personality-trait words. *Journal of Personality & Social Psychology,* 1968, *9,* 272–279.

Anderson, S. M., & Bem, S. L. Sex typing and androgyny in dyadic interaction: Individual differences in responsiveness to physical attractiveness. *Journal of Personality and Social Psychology,* 1981, *41,* 74–86.

Antunes, C.; Stolley, P.; Rosenshein, M.; Davies, J.;

Tonascia, J.; Brown, C.; Burnett, L.; Rutledge, A.; Pokempner, M.; & Garcia, R. Endometrial cancer and estrogen use. *New England Journal of Medicine*, 1979, *300*, 9–13.

Arafat, I. S., & Cotton, W. L. Masturbation practices of males and females. *Journal of Sex Research*, 1974, *10*, 293–307.

Ardrey, R. *The territorial imperative*. New York: Atheneum, 1966.

Argyle, M.; Lalljee, M.; & Cook, M. The effects of visibility on interaction in a dyad. *Human Relations*, 1968, *21*, 3–17.

Arkowitz, H.; Lichtenstein, E.; McGovern, K.; & Hines, P. The behavioral assessment of social competency in males. *Behavior Therapy*, 1975, *6*, 3–13.

Aronson, E., & Linder, D. Gain and loss of esteem as determinants of interpersonal attractiveness. *Journal of Experimental Social Psychology*, 1965, *1*, 156–171.

Aronson, E.; Willerman, B.; & Floyd, J. The effect of a pratfall on increasing interpersonal attractiveness. *Psychonomic Science*, 1966, *4*, 227–228.

Arvidsson, T., & Larsson, K. Seminal discharge and mating behavior in the male rat. *Physiology and Behavior*, 1967, *2*, 341–343.

Athanasiou, R.; Shaver, P.; & Tavris, C. Sex. *Psychology Today*, 1970 (July), 39–52.

Avers, C. J. *Biology of sex*. New York: Wiley, 1974.

Babcock, B. A.; Freedman, A. E.; Norton, E. H.; & Ross, S. C. *Sex discrimination and the law: Causes and remedies*. Boston: Little, Brown, 1975.

Baerends, G. P., & Baerends-Van Roon, J. M. An introduction to the study of the ethology of the cichlid fishes. *Behaviour*, supplement, 1950, *1*, 1–243.

Bancroft, J. *Deviant sexual behavior: Modification and assessment*. London: Oxford University Press, 1974.

Bandura, A. *Principles of behavior modification*. New York: Holt, Rinehart & Winston, 1969.

Bandura, A.; Ross, D.; & Ross, S. A. Vicarious reinforcement and imitative learning. *Journal of Abnormal and Social Psychology*, 1963, *63*, 601–607.

Bandura, A., & Walters, R. H. *Social learning and personality development*. New York: Holt, Rinehart & Winston, 1963.

Banta, T. J., & Hetherington, M. Relations between needs of friends and fiances. *Journal of Abnormal and Social Psychology*, 1963, *66*, 401–404.

Barbach, L. *For yourself: The fulfillment of female sexuality*. Garden City, N.Y.: Doubleday, 1975.

Barclay, A. M. Urinary acid phosphatase secretion in sexually aroused males. *Journal of Experimental Research in Personality*, 1970, *4*, 233–238.

Barclay, A. M. Linking sexual and aggressive motives: Contributions of "irrelevant" arousals. *Journal of Personality*, 1971, *39*, 481–492.

Bardwick, J. M. *Psychology of women: A study of biocultural conflicts*. New York: Harper & Row, 1971.

Barlow, D. *Sexually transmitted diseases*. New York: Oxford University Press, 1979.

Barlow, D., & Agras, W. S. Fading to increase heterosexual responsiveness in homosexuals. *Journal of Applied Behavior Analysis*, 1973, *6*, 355–367.

Barnes, C. G. *Medical disorders in obstetric practice*. 2d ed. Oxford: Blackwell Scientific Publications, 1965.

Barnes, R. D. *Invertebrate zoology*. Philadelphia: Saunders, 1963.

Baron, R. A. The reduction of human aggression: A field study of the influence of incompatible reactions. *Journal of Applied Social Psychology*, 1976, *6*, 260–274.

Baron, R. A. *Human aggression*. New York: Plenum, 1977.

Baron, R. A., & Bell, P. A. Sexual arousal and aggression by males: Effects of type of erotic stimuli and prior provocation. *Journal of Personality and Social Psychology*, 1977, *35*, 79–87.

Baron, R. A., & Byrne, D. E. *Social psychology: Understanding human interaction*. 3d ed. Boston: Allyn and Bacon, 1981.

Barros, R. *Sexual fantasy*. London: Luxor Press, 1970.

Barry, H.; Bacon, M. K.; & Child, I. L. A cross-cultural survey of some differences in socialization. *Journal of Abnormal and Social Psychology*, 1957, *55*, 327–332.

Bart, P. B. Depression in middle-aged women. In V. G. Gornick and B. K. Moran (eds.), *Women in a sexist society*. New York: Basic Books, 1971.

Bartell, G. D. Group sex among the mid-Americans. *Journal of Sex Research*, 1970, *6*, 113–130.

Bastock, M., & Manning, A. The courtship of *Drosophila melanogaster*. *Behaviour*, 1955, *8*, 85–112.

Bateman, A. J. Intra-sexual selection in *Drosophila*. *Heredity*, 1948, *2*, 349–368.

Bates, G. On the nature of the hot flash. *Clinical Obstetrics and Gynecology* 24 (1), 231–234, 1981.

Baumhover, A. H. Eradication of the screwworm fly. *Journal of the American Medical Association*, 1966, *196*, 150–158.

Baumrind, D. New directions in socialization research. *American Psychologist*, 1980, *35*, 639–652.

Beach, F. Effect of cortical lesions upon the copulatory behavior of male rats. *Journal of Comparative Psychology*, 1940, *29*, 193–244.

Beach, F. A review of physiological and psychological studies of sexual behavior in mammals. *Physiological Review*, 1947, *27*, 240–307.

Beach, F. A. Locks and beagles. *American Psychologist*, 1969, *24*, 971–989.

Beach, F. A. Coital behavior in dogs: VI. Long-term effects of castration upon mating in the male. *Journal of Comparative and Physiological Psychology*, 1970, *70*, 1–32.

Beach, F. A. Cross-species comparisons and human heritage. In F. A. Beach (ed.), *Human sexuality in four perspectives*. Baltimore: Johns Hopkins Press, 1977.

Beach, F. A., ed. *Sex and behavior*. New York: Wiley, 1965.

Beach, F. A.; Zitrin, A.; & Jaynes, J. Neural mediation of mating in male cats: II. Contributions of the frontal cortex. *Journal of Experimental Zoology*, 1955, *130*, 381–401.

Beamer, W.; Bermant, G.; & Clegg, M. Copulatory behavior of the ram, *Ovis aries*: II. Factors affecting copulatory satiation. *Animal Behavior*, 1969, *17*, 706–711.

Beardslee, D. C., & Fogelson, R. Sex differences in sexual imagery aroused by musical stimulation. In J. W. Atkinson (ed.), *Motives in fantasy, action and society*. Princeton, N.J.: Van Nostrand, 1958.

Bell, A. P. Childhood and adolescent sexuality. Address delivered at Institute for Sex Research, Indiana University, 1974.

Bell, A. P., & Weinberg, M. S. *Homosexualities*. New York: Simon & Schuster, 1978.

Bell, A. P.; Weinberg, M. S.; & Hammersmith, S. K. *Sexual preference: Its development in men and women*. Bloomington: Indiana University Press, 1981.

Bell, R. Q. Contributions of human infants to caregiving and social interaction. In M. Lewis & L. Orsenblum (eds.), *The effect of the infant on its caregiver*. New York: Wiley, 1974.

Bell, R. R. Sex as a weapon and changing sex roles. *Medical Aspects of Human Sexuality*, 1970, *4* (6), 102–105, 110–111.

Bell, R. R.; Turner, S.; & Rosen, L. A multivariate analysis of female extramarital coitus. *Journal of Marriage and the Family*, 1975, *37*, 375–383.

Belzer, E. G. Organic expulsions of women: A review and heuristic inquiry. *The Journal of Sex Research*, 1981, *17*, 1–12.

Bem, S. L. The measurement of psychological androgyny. *Journal of Consulting and Clinical Psychology*, 1974, *42*, 155–162.

Bem, S. L. Sex-role adaptability: One consequence of psychological androgyny. *Journal of Personality and Social Psychology*, 1975, *31*, 634–643.

Bem, S. L. On the utility of alternative procedures for assessing psychological androgyny. *Journal of Consulting and Clinical Psychology*, 1977, *45*, 196–205.

Bem, S. L. Gender schema theory: A cognitive account of sex typing. *Psychological Review*, 1981, *88*, 354–364.

Bem, S. L., & Lenney, E. Sex typing and the avoidance of cross-sex behavior. *Journal of Personality and Social Psychology*, 1976, *33*, 48–54.

Bem, S. L.; Martyna, W.; & Watson, C. Sex-typing and androgyny: Further explorations of the expressive domain. *Journal of Personality and Social Psychology*, 1976, *34*, 1016–1023.

Bentler, P. M., & Newcomb, M. D. Longitudinal study of marital success and failure. In M. Cook and G. Wilson (eds.), *Love and attraction*. Oxford: Pergamon Press, 1977.

Beral, V., & Kay, C. R. Morality among oral contraceptive users. *Lancet*, 1977, *2*, 726–731.

Berg, P. A., & Hyde, J. S. Race and sex differences in causal attribution of success and failure. Paper presented at meeting of the American Psychological Association, Washington, D.C., 1976.

Berkow, R. (ed.). *The Merck manual of diagnosis and therapy*. Rahway, N.J.: Merck Sharp & Dohme Research Laboratories, 1977.

Bermant, G., & Davidson, J. M. *Biological bases of sexual behavior*. New York: Harper & Row, 1974.

Bermant, G.; Lott, D.; & Anderson, L. Temporal characteristics of the Coolidge effect in male rat copulatory behavior. *Journal of Comparative and Physiological Psychology*, 1968, *65*, 447–452.

Bernard, J. Sex in remarriage. *Medical Aspects of Human Sexuality*, 1968, *2* (10), 54–61.

Bernstein, B. E. Effect of menstruation on academic performance among college women. *Archives of Sexual Behavior*, 1977, *6*, 289–297.

Berreman, G. D. Pahari polyandry: A comparison. *American Anthropologist*, 1962, *64*, 60–75.

Berscheid, E.; Dion, K.; Walster, E.; & Walster, G. Physical attractiveness and dating choice: A test of the matching hypothesis. *Journal of Experimental Social Psychology*, 1971, *7*, 173–189.

Berscheid, E., & Walster, E. *Interpersonal attraction*. Reading, Mass.: Addison Wesley, 1969.

Berscheid, E., & Walster, E. Beauty and the best. *Psychology Today*, 1972 (Oct.), 42–46.

Berscheid, E., & Walster, E. *Interpersonal attraction*. 2d ed. Reading, Mass.: Addison Wesley, 1978.

Bieber, I. A discussion of "Homosexuality: The ethical challenge." *Journal of Consulting and Clinical Psychology*, 1976, *44*, 163–166.

Bieber, I.; Dain, H. J.; Dince, P. R.; Drellich, M. G.; Grand, H. C.; Grundlach, R. H.; Kremer, M. W.; Rifkin, A. H.; Wilbur, C. B.; & Bieber, T. B. *Homosexuality: A psychoanalytic study*. New York: Random House, 1962.

Blank, L. Nudity as a quest for life the way it was before the apple. *Psychology Today*, 1969, *3*, 18–23.

Blau, S. Venereal diseases. In A. Ellis and A. R. Abarbanel (eds.), *The encyclopedia of sexual behavior*, vol. 2. New York: Hawthorne Books, 1961.

Blumstein, P., & Schwartz, P. Bisexuality: Some social psychological issues. *Journal of Social Issues*, 1977, *33* (2), 30–45.

Bodemer, C. W. *Modern embryology*. New York: Holt, Rinehart & Winston, 1968.

Boggan, E. C.; Haft, M. G.; Lister, C.; & Rupp, J. P. *The civil rights of gay people*. New York: Discus Books, 1975. (a)

Boggan, E. C.; Haft, M.; Lister, C; & Rupp, J. P. *The rights of gay people: The basic ACLU guides to a gay person's rights*. New York: Avon, 1975. (b)

Borgida, E., & White, P. Social perception of rape victims: The impact of legal reform. *Law and Human Behavior*, 1978, *2*, 339–351.

Bossart, W. H., & Wilson, E. O. The analysis of olfactory communication among animals. *Journal of Theoretical Biology*, 1963, *5*, 443–469.

Boswell, J. *Christianity, social tolerance, and homosexuality*. Chicago: University of Chicago Press, 1980.

Boyd, T. L. Learned helplessness in humans: A frustration-produced response pattern. *Journal of Personality and Social Psychology*, 1982, *42*, 738–752.

Boyden, T.; Carroll, J. S.; & Maier, R. A. Similarity and attraction in homosexual males: The effects of age and masculinity-femininity. *Sex Roles: A Journal of Research*, in press.

Brady, J. V. Emotional behavior. In J. Field; H. Magoun; & V. Hall (eds.), *Handbook of Physiology*, vol. 3. Washington, D.C.: American Philosophical Society, 1960.

Bragonier, J. R. Influence of oral contraception on

sexual response. *Medical Aspects of Human Sexuality*, 1976, *10* (10), 130–143.

Brehm, J. W., & Behar, L. B. Sexual arousal, defensiveness, and sex preference in affiliation. *Journal of Experimental Research in Personality*, 1966, *1*, 195–200.

Bremer, J. *Asexualization*. New York: Macmillan, 1959.

Bringle, R. G.; Roach, S.; Adler, C.; & Evenbeck, S. Correlates of jealousy. Paper presented at the annual meeting of the Midwestern Psychological Association, Chicago, 1977.

Bristowe, W. S. *The world of spiders*. London: Collins, 1958.

Brockopp, G. W., & Lester, D. The masturbator. *Crisis Intervention*, 1969, *1*, 10–13.

Broderick, C. B. Socio-sexual development in a suburban community. *Journal of Sex Research*, 1966, *2* (6), 1–24.

Broderick, C. B., & Bernard, J. *The individual, sex and society*. Baltimore: Johns Hopkins Press, 1969.

Brooks-Gunn, J., & Ruble, D. N. The menstrual attitude questionnaire. *Psychosomatic Medicine*, 1980, *42*, 503–511.

Broverman, D. M.; Klaiber, E. L.; & Vogel, W. Gonadal hormones and cognitive functioning. In J. E. Parsons (ed.), *The psychobiology of sex differences and sex roles*. Washington: Hemisphere, 1980.

Brown, J. L. *The evolution of behavior*. New York: W. W. Norton, 1975.

Brownell, K. D., & Barlow, D. H. Measurement and treatment of two sexual deviations in one person. *Journal of Behavior Therapy and Experimental Psychiatry*, 1976, *7*, 349–354.

Brownmiller, S. *Against our will: Men, women and rape*. New York: Simon & Schuster, 1975.

Brundage, L. W.; Derlega, V. J.; & Cash, T. F. The effects of physical attractiveness and need for approval on self-disclosure. *Personality and Social Psychology Bulletin*, 1977, *3*, 63–66.

Bryan, J. H. Apprenticeships and prostitution. *Social Problems*, 1965, *12*, 278–297.

Bryson, J. B. Situational determinants of the expression of jealousy. Paper presented at the annual meeting of the American Psychological Association, San Francisco, 1977.

Buck, R. W.; Miller, R. E.; & Caul, W. F. Sex, personality, and physiological variables in the communication of affect via facial expression. *Journal of Personality and Social Psychology*, 1974, *30*, 587–596.

Buck, R. W.; Savin, V. J.; Miller, R. E.; & Caul, W. F. Communication of affect through facial expressions in humans. *Journal of Personality and Social Psychology*, 1972, *23*, 362–371.

Buckner, H. The transvestite career path. *Psychiatry*, 1970, *33*, 381–389.

Buhrich, N., & Beaumont, T. Comparison of transvestism in Australia and America. *Archives of Sexual Behavior*, 1981, *10*, 269–279.

Buhrich, N., & McConaghy, N. The discrete syndromes of transvestism and transsexualism. *Archives of Sexual Behavior*, 1977, *6*, 483–495.

Bullough, V. *The history of prostitution*. Hyde Park, N.Y.: University Books, 1964.

Bullough, V. *Sexual variance in society and history*. New York: Wiley, 1976.

Burgess, A. W., & Holmstrom, L. L. Rape trauma syndrome. *American Journal of Psychiatry*, 1974, *131*, 981–986.

Burgess, A. W., & Holmstrom, L. L. Four- to six-year follow-up of rape victims. Address by A. W. Burgess, University of Illinois at Chicago Circle, May 15, 1978.

Burnside, I. M. Listen to the aged. *American Journal of Nursing*, 1975, *75*, 1801–1802.

Burton, F. D. Sexual climax in female *Macaca mulatta*. In *Proceedings of the Third International Congress of Primatology*, vol. 3. Basel: Karger, 1971.

Bush, P. *Drugs, alcohol and sex*. New York: Richard Marek, 1980.

Buss, A. H. Physical aggression in relation to different frustrations. *Journal of Abnormal and Social Psychology*, 1963, *67*, 1–7.

Butler, J. C.; Dale, P.; & Wagner, N. N. Sexuality during pregnancy and parturition. In R. Green (ed.), *Human sexuality: A health practitioner's text*. 2d ed. Baltimore: Williams & Wilkins, 1979.

Buunk, B. Anticipated sexual jealousy: Its relationship to self-esteem, dependency, and reciprocity. *Personality and Social Psychology Bulletin,* 1982, 310–316.

Byrne, D. A pregnant pause in the sexual revolution. *Psychology Today,* 1977, 11 (2), 67–68.

Byrne, D., & Buehler, J. A. A note on the influence of propinquity upon acquaintanceships. *Journal of Abnormal and Social Psychology,* 1955, 51, 147–148.

Byrne, D.; Ervin, C. R.; & Lamberth, J. Continuity between the experimental study of attraction and real-life computer dating. *Journal of Personality and Social Psychology,* 1970, 16, 157–165.

Byrne, D.; Fisher, J. D.; Lamberth, J.; & Mitchell, H. E. Evaluations of erotica: Facts or feelings? *Journal of Personality and Social Psychology,* 1974, 29, 111–116.

Byrne, D., & Lamberth, J. The effect of erotic stimuli on sex arousal, evaluative responses, and subsequent behavior. In *Technical Report of the Commission on Obscenity and Pornography,* vol. 8. Washington, D.C.: U.S. Government Printing Office, 1971.

Caird, W. K., & Wincze, J. P. *Sex therapy: A behavioral approach.* New York: Harper & Row, 1977.

Calhoun, A. W. *A social history of the American family,* vol. 1. 1917. Reprint ed.: New York: Barnes and Noble, 1960.

Calhoun, L. G.; Selby, J. W.; & King, H. E. The influence of pregnancy on sexuality: A review of current evidence. *The Journal of Sex Research,* 1981, 17, 139–151.

Callahan-Levy, C. M., & Messe, L. A. Sex differences in the allocation of pay. *Journal of Personality and Social Psychology,* 1979, 37, 443–446.

Campbell, M. F., & Harrison, J. H. eds. *Urology.* Philadelphia: Saunders, 1970.

Cantor, J. R. What is funny to whom? *Journal of Communication,* 1976, 26, 164–172.

Capranica, R. R. Auditory processing of vocal signals in Anurans. In D. H. Taylor and S. I. Gutt-

man (eds.), *The Reproductive Biology of Amphibians.* New York: Plenum, 1977.

Caprio, F. S. *The sexually adequate male.* New York: Citadel, 1952.

Carey, J. Changing courtship patterns in the popular song. *American Journal of Sociology,* 1969, 74, 720–731.

Carns, D. E. Talking about sex: Notes on first coitus and the double sexual standard. *Journal of Marriage and the Family,* 1973, 35, 677–688.

Carpenter, C. R. Sexual behavior of free-ranging rhesus monkeys (*Macaca mulatta*). *Journal of Comparative Psychology,* 1942, 33, 113–162.

Cartwright, R. D., & Ratzel, R. W. Effects of dream loss on waking behavior. *Archives of General Psychiatry,* 1972, 27, 277–280.

Cash, T. F.; Gillen, B.; & Burns, D. S. Sexism and "beautyism" in personnel consultant decision making. *Journal of Applied Psychology,* 1977, 62, 301–310.

Cattell, R. B.; Kawash, G. F.; & DeYoung, G. E. Validation of objective measures of ergic tension: Response of the sex erg to visual stimulation. *Journal of Experimental Research in Personality,* 1972, 6, 76–83.

Catterall, R. D. *A short textbook of venereology.* Philadelphia: J. B. Lippincott, 1974.

Cautela, J. R. Covert sensitization. *Psychological Record,* 1967, 20, 459–468.

Center for Disease Control, Morbidity and Mortality Weekly Report, 1980, 29 (37), 441–445.

Chang, J. *The Tao of love and sex.* New York: E. P. Dutton, 1977.

Chapman, A. J., & Gadfield, N. J. Is sexual humor sexist? *Journal of Communication,* 1976, 26, 141–153.

Cherniak, D., & Feingold, A. *Birth control handbook.* Montreal: Montreal Health Press, 1973.

Chesser, E. *Strange loves: The human aspects of sexual deviation.* New York: William Morrow, 1971.

Chevalier-Skolnikoff, S. Male-female, female-female, and male-male sexual behavior in the stumptail monkey, with special attention to the female orgasm. *Archives of Sexual Behavior,* 1974, 3, 95–116.

Christensen, H. T., & Johnson, K. P. *Marriage and the family.* New York: Ronald, 1971.

Citron, N. D. & Wade, P. J. Penile injuries from vacuum cleaners. *British Medical Journal,* 1980 (July), 26.

Clanton, G., & Smith, L. *Jealousy.* Englewood Cliffs, N.J.: Prentice-Hall, 1977.

Clark, K. B., & Clark, M. K. Racial identification and preference in Negro children. In T. Newcomb & E. Hartley (eds.), *Readings in social psychology.* New York: Holt, Rinehart & Winston, 1947.

Clark, R. A. The projective measurement of experimentally induced levels of sexual motivation. *Journal of Experimental Psychology,* 1952, 44, 391–399.

Clifford, E., & Crocker, E. C. Maternal responses: The birth of a normal child as compared to the birth of a child with a cleft. *Cleft Palate Journal,* 1971, 8, 298–306.

Clifford, R. E. Subjective sexual experience in college women. *Archives of Sexual Behavior,* 1978, 7, 183–197.

Clifton, A.; McGrath, D.; & Wick, B. Stereotypes of women: A single category? *Sex Roles,* 1976, 2, 135–148.

Cline, M. E.; Holmes, D. S.; & Werner, J. C. Evaluation of the work of men and women as a function of the sex of the judge and type of work. *Journal of Applied Social Psychology,* 1977, 7, 89–93.

Clore, G. L.; Wiggins, N. H.; & Itkin, S. Judging attraction from nonverbal behavior: The gain phenomenon. *Journal of Consulting and Clinical Psychology,* 1975, 43, 491–497.

Coe, W. R. Sexual phases in *Crepidula. Journal of Experimental Zoology,* 1936, 72, 455–477.

Cohen, J. The effects of oral contraceptives on sexual behavior. In R. Gemme & C. C. Wheeler (eds.), *Progress in sexology.* New York: Plenum, 1976.

Cohen, M. L.; Garafalo, R.; Boucher, R.; & Seghorn, T. The psychology of rapists. *Seminars in Psychiatry,* 1971, 3, 307–327.

Cohen, M. L.; Seghorn, T.; & Calmas, W. Sociometric study of the sex offender. *Journal of Abnormal Psychology,* 1969, 74, 249–255.

Cole, C. L. Cohabitation in social context. In R. W. Libby & R. N. Whitehurst (eds.), *Marriage and alternatives: Exploring intimate relationships.* Glenview, Ill.: Scott, Foresman, 1977.

Cole, T. M. Sexuality and the spinal cord injured. In R. Green (ed.), *Human sexuality: A health practitioner's text.* 2d ed. Baltimore: Williams and Wilkins, 1979.

Coleman, J. C. *Abnormal psychology and modern life.* Glenview, Ill.: Scott Foresman, 1972.

Coleman, J. S. *The adolescent society.* Glencoe, Ill.: The Free Press, 1961.

Comarr, A. Sexual function among patients with spinal cord injury. *Urologia Internationalis,* 1970, 25, 134–168.

Comfort, A. Likelihood of human pheromones. *Nature,* 1971, 230, 432–433.

Comfort, A. *The joy of sex.* New York: Crown, 1972.

Comfort, A. *Sexual consequences of disability.* Philadelphia: George F. Stickley, 1978.

Commission on Obscenity and Pornography. *The Report of the Commission on Obscenity and Pornography.* Washington, D.C.: U.S. Government Printing Office, 1970.

Comstock, G.; Chaffee, S.; Katsman, N.; McCoombs, M.; & Roberts, D. *Television and human behavior.* New York: Columbia University Press, 1979.

Connor, J. Olfactory control of aggressive and sexual behavior in the mouse (*Mus musclus L.*). *Psychonomic Science,* 1972, 27, 1–3.

Corzine, J., & Kirby, R. Cruising the truckers. *Urban Life,* 1977, 6 (2), 171–191.

Coult, A. D. Causality and cross-sex prohibitions. *American Anthropologist,* 1963, 65, 266–277.

Coyner, S. Women's liberation and sexual liberation. In S. Gordon & R. W. Libby (eds.), *Sexuality today and tomorrow.* North Scituate, Mass.: Duxbury Press, 1976.

Cozby, P. C. Self-disclosure: A literature review. *Psychological Bulletin,* 1973, 79, 73–91.

Crane, J. Aspects of social behavior in fiddler crabs, with special reference to *Uca maracoani* (Latreille). *Zoology,* 1958, 43, 113–130.

Crépault, C., & Couture, M. Men's erotic fantasies.

Archives of Sexual Behavior, 1980, *9*, 565–581.

Crooks, R., & Baur, K. *Our sexuality.* Menlo Park, Calif.: Benjamin/Cummings, 1980.

Cross, H. A.; Halcomb, C. G.; & Matter, W. W. Imprinting or exposure learning in rats given early auditory stimulation. *Psychonomic Science,* 1967, *7,* 233–234.

Cuber, J. F., & Harroff, P. B. *The significant Americans: A study of the sexual behavior of the affluent.* New York: Appleton-Century-Crofts, 1965.

Culp, O. S. Anomalies of male genitalia. *Medical Aspects of Human Sexuality,* 1974, *8* (9), 126–147.

Curtis, E. M. Oral-contraceptive feminization of a normal male infant. *Obstetrics and Gynecology,* 1964, *23,* 295–296.

Dailey, D. The pregnant male. *Journal of Sex Education and Therapy,* 1978, *4,* 43–44.

Daley, P. *The fantasy game: How male and female sexual fantasies affect our lives.* New York: Stein & Day, 1975.

Dalton, K. *The menstrual cycle.* New York: Pantheon Books, 1969.

Dalton, K. *Once a month.* London: Hunter House, 1979.

Daly, M., & Wilson, M. *Sex, evolution, and behavior.* 2d ed. Boston: Willard Grant, 1983.

Dan, A. J. Behavioral variability and the menstrual cycle. Paper presented at the meeting of the American Psychological Association, Washington, D.C., 1976.

Dank, B. M. Coming out in the gay world. *Psychiatry,* 1971, *34,* 180–197.

Darling, F. F. *A herd of red deer.* London: Oxford University Press, 1937.

Davenport, W. H. Sexual patterns and their regulation in a society of the Southwest Pacific. In F. A. Beach (ed.), *Sex and behavior.* New York: Wiley, 1965.

Davenport, W. H. Sex in cross-cultural perspective. In F. A. Beach (ed.), *Human sexuality in four perspectives.* Baltimore: Johns Hopkins Press, 1976.

Davidson, J. M. Characteristics of sex behavior in male rats following castration. *Animal Behavior,* 1966, *14,* 266–272.

Davis, K. E. Sex on campus: Is there a revolution? *Medical Aspects of Human Sexuality,* 1971, *5* (1), 128–142.

Davis, N. J. Prostitution: Identity, career, and legal-economic enterprise. In J. M. Henslin and E. Sagarin (eds.), *The sociology of sex: An introductory reader.* New York: Schocken, 1978.

Dearborn, L. W. Masturbation. In M. F. DeMartino (ed.), *Sexual behavior and personality characteristics.* New York: Grove Press, 1966.

Dearth, P. B. Viable sex education in the schools: Expectations of students, parents, and experts. *Journal of School Health,* 1974, *44,* 190–193.

Deaux, K. Honking at the intersection: A replication and extension. *Journal of Social Psychology,* 1971, *84,* 159–160.

Deaux, K. *The behavior of women and men.* Monterey, Calif.: Brooks/Cole Publishing, 1976.

Debrovner, C. H., & Shubin-Stein, R. Sexual problems in the infertile couple. *Medical Aspects of Human Sexuality,* 1975, *9* (1), 140–148.

De Lacoste-Utamsing, C., & Holloway, R. L. Sexual dimorphism in the human corpus callosum. *Science,* 1982, *216,* 1431–1432.

DeLora, J. S., & Warren, C. A. B. *Understanding sexual interaction.* Boston: Houghton Mifflin, 1977.

DeMartino, M. F. How women want men to make love. *Sexology,* 1970, no. 10, 4–7.

Dement, W. An essay on dreams. In *New directions in psychology,* vol. 2. New York: Holt, Rinehart & Winston, 1965.

Dement, W., & Wolpert, E. The relation of eye movements, bodily motility, and external stimuli to dream content. *Journal of Experimental Psychology,* 1958, *55,* 543–553.

Denfield, D. & Gordon, M. The sociology of mate swapping: Or the family that swings together clings together. *Journal of Sex Research,* 1970, *6,* 85–100.

Denko, J. D. Erotic enemas. *Medical Aspects of Human Sexuality,* 1976, *10* (12), 37–38.

Dennis, E. J., & Hester, L. L. Toxemia of pregnancy.

In D. N. Danforth (ed.), *Textbook of obstetrics and gynecology.* 2d ed. New York: Harper & Row, 1971.

Der-Karabetian, A., & Smith, A. Sex-role stereotyping in the United States: Is it changing? *Sex Roles,* 1977, *3,* 193–198.

Dermer, M., & Thiel, D. L. When beauty may fail. *Journal of Personality and Social Psychology,* 1975, *31,* 1168–1176.

Dewsbury, D. A. Effects of novelty on copulatory behavior: The Coolidge effect and related phenomena. *Psychological Bulletin,* 1981, *89,* 464–482.

Diamond, M. Transsexualism. *Medical Journal of Australia,* 1974, *12* (1), 51.

Diamond, M. New data supporting cortical asymmetry differences in males and females. *The Behavioral and Brain Sciences,* 1980, *3,* 233–234.

Diamond, M., & Karlen, A. *Sexual decisions.* Boston: Little, Brown, 1980.

Dickinson, R. L. *Human sex anatomy.* 2d ed. Baltimore: Williams and Wilkins, 1949.

Dick-Read, G. *Childbirth without fear.* 2d ed. New York: Harper & Row, 1944.

Diener, E., & DeFour, D. Does television violence enhance program popularity? *Journal of Personality and Social Psychology,* 1978, *36,* 333–341.

Dion, K. K.; Berscheid, E.; & Walster, E. What is beautiful is good. *Journal of Personality and Social Psychology,* 1972, *24,* 285–290.

Dion, K. K., & Dion, K. L. Self-esteem and romantic love. *Journal of Personality,* 1975, *43,* 39–57.

Dion, K. L., & Dion, K. K. Correlates of romantic love. *Journal of Consulting and Clinical Psychology,* 1973, *41,* 51–56.

Djerassi, C. *The politics of contraception.* New York: Norton, 1979.

Dmowski, W. P.; Gaynor, L.; Lawrence, M.; Rao, R.; & Scommegna, A. Artificial insemination homologous with oligospermic semen: Semen separation in albumin columns. *Fertility and Sterility,* 1979, *31,* 58–62.

Donnerstein, E. Pornography: Its effect on violence against women. In N. Malamuth and E. Donnerstein (eds.), *Pornography and Sexual Aggres-*sion. New York: Academic Press, in press.

Donnerstein, E.; Donnerstein, M.; & Evans, R. Erotic stimuli and aggression: Facilitation or inhibition. *Journal of Personality and Social Psychology,* 1975, *32,* 237–244.

Dormont, R. Ejaculatory anhedonia. *Medical Aspects of Human Sexuality,* 1975, *9* (2), 32–43.

Doty, R. L.; Orndorff, M. M.; Leyden, J.; & Kligman, A. Communication of gender from human axillary odors: Relationship to perceived intensity and hedonicity. *Behavioral Biology,* 1978, *23,* 373–380.

Dougherty, E. G. Comparative evolution and the origin of sexuality. *Systematic Zoology,* 1955, *4,* 145–169.

Douglass, C. P. Prenatal risks: An obstetrician's point of view. In S. Aladjem (ed.), *Risks in the practice of modern obstetrics.* St. Louis: Mosby, 1972.

Driori, D., & Folman, Y. Effects of cohabitation on the reproductive system, kidneys, and body composition of male rats. *Journal of Reproduction and Fertility,* 1964, *8,* 351–359.

Driscoll, R.; Davis, K. E.; & Lipetz, M. Parental interference and romantic love. *Journal of Personality and Social Psychology,* 1972, *24,* 1–10.

DuBois, C. *The people of Alor.* Minneapolis: University of Minnesota Press, 1944.

Duffy, J. Masturbation and clitoridectomy: A nineteenth-century view. *Journal of the American Medical Association.* 1963, *186,* 246–248.

Dutton, D. G. & Aron, A. P. Some evidence for heightened sexual attraction under conditions of high anxiety. *Journal of Personality and Social Psychology,* 1974, *30,* 510–517.

Eastman, W. F. First intercourse, *Sexual Behavior,* 1972, *2* (3), 22–27.

Edwards, D. A. Neonatal administration of androstenedione, testosterone, or testosterone propionate: Effects on ovulation, sexual receptivity, and aggressive behavior in female mice. *Physiology and Behavior,* 1971, *6,* 223–228.

Effects of sexual activity on beard growth in man. *Nature,* 1970, *227,* 869–870.

Efran, M. G. The effect of physical appearance on the judgment of guilt, interpersonal attraction, and severity of recommended punishment in a simulated jury task. *Journal of Research in Personality,* 1974, *8,* 45–54.

Egboh, E. O. Polygamy in Iboland. *Civilizations,* 1972, *22,* 431–444.

Ehrhardt, A. A., & Baker, S. W. Fetal androgens, human central nervous differentiation, and behavior sex differences. In R. C. Friedman; R. M. Richart; & R. L. VandeWiele (eds.), *Sex differences in behavior.* New York: Wiley, 1974.

Ehrhardt, A. A., & Meyer-Bahlburg, H. F. L. Effects of sex hormones on gender-related behavior. *Science,* 1981, *211,* 1312–1318.

Ehrlich, H., & Graeven, D. Reciprocal self-disclosure in a dyad. *Journal of Experimental Social Psychology,* 1971, *7,* 389–400.

Ehrlich, P. A., & Ehrlich, A. H. *Population, resources, environment.* 2d ed. San Francisco: Freeman, 1972.

Ehrmann, W. *Premarital dating behavior.* New York: Holt, Rinehart & Winston, 1959.

Eichenlaub, J. E. *The marriage art.* New York: Dell, 1961.

Eisenman, R. Sexual behavior as related to sex fantasies and experimental manipulation of authoritarianism and creativity. *Journal of Personality and Social Psychology,* 1982, *43,* 853–860.

Ekman, P. Universal facial expressions in emotion. *California Mental Health Research Digest,* 1970, *8,* 151–158.

Ekman, P. Biological and cultural contributions to body and facial movement. In J. Blacking (ed.), *The anthropology of the body.* A.S.A. Monograph 15. London: Academic Press, 1977.

Ekman, P., & Friesen, W. V. Nonverbal leakage and clues to deception. *Psychiatry,* 1969, *32,* 88–106.

Ekman, P., & Friesen, W. V. *Unmasking the face.* Englewood Cliffs, N.J.: Prentice-Hall, 1975.

Ekman, P.; Friesen, W. V.; & Ellsworth, P. *Emotion in the human face: Guidelines for research and an integration of findings.* New York: Pergamon Press, 1972.

Elias, J., & Gebhard, P. Sexuality and sexual learning in childhood. *Phi Delta Kappan,* 1969, *50,* 401–405.

Elias, J., & Gebhard, P. Sexuality and sexual learning in childhood. In A. M. Juhasz (ed.), *Sexual development and behavior.* Homewood, Ill.: Dorsey, 1973.

Ellis, A. *The art and science of love.* New York: Lyle Stuart, 1960.

Ellsworth, P. C.; Carlsmith, J. M.; & Henson, A. Staring as a stimulus to flight in humans: A series of field studies. *Journal of Personality and Social Psychology,* 1972, *21,* 302–311.

Eme, R. F. Sex differences in childhood psychopathology: A review. *Psychological Bulletin,* 1979, *86,* 574–595.

Enders, R. K. Reproduction in the mink. *Proceedings of the American Philosophical Society,* 1952, *96,* 691–755.

Epstein, A. W. Fetishism. *Journal of Nervous and Mental Disorders,* 1960, *130,* 107–119.

Ervin, C. V. Psychologic adjustment to mastectomy. *Medical Aspects of Human Sexuality,* 1973, *7* (2), 42–65.

Eskin, B. A. Aging and the menopause. In B. A. Eskin (ed.), *The menopause: Comprehensive management and current endocrine investigations.* New York: Masson, 1980.

Espenshade, T. J. The cost of children. In J. G. Wells (ed.), *Current issues in marriage and the family.* 2d ed. New York: Macmillan, 1979.

Evans, T. N. Infertility and other gynecologic problems. In D. N. Danforth (ed.), *Textbook of obstetrics and gynecology.* 2d ed. New York: Harper & Row, 1971.

Exline, R. V. Explorations in the process of person perception: Visual interaction in relation to competition, sex, and need for affiliation. *Journal of Personality,* 1963, *31,* 1–20.

Eysenck, H. J. Obscenity—officially speaking. *Penthouse,* 1972, *3* (11), 95–102.

Fabro, S. Passage of drugs and other chemicals into the uterine fluids and preimplantation blastocyst. In L. O. Boreus (ed.), *Fetal pharmacology.* New York: Raven Press, 1973.

Fagot, B. I., & Patterson, G. R. An *in vivo* analysis of reinforcing contingencies for sex-role behaviors in the pre-school child. *Developmental Psychology*, 1969, *1*, 563–568.

Falek, A. Ethical issues in human behavior genetics: Civil rights, informed consent, and ethics of intervention. In K. W. Schaie; V. E. Anderson; G. E. McClearn; & J. Money (eds.), *Developmental human behavior genetics*. Boston: D. C. Heath, 1975.

Fast, J. *Body language*. New York: Pocket Books, 1970.

Feigen, G. M. Injuries from anal coitus. In H. J. Lief (ed.), *Medical aspects of human sexuality*. Baltimore: Williams and Wilkins, 1975.

Feldman, H., & Feldman, M. Effect of parenthood on three points in marriage. Unpublished research report, Department of Human Development and Family Studies, Cornell University, Ithaca, N.Y. 1977.

Feldman, M. P., & MacCulloch, M. J. *Homosexual behavior: Therapy and assessment*. Oxford: Pergamon Press, 1971.

Feldman, Y., & Nikitas, J. Nongonococcal urethritis. *Journal of the American Medical Association*, 1981, *245*, 381–386.

Fenichel, O. On acting. *Psychoanalytic Quarterly*, 1946, *15*, 144–160.

Feshbach, N., & Sones, G. Sex differences in adolescent reactions toward newcomers. *Developmental Psychology*, 1971, *4*, 381–386.

Feshbach, S. Aggression. In P. H. Mussen (ed.), *Carmichael's manual of child psychology*, vol. 2, New York: Wiley, 1970.

Feshbach, S.; Malamuth, N.; & Drapkin, R. *The effects of aggression, inhibition, and aggression facilitation on sexual responsiveness*. Paper presented at the meeting of the International Society for Research on Aggression, Toronto, 1974.

Festinger, L. *A theory of cognitive dissonance*. New York: Harper & Row, 1957.

Festinger, L.; Schachter, S.; & Back, K. *Social pressures in informal groups: A study of a housing community*. New York: Harper & Row, 1950.

Fetal Alcohol Syndrome Work Group. *Facts about fetal alcohol syndrome*. Springfield, Ill.: 1980.

Fidell, L. Empirical verification of sex discrimination in hiring practices in psychology. *American Psychologist*, 1970, *24*, 1094–1098.

Finch, B. E. & Green, H. *Contraception through the ages*. Springfield, Ill.: Charles C Thomas, 1963.

Finkle, M. L., & Finkle, D. J. Sexual and contraceptive knowledge, attitudes and behavior of male adolescents. *Family Planning Perspectives*, 1975, *7* (6), 256–260.

Fisher, A. E. Maternal and sexual behavior induced by intracranial chemical stimulation. *Science*, 1956, *124*, 228–229.

Fisher, J. E.; O'Neal, E. C.; & McDonald, P. J. *Female competitiveness as a function of prior performance outcome, competitors' evaluation, and sex of competitor*. Paper presented at meeting of Midwestern Psychological Association, Chicago, 1974.

Fisher, Seymour. *Body Consciousness*. Glasgow: William Collins, 1976.

Fisher, W. A., & Byrne, D. *Individual differences in socialization to sex as mediators of responses to an erotic film*. Paper presented at meeting of the Midwestern Psychological Association, Chicago, 1976.

Fitting, M.; Salisbury, S.; Davis, N.; & Mayclin, D. Self-concept and sexuality of spinal-cord injured women. *Archives of Sexual Behavior*, 1978, *7*, 143–156.

Fitzgerald, R. G. Commentary on paper by Gillman and Gordon: Sexual behavior in the blind. *Medical Aspects of Human Sexuality*, 1973, *7* (6), 60.

Fiumara, N. J. Gonococcal pharyngitis. *Medical Aspects of Human Sexuality*, 1971, *5* (5), 194–209.

Fiumara, N. J. Differential diagnosis and treatment of venereally transmitted urethritis and vaginitis. *Medical Aspects of Human Sexuality*, 1976, *8* (3), 41–42.

Fleischman, A. R., & Fryd, D. S. The birth of an abnormal child. In B. L. Blum (ed.), *Psychological aspects of pregnancy, birthing, and bonding*. New York: Human Sciences Press, 1980.

Fletcher, J. *Situation ethics.* Philadelphia: Westminster Press, 1966.

Ford, C. S., & Beach, F. A. *Patterns of sexual behavior.* New York: Harper & Row, 1951.

Foster, A. L. Relationships between age and sexual activity in married men. *Journal of Sex Education and Therapy,* 1979, 5 (5), 21–26.

Fox, C. A. Some aspects and implications of coital physiology. *Journal of Sex and Marital Therapy,* 1976, 2 (3), 205–213.

Fox, C. A. Orgasm and fertility. In R. Gemme and C. C. Wheeler (eds.), *Progress in sexology.* New York: Plenum Press, 1977.

Fox, G. L. Sex-role attitudes as predictors of contraceptive use among unmarried university students. *Sex Roles,* 1977, 3 (3), 265–283.

Frank, S. *The sexually active man past forty.* New York: Macmillan, 1968.

Freeman, D. *Margaret Mead and Samoa: The making and unmaking of an anthropological myth.* Cambridge: Harvard University Press, 1983.

Freud, S. The transformation of puberty. In A. A. Brill (ed. and trans.), *The basic writings.* New York: Modern Library, 1938.

Freud, S. *The interpretation of dreams,* trans. A. A. Brill. 1900, Reprint ed.: New York: Modern Library, 1950.

Freund, K.; Sedlacek, F.; & Knob, K. A simple transducer for mechanical plethysmography of the male genital. *Journal for the Experimental Analysis of Behavior,* 1965, 8, 169–170.

Friday, N. *My secret garden: Women's sexual fantasies.* New York: Pocket Books, 1973.

Friedl, E. Women and men: *An anthropologist's view.* New York: Holt, Rinehart & Winston, 1975.

Friedman, A. *Hermaphrodeity: The autobiography of a poet.* New York: A. A. Knopf, 1973.

Frieze, I. H. *Changing self-images and sex-role stereotypes in college women.* Paper presented at meeting of American Psychological Association, Chicago, 1974.

Frisbie, L. Treated sex offenders and what they did. *Mental Hygiene,* 1959, 43, 263–267.

Fulton, G. *Sexual awareness.* Boston: Holbrook Press, 1974.

Gagnon, J. H. Female child victims of sex offenses. *Social Problems,* 1965, 13, 176–192. (a)

Gagnon, J. H. Sexuality and sexual learning in the child. *Psychiatry,* 1965, 28, 212–228. (b)

Gagnon, J. H., & Simon, W. *Sexual conduct: The social sources of human sexuality.* Chicago: Aldine, 1973.

Gagnon, J. H.; Simon, W.; & Berger, A. J. Some aspects of sexual adjustment in early and later adolescence. In J. Zubin and A. Freedman (eds.), *The psychology of adolescence.* New York: Grune & Stratton, 1970.

Gajdúsek, D. C. Physiological and psychological characteristics of Stone Age man. *Engineering and Science,* 1970, 33, 26–33.

Gallup, G. Pre-marital sex is no sin to most teens. Associated Press, 1978.

Galston, A. W. Here come the clones. *Natural History,* 1975, 84, 72–75.

Gardner, R. A., & Gardner, B. T. Teaching sign language to a chimpanzee. *Science,* 1969, 165, 664–672.

Garner, B., & Smith, R. W. Are there really any gay male athletes? An empirical survey. *Journal of Sex Research,* 1977, 13 (1), 22–34.

Garrett, T., & Wright, R. Wives of rapists and incest offenders. *Journal of Sex Research,* 1975, 11, 149–157.

Gartell, N. K.; Loriaux, D. L.; & Chase, T. N. Plasma testosterone in homosexual and heterosexual women. *American Journal of Psychiatry,* 1977, 10, 1117–1118.

Gaupp, L. A.; Stern, R. M.; & Ratliff, R. G. The use of aversion-relief procedures in the treatment of a case of voyeurism. *Behavior Therapy,* 1971, 2, 585–588.

Gebhard, P. H. Factors in marital orgasm. *Journal of Social Issues,* 1966, 22 (2), 88–95.

Gebhard, P. H. Postmarital coitus among widows and divorcees. In P. Bohannan (ed.), *Divorce and after.* Garden City, N.Y.: Doubleday, 1968.

Gebhard, P. H. Misconceptions about female prostitutes. *Medical Aspects of Human Sexuality,* 1969, 3 (3), 24–30.

Gebhard, P. H. Human sexual behavior: A summary statement. In D. S. Marshall & R. C. Suggs (eds.), *Human sexual behavior: Variations in the ethnographic spectrum.* New York: Basic Books, 1971.

Gebhard, P. H. Sexual behavior of the mentally retarded. In F. F. de la Cruz & G. D. LaVeck (eds.), *Human sexuality and the mentally retarded.* New York: Brunner/Mazel, 1973.

Gebhard, P. H. Fetishism and sadomasochism. In M. S. Weinberg (ed.), *Sex research.* New York: Oxford University Press, 1976.

Gebhard, P. H.; Gagnon, J. H.; Pomeroy, W. B.; & Christianson, C. V. *Sex offenders.* New York: Harper & Row, 1965.

Geer, J. H., & Fuhr, R. Cognitive factors in sexual arousal: The role of distraction. *Journal of Consulting and Clinical Psychology*, 1976, 44, 238–243.

Gendron, B. *Technology and the human condition.* New York: St. Martin's Press, 1977.

Gerall, A. A. Hormonal factors influencing masculine behavior of female guinea pigs. *Journal of Comparative and Physiological Psychology*, 1966, 62, 365–369.

Gerrard, M. Sex, sex guilt, and contraceptive use. *Journal of Personality and Social Psychology*, 1982, 42, 153–158.

Giambra, L. M. Daydreaming across the life span: Late adolescent to senior citizen. *International Journal of Aging and Human Development*, 1974, 5, 115–140.

Giambra, L. M., & Martin, C. E. Sexual daydreams and quantitative aspects of sexual activity: Some relations for males across adulthood. *Archives of Sexual Behavior*, 1977, 6, 497–505.

Gillen, B. Physical attractiveness: A determinant of two types of goodness. *Personality and Social Psychology Bulletin*, 1981, 7, 277–281.

Gilmartin, B. G. That swinging couple down the block. *Psychology Today*, 1975, 8 (9), 54.

Gilmartin, B. G. Swinging: Who gets involved and how. In R. W. Libby and R. N. Whitehurst (eds.), *Marriage and alternatives.* Glenview, Ill.: Scott, Foresman, 1977.

Gilmartin, B. G., & Kusisto, D. V. Some personal and social characteristics of mate-sharing swingers. In R. W. Libby and R. N. Whitehurst (eds.), *Renovating marriage.* Danville, Calif.:

Consensus Publications, 1973.

Ginsburg, K. N. The "meat-rack": A study of the male homosexual prostitute. In C. D. Bryant (ed.), *Sexual deviancy in social context.* New York: Franklin Watts, 1977.

Glasgow, R., & Arkowitz, H. The behavioral assessment of male and female social competence in dyadic heterosexual interactions. *Behavior Therapy*, 1975, 6, 488–498.

Glenn, N. D. The contribution of marriage to the psychological well-being of males and females. *Journal of Marriage and the Family*, 1975, 37, 594–601.

Glick, P. C., & Norton, J. *1979 Update: Marrying, divorcing and living together in the U.S. today.* Washington, D.C.: Population Reference Bureau, 1979.

Goffman, E. *Interaction ritual.* Garden City, N.Y.: Doubleday, Anchor, 1967.

Goldberg, P. Are women prejudiced against women? *Trans-action*, 1968, 5, 28–30.

Goldfoot, D. A.; Westerborg-van Loon, H.; Groeneveld, W.; & Koos Slob, A. Behavioral and physiological evidence of sexual climax in the female stump-tailed macaque (*Macacca arctoides*). *Science*, 1980, 208, 1477–1478.

Goldstein, B. *Human Sexuality.* New York: McGraw-Hill, 1976.

Goldstein, M. C. Stratification, polyandry, and family structure in central Tibet. *Southwestern Journal of Anthropology*, 1971, 27, 64–74.

Goldstein, M. C. *Tibetan polyandry revisited.* Paper presented at a meeting of the American Anthropological Association, Washington, D.C., 1976.

Goldstein, M. J.; Kant, H. S.; & Hartman, J. J. *Pornography and sexual deviance.* Berkeley: University of California Press, 1974.

Goleman, D., & Bush, S. The liberation of sexual fantasy. *Psychology Today*, 1977, 4 (10), 48–53, 104–107.

Goodlin, R. C. Routine ultrasonic examinations in obstetrics. *Lancet*, 1971 (September 11), 604–605.

Gordon, M., & Shankweiler, P. J. Different equals less: Female sexuality in recent marriage manuals. *Journal of Marriage and the Family*, 1971, *33*, 459–466.

Grant, M. *Eros in Pompeii*. New York: William Morrow, 1975.

Great Britain Committee on Homosexual Offenses and Prostitution. *The Wolfenden report*. New York: Stein & Day, 1963.

Green, R. *Sexual identity and conflict in children and adults*. Baltimore: Penguin Books, 1974.

Green, R. Adults who want to change sex; adolescents who cross dress; and children called "sissy" and "tomboy." In R. Green (ed.), *Human sexuality: A health practitioner's text*. Baltimore: Williams & Wilkins, 1975.

Green, R. Mythological, historical, and cross-cultural aspects of transsexualism. In J. L. McCary & D. R. Copeland (eds.), *Modern views of human sexual behavior*. Chicago: Science Research Associates, 1976.

Green, R. Sexual identity of 37 children raised by homosexual or transsexual parents. *American Journal of Psychiatry*, 1978, *135*, 692–697.

Greenbank, R. Are medical students learning psychiatry? *Pennsylvania Medical Journal*, 1961, *64*, 989–992.

Greenberg, J. S., & Archambault, F. X. Masturbation, self-esteem, and other variables. *Journal of Sex Research*, 1973, *9*, 41–51.

Greene, B. L.; Lee, R. R.; & Lustig, N. Consensus and unconscious factors in marital infidelity. *Medical Aspects of Human Sexuality*, 1974, *8* (9), 87–105.

Greenhouse, H. B. Penile erections during dreams. In R. L. Woods & H. B. Greenhouse (eds.), *The new world of dreams*. New York: Macmillan, 1974.

Griffiths, P. D.; Merry, J.; & Browning, M. Homosexual women: An endocrine and psychological study. *Journal of Endocrinology*, 1974, *63*, 549–556.

Griffitt, W. Response to erotica and the projection of response to erotica in the opposite sex. *Journal of Experimental Research in Personality*, 1973, *6*, 330–338.

Griffitt, W. Sexual experience and sexual respon-

siveness: Sex differences. *Archives of Sexual Behavior*, 1975, *4*, 529–540.

Griffitt, W.; May, J.; & Veitch, R. Sexual stimulation and interpersonal behavior: Heterosexual evaluative responses, visual behavior, and physical proximity. *Journal of Personality and Social Psychology*, 1974, *30*, 367–377.

Grossman, S. P. *A textbook of physiological psychology*. New York: Wiley, 1967.

Groth, A. N., & Burgess, A. W. Sexual dysfunction during rape. *New England Journal of Medicine*, 1977, *297*, 764–766.

Grumbach, M. The neuroendocrinology of puberty. *Hospital Practice*, 1980 (March), 51–60.

Grush, J. E. Attitude formation and mere exposure phenomena: A nonartifactual explanation of empirical findings. *Journal of Personality and Social Psychology*, 1976, *33*, 281–290.

Gurwitz, S. B., & Dodge, K. A. Adults' evaluations of a child as a function of sex of adult and sex of child. *Journal of Personality and Social Psychology*, 1975, *32*, 822–828.

Guttmacher, A. F. How can we best combat illegitimacy? *Medical Aspects of Human Sexuality*, 1969, *3* (3), 48–61.

Guyton, A. C. *Textbook of medical physiology*. 6th ed. Philadelphia: Saunders, 1981.

Hafez, E. S. E., & Schein, M. W. The behaviour of cattle. In E. S. E. Hafez (ed.), *The behaviour of domestic animals*. London: Bailliere, Tindall & Cassell, 1962.

Hageman, M. J. C. Male heterosexual prostitution. Paper presented at a meeting of the American Sociological Association, San Francisco, 1979.

Hahn, S. R., & Paige, K. E. American birth practices: A critical review. In J. E. Parsons (ed.), *The psychobiology of sex differences and sex roles*. New York: Hemisphere, 1980.

Halikas, J. A.; Goodwin, P. H.; & Guze, S. B. Marijuana effects: A survey of regular users. *Journal of the American Medical Association*, 1971, *217*, 692.

Hall, E. T. *The silent language*. New York: Fawcett, 1959.

Hamilton, E. Emotions and sexuality in the woman.

In H. A. Otto (ed.), *The new sexuality*. Palo Alto: Science and Behavior, 1971.

Hamilton, J. B. Demonstrable ability of penile erection in castrated men with markedly low titers of urinary androgen. *Proceedings of the Society for Experimental Biology and Medicine*, 1943, *54*, 309.

Hamilton, J. B.; Walter, R. O.; Daniel, R. M.; & Mestler, G. E. Competition for mating between ordinary and supermale Japanese medaka fish. *Animal Behavior*, 1969, *17*, 168–176.

Hand, J. R. Surgery of the penis and urethra. In M. F. Campbell & J. H. Harrison (eds.), *Urology*, vol. 3. Philadelphia: Saunders, 1970.

Handsfield, H. H. Incidence of asymptomatic gonorrhea. *Medical Aspects of Human Sexuality*, 1974, *8* (10), 111.

Hansell, S.; Sparacino, J.; & Ronchi, D. Physical attractiveness and blood pressure. *Personality and Social Psychology Bulletin*, 1982, *42*, 682–689.

Harbert, T. L.; Barlow, D. H.; Hensen, M.; & Austin, J. B. Measurement and modification of incestuous behavior: A case study. *Psychological Reports*, 1974, *34*, 79–86.

Hardin, G. *Birth control*. New York: Pegasus, 1970.

Hare-Mustin, R. T., & Broderick, P. C. The myth of motherhood: A study of attitudes toward motherhood. *Psychology of Women Quarterly*, 1979, *4* (1), 114–128.

Hariton, E. B. The sexual fantasies of women. *Psychology Today*, 1973, *6*, 39–44.

Harlen, A. *Sexuality and homosexuality: A new view*. New York: W. W. Norton, 1971.

Harlow, H. F. The heterosexual affectional system in monkeys. *American Psychologist*, 1962, *1*, 1–9.

Harlow, H. F., & Harlow, M. K. Social deprivation in monkeys. *Scientific American*, 1962, *207* (5), 136–146.

Harper, R. A. Extramarital sex relations. In A. Ellis & A. Abarbanel (eds.), *The encyclopedia of sexual behavior*, vol. 1. New York: Hawthorne Books, 1961.

Harris, L. ABC News—Harris Survey release. New York, March 6, 1979.

Harris, M. B. Mediators between frustration and aggression in a field experiment. *Journal of Experimental Social Psychology*, 1974, *10*, 561–571.

Harrison, A. A. *Individuals and groups: Understanding social behavior*. Belmont, Calif.: Wadsworth, 1976.

Harrison, A. A., & Saeed, L. Let's make a deal: An analysis of revelations and stipulations in lonely hearts advertisements. *Journal of Personality and Social Psychology*, 1977, *35*, 257–264.

Harrison, B. G. Feminist experiment in education. In J. Stacey; S. Bereaud; & J. Daniels (eds.), *And Jill came tumbling after: Sexism in American education*. New York: Dell, 1974.

Hart, B. L., & Jones, T. O. A. C. Effects of castration on sexual behavior of tropical male goats. *Hormones and Behavior*, 1975, *6*, 247–258.

Hart, G. *Sexual maladjustment and disease: An introduction to modern venereology*. Chicago: Nelson-Hall, 1977.

Hartrampf, C. R., Jr.; Scheflan, M.; & Black, P. W. The transverse abdominal island flap for reconstruction of the breast after mastectomy. *American Journal of Plastic and Reconstructive Surgery*, in press.

Hartup, W. W., & Zook, E. Z. Sex-role preferences in three- and four-year-old children. *Journal of Consulting Psychology*, 1960, *24*, 420–426.

Hass, A. *Teenage sexuality*. New York: Macmillan, 1979.

Hatcher, R. A.; Sewart, G. K.; Guest, F.; Finkelstein, R.; & Godwin, C. *Contraceptive Technology, 1976–1977*. 8th ed. New York: Irvington, 1976.

Hatcher, R. A.; Sewart, G. K.; Stewart, F.; Guest, F.; Stratton, P.; & Wright, A. H. *Contraceptive technology 1978–1979*. 9th ed. New York: Irvington, 1978.

Hatfield, E.; Sprecher, S.; & Traupmann, J. Men's and women's reactions to sexually explicit films: A serendipitous finding. *Archives of Sexual Behavior*, 1978, *7*, 583–592.

Heath, R. G. Pleasure and brain activity in man. *Journal of Nervous and Mental Disease* 1972, *154*, 3–18.

Heider, K. G. Dani sexuality: A low energy system. *Man,* 1976, *11,* 188–201.

Heim, N. Sexual behavior of castrated sex offenders. *Archives of Sexual Behavior,* 1981, *10,* 11–19.

Heiman, J. R. The physiology of erotica: Women's sexual arousal. *Psychology Today,* 1975, *8* (11), 90–94.

Heiman, J. R. A psychophysiological exploration of sexual arousal patterns in females and males. *Psychophysiology,* 1977, *14,* 266–274.

Hellerstein, H. K., & Friedman, E. H. Sexual activity and the postcoronary patient. *Medical Aspects of Human Sexuality,* 1969, *3* (3), 70–74.

Hellerstein, H. K., & Friedman, E. H. Sexual activity and the postcoronary patient. *Archives of Internal Medicine,* 1970, *125,* 987–999.

Helsing, K. J., & Szklo, M. Mortality after bereavement. *American Journal of Epidemiology,* 1981, *114,* 41–52.

Henriques, F. *Prostitution and society,* vol. 1. London: MacGibbon & Kee, 1962.

Hensen, D. E., & Rubin, H. B. Voluntary control of eroticism. *Journal of Applied Behavior Analysis,* 1971, *4,* 37–44.

Herbert, J. Hormones and reproductive behavior in rhesus and talapoin monkeys. *Journal of Reproduction and Fertility,* 1970, *11,* 119–140.

Herman, J., & Hirshman, L. Father-daughter incest. *Signs: Journal of Women in Culture and Society,* 1977, *2,* 735–756.

Herrell, J. M. Sex differences in emotional responses to "erotic literature." *Journal of Consulting and Clinical Psychology,* 1975, *43,* 921.

Herz, L. Predicting contraceptive choice: A joint consideration of an expectancy-value model and concepts from decision-making research. Ph.D. dissertation, Loyola University, Chicago, 1983.

Herz, L. *Young adult women's contraceptive decisions: A comparison of two predictive models of choice.* Ph.D. dissertation, Loyola University, Chicago, 1983.

Hess, E. H. Imprinting in birds. *Science,* 1964, *146,* 1128–1140.

Hess, E. H. Attitude and pupil size. *Scientific American,* 1965, *203* (4), 46–54.

Hess, E. H. Ethology. In A. M. Freeman & H. I. Kaplan (eds.), *Comprehensive textbook of psychiatry.* Baltimore: Williams & Wilkins, 1967.

Hess, E. H.; Seltzer, A. A.; & Schlein, J. M. Pupil responses of hetero- and homosexual males to pictures of men and women: A pilot study. *Journal of Abnormal Psychology,* 1965, *70,* 165–168.

Hilgard, E. R., & Bower, G. H. *Theories of learning.* 4th ed. Englewood Cliffs, N.J.: Prentice-Hall, 1975.

Hill, C.; Rubin, Z.; & Peplau, L. A. Breakups before marriage: The end of 103 affairs. In G. Levinger & O. Males (eds.), *Divorce and separation.* New York: Basic Books, 1979.

Hite, S. *The Hite report.* New York: Macmillan, 1976.

Hite, S. *The Hite report on male sexuality.* New York: A. A. Knopf, 1981.

Hobbs, D. F., & Cole, S. P. Transition to parenthood: A decade replication. *Journal of Marriage and the Family,* 1976, *38,* 723–731.

Hoffman-LaRoche, Inc. Radio-immunoassay for human chorionic gonadotropin for the detection of pregnancy. Nutley, N.J.: Roche Diagnostics, 1981.

Hogbin, H. I. Puberty to marriage: A study of the sexual life of the natives of Wogeo, New Guinea. *Oceania,* 1946, *16,* 185–209.

Hohn, E. O. The phalarope. *Scientific American,* 1969, *220* (6), 105–111.

Holden, C. Sex therapy: Making it as a science and an industry. *Science,* 1974, *186,* 330–334.

Holmes, D. L., & Morrison, F. J. *The child: An introduction to developmental psychology.* Monterey, Calif.: Brooks/Coles, 1979.

Holmstrom, L. L., & Burgess, A. W. *The victim of rape: Institutional reactions.* New York: Wiley, 1978.

Holroyd, J. C., & Brodsky, A. M. Psychologists' attitudes and practices regarding erotic and nonerotic physical contact with patients. *American Psychologist,* 1977, *32,* 843–849.

Hooker, E. The adjustment of the male, overt homosexual. *Journal of Projective Techniques*, 1957, *21*, 18–31.

Hooker, E. An empirical study of some relations between sexual patterns and gender identity in male homosexuals. In J. Money (ed.), *Sex research: New developments*. New York: Holt, 1965.

Horner, M. S. Toward an understanding of achievement-related conflicts in women. *Journal of Social Issues*, 1972, *28*, 157–176.

Hottes, J. H., & Kahn, A. Sex differences in a mixed-motive conflict situation. *Journal of Personality*, 1974, *42*, 260–275.

Howard, J. L.; Reifler, C. B.; & Liptzin, M. B. Effects of exposure to pornography. In *Technical report of the Commission on Obscenity and Pornography*, vol. 8. Washington, D.C.: U.S. Government Printing Office, 1971.

Howard, J. W., & Dawes, R. M. Linear prediction of marital happiness. *Personality and Social Psychology Bulletin*, 1976, *2*, 478–480.

Hraba J., & Grant, G. Black is beautiful: A reexamination of racial preference and identification. *Journal of Personality and Social Psychology*, 1970, *16*, 398–402.

Humphreys, L. *Tearoom trade: Impersonal sex in public places*. Chicago: Aldine, 1970, 1975.

Humphreys, L. Being odd against all odds. In R. C. Federico (ed.), *Sociology*. Reading, Mass.: Addison Wesley, 1979.

Hunt, M. *Sexual behavior in the 1970s*. Chicago: Playboy Press, 1974.

Hunt, M., & Hunt, B. *The divorce experience*. New York: Signet, 1977.

Hupka, R. B. The cultural determinants of jealousy. *Alternative Life Styles*, 1981, *4*, 3.

Hurowitz, L., & Gaier, E. L. Adolescent erotica and female self-concept development. *Adolescence*, 1976, *11*, 497–508.

Husted, J. Desensitization procedures in dealing with women's sexual dysfunction. *The Counseling Psychologist*, 1975, *5*, 30–37.

Huston, T. L. Ambiguity of acceptance, social desirability and dating choice. *Journal of Experimental Social Psychology*, 1973, *9*, 32–42.

Huston, T. L., & Cate, R. M. Social exchange in intimate relationships. In M. Cox & G. Wilson (eds.), *Love and attraction*. Oxford: Pergamon Press, 1979.

Hyde, J. S. *Understanding human sexuality*. New York: McGraw-Hill, 1979.

Hyde, J. S., & Rosenberg, B. G. *The psychology of women: Half the human experience*. Lexington, Mass.: D. C. Heath, 1976.

Hyde, M. O. *Speak out on rape*. New York: McGraw-Hill, 1976.

Immelmann, K. Ecological aspects of periodic reproduction. In Farner, D. S., & King, J. R. (eds.), *Avian Biology*, vol. 1. New York: Academic Press, 1971.

Imms, A. D. *Insect natural history*. 2d ed. London: Collins, 1956.

Imperato-McGinley, J.; Peterson, R. E.; Gautier, T.; & Sturla, E. Androgens and the evolution of male-gender identity among male pseudohermaphrodites with 5a-reductase deficiency. *New England Journal of Medicine*, 1979, *300*, 1233–1237.

Irons, W. The Yomut Turkmen: A study of social organization among a central Asian Turkic-speaking population. Anthropological Papers of the Michigan University Museum of Anthropology, 1975, *58*, 1–193.

Ivey, M. E., & Bardwick, Judith M. Patterns of affective fluctuation in the menstrual cycle. *Psychosomatic Medicine*, 1968, *30*, 336–345.

Jackson, R. Breast-feeding as contraceptive. *Medical Aspects of Human Sexuality*. 1976, *10* (11), 137.

Jacobs, P. A.; Brunton, M.; & Melville, M. M. Aggressive behavior, mental subnormality, and the XYY male. *Nature*, 1965, *208*, 1351–1352.

Jacobson, M., & Beroza, M. Chemical insect attractants. *Science*, 1963, *140*, 1367–1372.

Jaffe, Y.; Malamuth, N.; Feingold, J.; & Feshbach, S. Sexual arousal and behavioral aggression. *Journal of Personality and Social Psychology*, 1974, *30*, 759–764.

James, J. Prostitutes and prostitution. In E. Sagarin & F. Montanino (eds.), *Deviants: Voluntary actors in a hostile world*. Glenview, Ill.: General Learning Press, 1977.

James, J., & Meyerding, J. Early sexual experiences as a factor in prostitution. *Archives of Sexual Behavior*, 1977, *6*, 31–42.

James, W. H. The incidence of spontaneous abortion. *Population Studies*, 1970, *24*, 245.

James, W. H. Marital coital rates, spouses' ages, family size and social class. *Journal of Sex Research*, 1974, *10*, 205–218.

James, W. H. The honeymoon effect on marital coitus. *The Journal of Sex Research*, 1981, *17*, 114–123.

Janda, L. H., & Klenke-Hamel, K. E. *Human sexuality*. New York: Van Nostrand, 1980.

Janda, L. H.; O'Grady, K. E.; Nichelous, J.; Harsher, D.; Denny, C.; & Denner, K. Effects of sex guilt on interpersonal pleasuring. *Journal of Personality and Social Psychology*, 1981, *40*, 201–209.

Jenni, D. A., & Collier, G. Polyandry in the American jacana (*Jacana spinosa*). *Auk*, 1972, *89*, 743–765.

Jensen, G. D. Human behavior in private perspective. In J. Zubin & J. Money (eds.), *Contemporary sexual behavior*. Baltimore: Johns Hopkins Press, 1973.

Jobaris, R., & Money, J. Duration of orgasm. *Medical aspects of human sexuality*. 1976, *10* (7), 7–65.

Joffe, J. M. *Prenatal determinants of behavior*. Oxford: Pergamon Press, 1969.

Johnson, S. A. M. Syphilis of the scalp. *Medical Aspects of Human Sexuality*, 1978, *12* (12), 109.

Johnson, W. Key factors in the sex education of the mentally retarded. Paper presented at the Planned Parenthood Conference, Seattle, 1971.

Jolly, A. *The evolution of primate behavior*. New York: Macmillan, 1972.

Jones, H. B., & Jones, H. C. *Sensual drugs*. New York: Cambridge University Press, 1977.

Jones, I. H., & Frei, D. Provoked anxiety as a treatment of exhibitionism. *British Journal of Psychiatry*, 1977, *131*, 295–300.

Jones, W. H.; Hobbs, S. A.; & Hockenburg, D. Loneliness and social skills deficits. *Journal of Personality and Social Psychology*, 1982, *42*, 682–689.

Jost, A. Hormonal factors in the sex differentiation of the mammalian foetus. *Philosophical Transactions of the Society of London*, Ser. B, 1970, *259*, 119–131.

Kaats, G. R., & Davis, K. E. Effects of volunteer biases in studies of sexual behavior and attitudes. *Journal of Sex Research*, 1971, *7*, 26–34.

Kagan, J. Acquisition and significance of sex typing and sex role identity. In M. L. Hoffman & L. W. Hoffman (eds.), *Review of child development research*, vol. 1. New York: Russell Sage Foundation, 1964.

Kagan, J. *Change and continuity in infancy*. New York: Wiley, 1971.

Kahn, M. Non-verbal communication as a factor in marital satisfaction. *Dissertation Abstracts International*, 1970, *30* (10-B), 4794.

Kanin, E. J., & Parcell, S. R. Sexual aggression: A second look at the offended female. *Archives of Sexual Behavior*, 1977, *6*, 67–76.

Kantner, J. F., & Zelnik, M. Sexual experience of young unmarried women in the United States. *Family Planning Perspectives*, 1972, *4*, 9–18.

Kaplan, H. S. *The new sex therapy*. New York: Bruner/Mazel, 1974.

Kaplan, H. S. *Disorders of sexual desire*. New York: Simon & Schuster, 1979.

Karlen, A. *Sexuality and homosexuality*. New York: Norton, 1971.

Karpman, B. A case of pedophilia (legally rape) cured by psychoanalysis. *Psychoanalytic Review*, 1950, *37*, 235–276.

Katchadourian, H. A., & Lunde, D. T. *Fundamentals of human sexuality*. 3d ed. New York: Holt, Rinehart & Winston, 1980.

Kaufman, I. C., & Rosenblum, L. A. Depression in infant monkeys separated from their mothers. *Science*, 1967, *155*, 1030–1031.

Kegel, A. H. Sexual functions of the pubococcygeus muscle. *Western Journal of Surgery*, 1952, *60*, 521–524.

Keller, J. F.; Eakes, E.; Hinkle, D.; & Hughston, G. A. Sexual behavior and guilt among women: A cross-generational comparison. *Journal of Sex and Marital Therapy*, 1978, *4* (4), 259–265.

Kelley, K. Adolescent sexuality: The first lessons. In D. Byrne & W. A. Fisher (eds.) *Adolescents, sex, and contraception.* New York: McGraw-Hill, 1981.

Kerckhoff, A. C., & Davis, K. E. Value consensus and need complementarity in mate selection. *American Sociological Review*, 1962, *27*, 295–303.

Kessel, E. L. Mating activities of balloon flies. *Systematic Zoology*, 1955, *4*, 97–104.

Kessler, I. I. On the etiology and prevention of cervical cancer. A status report. *Obstetrics & Gynecological Survey*, 1979, *34*, 790–794.

Keverne, E. B. Sexual receptivity and attractiveness in the female rhesus monkey. *Advances in the Study of Behavior*, 1976, *7*, 155–200.

Kiesler, S. B., & Boral, R. L. The search for a romantic partner: The effects of self-esteem and physical attractiveness on romantic behavior. In K. J. Gergen & D. Marlowe (eds.), *Personality and social behavior.* Reading, Mass.: Addison Wesley, 1970.

Kilham, W., & Mann, L. Level of destructive obedience as a function of transmitter and executant roles in the Milgram Obedience Paradigm. *Journal of Personality and Social Psychology*, 1974, *29*, 696–702.

Kinsey, A. C.; Pomeroy, W. B.; & Martin, C. E. *Sexual behavior in the human male.* Philadelphia: Saunders, 1948.

Kinsey, A. C.; Pomeroy, W. B.; Martin, C. E.; & Gebhard, P. H. *Sexual behavior in the human female.* Philadelphia: Saunders, 1953.

Kirkham, G. Homosexuality in prison. In J. Henslin (ed.), *Studies in the sociology of sex.* New York: Appleton, 1971.

Kislack, J. W., & Beach, F. A. Inhibition of aggressiveness by ovarian hormones. *Endocrinology*, 1955, *56*, 684–692.

Klaus, M. H., & Kennell, J. H. *Maternal-infant bonding.* St. Louis: Mosby, 1976.

Kleinke, C. L.; Staneski, R. A.; & Berger, D. E. Evaluation of an interviewer as a function of interviewer gaze, reinforcement of subject gaze, and interviewer attractiveness. *Journal of Personality and Social Psychology*, 1975, *31*, 115–122.

Kleinman, S. Female premarital sexual careers. *Center for Youth Development and Research Quarterly Focus*, 1978 (Winter).

Kleitman, N. *Sleep and wakefulness.* Chicago: University of Chicago Press, 1963.

Klinger, E. *Structure and functions of fantasy.* New York: Wiley, 1971.

Klinghammer, E., & Hess, E. H. Imprinting in an altricial bird: The blond ring dove (*Streptopelia risoria*). *Science*, 1964, *146*, 265–266.

Knight, J. A. False pregnancy in a male. *Psychosomatic Medicine*, 1960, *22*, 260–266.

Knupfer, G.; Clark, W.; & Room, R. The mental health of the unmarried. *American Journal of Psychiatry*, 1966, *122*, 841–851.

Koch, P. B. A comparison of the sex education of primary-age children as expressed in art in Sweden and the United States. Paper presented to the Eastern Regional Meeting of the Society for the Scientific Study of Sex, 1978.

Koff, W. C. Marijuana and sexual activity. *Journal of Sex Research*, 1974, *10* (3), 194–204.

Kolodny, R. C.; Masters, W. H.; Johnson, V. E.; & Biggs, M. A. *Textbook of human sexuality for nurses.* Boston: Little, Brown, 1979.

Kolodny, R. C.; Masters, W. H.; Kolodner, R. M.; & Toro, G. Depression of plasma testosterone levels after chronic intensive marihuana use. *New England Journal of Medicine*, 1974, *290*, 872–874.

Konishi, M., & Nottebohm, F. Experimental studies on the autogeny of avian vocalization. In R. A. Hinde (ed.), *Bird vocalization.* New York: Cambridge University Press, 1969.

Kopera, A. A.; Maier, R. A.; & Johnson, J. E. Perception of physical attractiveness: The influence of group interaction and group coaction on ratings of the attractiveness of photographs of women. *Proceedings of the 79th Annual Convention of the American Psychological Association*, 1971, *6*, 317–318.

Kortlandt, A. Chimpanzees in the wild. *Scientific American*, 1962, *206* (5), 2–10.

Kraemer, D.; Moore, G.; & Kramen, M. Baboon infant produced by embryo transfer. *Science*, 1976, *192*, 1246–1247.

Krafft-Ebing, R. V. *Psychopathia sexualis*. 1886. Reprint ed.: New York: Pioneer, 1939.

Kreuz, L. E.; Rose, R. M.; & Jennings, J. Suppression of plasma testosterone levels and psychological stress. *Archives of General Psychiatry*, 1972, *26*, 479–482.

Kubie, J. L.; Cohen, J.; & Halpern, M. Shedding enhances the sexual attractiveness of oestradiol-treated garter snakes and their untreated penmates. *Animal Behavior*, 1978, *26*, 562–570.

Kubler-Ross, E. *On death and dying*. New York: Macmillan, 1969.

Kurland, M. Pedophilia erotica. *Journal of Nervous and Mental Disorders*, 1960, *131*, 394–403.

Kutner, S. J. Sex guilt and the sexual behavior sequence. *Journal of Sex Research*, 1971, *7*, 107–115.

Kutschinsky, B. The effect of pornography: A pilot experiment on perception, behavior, and attitudes. In *Technical Report of the Commission on Obscenity and Pornography*, vol. 8. Washington, D.C.: U.S. Government Printing Office, 1971.

Lamaze, F. *Painless childbirth*, trans. L. Celestin. Chicago: Regnery, 1970.

Landcaster, J. B. Sex and gender in evolutionary perspective. In H. Katchedourian (ed.), *Sex and its psychosocial derivatives*. Berkeley: University of California Press, 1979.

Lane, F. W. *Kingdom of the octopus*. London: Sheridan House, 1960.

Lanson, L. *From woman to woman*. New York: Knopf, 1975.

LaRocque, M. A., & Cosgrove, M. D. Priapism. *Medical Aspects of Human Sexuality*, 1976, *10* (6), 69–70.

Larsson, K. *Conditioning and sexual behavior in the male albino rat*. Stockholm: Almquist & Wiksell, 1956.

Larsson, K. Sexual activity in senile male rats. *Journal of Gerontology*, 1958, *13*, 136–139.

Lavrakas, P. J. Female preferences for male physiques. *Journal of Research in Personality*, 1975, *9*, 324–334.

Lavrakas, P. J., & Maier, R. A. Differences in human ability to judge veracity from the audio medium. *Journal of Research in Personality*, 1979, *13*, 139–153.

Lazarus, A. A. Psychological causes of impotence. In L. Gross (ed.), *Sexual behavior: Current issues*. Jamaica, N.Y.: Spectrum, 1974.

Leavitt, Fred. *Drugs and behavior*. Philadelphia: Saunders, 1974.

Leboyer, F. *Birth without violence*. New York: A. A. Knopf, 1975.

Lee, J. A typology of styles of loving. *Personality and Social Psychology Bulletin*, 1977, *3*, 173–182.

Lehfeldt, H. Artificial insemination. In A. Ellis & A. Abarbanel (eds.), *The encyclopedia of sexual behavior*, vol. 1. New York: Hawthorne, 1961.

Lehne, G. K. Homophobia among men. In D. S. David & R. Brannon (eds.), *The male sex role*. Reading, Mass.: Addison Wesley, 1976.

Leiblum, S. R. Common male errors in lovemaking. *Medical Aspects of Human Sexuality*, 1978, *12* (12), 71–91.

Leiser, B. M. *Liberty, justice and morals: Contemporary value conflicts*. 2d ed. New York: Macmillan, 1979.

Leitner, L. M., & Cado, S. Personal constructs and homosexual stress. *Journal of Personality and Social Psychology*, 1982, *43*, 869–872.

LeMagnen, J. Les pheromones olfaco sexuals chez le rat blanc. *Archives des Sciences Physiologiques*, 1952, *6*, 295–332.

Lerner, M. J.; Miller, D. T.; & Holmes, J. G. Deserving versus justice: A contemporary dilemma. In L. Berkowitz & E. Walster (eds.), *Advances in experimental social psychology*, vol. 12. New York: Academic Press, 1975.

Lester, D. *Unusual sexual behavior: The standard deviations*. Springfield, Ill.: Charles C Thomas, 1975.

Leventhal, G. S.; Karuza, J., Jr.; & Fry, W. R. Beyond fairness: A theory of allocation preferences. In G. Mikuls (ed.), *Justice and social interaction*. Bern: Huber, 1980.

Levin, Robert J., and Levin, Amy. ''Sexual pleasure: The surprising preferences of 100,000 women.'' *Redbook* (September 1975), 51–58.

Levine, J. B. The feminine routine. *Journal of Communication*, 1976, *26*, 173–175.

Levinger, G. A three-level approach to attraction: Toward an understanding of pair relatedness. In T. L. Huston (ed.), *Foundations of interpersonal attraction*. New York: Academic Press, 1974.

Levi-Strauss, C. *The elementary structures of kinship*. London: Eyre & Spottiswoode, 1969.

Levitt, E. E., & Klassen, A. D. Jr. *Public attitudes toward sexual behaviors: The latest investigation of the institute for sex research*. Bloomington: Indiana University Press, 1973.

Levy, J. Lateralization and its implications for variation in development. In E. Gollin (ed.), *Developmental plasticity: Behavioral aspects of variations in development*. New York: Academic Press, 1981.

Lewis, C. S. *The four loves*. New York: Harcourt, Brace & World, 1960.

Lewis, M., & Kagan, J. Studies in attention. *Merrill-Palmer Quarterly*, 1965, *2*, 95–127.

Lewis, O. *Tepoztlan: Village in Mexico*. New York: Holt, Rinehart & Winston, 1960.

Lewis, R. A.; Spanier, G. B.; Storm, V. L.; LeHecka, C. F. Commitment in married and unmarried cohabitation. *Sociological Focus*, 1977, *10*, 367–374.

Libby, R., & Nass, G. D. Parental views of teenage sexual behavior. *Journal of Sex Research*, 1971, *7*, 226–236.

Linde, R.; Doelle, G.; Alexander, N.; Kirchner, F.; Vale, W.; River, J.; & Rabin, D. Reversible inhibition of testicular steroidogenesis and spermatogenesis by a potent gonadotropin-releasing hormone in normal men. *The New England Journal of Medicine*, 1981, *305*, 663–667.

Lindsay, D. R.; Dunsmore, D. G.; Williams, J. D.; & Syme, G. J. Audience effects on the mating behavior of rams. *Animal Behavior*, 1976, *24*, 818–321.

Lindsay, D. R., & Ellsmore, J. The effect of breed, season and competition on mating behavior of rams. *Australian Journal of Experimental Agriculture and Animal Husbandry*, 1968, *8*, 649–652.

Linner, B., & Litell, R. J. *Sex and society in Sweden*. New York: Random House, 1967.

Lippes, I. J.; Tatum, H. J.; Maulid, D.; & Zielezny, M. A continuation of the study of post-coital IUDs. *Family Planning Perspectives*, 1979, *11*, 195.

Litman, R., & Swearington, C. Bondage and suicide. *Archives of General Psychiatry*, 1972, *27*, 80–85.

Lloyd, J. E. Aggressive mimicry in *Photuris*: Firefly femmes fatales. *Science*, 1965, *149*, 653–654.

Lloyd, J. E. Studies on the flash communication system in *Photuris* fireflies. *Miscellaneous Publications of the Museum of Zoology, University of Michigan*, 1966, *130*, 1–95.

Lobitz, W. C., & LoPiccolo, J. New methods in the treatment of sexual dysfunction. *Journal of Behavior Therapy and Experimental Psychiatry*, 1973, *3*, 265–272.

London, L. S. *Mental therapy: Studies in fifty cases*. New York: Couici-Friede, 1957.

LoPiccolo, J. Direct treatment of sexual dysfunctions. In J. LoPiccolo & L. LoPiccolo (eds.), *Handbook of sex therapy*. New York: Plenum, 1978.

LoPiccolo, J., & Heiman, J. Cultural values and the therapeutic definition of sexual function and dysfunction. *Journal of Social Issues*, 1977, *33* (2), 166–183.

LoPiccolo, L. Low sexual desire. In S. R. Leiblum & L. A. Pervin (eds.), *Principles and practice of sex therapy*. New York: Guilford, 1980.

Lott, A.; Aponte, J.; Lott, B.; & McGinley, W. The effect of delayed reward on the development of positive attitudes toward persons. *Journal of Experimental Social Psychology*, 1969, *5*, 101–113.

Lott, B. Behavioral concordance with sex role ideology related to play areas. *Journal of Personality and Social Psychology*, 1978, *36*, 1087–1100.

Luckey, E. B., & Bain, J. K. Children: A factor in marital satisfaction. *Journal of Marriage & The Family*, 1970, *32*, 43–44.

Lueck, J.; Brewer, J. I.; Aladjem, S.; & Novotny, M.

Observations of an organism found in patients with gestational trophoblastic disease and in patients with toxemia of pregnancy. *American Journal of Obstetrics and Gynecology*, 1983, *145*, 15–26.

Lukianowicz, N. Survey of various aspects of transvestism in the light of our present knowledge. *Journal of Nervous and Mental Disorders*, 1959, *128*, 36–64.

Luria, Z., & Rose, M. D. *Psychology of human sexuality.* New York: Wiley, 1979.

Lutwak-Mann, C. Drugs and the blastocyst. In L. O. Boreus (ed.), *Fetal Pharmacology.* New York: Raven, 1973.

McAdams, D. P. A thematic coding system for the intimacy motive. *Journal of Research in Personality*, 1980, 14, 413–432.

McAdams, D. P. Experiences of intimacy and power: Relationships between social motives and autobiographical memory. *Journal of Personality and Social Psychology*, 1982, *42*, 292–302.

McAdams, D. P., & Constantian, C. A. Intimacy and affiliation motives in daily living: An experience-sampling analysis. *Journal of Personality and Social Psychology*, 1982, *42*, 292–302.

McAdams, D. P., & Powers, J. Themes of intimacy in behavior and thought. *Journal of Personality and Social Psychology*, 1981, *40*, 573–587.

McAdams, D. P., & Vaillant, G. E. Intimacy motivation and psychosocial adjustment: A longitudinal study. *Journal of Personality Assessment*, in press.

McArthur, L. Z., & Resko, B. G. The portrayal of men and women in American television commercials. *Journal of Social Psychology*, 1975, *97*, 209–220.

McCaghy, C. H. Child molesting. *Sexual Behavior*, 1971, *1*, 16–24.

McCaghy, C. H., & Skipper, J. K. Lesbian behavior as an adaptation to the occupation of stripping. *Social Problems*, 1969, *17*, 262–270.

McCary, J. L. *Sexual myths and fallacies.* New York: Van Nostrand Reinhold, 1971.

McCary, J. L. Nymphomania: A case history. *Medical Aspects of Human Sexuality*, 1972, *6* (11), 192–202.

McCary, J. L. *Human sexuality.* 2d ed. Princeton, N.J.: Van Nostrand, 1973.

McCary, S. P. The interrelationship between sex variables and individuals' reported ages and sources of information for learning and experiencing sexual concepts. Ph.D. dissertation, University of Houston, 1976.

McClearn, G. Gene, generality and behavior research. In J. Hirsch (ed.), *Behavior genetic analysis.* New York: McGraw-Hill, 1967.

McClintock, M. K. Menstrual synchrony and suppression. *Nature*, 1971, *229*, 224–245.

Maccoby, E. E., & Jacklin, C. N. *The psychology of sex differences.* Stanford, Calif.: Stanford University Press, 1974.

MacDonald, A., & Games, R. Some characteristics of those who hold positive and negative attitudes towards homosexuals. *Journal of Homosexuality*, 1974, *1*, 9–27.

McDonald, D. F. Peyronie's disease. *Medical Aspects of Human Sexuality*, 1974, *8* (9), 155–171.

MacDonald, J. M. *Rape offenders and their victims.* Springfield, Ill.: Charles C Thomas, 1971.

MacDonald, J. M. *Indecent exposure.* Springfield, Ill.: Charles C Thomas, 1973.

MacDougold, D. Aphrodisiacs and anaphrodisiacs. In A. Ellis and A. Abarbanel (eds.), *The encyclopedia of sexual behavior*, vol. 1. New York: Hawthorne, 1961.

McGlone, J. Sex differences in brain asymmetry: A critical survey. *The Behavioral and Brain Sciences*, 1980, *3*, 215–263.

McGuire, R. J.; Carlisle, J. M.; & Young, B. G. Sexual deviation as conditioned behavior: A hypothesis. *Behavior Research and Therapy*, 1965, *2*, 185–190.

Machotka, P.; Pittman, F. S.; & Flomenhaft, K. Incest as a family affair. *Family Process*, 1967, *6*, 98–116.

McKee, J. P., & Sherriffs, A. C. The differential evaluation of males and females. *Journal of Personality*, 1957, *25*, 356–371.

Mackey, F. G. Sexuality and heart disease. In A.

Comfort (ed.), *Sexual consequences of disability*. Philadelphia: George F. Stickley, 1978.

McKinlay, S. M., & Jeffreys, M. The menopause syndrome. *British Journal of Preventive and Social Medicine*, 1974, *28* (2), 108.

Macklin, E. D. Heterosexual cohabitation among unmarried college students. *The Family Coordinator*, 1972, *21*, 463–472.

Macklin, E. D. Cohabitation in college: Going very steady. *Psychology Today*, 1974, *8* (6), 53–59.

McLane, M.; Krop, H.; & Mehta, J. Psychosexual adjustment and counseling after myocardial infarction. *Annals of Internal Medicine*, 1980, *92*, 514–519.

MacLean, P. D. New findings on brain function and socio-sexual behavior. In J. Zubin & J. Money (eds.), *Contemporary sexual behavior: Critical issues in the 1970s*. Baltimore: Johns Hopkins Press, 1973.

MacLeod, J. The semen quality in relation to male infertility. In C. Joel (ed.), *Fertility disturbances in men and women*. Basel, Switzerland: Karger, 1971.

McMullen, S., & Rosen, R. C. Self-administered masturbation training in the treatment of primary orgasmic dysfunction. *Journal of Consulting and Clinical Psychology*, 1979, *47*, 912–918.

MacNamara, D., & Sagarin, E. *Sex, crime and the law*. New York: The Free Press, 1977.

Mahoney, M. J., & Hobbins, J. C. Fetoscopy and fetal blood sampling. In A. Milunsky (ed.), *Genetic disorders and the fetus*. New York: Plenum, 1980.

Maier, N. R. F., & Thurber, J. A. Accuracy of judgments of deception when an interview is watched, heard, and read. *Personnel Psychology*, 1968, *21*, 23–30.

Maier, R. A., & Ernest, R. C. Sex differences in the perception of touching. *Perceptual and Motor Skills*, 1978, *46*, 577–578.

Maier, R. A., & Fox, V. Forced therapy of probated alcoholics. *Medical Times*, 1958, *86*, 1051–1054.

Maier, R. A., & Lavrakas, P. J. Lying behavior and evaluation of lies. *Perceptual and Motor Skills*, 1976, *42*, 575–581.

Maier, R. A.; Lavrakas, P. J.; Bentley, B.; & Parrella, G. Role of sex identification in perception of a social blunder. *Perceptual and Motor Skills*, 1977, *45*, 933–934.

Maier, R. A., & Lavrakas, P. J. Some personality correlates of attitudes about sports. *International Journal of Sports Psychology*, 1981, *12*, 19–22.

Maier, R. A., & Lavrakas, P. J. Attitudes toward women, personality rigidity, and idealized physique preferences in males. *Sex Roles: A Journal of Research*, in press.

Maier, R. A., & Maier, B. M. *Comparative animal behavior*. Belmont, Calif.: Brooks/Cole, 1970.

Maier, R. A., Jr. The relationship between perceived attractiveness and facial features of premature and full-term infants. Ph.D. thesis, Loyola University, Chicago, 1983.

Makepeace, J. M. Courtship violence among college students. *Family Relations*, 1981, *30*, 97–102.

Makosky, V. P. Fear of success, sex-role orientation of the task, and competitive conditions as variables affecting women's performance in achievement-oriented situations. Paper presented at meeting of the Midwest Psychological Association, Cleveland, 1972.

Malamuth, N. M. Rape fantasies as a function of exposure to violent sexual stimuli. *Archives of Sexual Behavior*, 1981, *10*, 33–47.

Malamuth, N. M.; Feshbach, S.; & Jaffe, Y. Sexual arousal and aggression. *Journal of Social Issues*, 1977, *33*, 110–131.

Malinowski, B. *The sexual life of savages in northwestern Melanesia*. New York: Harcourt, Brace, Jovanovich, 1929.

Mann, J.; Berkowitz, L.; Sidmar, J.; Starr, S.; & West, S. Satiation of the transient stimulating effect of erotic films. *Journal of Personality and Social Psychology*, 1974, *30*, 729–735.

Mantegazza, P. *Sexual relations of mankind* (trans. J. Bruce). New York: Anthropological Press, 1932.

Marks, I. M. Management of sexual disorders. In H. Leitenberg (ed.), *Handbook of behavior modification and behavior therapy*. Englewood Cliffs, N.J.: Prentice-Hall, 1976.

Marks, I.M., & Gelder, M. G. Transvestism and fetishism: Clinical and psychological changes during foradic aversion. *British Journal of Psychiatry,* 1967, *113,* 711–729.

Marmor, J. Homosexuality and sexual orientation disturbances. In B. G. Sadock; H. I. Kaplan; & A. M. Freedman (eds.), *The sexual experience.* Baltimore: Williams & Wilkins, 1976(a).

Marmor, J. Frigidity, dyspareunia, and vaginismus. In B. J. Sadock; H. I. Kaplan; & A. M. Freedman (eds.), *The sexual experience.* Baltimore, Williams & Wilkins, 1976(b).

Marmor, J; Finkle, A. L.; Lazarus, A. A.; Schumacher, S.; Auerbach, A.; Money, J.; & Norris, N. Viewpoints: Why are some orgasms better than others? *Medical Aspects of Human Sexuality,* 1971, *5* (3), 12–23.

Marmor, J., & Green, R. Homosexual behavior. In J. Money & H. Musaph, *Handbook of sexology.* New York: Elsevier North-Holland, 1977.

Marsden, H., & Bronson, F. Estrus synchrony in mice: Alteration by exposure to male urine. *Science,* 1964, *144,* 1469.

Marshall, A. J. *Bower-birds.* London: Oxford University Press, 1954.

Marshall, D. S. Sexual behavior on Mangaia. In D. S. Marshall & R. C. Suggs (eds.), *Human sexual behavior.* Englewood Cliffs, N.J.: Prentice-Hall, 1971.

Marshall, J., & Row, B. Psychological aspects of the basal body temperature method of regulating births. *Fertility and Sterility,* 1970, *21,* 14–19.

Marshall, P.; Surridge, D.; & Delva, N. The role of nocturnal penile tumescence in differentiating between organic and psychogenic impotence: The first stage of validation. *Archives of Sexual Behavior,* 1981, *10,* 1–10.

Marshall, W. L. The modification of sexual fantasies: A combined treatment approach to the reduction of deviant sexual behavior. *Behavior Research and Therapy,* 1973, *11,* 557–564.

Martinson, F. M. *Infant and child sexuality: A sociological perspective.* St. Peter, Minn.: Book Mark, 1973.

Martinson, F. M. Childhood sexuality. In B. B. Wolman & J. Money (eds.), *Handbook of human sexuality.* Englewood Cliffs, N.J.: Prentice-Hall, 1980.

Maslow, A. H. A theory of metamotivation: The biological rooting of value life. *Journal of Humanistic Psychology,* 1967, *7,* 93–127.

Maslow, A. H. *Toward a psychology of being.* 2d ed. Princeton, N.J.: Van Nostrand, 1968.

Masters, W. H., & Johnson, V. E. *Human sexual response.* Boston: Little, Brown, 1966.

Masters, W. H., & Johnson, V. E. *Human sexual inadequacy.* Boston: Little, Brown, 1970.

Masters, W. H., & Johnson, V. E. *Homosexuality in perspective.* Boston: Little, Brown, 1979.

Masur, F. T. Resuming sexual activity following myocardial infarction. *Sexuality and disability,* 1979, *2,* 98–114.

May, J. M. The psychology of why customers tip. *Institutions,* 1979, *33* (10), 33–34.

Mazur, T., & Money, J. Prenatal influences and subsequent sexuality. In B. B. Wolman & J. Money (eds.), *Handbook of human sexuality.* Englewood Cliffs, N.J.: Prentice-Hall, 1980.

Mead, B. T.; Zeller, W. W.; English, O. S.; Suarez, J. M.; & Cuber, J. F. Viewpoints: What impact does adultery generally have on a marriage? *Medical Aspects of Human Sexuality,* 1975, *9* (10), 122–142.

Mead, M. *Coming of age in Samoa.* New York: Morrow, 1929.

Mead, M. *Sex and temperament in three primitive societies.* New York: Mentor Books, 1950.

Mead, M. *Male and female.* New York: Mentor Books, 1955.

Medea, A., & Thompson, K. *Against rape.* New York: Farrar, Straus, and Giroux, 1974.

Mehrabian, A. Inference of attitudes from the posture, orientation, and distance of a communicator. *Journal of Consulting and Clinical Psychology,* 1968, *32,* 296–318.

Mehrabian, A. *Silent messages.* Belmont, Calif.: Wadsworth, 1971.

Mehrabian, A., & Ksionzky, S. *A theory of affiliation.* Lexington, Mass.: D. C. Heath, 1974.

Mellen, S. L. W. *The evolution of love.* Oxford: W. H. Freeman, 1981.

Merriam, A. P. Aspects of sexual behavior among the Bala (Basongye). In D. S. Marshall & R. C. Suggs (eds.), *Human sexual behavior: Varia-*

tions in the ethnographic spectrum. New York: Basic Books, 1971.

Messinger, J. C. Sex and repression in an Irish folk community. In D. S. Marshall & R. C. Suggs (eds.), *Human sexual behavior.* Englewood Cliffs, N.J.: Prentice-Hall, 1971.

Mettee, D., & Wilkins, P. When similarity "hurts": Effects of perceived ability and a humorous blunder on interpersonal attractiveness. *Journal of Personality and Social Psychology,* 1972, *22,* 246–258.

Meyer, A. W. *The rise of embryology.* Stanford, Calif.: Stanford University Press, 1939.

Meyer, J. K., & Reter, D. J. Sex reassignment: Follow-up. *Archives of General Psychiatry,* 1979, *36,* 1010–1015.

Meyer, T. P. The effects of sexually arousing and violent films on aggressive behavior. *Journal of Sex Research,* 1972, *8,* 324–333.

Michael, R. P.; Herbert, J.; & Welegalla, J. Ovarian hormones and the sexual behavior of the male rhesus monkey (*Macaca mulatta*). *Journal of Endocrinology,* 1967, *39,* 81–93.

Michael, R. P.; Keverne, E. B.; & Bonsall, R. W. Pheromones: Isolation of male sex attractants from a female primate. *Science,* 1971, *172,* 964–966.

Michael, R. P.; Setchell, K. D. R.; & Plant, T. M. Diurnal changes in plasma testosterone and studies on plasma corticosteroids in nonanaesthetized male rhesus monkeys (*Macaca mulatta*). *Journal of Endocrinology,* 1974, *63,* 325–335.

Michael, R. P.; Wilson, M.; & Plant, T. M. Sexual behavior of male primates and the role of testosterone. In R. P. Michael & J. H. Crook (eds.), *Comparative ecology and behavior of primates.* London: Academic Press, 1973.

Michelmore, S. *Sexual reproduction.* New York: Natural History Press, 1965.

Middlebrook, P. N. *Social psychology and modern life.* New York: A. A. Knopf, 1974.

Miller, C.; Byrne, D.; & Fisher, J. D. Preliminary scaling of 40 erotic slides for sexual arousal and disgust. Unpublished manuscript, Purdue University, 1976.

Miller, P. Y., & Simon, W. Adolescent sexual behavior: Context and change. *Social Problems,* 1974, *22,* 58–75.

Miller, W. R., & Lief, H. I. Masturbatory attitudes, knowledge, and experience: Data from the sex knowledge and attitude test (SKAT). *Archives of Sexual Behavior,* 1976, *5,* 447–467.

Millett, K. *Sexual politics.* Garden City, N.Y.: Doubleday, 1970.

Mitchell, J. *Psychoanalysis and feminism.* New York: Pantheon, 1974.

Mitchell, L.; Doctor, R. M.; & Butler, D. C. Attitudes of caretakers toward the sexual behavior of mentally retarded persons. *American Journal of Mental Deficiency,* 1978, *83,* 289–296.

Mobley, D. F. Relation of sexual habits to prostatitis. *Medical Aspects of Human Sexuality,* 1975, *8,* 75.

Mochi, U., & MacClintock, D. *A natural history of giraffes.* New York: Charles Scribner's Sons, 1973.

Moghissi, K. S. Accuracy of basal body temperature for ovulation detection. *Fertility and Sterility,* 1976, *27,* 1415–1421.

Mohr, J. W.; Turner, R. E.; & Ball, R. B. Exhibitionism and pedophilia. *Correct Psychiatry,* 1962, *8,* 172–186.

Money, J. Phantom orgasm in the dreams of paraplegic men and women. *Archives of General Psychiatry,* 1960, *3,* 373–382.

Money, J. Clitoral size and erotic sensation. *Medical Aspects of Human Sexuality,* 1970, 4, 95.

Money, J. Prefatory remarks on outcome of sex reassignment in 24 cases of transsexualism. *Archives of Sexual Behavior,* 1971, *1,* 163–165.

Money, J. Human behavior cytogenetics: Review of psychopathology in three syndromes—47, XXY, 47, XYY, and 45, X. *Journal of Sex Research,* 1975, *11,* 181–200.

Money, J. *Love and love sickness.* Johns Hopkins Press, 1980.

Money, J.; Clarke, F.; & Mazur, T. Families of seven male-to-female transsexuals after 5–7 years: Sociological sexology. *Archives of Sexual Behavior,* 1975, *4,* 187–197.

Money, J., & Ehrhardt, A. A. *Man and woman, boy and girl.* Baltimore: Johns Hopkins Press, 1972.

Morales, A.; Surridge, D. H. C.; Marshall, P. G.; & Fenemore, J. Nonhormonal pharmacological treatment of organic impotence. *Journal of Urology*, in press.

Morris, D. *The naked ape.* New York: McGraw-Hill, 1967.

Morris, J. *Living with lepchas.* London: William Heinemann, 1938.

Mosher, D. L. Measurement of guilt in females by self-report inventories. *Journal of Consulting and Clinical Psychology*, 1968, *32*, 690–695.

Mosher, D. L., & Cross, H. J. Sex guilt and premarital sexual experiences of college students. *Journal of Consulting and Clinical Psychology*, 1971, *36*, 27–32.

Mosher, D. L., & White, B. B. Effects of committed or casual guided imagery on females' subjective sexual arousal and emotional response. *The Journal of Sex Research*, 1980, *16*, 273–299.

Moss, H. A. Early sex differences and mother-infant interaction. In R. C. Friedman; R. M. Richart; & R. L. Vande Wiele (eds.), *Sex differences in behavior.* New York: Wiley, 1974.

Mottebohm, F. Ontogeny of bird song. *Science*, 1970, *167*, 950–956.

Moulton, J.; Robinson, G. M.; & Elins, C. Psychology in action: Sex bias in language use: "Neutral" pronouns that aren't. *American Psychologist*, 1978, *33* (11), 1032–1036.

Mozes, E. B. The technique of wooing. *Sexology*, 1959, 756–760.

Mulvill, D. J. Crimes of violence: A staff report to the National Commission on the Causes and Prevention of Violence. Washington, D.C.: U.S. Government Printing Office, 1969.

Munjack, D. J., & Kanno, P. H. Retarded ejaculation: A review. *Archives of Sexual Behavior*, 1979, *8*, 139–144.

Munjack, D. J., & Oziel, L. J. *Sexual medicine and counseling in office practice.* Boston: Little, Brown, 1980.

Murdock, G. P. *Social structure.* New York: The Free Press, 1949.

Murdock, G. P. *Ethnographic atlas.* Pittsburgh: University of Pittsburgh Press, 1967.

Murdock, G. P., & Provost, C. Factors in the division of labor by sex: A cross-cultural analysis. *Ethnology*, 1973, *12*, 203–225.

Murray, F. S., & Beran, L. C. A survey of nuisance calls received by males and females. *Psychological Record*, 1968, *18*, 107–109.

Murray, H. A. *The thematic apperception test: Manual.* Cambridge: Harvard University Press, 1943.

Murstein, B. A theory of marital choice and its applicability to marriage adjustment. In B. Murstein (ed.), *Theories of attraction and love.* New York: Springer, 1971.

Murstein, B. Physical attractiveness and marital choice. *Journal of Personality and Social Psychology*, 1972, *22*, 8–12.

Mussen, P. H., & Jones, M. C. The behavior-inferred motivations of late- and early-maturing boys. *Child Development*, 1958, *29*, 61–67.

Nadler, A.; Shapiro, R.; & Itzhak, S. Good looks may help: Effects of helper's physical attractiveness and sex of helper on males' and females' help-seeking behavior. *Journal of Personality and Social Psychology*, 1982, *42*, 90–99.

Nadler, R. P. Approach to the psychology of obscene phone calls. *New York State Journal of Medicine*, 1968, *68*, 521–526.

Naeye, R. L. Coitus and associated amniotic-fluid infections. *New England Journal of Medicine*, 1979, *301*, 1198–1200.

Napolitani, C., & Pellegrino, V. *Living and loving.* New York: Rawson Association, 1977.

Nass, G. D.; Libby, R. W.; & Fisher, M. P. *Sexual choices: An introduction to human sexuality.* Monterey, Calif.: Wadsworth, 1981.

Neel, J. V. Lessons from a "primitive" people. *Science*, 1970, *170*, 3960.

Nelson, J. B. *Embodiment: An approach to sexuality and Christian theology.* Minneapolis: Augsburg, 1978.

Netter, F. H. *Reproductive system.* Summit, N.J.: CIBA Pharmaceutical Products, 1961.

Neubardt, S. Anal coitus. In H. J. Lief (ed.), *Medical aspects of human sexuality.* Baltimore: Williams & Wilkins, 1975.

Newcomer, V. D. Scabies. *Medical Aspects of Human Sexuality*, 1976, *10* (6), 67–68.

Newsom, J., & Newsom, E. *Four years old in an urban community*. London: George Allen and Unwin, 1968.

Newth, D. R. Embryology and development, animal. *Encyclopaedia Britannica*, 1973.

Newton, N. Interrelationships between sexual responsiveness, birth, and breast feeding. In J. Zubin & J. Money (eds.), *Contemporary sexual behavior: Critical issues in the 1970s*. Baltimore: Johns Hopkins Press, 1973.

Nguyen, T.; Heslin, R.; & Nguyen, M. L. The meaning of touch: Sex differences. *Journal of Communication*, 1975, *25*, 92–103.

Noller, P. Gender and marital adjustment level differences in decoding messages from spouses and strangers. *Journal of Personality and Social Psychology*, 1981, *41*, 272–278.

Noss, J. B. *Man's religions*. 3d ed. New York: Macmillan, 1963.

Novak, E. R.; Jones, G. S.; & Jones, H. W. *Novak's textbook of gynecology*. 9th ed. Baltimore: Williams & Wilkins, 1975.

Noyes, R. W. Perspectives in human fertility. In M. Diamond (ed.), *Perspectives in reproduction and sexual behavior*. Bloomington: University of Indiana Press, 1968.

Nyberg, K. L., & Alston, J. P. Analysis of public attitudes toward homosexual behavior. *Journal of Homosexuality*, 1976, *2* (2), 99–107.

Offir, C. Don't take it lying down. *Psychology Today*, 1975, *8* (1), 73.

Offit, A. *The sexual self*. New York: Ballantine, 1977.

Olds, J. Pleasure centers in the brain. *Scientific American*, 1956, *195* (4), 105–117.

Olds, J. Self-stimulation of the brain. *Science*, 1958, *127*, 315–323.

Oliven, J. F. *Clinical sexuality*. Philadelphia: J. B. Lippincott, 1974.

Ommanney, F. D., & the editors of Time-Life Books. *The fishes*. New York: Time, 1963.

O'Neill, N., & O'Neill, G. *Open marriage*. New York: Avon, 1972.

Ovid. *The art of love*. New York: Grosset & Dunlap, 1959.

Packer, H. L. *The limits of the criminal sanction*. Stanford, Calif.: Stanford University Press, 1968.

Paige, K. E. Effects of oral contraceptives on affective fluctuations associated with the menstrual cycle. *Psychosomatic Medicine*, 1971, *33*, 515–537.

Paige, K. E. Women learn to sing the menstrual blues. *Psychology Today*, 1973, *7* (4), 41.

Paige, K. E. The declining taboo against menstrual sex. *Psychology Today*, 1978, *12* (7), 50–51.

Palson, C., & Palson, R. Swinging in wedlock. *Society*, 1972, *9*, 43–48.

Parker, G. A.; Baker, R. R.; & Smith, V. G. F. The origin and evolution of gamete dimorphism and the male-female phenomenon. *Journal of Theoretical Biology*, 1972, *36*, 529–553.

Parkes, A. S., & Bruce, H. J. Olfactory stimuli in mammalian reproduction. *Science*, 1961, *134*, 1049–1054.

Pauly, I. B. Male psychosexual inversion. *Archives of General Psychiatry*, 1965, *13*, 172–179.

Pauly, I. B. Female transsexualism: Part I. *Archives of Sexual Behavior*, 1974, *3*, 487–508. (a)

Pauly, I. B. Female transsexualism: Part II. *Archives of Sexual Behavior*, 1974, *3*, 509–526. (b)

Payne, R. S., & McVay, S. 1971 songs of humpback whales. *Science*, 1971, *173*, 583–597.

Penfield, W., & Rasmussen, T. *The cerebral cortex of man*. New York: Macmillan, 1950.

Pepelko, W., & Clegg, M. Studies of mating behavior and some factors influencing the sexual response in the male sheep, *Ovis aries*. *Animal Behavior*, 1965, *13*, 249–259.

Peplau, L. A. What homosexuals want. *Psychology Today*, 1981, *14* (3), 28–38.

Peplau, L. A.; Rubin, Z.; & Hill, C. T. Sexual intimacy in dating relationships. *Journal of Social Issues*, 1977, *33* (2), 86–109.

Perry, J., & Whipple, B. Diagnostic, therapeutic and research applications of the vaginal myograph. Paper presented at the meeting of the American

Association of Sex Educators, Counselors, and Therapists, Washington, D.C., 1980.

Perry, J., & Whipple, B. Pelvic muscle strength of female ejaculations: Evidence in support of a new theory of orgasm. *The Journal of Sex Research,* 1981, *17,* 22–39.

Peters, R. *Mammalian communication: A behavioral analysis of meaning.* Monterey, Calif.: Brooks/Cole, 1980.

Peterson, K., & Curran, J. P. Trait attribution as a function of hair length and correlates of subjects' preferences for hair style. *Journal of Psychology,* 1976, *93,* 331–339.

Pfeiffer, E., & Davis, G. C. Determinants of sexual behavior in middle and old age. *Journal of the American Geriatric Society,* 1972, *20,* 151–158.

Pfeiffer, E., Verwoerdt, A., & Wang, H. Sexual behavior in aged men and women: I. Observations on 254 community volunteers. *Archives of General Psychiatry,* 1968, *19,* 753–758.

Pheterson, G. I.; Kiesler, S. B.; & Goldberg, P. A. Evaluation of the performance of women as a function of their sex, achievement, and personal history. *Journal of Personality and Social Psychology,* 1971, *19,* 114–118.

Phoenix, C. H.; Goy, R. W.; Gerall, A. A.; & Young, W. C. Organizing action of prenatally administered testosterone proprionate on the tissue mediating behavior in the female guinea pig. *Endocrinology,* 1959, *65,* 369–382.

Piemme, T. E. Factors contributing to VD epidemic. *Medical Aspects of Human Sexuality,* 1974, *8* (8), 117.

Pierce, J., & Nuttall, R. Self-paced sexual behavior in the female rat. *Journal of Comparative and Physiological Psychology,* 1961, *54,* 310–313.

Piotrow, P. T.; Rinehart, W.; & Schmidt, J. C. IUDs—Update on safety, effectiveness, and research. Population Reports, 1979, series B, no. 3.

Ploog, D. W.; Blitz, J.; & Ploog, F. Studies on the social and sexual behavior of the squirrel monkey (*Samiri sciureus*). *Folia Primatology,* 1963, *1,* 29–66.

Pocs, A., & Godow, A. G. The shock of recognizing parents as sexual beings. In D. Byrne & L. A. Byrne (eds.), *Exploring human sexuality.* New York: Crowell, 1977.

Polatin, P., & Douglas, D. B. Spontaneous orgasm in a case of schizophrenia. *Psychoanalytic Review,* 1953, *40,* 17–26.

Pomeroy, W. B. Human sexual behavior. In N. L. Farberow (ed.), *Taboo topics.* New York: Atherton, 1963.

Pomeroy, W. B. *Doctor Kinsey and the Institute for Sex Research.* New Haven, Conn.: Yale University Press, 1972.

Ponse, B. *Identities in the lesbian world: The social construction of self.* Westport, Conn.: Greenwood Press, 1978.

Popper, A., & Fay, R. Sound detection and processing by teleost fishes: A critical review. *Journal of the Acoustical Society of America,* 1973, *53,* 1515–1529.

Posavac, E. Dimensions of trait preferences and personality type. *Journal of Personality and Social Psychology,* 1971, *19,* 274–281.

Potts, M.; Clair, B.; van der Vlugt, T.; Piotrow, P. T.; Gail, L. J.; & Huber, S. C. Advantages of orals outweigh disadvantages. *Population Reports,* 1975, series A (2), 29–51.

Price, J. H. Update: Toxic shock syndrome. *The Journal of School Health,* 1981, *51* (3), 143–145.

Prince, V., & Bentler, P. M. Survey of 504 cases of transvestism. *Psychological Reports,* 1972, *31,* 903–917.

Pulaski, M. A. S. The rich rewards of make believe. *Psychology Today,* 1974, *7* (8), 68–74.

Queen, S. A., & Habenstein, R. W. *The family in various cultures.* Philadelphia: J. B. Lippincott, 1974.

Quinn, J. T.; Harbinson, J. J.; & McAllister, H. An attempt to shape penile response. *Behavior Research and Therapy,* 1970, *8,* 212–216.

Rabb, G. B., & Rabb, M. S. Observations on breeding development of the Surinam toad, *Pipa pipa. Copeia,* 1960, *4,* 636–642.

Raboch, J.; Mellan, J.; & Starka, L. Klinefelter's syndrome: Sexual development and activity. *Archives of Sexual Behavior,* 1979, *8,* 333–339.

Raboch, J., & Starka, L. Coital activity of men and the levels of plasmatic testosterone. *Journal of Sex Research,* 1972, *8,* 219–224.

Rachman, S. Sexual fetishism: An experimental analogue. *Psychological Record,* 1966, *16,* 293–296.

Rainwater, L. *Family design: Marital sexuality, family size and contraception.* Chicago: Aldine, 1965.

Ramey, J. *Intimate friendships.* Englewood Cliffs, N.J.: Prentice-Hall, 1976.

Rawson, P. *Primitive erotic art.* London: Weidenfeld and Nicolson, 1973.

Reeder, S. R.; Mastroianni, L.; Martin, L. L.; & Fitzpatrick, E. *Maternity nursing.* 15th ed. Philadelphia: J. B. Lippincott, 1983.

Reedy, M. N. What happens to love? Love, sexuality and aging. In R. L. Solnick (ed.), *Sexuality and aging.* 2d ed. Los Angeles: University of Southern California Press, 1978.

Reik, T. *A psychologist looks at love.* New York: Rinehart, 1944.

Reiss, A. J. The social integration of queers and peers. *Social Problems,* 1961, *9,* 102–120.

Reiss, I. L. *Premarital sexual standards in America.* New York: The Free Press, 1960.

Reiss, I. L. The sexual renaissance in America. *Journal of Social Issues,* 1966, *2,* 1–140.

Reiss, I. L. Heterosexual relationships. In R. Green (ed.), *Human sexuality: A health practitioner's text.* Baltimore: Williams & Wilkins, 1974.

Renshaw, D. C. Impotence in diabetics. *Diseases of the Nervous System,* 1975, *36* (7), 369–371.

Renshaw, D. C. The symptoms of insomnia. *Continuing Education,* 1976, *2,* 103–112.

Resko, J. A., & Phoenix, C. H. Sexual behavior and testosterone concentrations in the plasma of the rhesus monkey before and after castration. *Endocrinology,* 1972, *91,* 499–503.

Resnick, J. Eroticized repetitive hangings. *American Journal of Psychotherapy,* 1972, *26,* 4–21.

Reuben, D. *Everything you always wanted to know about sex.* New York: David McKay, 1969.

Rice, B. Rx: Sex for senior citizens. *Psychology Today,* 1974, *8* (1), 18–20.

Rich, A. *Of woman born.* New York: Norton, 1976.

Riger, S.; LeBailly, R. K.; & Gordon, M. T. Community ties and urbanites' fear of crime: An ecological investigation. *American Journal of Community Psychology,* in press.

Rimm, D., & Somerville, J. W. *Abnormal psychology.* New York: Academic Press, 1977.

Rinehart, W., & Piotrow, P. T. OCs—Update on usage, safety, and side effects. *Population Reports,* 1979, series A (5), 134–186.

Robbins, M. B., & Jensen, G. D. Multiple orgasms in males. In R. Gemme & C. Wheeler (eds.), *Progress in sexology.* New York: Plenum, 1977.

Roberts, D. F. Incest, inbreeding, and mental abilities. *British Medical Journal,* 1967, *4,* 336–337.

Roberts, E. J.; Kline, D.; & Gagnon, J. *Family life and sexual learning.* Cambridge, Mass.: Population Education, 1978.

Robertson, D. R. Social control of sex reversal in a coral-reef fish. *Science,* 1972, *177,* 1007–1009.

Roebuck, J., & Spray, S. L. The cocktail lounge: A study of heterosexual relations in a public organization. *American Journal of Sociology,* 1967, *72,* 388–395.

Roeder, K. D. An experimental analysis of the sexual beh vior of the praying mantis. *Biological Bulletin,* 1935, *69,* 203–220.

Rogel, M. J. A critical evaluation of the possibility of higher primate reproductive and sexual pheromones. *Psychological Bulletin,* 1978, *85,* 810–830.

Rogers, C. R. *Client-centered therapy: Its current practice, implications and theory.* Boston: Houghton Mifflin, 1951.

Rollins, B., & Feldman, H. Marital satisfaction through the life span. *Journal of Marriage and the Family,* 1970, *32,* 20–27.

Rosaldo, M. Z. Woman, culture, and society: A theoretical overview. In M. Z. Rosaldo & L. Lamphere (eds.), *Woman, culture and society.* Stanford, Calif.: Stanford University Press, 1974.

Rose, R. M. Testosterone, aggression, and homosexuality: A review of the literature and implications for future research. In E. J. Sachar (ed.), *Topics in psychoendocrinology.* New York: Grune and Stratton, 1975.

Rosebury, T. *Microbes and morals: The strange story of venereal disease.* New York: Viking Press, 1971.

Rosen, D. H. *Lesbianism: A study of female homosexuality.* Springfield, Ill.: Charles C Thomas, 1974.

Rosenbaum, S. Pretended orgasm. *Medical Aspects of Human Sexuality,* 1970, *4* (6), 84–96.

Rosenthal, R.; Archer, D.; DiMatteo, M. R.; Koivwmaki, J. M.; & Rogers, P. L. Body talk and tone of voice: The language without words. *Psychology Today,* 1974, *7* (9), 64–68.

Rossi, A. S. The biosocial side of parenthood. *Human Nature,* 1978, *1,* 72–79.

Rossman, P. The pederasts. *Society,* 1973, *29,* 22–24.

Roszak, T. *The making of a counter-culture.* Garden City, N.Y.: Doubleday, 1969.

Rowland, K. F., & Haynes, S. N. A sexual enhancement program for elderly couples. *Journal of Sex and Marital Therapy,* 1978, *4,* Summer issue.

Roy, D. Sex in the factory: Informal heterosexual relations between supervisors and work groups. In C. D. Bryant (ed.), *Deviant behavior: Occupational and organizational bases.* Skokie, Ill.: Rand McNally, 1974.

Rubenstein, J. S.; Watson, F. G.; Drolette, M. E.; & Rubenstein, H. S. Young adolescents' sexual interests. *Adolescence,* 1976, *9,* 487–496.

Rubin, E.; Lieber, C. S.; Altman, K.; Gordon, G. G.; & Southren, A. L. Prolonged ethanol consumption increases testosterone metabolism in the liver. *Science,* 1976, *191,* 563–564.

Rubin, I. *Sexual life after sixty.* New York: London, 1965.

Rubin, L. B. *Worlds of pain: Life in the working-class family.* New York: Basic Books, 1976.

Rubin, Z. Measurement of romantic love. *Journal of Personality and Social Psychology,* 1970, *16,* 265–273.

Rubin, Z. *Liking and loving: An invitation to social psychology.* New York: Holt, Rinehart, & Winston, 1973.

Rubin, Z. From liking to loving: Patterns of attraction in dating relationships. In T. L. Huston (ed.), *Foundations of interpersonal attraction.* New York: Academic Press, 1974.

Rugoff, M. *Prudery and passion.* New York: Putnam, 1971.

Russell, C. S. Transition to parenthood: Problems and gratifications. *Journal of Marriage and the Family,* 1974, *36,* 294–301.

Russell, D. *The politics of rape: The victim's perspective.* New York: Stein & Day, 1975.

Russell, M. J.; Switz, G. M.; & Thompson, K. Olfactory influences in the human menstrual cycle. Paper presented at the meeting of the American Association for the Advancement of Science, San Francisco, 1978.

Sade, D. S. Inhibition of son-mother mating among free-ranging rhesus monkeys. *Science and Psychoanalysis,* 1968, *12,* 18–37.

Sadock, B. J., & Spitz, H. J. Group psychotherapy of sexual disorders. In B. J. Sadock, H. I. Kaplan, & A. M. Freedman (eds.), *The sexual experience.* Baltimore: Williams & Wilkins, 1976.

Sadoff, R. L. Sex and the law. In B. J. Sadock, H. I. Kaplan, & A. M. Freedman (eds.), *The sexual experience.* Baltimore: Williams & Wilkins, 1976.

Sagarin, E. Power to the peephole. *Sexual Behavior,* 1973, *3,* 2–7.

Saghir, M.; Robins, E.; & Walbran, B. Homosexuality. *Archives of General Psychiatry,* 1969, *21,* 219–229.

Salmon, U. J., & Geist, S. H. Effects of androgens upon libido in women. *Journal of Clinical Endocrinology and Metabolism,* 1943, *3,* 235–238.

Sanford, F. H. *Psychology: A scientific study of man.* 2d ed. Belmont, Calif.: Wadsworth, 1965.

Sanger, M. *Margaret Sanger: An autobiography.* New York: W. W. Norton, 1938.

Sarrel, P., & Masters, W. H. Sexual molestation of men by women. *Archives of Sexual Behavior,* 1982, *11,* 117–131.

Sarrel, P., & Sarrel, L. The Redbook report on sexual relationships. *Redbook*, 1980, *155* (6), 73–80.

Savicki, V. Outcomes of nonreciprocal self-disclosure strategies. *Journal of Personality and Social Psychology*, 1972, *23*, 271–276.

Savory, T. Courtship behavior of arachnids. *Natural History*, 1965, *74* (5), 52–56.

Saxton, P. *The feminized male*. New York: Random House, 1970.

Schaller, G. B. *The mountain gorilla: Ecology and behavior*. Chicago: University of Chicago Press, 1963.

Schein, M. W. The physical environment and behavior. In E. S. E. Hafez (ed.), *The behavior of domestic animals*. Baltimore: Williams & Wilkins, 1965.

Schmidt, G., & Sigusch, V. Sex differences in response to psychosexual stimulation by films and slides. *Journal of Sex Research*, 1970, *6*, 268–283.

Schmidt, G., & Sigusch, V. Patterns of sexual behavior in West German workers and students. *Journal of Sex Research*, 1971, *7*, 89–106.

Schoedel, J.; Frederickson, W. A.; & Knight, J. M. An extrapolation of the physical attractiveness and sex variables within the Byrne attraction paradigm. *Memory and Cognition*, 1975, *3*, 527–530.

Schoettle, H. E. T., & Schein, M. W. Sexual reactions of male turkeys to deviations from a normal female head model. *Anatomical Record*, 1959, *134*, 635 (abstract).

Schofield, C. B. *Sexually transmitted diseases*. New York: Churchill Livingstone, 1979.

Schofield, M. *The sexual behavior of young adults*. Boston: Little, Brown, 1973.

Schon, M., & Sutherland, A. M. The role of hormones in human behavior: III. Changes in female sexuality after hypophysectomy. *Journal of Clinical Endocrinology and Metabolism*, 1960, *20*, 833–841.

Schoof-Tams, K.; Schlaegel, J.; & Walczak, L. Differentiation of sexual morality between 11 and 16 years. *Archives of Sexual Behavior*, 1976, *5*, 353–370.

Schram, D. D. Rape. In J. R. Chapman & M. Gages (eds.), *Victimization of women*. Beverly Hills, Calif.: Sage, 1978.

Schreiner, L., & Kling, A. Behavioral changes following rhinencephalic injury in cat. *Journal of Neurophysiology*, 1953, *16*, 643–659.

Schull, W. J., & Neel, J. V. *The effects of inbreeding on Japanese children*. New York: Harper & Row, 1965.

Schultz, D. A. *Human sexuality*. Englewood Cliffs, N.J.: Prentice-Hall, 1979.

Schwartz, M. F., & Bauman, J. E. Hyperprolactinemia and sexual dysfunction in men. Paper presented at the annual meeting of the Society for Sex Therapy and Research, New York, 1981.

Schwartzkopff, J. Auditory communication in lower animals: Role of auditory physiology. *Annual Review of Psychology*, 1977, *28*, 61–84.

Scott, F. B.; Fishman, I. J.; & Light, J. K. An inflatable penile prosthesis for treatment of diabetic impotence. *Annals of Internal Medicine*, 1980, *92*, 340–342.

Seaman, B., & Seaman, G. *Women and the crisis in sex hormones*. New York: Bantam, 1978.

Seavey, C. A.: Katz, P. A.; & Zalk, S. R. Baby X: The effect of gender labels on adult responses to infants. *Sex Roles*, 1975, *1* (2), 103–109.

Segner, L. L. Two studies of the incest taboo. *Dissertation Abstracts*, 1968, *29B*, 796.

Semans, J. Premature ejaculation: A new approach. *Southern Medical Journal*, 1956, *49*, 353–357.

Serber, M. Videotape feedback in the treatment of couples with sexual dysfunction. *Archives of Sexual Behavior*, 1974, *3*, 377–380.

Shaffer, D. R. & Wegley, C. Success orientation and sex-role congruence as determinants of the attractiveness of competent women. *Journal of Personality*, 1974, *42*, 586–600.

Shah, F., & Zelnik, M. Sexuality in adolescence. In B. B. Wolman & J. Money (eds.), *Handbook of human sexuality*. Englewood Cliffs, N.J.: Prentice-Hall, 1980.

Shapiro, H. I. *The birth control book*. New York: St. Martin's Press, 1977.

Shepher, J. Mate selection among second generation kibbutz adolescents and adults: Incest avoidance and negative imprinting. *Archives of Sexual Behavior*, 1972, 1, 293–307.

Sherfey, M. J. *The nature and evolution of female sexuality.* New York: Random House, 1972.

Sheridan, M. D. Final report of a prospective study of children whose mothers had rubella in early pregnancy. *British Medical Journal*, 1964, 2, 536–539.

Shields, S. A. Ms. Pilgrim's progress: The contribution of Leta Stetter Hollingworth to the psychology of women. *American Psychologist*, 1975, 30, 852–857.

Shirer, W. L. *The collapse of the third republic.* New York: Pocket Books, 1971.

Siegel, P. B. Genetics of behavior: Selection for mating ability in chickens. *Genetics*, 1965, 52, 1269–1277.

Sigall, H., & Aronson, E. Liking for an evaluator as a function of her attractiveness and nature of the evaluations. *Journal of Experimental Social Psychology*, 1969, 5, 93–100.

Sigall, H., & Ostrove, N. Beautiful but dangerous: Effects of offender attractiveness and nature of the crime on juridic judgment. *Journal of Personality and Social Psychology*, 1975, 31, 410–414.

Silber, S. J., & Cohen, R. Normal intrauterine pregnancy after reversal of tubal sterilization in the wife and vasectomy in the husband. *Fertility and Sterility*, 1978, 30, 606–608.

Silny, A. J. Sexuality and aging. In B. B. Wolman & J. Money (eds.), *Handbook of human sexuality.* Englewood Cliffs, N.J.: Prentice-Hall, 1980.

Silverberg, E. Cancer statistics, 1981. *Ca-A Cancer Journal for Clinicians*, 1981, 1 (1), 13–28.

Silverman, I. J. A survey of cohabitation on two college campuses. *Archives of Sexual Behavior*, 1977, 6, 11–20.

Simonds, P. E. *The social primates.* New York: Harper & Row, 1974.

Singer, J. *The inner world of daydreaming.* New York: Harper & Row, 1975.

Singer, J., & Singer, I. The types of female orgasm. *Journal of Sex Research*, 1972, 8, 255–267.

Sintchak, G. H., & Geer, J. H. A vaginal plethysmo-graph system. *Psychophysiology*, 1975, 12, 113–115.

Skipper, J. K., & McCaghy, C. H. Stripteasers. *Social Problems*, 1970, 17, 391–405.

Slater, P. *Footholds: Understanding the shifting family and sexual tensions in our culture.* New York: Dutton, 1977.

Sloane, P., & Karpinski, E. Effects of incest on participants. *American Journal of Orthopsychiatry*, 1942, 12, 666–673.

Slovenko, R. *Sexual behavior and the law.* Springfield, Ill.: Charles C Thomas, 1965.

Smedley, A. Birom cicibeism. Paper presented to the meeting of the American Anthropological Association, Washington, D.C., 1976.

Smith, E. A follow-up study of women who request abortion. *American Journal of Orthopsychiatry*, 1973, 43, 574–585.

Smith, G. P. For unto us a child is born—legally. *American Bar Association Journal*, 1970, 56, 143–145.

Smith, J. M. *The evolution of sex.* Cambridge: Cambridge University Press, 1978.

Snyder, F. *Sleep.* Philadelphia: J. B. Lippincott, 1969.

Socarides, C. W. The development of fetishistic perversion. *Journal of the American Psychoanalytic Association*, 1960, 8, 281–311.

Socarides, C. W. *Beyond sexual freedom.* New York: Quadrangle, 1975.

Solomon, P., & Patch, V. D. *Handbook of psychiatry.* Los Altos, Calif.: Lang Medical Publications, 1974.

Sørensen, T., & Hertoft, P. Male and female transsexualism: The Danish experience with 37 patients. *Archives of Sexual Behavior*, 1982, 11, 133–155.

Sorenson, R. C. *Adolescent sexuality in contemporary America.* New York: World, 1973.

Spanier, G. B. Sources of sex information and premarital sexual behavior. *Journal of Sex Research*, 1977, 13, 73–88.

Spark, Richard F.; White, Robert A.; & Connolly, Peter B. Impotence is not always psychogenic. *Journal of the American Medical Association*, October 3, 1980, 243 (8), 1558.

Spence, J. T. The Thematic Apperception Test and attitudes toward achievement in women: A new look at the motive to avoid success and a new method of measurement. *Journal of Consulting and Clinical Psychology,* 1974, *42,* 427–437.

Spence, J. T.; Helmreich, R.; & Stapp, J. Likability, sex-role congruence of interest, and competence: It all depends on how you ask. *Journal of Applied Social Psychology,* 1975, *5,* 93–109. (a)

Spence, J. T.; Helmreich, R.; & Stapp, J. Ratings of self and peers on sex-role attributes and their relation to self-esteem and conceptions of masculinity and femininity. *Journal of Personality and Social Psychology,* 1975, *32,* 29–39. (b)

Spreitzer, E., & Riley, L. E. Factors associated with singlehood. *Journal of Marriage and the Family,* 1974, *36,* 533–542.

Sprey, J. Extramarital relationships. *Sexual Behavior,* 1972, *2* (8), 34–40.

Stamm, R. A. Aspekte des Paarverhaltens von *Agapornis personata* Reichenow. *Behaviour,* 1962, *19,* 1–56.

Steen, E. B., & Montagu, A. *Anatomy and physiology,* vol. 2. New York: Barnes & Noble, 1959.

Stein, M. L. *Friends, lovers, slaves.* New York: Berkeley, 1974.

Stein, P. *Single.* Englewood Cliffs, N.J.: Prentice-Hall, 1976.

Stephan, W.; Berscheid, E.; & Walster, E. Sexual arousal and heterosexual perception. *Journal of Personality and Social Psychology,* 1971, *20,* 93–101.

Stephens, W. N. A cross-cultural study of modesty and obscenity. *Technical Report of the Commission on Obscenity and Pornography.* Washington, D.C.: U.S. Government Printing Office, 1971, *11,* 405–451.

Sternglanz, S. H., & Serbin, L. A. Sex-role stereotyping in children's television programs. *Developmental Psychology,* 1974, *10,* 710–715.

Stock, W. E., & Geer, J. H. A study of fantasy-based sexual arousal in women. *Archives of Sexual Behavior,* 1982, *11,* 33–47.

Stoller, R. J. Transvestites' woman. *American Journal of Psychiatry,* 1967, *124,* 333–339.

Stoller, R. J. Male childhood transsexualism. *Journal of the American Academy of Child Psychiatry,* 1968, *7,* 193–209.

Stoller, R. J. Etiological factors in female transsexualism. *Archives of Sexual Behavior,* 1972, *2,* 47–64.

Stoller, R. J. Sexual deviations. In F. A. Beach (ed.), *Human sexuality in four perspectives.* Baltimore: Johns Hopkins Press, 1976.

Stoller, R. J. Erotic vomiting. *Archives of Sexual Behavior,* 1982, *11,* 361–35.

Stone, A. *The practice of contraception.* Baltimore: Williams & Wilkins, 1931.

Storms, M. D. Theories of sexual orientation. *Journal of Personality and Social Psychology,* 1980, *38,* 783–792.

Storms, M. D. A theory of erotic orientation development. *Psychological Review,* 1981, *88,* 340–353.

Straus, M. A.; Gelles, R. J.; & Steinmetz, S. K. *Behind closed doors.* Garden City, N.Y.: Doubleday, Anchor, 1980.

Streissguth, A. P. Maternal drinking and the outcome of pregnancy: Implications for child mental health. *American Journal of Orthopsychiatry,* 1977, *47,* 422–431.

Suchner, R. W. Sex ratios and occupational prestige: Three failures to replicate a sexist bias. *Personality and Social Psychology Bulletin,* 1979, *5,* 236–239.

Sue, D. Erotic fantasies of college students during coitus. *Journal of Sex Research,* 1979, *15,* 299–305.

Suitters, B. *The history of contraceptives.* London: International Planned Parenthood Foundation, 1967.

Sussman, N. Sex and sexuality in history. In B. J. Sadock, H. I. Kaplan, & A. M. Freedman (eds.), *The sexual experience.* Baltimore: Williams & Wilkins, 1976.

Sussman, N. M., & Rosenfeld, H. M. Influence of culture, language, and sex on conversational distance. *Journal of Personality and Social Psychology,* 1982, *42,* 66–74.

Sutherland, S., & Scherl, D. L. Patterns of responses

among victims of rape. *American Journal of Orthopsychiatry*, 1970, *49*, 503–511.

Symons, D. *The evolution of human sexuality*. New York: Oxford University Press, 1979.

Taleisnik, S., Caligaris, L. & Astrada, J. J. Effect of copulation on the release of pituitary gonadotropins in male and female rats. *Endocrinology*, 1966, *79*, 49–54.

Talese, G. *Thy neighbor's wife*. New York: Doubleday, 1980.

Tannahill, Reay. *Sex in history*. New York: Stein & Day, 1980.

Tannenbaum, P. H. Emotional arousal as a mediator of communication effects. *Technical Reports of the Commission on Obscenity and Pornography*, vol. 8. Washington, D.C.: U.S. Government Printing Office, 1970.

Tanner, J. M. Puberty. In A. McLaren (ed.), *Advances in reproductive physiology*, vol. 2. New York: Academic Press, 1967.

Tanowitz, H. B. Parasitic gynecologic diseases. *Medical Aspects of Human Sexuality*, 1974, *8* (9), 45–63.

Tavris, C. The sex lives of happy men. *Redbook Magazine*, 1978, *150* (5), 109, 193–199.

Tavris, C., & Offir, C. *The longest war: Sex differences in perspective*. New York: Harcourt, Brace, Jovanovich, 1977.

Tavris, C., & Sadd, S. *The Redbook report on female sexuality*. New York: Delacorte Press, 1977.

Taylor, G. R. *Sex in history*. New York: Vanguard, 1954.

Taylor, J., & Deaux, K. When women are more deserving than men: Equity, attribution, and perceived sex differences. *Journal of Personality and Social Psychology*, 1973, *28*, 360–367.

Taylor, S. P., & Epstein, S. Aggression as a function of the interaction of the sex of the aggressor and the sex of the victim. *Journal of Personality*, 1967, *35*, 473–486.

Télégdy, G. Prenatal androgenization of primates and humans. In J. Money & H. Musaph (eds.), *Handbook of sexology*. New York: Exerpta Medica, 1977.

Teleki, G. The omnivorous chimpanzee. *Scientific American*, 1973, *228* (1), 32–42.

TeLinde, R. W. *Operative gynecology*. Philadelphia: J. B. Lippincott, 1953.

Tennov, D. *Love and limerence*. New York: Stein & Day, 1978.

Tharp, G. D. *Experiments in physiology*. 4th ed. Minneapolis: Burgess, 1980.

Thigpen, C. H., & Cleckley, H. M. *Three faces of Eve*. New York: McGraw-Hill, 1957.

Thompson, N.; Schwartz, D.; McCandless, B.; & Edwards, D. Parent-child relationships and sexual identity in male and female homosexuals and heterosexuals. *Journal of Consulting and Clinical Psychology*, 1973, *41*, 120–127.

Thorp, L. P.; Katz, B.; & Lewis, R. T. *Psychology of abnormal behavior*. New York: Ronald, 1961.

Tietze, C. History of contraceptive methods. *Journal of Sex Research*, 1965, *1*, 69–85.

Tietze, C. Induced abortion. In J. Money & H. Musaph (eds.) *Handbook of sexology*. New York: Elsevier North-Holland, 1977.

Tittle, C. Inmate organization. *American Sociological Review*, 1969, *34*, 492–505.

Tollison, C. D., & Adams, H. E. *Sexual disorders: Treatment, theory, and research*. New York: Gardner, 1979.

Tollison, C. D.; Nesbitt, J. G.; & Frye, J. D. Comparison of attitudes toward sexual intimacy in prostitutes and college coeds. *Journal of Social Psychology*, 1975, *6*, 316–318.

Touhey, J. C. Effects of additional women professionals on ratings of occupational prestige and desirability. *Journal of Personality and Social Psychology*, 1974, *29*, 86–89.

Trainer, J. B. *Physiologic foundations for marriage counseling*. St. Louis: Mosby, 1965.

Tripp, C. A. *The homosexual matrix*. New York: McGraw-Hill, 1975.

Trudgill, E. *Madonnas and magdalens: The origins and development of Victorian sexual attitudes*. New York: Holmes & Meier, 1976.

Udry, J. A., & Morris, N. M. Distribution of coitus in the menstrual cycle. *Nature*, 1968, *220*, 593–596.

Udry, R. J. Sex and family life. *The Annals of the American Academy of Political and Social Science*, 1968, *376*, 25–35.

Ueno, M. *Sex and your heart.* New York: Award Books, 1968.

Unger, K. W. Medical problems caused by homosexual relations. *Medical Aspects of Human Sexuality*, 1975, *9* (2), 152.

United States, Bureau of the Census. Marital status and living arrangements. March 1978. *Current Population Reports*, series P-20, no. 338. Washington, D.C.: U.S. Government Printing Office, 1979.

United States, Department of Health, Education and Welfare. *Herpes Simplex Type 2.* No. 00-2797. Washington, D.C.: U.S. Government Printing Office, 1980.

United States Public Health Service, Center for Disease Control. *VD fact sheet for 1976.* HEW publication no. 77-8195. Washington, D.C.: U.S. Government Printing Office, 1976.

Valins, S. Cognitive effects of false heart-rate feedback. *Journal of Personality and Social Psychology*, 1966, *4*, 400–408.

Vance, E. B., & Wagner, N. N. Written descriptions of orgasm: A study of sex differences. *Archives of Sexual Behavior*, 1976, *5*, 87–98.

Van de Castle, R. L. *The psychology of dreaming.* Morristown, N.J.: General Learning Press, 1971.

Vandenbergh, J., & Vessey, S. Seasonal breeding of free-ranging rhesus monkeys and related ecological factors. *Journal of Reproduction and Fertility*, 1968, *15*, 71–79.

van Lawick-Goodall, J. The behaviour of free-living chimpanzees in the Gombe Stream Reserve. *Animal Behaviour Monographs*, 1968, *1*, 161–311.

Vatsyayana. *The Kama Sutra,* trans. R. F. Burton & F. F. Arbuthnot. New York: G. P. Putnam's Sons, 1963.

Vaughan, D. Uncoupling: The process of moving from one lifestyle to another. *Alternative Lifestyles*, 1979, *2* (4), 415–442.

Vaughan, E., & Fisher, A. E. Male sexual behavior induced by intracranial electrical stimulation. *Science*, 1962, *137*, 758–760.

Vellois, H. V. The social life of early man: The evidence of skeletons. In S. L. Washburn (ed.), *Social life of early man.* Chicago: Aldine, 1961.

Vetter, H. J. *Psychology of abnormal behavior.* New York: Ronald Press, 1972.

Victor, J. S. *Human sexuality: A social psychological approach.* Englewood Cliffs, N.J.: Prentice-Hall, 1980.

Vogel, S. R.; Broverman, I. K.; Broverman, D. M.; Clarkson, F. E.; & Rosenkrantz, P. S. Maternal employment and perception of sex roles among college students. *Developmental Psychology*, 1970, *3*, 384–391.

Vogelmann-Sine, S., Ervin, E. D.; Christensen, R.; Warmsun, C. H.; & Ullmann, L. P. Sex differences in feelings attributed to a woman in situations involving coercion and sexual advances. *Journal of Personality*, 1979, *47*, 420–431.

Wabrek, A. J., & Wabrek, C. J. A primer on impotence. *Medical Aspects of Human Sexuality*, 1976, *10* (11), 102–114.

Wachtel, S. S.; Koo, G. C.; Breg, W. R.; Thaler, H. T.; Dillard, G. M.; Rosenthal, I. W.; Dosik, H.; Gerald, P. S.; Saenger, P.; New, M.; Lieber, E.; & Miller, O. J. Serologic detection of a Y-linked gene in XX males and XX true hermaphrodites. *New England Journal of Medicine*, 1976, *295*, 750–751.

Wagner, N., & Solberg, D. Pregnancy and sexuality. *Medical Aspects of Human Sexuality*, 1974, *8* (3), 44–79.

Wagner, N. M. Sexual activity and the cardiac patient. In R. Green (ed.), *Human sexuality: A health practitioner's text.* Baltimore: Williams & Wilkins, 1975.

Walen, S.; Hauserman, N. M.; & Lavin, P. J. *Clinical guide to behavior therapy.* Baltimore: Williams & Wilkins, 1977.

Wallace, D. H., & Wehmer, G. Evaluation of visual erotica by sexual liberals and conservatives. *Journal of Sex Research*, 1972, *8*, 147–153.

Wallace, R. A. *How they do it.* New York: William Morrow, 1980.

Walstedt, J. J.; Geis, F. L.; & Brown, V. Influence of television commercials on women's self-confidence and independent judgment. *Journal of Personality and Social Psychology*, 1980, *38*, 203–210.

Walster, E. The effect of self-esteem on romantic liking. *Journal of Experimental and Social Psychology*, 1965, *1*, 184–197.

Walster, E.; Aronson, V.; Abrahams, D.; & Rottman, L. Importance of physical attractiveness in dating behavior. *Journal of Personality and Social Psychology*, 1966, *4*, 508–516.

Walster, E.; Walster, G. W.; Piliavin, J.; & Schmidt, L. Playing hard to get: Understanding an elusive phenomenon. *Journal of Personality and Social Psychology*, 1973, *26*, 113–121.

Walters, D. R. *Physical and sexual abuse of children.* Bloomington: Indiana University Press, 1975.

Warden, A. N., & Leahy, J. S. The behavior of rabbits. In E. S. E. Hafez (ed.), *The behavior of domestic animals.* London: Bailliere, Tindall & Cassell, 1962.

Warren, C. A. B. *Identity and community in the gay world.* New York: Wiley, 1974.

Wasserman, G. The nature and function of early mother-infant interaction. In B. L. Blum (ed.), *Psychological aspects of pregnancy, birthing, and bonding.* New York: Human Sciences Press, 1980.

Waterman, C. K., & Nevid, J. S. Sex differences in the resolution of the identity crisis. *Journal of Youth and Adolescence*, 1977, *6*, 337–342.

Watson, M.A. Sexually open marriage: Three perspectives. *Alternative Lifestyles*, 1981, *4*, 3–21.

Waxenberg, S. E.; Drellich, M. G.; & Sutherland, A. M. The role of hormones in human behavior: I. Changes in female sexuality after adrenalectomy. *Journal of Clinical Endocrinology and Metabolism*, 1959, *19*, 193–202.

Weatherly, D. Self-perceived rate of physical maturation and personality in late adolescence. *Child Development*, 1964, *35*, 1197–1210.

Weg, R. B. The physiology of sexuality in aging. In R. L. Solnick (ed.), *Sexuality and aging.* Los Angeles: University of Southern California Press, 1978.

Weidner, G., Istvan, J., & Griffitt, W. Beauty in the eyes of horny beholders. Paper presented at the meeting of the Midwestern Psychological Association, Chicago, 1979.

Weinberg, K. *Incest behavior.* Secaucus, N.J.: Citadel, 1976.

Weinberg, M. Sexual modesty, social meaning and the nudist camp. *Social Problems*, 1965, *12*, 311–318.

Weinberg, M. S., & Williams, C. *Male homosexuals: Their problems and adaptations.* New York: Oxford University Press, 1974.

Weinberg, S. K. *Incest behavior.* New York: Citadel, 1955.

Weiss, H. D. Mechanism of erection. *Medical Aspects of Human Sexuality*, 1973, *7*, 21–40.

Weiss, R. S. *Marital separation.* New York: Basic Books, 1975.

Weissman, P. Some aspects of sexual activity in a fetishist. *Psychoanalytic Quarterly*, 1957, *26*, 494–507.

Weitz, S. *Sex roles.* New York: Oxford University Press, 1977.

Weitzman, L. J.; Eifler, D.; Hokada, E.; & Ross, C. Sex role socialization in picture books for preschool children. *American Journal of Sociology*, 1972, *77*, 1125–1150.

Welty, J. C. *The life of birds.* New York: A. A. Knopf, 1963.

Wendrich, D. H. Comments on the origin and evolution of sex. In D. H. Wendrich (ed.), *Sex in micro-organisms.* Washington: American Association for the Advancement of Science, 1954.

Westoff, C. F. Coital frequency and contraception. *Family Planning Perspectives*, 1974, *6* (3), 136–141.

Westoff, C. F., & Jones, E. F. The secularization of U.S. Catholic birth control practices. *Family Planning Perspectives*, 1977, *9*, 203–207.

Westoff, L. A., & Westoff, C. F. *From now to zero: Fertility, contraception and abortion in America.* Boston: Little, Brown, 1971.

Whalen, R. E. Brain mechanisms controlling sexual behavior. In F. A. Beach (ed.), *Human sexuality in four perspectives.* Baltimore: Johns Hopkins Press, 1976.

Whitam, F. L. The homosexual role: A reconsideration. *Journal of Sex Research*, 1977, *13* (1), 1–11.

White, C. B. Sexual interest, attitudes, knowledge, and sexual history in relation to sexual behavior in the institutionalized aged. *Archives of Sexual Behavior*, 1982, *11*, 11–21.

White, L. A. The definition and prohibition of incest. *American Anthropologist*, 1948, *50*, 416–435.

White, L. A. Erotica and aggression: The influence of sexual arousal, positive affect, and negative affect on aggressive behavior. *Journal of Personality and Social Psychology*, 1979, *37*, 591–601.

White, M. *Animal cytology and evolution.* New York: Cambridge University Press, 1954.

White, S. E., & Reamy, K. Sexuality and pregnancy: A review. *Archives of Sexual Behavior*, 1982, *11*, 429–444.

Whitten, W. K.; Bronson, F.; & Greenstein, J. Estrus-inducing pheromone of male mice: Transport by movement of air. *Science*, 1968, *161*, 584–585.

Wickler, W. *The sexual code: The social behavior of animals and men.* New York: Doubleday, 1972.

Wickramasekera, I. A technique for controlling a certain type of sexual exhibitionism. *Psychotherapy: Theory, Research and Practice*, 1972, *9*, 207–210.

Widmayer, S. M., & Field, T. M. Effects of Brazelton demonstrations on early interactions of preterm infants and their teenage mothers. *Infant Behavior and Development*, 1980, *3*, 79–91.

Wiener, H. External chemical messengers: I. Emission and reception in man. *New York State Journal of Medicine*, 1966, *66*, 3153–3170.

Wiggins, J. S., Wiggins, N., & Conger, J. C. Correlates of heterosexual somatic preference. *Journal of Personality and Social Psychology*, 1968, *10*, 82–90.

Williams, J. H. Sexuality in marriage. In B. B. Wolman & J. Money (eds.), *Handbook of human sexuality.* Englewood Cliffs, N.J.: Prentice-Hall, 1980.

Williams, J. H. Psychology of women. 2d ed. New York: Norton, 1983.

Williams, L. *Der Affe wie ihn keiner kennt.* Wien: Molden, 1968.

Williamson, R. L. Marriage and family relations. New York: Wiley, 1966.

Wilson, E. O. *Sociobiology: The new synthesis.* Cambridge, Mass.: Belknap Press, 1975.

Wilson, G. T., & Lawson, D. M. Expectancies, alcohol and sexual arousal in male social drinkers. *Journal of Abnormal Psychology*, 1976, *85*, 587–594.

Wilson, G. T., & Lawson, D. M. Expectancies, alcohol and sexual arousal in women. *Journal of Abnormal Psychology*, 1978, *87*, 358–367.

Winchester, A. M. *The nature of human sexuality.* Columbus: Charles Merrill, 1973.

Winick, C., & Kinsie, P. M. Prostitution. *Sexual Behavior*, 1971, *3*, 36–39.

Winick, M. Nutrition and brain development. In G. Serban (ed.), *Nutrition and mental functions.* New York: Plenum, 1975.

Witkin, H.; Mednick, S.; Schulsinger, F.; Bakkestrom, E.; Christiansen, K. O.; Goodenough, D.; Hirshhorn, K.; Lundsteen, C.; Owen, D. R.; Philip, J.; Rubin, D. B.; & Stocking, M. Criminality in XYY and XXY men. *Science*, 1976, *196*, 547–555.

Wolf, A. P. Childhood association and sexual attraction. *American Anthropologist*, 1970, *72*, 503–515.

Wolf, D. G. *The lesbian community.* Berkeley and Los Angeles: University of California Press, 1979.

Wolfson, C. Shared-caregiving fathers in intact families: An exploration of personality characteristics, motivation and antecedents. Ph.D. dissertation, Loyola University, Chicago, 1982.

Wolpe, J. *Psychotherapy by reciprocal inhibition.* Stanford, Calif.: Stanford University Press, 1958.

Wolpe, J. *The practice of behavior therapy.* 2d ed. New York: Pergamon, 1973.

Wood-Gush, D. G. M. Genetic and experiential factors affecting the libido of cockerels. *Proceedings of the Royal Society of Edinborough*, 1958, *27*, 6–7.

Woods, N. F. *Human sexuality in health and illness*. St. Louis: Mosby, 1975.

Woolsey, C. N. Organization of somatic sensory and motor areas of the cerebral cortex. In H. F. Harlow & C. N. Woolsey (eds.), *Biological and biochemical bases of behavior*. Madison: University of Wisconsin Press, 1958.

Wyden, R., & Wyden, B. *Growing up straight*. New York: Signet Books, 1968.

Yalom, I. D. Aggression and forbiddenness in voyeurism. *Archives of General Psychiatry*, 1960, *3*, 305–319.

Yankelovich, D. The new morality. *Time*, 1977, *110* (31), 111–116.

Yerkes, R. M. The mind of the gorilla: III. Memory. *Comparative Psychology Monographs*, 1928, *5*, 1–92.

Yerkes, R. M. Sexual behavior in the chimpanzee. *Human Biology*, 1939, *2*, 78–110.

Yllo, K. Nonmarital cohabitation: Beyond the college campus. *Alternative Lifestyles*, 1978, *1*, 37–55.

Yorburg, B. *Sexual identity*. New York: Wiley, 1975.

Yorukoglu, A., & Kemph, J. P. Children not severely damaged by incest with a parent. *Journal of the American Academy of Child Psychiatry*, 1966, *5*, 111–124.

Young, W. Prostitution. In J. D. Douglas (ed.), *Observation of defiance*. New York: Random House, 1970.

Young, W. C. The hormones and mating behavior. In W. C. Young (ed.), *Sex and internal secretions*. Baltimore: Williams & Wilkins, 1961.

Young, W. C., & Fish, W. R. The ovarian hormones and spontaneous running activity in the female rat. *Endocrinology*, 1945, *36*, 181–189.

Zacharias, L., & Wurtman, R. J. Blindness: Its relation to age at menarche. *Science*, 1964, *144*, 1154–1155.

Zajonc, R. B. Attitudinal effects of mere exposure. *Journal of Personality and Social Psychology Monograph Supplement*, 1968, *9*, 1–27.

Zelnik, M., & Kantner, J. F. Sexual and contraceptive experience of young unmarried women in the United States, 1976 and 1971. *Family Planning Perspectives*, 1977, *9*, 55–71.

Zelnik, M., & Kantner, J. F. Contraceptive patterns and premarital pregnancy among women aged 15–19 in 1976. *Family Planning Perspectives*, 1978, *10* (3), 135–142.

Zelnik, M.; Kim, J.; & Kantner, J. F. Probabilities of intercourse and conception among U.S. teenage women, 1971 and 1976. *Family Planning Perspectives*, 1979, *11*, 177–183.

Zelnik, M., & Shah, F. Sexuality in adolescence. In B. B. Wolman & J. Money (eds.), *Handbook of human sexuality*. Englewood Cliffs, N.J.: Prentice-Hall, 1980.

Ziegler, F. J.; Rodgers, D. A.; & Prentiss, R. J. Psychosocial responses to vasectomy. *Archives of General Psychiatry*, 1969, *31*, 46–54.

Zilbergeld, B. *Male sexuality: A guide to sexual fulfillment*. Boston: Little, Brown, 1978.

Zilbergeld, B., & Evans, M. The inadequacy of Masters and Johnson. *Psychology Today*, 1980, *13*, (8), 29–43.

Zuckerman, M.; Tushup, R.; & Finner, S. Sexual attitudes and experience: Attitude and personality correlates and changes produced by a course of sexuality. *Journal of Consulting and Clinical Psychology*, 1976, *44*, 7–19.

Zuckerman, M., & Wheeler, L. To dispel fantasies about the fantasy-based measure of fear of success. *Psychological Bulletin*, 1975, *82*, 932–946.

NAME INDEX

Abarbanel, A. R., 456
Abel, G. G., 417
Abramson, P. R., 132
Adams, H. E., 70, 375, 379, 385, 388, 393, 395, 402, 403, 404, 407, 412, 413, 414, 424, 434, 436, 454, 455, 456, 462
Addiego, F., 90
Adler, C., 209
Aiman, J., 393
Aladjem, S., 238
Alexander, N., 265
Allen, C., 257
Allen, D. M., 257, 439
Almouist, J. O., 335
Alston, J. P., 371
Altman, K., 111
Amelar, R. D., 222
American Law Institute, 148, 440
American Psychological Association, 33, 40n
Amir, M., 416, 420, 422
Anderson, J., 229
Anderson, N., 178
Anthunes, C., 343
Aponte, J., 174
Arafat, I. S., 130
Archambault, F. X., 132
Arkowitz, H., 193
Aron, A. P., 177
Aronson, E., 174, 175, 178
Arvidsson, T., 107
Athanasiou, R., 111
Auerbach, A., 99
Augustine, 359
Aurelius, Marcus, 5–6
Austin, J. B., 406

Babcock, B. A., 440
Back, K., 174
Bacon, M. K., 306
Bain, J. K., 325
Baker, S. W., 286
Bakkestrom, E., 486
Ball, R. B., 398
Bancroft, J., 379
Bandura, A., 287, 314

Barbach, L., 52
Bardwick, J. M., 79, 343
Barlow, D. H., 406, 409n, 417, 479
Baron, R. A., 172, 187n, 423
Barros, R., 122, 404, 426
Barry, H., 306
Bart, P. B., 343
Bartell, G. D., 33, 333, 334
Bates, G., 343
Bauman, J. E., 453
Baur, K., 89, 101n, 482
Beach, F. A., 15, 18, 19, 20, 21, 36, 49, 68, 71, 78, 95, 110, 133, 147, 156, 157, 165, 184, 224, 226, 286, 293, 301, 328, 329, 366
Beaumont, T., 413
Bell, A. P., 28–29, 362, 363, 364, 365, 366, 369, 370, 373
Bell, R. Q., 246
Bell, R. R., 197
Belzer, E. G., 90
Bem, S., 308, 309
Bentler, P. M., 336, 389
Bentley, B., 178, 187n
Beral, V., 262
Beran, L. C., 387
Berg, P. A., 305
Berger, A. J., 132
Berger, D. E., 182
Berkow, R., 480
Bermant, G., 73, 108, 335, 485
Bernard, J., 292, 336
Bernstein, B. E., 80
Beroza, M., 172
Berreman, G. D., 328, 329
Berscheid, E., 167, 171, 205, 207, 443
Biaggs, M. A., 350, 352, 353
Bieber, I., 368, 377
Bieber, T. B., 368, 377
Black, Eve, 427, 428
Blanchard, E. B., 417
Blank, L., 386
Blau, S., 474, 476, 480
Blumstein, P., 370
Bodemer, C. W., 230
Boggan, E. C., 390
Bonnemains, Madame de, 105

Bonsall, R. W., 173
Boral, R. L., 201
Borgida, E., 422
Boswell, J., 381n
Boucher, R., 418
Boulanger, Georges, 105
Bow, Clara, 12
Bower, G. W., 314
Boyar, R. M., 393
Boyd, T. L., 284
Boydon, 362
Brady, Ian, 411
Bragonier, J. R., 262
Breg, W. R., 279
Bremer, J., 108
Brewer, J. L., 238
Bringle, R. G., 209
Brockopp, G. W., 387
Broderick, C. B., 292
Broderick, P. C., 229
Brodsky, A. M., 467
Bronson, F., 173
Brooks-Gunn, J., 80
Broverman, D. M., 73, 290
Broverman, I. K., 290
Brown, C., 343
Brown, V., 286
Brownell, K. D., 409n
Browning, M., 368
Brownmiller, S., 414, 422, 424
Bruce, H. J., 233
Brundage, L. W., 193
Brunton, M., 486
Bryan, J. H., 437
Bryant, Anita, 372
Bryson, J. B., 209
Buehler, J. A., 174
Buhrich, N., 413
Burgess, A. W., 416, 419, 420, 421, 422
Burnett, L., 343
Burns, D. S., 171
Burnside, I. M., 345
Burton, F. D., 95
Bush, P., 113, 126
Bush, S., 126
Butler, D. C., 353
Butler, J. C., 238

539

SUBJECT INDEX

(Terms in bold face are defined in the glossary.)